Handbook of
COMMERCIAL
POLICY

Handbook of
COMMERCIAL POLICY

Volume 1A

Edited by

KYLE BAGWELL
Stanford University
Stanford, CA, USA

ROBERT W. STAIGER
Dartmouth College
Hanover, NH, USA

ELSEVIER

Amsterdam • Boston • Heidelberg • London • New York • Oxford
Paris • San Diego • San Francisco • Singapore • Sydney • Tokyo
North-Holland is an imprint of Elsevier

North-Holland is an imprint of Elsevier

Radarweg 29, PO Box 211, 1000 AE Amsterdam, The Netherlands
The Boulevard, Langford Lane, Kidlington, Oxford OX5 1GB, United Kingdom

Notices
Knowledge and best practice in this field are constantly changing. As new research and experience broaden
our understanding, changes in research methods, professional practices, or medical treatment may become
necessary.
Practitioners and researchers must always rely on their own experience and knowledge in evaluating and
using any information, methods, compounds, or experiments described herein. In using such information or
methods they should be mindful of their own safety and the safety of others, including parties for whom they
have a professional responsibility.
To the fullest extent of the law, neither the Publisher nor the authors, contributors, or editors, assume any
liability for any injury and/or damage to persons or property as a matter of products liability, negligence or
otherwise, or from any use or operation of any methods, products, instructions, or ideas contained in the
material herein.

British Library Cataloguing-in-Publication Data
A catalogue record for this book is available from the British Library

Library of Congress Cataloging-in-Publication Data
A catalog record for this book is available from the Library of Congress

ISBN: 978-0-444-63280-7 (Vol. 1A)
ISBN: 978-0-444-63922-6 (Vol. 1B)
Set record (1A and 1B): 978-0-444-63921-9

For information on all North-Holland publications
visit our website at https://www.elsevier.com/

Working together
to grow libraries in
developing countries

www.elsevier.com • www.bookaid.org

Publisher: Zoe Kruze
Acquisition Editor: Kirsten Shankland
Editorial Project Manager: Hannah Colford
Production Project Manager: Radhakrishnan Lakshmanan
Cover Designer: Maria Inês Cruz

Typeset by SPi Global, India

INTRODUCTION TO THE SERIES

The aim of the *Handbooks in Economics* series is to produce Handbooks for various branches of economics, each of which is a definitive source, reference, and teaching supplement for use by professional researchers and advanced graduate students. Each Handbook provides self-contained surveys of the current state of a branch of economics in the form of chapters prepared by leading specialists on various aspects of this branch of economics. These surveys summarize not only received results but also newer developments, from recent journal articles and discussion papers. Some original material is also included, but the main goal is to provide comprehensive and accessible surveys. The Handbooks are intended to provide not only useful reference volumes for professional collections but also possible supplementary readings for advanced courses for graduate students in economics.

Kenneth J. Arrow and Michael D. Intriligator

CONTENTS

PREFACE

The *Handbook of Commercial Policy* surveys recent developments in the study of commercial policy. Economic research on commercial policy has flourished in the past two decades. Using new theoretical models, empirical methodologies, and data sources, important recent research offers valuable new insights regarding the determinants and effects of unilateral trade policies. In turn, this work feeds into a primary focus of modern commercial policy research that concerns the role of trade-agreement rules in shaping trade-policy conduct. From this general perspective and motivated by the success of the General Agreement on Tariffs and Trade (GATT) and its successor organization, the World Trade Organization (WTO), a vibrant area of recent research studies the purpose and design of trade agreements. The GATT/WTO has in effect served as the constitution of the postwar international trading system, and an important objective of recent research is to interpret and evaluate the key GATT/WTO design features. Another central feature of the modern trading environment is the rising prominence of preferential trading agreements (PTAs). A large set of recent research also offers new theoretical and empirical insights regarding the implications of PTAs for member and nonmember countries and for the multilateral trading system more generally.

The primary objective of this handbook is to provide a comprehensive survey of a large body of frontier economic research on commercial policy. The handbook will be an important resource for research economists already working in commercial policy, and it will also provide an essential guide to state-of-the-art research in commercial policy for economists and graduate students who are new to the field. While the handbook does not aim to provide a comprehensive treatment of the legal design of trade agreements, it also provides some legal background on trade agreements that will be useful for research economists.

The *Handbook of Commercial Policy* is organized into three parts that are contained in two volumes. The first volume holds the first two parts of the handbook. The first part has four separate chapters covering economic research that describes the broad set of basic empirical facts regarding the pattern and evolution of commercial policy, the unilateral determinants of commercial policy in developed and in developing countries, the effects of commercial policy intervention on economic magnitudes of interest, and quantitative models of commercial policy. The second part contains four separate chapters providing the relevant legal background for economic research on multilateral and preferential trade agreements and covering economic research on cross-cutting issues relating to the purpose and design of trade agreements. The second volume contains the third part of the handbook, which entails nine separate chapters covering economic research on key issue areas relevant to trade agreements in the modern global economy. The specific issue areas covered here are: enforcement and dispute settlement, escape clauses, dumping and anti-dumping duties, subsidies and countervailing duties, nontariff measures, preferential trade agreements, special and differential treatment for developing countries, intellectual property rights and the WTO, and issue linkages.

We are deeply grateful to the authors of these chapters for their hard work and exceptional contributions. As a result of their efforts and expertise, this handbook will play a valuable role for economic research on commercial policy by organizing a large body of existing research, identifying key open questions, and stimulating important new research.

We also gratefully acknowledge the work of those associated with the Elsevier *Handbooks in Economics* series, including Founding Editors Kenneth J. Arrow and Michael D. Intriligator, current Editors Julio Rotemberg and Michael Woodford, Editorial Project Manager Hannah Colford, Acquisitions Editor Kirsten Shankland, and Project Manager Radhakrishnan Lakshmanan. We are especially grateful to Scott Bentley for his encouraging response to this project during an initial meeting at Stanford and for his guidance of the project throughout the early stages. We also thank Dartmouth College, which provided generous financial support and facilities for a conference in which initial drafts of chapters were presented. For their valuable comments, we also thank the chapter discussants—Manuel Amador, Mostafa Beshkar, Emily Blanchard, Bruce Blonigen, Eric W. Bond, Chad P. Bown, Lorenzo Caliendo, Paola Conconi, Arnaud Costinot, Meredith Crowley, Avinash Dixit, Caroline Freund, Penny Goldberg, Bernard Hoekman, Doug Irwin, Brad Jensen, Pravin Krishna, Nuno Limao, Rodney Ludema, Giovanni Maggi, Petros C. Mavroidis, Anna Maria Mayda, Phil McCalman, Peter Neary, Marcelo Olarreaga, Emanuel Ornelas, Jee-Hyeong Park, Nina Pavcnik, Michele Ruta, Kamal Saggi, Peter Schott, Joel Watson, Alan Winters, and Mark Wu—and other conference participants. Finally, we are grateful to Christianne Wohlforth, whose organizational expertise was instrumental in the success of the handbook conference.

Kyle Bagwell and Robert W. Staiger

CONTRIBUTORS

K. Bagwell
Stanford University, Stanford, CA; NBER, Cambridge, MA, United States

M. Beshkar
Indiana University, Bloomington, IN, United States

B.A. Blonigen
University of Oregon, Eugene, OR, United States

E.W. Bond
Vanderbilt University, Nashville, TN, United States

C.P. Bown
Peterson Institute for International Economics, Washington, DC, United States; CEPR, London, United Kingdom

M.A. Crowley
University of Cambridge, Cambridge; CEPR, London, United Kingdom

J. Ederington
University of Kentucky, Lexington, KY, United States

P.K. Goldberg
Yale University, New Haven, CT, United States

G.M. Grossman
Princeton University, Princeton, NJ, United States

G.M. Lee
School of Economics, Singapore Management University, Singapore, Singapore

N. Limão
University of Maryland, College Park, MD, United States

G. Maggi
Yale University, New Haven, CT; NBER, Cambridge, MA, United States

P.C. Mavroidis
Edwin B. Parker Professor of Law at Columbia Law School, New York City, NY, United States

J. McLaren
University of Virginia, Charlottesville, VA, United States

E. Ornelas
Sao Paulo School of Economics-FGV, São Paulo, Brazil; London School of Economics and Centre of Economic Performance; Centre for Economic Policy Research, London, United Kingdom; CESifo, Munich, Germany

R. Ossa
University of Chicago, Booth School of Business, Chicago, IL; NBER, Cambridge, MA, United States

J.-H. Park
Seoul National University, Seoul, Republic of Korea

N. Pavcnik
Dartmouth College, Hanover, NH, United States

T.J. Prusa
Rutgers University, New Brunswick, NJ, United States

M. Ruta
World Bank, Washington, DC, United States

K. Saggi
Vanderbilt University, Nashville, TN, United States

R.W. Staiger
Dartmouth College, Hanover, NH; NBER, Cambridge, MA, United States

A.O. Sykes
Stanford University, Stanford, CA, United States

PART I

Commercial Policy: Empirical Facts, Determinants and Effects

CHAPTER 1

The Empirical Landscape of Trade Policy

C.P. Bown*,‡, M.A. Crowley†,‡
*Peterson Institute for International Economics, Washington, DC, United States
†University of Cambridge, Cambridge, United Kingdom
‡CEPR, London, United Kingdom

Contents

Handbook of Commercial Policy, Volume 1A
ISSN 2214-3122, http://dx.doi.org/10.1016/bs.hescop.2016.04.015

Abstract

This chapter surveys empirically the broad features of trade policy in goods for 31 major economies that collectively represented 83% of the world's population and 91% of the world's GDP in 2013. We address five questions: Do some countries have more liberal trading regimes than others? Within countries, which industries receive the most import protection? How do trade policies change over time? Do countries discriminate among their trading partners when setting trade policy? Finally, how liberalized is world trade? Our analysis documents the extent of cross-sectional heterogeneity in applied commercial policy across countries, their economic sectors, and their trading partners, over time. We conclude that substantial trade policy barriers remain as an important feature of the world economy.

Keywords

Tariffs, MFN, Preferences, Quantitative restrictions, Temporary trade barriers, Antidumping, Safeguards, Nontariff barriers

JEL Classification codes

F02, F13, F14, F15, H21, H23, K33, L5, N4, N70

1. INTRODUCTION

This chapter surveys the broad features of and developments in the use of trade policy across countries, within countries, and over time. Our goal is to describe and, whenever possible, quantify the extent of cross-sectional heterogeneity in applied commercial policy across countries, their economic sectors, and their trading partners, over time.[a] We construct a relatively comprehensive picture of trade policy for 31 economies that represented 83% of the world's population and 91% of the world's GDP in 2013. Our main conclusion is that substantial trade policy barriers remain as an important feature of the world economy today.

As a starting point, we must define what we mean by a trade policy "barrier." As we will illustrate, there is an ever-increasing set of policy instruments that both researchers

---

[a] This paper builds from a number of previous *Handbook* chapters describing various elements of how trade policy is used in practice, and notably Feenstra (1995), Rodrik (1995), Staiger (1995), and Maggi (2014).

and trade negotiators would like to better understand because they are perceived to have a trade-restricting effect. Until recently, researchers have had little information about border policy instruments. Indeed, as Anderson and van Wincoop noted: "[t]he grossly incomplete and inaccurate information on policy barriers available to researchers is a scandal and a puzzle" (Anderson and van Wincoop, 2004, p. 693). The good news is that research no longer needs to operate behind a veil of ignorance created by the lack of information on border barriers; product-level data on many of the important trade policy instruments imposed at the border are now routinely being made available for most economies in the world.[b]

The picture of the empirical landscape of trade policy that emerges is complex, with substantial variation along some dimensions and little variation along others. We frame our assessment of this trade policy variation by centering our analysis around five main questions:

1. Do some countries have more liberal trading regimes than others?
2. Within countries, which industries receive the most import protection?
3. How do trade policies change over time?
4. Do countries discriminate across their trading partners when setting trade policy?
5. How liberalized is world trade?

As we examine each question, we document heterogeneity in trade policy arising along important dimensions.[c] Whenever possible, we also comment on the factors that are understood as driving this variation. Here, we offer five brief answers, with a promise to expand on them in the coming pages.

Question 1: Do some countries have more liberal trading regimes than others?

Yes, there are large differences across countries in the average level of import tariffs. High-income countries have more liberal regimes than middle income countries which, in turn, have more liberal regimes than low income countries. To this broad picture we add two more subtle observations. High-income countries appear even more open when we expand the set of policies to include preferential tariffs on imports that they offer to selected trading partners. On the other hand, both high-income and emerging economies appear less open when we expand the set of policies beyond tariffs to include policies such as temporary trade barriers and quantitative restrictions.

Question 2: Within countries, which industries receive the most import protection?

With respect to import tariffs, agricultural products and foodstuffs are protected almost everywhere, regardless of a country's level of development. Textiles, apparel

---

[b] Our survey is limited to policy barriers to goods trade only and thus does not address services.

[c] An alternative approach that we do not pursue is the theoretically-grounded Trade Restrictiveness Index (TRI) measures of Anderson and Neary (1992, 1996). The TRI collapses within-country, cross-sector variation into a single measure that can be compared across countries; it has been implemented empirically, for example, in Kee et al. (2009). However, the TRI does not capture many of the aspects of the intertemporal and cross-trading partners variation in trade policy that we describe throughout this chapter.

and footwear are more protected than other manufactured goods. Minerals and fuels tend to face few import barriers. Furthermore, import tariffs on final goods are higher than those on intermediates in all sectors, everywhere. When expanding the policy set beyond tariffs, however, the sector-level variation in import protection levels becomes much more muddled.

Question 3: How do trade policies change over time? Are countries consistently liberalizing, or are there reversals?

Over the last 20 years, tariffs have been trending down around the world. Among high-income countries, changes in applied tariffs are mostly stable around this trend; there is a bit more fluctuation for lower income countries. However, this broad trend is partially deceiving for many high income and emerging economies; they have switched from tariffs toward antidumping and safeguards policies to implement higher frequency changes to their levels of import protection.

Question 4: Do countries discriminate across their trading partners when setting trade policy? If so, by how much?

The short answer to the first part of this question is yes. Many countries discriminate across trading partners by offering *lower* levels of import protection—ie, lower applied tariffs that provide more favorable market access to preferred trading partners relative to the nondiscriminatory tariffs offered under multilateral agreements. On the other hand, many countries discriminate across trading partners by imposing *higher* levels of import protection—ie, antidumping import restrictions designed to limit the market access of particular trading partners, including new entrants such as China. Answering the second part of this question is much more difficult.

Question 5: How liberalized is world trade?

In historical context, the answer is probably a lot relative to previous eras. However, it is much less liberalized than many economists probably realize, especially when taking into account border barriers beyond tariffs. Finally, very little is known about how "liberalized" world trade is once we expand the analysis and consider potential trade-restricting effects of behind-the-border policies.

In our attempts to answer these five questions, three important themes emerge.

First, trade is restricted through the use of many different policy tools. The fundamental dichotomy in the lexicon of import policies has been between price-based measures (import tariffs) and quantity-based measures (quotas). However, a variety of specialized categories have arisen within these broad classes. The development of trade agreements has played an important role in both constraining access to certain policies, and yet also making other policies more readily available under certain types of legal-economic conditions. The result is an extensive variety of policies in use at any moment in time. Moreover, across countries and sectors, the trade regime can exhibit extensive heterogeneity in the level of restrictiveness. Including all border policy barriers is thus likely to be important; for example, in their major contribution to estimating the *combined* restrictiveness of various trade policies using data from the late 1990s and early 2000s, Kee et al. (2009) conclude that restrictiveness measures that include nontariff barriers are 87% higher on average than measures based on tariffs alone.

A second emerging theme is that history tends to repeat itself. While some of the most popular forms of border policies have changed over the decades since World War II, some of the same sectors remain protected or have repeated episodes of protection. Furthermore, the circumstances in which countries raise their barriers to trade resurface time and again.

The third theme is that the reduction of traditional border barriers and integration of economic activity, even though arguably incomplete, has opened up new areas of policy conflict that are expected to grow in importance. Bilateral frictions between trading partners have moved beyond tariffs and quotas to the international externalities associated with domestic policies—ie, domestic tax and subsidy regimes, health and safety standards for products, as well as labor and environmental regulations. In order to survey the empirical landscape of these "behind-the-border" policies that potentially restrict trade, we use case studies to highlight important themes. Partly because of the lack of internationally comparable data on domestic policies, rigorous empirical work in this area is very thin. While this area is of increasing importance, the literature is unsettled as to the positive and normative understanding of the extent to which regulatory policies unduly inhibit trade and what, if anything, trade agreements could or should do about it.

As we catalogue and describe what is known about trade policy in 2013 and 2014— the most recent years for which we observe near-complete data reporting—one objective is to correct the widely-held misunderstanding that trade is already free from policy impediments. Among academic economists, there remains considerable disagreement about the quantitative importance of different types of trade barriers. While firm-level studies infer that sizeable additional costs associated with *international* commerce relative to domestic commerce must exist,[d] an open question is whether these important trade costs are due to trade policy or to something else. Anderson and van Wincoop (2004), through a combination of direct observation and inferences from a gravity trade model, quantify the representative border-related trade costs for an industrialized country at 44% ad valorem and the representative transportation costs at 21%. In contrast, Hummels (2007, p. 136) suggests that the importance of policy barriers has been completely eclipsed by real transportation costs: "For the median individual shipment in US imports in 2004, exporters paid $9 in transportation costs for every $1 they paid in tariff duties."

---

[d] For example, Bernard et al. (2007) and Eaton et al. (2011) have documented that only a small fraction of a country's manufacturing firms tend to engage internationally, with 18% of US firms exporting in 2002 and 15% of French firms exporting in 1986, respectively.

Although we are not be able to quantify the relative contributions of different forms of trade costs, we do hope to illustrate why many summary measures of trade policy are not appropriate for understanding the full economic importance of policy barriers to trade. Three simple examples help to illustrate the point. First, the real world consists of significant nontariff policy instruments; these include a number of border policies that, while *technically* applied as a tariff, are typically not captured in the reported data of "headline" measures of tariffs. Second, trade policy is commonly applied in a nonuniform manner across trading partners. Third, applied trade policy can vary considerably over time, especially in response to the business cycle, movements in the real exchange rate, or due to trade volume shocks; nevertheless, these policy changes are not made through applied ad valorem import tariffs, but via some other, less transparent, policy tool.

In the coming sections, we document that policy barriers to trade still exist; they vary considerably across products, trading partners and time; they take many forms; and they arise under legal frameworks (established by international trade agreements) that can result in subtle differences in both the frequency of their use and of their trade-reducing potential.

Section 2 begins by analyzing the focal policy of the trading system—the import tariff. This section examines different dimensions of tariff data for our sample of 31 economies to provide an initial response to each of our chapter's first four questions. We introduce the most-favored-nation (MFN) ad valorem import tariff—ie, the "headline" border policy instrument that countries impose under the WTO. While applied tariff levels are relatively low in historical terms, significant cross-country heterogeneity remains; furthermore, the negative correlation between applied tariffs and income per capita is even more pronounced once we consider the countries' "legal" commitments that are the upper limits for their tariffs. Next, we characterize cross-sectional variation in applied tariffs across sectors and inter-temporal variation across countries over 1993–2013. We then introduce which countries and sectors apply *specific*—or per unit—duties, and we describe what makes them distinct from ad valorem tariffs. Finally, we characterize the lower-than-MFN tariffs that countries apply under a variety of preferential trade arrangements. Because these allow countries to take on additional liberalization, we illustrate the extent to which countries apply tariffs so as to discriminate among trading partners.

In Section 3 we introduce the other major (nontariff) border barriers, and we use them to further inform our chapter's main themes.[e] Contemporary use of temporary

---

[e] One set of border policies that we do not directly address are export policies, and in particular export taxes or export quotas. Some discussion of export subsidies will arise in Section 5 by implication of our discussion of domestic subsidies, especially where they impact two exporting countries competing in a third market. On subsidies more generally, see Lee (2016). Export restrictions are of particular historical importance in global energy (oil, natural gas) and commodity food markets. For a discussion, see Ederington and Ruta (2016).

trade barrier policies—such as antidumping, safeguards, and countervailing duties—by emerging economies in particular has been increasing, and these import restrictions are characterized by both heterogeneity across economic sectors and discriminatory use against particular exporting country trading partners. We then turn to a description of other nontariff policies, such as quotas, price undertakings, voluntary export restraints, and other administrative hurdles (customs valuation and import licensing) that governments can manipulate to restrict trade at the border.

Once we have described the contemporary landscape of border policies, Section 4 examines the longer-term evolution of import tariffs and other border barriers in order to put the current system into better historical context. We start with information on the evolution of tariffs from the late 1940s through the late 1990s. Moreover, we provide a brief history of the ebb and flow in the use of a number of special import restrictions over this longer time horizon. This includes import restrictions to safeguard the balance of payments; the discriminatory treatment of Japan despite its GATT accession in 1955; the multifiber arrangement (MFA) and other voluntary export restraints; the sectoral carve out for agriculture; and special and differential treatment for developing countries. This section not only clarifies how the current landscape of trade policy arose, but it also allows us to emphasize our second theme of history frequently repeating itself, albeit through different policy tools, by different countries, or against different trading partners. Finally, this section helps provide a partial answer to our fifth question, "how liberalized is world trade?" In comparing the border barriers of today with the border barriers of the past, the current system is one that appears relatively open.

Section 5 then returns to the contemporary landscape by introducing a set of "behind-the-border" policies that have the ability to substantially impact international commerce. These include domestic subsidies and taxes, as well as standards and regulations. A comprehensive characterization of such data is notoriously difficult and fraught with measurement concerns; thus we survey case studies from recent policy conflicts in order to highlight important areas. Our survey covers roughly 10% of the population of formal trade disputes arising during the WTO's first 20 years. We conclude that the next major frontier for the world trading system involves how it confronts the trilemma of respecting local tastes and objectives in domestic policy, internalizing cross-border policy spillovers that operate through trade flows, and facilitating greater trade integration to sustainably maximize the value of the world's productive resources.

Finally, Section 6 concludes with a brief discussion of how our results may also inform other areas of research in international economics beyond studies of commercial policy.

2. IMPORT TARIFFS

The natural place to begin an empirical analysis of contemporary trade policy is with the import tariff, the most prevalently applied trade policy which is used under both multilateral trade agreements such as the GATT/WTO as well as under preferential trading arrangements (PTAs). This section uses tariffs to provide a first round of answers to each of our five major questions: Do some countries have lower tariffs than others? Within countries, which sectors receive the most tariff protection? How do tariffs change over time? Do countries set tariffs so as to discriminate among their trading partners? Finally, how liberalized are tariffs?

Much of our formal analysis in this section relies on cross-country and inter-temporal data comparisons where, for reasons of data quality, we do not attempt to be comprehensive. Instead, we focus on a sample of 31 economies listed in Table 1.[f] These major economies were not chosen randomly—they include the Group of 20 (G20) economies plus an additional set of developing countries each with 2013 populations of over 40 million. Collectively in 2013, these 31 economies represented 83% of the world's population, 91% of GDP, 80% of imports, and 79% of exports. Fig. 1 illustrates their geographic diversity.[g]

We begin in Section 2.1 by introducing and describing *ad valorem* import tariffs under the WTO. In the contemporary data, we find the tariffs that countries apply are relatively low on average. However, for many countries, these applied tariffs are substantially lower than the maximum tariffs allowed under the WTO, implying that trade is much less liberalized when viewed through the lens of the tariffs that countries are legally permitted to apply. There are also surprisingly large differences across countries in the average level of tariffs: high-income countries have more liberal trade regimes than middle income countries which, in turn, have more liberal regimes than low income countries. Across the board, countries tend to charge higher tariffs in the agricultural sector, in manufacturing industries such as textiles, apparel, and footwear, and in final goods relative to intermediate inputs. Finally, over the most recent 20 year period (1993–2013), we find a general downward trend in tariffs for many, but not all, countries. Furthermore, while applied tariffs for high-income countries exhibit little variation at the annual frequency over the period, there is slightly more variation for lower-income countries.

---

[f] Here and throughout we refer to economies and countries interchangeably even though we will generally rely on information about the European Union collectively as opposed to its member states individually. Since these countries have a common trade policy set by the European Commission, we treat them as one economy. The 28 member countries of the EU as of 2013 included Austria, Belgium, Bulgaria, Croatia, Republic of Cyprus, Czech Republic, Denmark, Estonia, Finland, France, Germany, Greece, Hungary, Ireland, Italy, Latvia, Lithuania, Luxembourg, Malta, Netherlands, Poland, Portugal, Romania, Slovakia, Slovenia, Spain, Sweden and the United kingdom.

[g] Sub-Saharan Africa is under-represented in the sample of 31 economies utilized in the empirical analysis. Nevertheless, the tariff characteristics for African countries more generally, and that we detail later, are well captured by the countries included in the analysis, and especially Democratic Republic of Congo, Ethiopia (a WTO nonmember), Kenya, Nigeria, and Tanzania. Bown (2015) provides additional descriptive analysis of the tariffs for developing countries, including African countries.

Table 1 MFN ad valorem import tariffs for selected economies, 2013

Country/ territory	MFN applied rate, simple average	WTO binding rate, simple average	Binding coverage	Coverage of applied duties >15%	Coverage of binding rates >15%	Maximum MFN applied rate
	(1)	(2)	(3)	(4)	(5)	(6)
G20[a] High income						
Australia	2.7	10.0	97.0	0.1	13.4	140.0
Canada	4.2	6.8	99.7	6.8	7.3	484.0
European Union	5.5	5.2	100.0	5.1	4.8	511.0
Japan	4.9	4.7	99.6	3.7	3.7	736.0
Korea	13.3	16.6	94.6	10.4	20.5	887.0
Saudi Arabia	4.8	11.2	100.0	0.2	1.1	298.0
United States	3.4	3.5	100.0	2.7	2.7	350.0
G20[a] Emerging						
Argentina	13.4	31.9	100.0	36.0	97.8	35.0
Brazil	13.5	31.4	100.0	36.2	96.4	55.0
China	9.9	10.0	100.0	15.6	16.4	65.0
India	13.5	48.6	74.4	19.0	71.5	150.0
Indonesia	6.9	37.1	96.6	1.7	90.7	150.0
Mexico	7.9	36.2	100.0	15.7	98.7	210.0
Russia	9.7	7.7	100.0	10.1	2.1	441.0
South Africa	7.6	19.0	96.1	20.7	39.6	>1000
Turkey	10.8	28.6	50.3	13.6	28.9	225.0
Developing, other[b]						
Bangladesh	13.9	169.2	15.5	41.2	15.1	25.0
Burma	5.6	84.1	17.8	5.0	14.6	40.0
Colombia	8.8	42.1	100.0	2.1	98.0	98.0
DR of the Congo (2010)	11.0	96.2	100.0	28.5	98.9	20.0
Egypt (2012)	16.8	36.9	99.3	19.2	70.7	>1000
Ethiopia[c] (2012)	17.3	—[d]	—[d]	50.8	—[d]	35.0
Iran[c] (2011)	26.6	—[d]	—[d]	45.7	—[d]	400.0
Kenya	12.7	95.1	14.8	41.4	14.8	100.0
Nigeria	11.7	118.3	19.1	39.0	19.1	35.0
Pakistan	13.5	60.0	98.7	36.0	94.9	100.0
Philippines	6.3	25.7	67.0	3.2	56.0	65.0
Tanzania	12.8	120.0	13.3	41.8	13.3	100.0

Continued

Table 1 MFN ad valorem import tariffs for selected economies, 2013—cont'd

Country/ territory	MFN applied rate, simple average	WTO binding rate, simple average	Binding coverage	Coverage of applied duties >15%	Coverage of binding rates >15%	Maximum MFN applied rate
	(1)	(2)	(3)	(4)	(5)	(6)
Thailand	11.4	27.8	75.0	25.5	66.0	226.0
Ukraine	4.5	5.8	100.0	2.7	3.8	59.0
Vietnam	9.5	11.5	100.0	24.8	27.7	135.0

Notes: Tariff data taken from WTO, 2014. World Tariff Profiles 2014. WTO, UNCTAD, and ITC, Geneva. Columns (1), (2), and (6) are ad valorem rates, and columns (3), (4), and (5) are shares of import products. Parentheses indicate data availability for year other than 2013.
[a]G20 = Group of 20.
[b]Selected other developing countries chosen as those with 2013 populations greater than 40 million.
[c]Indicates WTO nonmember.
[d]Indicates legal bindings not relevant for WTO nonmembers.

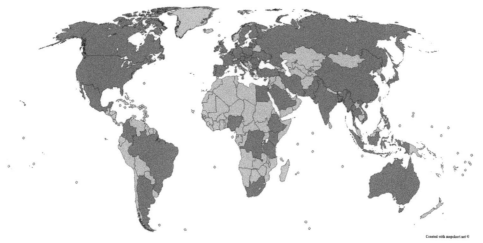

Fig. 1 Geographic coverage of the 31 economies in the empirical exercise.
Constructed by the authors. Dark gray countries are included in the empirical exercise.

In Section 2.2, we document the frequency with which countries apply specific duties, or per unit import tariffs, under the WTO. These sorts of tariffs arise disproportionately in a number of high and middle-income economies and are mostly limited to sectors such as agriculture, textiles and apparel, and footwear. We then motivate why it is important to consider specific duties distinctly from ad valorem tariffs. The ad valorem equivalent of a specific duty can vary—either over time or with respect to its discriminatory effect across trading partners—in ways that are distinctive from tariffs applied in ad valorem form.

Section 2.3 then examines the characteristics of the bilateral tariffs that countries charge under various preferential trading arrangements; this allows us to assess the extent to which countries apply tariffs which discriminate among trading partners. We find that countries vary considerably with respect to how many products are eligible for tariff preferences, how many preferences are offered, and how large tariff preference margins are. High-income countries have relatively few products on which they could offer preferential tariffs because so many of their tariffs are already set at zero. While high-income countries are rather generous in offering favorable treatment when possible, the resulting tariff preference margins that they can offer are nonetheless expectedly low. Lower income countries have more potential products over which they could offer preferences. However, because they offer preferences for fewer products and the preference margins are relatively high, trade diversion (Viner, 1950) associated with preferential tariffs is perhaps a more significant concern for lower income countries.

2.1 MFN (Most-Favored-Nation) Ad Valorem Import Tariffs Under the WTO

The WTO had 161 members as of 2015. This means that the WTO rules governing import restrictions apply to almost all countries that are engaged in international trade; indeed, 29 out of the 31 economies of Table 1 are WTO members. The vast majority of tariffs are applied in the *ad valorem* form that we describe in this section; the alternative is for the rate to be defined as a specific, or per unit, duty. As specific duties capture a few additional subtle distinctions, we introduce them separately below. Finally, and as we discover below in our analysis of tariffs under PTAs in Section 2.3, the applied ad valorem import tariff under the WTO is the border tax applied to an overwhelming share of traded products in the global system.

2.1.1 MFN Applied Rates, Tariff Bindings/Caps, and Binding Commitments

Are today's tariffs liberalized under the WTO? Furthermore, do some countries seem to have lower tariffs than others under the WTO? We examine these questions not only for applied tariffs, but also by describing the maximum tariffs that countries can *legally* apply under WTO rules. We begin by briefly introducing the basic WTO legal requirements associated with membership and defining some terminology.

Membership in the WTO requires that countries take on three main commitments with respect to their tariffs. First is the commitment that they apply the tariff at the same rate against imports from all other WTO members through the most-favored-nation (MFN) principle of nondiscrimination. Second, a WTO member chooses the set of products—up to 100% of products defined under the Harmonized System—over which it agrees to take on some legally binding commitment—a cap above which it promises not to raise its applied tariff. Third, for each of those products with some legally binding commitment, the member chooses an exact value for this upper limit. This upper limit is referred to as the "tariff binding" or "tariff cap." A country's MFN applied rate must therefore be less than or equal to the tariff binding in order to be legal under the WTO.[h] Finally, the difference between the tariff binding rate and the MFN applied rate is frequently referred to as the tariff binding "overhang" or alternatively, the "water" in the tariff binding.

The first column of Table 1 presents the simple average of the MFN applied ad valorem import tariff rate for our sample of major economies in 2013, only two of which were not members of the WTO.[i] The United States, for example, applied an MFN tariff to imports from other WTO members at a simple average rate across the roughly 5200 6-digit Harmonized System (HS06) products of 3.4% in 2013. Among the high-income G20 members, Australia had the lowest average MFN applied tariff (2.7%) and Korea had the highest (13.3%). The emerging economy members of the G20 tend to have slightly higher MFN applied import tariffs, ranging from Indonesia (6.9%) to India (13.5%). The other developing countries in the sample that were WTO members by 2013 had applied MFN tariffs that were even slightly higher than the typical G20 rates, ranging from an average of 5.6% (Burma) to 16.8% (Egypt). Finally, the WTO nonmember countries, such as Ethiopia and Iran, had average MFN applied rates that were substantially higher.[j]

[h] To summarize, the MFN commitment is a principle to which all WTO members must abide, subject to a number of well-defined exceptions that we describe later. On the other hand, WTO members establish their second (set of products with any cap) and third (level of the binding tariff) commitments individually. These second and third commitments have resulted from either decades of interaction with other WTO members under GATT negotiating rounds or the negotiated process of accession.

[i] More details on these data are described in Data Appendix. First, the applied tariffs are the tariffs that governments set, and the measure derives from policy data that either the government reports itself (to the WTO) or which are collected via official government publications by other international organizations; typically these are reported on an annual basis. Put differently, these measures of tariffs are *not* imputed from data on customs revenue collections. Furthermore, these applied tariff measures do *not* include other border charges or taxes, including safeguards tariffs and antidumping duties that we describe in Section 3.1. Second, throughout this analysis we only utilize simple average tariffs; the alternative of constructing trade-weighted average tariffs can lead to the well-known problem of downward bias due to products with high tariffs receiving low weights (because of small import volumes). The intuition is provided by the limiting example of a prohibitive tariff level which receives zero weight in the averaging calculation. Third, the calculations in Table 1 derive from data that does include consideration of ad valorem equivalent estimates for products over which the import tariff that the country applies is a specific duty. We describe data on the prevalence of import tariffs applied as specific duties in Section 2.2. In other areas of this chapter—such as when we wish to focus on changes in tariffs arising from *policy decisions*—we deliberately drop from consideration the products for which tariffs are applied as specific duties.

[j] We note that an MFN tariff is somewhat of a legally meaningless concept for countries such as Ethiopia and Iran as they are not WTO members and are thus not bound by the multilateral agreement. This similarly holds for the "MFN" tariffs (reported later) applied prior to GATT/WTO membership for countries that ultimately become members. An open research question is the extent to which countries impose tariffs on an MFN basis when they are not legally bound to do so. Furthermore, our use of the word "legal" to describe WTO tariff commitments refers to treaty obligations that countries voluntarily assume, as enforcement of WTO "law" is by the mutual agreement of all parties, as is described in greater detail elsewhere in this volume (Mavroidis, 2016).

Overall, applied ad valorem import tariffs exhibit substantial heterogeneity across countries. High-income economies apply much lower tariffs than middle income countries. Furthermore, poor countries apply tariffs that are even higher than the middle income countries.

The MFN tariff rates that countries apply are not necessarily the same as the tariffs that countries have legally committed to under the WTO as they can be lower. The third column in Table 1 lists the share of imported products over which the country has agreed to take on a tariff commitment. The United States, the EU, Saudi Arabia, Argentina, Brazil, China, Mexico, Russia, Democratic Republic of Congo, and Vietnam have agreed to bind tariffs for 100% of their imported products. For countries that have not agreed to bind all of their products at some upper limit, the remaining products have tariff upper limits that are "unbound," ie, potentially infinite. For example, India and Turkey have 25% and 50% of their imported products with MFN tariffs that are unbound, respectively.[k] Finally, the lower third of the table reveals that poorer countries like Bangladesh, Burma, Kenya, Nigeria and Tanzania have more than 80% of their imported products with tariffs that remain unbound.

The second column in Table 1 reveals that even for the economies that have agreed to bind the vast majority of their tariffs under the WTO, there is wide variation in the average upper limit that the country has agreed to take on. For example, while the first column identifies 14 different economies that *applied* their MFN tariffs at rates that average less than 10%, only Canada, China, the EU, Japan, Russia, Ukraine, and the United States have undertaken WTO legal commitments to *keep* those tariffs at an average of 10% or less. And while average applied and WTO binding rates are almost identical for China, the EU, Japan, Russia, and the United States, most emerging economies and developing countries have average WTO binding rates that are significantly higher than their average applied MFN rates.[l] Within the G20 emerging economies, the existence of this binding overhang is particularly prominent, as average bindings may be 2–5 times higher than applied rates. For other developing countries listed in Table 1, such as Bangladesh and Nigeria, the average binding commitment is more than 100 percentage points higher than the MFN applied rate in 2013.

---

[k] On the other hand, and as we introduce in Section 2.3, Turkey has a customs union with the European Union and thus its applied MFN tariffs are tied to the EU's applied tariffs. Thus, the fact that the EU has bound 100% of its tariffs may serve as a de facto anchor (in lieu of a WTO binding legal commitment) for Turkey as well.

[l] Average applied rates are higher than average binding rates for an economy like the European Union in Table 1 because of a combination of the procedure of averaging from product-level data and of the computation of ad valorem equivalents for products' rates applied as specific duties (in a given year, reflecting current prices) vs binding rates. For Russia, an additional contributor to the fact that its applied MFN rates were higher than its binding rates is likely due to its relatively recent WTO accession and it has not yet fully phased in all of its associated applied MFN tariff reductions.

Average import tariff bindings exhibit even more variation across countries than applied tariffs. High-income economies have comprehensive tariff binding coverage for their products, low legally binding tariff commitments, low applied rates, and little tariff overhang. Poorer countries have many more products with import tariffs that are unbound, and their binding tariff commitments are significantly higher than their applied rates. For middle income and poor countries under the WTO, although many are currently applying a fairly liberal tariff regime, they are not legally committed to maintaining this liberal regime under the WTO.

For countries with low tariffs on average, are tariffs set at universally low levels across products? The last three columns in Table 1 provide a summary answer to this question by reporting the share of products covered by tariffs of 15% or more, or "tariff peaks." For example, even though the United States has an applied MFN tariff that averages 3.4%, 2.7% of its imported products in 2013 faced MFN applied tariffs of 15% or more. The peak US tariff was 350%. Canada had nearly 7% of its imported products with tariffs of over 15%, with a peak rate of 484%. For emerging and developing countries, even larger shares of imported products are subject to these tariff peaks. Most every country has some sensitive products over which it retains very high tariffs.

We conclude this section with a brief discussion of our first broad finding, which is that there can be surprisingly large differences across countries in the average level of tariffs. Overall, both applied tariffs and tariff binding levels are negatively correlated with GDP per capita.

A first important research question is thus why tariffs are so much higher for lower income countries in particular. One long-standing explanation for why developing countries set higher tariffs is that collecting government revenue at the border may be more efficient administratively than other forms of taxation. For example, Keen (2008) reports import tariffs account for 20% or more of tax revenues in many developing countries, and Baunsgaard and Keen (2010) find that low-income countries undergoing trade reforms have been only partly successful (20–25%) at recovering lost tariff revenue by switching to other sources of taxation.[m] Country-level differences are likely explained not only by fiscal concerns, but also by the transparency of the country's government, its form of governance, and its responsiveness to public welfare (Gawande et al., 2006, 2009; Mitra et al., 2002).

---

[m] As a point of comparison, consider the importance of customs revenue in total fiscal revenue in the United States before the ratification of the 16th Amendment in 1913 which made constitutional the US federal income tax. Data from International Historical Statistics (Palgrave Macmillan, 2013) reports that customs revenue made up an average of 47% of total federal tax revenue collections during the decade of 1900–09. On the other hand, after both the income tax and the beginnings of the GATT tariff liberalization, customs revenue made up an average of less than 1% of US total federal tax revenue collections during the decade of 1950–59.

A second important research question involves the potential implications of lower-income country decisions to retain sizeable differences between binding and applied tariff rates. A nascent research literature suggests that such differences may affect a country's ability to reduce the sort of trade policy uncertainty that leads to inefficient levels of firm investment, output, and exporting (Handley and Limão, 2014, 2015; Handley, 2014; Crowley et al., 2016).

2.1.2 MFN Applied Tariffs Across Sectors

The second main question of our chapter asks if tariffs are set at different rates across sectors within countries. Here, we begin by inquiring whether there are some sectors that uniformly receive more import protection than others, and if there are patterns to this variation across countries.

Fig. 2 provides detail on the average applied MFN rates and legal bindings by industry for three groups of policy-imposing countries—the G20 high-income, the G20

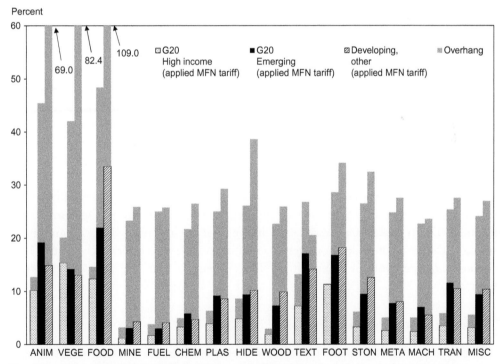

Fig. 2 Average applied MFN tariffs in 2013 and tariff bindings, by industry and country group. *Constructed by the authors from tariff data at the HS-06 level from the WTO and UNCTAD/TRAINS. Tariff "overhang" (or water) defined as the difference between the country's tariff binding legal commitment and its applied MFN rate. Country groupings based on Table 1.*

emerging, and the other developing countries as classified in Table 1. We break up the universe of imported goods in the Harmonized System into sixteen different sectors.[n]

The figure illustrates a number of relatively clear patterns to the cross-sectoral variation in applied tariff levels. First, high-income countries have lower average applied MFN tariffs than emerging economies and other developing countries almost universally across sectors; sector-by-sector, higher-income economies have lower tariffs than emerging economies which, in turn, have lower tariffs than poorer developing countries. Second, across country groupings, the average applied MFN tariffs are also typically higher in sectors such as agriculture (animals, vegetables, and foodstuffs), textiles and apparel, and footwear. Third, while the high-income economies have relatively little binding overhang in any sector, there is evidence of significant overhang for emerging and developing countries across all sectors. However, the greatest amount of overhang is in agriculture, suggesting that this is the sector in which emerging and developing economies have the greatest discretion to raise applied tariffs from 2013 levels while maintaining their WTO commitments.[o] For high-income economies in agriculture, we return to this issue in our discussion of specific duties and quantitative restrictions below.

Fig. 3 presents an alternative approach to the tariff data by examining the share of HS06 imported products within a sector for which the MFN applied rate is defined as being a tariff peak, or a tariff applied at or above the threshold level of 15%. For high-income economies, nearly 30% of products in the foodstuffs sector had an applied MFN tariff in 2013 of 15% or more. Similar peak tariffs can be found for high-income economies in 18% of products in the animal sector, 15% in footwear, 13% in vegetables, and 6% in textiles and apparel. The distribution of peak tariffs across sectors is quite similar for emerging and developing countries; it is simply that in emerging and developing countries the share of products within each sector that has such high tariffs is significantly larger. Nearly 70% of footwear products in developing countries had applied MFN tariffs at rates that are higher than 15% in 2013.

Recent empirical research has sought to explain aspects of the considerable cross-sectional variation in MFN applied tariffs and WTO tariff bindings. One important example is Broda et al. (2008), which exploits the variation in applied rates to assess implications of the terms-of-trade theory across a number of different empirical contexts. They examine tariff variation for a number of WTO *nonmember* countries and conclude that market power helps to explain applied tariffs for countries unconstrained by trade

---

[n] Industry classification is given in Table A.1.

[o] Some countries have used this flexibility to make relatively high frequency—eg, weekly and monthly—changes within years (and thus potentially not captured in the annual data) to applied MFN tariffs on agricultural products, perhaps in light of both political economy concerns and the uncertainty of yields due to weather-related shocks and growing seasons. Recent WTO disputes challenging such policies imposed by Chile and Peru are described in Bagwell and Sykes (2005a) and Saggi and Mark (2016), respectively. On agricultural tariffs more generally, see Hoekman et al. (2002, 2004).

Percent of
HS06 products

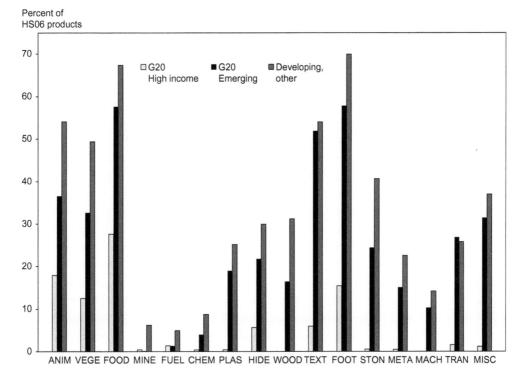

Fig. 3 Applied MFN tariff peaks in 2013, by industry and country group.
Constructed by the authors from tariff data at the HS-06 level from the WTO and UNCTAD/TRAINS. A tariff peak is defined as an HS-06 product with an applied MFN tariff greater than 15%. Country groupings based on Table 1.

agreements.[p] An alternative theoretical explanation for cross-sectoral variation in applied tariffs is political economy, for which the Grossman and Helpman (1994) structural model of lobbying and endogenous import protection provides a rich set of empirically testable predictions. However, much of the literature seeking to empirically test the Grossman–Helpman model has focused on the sector-level variation in *nontariff* policies—of the sort that we introduce and describe in Section 3.[q]

---

[p] Other research exploring the empirical relevance of the terms-of-trade theory for negotiated trade agreements using applied and bound tariffs includes Bagwell and Staiger (2011), Ludema and Mayda (2013), Nicita et al. (2014), and Beshkar et al. (2015). Bown (2015) provides both a survey of these papers and an empirical assessment of some of their implications for the applied and bound tariffs of developing countries.

[q] This literature is surveyed in McLaren (2016). Exceptions for research providing estimates of the Grossman–Helpman model on *tariff* policies include Mitra et al. (2002) for Turkey, Bown and Tovar (2011) for India, and Gawande et al. (2009) for a cross section of countries.

2.1.3 MFN Applied Tariffs Within Sectors by End-Use

Within sectors, do countries also apply different tariffs to products depending on what "consumers" use them for? Our next diagnostic maps HS06 products into two categories from the UN Broad Economic Categories (BEC): final goods (for consumption) and intermediate inputs.[r]

Fig. 4 provides some evidence of "tariff escalation"—ie, countries tend to apply higher import tariffs on final goods than they apply on intermediate inputs. The purpose may be to increase domestic value-added into production (and exports) or to affect inclusion in international supply chains. Overall, MFN applied tariffs on final goods average 70–75% higher for the G20 high income and emerging economies (and more than 90% higher for other developing countries) than the average MFN tariffs that those same countries apply to products classified as intermediate inputs. The evidence of tariff escalation is fairly strong across almost all sectors and country groups as average applied MFN tariffs on final goods are significantly higher than those on intermediate inputs.

Finally, we note the existence of one additional source of tariff discrimination within certain products— ie, intermediate inputs—that is contingent on the final geographic consumption location (domestic or foreign) of the ultimate final output. Consider the tariff rate on intermediate inputs in a country which uses a "dual import" or "duty drawback" tariff regime. Such regimes apply different MFN tariff rates for the same imported intermediate input (and from the same foreign source) depending on whether the ultimate *consumer* of the final processed good embodying that input is domestic or foreign. Under such regimes, imported inputs into a final product designated for export are allowed to enter the economy duty-free (or with the applied MFN tariff being refunded), whereas the same inputs face the normal MFN applied tariff if the input is used to produce a good that could be consumed domestically. With China arising as a prominent example of an export-led major economy that utilizes such a special import tariff system, researchers are increasingly studying the implications of this form of applied tariff discrimination.[s]

2.1.4 Changes to MFN Applied Tariffs Over Recent History

Our third major question involves whether governments make significant changes to their applied tariffs over time. Here, we examine the extent to which tariffs have changed

---

[r] For ease of exposition, we strip out BEC categories of "mixed use."

[s] A constraining feature of such regimes is that they must be designed so as to satisfy the WTO rules that limit export subsidies; for a discussion, see ITC (2009). Sometimes these systems are administered via a geographic area being designated as an export processing zone; in other instances, the regimes may not be constrained by geography but only by the willingness and ability of firms to comply with national legal requirements such as customs declarations. See Madani (1999) for an overview of export processing zones. Recent research analyzes the productivity implications of these dual tariff structures (Yu, 2015) or the implications for domestic factor demands (Brandt and Morrow, 2015).

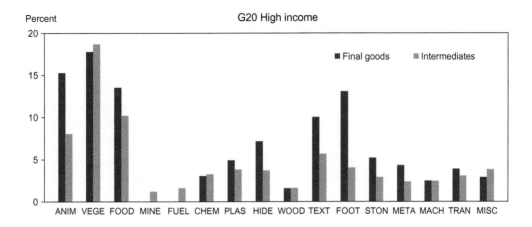

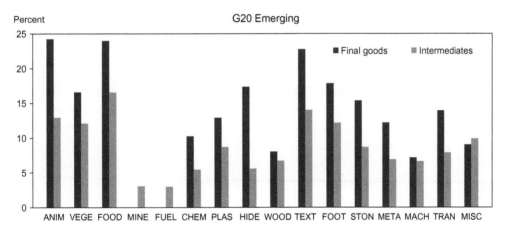

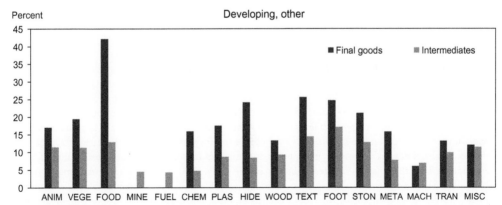

Fig. 4 Tariff escalation: Average applied MFN tariffs in 2013, by end use categories, industry and country group.
Constructed by the authors from tariff data at the HS-06 level from the WTO and UNCTAD/TRAINS. End use categories for each HS06 product taken from the BEC, with mixed use goods dropped. Country groupings based on Table 1.

over the most recent 20 year period, beginning with the ending of the GATT period through 2013.[t] We first examine changes arising as long differences before turning to higher frequency data.

Table 2 presents average applied MFN tariffs for our sample of countries for three key years chosen to reveal the impacts of important institutional milestones arising across three decades: 1993, 2003, and 2013.[u] The table also provides information on when (if ever) the country became a member of the GATT, as well as when (if ever) the country became a member of the WTO.

For countries that were members of the GATT, the 1993 data in Table 2 reflects their applied MFN GATT tariffs *before* they implemented any changes resulting from the Uruguay Round of negotiations that ushered in the WTO. By 2003, the countries that joined the WTO at its 1995 inception had phased in most of their Uruguay Round tariff liberalization commitments; thus a comparison of 1993 and 2003 for such countries provides a first-order assessment of the impact of the Uruguay Round on average applied MFN tariffs. For countries that acceded to the WTO somewhat later, comparisons of the tariff data can provide information on pre-WTO and post-WTO accession applied MFN tariffs.

Table 2 evidence on changes to applied MFN tariffs for the G20 high-income economies over this extended period is mixed. Long-standing GATT/WTO members such as the European Union, Japan and the United States already had relatively low MFN applied rates at the end of the GATT period in 1993 at 7.0%, 4.4%, and 5.6%, respectively. These economies cut their average applied tariffs by another 1–3 percentage points as a result of the Uruguay Round; and, given their low initial applied levels, low tariff bindings, and resulting lack of overhang (see again Table 1), applied MFN tariffs for these economies were virtually unchanged between 2003 and 2013. For Australia and Canada, average applied MFN tariff cuts over the 20 year period have been larger. Korea's average

---

[t] In Section 4 we address the question for tariffs over a longer period dating back to 1947 for a smaller selection of countries.

[u] We examine this particular period for two reasons. First, we are interested in the highest quality (across country) data on MFN applied tariffs for a consistent classification scheme, and the Harmonized System (HS) went into effect in 1988. Thus any attempts to assess changes in tariffs for a period before and after 1988 will have to confront serious concordance issues that will differ country-by-country, but which will make averaging or examining product level changes nontrivial. Second, despite the HS beginning in 1988, data for many countries in our sample does not become routinely available until the early 1990s. Nevertheless, picking 1993 as a common starting point does miss out on some countries' substantial tariff liberalization periods that may have already begun in the early 1990s (India), 1980s (Argentina, Brazil, Colombia, Mexico), or even earlier. Furthermore, applied MFN tariff data is not available for all countries in all years in the sample. Finally, the data for 2013 in Table 2 may differ from Table 1 as we are now limiting our consideration of products to which the tariff is applied on an ad valorem basis, so as to focus on policy changes and not changes in ad valorem equivalent rates that may arise for specific duties due to changes in underlying prices.

Table 2 Average applied MFN ad valorem import tariffs for selected economies: 1993, 2003, and 2013

	GATT membership year	WTO membership year	Simple average applied MFN tariff for		
			1993	2003	2013
G20 High income					
Australia	1948	1995	8.8	4.2	2.7
Canada	1948	1995	9.0	5.1	3.7
European Union	—[a]	1995	7.0	4.4	4.4
Japan	1955	1995	4.4	3.2	3.0
Korea	1967	1995	11.7[b]	11.6	12.2
Saudi Arabia	NM	2005	12.1[b]	6.0	4.6
United States	1948	1995	5.6	3.7	3.5
G20 Emerging					
Argentina	1967	1995	11.2	14.2	13.4
Brazil	1948	1995	14.0	13.5	13.5
China	NM	2001	39.1	11.4	9.6[b]
India	1948	1995	56.3[b]	26.5	13.3
Indonesia	1950	1995	17.9	6.9	6.7
Mexico	1986	1995	13.7[b]	18.0	7.7[b]
Russia	NM	2012	7.8	10.7[b]	8.9
South Africa	1948	1995	16.0	5.6	7.4
Turkey	1951	1995	9.3	10.0	10.8
Developing, other					
Bangladesh	1972	1995	82.8[b]	19.5	14.0
Burma	1948	1995	–	5.5	5.6[b]
Colombia	1981	1995	12.3[b]	12.3	6.8
DR of the Congo	NM	1997	–	12.0	11.0[b]
Egypt	1970	1995	34.6[b]	26.9	16.8[b]
Ethiopia	NM	NM	28.9[b]	18.8[b]	17.3[b]
Iran	NM	NM	–	27.3	26.6[b]
Kenya	1964	1995	35.2[b]	15.2[b]	12.8
Nigeria	1960	1995	34.4[b]	28.6	11.7
Pakistan	1948	1995	50.8[b]	17.1	13.5
Philippines	1979	1995	22.9	4.7	6.3
Tanzania	1961	1995	20.3	13.6	12.8
Thailand	1982	1995	45.7	15.4	10.4
Ukraine	NM	2008	7.0[b]	7.0[b]	4.5
Vietnam	NM	2007	14.1[b]	16.8	9.4

Constructed by the authors with applied ad valorem duties data at the HS06 level taken from WTO and UNCTAD/ TRAINS. For the purposes of this table, ad valorem equivalent rates of tariffs applied as specific duties are omitted from the calculations. G20 = Group of 20. NM indicates GATT or WTO nonmember.
[a]Different European Union member states became GATT Contracting Parties in different years.
[b]Data for that year not available and so chosen as the closest available year.

applied MFN import tariff is actually higher in 2013 than it was in 1993. Finally, Saudi Arabia's tariff by 2013 is roughly one third of its 1993 level, which largely reflects the commitments it undertook as part of its 2005 WTO accession.

Table 2 reveals even more heterogeneity in the changes in average MFN applied tariffs across the G20 emerging economies taking place between 1993 and 2013. China and India began the early 1990s with extremely high applied tariffs that still averaged 56.3% and 39.1%, respectively. These countries subsequently underwent tariff liberalization reforms; by 2013, their MFN applied rates has been reduced to only 9.6 and 13.3%, on average. Indonesia, Mexico, and South Africa also had much lower applied MFN tariffs in 2013 relative to 1993. On the other hand, Argentina, Brazil, and Turkey began the period with mid-range applied MFN tariffs that have not changed much since. Finally, while Russia's applied MFN import tariffs were also mostly unchanged over these decades, Russia entered the WTO in 2012 and bound 100% of its tariffs at relatively low rates (see again Table 1, column 2); some of its applied tariff reductions are thus still being phased in.

Finally, the lower third of Table 2 indicates that the sample of developing countries has, for the most part, engaged in a general period of tariff liberalization over these 20 years. For all of the countries with available data, applied MFN tariffs in 2013 were significantly lower than they were in 1993. A number of these developing countries cut their average applied MFN tariffs by 20 percentage points or more from their levels in the early 1990s, when the average applied MFN tariff for Nigeria was 34.4%, for Kenya was 35.2%, for Thailand was 45.7%, for Pakistan was 50.8%, and for Bangladesh was 82.8%.

While the data in Table 2 suggest that tariffs were generally lower (or at least not much higher) in 2013 relative to 1993 for most of these 31 economies, our next investigation involves the inter-temporal path of this liberalization. In the higher frequency data, does liberalization appear to take place gradually, or were tariff cuts implemented in large increments? Whether continuous or discrete, was the liberalization a continual down-ward process or were there significant fluctuations so that tariffs fell initially, then increased (as policies were reversed), before falling again?

Fig. 5 plots the year-to-year change in the level of average applied MFN tariff rates across the three country groups over the WTO period of 1996–2013.[v] The annual changes for the United States, for example, are visually indistinguishable from zero during this period. In 1995, the United States began with extremely low applied MFN tariffs, applied MFN tariffs declined by an average of only 0.3 percentage points each in 1996, 1997, 1998, and 1999 as the United States implemented its Uruguay Round commit-ments, and there is little annual change to the US average applied MFN tariff after 2000. The same basic pattern holds for Australia, Canada, the EU and Japan. Korea is

---

[v] Again, in any given year, data for an entire country may be missing; in such cases the years that rely on such data are not plotted in the figure. To the extent that there are missing data in years that countries make substantial tariff changes, Fig. 5 would understate the extent of inter-temporal variation in applied tariffs.

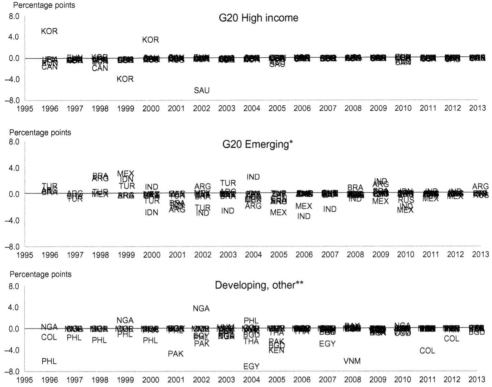

Fig. 5 Annual changes in average applied MFN tariffs 1996–2013, by country group.
Constructed by the authors as the annual difference in the simple average MFN applied tariffs, with tariff data taken from WTO and UNCTAD/TRAINS. Data not comprehensively available for this period: missing are data for 6% of annual observations for high-income economies, 25% of observations for emerging economies, and 40% of observations for developing countries. For ease of exposition, not shown are known outliers defined as annual changes greater than (in absolute value) 8 percentage points. *One outlier is India (−10.8 percentage points in 2005). **A second outlier is Pakistan (−22.0 percentage points in 1999).

the main high-income country exception during this period; its average applied MFN tariff increased by 5.2 percentage points in 1996 immediately preceding the Asian Financial Crisis, declined by 3.9 percentage points in 1999, increased by 3.5 percentage points in 2000, and only since has remained relatively stable, albeit at a high (relative to the other high-income G20 economies) average level.

For G20 emerging and other developing economies, Fig. 5 indicates more variation in the annual changes in average applied MFN tariffs. For example, the average applied MFN tariffs in Argentina and Brazil increased by 2.4 and 2.8 percentage points, respectively, in 1998, in part to address a recession associated with the contagion of the Asian Financial Crisis that had spread to Brazil. Argentina and Brazil then cut those tariffs by an average of 2.3 and 1.4 percentage points, respectively, in 2001, in the lead-up to

Argentina's abandonment of its fixed exchange rate regime and default in 2002. Turkey similarly had fluctuations in its average applied MFN tariff that were greater than 1 percentage point per year for 4 out of 5 years during 1999–2003 in the face of its own financial crisis. Of all of the major emerging economies, however, India had the greatest year-to-year fluctuations during this period. In 10 out of the 11 years between 2000 and 2010 India's average applied MFN tariffs changed by at least 1 percentage point—in some years it increased and in others it fell. For the other developing countries presented in the lower panel of Fig. 5, there is evidence of more variation in applied tariffs; nevertheless, the largest annual changes are primarily episodes of tariff cuts, some of which were associated with WTO accession (eg, Vietnam in 2008). While there is more variation in the higher frequency data for lower income countries compared to high-income countries, it is safe to conclude that there is not widespread evidence of frequent and large annual fluctuations in applied MFN tariffs taking place during this period for these countries under the WTO.

To summarize this section, overall, there is much more heterogeneity across countries as to the *changes* to their levels of average applied MFN tariffs that took place between 1993 and 2013. Interestingly, there is even substantial heterogeneity across countries within a given level of economic development, especially for the middle income countries. This is suggestive of the strong influence of country-specific factors affecting the timing of major changes to applied tariffs during these 20 years. Second, in most of these major economies, there were not large changes in average applied MFN tariffs on an annual basis during this period. There have been a few exceptions; many of the instances in which there was a sizeable *increase* can be tied to particularly acute economic crisis, and some instances in which there was a sizeable *decrease* can be tied to the timing of a country's applied tariff cuts to abide by WTO accession commitments.

In the remainder of this section, we briefly describe three different strands of the formal research literature examining patterns in the intertemporal changes in applied MFN tariffs.

The first strand examines the role of economy-wide shocks on government decisions to change the level of a country's import protection. Dating back to at least the Great Depression in the 1930s, there is a presumption that macroeconomic shocks can have significant effects on trade policy. Indeed, Irwin (2012) attributes much of the protectionism arising after the onset of the Great Depression to the inflexibility of exchange rates due to the gold standard; sharp real exchange rate appreciations that decrease the relative price of imports across the board may intensify import competition facing domestic producers and increase demands to raise applied tariffs.[w]

---

[w] There is also an historical literature, likely motivated by the 1929 stock-market crash and the US imposition of the Smoot–Hawley tariffs in 1930 (see also Irwin, 2011), that US tariffs are countercyclical (Bohara and Kaempfer, 1991; Cassing et al., 1986) and rise following periods of recession (negative or weak real GDP growth, increases in unemployment), high inflation, etc.

One potentially surprising outcome arising from Fig. 5, however, involves the Great Recession period of 2008–09. The evidence from this figure is that there was not a significant increase in average applied tariffs, despite the massive and simultaneous macroeconomic contraction that took place globally. Research that has begun to examine changes in applied MFN tariffs during the 2008–09 crisis includes Kee et al. (2013), Rose (2013), Gawande et al. (2015), and Foletti et al. (2011). Nevertheless, the fact that applied MFN tariffs did not increase significantly during the Great Recession does not necessarily imply that import protection overall is no longer sensitive to macroeconomic fluctuations. The "success" of WTO disciplines on tariff bindings in particular may have pushed countries to increase import protection during this period through other trade policy instruments, such as those that we introduce below in Section 3.1.[x]

A second strand examines the role of PTAs on changes to applied MFN tariffs, and whether preferential tariff liberalization serves as a "stumbling block" or a "building block" to future MFN applied tariff cuts (Bhagwati, 1991). Many of the PTAs described later in Section 2.3 also motivate 1993–2013 as being a useful period to study this question.

The evidence thus far of the impact of preferential tariff cuts on applied MFN tariff cuts has been mixed. Limão (2006) and Karacaovali and Limão (2008) examine the PTAs in effect as of the mid-1990s for the United States and European Union, respectively, and find stumbling block evidence that they significantly limited the MFN tariff cutting arising under the Uruguay Round. On the other hand, Estevadordal et al. (2008) present building block evidence from a set of Latin American countries that cut tariffs preferentially via free trade agreements in the 1990s and followed those up by then reducing their applied MFN tariffs.[y]

A third strand seeks to utilize any (plausibly) *exogenous* episodes of MFN applied tariff liberalization so as to exploit the unexpected nature of the shock. One episode worth highlighting is India's unilateral liberalization of the early 1990s (see again Table 2), which is an environment that has turned out to be a useful laboratory for conducting this sort of research.

---

[x] To foreshadow our discussion later, Bown and Crowley (2013a, 2014) consider the time-varying constraints on a country's applied MFN tariffs imposed by WTO tariff binding commitments as a contributing factor behind the substitution toward use of other trade policies in response to aggregate-level fluctuations, including during the 2008–09 crisis. On the other hand, another contributing explanation for the lack of responsiveness of import protection to macroeconomic shocks may be the lack of theoretical guidance for estimation, as there is not a robust theoretical literature linking business cycles and import protection. An exception is Bagwell and Staiger (2003).

[y] See also Limão (2007) for a theoretical motivation for the US results, as well as additional empirical evidence from the ASEAN Free Trade Agreement (described later) from Calvo-Pardo et al. (2011) and the Central American Free Trade Agreement-Dominican Republic (CAFTA-DR) from Tovar (2012).

Topalova and Khandelwal (2011) have examined the environment and empirically established that the MFN tariffs that India applied during the late 1990s were unrelated to standard political-economy determinants of its trade policy.[z] This important empirical result established India's IMF-mandated tariff cuts associated with its 1991–92 macroeconomic crisis and stand-alone agreement as an environment suited to assess a number of important research questions related to the impact of globalization on incentives and micro-level economic activity.[aa]

2.2 MFN Specific Duties Under the WTO

While the vast majority of import tariffs are applied as ad valorem duties, there are a number of important instances in which countries apply trade policy through specific, or per-unit duties. We first document the countries and sectors in which such duties continue to be applied. We then explore how a country's decision to apply an import tariff as a specific duty instead of an ad valorem duty can also affect our answers to questions regarding how the restrictiveness of an import tariff *changes* over time and whether a country's tariff discriminates *between* trading partners.[ab]

First consider countries' applied MFN tariffs imposed as specific duties. While the WTO (2014) reports that in most countries the share of product lines with non-ad valorem tariffs is zero, a number of major economies constitute sizeable exceptions. Fig. 6 reveals that specific duties remained a significant part of the applied MFN tariff policy arsenal in 2013 for many of the 31 major economies in our sample. Indeed, Russia had more than 11% of its product lines set as specific duties in 2013; Thailand, the United States, the EU, and India also apply specific duties to 5% or more of their imported products.[ac]

---

[z]   Bown and Tovar (2011) use an alternative approach and find supporting evidence of this result by showing how India's applied MFN tariffs set in 1990 are consistent with the structural framework of the Grossman and Helpman (1994) model, but that the MFN applied tariffs in 2000–02 then become inconsistent with the model.

[aa]   The Indian empirical environment in the 1990s has been used to study the impact of globalization on schooling and human capital acquisition (Edmonds et al., 2010), firm productivity (Krishna and Mitra, 1998; Topalova and Khandelwal, 2011), use of intermediate inputs (Goldberg et al., 2010a) product switching (Goldberg et al., 2010b), and customs evasion (Mishra et al., 2008), amongst others. Much of this literature is reviewed in detail in Goldberg and Pavcnik (2016).

[ab]   We do not analyze computed *levels* of ad valorem equivalent estimates (AVEs) of the specific duties described here because the AVEs would be time varying for reasons unrelated to changes in policy. UNCTAD (via TRAINS) frequently provides ad valorem equivalent estimates for products with MFN tariffs applied as specific duties, using a number of different methodologies. These have been made freely available from the World Bank via the World Integrated Trade Solution (WITS) web-based software platform.

[ac]   Of the WTO member countries not included in our sample, Switzerland is the only one with a higher share of imported products subject to specific duties than Russia in 2013, at 78.3%. Belarus and Kazakhstan have a customs union with Russia and thus roughly the same share of products subject to specific duties. Other countries with shares larger than 5% of imported products not shown in Fig. 6 include Norway (7.8), Zimbabwe (6.4), Uzbekistan (5.8), and Israel (5.0).

Percent of
HS06 products

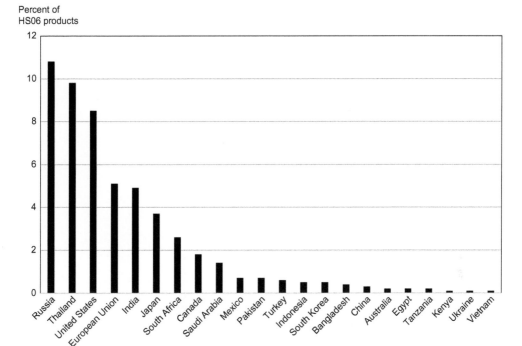

Fig. 6 Import products with MFN tariffs applied as specific duties in 2013, by country.
Constructed by the authors from WTO, 2014. World Tariff Profiles 2014. Geneva, WTO, UNCTAD, and ITC. Includes 31 economies from sample of Table 1; the remaining nine countries from Table 1 each had zero HS06 products with MFN tariffs applied as specific duties in 2013.

Fig. 7 further identifies the sectoral distribution of MFN tariffs applied as specific duties across our three country groupings. For the high-income economies, specific duties are overwhelmingly found in agriculture—more than 10% of animal products, more than 15% of vegetables, and nearly 25% of foodstuffs report MFN tariffs being applied as specific duties. A smaller, though still nontrivial, incidence of specific duties is found in sectors such as footwear, textiles and clothing, and fuel. For the United States, MFN tariffs are applied as specific duties for nearly 50% of vegetables and foodstuffs, 27% of animal products, 10% of minerals, 16% of fuels, 9% of textiles and apparel, 21% of footwear, and 18% of miscellaneous products.

Second, and as we further describe in Section 3, MFN applied tariffs are not the only instrument of trade policy in which specific duties are found to arise; they are also a somewhat common outcome of temporary trade barrier investigations. In some instances, a newly imposed antidumping or safeguard restriction may result in a new and additional specific duty, even though the benchmark trade policy had been applied as an ad valorem import duty.

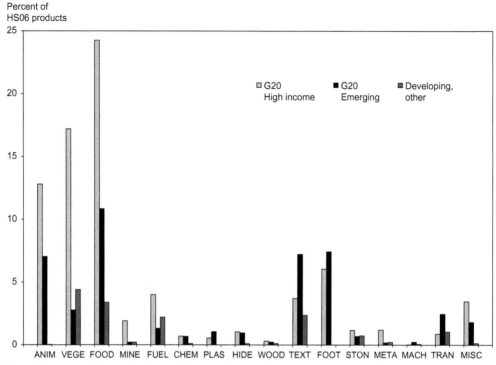

Percent of
HS06 products

Fig. 7 Import products with MFN tariffs applied as specific duties in 2013, by industry and country group. *Constructed by the authors from tariff data at the HS-06 level from the WTO and UNCTAD/TRAINS. Country groupings based on Table 1 and includes all countries, even those revealed in Fig. 6 as having zero MFN tariffs applied as specific duties.*

An open research question is what explains the cross-country and sectoral variation in MFN tariffs applied as specific duties, and in particular, the relatively high incidence in agriculture, textiles and clothing, and footwear in high-income economies. Given that the US applied specific duties much more prevalently across products during the pre-GATT period (Irwin, 1998a,b), this may be equivalent to asking why specific duties applied in the 1940s in these sectors were less likely (than those applied in other sectors) to be converted to ad valorem rates.[ad]

[ad] An approach structured similar to Ludema and Mayda (2013) may provide a partial explanation. The Ludema–Mayda result is that high import tariffs in certain sectors (eg, agriculture, textiles and apparel, and footwear, see again Fig. 2) can be linked to diffuse exporting interests in the rest of the world; the implication is that the lack of exporter concentration has led to fewer demands under GATT negotiating rounds that importers lower their tariffs. With respect to an explanation for the pattern of specific duties, perhaps the free rider problem not only resulted in these sectors maintaining high levels of applied tariffs, but it also meant that negotiators never got around to bargaining to convert the form of the policy from a specific duty to an ad valorem rate.

We conclude with a brief discussion of reasons why the existence of specific duties remains important, especially for two of the thematic questions of our chapter.[ae]

The first involves the role of prices and *changes* in the trade-restrictiveness of different forms of tariffs—ie, ad valorem vs specific rates—even when policymakers do not make changes to their applied levels. The US experience with the Smoot–Hawley tariffs of 1930 over the period of the Great Depression demonstrates the changes that can occur with specific duties. Because many Smoot–Hawley tariffs were specific duties, their trade-restrictiveness *increased* over the 1930s in the face of deflation and falling domestic prices. Conversely, the high ad valorem equivalent rate of these specific duties in the early 1940s implies that much of the subsequent tariff "liberalization" of US import markets during the 1940s arose not because of particular policy decisions to cut tariffs, but simply because inflation increased, thereby reducing the ad valorem equivalent of the imposed specific duty (Crucini, 1994; Irwin, 1998a,b).

Fig. 7 suggests that, for high-income economies and agricultural markets, the trade restrictiveness of tariffs imposed as specific duties will increase during deflationary periods, which is (not coincidentally) when the sector is more likely to be injured and seeking additional protection from import competition. This suggests a potential explanation for the puzzling existence of particularly large amounts of binding overhang for agricultural goods in the developing and emerging economies (see again Fig. 2) that apply tariffs as ad valorem duties in agricultural products. Unlike high-income countries with specific duties, the *form* of the applied tariffs in lower income countries implies that they do not have a natural buffer against negative world price shocks.

Second, specific duties implicitly discriminate between trading partners (in ways that an ad valorem tariff would not) without violating the MFN rule when there are heterogeneous varieties of differentiated products included in the same tariff code. Consider, for example, two varieties of shoes from two different countries that fall within the same product category and which therefore face the same applied MFN tariff rate. Suppose those two varieties of shoes have different prices because of quality differences (Schott, 2004). The ad valorem equivalent of a $2 specific duty on a $10 pair of shoes (say, from China, Indonesia, or Vietnam) is 20%, whereas the ad valorem equivalent on a $100 pair of shoes (say, from Italy) is only 2%. While the ad valorem equivalent of an MFN-consistent specific duty is clearly discriminatory across trading partners, it is permissible under the WTO.[af]

[ae] A final issue that we do not address here is that the application of a specific duty and ad valorem duty can differ in their efficiency as a form of taxation. This is particularly the case under different market structures, as has been discussed in the public finance literature (Delipalla and Keen, 1992 and Keen, 1998).

[af] The use of specific duties at the conclusion of "safeguard" investigations—see Section 3.1—is particularly noteworthy because this policy was designed by the WTO Agreements to be less discriminatory than other policy tools, like antidumping. In practice, the use of safeguards is a politically useful way for governments to discriminate between foreign suppliers, such as against varieties from a low-priced trading partner while minimizing the impact on a high-priced trading partner. See, for example, Turkey's safeguards on imports of footwear described in Bown et al. (2015).

2.3 Ad Valorem Import Tariffs Under Preferential Trading Arrangements

Lower tariffs can create trade, but when a country offers lower tariffs preferentially and selectively so as to discriminate between trading partners, the result can also be a distortion of trade. Here, we provide an investigation into our fourth thematic question: when setting tariffs, do countries discriminate in important ways across their trading partners?

This question is both important and difficult to answer. First, the number of preferential trading arrangements (PTAs) in existence has exploded since the early 1990s; yet, as we established in Section 2.1.4, this period also coincides with a broad decline in applied MFN tariffs for many countries. Second, the WTO (2011) has found that the share of intra-PTA trade in world trade has nearly doubled from 18% in 1990 to 35% in 2008; including intra-EU trade in these calculations leads to an increase from 28% in 1990 to 51% in 2008. Yet, in a detailed study of PTAs involving 85 countries and 90% of world trade in 2007 that matches bilateral imports to tariffs at the product level, the WTO (2011) also reports that only 16% of global trade was eligible for any preferential tariffs (30% if intra-EU trade is included). Put differently, this would imply that 84% (70%) of world merchandise trade was still taking place on an MFN basis. How can this seeming contradiction between the rise of PTAs, the rise of intra-PTA trade, and yet the continued importance of MFN tariffs, be reconciled?

We begin in Section 2.3.1 by defining and then introducing the different forms of PTAs that have arisen across the trading system. The many different arrangements that countries use to implement a lower tariff toward a particular trading partner—arrangements which comply with basic GATT/WTO exceptions to the MFN principle of nondiscrimination—include free trade agreements, customs unions, unilateral preference schemes, and the lesser-known partial scope agreements.[ag]

Section 2.3.2 provides more detail on the potential economic significance of tariff preferences arising under these PTAs. We begin by characterizing the scope of products for which countries can and do offer tariff preferences (given their MFN tariffs), the size of the discriminatory preference margins that are granted, and the trading partners to which they are being offered. Our product-level bilateral tariff preference data is sufficiently rich that we can examine the bilateral tariff rates offered by 27 of our economies to the 30 trading partners in our sample.[ah]

While we document considerable variation across countries, a number of interesting patterns emerge. First, high-income countries, which generally have very low MFN

[ag] These exceptions include the original GATT 1947's Article XXIV and the 1979 "Enabling Clause" that permits nonreciprocal and noncomprehensive preferential tariff coverage for developing countries involved in PTAs.

[ah] Bilateral tariff data is not available for four of the countries in our analysis. Furthermore, for tractability, we restrict the analysis to variation across 30 trading partners. This obviously misses additional variation associated with other trading partners.

tariffs, have relatively fewer products over which they can offer any preferential tariffs. These countries tend to offer preferential treatment to *many* trading partners where they can; however, their tariff preference margins are typically quite small because their applied MFN tariffs are already so low. On the other hand, lower income countries have many more products for which they could offer preferential tariffs, and yet the patterns to their offerings are much different. Developing countries do sometimes offer lower tariffs; the main distinction is that their offerings are much more limited—to fewer selected partners and/or over fewer selected products. Not surprisingly, for the products in which developing countries do offer lower-than-MFN tariffs to someone, the tariff preference margin can actually turn out to be quite high. Finally, we document patterns in the *recipients* of these tariff preferences. Developing country exporters are the most frequent recipients. Whether high-income country exporters receive lower-than-MFN tariffs varies widely across preference-offering countries; nevertheless, there are many fewer examples of lower-income countries granting tariff preferences to high-income countries.

Finally, in Section 2.3.3 we detail the tariff preferences offered by one country in particular. We utilize the United States to highlight additional margins along which countries can be shown to discriminate with respect to their applied preferential tariff policies.

2.3.1 Major Economies and Their Preferential Trading Arrangements

We begin with a brief definition of each of the four major types of PTAs. A free trade agreement is typically a reciprocal agreement in which two or more countries offer zero tariffs to one another for virtually all products. A customs union is an FTA with the additional feature that the members of the FTA have a common external trade policy, including a commonly applied MFN tariff, on imports from all nonmembers. Unilateral preferences are an arrangement whereby one country—typically a high-income country—offers lower-than-MFN tariffs to one or more developing countries for a selection of imported products. A partial scope agreement is an arrangement whereby two or more developing countries offer one another lower-than-MFN tariffs for a selection of imported products. For these last two forms of PTAs, in practice, the selection can be much less than 100% of products.

As of 2015, more than 250 regional trade agreements (free trade agreements, customs unions, partial scope agreements) covering international trade in goods were in force (WTO, 2015c); additionally, WTO members were offering nearly 30 different unilateral preference programs (WTO, 2015a).[ai]

[ai] Given that multiple agreements or preference schemes frequently apply to the same bilateral tariff relationship for a given product, it is difficult to interpret the economic meaning of the raw number of agreements or programs in effect. For example, within the regional trade agreement figures, Thailand is part of the original ASEAN agreement; ASEAN has an FTA with Australia, and Thailand has its own bilateral FTA with Australia. A separate example of redundancy in unilateral programs is some preference-offering countries make exporters from a certain country eligible for multiple unilateral schemes.

Table 3 lists a number of prominent examples of different types of PTAs between countries in our 31 economy sample. The most common form of preferential arrangement is a free trade agreement (FTA). The United States is involved in a number of FTAs, including NAFTA (with Canada and Mexico), and bilateral FTAs with Australia, Colombia, and Korea. The European Union with its 28 member countries is an example of a customs union. The EU also has a separate customs union with Turkey (sharing a common external MFN tariff toward third countries), and the EU has a number of FTAs (not customs unions) with other countries including Colombia, Egypt, Korea, Mexico, and South Africa.

Groups of developing and emerging economies have also formed FTAs or customs unions between themselves— ie, without involvement of high-income economies. The Southern Common Market (MERCOSUR) is a customs union between Argentina, Brazil, Paraguay and Uruguay. A prominent example of a primarily developing economy FTA is the Association of Southeast Asian Nations (ASEAN) which involves Brunei, Burma, Cambodia, Indonesia, Laos, Malaysia, Philippines, Singapore, Thailand, and Vietnam. ASEAN has also negotiated FTAs with Japan, Australia, China, India and Korea through what are frequently referred to as "hub and spoke" agreements— eg, Japan, China, and Korea each had a bilateral FTA with ASEAN but they did not (as of 2015) have separate free trade agreements in force with each other.[aj] Furthermore, the East African Community is a customs union between Burundi, Kenya, Rwanda, Tanzania, and Uganda. The Common Market for Eastern and Southern Africa (COMESA) is an FTA between 19 countries in Africa (including DR Congo, Egypt, Ethiopia and Kenya) that launched a customs union in 2009.

Partial scope arrangements (PSAs) are the least common form of PTA and they have arisen among low- and middle-income economies. A country involved in a PSA typically submits a list of products—ranging from a few dozen to a few hundred—over which it offers preferential tariffs to all other signatories to the agreement. One example of a partial scope agreement is the Asia-Pacific Trade Agreement (APTA) in which Bangladesh, China, India, Laos, Korea, and Sri Lanka participate. Further, the Global System of Trade Preferences (GSTP) has 43 participants including Argentina, Brazil, Egypt, India, Indonesia, and Nigeria. Finally, MERCOSUR has also negotiated a less-than-comprehensive (bilateral) partial scope agreement with India.

The lower rows of Table 3 list economic development-oriented unilateral preference schemes in force as of 2015. Seven different economies offered preferences to developing economies via their unique implementation of the Generalized System of Preferences (GSP). Under these schemes, a preference-granting country decides unilaterally what trading partners and what products will be offered favorable tariff treatment. Furthermore, the

---

[aj]   However, Korea and China did offer some preferences toward one another as they were both signatories to the Asia-Pacific Trade Agreement (APTA), a partial scope agreement. China and Korea announced the formation of a new FTA in June 2015, but it was not yet in force by the end of the year.

Table 3 Major preferential trade arrangements in force in 2015

Type of arrangement	Number in force	Major examples
Free Trade Agreement (FTA)	233	North American Free Trade Agreement (NAFTA) US–Australia, US–Colombia, Korea–US Canada–Colombia, Canada–Korea EU–Colombia and Peru, EU–Egypt, EU–Korea, EU–Mexico, EU–South Africa, EU–Ukraine Association of Southeast Asian Nations (ASEAN) FTA ASEAN–Japan, ASEAN–Australia–New Zealand, ASEAN–China, ASEAN–India, ASEAN–Korea India–Japan Japan–Australia, Japan–Indonesia, Japan–Mexico, Japan–Philippines, Japan–Thailand, Japan–Vietnam Korea–Australia, Korea–India Pakistan–China Thailand–Australia Turkey–Egypt Turkey–Korea Ukraine–Russia
Customs Union (CU)	19	European Union (EU) EU–Turkey MERCOSUR (Southern Common Market) East African Community Common Market for Eastern and Southern Africa (COMESA)
Partial Scope Agreement (PSA)	14	Asia-Pacific Trade Agreement (APTA) Global System of Trade Preferences (GSTP) Latin American Integration Association (ALADI) MERCOSUR–India

Unilalteral Preference Scheme	28	Generalized System of Preferences (GSP) schemes:
		     Australia, Canada, European Union, Japan, Russia,
		 Turkey, United States
		 Duty-free treatment for certain less developed countries (LDCs):
		     China, Korea, India, Thailand
		 Other examples:
		     African Growth and Opportunities Act (AGOA)–US
		     Trade preferences for Pakistan–EU

Constructed by the authors from WTO, 2015a. Database on preferential trade arrangements. Available from: http://ptadb.wto.org/default.aspx (accessed 30 December); WTO, 2015c. Regional trade agreements information system. Available from: http://rtais.wto.org/UI/PublicMaintainRTAHome.aspx (accessed 30 December). The list of "major examples" is not comprehensive as it omits preferential trade arrangements that do involve at least two of the major economies listed in Table 1.

United States and European Union offer other unilateral preference programs in addition to GSP, such as the African Growth and Opportunities Act (AGOA) offered by the United States, and an additional set of tariff preferences (covering 75 products) that the EU offered to Pakistan in response to devastating floods in 2010. China, Korea, India and Thailand also have programs whereby they offer tariff preferences over a specified set of products but only to a smaller set of imports arising from least developed countries (LDCs).[ak]

2.3.2 Preferential Tariffs Across Countries

Table 4 summarizes information on bilateral tariffs that 27 of our major economies apply toward their trading partners as of 2014. It addresses the question: how much do countries discriminate among trading partners through their application of lower-than-MFN tariffs? We capture the extent of the favorable tariff treatment along two dimensions: (1) a quantity dimension, which we capture as the share of imported products that receive a tariff reduction; and (2) a price dimension, which is the depth of the tariff reduction relative to the applied MFN tariff for a particular product.

To interpret Table 4, we begin by assessing the tariff information for the European Union.[al] As we observed in Table 3, the EU has FTAs with many countries, including Colombia, Egypt, Mexico, South Africa, and Korea. Furthermore, the EU offers a number of unilateral preference programs and its own GSP program. One interesting point of comparison is that the EU's list of GSP-eligible countries has historically included China, which has not been a recent GSP recipient under the US program that we introduce later.[am] Finally, the EU has also formed a customs union with a nonmember Turkey and thus the two share a common external applied MFN tariff vis-à-vis imports from third countries.[an]

[ak] The United States and EU had other preference programs to primarily least developed and small economies in effect that are not described here as they do not apply to the exporting countries in our sample. For a more complete analysis of such programs, see Ornelas (2016).

[al] Recall that the 28 current countries that are EU members not only have a common internal market with zero tariffs toward trade from one another (an FTA), but they have also ceded their national trade policy to a collectivized central authority (the European Commission) in Brussels that sets its common external trade policy vis-à-vis the rest of the world (thus creating a customs union). The post-World War II integration of Europe proceeded from the Treaty of Paris in 1951, to the Treaty of Rome in 1957 which established an internal FTA and customs union between six countries, to subsequent accessions over time before reaching the current 28 countries. Most recently the EU integration process has deepened beyond trade policy to cover factor markets and notably many forms of domestic regulations.

[am] The European Commission did finally graduate China from its GSP program as of 2015.

[an] The EU–Turkey customs union is much less complete than the EU's "internal" customs union based on a number of different measures. First, recall from Table 1 that the economies have undertaken different levels of tariff binding commitments at the WTO. Second, their average applied MFN rates are different because agriculture is excluded entirely, and there are special provisions for steel, textile, and apparel products. Third, as described later in Section 3.1, the EU and Turkey each also administer their own temporary trade barrier policies of antidumping, countervailing duties, and safeguards and in some instances even apply these toward imports from each other (Bown, 2014b).

Table 4 Bilateral import tariff characteristics under PTAs for selected economies, 2014

Country	All products MFN applied tariff	Preference possible (PP) products with nonzero applied MFN tariffs						
		PP products (% of all HS06 products)	Products given preferences (% of all PP products)	Products given preferences (% of all products)	MFN applied tariff, all PP products	MFN applied tariff, preference given	Bilateral applied tariff, preference given	Bilateral tariff preference margin, preference given
	(1)	(2)	(3)	(4)	(5)	(6)	(7)	(8)
G20 High income								
Australia	2.7	52.5	39.8	20.9	5.1	5.0	0.6	4.4
Canada	2.2	31.3	58.8	18.4	7.1	6.7	1.5	5.2
European Union	5.6	76.0	78.7	59.8	7.3	6.6	1.8	4.8
Japan	2.8	47.5	64.4	30.6	5.8	5.2	0.8	4.4
Saudi Arabia	4.7	89.7	3.6	3.2	5.3	5.3	0.0	5.3
United States	2.9	58.0	59.7	34.6	5.1	4.2	0.1	4.1
G20 Emerging								
Argentina	13.6	96.7	10.0	9.7	14.1	13.5	2.5	11.0
Brazil	13.6	96.8	10.2	9.9	14.0	13.7	3.9	9.8
China	9.6	93.6	52.8	49.4	10.3	9.3	0.7	8.6
India	12.4	97.3	3.6	3.5	12.7	15.0	9.2	5.8
Indonesia	7.2	90.6	23.7	21.5	8.0	7.2	0.6	6.6
Mexico	7.4	57.0	20.3	11.6	12.9	12.6	2.5	10.1
Russia	8.8	89.4	20.2	18.1	9.9	11.1	5.7	5.4
South Africa	7.5	43.7	6.8	3.0	17.3	17.3	2.1	15.2
Turkey	10.8	80.4	67.1	53.9	13.4	5.6	1.9	3.7

Continued

Table 4 Bilateral import tariff characteristics under PTAs for selected economies, 2014—cont'd

	All products	Preference possible (PP) products			Preference possible (PP) products with nonzero applied MFN tariffs			
Country	MFN applied tariff	PP products (% of all HS06 products)	Products given preferences (% of all PP products)	Products given preferences (% of all products)	MFN applied tariff, all PP products	MFN applied tariff, preference given	Bilateral applied tariff, preference given	Bilateral tariff preference margin, preference given
	(1)	(2)	(3)	(4)	(5)	(6)	(7)	(8)
Developing, other								
Bangladesh	14.6	93.5	2.0	1.9	15.6	22.6	21.2	1.4
Burma	5.6	96.9	4.6	4.5	5.8	13.4	4.9	8.5
Colombia	6.3	54.2	18.7	10.1	11.7	11.9	1.9	10.0
Egypt	16.8	90.6	10.7	9.7	18.6	18.6	5.6	13.0
Ethiopia	17.3	95.7	7.1	6.8	18.1	18.1	16.3	1.8
Kenya	12.8	63.8	10.7	6.8	20.0	20.0	0.7	19.3
Pakistan	13.4	94.3	5.2	4.9	14.2	15.1	13.1	2.0
Philippines	6.3	98.2	13.8	13.6	6.4	6.4	0.6	5.8
Thailand	10.7	78.3	17.6	13.8	13.6	13.5	0.3	13.2
Tanzania	12.8	63.8	3.6	2.3	20.1	20.1	0.0	20.1
Ukraine	4.4	63.8	3.6	2.3	6.9	6.9	0.0	6.9
Vietnam	9.3	64.9	22.5	14.6	14.4	15.3	4.8	10.5

Constructed by the authors with bilateral tariff data at the HS06 level for each importing economy vis-à-vis its 30 trading partners listed in Table 1. Data does not include ad valorem equivalent estimates for tariffs applied as specific duties. For countries for which 2014 data is not available, comprehensive data from the nearest available year was utilized. Not included are DR Congo, Iran, Korea, and Nigeria, for which bilateral tariff preference data were incomplete. G20 = Group of 20. Columns (1), (5), (6), (7), and (8) are simple averages of ad valorem rates; column (2) is share of all import products; column (3) is share of all PP products; and columns (3) and (4) are shares of all product-trading partner pairings.

Beginning with column (1), recall the EU's simple average applied MFN tariff rate was 5.6%.[ao] Column (2) indicates that 76.0% of all HS06 products have nonzero MFN applied tariffs and are thus what we define as products that are "preference possible." Column (3) introduces the trading partner dimension and reports that the EU granted preferences for 78.7% of the preference possible goods to these 30 exporting countries. Overall, column (4) reports that the EU offers a lower-than-MFN tariff for 59.8% of all HS06 products entering the EU from these 30 partners. These statistics for the EU suggests a broad application of preferential tariffs.

Since the EU's lower-than-MFN offerings do not cover 100% of preference possible products, an interesting follow-up question arises. Does the EU typically grant preferences in products that have high or low applied MFN tariffs? Compare column (5), which reports the average applied MFN tariff for the EU's preference possible products (7.3%) with column (6), which reports the average applied MFN tariff for the selected group of products (and trading partner pairs) for which the EU offers (6.6%). Perhaps not surprisingly, the EU offers bilateral preferences in products for which the average applied MFN tariff is already relatively low.[ap] This is consistent with expectations that the EU would find it more difficult to offer preferences in products that start with relative high applied MFN tariffs.

Along the price dimension, how "deep" are the EU's tariff preferences? First note that, unlike many other high-income economies, the EU frequently does not cut its lower-than-MFN tariff all the way to zero; ie, column (7) indicates that the average applied bilateral tariff (when a tariff preference is offered) remains at 1.8%. The EU's average preference margin is thus 4.8%, or the difference between columns (6) and (7).

More generally, Table 4 reveals a number of stylized facts on the scope and the depth of preferential tariff offerings across countries.

First, consider the scope of preference possible products and the breadth of preferential tariff offerings. For high-income economies, although there are few products overall in which they can offer tariff preferences, they tend to offer preferences for relatively large shares of these goods. While the EU is at the high end, Australia, Canada, Japan and the US offer bilateral tariff preferences for between 18% and 35% of all products. On the

---

[ao] Due to the limited availability of ad valorem equivalent estimates for the bilateral (and some of the applied MFN) tariffs applied as specific duties, this section only relies on the products for which tariffs are imposed as ad valorem duties. Because the HS06 products with tariffs applied as specific duties have higher (on average) ad valorem equivalent estimates than the HS06 products with tariffs applied as ad valorem duties (see discussion in Section 2.2), these data on average tariffs will differ from other parts of this chapter. We would expect the differences (or potential mis-measurement) to be larger for the economies that are major users of specific duties, such as Russia, United States, EU, Japan and India, and in sectors where specific duties are more prominent, including agriculture, footwear, textiles and apparel.

[ap] While not shown in Table 4, the EU's average applied MFN tariff for the 21% of products and trading partners in the sample that were not granted a preference was 10.1%.

other hand, the breadth of preferential tariff offerings is comparatively modest in middle and low income countries, despite them having so many more preference possible products to potentially offer. Although many lower income countries could offer preferences in more than 90% of products, they typically offer bilateral tariff preferences in 5–20% of these goods. Among developing and emerging economies, the main exceptions are China, Indonesia, and Turkey, each of which offers lower-than-MFN tariffs on substantially more products.

Second, consider the depth of the bilateral tariff preference offerings. For high-income economies, conditional on a preference being granted, the average bilateral preference margin is only in the range of 4–5 percentage points. In contrast, when poorer countries offer bilateral tariff preferences, the bilateral tariff preference margin is typically much higher (column 8). The average bilateral tariff preference margin offered by China is 8.6 percentage points, by Mexico is 10.1 percentage points, by Argentina is 11.0 percentage points, and by South Africa is 15.2 percentage points. For other poorer countries, the average bilateral tariff preference margin can be as high as 19–20 percentage points (Kenya, Tanzania). Thus even though these lower income countries offer lower-than-MFN tariffs to many fewer product-trading partner pairs, when they do offer such a preference, the margin can be quite large.

Finally, to whom do these countries offer bilateral tariff preferences? Fig. 8 illustrates the export recipients in 2014; consider again the data for the European Union. The EU offered a bilateral tariff preference to developing country exporters in 89% of these preference possible products and to middle income countries in 95% of products.[aq] On the other hand, it offered a tariff preference to high-income countries in only 32% of available products.

In general, high-income economies in Fig. 8 tend to provide the largest share of their realized offerings of preference possible products to developing countries, primarily through GSP-type programs (see again Table 3) but also increasingly through FTAs. With the exception of Australia, high-income economies offer the fewest preferences to other high-income economies; they offer much more to emerging and developing countries. Indeed, Japan (and Saudi Arabia) offered zero tariff preferences to other high-income economies in these data. However, this pattern may also change if the Trans-Pacific Partnership (TPP) (which includes Australia, Canada, Japan, and the United States) and the Transatlantic Trade and Investment Partnership (which includes

---

[aq] Note that this ordering is reversed for most of the other high-income countries which tend to offer preferences in more products to poorer countries. The EU's results stem from its FTAs with Mexico and South Africa, and its customs union with Turkey. Furthermore, unlike the United States in 2014, for example, the EU also offered GSP eligibility to Argentina, China and Russia. These countries were removed from the EU GSP program in 2015.

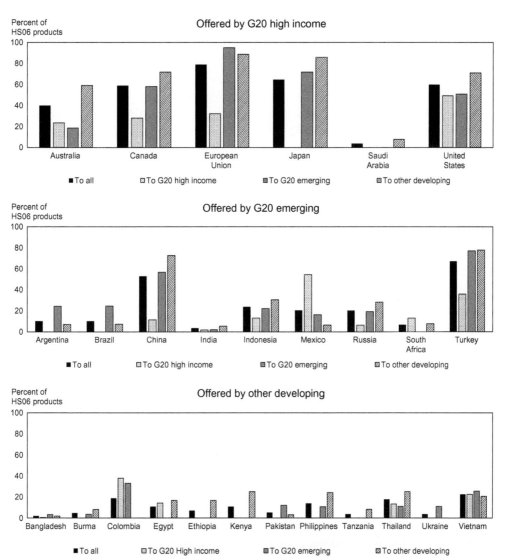

Fig. 8 Bilateral tariff preference offerings by policy-imposing economy, 2014.
Constructed by the authors with bilateral tariff data (policy-imposing economy vis-à-vis 30 trading partners listed in Table 1) at the HS06 level from UN International Trade Center. Data illustrates percent of the "preference possible" HS06 products for which the policy-imposing economy offers bilateral tariffs to exporting countries in each group. For list of exporting countries in each group (G20 high income, G20 emerging, and other developing) see Table 1.

the EU and United States) negotiations result in FTAs that include the standard comprehensive reciprocal tariff reductions between members.

Fig. 8 also reveals substantial variation for the bilateral preferences offered by emerging economies. India has the most preference possible products and yet offers the fewest preferences overall (see again column 3 of Table 4). Argentina and Brazil also tend to offer relatively few bilateral preferences to the countries in this sample; on the other hand, China and Turkey offered the most preferences in the set of emerging economies and have levels of offerings comparable to some high-income countries. Mexico stands out by way of the concentration of its tariff preferences toward high-income economy exporters—recall its NAFTA participation (with the United States and Canada) and its bilateral FTAs with the EU and Japan.

The lowest panel of Fig. 8 reveals the pattern of bilateral tariff preferences that developing countries offered in 2014. Overall, they offered fewer bilateral preferences across all exporter recipient groups. Their limited preferential offerings go toward other developing countries; these frequently arise through PSAs, or in the case of African countries, through customs unions like the East African Community or COMESA. Colombia, Egypt and the countries involved in ASEAN are the only ones offering tariff preferences to high-income economy exporters, and these are primarily through FTAs.

Before concluding this section, we briefly describe research that has begun to explore the *determinants* of bilateral tariffs. In particular, Blanchard et al. (2016) focus on global supply chain determinants and use a sample of 14 high-income and emerging economies over 1995–2009. They find that bilateral final goods tariffs are decreasing in the amount of domestic value added embodied in foreign production and the amount of foreign value added embodied in domestic production. In related work, Blanchard and Matschke (2015) examine US bilateral tariff preferences and find that US multinational affiliates' offshoring behavior impacts the likelihood of a trading partner being granted such as preference. Overall, however, the existing literature in this area is quite thin, which is somewhat surprising given the substantial increase in preferential tariff offerings arising since the early 1990s. However, the tremendous variation in the data shown here suggests this as a potentially fruitful environment for additional research.[ar]

2.3.3 Tariff Preferences Offered by the United States

Here, we extend the analysis to provide a more detailed assessment of the variation in the United States' preferential tariff offerings under its various PTAs. Fig. 9 breaks out

[ar] There is a larger literature on the determinants of preferential trading arrangements at the aggregate level; see, for example, Baier and Bergstrand (2004) and Baier et al. (2014). Furthermore, there are also expansive literatures on the impact of preferential tariffs—both on trade flows and on other trade policy-setting behavior. Limão (2016) surveys the literature on preferential trading arrangements. For the impact of tariff preferences arising under unilateral preference programs such as GSP; see Ornelas (2016). For a broader comparison of the WTO and PTAs, see Bagwell et al. (2016).

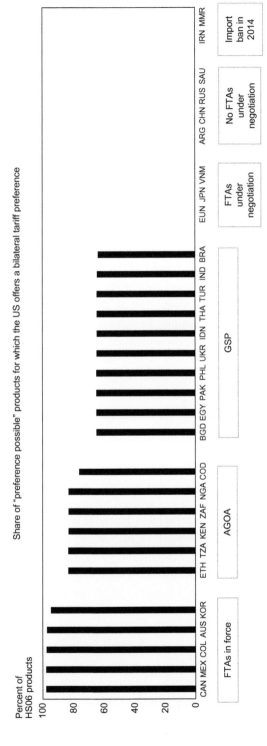

Fig. 9 United States's bilateral tariff preferences toward major economies, 2014.

Constructed by the authors with bilateral tariff data at the HS06 level from UN International Trade Center. "Preference possible" products, defined as HS06 products with nonzero applied MFN tariffs in 2014 (58.0% of US imported products), not including products with tariffs applied as specific duties. For country acronyms, see Table A.2.

bilaterally the United States' share of these preference possible products for which it actually granted a lower-than-MFN tariff in 2014. As previously observed in Table 3, the United States offers some bilateral tariff preferences to countries via free trade agreements including NAFTA (with Canada and Mexico), and bilateral FTAs with Australia, Colombia and Korea. The United States offered a lower-than-MFN tariff in 2014 for close to 100% of preference possible products to each of these countries. In the few instances in which a product was not offered a bilateral tariff preference, it is typically associated with the more recent agreements (Colombia, Korea) that were not yet fully phased in.

US trading partners also receive lower-than-MFN applied tariffs under unilateral preference offerings. In 2014, the United States offered tariff preferences to trading partners under a number of different unilateral programs; for the trading partners in our sample, this includes the African Growth and Opportunity Act (AGOA) and the Generalized System of Preferences (GSP). Fig. 9 indicates differences in the comprehensiveness (product coverage) across the different US programs. For example, the US offered tariff preferences for more than 80% of possible products for African countries such as Kenya or Tanzania (which are eligible for AGOA) and only 65% of possible products for Bangladesh or Pakistan (which are eligible for GSP), despite these countries all having comparable levels of income per capita. Furthermore, because the United States exercises discretion by excluding certain products from certain countries (that are both otherwise part of the program) from being GSP eligible, the United States offers Brazil, India, Indonesia, Thailand, Turkey, and Ukraine slightly fewer tariff preferences than other GSP-eligible countries.

Importantly, there are also major trading partners to which the United States offered no special tariffs in 2014. These include three of the top five sources for its imports—China, the EU, and Japan. Collectively, these three economies alone accounted for over 43% of total US goods imports; by itself, this explains why such a large share of US trade continues to arrive under MFN tariffs. This may partially explain why countries were seeking comprehensive new free trade agreements with the United States in 2014 via the Trans-Pacific Partnership (TPP) negotiations (which includes Japan, as well as Vietnam) and the Transatlantic Trade and Investment Partnership (TTIP) negotiations with the European Union. Other major countries to which the United States did not offer preferences in 2014 include Argentina, Russia and Saudi Arabia. Argentina and Russia had previously been part of the US GSP program for a number of years; both were recently removed from eligibility. Finally, the United States not only did not offer Burma and Iran any bilateral tariff preferences in 2014, they were not even granted the US's applied MFN tariff rate (despite Burma being a WTO member); the United States had an import ban from both countries in effect in 2014.

Before concluding our discussion of preferential tariffs, we make two additional points regarding US tariff preferences that we are not able to capture in the data utilized here.

First, our description of US tariff preferences has focused exclusively on the supply (offerings) side. Even our data on bilateral tariff offerings are incomplete as they exclude reference to the fact that the United States also imposes upper limits (quantitative restrictions) on how much can be imported under some of these unilateral preferences. The focus on bilateral tariff offerings also does not assess the equilibrium take-up of preferences, as it does not consider demand-side factors. For example, preference utilization rates describe the equilibrium outcome whereby exporters actually claim the preferential tariff rate on the customs declaration form, in lieu of simply continuing to pay the (potentially higher) applied MFN tariff.[as]

Finally, like other areas of trade policy, there is additional variation to US tariff preference offerings *over time* as well as across trading partners and products, especially associated with the preferences that arise under the discretionary unilateral programs. The list of products for which the US offers preferences can change from year to year; furthermore, as we have seen from Fig. 9, certain GSP-eligible exporting countries may have their particular export products *excluded* from GSP in a given year that are otherwise GSP eligible. Trading partners can also "graduate" from a given GSP scheme over time, especially after exceeding certain income-per-capita thresholds. For example, the US graduated Bulgaria and Romania from its GSP program in 2007 (upon their accession to the European Union) and Russia in 2014. Finally, countries can also be kicked out of GSP for political reasons. For example, the United States removed Argentina from its GSP program beginning in 2012 due to Argentina's failure to pay roughly $300 million in damages since 2005–06 that it owed US investors arising under a foreign direct investment dispute (USTR, 2012). Overall, there should appear to be much more trade policy uncertainty associated with a US tariff preference arising under GSP than a US tariff preference arising under one of its free trade agreements.

2.4 Other Import Tariffs Beyond MFN and Bilateral Tariff Preferences

Before moving on to other trade policy instruments, we conclude this section with three other examples of ad valorem tariffs that are not captured by the data on either applied MFN tariffs or the bilateral tariffs arising under preferential trading arrangements. We use the example of the United States' trade policy to explain how each example can and has arisen.

First, consider a trading partner that is both not a member of the WTO (so it is not guaranteed an MFN tariff) and is also not part of any preferential trading agreement. For such exporting countries, the United States has a special category in its tariff schedule

---

[as]   Under the US GSP program, quantitative restrictions are referred to as competitive needs limits (CNLs), see Blanchard and Hakobyan (2015) for an analysis. Hakobyan (2015) provides a study of the utilization rates for preferences under the US GSP program. Keck and Lendle (2014) analyze preference utilization rates in a cross-country study involving the United States, EU, Canada and Australia.

referred to as "Column 2" tariffs. These applied tariffs are typically much higher than the MFN rates. In 2014, the US imposed these tariffs on imports from North Korea and also from Cuba (despite Cuba being a WTO member country).

Second, there are instances under both the WTO and some preferential trading arrangements in which countries can be authorized to legally impose (higher) retaliatory tariffs after the adjudication of a formal dispute if the defendant country refuses to comply with a ruling. In these instances, the complaining country in a dispute can be granted the right to raise its bilateral tariff (on imports arising from the defendant country) to some level that is higher than the MFN binding rate. Indeed, the United States has implemented WTO-authorized retaliatory tariffs of 100% on imports from the European Union in the wake of disputes involving bananas and hormone-treated beef; in some instances, retaliatory tariffs have remained in place for years. Mexico, the EU, and other countries have similarly been authorized to raise tariffs on imports from the United States after disputes.[at]

Third, in some instances the applied bilateral ad valorem import tariff is irrelevant because there is an imposed import ban in effect; ie, a quota, or a quantitative restriction sets imports equal to zero. For example, the United States had a ban on imports from Burma and from Iran in 2014.

Overall, while these examples focus on the United States, these sorts of additional considerations can affect any country's applied level of tariff protection, and they have the potential to introduce additional variation to measures of import protection—even beyond those already captured by the tariff policies described in the preceding sections—across sectors, trading partners, and time.

3. BORDER POLICIES BEYOND IMPORT TARIFFS

This section looks past import tariffs to introduce other commercial policies that affect imports at the border. These include the temporary trade barrier policies of antidumping, countervailing duties and safeguards; quantitative restrictions, quotas, and tariff-rate quotas; negotiated arrangements with exporters such as price undertakings and voluntary export restraints (VERs); the allocation of import licences, and the valuation of customs transactions. We briefly describe the contemporary landscape of each policy individually, though one theme that will emerge from our discussion of the empirical research on the determinants of these policies is the substitutability of these instruments with the applied import tariffs described in Section 2, as well as with each other.

[at] See, for example, the collection of research in Bown and Pauwelyn (2010) regarding the retaliation in WTO disputes arising between 1995 and 2008. For a broader introduction to WTO dispute settlement, see Mavroidis (2016).

For some of the policies, the existing data sources are comprehensive and rich; this allows us to address empirically some of our chapter's main questions. For the temporary trade barrier policies, we examine cross-country differences in the import coverage of these barriers. Within countries, we examine sectoral differences in import protection under these policies and compare sectors with temporary trade barriers to those with high applied tariffs. Furthermore, the levels of these barriers change considerably over time. Finally, they exhibit significant discrimination across trading partners.

Before turning to a description of the policies, we note that, collectively, these non-tariff border policies have been the focus of seminal empirical studies of theories of trade policy determination. Indeed, the modern literature on endogenous import protection focused on these nontariff policies because the *negotiated* (MFN) import tariffs (described in Section 2) that the major GATT/WTO members applied were inappropriate for studies of optimal, unconstrained policymaking behavior. Many of the policy instruments described next (and perhaps some from Section 5) are important components of the measures of "trade policy"—frequently defined as sector-level coverage ratios—used in Trefler (1993), Goldberg and Maggi (1999), and Gawande and Bandyopadhyay (2000).[au]

3.1 Temporary Trade Barriers of Antidumping, Countervailing Duties, and Safeguards

The first set of trade policy instruments that we consider are antidumping, countervailing duties, and safeguards. These are collectively referred to as temporary trade barriers (TTBs) based on the common property that legally each has a temporary life span. Later we assess both their collective use—motivated by evidence of how they have been used as substitute policy instruments—and we also disentangle their individual use in order to show their relative importance, since the GATT/WTO does impose distinct legal conditions under which use of each can be permitted. While all three require evidence of injury to the domestic, import-competing industry, antidumping also requires evidence that this was caused by low-priced (dumped) imports, countervailing duties require evidence that this was caused by foreign-government subsidized imports, and safeguards require evidence that injury was caused by an unexpected import surge.[av] Overall, according to metrics such as frequency of use and import coverage, the most empirically important of the policies is antidumping. Nevertheless, safeguards use has been important for certain countries and especially during certain periods, and there is also some evidence that countervailing duty use may be increasing for some countries over time.

[au] More recent research has utilized these data for other purposes, including studies such as Broda et al. (2008) and Blanchard et al. (2016), so as to validate their primary results (that focus on determinants of applied tariffs) with empirical analysis of other border barriers.

[av] For a comprehensive survey of economics research on antidumping, see Blonigen and Prusa (2016); on countervailing duties and subsidies, see Lee (2016); and on safeguards, see Beshkar and Bond (2016).

The data on TTBs is sufficiently comprehensive—at least relative to the other border policies we examine in Section 3—that we are also able to present measures that illustrate policy variation and thus which can address some of our chapter's main questions.[aw]

Table 5 summarizes TTB use by our 31 economies over 1995–2013. It also includes information on when the economy implemented its antidumping law, and when it initiated its first antidumping investigation. We choose the 1995–2013 period for a number of reasons. First, it is a period that our data most accurately captures the "stock" of TTB policies in effect.[ax] Second, 1995 initiated common rules for TTB use for all WTO members.[ay] Third, by 1995 we observe a common external trade policy for customs union partners such as EU–Turkey and Argentina–Brazil and thus can more easily examine potential differences in TTB use between partners.

For interpretive purposes, consider the import coverage of the TTBs that the United States had in effect over 1995–2013. The first four columns of Table 5 reveal information on the cumulative share of imported products over which the United States imposed some sort of TTB policy during the period. The United States imposed some TTB policy on 10.6% of all HS06 imported products at some point during 1995–2013. Among the four different TTB policies in use by the United States during this period, antidumping has been most prevalently applied (covering 9.0% of all products), followed by countervailing duties (5.1%), the global safeguard (2.8%), and the China-specific transitional safeguard (less than 0.1%). The fact that individual TTB policies for the US aggregate to more than 10.6% of total imports reflects both the *substitutability* of these policy instruments—eg, the United States has applied different TTB policies to the same products at different points in time—as well as the *redundancy* of these policy instruments—eg, the United States frequently applies two different TTB policies, such as an antidumping duty and a countervailing duty, to the

---

[aw] The empirical analysis in this section updates and extends much of the information initially presented in Bown (2011b), which also provides more detail on the underlying methodology, using more recent data from the World Bank's Temporary Trade Barriers Database (Bown, 2014a). Additional detail on the database is provided in Data Appendix. Our analysis below is not comprehensive, however, and there are at least three other important aspects of TTB use that we mention briefly here. First, and as we describe elsewhere in this chapter, these policies are applied not only as ad valorem duties, but also frequently as specific duties, price undertakings, quotas, and tariff rate quotas. Second, our import coverage ratio measures do not address potentially significant variation in the restrictiveness of the policies; here we only note that even when these policies are imposed as ad valorem import duties, they are sometimes set at prohibitive levels of greater than 100%, 500%, or 800%. Third, while the "stock" measures introduced later are affected by the duration of the imposed policy—recall that WTO rules for each of them are that they are supposed to be "temporary" (ie, duration of less than 3–5 years)—there are numerous examples of duties covering some products that have been imposed for 20–30 years or longer. The data required to explore each of these points empirically is readily available in Bown (2014a).

[ax] For the United States and EU especially, the early 1990s featured antidumping duties still in effect from the 1980s and earlier but for which we do not have the HS codes because they were imposed under different product classification schemes.

[ay] Under the GATT, the rules for certain TTBs were different depending on whether a GATT member was a signatory to the plurilateral Antidumping Code and Subsidies Code.

Table 5 Import product coverage by temporary trade barriers over 1995–2013, by country and policy

	AD law/ initiation	Cumulative coverage by TTB ever in effect during 1995–2013					Annual coverage by TTB in effect 1995–2013				Annual coverage by new TTB investigation 1995–2013			
		All TTBs	AD only	CVD only	SG only	CSG only	Mean	St. Dev.	Min.	Max.	Mean	St. Dev.	Min.	Max.
G20 High income														
Australia	1906/na	2.5	2.5	0.5	0.0	0.0	0.8	0.2	0.4	1.2	0.2	0.1	0.1	0.4
Canada	1904/na	3.4	3.4	1.5	0.0	0.0	1.6	0.3	1.2	2.2	0.3	0.3	0.0	1.1
European Union	1968/1968–69	8.1	6.6	1.4	1.6	0.0	2.8	0.5	2.1	3.6	0.6	0.5	0.1	2.2
Japan	1920/1982	0.3	0.1	0.1	0.0	0.0	0.1	0.1	0.0	0.2	0.0	0.0	0.0	0.1
Korea	1963/1986	1.6	1.4	0.0	0.1	0.0	0.6	0.2	0.2	0.8	0.1	0.2	0.0	0.6
Saudi Arabia	na/na	na	na	na	na	na	na	na	na	na	na	na	na	na
United States	1916/1922	10.3	9.0	5.1	2.8	0.0	4.9	1.1	3.3	6.8	0.9	0.8	0.1	3.9
G20 Emerging														
Argentina	1972/na	4.8	4.6	0.1	0.5	0.0	2.2	0.6	1.2	3.2	0.5	0.4	0.0	1.3
Brazil	1987/1988	2.8	2.4	0.2	0.3	0.0	1.2	0.4	0.4	1.9	0.3	0.2	0.0	0.6
China	1997/1997	3.1	2.1	0.2	1.3	0.0	1.1	0.7	0.0	2.0	0.2	0.4	0.0	1.8
India	1985/1992	8.0	7.6	0.0	0.9	0.3	3.4	2.2	0.2	6.6	0.9	0.7	0.1	2.4
Indonesia	1995/1996	2.1	1.1	0.0	1.1	0.0	0.6	0.6	0.0	1.8	0.2	0.3	0.0	1.2
Mexico	1986/1987	22.9	22.8	0.6	0.0	0.0	17.5	10.0	1.0	23.7	0.2	0.1	0.0	0.4
Russia	na/na	na	na	na	na	na	na	na	na	na	na	na	na	na
South Africa	1914/1921	2.1	2.1	0.1	0.0	0.0	1.0	0.4	0.3	1.7	0.1	0.1	0.0	0.6
Turkey	1989/1989	4.2	2.5	0.0	1.6	0.1	2.9	2.0	0.6	5.9	0.4	0.5	0.0	1.8

Continued

Table 5 Import product coverage by temporary trade barriers over 1995–2013, by country and policy—cont'd

AD law/ initiation	Cumulative coverage by TTB ever in effect during 1995–2013					Annual coverage by TTB in effect 1995–2013				Annual coverage by new TTB investigation 1995–2013			
	All TTBs	AD only	CVD only	SG only	CSG only	Mean	St. Dev.	Min.	Max.	Mean	St. Dev.	Min.	Max.
Developing, other													
Colombia 1990/1991	2.3	1.2	0.0	0.1	1.5	0.6	0.5	0.1	1.9	0.2	0.4	0.0	1.8
Egypt na/na	na	na	na	3.6	na	na	na	na	na	na	na	na	na
Pakistan 1983/2002	0.4	0.4	0.0	0.0	0.0	0.2	0.1	0.0	0.3	0.1	0.1	0.0	0.3
Philippines 1994/1994	0.5	0.3	0.0	0.2	0.0	0.2	0.1	0.1	0.7	0.1	0.1	0.0	0.4
Thailand 1994/1994	0.6	0.6	0.0	0.1	0.0	0.3	0.2	0.0	0.7	0.4	0.5	0.0	1.0
Ukraine na/na	na	na	na	0.1	na	na	na	na	na	na	na	na	na

Coverage indicates share of a country's HS06 import product lines, constructed by the authors with data from Bown, C.P., 2014a. Temporary trade barriers database. The World Bank. Available from: http://econ.worldbank.org/ttbd/ (accessed 25.07.14).

Notes: na indicates policy data not available, though the country is a known user of TTBs more generally. TTB, temporary trade barrier; AD, antidumping; CVD, countervailing duty; SG, global safeguard; CSG, China-specific transitional safeguard; and G20, Group of 20. AD law is year of implementation of the country's antidumping regime, and initiation refers to the year of initiation of the country's first antidumping investigation. Data for Bangladesh, Burma, DR of the Congo, Ethiopia, Iran, Kenya, Nigeria, Tanzania, and Vietnam omitted.

same product and trading partner at the same time. The last columns indicate that, on average over 1995–2013, the United States had 4.9% of imported products covered by an imposed TTB in any year, and the maximum coverage was at 6.8% in 2012. Finally, the mean share of imported products in a year that were subject to a new US TTB investigation—and that could potentially lead to new import restrictions—was 0.9%. The maximum share of imports subject to new TTB investigations was 3.9% of products in 2001, when the United States initiated a wide-ranging safeguard investigation over steel.

Is there a pattern to which countries tend to utilize TTBs as import protection? To summarize Table 5, while some countries certainly use TTBs more than others, the overall country-level pattern is not as clear as the import tariffs covered in Section 2.1. First, significant users of TTBs include a mix of high-income (US, EU) and emerging (Argentina, Brazil, China, India, Mexico, and Turkey) economies; many of the emerging economies only began using TTBs in the late 1980s or early 1990s. Second, not all WTO members use TTBs.[az] Most of the poorest developing countries in our sample do not use TTBs, and thus are not listed. While most of the high-income and emerging economies have become users of TTBs over time—albeit at different levels and frequencies—there are some high-income economies which only rarely apply them. For example, Japan is a rare user even though its antidumping law dates to 1920. Furthermore, there are some countries—eg, Australia, Canada, and even South Africa—who were major users of TTBs historically but whose use during 1995–2013 has declined relative to earlier decades. Finally, customs union partner pairs that share a common applied MFN tariff—eg, EU–Turkey, Argentina–Brazil—retain the legal authority to implement their TTB policies independently and clearly do so.

Before moving on to our next question of interest, we pause briefly to note that the composition of antidumping, safeguards and countervailing duties used by different countries is not systematic. While the United States has implemented each of the three major TTB policies with a significant share of import coverage during this period, most of the TTB users tend to rely primarily on antidumping, with a more limited use of safeguards.[ba] Countervailing duty laws, on the other hand, have only recently been adopted by a number

---

[az] The table lists the data for the users of the policies that are "known" users; users are known even if detailed data on their use is not available from Bown (2014a) due to the WTO's minimum reporting requirements. Countries are listed if they are known users of the policy even if the details of the data on their policy use are not available (na). For an exploratory analysis of why countries adopt antidumping laws, for example, see Vandenbussche and Zanardi (2008).

[ba] Significant users of safeguards in our sample of economies, for example, include Argentina, Brazil, Egypt, the EU, China, India, Indonesia, and Turkey—though for the United States, EU, and China, the significant safeguards use during this period was dominated by the almost simultaneous safeguards imposed over an overlapping set of steel products in 2001–03. For a discussion of the US safeguard on steel, and a comparison to the similarities on prior United States use of antidumping and countervailing duties products during the 1990–2003 period, see Bown (2013b). On the other hand, Blonigen et al. (2013) use the US steel industry to examine the nonequivalent market power effects of quotas and tariffs arising in the industry, some of which arose through TTB policies.

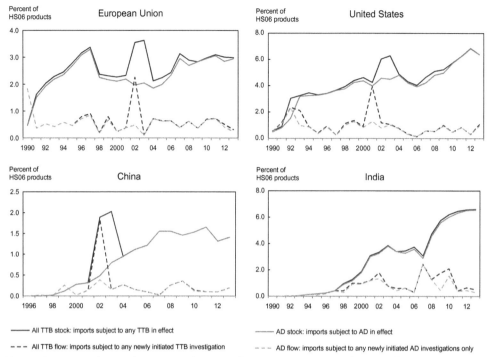

Fig. 10 Import products subject to newly initiated TTB investigations and imposed import restrictions for selected economies, 1990–2013.
Share of HS06 import protects subject to TTBs. Constructed by the authors from temporary trade barrier (TTB) data at the HS-06 level from Bown, C.P., 2014a. Temporary trade barriers database. The World Bank. Available from: http://econ.worldbank.org/ttbd/ (accessed 25.07.14); TTBs include antidumping, countervailing duties, global safeguards, and China-specific transitional safeguards.

of economies and are only starting to be implemented; as such, their import coverage has been fairly limited to high-income economies including the United States, EU and Canada. The China-specific transitional safeguard mechanism that was introduced as part of China's WTO Accession Protocol in 2001 has not been frequently utilized.[bb]

Next, do countries make significant changes to the levels of their TTB import protection over time? Fig. 10 presents a measure of the time path of TTB use for the EU, the United States, China and India over a slightly longer time period of 1990–2013. The figure plots four series of data—for all TTB policies (and antidumping only), a "flow" measure of the share of HS06 import products each year subject to a newly-initiated TTB investigation that could result in a new import restriction; and for all TTB policies

---

[bb] Notwithstanding the somewhat infamous use of this policy by the United States on imports of tires in 2009, the peak use was by Colombia, briefly, over a set of textile and apparel products in 2005. For a discussion of the United States safeguard on tires, see Charnovitz and Hoekman (2013). For the China safeguard more broadly, see Bown (2010) and Bown and Crowley (2010).

(and antidumping only), a "stock" measure of the share of HS06 import products each year subject to an imposed import restriction.

Fig. 10 illustrates interesting features on the use of these TTBs over time. First, there are spikes for the United States in 1992 and 2001 and for the EU in 2001; empirical evidence described in more detail later links significant increases in TTB use to recessionary periods (especially unemployment rate increases) as well as real exchange rate appreciations. Second, India began using TTBs in 1992 and China in 1997; import coverage levels for India exhibit a consistently upward trend. Third, for China, the EU, and the United States, the significant deviation in 2001–03 between the "all TTB" series and "antidumping only" series reflects the previously discussed global safeguards that each applied over steel products. Fourth, there is a slight increase for these economies in the "flow" of products subject to new TTB investigations during the Great Recession period of 2008–09, but it is not nearly as sizeable as in other periods of macroeconomic downturn.

To what extent has research linked changes in TTB levels to macroeconomic shocks such as real exchange rate appreciations and increases in the unemployment rate? Furthermore, can this partially explain why applied MFN tariffs were not responsive to the massive aggregate-level fluctuations taking place during the Great Recession, as discussed in Section 2.1? Knetter and Prusa (2003) and Irwin (2005) provide evidence from data through the 1990s that exchange rate appreciation significantly impacts antidumping use for a number of high-income economies. More recently, Bown and Crowley (2014) and Limão (2006) confirm these results in the more comprehensive TTB data in cross-country samples of five high-income economies and 13 emerging economies, respectively, covering the period of 1988–10. They find for the EU and the United States, the flexibility of the real exchange rate, and in particular the sharp depreciations that subsequently took place (after initial sharp appreciations in 2009) likely contributed to the dampening pressure on demands for import protection during the Great Recession. Second, over time, the emerging economies' collective TTB responsiveness to macroeconomic shocks (including also changes in the unemployment rate and real GDP growth) has been increasing, and thus mimicking the TTB counter-cyclical responsiveness of high-income economies. Finally, there is some evidence from emerging economies that as the tariff binding overhang diminishes over time, countries substitute away from adjusting their MFN applied tariffs and toward implementing TTBs.

The next of our major questions is whether, when countries apply import protection via TTBs, they do so differentially across sectors. Fig. 11 illustrates the breakdown for the major TTB users and presents clear evidence of significant variation across industries.[bc]

[bc] In particular, we provide figures for countries for which 2.8% or more of their HS06 lines were subject to a TTB during this period. We also group countries somewhat differently so as to make more direct comparisons between certain pairings that might be expected to have common determinants of policy, including those arising for institutional reasons under an FTA or customs union.

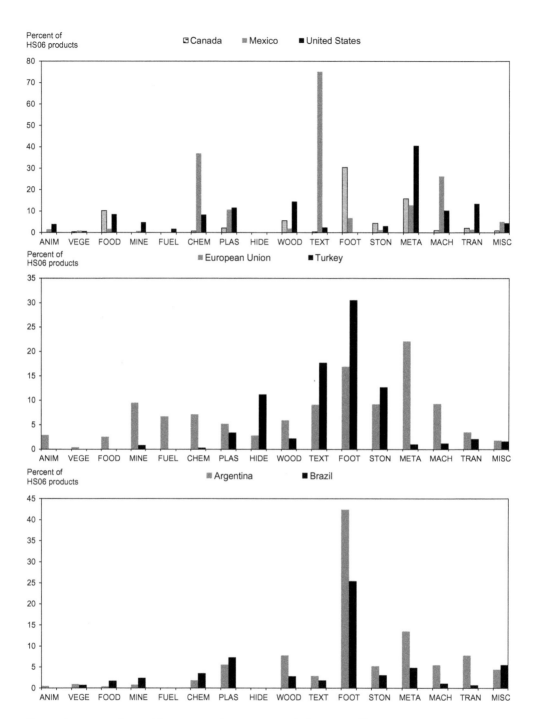

Fig. 11 Import products with an imposed temporary trade barrier in effect over 1995–2013, by policy-imposing economy and industry.

Constructed by the authors from temporary trade barrier (TTB) data at the HS-06 level from Bown, C.P., 2014a. Temporary trade barriers database. The World Bank. Available from: http://econ.worldbank.org/ ttbd/ (accessed 25.07.14); TTBs include antidumping, countervailing duties, global safeguards, and China-specific transitional safeguards. Notes: during this period Canada, Mexico, and the United States had a common FTA (NAFTA), European Union and Turkey had a customs union (common external applied MFN tariff), and Argentina and Brazil had a customs union (common external applied MFN tariff).

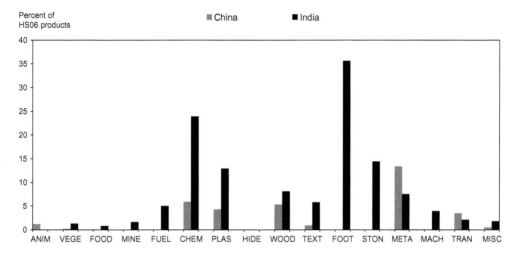

Percent of
HS06 products

■ China   ■ India

Fig. 11—Cont'd

Furthermore, do countries apply TTBs in the same sectors in which they have high tariffs? A comparison of Fig. 11 with Figs. 2, 3, and 7, suggests no clear pattern as to whether TTBs were more or less likely to arise in the sectors that were still subject to high average tariffs, high incidence of tariff peaks, or high frequency of specific duties. For example, agriculture during 1995–2013 was not a frequent target of TTBs across using countries. For other sectors, such as textiles and apparel and footwear, there is more variation across countries. The United States has relatively high MFN applied tariffs in those sectors and has not used TTBs. On the other hand, Argentina, Brazil, India, Mexico and Turkey had these sectors protected by relatively high MFN applied tariffs and a relatively high import coverage by TTBs. One rationale for these countries, as we describe next, is frequently to address increased import competition in these sectors from other emerging economies, especially China (Bown, 2013a). Finally, chemicals and metals are relatively low tariff sectors but high TTB sectors, especially in high-income economies. This is consistent with use in earlier decades as we further detail later in Section 4. Contributing explanations include that these are high fixed cost, concentrated industries; this may affect an industry's ability to organize politically and file petitions for TTB protection under these laws.

Here, we briefly point to two recent approaches that researchers have used to explain elements of the cross-sectional variation in TTB use within countries. First, Bown and Crowley (2013b) examine US TTB use at the industry-trading partner level over 1997–2006 in order to assess whether import protection responds to terms-of-trade pressure, in the spirit of the repeated game model of Bagwell and Staiger (1990). Because US applied MFN tariffs are constrained due to WTO tariff bindings, the Bown–Crowley approach can be interpreted as providing evidence consistent with the terms-of-trade theory that levels of import protection increase in the face of trade volume surges, especially in sectors with import demand and export supply that are relatively inelastic. Second, Bown and Tovar (2011) examine India's applied TTBs and the Grossman and Helpman (1994) model of endogenous trade policy formulation. Their empirical results are consistent with the Grossman–Helpman theory when using India's applied MFN tariffs in 1990, inconsistent with the theory for applied MFN tariffs *only* in 2000–02, but consistent again with the theory when using India's TTBs *in addition to* the applied MFN tariffs in 2000–02. This evidence suggests that, over time, India unwound some of its applied tariff reductions by substituting toward antidumping and safeguard policies.

The last of our thematic questions is whether, when countries apply import protection through TTBs, their applied policies discriminate among different trading partners. While there are different ways to examine this issue, Table 6 presents two measures—the trade-weighted share of the exporting country's total exports to the G20 economies over which the G20 economy had a TTB imposed, and the estimated value of those TTB-impacted exports to the G20 economy.[bd] We compute these two measures both in 2013 for the G20 economies and then, for rough comparison purposes, also in 1995 for the "G4" economies of Australia, Canada, the EU and the United States— the major TTB users at the time.

To interpret Table 6, consider an exporter like China. In 2013, 7.1% of China's exports to the G20 economies were subject to a TTB, and this is estimated to cover roughly $100 billion of its exports to those economies. In 1995, only 2.9% of China's exports to the G4 economies were subject to a TTB, and this was estimated to cover only $3.3 billion (in constant 2013 dollars) of its exports to those four economies.

Table 6 thus clearly reveals that TTBs are not applied uniformly across exporters. First is the sheer scale with which the value of China's exports were subject to G20 TTBs in 2013 relative to all other exporting countries—in value terms, China has almost 10 times more TTB-affected exports than the second most-impacted exporter, Korea, which had roughly $14 billion of affected exports. The United States comes in third at $12.6

[bd] These data are derived from dynamic import coverage ratios following the methodology described and applied in Bown (2011b, 2013a). The main requirement is an assumption on counterfactual import growth for products from trading partners subject to an imposed TTB during the period that the TTB was in effect. The current data relies on the relatively conservative assumption that TTB-impacted products would have grown at the average rate of import growth for non-TTB impacted products.

Table 6 Exporting countries most exposed to foreign-imposed TTBs, 2013 and 1995

#	Exporter	TTB-affected share of 2013 exports to G20 (%)	#	Exporter	TTB-affected value of 2013 exports to G20 (billions of 2013 dollars)	#	Exporter	TTB-affected share of 1995 exports to G4 (%)	#	Exporter	TTB-affected value of 1995 exports to G4 (billions of 2013 dollars)
1.	Latvia	17.7	1.	China	100.3	1.	Korea	7.6	1.	Japan	7.7
2.	China	7.1	2.	Korea	14.0	2.	Venezuela	6.2	2.	Korea	4.6
3.	Ukraine	5.7	3.	United States	12.6	3.	Ukraine	5.7	3.	China	3.3
4.	Kuwait	5.1	4.	Japan	4.4	4.	Lithuania	4.4	4.	United States	1.8
5.	Korea	3.9	5.	India	3.5	5.	China	2.9	5.	Thailand	0.9
6.	Argentina	3.8	6.	Thailand	3.5	6.	Thailand	2.8	6.	Brazil	0.7
7.	Moldova	3.7	7.	Indonesia	2.9	7.	Japan	2.6	7.	Malaysia	0.6
8.	Indonesia	3.1	8.	Russia	2.5	8.	Brazil	2.2	8.	Canada	0.6
9.	India	2.7	9.	Mexico	2.5	9.	Turkey	1.9	9.	Hong Kong	0.5
10.	Russia	2.3	10.	Germany	2.5	10.	Russia	1.8	10.	Germany	0.5
11.	Slovenia	2.3	11.	Argentina	1.9	11.	Egypt	1.6	11.	Russia	0.4
12.	Thailand	2.3	12.	Ukraine	1.7	12.	Hong Kong	1.5	12.	Turkey	0.4
13.	Macedonia	2.1	13.	Malaysia	1.6	13.	Malaysia	1.4	13.	Singapore	0.4
14.	Trin. and Tobago	2.1	14.	Vietnam	1.3	14.	Saudi Arabia	0.9	14.	Netherlands	0.2
15.	U.A.E.	1.6	15.	Brazil	0.8	15.	Poland	0.8	15.	United Kingdom	0.2
16.	Oman	1.6	16.	Italy	0.8	16.	Singapore	0.8	16.	Italy	0.2
17.	Poland	1.6	17.	Canada	0.6	17.	Australia	0.5	17.	Venezuela	0.2
18.	Kenya	1.5	18.	U.A.E.	0.6	18.	United States	0.5	18.	Poland	0.2
19.	Vietnam	1.3	19.	France	0.6	19.	Argentina	0.5	19.	France	0.2
20.	United States	1.3	20.	Singapore	0.5	20.	South Africa	0.5	20.	Ukraine	0.2

Trade-weighted shares of imports subject to foreign-imposed TTBs, constructed by the authors using HS-06 level data from Bown, C.P., 2014a. Temporary trade barriers database. The World Bank. Available from: http://econ.worldbank.org/ttbd/ (accessed 25.07.14) matched to UN Comtrade import data and using the methodological approach of Bown (2011b, 2013a). G20 = Group of 20 economies listed in Table 1. G4 = Australia, Canada, European Union, and United States only.

billion.[be] Furthermore, a number of other emerging, developing, and "transition" economies also have a substantial share of their exports affected by foreign-imposed TTBs. While not shown here, some of this can be tied to the fact that some of the major new users of TTB policies are other emerging economies, thus revealing TTBs as an instrument through which "South–South" protectionism is arising (Bown, 2013a). Third, China, Ukraine, Moldova, Russia and Macedonia are all former "nonmarket" economies (NMEs); there are special rules available for countries to impose antidumping in particular against NMEs during this period which may make it arguably easier legally to apply such import restrictions to them.

Can the main export targets of TTB use change over time? In 1995 the main TTB policy in use (antidumping) was primarily targeting the newly industrializing Asian economies of Japan and Korea. Indeed, Japan went from having $7.7 billion of exports to the G4 in 1995 being subject to TTBs (roughly 2.6% of its total exports to those economies), to only $4.4 billion in 2013, and it is now not even among the top 20 targeted countries as a share of the country's total exports. And while Korea was still the second largest exporter in 2013 when calculated in value terms, the share of its exports subject to TTBs in these two sets of important markets is only roughly half as large in 2013 as it was in 1995. This anecdotal evidence for Japan and Korea at least suggests that highly-impacted exporters—including China today—may be able to "graduate" from being targets of foreign TTB use over time.

3.2 Quantitative Restrictions, Import Quotas, and Tariff Rate Quotas

Import quotas—defined as a limit on the number of units of a product that may enter a country—are generally forbidden under the original GATT through Article XI. A long line of economic research has shown that the administration of a quota affects the allocation of welfare and the costs that the quota imposes on different societal groups. If a domestic government auctions off licenses to import the good, then the difference between the item's price under free trade and the domestic price of the good under the quota is a "quota rent" which is collected by the importing country's government. If the government gives away licenses to import under the quota, it transfers the value of this potential (auctioned license) revenue to whomever receives the licenses—a foreign government, a foreign export licensing board, or foreign producers. In this process, there is great scope for corruption; concern regarding corruption is one of the reasons why ad valorem tariff policies have long been encouraged as the "preferred" form of border

---

[be] While Latvia had a larger share of its exports subject to G20-imposed TTBs than China in 2013, because it is such a small exporting country, when measured in dollar terms it was not in the top 20 most affected exporters.

barrier.[bf] While the inherent assumption in the preceding examples was that the world market price was below the domestic price, so that the entire quota was filled, in practice, nonbinding quotas with unfilled allotments are not uncommon. In these cases, the quota fill rate, the ratio of actual imports to quota-allowed imports, can serve as a measure of the restrictiveness of the policy.

Countries today continue to apply quantitative restrictions on imports in a few different areas under the WTO system.

First, a number of countries continue to maintain quantitative restrictions in their agricultural sector. Some countries have articulated—as part of their legal commitment to the WTO—a minimum volume of imports of a product for which they offer one (lower) tariff rate; any additional imports arising beyond that minimum volume face a higher tariff rate. These are referred to as tariff rate quotas (TRQs). Take, for example, the United States, which continues to maintain a TRQ for sugar with an in-quota specific duty of 0.625 cents per pound and out-of-quota specific duty of over 20 times that—ie, of 15.36 (raw sugar) or 16.21 (refined sugar) cents per pound. Overall, in the United States in 2013, 4.5% of agricultural products remained subject to quantitative restrictions (through tariff rate quotas). TRQs are also prominent in agriculture in a number of other high-income economies: for the EU, 11.3% of agricultural products were still subject to TRQs, in Canada 9.5%, and in Japan 6.2% (WTO, 2014).

Second, quantitative restrictions remain an especially prevalent outcome in safeguard investigations, including many imposed by emerging and developing countries. Overall, 30% of the import restrictions that WTO members imposed under the Agreement on Safeguards between 1995 and 2014 involved quotas.

Do countries impose quotas so as to discriminate among trading partners? Indeed, the administration of quotas frequently allocates the import licenses under an historical market share rule; typically a firm or country's average market share over the prior 3 years.[bg] Bown and McCulloch (2003) examine the WTO safeguards imposed over 1995–2000

[bf] More generally, the empirical relevance of the distinction between tariffs and quotas depends on the production technology in an industry and its market structure. Since Bhagwati (1965), economists have understood the general equivalence of tariffs and quotas in perfectly competitive markets with a competitive allocation of quota rights. Interestingly, since its inception in 1947, the GATT/WTO system has pushed for members to adopt tariffs rather than quotas. Important theoretical differences between tariffs and quotas have focused on deviations from the assumption of perfect competition (Panagariya, 1981, 1982) or wasteful resources devoted to gaining import licenses (Krueger, 1974).

[bg] In particular, a quota might allocate a value-based measure of domestic market share to all foreign producers—eg, 50%—and then further divide the aggregate quota to historical exporters based on historical market shares. This system has the advantage of dramatically reducing competitive pressure on domestic producers, partially placating major foreign producers, while facing minimal resistance from the major losers, ie, disorganized consumers and potential new entrants from foreign countries. This system nominally satisfies nondiscrimination by providing market access to historical exporters, but prevents new market entrants that have the potential to put downward pressure on consumer prices.

and highlight the discriminatory nature of quota allocations. For example, quantitative restrictions which base within-quota shares on historical market presence discriminate against new entrants.

Finally, the most significant quota system of the last half-century, the multifiber arrangement (MFA)— that we address in Section 4—was dismantled in 2004. A number of studies have focused on different aspects of the MFA (Brambilla et al., 2010; Harrigan and Barrows, 2009; Dean, 1995; Khandelwal et al., 2013), and especially the implications of its expiration.

3.3 Price Undertakings and Voluntary Export Restraints

A second form of quantitative restriction is a voluntary agreement by exporters to raise their prices and/or restrain their export volumes. These policies are referred to as price undertakings or voluntary export restraints (VERs), and while they share many common economic features; they are currently treated in different ways under the WTO. For while VERs were supposedly banned in the Agreement on Safeguards established in 1995, price undertakings are encouraged as an outcome in the 1995 WTO Agreement on Antidumping.[bh]

Not surprisingly, given the high frequency of antidumping use across countries, price undertakings are also a relatively common outcome of the investigations. Consider, for example, the data on antidumping outcomes for the European Union. Overall, approximately 20% of EU antidumping investigations that found evidence of dumping by foreign exporters over 1989–2011 resulted in a negotiated price undertaking. These arrangements typically consist of a minimum import price and a market share allotment.[bi] Thus, the impact of an undertaking, like that of a quota, will depend on the competitive structure of the industry with considerable scope for losses to consumers if the market is imperfectly competitive.

Table 7 summarizes the EU's application of different *forms* of import barriers arising as the outcomes of antidumping investigations over 1989–2011. Each entry is the percent of total antidumping measures, by export origin, implemented in the form listed.[bj] The EU imposed almost two thirds of antidumping measures as ad valorem duties and roughly 10% as specific duties; as noted earlier, these specific duties can also discriminate between trading partners and in particular against those producing lower-priced varieties.

[bh] Bown (2002b) presents a discussion. As we further describe later in Section 4, one of the political motivations for the attempts to ban VERs was that they had become a common outcome to US safeguard and antidumping investigations in the 1970s through early 1990s, especially with respect to bilateral frictions that the United States had at the time with Japan (Bown and McCulloch, 2009).

[bi] However, these are nontransparent in that official EU publications do not report the negotiated prices or market shares. Rather, official *Decisions* and *Regulations* report the names of the lead foreign negotiating authority (for example, a foreign Chamber of Commerce or industry association) and all firms that are participating in the undertaking. This set-up leaves the Commission with flexibility to adjust minimum import prices and market shares as the situation warrants.

[bj] During this period, according to the Temporary Trade Barriers Database, the EU implemented a total of 492 antidumping measures. In roughly 5% of cases, the form of the final antidumping measure is unknown.

Table 7 European Union border barriers resulting from imposed antidumping, 1989–2011

	All countries	Export Origin G20 high income	G20 emerging	Developing
Tariffs				
Ad valorem duty	65.0	75.3	68.2	56.5
Specific duty	9.6	9.6	12.0	6.2
Price undertakings				
Price undertaking	13.2	6.8	6.6	24.9
Price undertaking/Ad val. duty	4.9	2.7	2.5	9.6
Duty if min. price breached	2.2	4.1	2.5	1.1
Other (outcome unknown)	5.1	1.5	8.2	1.7

Constructed by the authors with data from Bown, C.P., 2014a. Temporary trade barriers database. The World Bank. Available from: http://econ.worldbank.org/ttbd/ (accessed 25.07.14). Entries are share of imposed border restrictions resulting in that type of imposed border barrier.

Next consider the breakdown of the form of antidumping measures by export origin. Broadly, the EU tends to favor ad valorem import tariffs to restrict imports from high-income and emerging economies. In contrast, the EU negotiates a price undertaking in roughly 35% of the instances in which it imposes an antidumping measure against a developing country. This result could be another means to discriminate between trading partners (against new entrants). On the other hand, price undertakings may actually be preferred by the exporters if the alternative is an EU antidumping import tariff because, with a price undertaking, at least the exporter receives any "quota rents" associated with the restriction.

Two final examples illustrate the continued economic relevance of these "voluntary" policies. Consider first the price undertaking that the EU negotiated with China regarding imports of solar panels. At the time, this was an important trade policy event from China's perspective as solar panels comprised 7% of *total* Chinese exports to the EU in 2012.[bk] Second, while VERs are not commonly in current use, they were used in a major industry as recently as 2008. Upon the expiration of the MFA in 2005, the United

[bk] Interestingly, the cumulative abnormal return of Chinese solar panel producers to the European Commission's decision to institute a price undertaking was, on average, negative (Crowley and Song, 2015). Although a quota could, in theory, improve profitability of exporters by facilitating collusive price increases, it seems that for Chinese solar panel producers, the loss of future sales growth in Europe more than offset any gains associated with the elimination of aggressive price competition insured by the undertaking's minimum import price. This is in sharp contrast to the investor response to the announcement of the 1981 US automobile voluntary export restraint. The announcement of that VER, which gave the right to issue export licenses to the United States to Japanese authorities, sent the stock prices of Japanese automobile producers up (Ries, 1993), a phenomenon that demonstrated how import quotas facilitate collusive behavior in an oligopolistic market (Harris, 1985; Krishna, 1989). By establishing the restriction as a count of units rather than as a market share, the US government also provided an incentive for Japanese exporters to improve quality and increase price-cost markups (Berry et al., 1999; Goldberg, 1995; Feenstra, 1988).

States and EU quickly negotiated a set of VERs for China's exports of textiles and apparel to their markets for the period covering 2005–08.[bl]

3.4 Import Licensing, Customs Valuation, and Trade Facilitation

The final two border "policies" that we introduce include additional ways that governments can manipulate administrative hurdles to impact trade. A government may impose additional requirements that traders have official import licences in order to sell goods in its market, and then impose barriers to the acquisition of such licences. Furthermore, while the GATT and WTO contain substantial legal provisions instructing authorities on how to evaluate merchandise for assessment of duties, governments may also deliberately distort customs valuation procedures to restrict trade.

While we are unaware of any comprehensive attempts to catalogue import licensing requirements or variation in customs valuation procedures, thus making it difficult to assess their more general impact, there are certainly case studies revealing instances in which each has likely had a significant impact on international trade. The WTO has an Agreement on Import Licensing Procedures, and a prominent recent concern has arisen over Argentina's institution of import licensing requirements for hundreds of products beginning in 2012. In particular, the EU, the United States and Japan have used the WTO's formal dispute settlement process to challenge Argentina's requirements for the declarations needed for import approval, the variety of licences required for the importation of certain goods, and the substantial delay in granting the approval to import. Overall, WTO (2015b) indicates that in at least 44 formal disputes initiated between 1995 and 2015, the complaining country alleged that the responding country violated some element of the WTO's Agreement on Import Licensing. In at least 17 formal WTO disputes during the period, the complaining country alleged that the respondent violated some element of the GATT/WTO provisions on customs valuation.

There is a small but growing empirical literature examining how these administrative channels affect trade; indeed, governments have recently put a priority on them through the WTO's newly negotiated Trade Facilitation Agreement. The World Bank's *Doing Business* reports are the best known source of comprehensive data about time delays and related problems associated with moving goods across a border. Djankov et al. (2010), for example, use these data to estimate a gravity model of trade and find that each additional day of delay before shipment reduces trade by more than 1%. Furthermore, Volpe et al. (2015) utilize detailed export transaction data from Uruguay to estimate the impact of customs delays on firm exports. Finally, research using data on customs

---

[bl] For a discussion, see Bown (2010, pp. 307–311). The leverage that the United States and EU arguably had with China was that they could have imposed the China-specific transitional safeguard—eg, an import tariff—to curtail China's export growth. By agreeing to the VERs, China was able to keep the quota rents associated with the (potentially inevitable) border restrictions.

valuation to examine bureaucratic corruption and tariff evasion includes Javorcik and Narciso (2008) for Eastern Europe and Mishra et al. (2008) for India.

4. THE HISTORICAL EVOLUTION OF BORDER BARRIERS UNDER THE GATT

Focussing thus far on trade barriers imposed at the border, we have characterized the contemporary landscape of trade policy as both having significant heterogeneity in applied tariffs, but also as being littered with numerous other border barriers. Collectively and cumulatively, the status quo is of trade policy marked by variation across countries, products, and trading partners. But how did the international trading system arrive at this point? With only a few exceptions, our discussion of history thus far has been limited to the evolution of trade policy since the 1995 inception of the WTO. Here, we briefly appeal to a longer view of the history of the multilateral trading system by focusing on major trade policy developments taking place over the period spanning 1947–94, covering the full GATT era.

We begin with the level of tariffs for the major economies at the outset of the GATT negotiations in 1947 that established the new multilateral trading system.[bm] After reporting on the subsequent evolution of applied tariffs, we introduce the major exceptions to the GATT rule that countries should limit the form of their import protection to their applied MFN tariffs and we assess recently released data from the GATT Archives on their use. One key observation is that protectionist forces have been pushing back against trade liberalization since the inception of the multilateral system. Amidst a general decline in tariffs, new trade restrictions emerged. Thus still open questions for researchers to pursue include quantifying the importance of this push-back and further clarifying how it relates to the policy substitution that we documented in Section 3 as having arisen today.

The GATT members introduced a number of contingency clauses regarding the use of trade restrictions when they drafted the agreement because they understood that changing economic conditions might force countries to face pressure to renege on their tariff commitments. We have already observed the current incarnation of a number of these provisions, such as antidumping and safeguards, as they have been part of the GATT since its origin. In other instances, the exceptions that we introduce later arose on an ad hoc basis and were not anticipated when the GATT was written. In a few others, their use waned and they have largely disappeared from the current policy landscape.

In keeping with our organizational structure, we use the lens of policy instruments to describe the major trade policy developments arising during the GATT era. We begin by

---

[bm] The historical context matters, as the GATT system arose and was shaped by a number of major geo-political events. These include the catastrophic economic policies of the 1930s Great Depression era, the devastation of Western Europe and Japan during World War II, and the rise of the Cold War between the United States and Soviet Union. See, for example, Irwin et al. (2008) for the negotiating origins of the GATT.

examining the procedures by which countries could increase their MFN tariffs through renegotiations, before we push beyond applied tariffs to other border barriers. We also introduce an emergency import restriction necessitated by the fixed exchange rate regime of the postwar era that countries could implement to address a macroeconomic (balance of payments) crisis.

We also highlight other exceptions and carve outs that arose during the GATT period, some of which cannot be tied to any singular policy instrument or exception. In particular, the GATT had to accommodate the contentious integration of major new members such as Japan into the system; it responded to demands from developing countries for special and differential treatment; it sought to retain relevance despite major economies brokering side deals that resulted in entire sectors (textiles and apparel, agriculture) being pulled out of certain elements of the system; it oversaw the rise of less transparent and less market-oriented "grey area" measures such as voluntary export restraints; and it witnessed the increased use of antidumping by high-income economies, a temporary trade barrier policy that has since exploded in use globally.

In a final section we draw a few implications from this era for contemporary research and policy. Some of the policies of importance were only temporary; others have arguably had effects that persist to this day. Along the way, we also highlight both our main themes and important venues for additional research, especially given the troves of historical data, digitization, and electronic archives increasingly being made publicly available to researchers.[bn]

4.1 Pre-GATT 1947 Tariff Levels and Tariff Trends Over the GATT Period

The GATT negotiations began in 1947 with 23 countries—referred to as "Contracting Parties"—ultimately signing the agreement. The initial activity consisted of a round of reciprocal tariff cutting negotiations between those countries, as well as the establishment of a set of principles, rules and exceptions, set out as distinct "Articles" in the agreement, that together launched the new multilateral trading system.[bo] The United States, Canada, Australia, the countries of Western Europe, and the other Contracting Parties then repeatedly convened under GATT negotiating rounds over the next five decades to bargain for additional tariff reductions and sometimes consider adoption of new rules.[bp] Eight different negotiating rounds were initiated and concluded between 1947 and 1994.

For a number of reasons, very little is known about the exact levels of import tariffs that countries applied in 1947, immediately prior to the first set of GATT tariff-cutting

---

[bn] Data Appendix includes a detailed introduction and discussion of the GATT archival data utilized in this Section.

[bo] For a description of the key GATT Articles—the rules and exceptions—that we have introduced and referenced throughout this chapter, see Table A.3.

[bp] Bagwell et al. (2015), for example, present a micro-level empirical bargaining investigation of the negotiations that took place during the GATT's (third) set of negotiations, referred to as the "Torquay Round" of 1950–51.

Percent

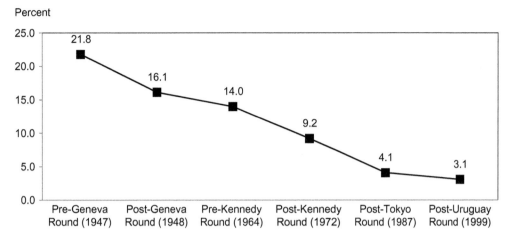

Fig. 12 Estimates of average tariffs for the United States, Western Europe, and Japan, 1947–99. *Bown, C.P., Irwin, D.A., 2015. The GATTs starting point: tariff levels circa 1947. NBER Working Paper No. 21782, fig. 1, based on backcast estimates for 1947 average tariffs, computed from data on simple average tariffs in effect at the beginning of the Kennedy Round (1964), and reports on the size of average tariff cuts arising during the initial GATT negotiating rounds.*

negotiations. Bown and Irwin (2015) suggest that the average applied import tariff in 1947 was likely around 22% for the United States, Japan, and the major countries of Western Europe.[bq]

While the exact starting point for tariff negotiations may not be known, there is a consensus on the evolution of average applied imports tariffs for these major economies over the subsequent decades. Overall, Fig. 12 presents the path of average tariffs for these major countries between 1947, beginning at roughly 22%, and 1999, by which time most of the GATT's Uruguay Round tariff reduction commitments had been phased in, at roughly 3%.

[bq] A separate issue is the extent to which applied import tariffs were even the major policy constraint on trade flows at the time; eg, Curzon (1965, pp. 80–81) points out that quotas and foreign exchange controls were major impediments to trade for many countries during this era. Nevertheless, Bown and Irwin (2015) suggest a number of reasons why even calculating average tariffs for 1947 is difficult. First, there was a lack of transparency across countries about their applied tariff policies; ie, data unavailability. Second, even if data were available, there was no common tariff classification scheme across countries, making it potentially difficult to make meaningful cross-country comparisons of simple average tariffs. Third, alternative measures of trade-weighted average tariffs, while readily calculable from available data, suffer from potentially severe biases associated with high tariffs leading to low import volumes and thus under weighting. Fourth, the frequency of tariffs being applied as specific duties is known to have been a major measurement issue for United States tariffs during the period (eg, Irwin, 1998a,b; Crucini, 1994); and while the prevalence of specific tariff use for other countries during this period is unknown, it is expected to potentially also play a major complicating role. Note that Ossa (2014) adopts a distinct approach that relies on quantitative modeling techniques to construct counterfactual estimates for the size of Nash (noncooperative) tariffs in a model featuring seven regions (including the United States, EU, Japan, China, India, Brazil, and rest of the world). He computes the median tariff to be 58.1%, which is somewhat higher than estimates of the pre-GATT levels of average applied tariffs described earlier.

However, the remainder of this section showcases a number of ways by which this headline result, of a broad downward trend in average tariffs for the major economies, is nevertheless incomplete. First, this figure reveals nothing about the applied tariffs for countries other than the United States, Japan, and Western Europe, most of which have quite different end points (see again Table 1) as well as tariff liberalization experiences getting there.[br] Second, even for the major economies, the average tariff fails to capture what was happening with other border barriers during this period.

4.2 Changing Tariff Rates Under the GATT

Two distinct legal provisions in the original GATT permitted countries to increase their tariffs after negotiations with key trading partners. The first was for permanent changes to the tariff (Article XXVIII), and thus was a renegotiation of binding commitments. The other allowed a temporary increase to the tariff (Article XIX) in light of unforeseen, but temporary, events. One common feature of both is that tariff-changing countries were required to provide *compensation* to the affected trading partners. This compensation could take the form either of a mutually agreeable tariff reduction in some other sector or of the affected trading partner being permitted to raise its tariff in some other sector in response. A second common feature is that, unlike other GATT provisions introduced later, these changes to tariffs were meant to apply only to limited and well-defined *products*, and not entire sectors or bundles of imports.[bs]

Over the entire GATT period of 1947–94, countries invoked Article XIX on 150 different occasions to increase their tariffs temporarily and Article XXVIII on 275 occasions to increase their tariff bindings permanently (WTO, 1995). While there is little empirical research examining use of these provisions, access to some newly available archival data from the 1950s allows us to investigate patterns to some of the new import restrictions triggered right after the GATT's inception.[bt] For example, the early GATT

[br] The WTO (2007) provides an important survey of the first 60 years of the GATT/WTO system and includes additional, country-specific descriptions of tariff data over the decades for a number of countries not covered in depth here, such as Brazil, India, Senegal, Nigeria, Argentina and Korea (pp. 211–219).

[bs] For example, an Article XIX action typically involved a tariff line or group of products like "hatter's fur" (US, 1951), "strawberries" (Canada, 1957) or "hard coal" (West Germany, 1957) rather than a broad industrial classification like "chemicals" or "machinery."

[bt] Bown (2004) examines invocations of Article XIX and XXVIII over the 1973–94 period in one of the relatively few empirical studies seeking to explain why countries used these provisions to implement additional import protection. The evidence there is consistent with a theory that countries invoked these exceptions when they needed to make changes to their trade policies between negotiating rounds and wanted to do so in accordance with GATT rules so as to avoid a dispute and potentially more severe retaliation by affected trading partners. For a theoretical exploration of the different GATT rules on *compensation* under Article XIX and XXVIII vs under dispute settlement (GATT Article XXIII), see Bown (2002a). A case study of US import policy in the 20th century by Baldwin (1985) suggests that the United States' use of Article XIX cycled with changes in US trade law. The US law regarding safeguards varied in the stringency of qualifying criteria over decades with the result that safeguards were never used under the 1962 US Trade Act but were far more common after reforms to the law in 1974.

negotiations for tariff reductions could have significantly over-estimated the amount of tariff-cutting liberalization that government might be able to sustain, thus triggering the need to raise tariffs.

We begin with the permanent tariff increases triggered under Article XXVIII. Between 1950 and 1959, the GATT Contracting Parties invoked Article XXVIII only 70× (WTO, 1995). Thus it appears that formal actions to raise tariffs permanently under Article XXVIII were relatively rare, and when they arose, the requests were scattered across countries and sectors. The lack of major permanent tariff increases, at least for the major GATT members, is consistent with the downward trend in average applied tariffs for these countries over the GATT period (see again Fig. 12).

Next, consider the frequency with which countries resorted to *temporary* escape from their tariff commitments (Article XIX). A distinctive element of this channel is the mandate that, in order to justify use of Article XIX, governments were required to provide some evidence of unforeseen events having taking place, and that increased imports of the product were causing injury to the domestic, import-competing industry. Notably, the Article XIX provision has subsequently been transformed into the WTO's Agreement on Safeguards. We have presented cross-country data on safeguards use over 1995–2013 in substantial detail in Section 3.1.

Overall, countries triggered temporary tariff increases in only 19 instances under Article XIX over 1950–59; the United States requested slightly more than half.[bu] Fig. 13 displays Article XIX use over 1950–59 so as to make comparisons to safeguard use in more recent decades. The figure presents the share of all cases that high-income and developing countries triggered in the different periods by sector.[bv] There has been a dramatic change in the sectoral distribution of safeguard use over time. In the 1950s, high-income countries utilized safeguards in a wide variety of sectors, including footwear, minerals, transportation equipment, textiles, and plastics. More recently, they have used safeguards primarily to restrict trade in metals. The pattern of concentration across industries for developing countries is reversed; two thirds of safeguards in the 1950s were in one sector (machinery); more recently developing countries have implemented safeguards more diffusely across a number of industries, including chemicals, plastics, wood products, textiles, stone, metals, and machinery.

In summary, actions to raise tariffs in the first decade of the GATT appear to have been in disperse product categories across a wide variety of countries. Unlike other policy tools discussed later, Article XIX and XXVIII were not used to dramatically reduce imports at the aggregate level or to dramatically reduce trade in an entire sector of the economy.

[bu] Data on Article XIX investigations between 1950 and 1959 was collected from the GATT digital archive at Stanford University and each verbal description of a product was matched to the modern HS06 product classification.

[bv] The definition of core European countries is West Germany, France, the Netherlands, Belgium, the United Kingdom, and Italy.

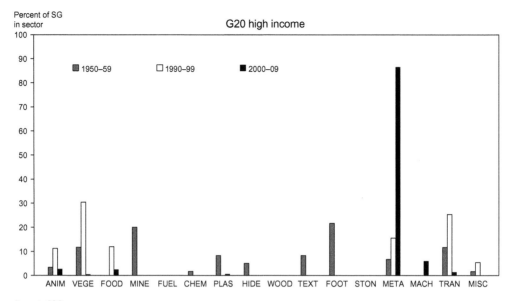

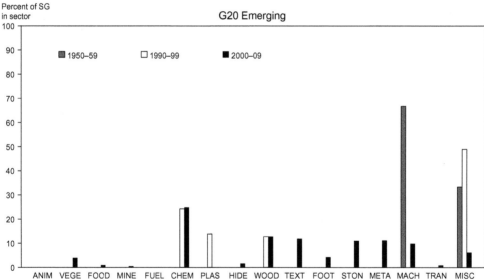

Fig. 13 Temporary import protection actions under Article XIX and WTO agreement on safeguards: Share of total investigations by sector by decade.

Constructed by the authors from Bown, C.P., 2014a. Temporary trade barriers database. The World Bank. Available from: http://econ.worldbank.org/ttbd/ (accessed 25.07.14) and L: series reports from 1950 to 1959 in the GATT digital archive. The share reported for each decade is the count of safeguards investigations by HS06 product and export origin within one of 16 industrial sectors divided by the count of safeguards investigations by HS06 and export origin summed over all industrial sectors.

4.3 GATT Exceptions and the Rise of Major Carve-Outs

In this section we briefly introduce a number of major exceptions to the general application of the GATT rules and procedures that resulted in important "carve outs" from liberal trade during 1947–94. These take on a number of different forms.[bw]

4.3.1 Emergency Import Restrictions to Address Balance of Payments Problems

From the end of World War II until 1971, the major economies participated in the Bretton Woods system of fixed exchange rates in which countries pegged their currencies to the US dollar.[bx] Understanding that macroeconomic forces could lead to an overvalued currency, and that this could lead to a balance of payments (BOP) deficit and the loss of foreign currency reserves, the GATT included Article XII, which explicitly permitted government use of import restrictions to defend a currency's peg and prevent a forced devaluation.[by] Balance of payments actions were rarely used by the major economies after the system of flexible exchange rates was introduced in 1971.[bz] However, when BOP actions were taken during the GATT's first 25 years to address a fundamental macroeconomic imbalance, they tended to be broad-based import restrictions of sizeable magnitudes. This is quite distinct from the product-specific (Article XIX, XXVIII, or antidumping) exceptions or even sector-specific exceptions introduced later regarding textiles and apparel, and agriculture.

To give one example, in January 1952, the government of the United Kingdom was forecasting a balance of payments deficit for 1952 of about £500 million. The Chancellor of the Exchequer circulated a top secret Cabinet memo which declared: "The gold and dollar reserves continue to fall at an alarming rate... unless we tackle this situation... by the middle of the year we shall not be able to hold the pound at $2.80... Unless we stem this tide, it will swallow us up, and we shall reach a point at which we can no longer buy the basic food and raw materials on which this island depends..." (Butler, 1952). By early March, the UK suspended or restricted imports on an enormous variety of foodstuffs and manufactured goods— including cheese, cloth, dishwashing machines, roof tiles, metal buckets, fish hooks, and umbrellas—with the objective of reducing imports in 1952 by "about 10 per cent of the value of imports in the year 1951." (UK, 1952)

[bw] This section deliberately omits reference to preferential trading arrangements; see again our earlier discussion in Section 2.3. The one major example of a successful and sustained PTA established early in the GATT era was the European Economic Community. Other major PTA examples such as CUSFTA/NAFTA, MERCOSUR, and ASEAN were all established at the tail end of the GATT period.

[bx] In 1971, the Bretton Woods system effectively collapsed when the United States abandoned the gold standard.

[by] Irwin (2012) describes how the mismanagement of currencies contributed to the disastrous trade policy environment of the 1930s and thus to the deepening and persistence of the Great Depression.

[bz] BOP consultations and import restrictions continued in the 1970s and 1980s for many small and low-income countries that pegged their currencies to a major currency after the collapse of Bretton Woods.

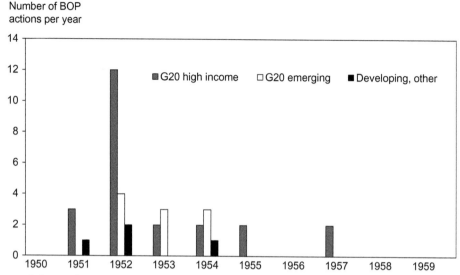

Fig. 14 Balance of payment import restrictions under Article XII, 1950–59.
Constructed by the authors from the L: reports from 1950 to 1959 in the GATT digital archive.

Fig. 14 presents data on the number of import restrictions necessitated by BOP problems between 1950 and 1959.[ca] While the absolute number may be small in any given year, the actions taken as a fraction of the total GATT membership at the time were sometimes substantial. For example, in 1952, *nearly half* of the initial 23 GATT Contracting Parties—Australia, Brazil, Chile, Finland, France, New Zealand, Pakistan, Rhodesia, Sweden, South Africa and the United kingdom—imposed import restrictions for balance of payments problems.

4.3.2 Japan's GATT Accession and the "Temporary" Article XXXV Exception

Two major economies were not included as part of the original 23 Contracting Parties that negotiated the launching of the GATT at the end of World War II—West Germany and Japan. Both were eventually allowed entry—West Germany acceded in 1951 and Japan acceded in 1955.[cb]

However, Japan's accession to the GATT, and its reindustrialization and export-led growth strategy, led to a major period of adjustment for many other GATT members.

[ca] These data on the number of reports to the GATT of import restrictions necessitated by BOP problems are collected from the GATT Digital Archive.
[cb] As we have already discussed, during the period in which West Germany was becoming a formal part of the GATT system, it was also involved in substantial efforts at Western European integration, including the ECSC in 1951 and the 1957 establishment of the European Economic Community and customs union. See again Section 2.3.

Indeed, upon Japan's GATT entry in 1955, more than 50 countries invoked the GATT's Article XXXV exception which allowed them to refuse to apply the Agreement's legal obligations to their trade with Japan. The implication was that most of the GATT membership set a higher tariff on imports from Japan, even after it joined the GATT, than the MFN tariff they applied to imports from all other members.[cc]

The length of this temporary nonapplication of the GATT varied substantially. Australia, Belgium, France, Netherlands, and the United Kingdom did not recognize Japan's full membership into the GATT for nearly a decade (until 1963 or 1964). Others did not revoke their Article XXXV exception, and thus reduce their tariff on imports from Japan to MFN levels, until the 1970s or later.

4.3.3 The Rise of Voluntary Export Restraints, Including the Multifiber Arrangement

Unlike much of the GATT membership, the United States championed Japan's accession to the GATT and offered Japanese exporters MFN tariff treatment in the US market. However, industries in the United States also faced acute pressure as they struggled to adjust to suddenly increasing imports from Japan. This led the US government to use a number of *other* policy instruments to slow down Japan's export growth; the most prolific of these were in the form of negotiated voluntary export restraints, the policy that we introduced conceptually in Section 3.3.

One major set of quotas and VERs arose in the face of increased imports of textiles and apparel from Japan; this led first to the Short Term arrangement covering cotton textiles (1961–62), followed by the Long Term arrangement covering cotton textiles (1962–74), and ultimately the multifiber arrangement (MFA) that remained in place between 1974 and 2004.

The textile and apparel sector turned out to be the tip of the iceberg for the VERs that the United States negotiated with Japan. For example, in the decade between 1975 and 1984, the United States had at least six different sectors in which its safeguard (Article XIX) investigations ultimately resulted in VERs with Japan, including autos, televisions, steel and footwear (Bown and McCulloch, 2009). Furthermore a set of US antidumping investigations begun in 1985 over DRAMS and other semiconductors also resulted in VERs with Japan.

To be clear, there was no GATT legal exception or provision that expressly authorized VERs—indeed, they were often referred to as "grey-area" measures, and as we described earlier, this outcome has been banned for safeguard investigations under the WTO's Agreement on Safeguards. Under the GATT, VERs arose on an ad hoc basis, and they were frequently the result of negotiations that had developed after the United

---

[cc] On the other hand, Japan did not invoke the Article XXXV exception and thus granted MFN tariff treatment to all GATT members, including the ones that invoked Article XXXV.

States had a domestic industry trigger one of the other potential GATT exceptions, such as a safeguard (Article XIX) or antidumping (Article VI) investigation.

4.3.4 Agriculture

From the GATT's inception, the agricultural sector was treated as unique and thus one for which the GATT rules and obligations would not comprehensively apply. Two of the primary proponents for such an approach were the United States and the countries of Western Europe. Indeed, the United States had requested and was granted a waiver (under Article XXV) in 1955 that even the basic GATT provisions on tariffs (Article II) and quantitative restrictions (Article XI) not be applied to its agricultural sector. Europe was also not in favor of applying basic GATT tenets to the agricultural sector; beginning in the late 1950s, the EEC was busy developing its Common Agricultural Policy (CAP) of integrating European agricultural markets; policies included high border barriers as well as establishing a complex system of subsidy programs.[cd]

Without understating the importance of the sector, we limit further discussion here to two additional points. First, although agriculture was seen as special during the period, a number of formal and contentious trade disputes concerning the sector arose under the GATT. In particular, the United States and EEC formally confronted each other on a number of different occasions.[ce] Second, while agriculture was formally brought back into the multilateral system through the WTO Agreement on Agriculture in 1995, it remains a sector marked by high levels of import protection. As we have already observed via Figs. 2, 3, and 7, contemporary tariffs (applied rates and bindings) in the sector remain high, with a high incidence of both tariff peak products and tariffs applied as specific duties, and some countries continue to implement quotas in the sector (Section 3.2). Furthermore, and as we will discover in Section 5, agriculture is a sector characterized by significant *domestic* policy interventions, such as subsidies, crop insurance, and other price (and income) support schemes, and is one in which special trade rules for health and safety (through the WTO Agreement on Sanitary and Phytosanitary Measures) frequently apply.

4.3.5 Special and Differential Treatment for Developing Countries

The GATT was a voluntary agreement. Countries individually decided how much tariff cutting they would attempt to extract from trading partners via the repeated rounds of multilateral negotiations and, in return, how much tariff-cutting they would agree to

---

[cd] For an introduction to agricultural issues in the GATT and WTO, see Hoekman and Kostecki (2009, pp. 270–303). For historical data dating back to 1955 on agricultural distortions in major markets, see Anderson and Nelgen (2013).

[ce] Disputes arose in a challenge to the CAP in 1962, and in bilateral skirmishes in products including dairy, processed fruits and vegetables, animal feed proteins, sugar, poultry, as well as the infamous "chicken war" (Hudec, 1993).

undertake at home. A number of major developing countries helped to found the GATT in 1947, including Brazil, Burma, India, Pakistan, South Africa, Sri Lanka, and Zimbabwe. In the 1950s and 1960s, the GATT membership expanded to include a number of developing countries after they gained independence from colonial rule. Nevertheless, during most of the GATT period, many developing countries did not pursue export-oriented trade and development strategies, but instead chose to pursue import-substitution regimes.

The original GATT 1947 introduced special and differential treatment (SDT) for developing countries via Article XVIII. In the 1960s, the GATT adopted its Part IV "Chapter on Trade and Development" which specified additional principles by which high-income countries were encouraged to reduce trade barriers in products of particular interest to developing countries. Finally, in the 1970s major economies like the European Economic Community and United States implemented lower-than-MFN tariffs on imports of many products from developing countries under the Generalized System of Preferences (GSP). This exception to MFN was brought into the GATT system legally with the adoption of the Enabling Clause in 1979.

Looking back at this historical episode, however, the consensus is that the GATT period was not a successful one for integrating developing countries into the multilateral trading system. One explanation offered by economists is that all of the exceptions associated with SDT combined to result in a strong *disincentive* for developing countries to engage the same "reciprocity" process that was the mechanism that arguably made the GATT such a success for the high-income countries. Because developing countries had been offered export market access (via unilateral preferences) "for free," developing countries did not have to simultaneously reform their import-competing sectors; this is what high-income countries had been required (by general equilibrium market forces) to do in exchange for the reciprocal market access that had been granted to their exporters.[cf]

Second, because developing countries did not offer any market access of their own in exchange for special tariff cuts, they could not influence either the products or the countries from which they would receive these tariff cuts. And, as we observed already via Figs. 9 and 8, countries typically did not offer unilateral tariff cuts for 100% of their imported products even to developing country exporters under PTAs. Furthermore, the comparative advantage of most developing countries had them involved in globally diffuse export sectors; the result was low-income countries had great difficulty in organizing negotiations among themselves to coordinate tariff liberalization "requests" being made of major importing countries (Ludema and Mayda, 2013).

[cf] McCulloch and Pinera (1976) offer an early skeptical view of the benefits of GSP, for example. Subramanian and Wei (2007) provide empirical evidence that the GATT had relatively little impact on developing country trade, potentially due to the asymmetries implied by such preferences. See also Staiger (2006), Bagwell and Staiger (2014), and Ornelas (2016).

Overall, developing countries were not successful at getting their true export interests reflected as part of negotiated bargains. As such, one legacy of the GATT period is that agriculture, textiles and apparel, and footwear—sectors of production and export interest for developing countries—were essentially excluded from much of the trade liberalization that took place.

4.3.6 Antidumping in Historical Perspective

The last trade policy exception from the GATT period that we introduce is antidumping.[cg] As described in Section 3.1, the GATT system permitted countries to impose antidumping import restrictions against products sold at low (dumped) prices if such imports caused injury to the domestic, import-competing industry. Today antidumping is in use by a wide range of high-income and emerging economies.

Prior to the 1990s, only four economies—Australia, Canada, the EEC and the United States—used antidumping import restrictions with any regularity.[ch] In the 1980s, for example, the United States began to use antidumping with increased frequency to address the import growth in a number of different sectors from Japan, as well as some of the other newly industrializing economies of East Asia, such as Korea and Taiwan.[ci]

Here, we take advantage of newly compiled data on historical use of antidumping by the GATT's high-income economies so as to compare their use of the policy during the 1970s with their more contemporary use. Fig. 15 depicts the share of antidumping investigations across industrial sectors for three different decades.[cj]

Interestingly, the figure reveals a number of similarities arising for antidumping use by both the United States and Europe. In the 2000s, the industry demands for new import restrictions were mostly concentrated into the metals (steel) sector. However, this was not always the case. In the 1970s, less than 25% of US antidumping investigations were in the metal sector. In both economies in the 1970s, antidumping use was much more evenly dispersed across sectors, including chemicals, machinery, plastics, stone, and transportation equipment.

[cg] Under the GATT 1947, both antidumping and countervailing duties were permitted under Article VI. Additional provisions for these policies were put forward through "plurilateral codes" as a result of the GATT's Tokyo Round of negotiations in 1979.

[ch] South Africa was also a major user of antidumping during the period between 1921 and the 1970s; for a discussion, see Edwards (2011).

[ci] See Irwin (2005) for a presentation of the historical use of antidumping by the United States. Blonigen and Prusa (2016) survey the literature on antidumping; most of the early empirical research in particular that had arisen in the 1980s and 1990s had focused on the United States and, to a lesser extent, the European Economic Community.

[cj] Data used to construct these figures for 1970–79 come from the GATT digital archive series COM.AD, and for 1990–2000 from the Temporary Trade Barriers Database. For the 1970s, we mapped the verbal descriptions of products involved into HS06 product categories.

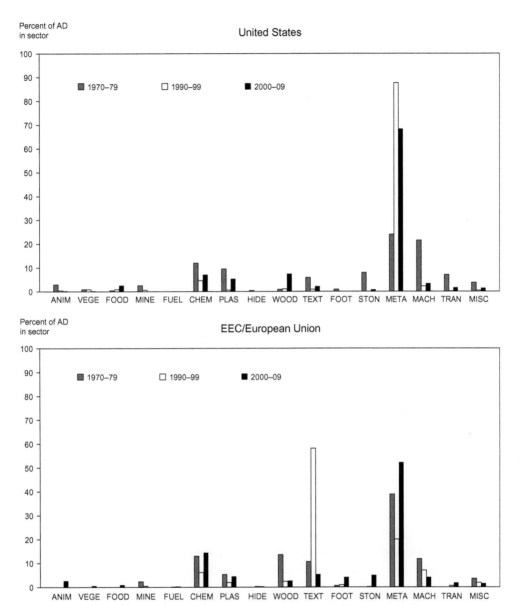

Fig. 15 Article VI and agreement on antidumping: Share of antidumping investigations by sector by decade.

Constructed by the authors from Bown, C.P., 2014a. Temporary trade barriers database. The World Bank. Available from: http://econ.worldbank.org/ttbd/ (accessed 25.07.14) and COM.AD reports from 1970 to 1979 in the GATT Digital Archive. The share reported for each decade is the count of antidumping investigations by HS06 product and export origin within one of 16 industrial sectors divided by the count of antidumping investigations by HS06 and export origin summed over all industrial sectors.

4.4 Implications for the Contemporary Landscape of Trade Policy

We summarize our brief history of the GATT period with four important observations that build upon our chapter's main themes.

First, for the GATT period, an empirical analysis focused exclusively on applied tariffs may result in a serious mischaracterization of the landscape of trade policy. Whether it was the implementation of quantitative restrictions to protect the balance of payments due to aggregate-level shocks in the 1950s, the imposition of Article XIX (safeguard) exceptions, the exemption of Japan from MFN tariff treatment for a decade (*after* its GATT accession), the rise of sector-wide voluntary export restraints (the MFA), the proliferation of VERs in other major sectors and markets (US steel, autos, footwear), or the inception of antidumping; from the GATT's earliest years, the full story of border barriers under the multilateral trading system requires much more than examining measures of applied tariff rates.

Second, there can be substantial shifts away from one border policy tool and toward another, even within countries and potentially within sectors, over the decades. For example, consider the United States, and the textiles and apparel industry. The United States used both temporary (Article XIX) and permanent (Article XXVIII) actions to restrict imports of textiles and apparel in the 1950s. However, with the subsequent establishment of the short- and long-term arrangements on cotton textiles and then the MFA, beginning in 1961, the next four decades featured a notable absence of US special import restrictions in these sectors under its antidumping and safeguard policies.

Third, while each of these policy instruments has had at least one episode of major use, sometimes particular policies fall out of favor. This can occur for a variety of different reasons. For VERs, the new rules developed under the WTO Agreement on Safeguards, which were negotiated by the same countries that utilized this policy in the 1980s, were explicitly written to discourage their use. In this case, it appears that governments were tying their own hands to reduce the use of a policy that they understood had undesirable costs. However, these same governments appear to have turned to something else (eg, antidumping and price undertakings) when new demands for protection arose. For the balance of payment exceptions, however, the demand was largely eliminated with the collapse of the Bretton Woods system of fixed exchange rates.

Fourth, given the relative substitutability of many of these policy instruments, and perhaps due to the fact that many of the "problems" that trade policy is seen to solve remain the same (eg, competitive adjustment due to new market entrants, macroeconomic shocks, exchange rate misalignment for currencies that are not truly floating, etc.), it also turns out that history tends to repeat itself. Frequently the story-line stays the same, it is simply the countries, sectors, governments, or particular policy instruments that change.

We conclude this section by highlighting some of the parallels between what is perhaps the most significant trade policy "issue" of the most recent period—ie, the integration of China into the global trading system—with events that took place in the 1950s. First, the 2001 WTO accession of China mirrors certain aspects of the 1955 GATT accession of Japan. For example, while the GATT membership in the 1950s adjusted to Japan's entry by either raising tariffs (above otherwise mandated MFN levels) by invoking Article XXXV or negotiating VERs, the WTO membership in the 2000s adjusted to China's entry by imposing product-specific import restrictions like antidumping (see again Section 3.1 and Table 6).

Second, the 1950s and the 2000s also featured significant concerns over macroeconomic imbalances with implications for trade policy.[ck] In the 1950s, under the Bretton Woods system, many countries implemented import restrictions for balance of payment purposes. In the 2000s, under a system of flexible exchange rates for major currencies (dollar, euro, yen) and fixed or managed exchange rates for others (renminbi), interest has returned to using import policy to address macroeconomic imbalances, including those associated with China's current account surplus and its potentially "undervalued" currency. Economics has no universally-accepted definition of what constitutes an "undervalued" currency and, even if one were developed, it is unclear whether the WTO would have the institutional capacity to effectively monitor and enforce currency values. Nevertheless, an evocative academic debate arose during the 2000s regarding the appropriate role for including currency manipulation provisions into trade agreements.[cl]

5. BEHIND-THE-BORDER POLICIES

This section returns to *contemporary* economic policies and pushes beyond border barriers to introduce some of the domestic laws and regulations that can also significantly impact international commerce. "Behind-the-border" (BTB) policies start with straightforward domestic taxes and subsidies; these policies mostly become relevant when their *application* discriminates between domestic- and foreign-produced varieties of substitutable goods. However, concerns over BTB policies quickly move beyond taxes and subsidies and

---

[ck] To be clear, the 1950s were not the only episode during the GATT era in which macroeconomic shocks triggered major trade policy actions. See, for example, the Nixon-era US import surcharge in response to the Bretton Woods collapse in 1971 (Irwin, 2013), or the pressure on US trade policy in the 1980s due to the over-valued dollar prior to the Plaza Accord.

[cl] See Mattoo and Subramanian (2009) for arguments in favor of bringing the issue of currency undervaluation into the WTO; Staiger and Sykes (2010) describe a number of difficulties arising with such a proposal. The gradual appreciation of the Chinese renminbi against major currencies since 2005 served to decrease some of the intensity of the debate around the issue.

increasingly include competition policy, foreign investment regulations and local content requirements, labor and environmental regulations, other production process standards designed to protect animal or plant health, product standards to ensure consumer safety, and product labeling that is a response to consumer demands for information.

We bring BTB policies into our analysis for three reasons.

First, economic theory shows that the effects of an import tariff can be replicated through the appropriately chosen combination of a domestic consumption tax and a domestic production subsidy. Thus, if left unconstrained, we expect governments to implement such domestic policies, if only to simply replace dismantled import tariffs. Just like the various motives to impose tariffs in the first place, these taxes and subsidies may be due to government incentives to shift costs onto trading partners (eg, Bagwell and Staiger, 1999, 2001) or because of commitment problems with respect to their private sectors (Maggi and Rodriguez-Clare, 1998; Limão and Tovar, 2011).

Second, while our description later focuses on contemporary BTB policies, the trade restrictiveness concerns over BTB policies are not merely theoretical; governments have long confronted the possibility of policy substitution by addressing the issue through trade agreements. Even the original GATT 1947 did not ignore BTB policies; it included the nondiscrimination principle of national treatment (Article III) which states explicitly that, aside from the import tariff that a good must pay to cross the border, imports could not be subject to additional forms of regulatory or tax discrimination (Horn, 2006). However, the GATT also explicitly allowed governments to impose BTB policies (that might affect trade) through Article XX's "General Exceptions" for conservation of exhaustible natural resources, public (animal, plant, and human) health, public morals, etc. The establishment of the WTO in 1995 created further Agreements attempting to clarify some of the characteristics for permissible BTB policy interventions, including those concerning animal, plant, or human health (Sanitary and Phytosanitary—SPS—measures) and also product standards (technical barriers to trade— TBT—measures). Furthermore, the United States and EU especially have negotiated a number of PTAs since the early 1990s that go even further, often resulting in negotiations over BTB policies themselves.

Third, the trade restrictiveness of BTB policies ultimately ties back into our chapter's five main questions. Even though we have established that tariffs and other nontariff border barriers have not been eliminated for all countries and in all sectors, in some countries and in some sectors border barriers are low. In such cases, logical follow-up questions include, how "liberalized" is world trade with respect to BTB policies? Is there significant variation for levels of import protection arising from BTB policies across countries and industries? Furthermore, do countries use BTB policies to discriminate among trading partners, and do they change the trade restrictiveness of such policies much over time?

To establish expectations, the existing literature and data sources are not sufficiently developed so as answer any of these five questions. Unlike our approach in Sections 2 or 3, we do not utilize formal data or any summary measures of BTB policies to shed light on these questions.[cm]

Instead, our specific approach is to characterize the contemporary landscape of BTB policies through a survey of case studies of particularly contentious domestic policies that have been the subject of formal WTO disputes.[cn] While the case studies are not comprehensive, they are arguably representative of the BTB policies most frequently challenged under the WTO. They cover roughly 50 formal WTO disputes over BTB policies, or 10% of the population of all WTO disputes arising between 1995 and 2015.[co] And for most of the case studies on BTB policies, we are able to explicitly direct the interested reader to additional research from a now established and growing literature whereby economists have been paired with legal scholars to provide a jointly-written, detailed analyses of the domestic policies, markets, and jurisprudence arising under the individual WTO dispute.[cp] Tables 8–11, in each of the four sections, provide explicit references to the published dispute-specific introductions to the policies and the more detailed analyses.

By introducing these conflicts over BTB policies, we demonstrate that the next major area for the world trading system involves confronting the balance of respecting local preferences, internalizing cross-border policy externalities that arise through trade, and yet integrating economic activity across borders so as to make the most productive use of global resources. And yet not surprisingly, our main result from this section is that much more theoretical, empirical, and quantitative research is needed before we can systematically characterize in any meaningful way the trade restrictiveness, or levels of import protection, associated with BTB policies. Our discussion tends to

---

[cm] Ederington and Ruta (2016) survey the limited data on BTBs that has been made available to researchers thus far; we do not repeat the exercise here due to space constraints. As of the time of writing, and unlike policies covered in Section 2 and some of Section 3, there are no comprehensive data sets on BTB policies. There have been a few piecemeal approaches that have served as first steps. One has been to survey firms and traders as to which nontariff barriers exporters feel most impede their ability to trade. Other and more comprehensive approaches at data collection are ongoing, including efforts by international organizations such as UNCTAD and the World Bank, that review domestic laws and regulations and categorize them according to an established template of well-defined categories of nontariff measures (NTMs). These NTMs are then also mapped to HS06 products based on the descriptions of the products mentioned in the laws and regulations. While such efforts at data collection and construction are surely a step in the right direction, other significant efforts will be required before these data can be used to address the main questions of this chapter.

[cn] See Bown and Pauwelyn (2010) for a survey of WTO disputes.

[co] For context, the temporary trade barriers (antidumping, countervailing, and safeguards) described in Section 3.1 were the most frequently disputed border policy during the period. Applied TTBs were the topic of more than 175 disputes—ie, more than 35% of all WTO disputes (Bown, 2014a).

[cp] Beginning in 2001, in a project initially sponsored by the American Law Institute, Henrik Horn and Petros Mavroidis initiated a program that annually convened a set of economists and legal scholars so as to provide reports assessing the new case law arising from the WTO's Appellate Body (and unappealed Panel Reports). These joint assessments have subsequently been published annually by Cambridge University Press, primarily through special issues of the *World Trade Review*. In 2011, one of the coauthors of this chapter (Bown) took over codirecting the project (from Horn) with Mavroidis. After more than 15 years, the result is a body of work covering more than 100 WTO legal decisions.

Table 8 Disputed behind-the-border policies predominantly affecting supply, 1995–2015

Behind the border policy	WTO dispute (complaining countries)	Legal-economic research
Subsidies/Taxes		
US and EU subsidies to Boeing and Airbus for large civil aircraft	US–Large Civil Aircraft (EU) EU–Large Civil Aircraft (US) US–Tax Incentives (EU)	Hahn and Mehta (2013) and Neven and Sykes (2014)
Brazil and Canada subsidies to Embraer and Bombardier for regional aircraft	Canada–Aircraft (Brazil) Brazil–Aircraft (Canada)	Howse and Neven (2005a)
China's value-added tax exemption for domestically produced aircraft	China–Tax Measures Concerning Certain Domestically Produced Aircraft (US)	
US cotton farming subsidies	US–Upland Cotton (Brazil)	Sapir and Trachtman (2008)
EU subsidy regime for sugar	EU–Export Subsidies on Sugar (Australia, Brazil, Thailand)	Hoekman and Howse (2008)
US tax exemptions for Foreign Sales Corporations (FSC) regarding their export-related foreign trade income	US–FSC (EU)	Howse and Neven (2005b)
Korea subsidies to semiconductor producers targeted by foreign countervailing measures	Japan–DRAMs (Korea)[a] EU–Countervailing Measures on DRAM Chips (Korea)[a] US–Countervailing Duty Investigation on DRAMs (Korea)[a]	Francois and Palmeter (2008), Prusa (2008), and Crowley and Palmeter (2009)
China subsidies to clean energy products targeted by US countervailing measures	US–Countervailing Measures (China)[a]	Brewster et al. (2016)

Constructed by the authors.
[a]Indicates dispute concerned the trading partner's countervailing duty trade policy response to the subsidy and not the underlying subsidy itself.

disproportionately feature BTB policies that high-income economies impose and that are potentially affecting trade in major sectors of interest to these economies, such as aircraft, semiconductors, clean energy, autos, agriculture, foodstuffs, and also cigarettes and alcohol.[cq] While these features may motivate BTB policies as worthy of additional research

[cq] In their survey of all border and BTB policies subject to WTO disputes over 1995–2011, Bown and Reynolds (2015) find that WTO disputes collectively investigated nearly $1 trillion in goods imports, an average of $55 billion per year, or roughly 0.5% of world imports in 2011.

Table 9 Other disputed behind-the-border policies predominantly affecting supply, 1995–2015

Behind the border policy	WTO dispute (complaining countries)	Legal-economic research
Services and distribution (competition policy)		
Canadian Wheat Board export regime and regulations on distribution of grain imports	Canada–Wheat Exports and Grain Imports (US)	Hoekman and Trachtman (2008)
China regulations on distribution of imported audio-visual, music, and reading products	China–Publications and Audiovisual Products (US)	Conconi and Pauwelyn (2011)
Japan regulations of distributors and retailers affecting the photographic film (Kodak/Fuji) market	Japan–Film (US)	
EU Third Energy Package Directives and Regulations unbundling vertically-integrated provision (production, supply, and transmission) of natural gas or electricity	EU–Certain Measures Relating to the Energy Sector (Russia)	
Animal health and product standards		
India import measures on US poultry products due to Avian Influenza	India–Agricultural Products (US)	Bown and Hillman (2016)
US import measures on Argentine beef after foot and mouth disease outbreak	US–Animals (Argentina)	
Russia import measures on EU pork products after African Swine Fever outbreak	Russia–Pigs (EU)	
Korea import measures on Canada beef after mad cow disease (BSE) outbreak	Korea–Bovine Meat (Canada)	
Other environmental regulations		
US import measures on shrimp caught without using sea turtle excluder devices	US–Shrimp (India, Malaysia, Pakistan, Philippines, Thailand)	Howse and Neven (2003)
EU import measures on seals and related products	EU–Seal Products (Canada, Norway)	Levy and Regan (2015) and Conconi and Voon (2016)
Brazil import measures on retreaded tires out of fear of spread of mosquito-transmitted diseases	Brazil–Retreaded Tyres (EU)	Bown and Trachtman (2009)

Continued

Table 9 Other disputed behind-the-border policies predominantly affecting supply, 1995–2015—cont'd

Behind the border policy	WTO dispute (complaining countries)	Legal-economic research
Japan import measures on apples over concerns about the risk of transmission of fire blight bacterium	Japan–Apples (US)	Neven and Weiler (2006)
China export quotas on certain rare earths and raw materials allegedly to conserve natural resources	China–Raw Materials (EU, US, Mexico) China–Rare Earths (EU, Japan, US)	Bronckers and Maskus (2014) and Bond and Trachtman (2016)
US Clean Air Act rule to differentially treat imported and domestic gasoline for air pollution prevention	US–Gasoline (Brazil, Venezuela)	
Russia older motor vehicle recycling fee promoting purchase of environmentally friendly autos	Russia–Motor Vehicles (EU, Japan)	
Labor regulations		
Guatemala failure to enforce its own labor laws related to the right of association, the right to organize and bargain collectively, and acceptable conditions of work	Guatemala–Issues Relating to the Obligations Under Article 16.2.1(a) of the CAFTA-DR (US)[a]	

[a]Not a WTO dispute, as the US dispute against Guatemala was adjudicated under the Central American Free Trade Agreement Dominican Republic (CAFTA-DR).
Constructed by the authors.

scrutiny, we must caveat that one should not conclude that import protection through BTB policies is thus more likely to arise in these particular countries and sectors. In a final section later, we return to these and other caveats regarding the interpretation of these results given sample selection bias due to the endogeneity of the dispute settlement process, as well as how the trade restrictiveness of BTB policies also interacts with levels of import protection through border barriers.

5.1 Behind-the-Border Policies Affecting Supply

This section introduces a number of domestic policies that primarily affect the supply side of the market— either by lowering domestic firms' costs or by raising a foreign rival's costs by potentially forcing them to undertake additional investment to meet a standard or regulation.

Table 10 Disputed behind-the-border policies predominantly affecting demand, 1995–2015

Behind the border policy	WTO dispute (complaining countries)	Legal-economic research
Subsidies/taxes		
Canada, Chile, Japan, Korea, and Philippines each with domestic tax regime discriminating in favor of locally-produced alcohol relative to foreign-produced varieties: • Canada (wine and beer) • Chile (pisco) • Japan (sochu) • Korea (soju) • Philippines (distilled spirits)	Canada–Tax Exemptions and Reductions for Wine and Beer (EC) Chile–Alcoholic Beverages (EC, US) Japan–Alcoholic Beverages II (Canada, EC, US) Korea–Alcoholic Beverages (EC, US) Philippines–Distilled Spirits (EC, US)	Neven and Trachtman (2013)
Foreign investment and local content requirements		
Brazil, Canada, China, India, Indonesia, and Philippines regulations in the auto sector with local content requirements	Brazil–Certain Automotive Investment Measures (EU, Japan, US) Indonesia–Autos (EU, Japan, US) Canada–Autos (Japan) India–Autos (EU, US) Philippines–Motor Vehicles (US) China–Auto Parts (Canada, EU, US)	Bagwell and Sykes (2005b) and Wauters and Vandenbussche (2010)
Canada regulations for renewable energy generation and local content requirements	Canada–Renewable Energy (Japan)	Charnovitz and Fischer (2015) and Rubini (2015)
EU regulations for renewable energy generation and local content requirements, subsidies for solar energy consumption	EU–Certain Measures Affecting the Renewable Energy Generation Sector (China)	
China Special Fund for Industrialization of Wind Power Equipment and contingencies for local content requirements	China–Measures concerning wind power equipment (US) US–Countervailing Measures (China)[a]	Brewster et al. (2016)
India Jawaharlal Nehru National Solar Mission for solar cells and solar modules and local content requirements	India–Solar Cells (US)	

[a]indicates dispute concerned the trading partner's countervailing duty trade policy response to the subsidy and not the underlying subsidy itself.
Constructed by the authors.

Table 11 Other disputed behind-the-border policies predominantly affecting demand, 1995–2015

Behind the border policy	WTO Dispute (Complaining Countries)	Legal-economic research
Public health, consumer safety, and product standards		
EU import measures on food and agricultural products containing genetically modified organisms (GMOs)	EU–Approval and Marketing of Biotech Products (US, Argentina, Canada)	Howse and Horn (2009)
US Family Smoking Prevention Tobacco Control Act of 2009 that bans most all flavored cigarettes (like cloves) but not menthol	US–Clove Cigarettes (Indonesia)	Howse and Levy (2013) and Broude and Levy (2014)
US regulations and federal laws banning cross-border internet gambling, such as the Wire Act, Travel Act, and the Illegal Gambling Business Act	US–Gambling (Antigua and Barbuda)	Irwin and Weiler (2008)
France import measures on asbestos	EU–Asbestos (Canada)	Horn and Weiler (2003)
US import measures on Mexico's commercial trucking services due to public health and safety concerns	US–Cross-Border Trucking Services (Mexico)[a]	
EU import measures on hormone-treated beef (precautionary principle)	EU–Hormones (Canada, US)	
Korea import measures and additional testing requirements on agricultural products from Japan after Fukushima nuclear event	Korea–Radionuclides (Japan)	
Consumer product labeling and intellectual property rights		
US dolphin-safe tuna labeling	US–Tuna II (Mexico)	Howse and Levy (2013) and Crowley and Howse (2014)
US country of origin labeling (COOL) requirement for the tracking of cows and pigs (and beef and pork) intended for the US market along the global supply chain	US–COOL (Canada, Mexico)	Howse and Levy (2013) and Mavroidis and Saggi (2014)
EU regulation related to the protection of geographical indications and designations of origin on agricultural products and foodstuffs	EU–Trademarks and Geographical Indications (Australia, US)	
Australia laws and regulations that impose restrictions on trademarks, geographical indications, and other plain packaging requirements on tobacco products	Australia–Tobacco Plain Packaging (Dominican Republic, Honduras, Indonesia, Ukraine)	

Constructed by the authors.
[a]not a WTO dispute, as Mexico dispute against the US adjudicated under NAFTA.

5.1.1 Domestic Subsidies: Aircraft, Agriculture, Semiconductors, and Clean Energy

We begin with examples of domestic subsidies impacting production. In some sectors, the subsidies could be motivated on efficiency grounds as designed to confront external-ities, or imperfect markets; in others, the subsidies may only be motivated as a second-best form of income redistribution for a politically-motivated government with an incom-plete set of policy instruments.

Domestic subsidies abound in the civil aircraft industry and date back to the GATT period and even arguably predate the eventual rivalry between US-based Boeing and Europe-based Airbus. Subsidies, tax exemptions, and other forms of policy intervention in this market have triggered attempts to design international rules since at least the 1970s.[cr]

Consider a production subsidy that a European government grants to Airbus. Such a subsidy increases domestic production in Europe and, all else equal, leads to a decrease in European imports of aircraft from Boeing. In 2004, the US government filed a WTO dispute over European subsidy policies. Table 8 indicates that the EU filed a similar (and almost simultaneous) dispute challenging US subsidies to Boeing. Admittedly, the policies under dispute are much more complex than simple production subsidies; they include tax exemptions offered at the subfederal level (eg, by Washington state to Boeing); EU "launch-aid" to help overcome the start-up costs of developing new models; the civil aircraft subsidy spillovers arising from US government military contracts to Boeing, given that military aircraft technology has "dual use" (for civil aircraft) appli-cations; and export–credit and guarantee arrangements offered to (consumer) airlines.

Civil aircraft subsidies can have additional strategic effects given the unique nature of the global duopoly; ie, the two producers not only compete for sales in each others' mar-ket, but for sales in third country markets.[cs] Table 8 indicates a very similar set of disputes has played out between Canada and Brazil in a separate segment of the civil aircraft market; each country challenged the other for subsidizing smaller aircraft (regional jet) producers Embraer and Bombardier, respectively. Finally, and while admittedly more of a demand-side policy, the United States recently challenged China with providing a subsidy (value-added tax exemption) for its domestically-produced aircraft.

Agriculture is another sector in which domestic subsidies frequently arise, albeit in different forms.[ct] The EU's Common Agricultural Policy has a long history of BTB

[cr] The GATT's Tokyo Round of negotiations produced a plurilateral code in 1979 that applied to inter-national trade in civil aircraft.

[cs] The Boeing-Airbus storyline helped motivate the substantial strategic trade policy literature that arose in the 1980s; for a survey, see Brander (1995). Irwin and Pavcnik (2004) provide an empirical study of the Boeing-Airbus rivalry and policies of the 1990s.

[ct] Agriculture is perhaps the one sector for which there exists more systematic provision of data for a num-ber of BTB policies. For example, the OECD has routinely produced a cross-country database on "producer and consumer support estimates" for agricultural support payments. Furthermore, Kym Anderson has worked with the World Bank to produce a historical database of distortions to agricultural incentives covering the period of 1955–2011 (Anderson and Nelgen, 2013). For a survey of the political economy of agricultural policy, see Anderson et al. (2013).

policies sparking disputes; one example was its domestic price support system for sugar. Australia, Brazil, and Thailand—other major exporters of sugar—ultimately challenged EU subsidies that had transformed it from a net importer to a net exporter of sugar, with the excess supply dumped onto export markets. Similarly, US agricultural policy, and various iterations of the US Farm Bill legislation in particular, has also been subject to considerable international scrutiny. For example, in 2002 Brazil brought a formal WTO dispute against US cotton subsidies. In both the EU and US disputes, the complaining countries' concerns with the subsidy were less over their impact for lost sales to the policy-imposing country's own market, and instead for lost sales competing with EU sugar or US cotton exports in third country markets.

Two additional industries—semiconductors and clean energy products—further highlight the complexities of subsidies arising as part of national industrial policies.

Semiconductors have been subject to considerable government intervention since at least the 1980s; indeed, our discussion of border barriers in the last section illustrated the industry as one in which antidumping and VERs were prevalent between the United States and Japan.[cu] More recently a leading Korean producer, Hynix, which accounted for 4% of *total* Korean exports globally, became financially insolvent. In October 2001 and again in December 2002, Hynix's creditors organized financial bail-outs designed to save the company. The United States, EU and Japan, major importers and producers of semiconductors at the time, each asserted that the Korean government had subsidized the industry by orchestrating the bailouts, and they then each responded by imposing countervailing duties on Korean semiconductor exports to their markets.

This kind of dispute introduces another channel through which BTB policies can be impacted by WTO legal decisions; this is due to a particular way that certain areas of the WTO Agreements are structured. While the primary "policy" triggering the friction between the United States, EU, Japan and Korea was Korea's (BTB) subsidy, the subject of the WTO dispute was the United States and Japanese countervailing duty policies in *response* to the Hynix bailout; not the bailout itself. In this kind of a dispute, for example, the WTO could not rule that Korea should reform its subsidy policy, it could, at most, direct the United States or Japan to reform how their countervailing duty policies addressed the Korean subsidy (Hynix bailout) policy. However, any adjustments to the rules for when it is permissible for a trading partner to implement countervailing duties would be expected to *indirectly* affect how a country like Korea implements its subsidy policies in the first place.

Finally, recent disputes over BTB policies have arisen in a number of interrelated markets for clean energy products. Here, we describe solar panels, though similar

---

[cu] Irwin and Klenow (1994) provide an empirical study of the semiconductor industry and learning-by-doing spillovers over the 1974–92 period.

BTB policies are affecting markets for wind towers and wind turbines.[cv] Solar panels are potentially distinct from a number of other sectors in that their *consumption*—ie, a shift toward clean energy production and away from more polluting fossil fuels—may be associated with positive externalities that may even be global in scope, considering climate change. Beginning in 1999, European governments implemented consumption subsidies to stimulate demand for solar energy resulting in an increase in solar generating capacity; for example, in Germany by 2014, installed solar capacity was larger than natural gas, hard coal, and brown coal (Burger, 2014).

Although the European consumption subsidy was partially intended to benefit the German firms instrumental in the technological development of solar panels, by 2012, China's solar panel exporters had captured 80% of the European market. This prompted new EU import restrictions of solar panels from China under its antidumping policy. In essence, the *nondiscriminatory* nature of the original European consumption subsidies helped trigger such an increase in imports that the EU government came under political pressure to apply new border barriers.

The effect of the European policies has spilled over into other countries' policies and into upstream (input) markets. First, the Chinese government responded to the decline in exports to the EU by implementing its own BTB policies, including by introducing a regulation to force industry consolidation in 2013 as well as a program of consumption subsidies. Second, China also adjusted its border policies by imposing antidumping duties on imports of solar grade polysilicon—a key input for solar panel production—from the United States, EU and Korea beginning in 2013. Third, the United States also adjusted its border policies in the solar panel market when a subsidiary of a German firm, Solar World AG, filed a series of TTB cases against imports from China and Taiwan (but not Germany) beginning in 2011; they have subsequently resulted in the United States imposing new antidumping and countervailing duties against these countries.[cw] Finally, there has also been a WTO dispute over solar panels, though it only indirectly concerns the underlying Chinese BTB policy. Similar to the semiconductors example, China filed a WTO dispute over the US applied countervailing duty that was the policy response to the Chinese subsidies.

These last examples in particular raise a host of questions for research on the design of international institutions to coordinate BTB policy actions that might address various types of market failures, as well as local and global, nonpecuniary externalities, including climate change.

[cv] This section draws from Crowley and Song (2015). Cosar et al. (2015) provide an empirical study of the European wind turbine industry.
[cw] India also initiated an antidumping investigation into imported solar cells from China, Taiwan, United States and Malaysia in 2012.

5.1.2 Other Supply-Side Policies: Competition, Production Standards, Environment and Labor

Next turn to Table 9, which provides examples of other supply-side policies subject to WTO dispute. The public policy motive behind these policies are frequently even more complex than subsidies; furthermore, the manner by which these BTB policies potentially discriminate between domestic and foreign-produced varieties can also be much more subtle.

First, a number of WTO disputes have arisen in the area of competition policy, perhaps partly because there is no agreement fully articulating the scope of international cooperation for antitrust authorities. The United States has used the WTO to file disputes against Canada, Japan, and China, for example, and in each case one of the key allegations was that US producers were unable to sell their products to foreign consumers because of bottlenecks in the distribution networks arising from excessive domestic market power. The United States alleged that the concentration of the domestic industry resulted in discrimination against US exports of wheat, photographic film (Kodak), and audio-visual products (Hollywood movies), respectively. On the other hand, Russia has challenged the EU's attempts at "unbundling" vertically integrated providers of natural gas and electricity that would expectedly change the market structure facing energy service providers and which might *increase* the level of competition.

Another increasingly contentious area of domestic policy involves production process standards. Consider, for example, India's set of import restrictions on US poultry products; the policy was motivated out of the concern that the existence of the avian influenza (AI) virus in the US would affect the US process of producing poultry and thus result (through trade) in the virus being transmitted to India's domestic poultry industry. The main US allegation was that India's import ban on US poultry products was being justified by the application of domestic standards that were "too restrictive" in light of *international* scientific standards.

As this example illustrates, a key aspect of the BTB policies over standards is the regulatory *justification*—ie, scientific evidence, public health concern, or even ethical or moral outrage— behind the policy *application*; ie, the policy application frequently takes the form of a blunt import ban (thus arising through a *border* policy). It is typical for foreign suppliers to allege that such standards are either too restrictive (in light of scientific evidence) or are applied in a way that discriminates against foreign relative to domestic production, potentially by forcing them to undertake additional costly investment to meet compliance requirements.[cx] Thus, any process by which to evaluate whether

---

[cx]   Staiger and Sykes (2011) provide a model in order to show how a government may have an incentive to "over-regulate"—ie, impose standards that while nondiscriminatory are nevertheless "too high" from a global perspective—because it can shift some of the costs of those standards onto trading partners by reducing their terms of trade.

a domestic standard is too restrictive mandates a commonly accepted benchmark for purposes of comparison.

The WTO system has outsourced this benchmarking to scientists organized under international standards-setting agencies; for the case of food safety to Codex Alimentarius, for animal health (eg, the AI-example above) to the World Animal Health Organization (OIE), and for plant health to the International Plant Protection Convention (IPPC). Table 9 documents a number of disputes arising in these areas, including over animal health and safety standards; in addition to the Indian AI-policies on poultry, similar thematic disputes have taken place over US policies on beef (related to foot and mouth and disease in Argentina), Korean policies on beef (related to mad cow disease in Canada), and Russian policies on pork (related to African Swine Fever in the EU).

The WTO has considered challenges to a number of other environment-related policies that also affect production processes or standards. One example is the US mandate that wild-caught shrimp must use nets that protect endangered sea turtles from being caught inadvertently. The EU had its ban on imports of seal products challenged by Canada and Norway; one of the claims of the exporters was that the EU policy was applied in a discriminatory manner because it exempted certain EU-based producers (indigenous communities) of seal products. Finally, one of the very first disputes filed with the WTO involved Brazil and Venezuela challenging provisions of the US Clean Air Act as requiring different standards for imported vs domestically-produced gasoline.

Finally, the United States has also initiated a dispute over a trading partner's domestic labor market policies. The United States alleged that Guatemala was not enforcing its own labor laws regarding unionization, collective bargaining, and work conditions for workers in major export sectors, including shipping, apparel, steel and agriculture.[cy] To date, labor standards disputes remain relatively rare; indeed, this particular dispute was not initiated under the WTO, which does not include labor provisions, but under a free trade agreement that does contain such provisions.

5.2 BTB Policies Affecting Demand

We next turn to case studies of demand-side policies that can also have a trade-restricting effect, typically of negatively impacting imports.

5.2.1 Taxes, Foreign Investment Measures, and Local Content Requirements

The most straightforward example of a demand-side, behind-the-border policy is a domestic consumption tax that discriminates by incentivizing consumption of local varieties relative to consumption of imported varieties of substitute goods.

[cy] This is an example, however, in which the domestic policy is being challenged because it is lowering domestic firms' costs (in industries that export to the United States) and not raising foreign firms' costs (in US industries attempting to export to Guatemala).

A relatively common theme for a WTO dispute has involved alcohol, and the allegation that governments impose discriminatory consumption taxes on different varieties. The lower tax on the domestic variety stimulates demand facing the domestic industry relative to the taxed foreign variety; specific examples listed in Table 10 include beer and wine in Canada, pisco in Chile, sochu in Japan, soju in Korea, or distilled spirits in the Philippines. The government defense typically attempts to justify the tax differential by claiming that its locally-produced variety is not a "like product" or a "directly competitive or substitutable product" relative to the imported varieties.

A second and more subtle example of an indirect consumption tax commonly arises through regulations to foreign direct investment; governments frequently create tax incentives for such investment that are *conditional* on local content requirements being met. As Table 10 indicates, automobiles are a common sector in which countries attempt to encourage foreign investment but also mandate local content requirements. The policy is typically structured so that the government incentivizes (with subsidies or other general tax exemptions) foreign automakers to establish a local production facility, and the preferential tax treatment is applied conditional on the resulting local production of autos containing sufficient domestic content (eg, locally produced auto parts). Some of the effect of the foreign investment subsidy is then passed on—via the local content requirement—to indirectly subsidize consumption of locally-produced inputs relative to foreign-produced inputs (Bagwell and Sykes, 2005b). In the auto sector alone, the EU, Japan, and the United States have brought disputes against at least six other WTO members (Brazil, Canada, China, India, Indonesia, and Philippines) with foreign investment regimes alleged to contain local content requirements.

More recently, the renewable energy sector—eg, wind turbines and towers, solar panels—has also faced a number of WTO challenges to foreign direct investment regulations for their inclusion of local content requirements. The allegation is that such requirements artificially stimulate demand for locally-sourced inputs and upstream industries and thus discriminate against imported inputs. Examples from these sectors include regulations imposed by Canada, the EU, China, and India and disputes brought by Japan, China and the United States.[cz]

5.2.2 Other Demand Policies: Consumer Safety, Product Labeling, and IPRs

Table 11 presents our final examples of potentially trade-restricting demand-side policies, including product standards for consumer safety, consumer product labeling, trademarks, and other regulations related to intellectual property rights (IPRs) enforcement.

Consumer product safety standards are similar to the production standards described earlier, in that foreign exporters typically allege that the standard is either too restrictive,

---

[cz]   Some of these disputes also concern the consumption subsidies and other BTB policies described earlier in the market for solar panels.

and not justified in light of scientific evidence and international standards, or it is being applied in a manner than discriminates against imports. Perhaps the highest-profile examples of such disputed policies are the EU's "Frankenstein food" regulations applied to hormone-treated beef and to food and agricultural products containing genetically modified organisms (GMOs). The United States and other countries appealed to the lack of scientific evidence supporting EU attempts to justify these policies through the "precautionary principle," or that the long-term effects of such product characteristics on human, animal, and plant health, as well as the environment, were unknown. As indicated earlier, the WTO relies on Codex Alimentarius as the international organization in charge of establishing scientific standards for food safety; as such, its standards play an important benchmarking role against which to compare any country's chosen level of domestic standards.

Table 11 indicates a number of other countries have also faced challenges to their public health policies on consumer safety standards. There have been WTO challenges to the US bans on clove cigarettes, Internet gambling, and Mexican commercial trucking services. Japan has also challenged Korea's restrictions on imported agricultural products after the Fukushima nuclear incident.

Foreign exporters are increasingly challenging consumer product labels by alleging that the label increases demand for the domestic variety at the expense of foreign varieties. The consumer labels sometimes arise from a domestic legal requirement regarding a consumer's "right to know," and often mandate that firms provide information about certain product attributes. Furthermore, the schemes can be mandatory or voluntary.

Failure to satisfy the mandatory labeling requirements means a product cannot be sold. Discrimination against foreign products could arise, for example, if it is more costly to label imported products. Table 11 documents how Mexico and Canada recently challenged a US country of origin labeling (COOL) scheme that required cows and pigs, as well as the resulting beef and pork products, be traceable to their source country. The allegation was that the US policy discriminated against imported inputs by imposing additional costs on US meatpackers that sourced cows and pigs (as inputs) from Mexico or Canada.

Under a voluntary scheme, a good can still be sold if it fails to satisfy a label's requirements, it is simply that demand may collapse if the label is informative about some minimum threshold for a product attribute. As an example, Mexico used the WTO to challenge a US law which enforced a voluntary labeling scheme for "dolphin safe" canned tuna by arguing that the label reduced demand for the Mexican variety and thus discriminated against Mexican exports.

Finally, some consumer labels have been challenged in disputes over IPRs, but the underlying issue is essentially the same—a label shifts demand for a foreign, imported product in a way that hurts its producer. Cases regarding "geographical indicators" are similar to mandatory and voluntary labeling; the alleged intent is to increase demand for one variety of a good (eg, cheese from Parma, Italy) and reduce demand for other varieties (a similar-tasting cheese made in the United States). Australia and the US challenged EU efforts to establish geographical indicators or trademarks for a number of its agricultural products—parmesan cheese, feta cheese, kalamata olives, etc.—based on where the product originated. In another case, Australia attempted to reduce consumer demand for all varieties of cigarettes by requiring plain packaging on cigarette boxes. The exporters claimed that the Australian public health policy had reduced the value of their intellectual property; ie, the value of their trademark was reduced due to the regulation *limiting* the ability of cigarette makers to differentiate their product through labeling.

5.3 Final Caveats on BTB Policies

Our case studies highlight a number of the complexities that researchers inevitably face in bringing scrutiny to bear on BTB policies. These include attempts to disentangle which elements of BTB policies are potentially "legitimate"—from a global, efficiency-enhancing perspective in light of the relevant market failures—from "illegitimate" elements that result in mainly (uncompensated) cost-shifting or profit-shifting across countries. We conclude with a brief discussion of some of the limitations of our approach.

First, a discussion of hand-picked case studies is certain to be fraught with sample selection concerns.[da] For example, most of the disputes over BTB policies have arisen in large and disproportionately high-income economies with democratic political systems in which policies are developed (and applied) under conditions of relative transparency (Canada, EU, United States, Japan, etc.). Furthermore, these economies also have relatively low levels of tariffs (see again Section 2); this raises the question of whether the BTB policy under scrutiny was there all along, and only worth challenging once the border barriers had first been liberalized, or whether the BTB policy only arose after the border barrier was dismantled.[db]

Second, we have attempted in our analysis to refrain from passing judgment on any particular BTB policy; ie, our selection of BTB policies should not be construed as a commentary on their trade restrictiveness or on any particular WTO legal decision. Indeed, a close read of more than 20 years and 100 WTO legal decisions indicates a surefire tension that has arisen but which also speaks again to the complexities involved in research in this area. On one hand, the WTO's Dispute Settlement Body (DSB) almost never questions

---

[da] An example of research examining the specific trade concerns (STCs) that governments have brought to the WTO under the SPS or TBT committees is Fontagné et al. (2015). More generally, Bown (2009, chapters 3 and 4) surveys the early research on some determinants of which policies governments choose to challenge under the WTO, and also finds that high-income countries are mostly behind the challenges to BTB policies.

[db] Another limitation of our approach is that it does not attempt to provide even a cross-section of imposed BTB policies in existence at any moment in time—ie, some of the BTB policies highlighted here may no longer be in effect. See also the survey and compilation of policies provided in WTO (2012).

the legitimacy of the respondent country's underlying domestic policy under dispute; ie, the WTO approach seems to respect national sovereignty and its member governments' right to regulate to address market failures and externalities. On the other hand, in almost every dispute, the DSB also finds that the respondent country has done something fundamentally wrong via the manner though which it has *applied* its BTB policy.

6. CONCLUSION

We have presented a portrait of the complexity of international commercial policy as of 2013–14 and have provided answers to some of our chapter's fundamental questions regarding variation in the levels of import protection in place today—across countries, within countries across sectors, over time, and vis-à-vis different trading partners in a discriminatory manner. However, most of our main questions remain only partially answered. The inability of the current literature to completely assess these questions— especially with respect to the overall restrictiveness of policy, but also with respect to the trade restrictiveness of the "newest" policies of interest that are behind-the-border— provides an opportunity. Indeed, with increasing access to policy data, a long-term research agenda directed toward an improved understanding of trade policy is not only likely to bear fruit scientifically, but it is also likely to result in large societal payoffs.

Before concluding, we take the opportunity to suggest additional ways through which these newly available policy data sources may improve our understanding of other areas of the international economy.

Over the last decade, empirical research on firms engaged in international trade has exploded. This includes firms involved in multicountry production through foreign direct investment, and in cross-border production structures and global supply chains. Scholars have provided a sound understanding of many of the differences between manufacturing firms that operate domestically and those that engage globally.

However, while these firm-level studies are informed by a wealth of data on the destinations for their outputs, origin of inputs, prices, quantities, worker matching, revenues, debts, firm-to-firm relations, etc.—they most often treat the policy environment as an afterthought. The richness of changes in the trade policy barriers, which we have documented result in considerable heterogeneity over time, across destinations, and products, are typically swept up in these studies into an economy-wide trade cost or a product-specific fixed effect.

Furthermore, there have also been substantial developments in empirical research into firm-pricing behavior (domestically and internationally), the importance of the relationship between the parties in international trade transactions, and the extent to which exchange rates pass through into transaction-level prices. This literature has deepened our understanding of the substantial differences in the prices of tradeable goods across borders. However, very little research on product-specific trade policy changes—many of which have magnitudes that dwarf the annual changes to exchange rates—has been undertaken in a way that would inform our understanding of the remaining pricing puzzles.

The fact that fewer than 20% of manufacturing firms in major economies export anything to anyone suggests that policy barriers to trade continue to matter. Similarly, increasingly disaggregated, high-frequency data on the prices of traded goods indicates that cross border price differences remain sizeable. Is there more that can be learned by incorporating similarly detailed trade policy data into microeconomic studies of firms and international pricing? Our hope is that this chapter sparks research ideas about how to take advantage of the rich variation in policy data to learn more about these other important questions facing the global economy.

To wrap up our analysis, we make a final, more practical, point regarding the increasing availability of trade policy data. Although a wealth of policy data is now almost continuously becoming available, because these data are still relatively new, in many instances, the data are not yet "clean." Thus working with such data will require researchers to make some human capital investment into the details of the policies themselves so that they can check and verify the accuracy of newer datasets. A basic knowledge of trade agreements and the relevant domestic institutions is extremely helpful to understand the structure of data reporting and the potential substitutability of policy tools. In our view, the opportunities provided by this newfound data availability far outweigh the costs of this one-time investment.

To assist economists embarking on research in trade policy, we include two additional resources. First, we provide a Data Appendix with an in-depth description of the underlying sources for the data that we utilize in our empirical exercises. Second, and as our discussion of the landscape of trade policy has revealed, a large amount of policy data is collected and referred to by distinct GATT legal provisions that are known as "Articles." For ease of reference, in Table A.3, we provide a summary which links each of the key GATT Articles that we have utilized in the chapter to the main economic policies, exceptions, or concepts that they address.

A. DATA APPENDIX

This section introduces the main sources of the underlying data sets for the various trade policy instruments that we have utilized in the empirical analysis.

A.1 Tariff Data

In Section 2 we first utilized data on product-level MFN tariffs. These data arise from a number of different sources, including the WTO's Integrated Database (IDB), WTO's Consolidated Tariff Schedules (CTS), UNCTAD's Trade Analysis Information System (TRAINS) database, as well as from the International Trade Centre (ITC) in Geneva. In some instances, the ITC may be the first source of the raw data (even if it is ultimately attributed to UNCTAD/TRAINS), as one UN agency sends it to another for further cleaning and processing before making it available to the public. Data on WTO tariff binding commitments is made available through WTO's CTS; these bindings are essentially unchanged since the negotiation of the Uruguay Round in 1995, with the exception of new accession countries for whom binding rates were established at the date of their accession. Data from each of the other sources is on MFN *applied* rates.

In terms of the classification, it is important to note that the Harmonised System only began in 1988 and was slowly adopted by countries starting thereafter. As such, a common product-level classification scheme across countries—an important necessary condition for meaningful construction of clean measures for simple average tariffs, for example—is only potentially available beginning in 1988. Next, the "products" in these data series are only comparable across countries at the 6-digit Harmonised System (HS06) level, and there are roughly 5200 HS06 products in existence at any moment in time.[dc] These tariff data are also frequently available at the "tariff-line" level—eg, 8-digit, 10-digit, etc.—ie, under the national customs authority's own scheme for how it chooses to differentiate product varieties beyond the HS06 level, over which it has authority. To the extent that data are reported at the HS06 level, they have been averaged from the underlying level in some way, typically as a simple average.

The tariff data from the WTO, UNCTAD, and the ITC has been made freely available to the public over the last few years through a consortium arrangement that also includes the World Bank and the wing of the United Nations statistical division that collects and reports commodity-level trade data. In addition to financial support, the World Bank's substantive contribution to the arrangement has been to develop and provide technical support and an on-line software platform called World Integrated Trade Solution (WITS) for public dissemination of the data. To be clear, the World Bank's WITS is not the underlying source for any of the data—it is merely the platform by which the data has been made available from the WTO, UNCTAD or ITC to the general public.[dd] WITS makes available on its website a user's manual that provides details on

---

[dc] Revisions to the Harmonized System, affecting upwards of 200 products each time, were undertaken in 1996, 2002, 2007, and 2012.

[dd] One concern with the current, decentralized arrangement is whether it creates the right incentive structure to make and implement fixes of importance to scholars; eg, when users discover data problems in historical data. That is, typically the World Bank (WITS) is not in a position to fix the publicly provided data because it did not collect the data in the first place. Furthermore, because these UN agencies (and even the WTO) have both tight budget constraints (for data production) and whose mandate is more focused on contemporary policy rather than historical policy—even if by "history," we are referring to only 2 or 3 years in the past—they may not face the proper incentives to bear the costs of implementing major fixes to the historical data that may be incomplete or incorrect.

the underlying sources of data, the descriptions of the different types of policy data made available, as well as other useful information. Through the arrangement, WITS also provides HS06 level bilateral import and export data that is collected by UN Comtrade. Furthermore, in recent years, the WTO, UNCTAD and the ITC have made varying efforts to release the raw data directly to the public via their own websites as well.

The raw data from the WTO and ITC typically do not contain information on estimated ad valorem equivalents for all of the tariffs applied as specific duties that we analyze in Section 2.2. In the data sets made available through WITS, UNCTAD has undertaken efforts to construct ad valorem equivalent estimates for the tariffs imposed as specific duties. At least four different calculations for the AVEs are provided, each based on a different methodology. However, these data are not as comprehensively available as the raw data. In some years, for example, they are completely missing. Furthermore, their values will expectedly vary significantly over time, of course, due to changes in prices, even when the applied tariff policies themselves have not changed.

The Section 2 analysis relied on preferential tariff data that was also, for the most part, collected by the ITC and UNCTAD. That data is also typically made publicly available through WITS, and in many instances, UNCTAD will compute AVE estimates for the products with preferential tariffs applied as specific duties. However, it has been our experience that the raw preferential tariff data made available in WITS is much more problematic—in terms of comprehensiveness of coverage—than the applied MFN tariff data. For example, in certain years no preferential tariff data may be available for an entire country. In other years, some, but not all, of a country's preferential tariffs will be recorded. Clearly these data need to be cleaned by researchers and cross-validated against other external sources (at a minimum, which catalog the existence of preferential trade agreements, such as WTO, 2015c,a). Much of the preferential tariff data that we utilize in this chapter for the year 2014 was actually acquired directly from ITC.

We repeat here three important points made in the chapter regarding the MFN and preferential applied tariff data in particular. First, the applied tariffs are those that governments set, and our measure derive from either what a government reports (to the WTO, for applied MFN rates) or which these UN agencies collect and compile from official government sources, and typically these are reported on an annual basis. Furthermore, the applied tariff data does *not* include other border charges or taxes, including safeguards tariffs and antidumping duties. (To the extent that these are applied in a particular context, they would need to be added onto the existing level of the applied MFN or bilateral tariff.) Second, throughout the chapter and for consistency, the statistics that we report utilize simple averaging for the tariffs; the alternative of constructing trade-weighted average tariffs can lead to the well-known problem of downward bias due to products with high tariffs receiving low weights (because of small import

Table A.1 Industry classification used in the analysis

Acronym	Industry	Harmonized System 2-digit (HS02) Sections
ANIM	Animal products, live animals	01–05
VEGE	Vegetable products	06–15
FOOD	Prepared foodstuffs, beverages, spirits, vinegar, tobacco products, edible fats	16–24
MINE	Mineral products	25–26
FUEL	Mineral fuels	27
CHEM	Chemicals	28–38
PLAS	Plastics and rubber	39–40
HIDE	Hides, skins, leather, etc	41–43
WOOD	Wood and articles of wood, pulp and paper	44–49
TEXT	Textiles, fibers, apparel, etc.	50–63
FOOT	Footwear, headgear, umbrellas, feathers, etc	64–67
STON	Stone, cement, plaster, ceramics, glassware, pearls, etc	68–71
META	Base metals and articles of base metal	72–83
MACH	Machinery, mechanical appliances, electrical equipment	84–85
TRAN	Transportation: vehicles, aircraft, vessels	86–89
MISC	Miscellaneous	90–97

volumes). Third, sometimes the underlying data that we utilize to construct measures of average tariffs (eg, at the country or sector level) may utilize ad valorem equivalent estimates for products over which the import tariff that the country applies is a specific duty. In other instances it may not; as we indicated in the chapter, our decision of whether or not to include them depended on the context.

A.2 Temporary Trade Barriers (Antidumping, Safeguards, and Countervailing Duties) Data

The analysis of temporary trade barriers in Section 3.1 is based on the data collected annually and made publicly available through the World Bank's Temporary Trade Barriers Database (Bown, 2014a). The data was first made freely available to the public over the Internet in 2005; since 2009, it has been updated at least at the annual frequency.[de]

[de] Bown (2011a) provides a discussion of its use during the 2008–10 crisis, during 2009–10 it was updated and released on a quarterly basis. The project was conceived in the early 2000s because countries reported so little information about their temporary trade barriers use to the WTO, that it was insufficiently detailed for research purposes. Yet governments did report the information publicly, through official publications; this only required collating the information from national sources into a common format.

The Temporary Trade Barriers Database website also posts a complete users manual describing the data sources and all of the available variables utilized here and others made available (but not utilized here).

The raw data on antidumping and countervailing duties in the Temporary Trade Barriers Database are collected directly from official government sources; ie, it is important to note that these are not based on what countries report to the WTO. As such, the database includes much additional detail that the WTO has historically been unable to provide—because it relies on self-reporting by members—including product-level tariff codes for products subject to the policies, the dates of key aspects of the investigations (initiation, preliminary decisions, final decisions, policies imposed, and policies removed wherever possible), the trading partners investigated, the type of border barrier imposed (ad valorem duty, specific duty, price undertaking, etc) as well as its level. Finally, and where available, the database also includes information on the domestic firms, industry associations, or labor groups behind the petition initiating the investigation, and it also has firm-specific trade barriers for the foreign firms (and their names) when cases result in different levels of the new barriers applying to different firms within the same country.

Finally, the information on the use of safeguards compiled into the Temporary Trade Barriers Database is gathered from information on what government's report to the WTO Committee on Safeguards. Under this particular policy, governments have been mandated to report sufficiently detailed information on the HS codes associated with their product-level trade restrictions, as well as the other key pieces of information, including exemptions for trading partners excluded from application of the policy. The safeguards policy is distinct from the WTO's reporting requirements for antidumping and countervailing duties.

A.3 Historical Data from the GATT Archives

Data on the GATT-era (1947–94) use of safeguards (Article XIX), antidumping (Article VI), and import restrictions related to balance of payments difficulties (Article XII) were compiled from information in hundreds of documents housed in the Stanford GATT digital archive. The selection of years for the figures presented was driven by the availability of reports in the digital archive. Notably, documents for different policy instruments in several decades have yet to be uploaded to the archive.

The archive organizes documents according to the nomenclature that was used by the GATT. Thus, work of the Committee on Anti-Dumping Practices is reported in a series beginning COM.AD, work of the Committee on Government Procurement is reported in a series beginning GPR, etc. Somewhat confusingly, some document series include reports on a wide array of issues. At the same time, some policies are reported in multiple document series and it appears that there is no overlap; ie, if a tariff increase is reported in one series, the same increase does not appear to be reported in other series.

The information on antidumping described in Section 4.3.6 was collected from a series of approximately 270 documents reported by the GATT's Committee on Anti-Dumping Practices between 1970 and 1979. During this period, the Committee issued 86 basic documents/reports, but with various addendum included. Periodic reports issued by this committee include lists of all countries that reported antidumping activity in the relevant period, the trading partners affected by the antidumping case, verbal descriptions of the products involved, and information about provisional and final antidumping measures imposed. In some cases, countries have reported the removal of duties, the termination of investigations that did not result in duties, and the outcomes of negotiated settlements like price undertakings. We then concorded these verbal product descriptions to modern HS product classifications. While the information is similar to what is reported to the WTO in the modern era, it appears to be less systematically reported. Moreover, it does not include information on values of trade, prices of goods, or magnitude of antidumping duties.

Information on safeguards (Article XIX) for 1950–59 utilized in Section 4.2 is reported in the L: General Series (Limited Distribution) and the GATT/CP series. In this period, there are almost 1500 individual documents in the L: series and over 900 individual documents in the GATT: series. Only a small fraction of these documents relate to Article XIX actions so significant effort must go into identifying the relevant documents for Article XIX and then extracting the information contained in the documents. As with antidumping, we recorded data on the country imposing the measure, the product(s) involved, that date the investigation began, and the final policy outcome.

Information on changes in import restrictions to address BOP problems used in Section 4.3.1 is also reported in the L: General Series. From these reports, we recorded the country imposing the measures and the date of implementation. These reports also include long lists of products whose importation has been banned or restricted in an effort to reduce the country's trade deficit.

Finally, we recorded data on permanent renegotiations of tariff rates under Article XXVIII that were reported in the L: General Series between 1950 and 1959. However, we do not report this information in the chapter because this series of reports seems to cover only a small subset of all Article XXVIII actions. In particular, *GATT Analytical Index* (WTO, 1995) provides summary information on actions taken by countries during the period 1947–94 and indicates that most Article XXVIII renegotiations were recorded in a series of documents classified as SECRET. The SECRET document series is not (currently) included in the GATT Digital Archive.

Table A.2 Country classification used in the analysis

Acronym	Country	Acronym	Country	Acronym	Country
ARG	Argentina	IDN	Indonesia	RUS	Russia
AUS	Australia	IND	India	SAU	Saudi Arabia
BGD	Bangladesh	IRN	Iran	THA	Thailand
BRA	Brazil	JPN	Japan	TUR	Turkey
CAN	Canada	KEN	Kenya	TZA	Tanzania
CHN	China	KOR	Korea	UKR	Ukraine
COD	DR Congo	MEX	Mexico	USA	United States
COL	Colombia	MMR	Burma	VNM	Vietnam
EGY	Egypt	NGA	Nigeria	ZAF	South Africa
ETH	Ethiopia	PAK	Pakistan		
EUN	European Union	PHL	Philippines		

Table A.3 Topics of major GATT articles and WTO agreements

GATT 1947 (article)	Topic	WTO agreements (in addition to GATT 1947)
Article I	Most-favored nation (MFN) treatment of nondiscrimination across trading partners	
Article II	Tariff binding commitment submissions (schedule of concessions)	
Article III	National treatment (nondiscrimination between domestic and foreign-produced goods in terms of domestic policies)	
Article XX	General exceptions (for domestic policies)	Agreement on Sanitary and Phytosanitary (SPS) Measures. Agreement on Technical Barriers to Trade (TBT)
Article VI	Antidumping and Countervailing Duties	Agreement on Antidumping
Article XVI	Granting of Subsidies	Agreement on Subsidies and Countervailing Measures
Article XI	Elimination of Quantitative Restrictions	
Article XII	Exceptions to protect the Balance of Payments	
Article XVIII	Special and differential treatment for developing countries	
Article XIX	Temporary safeguards/escape clause (protection for particular products)	Agreement on Safeguards
Article XXII	Dispute settlement procedures	Dispute Settlement Understanding (DSU)
Article XXIII		
Article XXIV	MFN exception for customs unions and free-trade areas	
Article XXV	Other waivers of GATT provisions	
Article XXVIII	Permanent renegotiation of tariffs	
Article XXXV	Non-application of the entire agreement between particular countries	

Constructed by the authors.

ACKNOWLEDGMENTS

The authors acknowledge financial support from the World Bank's Multi-Donor Trust Fund for Trade and Development, the Strategic Research Partnership on Economic Development, and the Student Summer Bursary of the Faculty of Economics at the University of Cambridge. The authors thank Kyle Bagwell, Caroline Freund, Michele Ruta, and Robert Staiger for detailed comments on an earlier draft, as well as suggestions from Mostafa Beshkar, Emily Blanchard, Bruce Blonigen, Avinash Dixit, Bernard Hoekman, Rod Ludema, Penny Goldberg, Ohyun Kwon, Will Martin, Phil McCalman, Nina Pavcnik, Alan Sykes, and Alan Winters. Aksel Erbahar, Carys Golesworthy, Semira Ahdiyyih, and Karthik Raghavan provided outstanding research assistance. C.P.B. thanks the World Bank's Development Research Group for its hospitality during the period in which most of the work on this chapter was completed.

REFERENCES

Anderson, J.E., Neary, J., 1992. Trade reform with quotas, partial rent retention, and tariffs. Econometrica 60 (1), 57–76.

Anderson, J.E., Neary, J., 1996. A new approach to evaluating trade policy. Rev. Econ. Stud. 63 (1), 107–125.

Anderson, J.E., van Wincoop, E., 2004. Trade costs. J. Econ. Lit. 42 (3), 691–751.

Anderson, K., Nelgen, S., 2013. Updated national and global estimates of distortions to agricultural incentives, 1955 to 2011. The World Bank. Available from: http://www.worldbank.org/agdistortions.

Anderson, K., Rausser, G., Swinnen, J., 2013. Political economy of public policies: insights from distortions to agricultural and food markets. J. Econ. Lit. 51 (2), 423–477.

Bagwell, K., Staiger, R.W., 1990. A theory of managed trade. Am. Econ. Rev. 80 (4), 779–795.

Bagwell, K., Staiger, R.W., 1999. An economic theory of GATT. Am. Econ. Rev. 89 (1), 215–248.

Bagwell, K., Staiger, R.W., 2001. Domestic policies, national sovereignty and international economic institutions. Q. J. Econ. 116 (2), 519–562.

Bagwell, K., Staiger, R.W., 2003. Protection and the business cycle. Adv. Econ. Anal. Policy. 3 (1). Article 3.

Bagwell, K., Staiger, R.W., 2011. What do trade negotiators negotiate about? Empirical evidence from the World Trade Organization. Am. Econ. Rev. 101 (4), 1238–1273.

Bagwell, K., Staiger, R.W., 2014. Can the Doha round be a development round? Setting a place at the table. In: Feenstra, R.C., Taylor, A.M. (Eds.), Globalization in an Age of Crisis: Multilateral Economic Cooperation in the Twenty-First Century. University of Chicago Press for the NBER, Chicago, IL, pp. 91–124.

Bagwell, K., Sykes, A.O., 2005a. Chile–Price band system and safeguard measures relating to certain agricultural products. In: Horn, H., Mavroidis, P.C. (Eds.), The WTO Case Law of 2002. Cambridge University Press, Cambridge, UK.

Bagwell, K., Sykes, A.O., 2005b. India–Measures affecting the automotive sector. In: Horn, H., Mavroidis, P.C. (Eds.), The WTO Case Law of 2002. Cambridge University Press, Cambridge, UK.

Bagwell, K., Staiger, R.W., Yurukoglu, A., 2015. Multilateral trade bargaining: a first look at the GATT bargaining records. NBER Working Paper No. 21488.

Bagwell, K., Bown, C.P., Staiger, R.W., 2016. Is the WTO passé? J. Econ. Lit.

Baier, S.L., Bergstrand, J.H., 2004. Economic determinants of free trade agreements. J. Int. Econ. 64 (1), 29–63.

Baier, S.L., Bergstrand, J.H., Mariutto, R., 2014. Economic determinants of free trade agreements revisited: distinguishing sources of interdependence. Rev. Int. Econ. 22 (1), 31–58.

Baldwin, R., 1985. The Political Economy of US Import Policy. The MIT Press, Cambridge, MA, USA.

Baunsgaard, T., Keen, M., 2010. Tax revenue and (or?) trade liberalization. J. Public Econ. 94 (9-10), 563–577.

Bernard, A.B., Jensen, J., Redding, S.J., Schott, P.K., 2007. Firms in international trade. J. Econ. Perspect. 21 (3), 105–130.

Berry, S., Levinsohn, J., Pakes, A., 1999. Voluntary export restraints on automobiles: evaluating a trade policy. Am. Econ. Rev. 89 (3), 400–430.

Beshkar, M., Bond, E.W., 2016. The escape clause in trade agreements. In: Bagwell, K., Staiger, R.W. (Eds.), The Handbook of Commercial Policy, vol. 1B. Elsevier, Netherlands, pp. 69–106.

Beshkar, M., Bond, E.W., Rho, Y., 2015. Tariff binding and overhang: theory and evidence. J. Int. Econ. 97 (1), 1–13.

Bhagwati, J., 1965. On the equivalence of tariffs and quotas. In: Baldwin, R.E., Bhagwati, J., Caves, R.E., Johnson, H.G. (Eds.), In Trade, Growth and the Balance of Payments: Essays in Honor of G. Haberler. Rand McNally, Chicago.

Bhagwati, J., 1991. The World Trading System at Risk. Princeton University Press, Princeton.

Blanchard, E.J., Hakobyan, S., 2015. The US generalised system of preferences in principle and practice. World Econ. 38 (3), 399–424.

Blanchard, E.J., Matschke, X., 2015. U.S. multinationals and preferential market access. Rev. Econ. Stat. 97 (4), 839–854.

Blanchard, E.J., Bown, C.P., Johnson, R.C., 2016. Global supply chains and trade policy. NBER Working Paper No. 21883.

Blonigen, B.A., Prusa, T.J., 2016. Dumping and antidumping duties. In: Bagwell, K., Staiger, R.W. (Eds.), The Handbook of Commercial Policy, vol. 1B. Elsevier, Netherlands, pp. 107–159.

Blonigen, B.A., Liebman, B.H., Pierce, J.R., Wilson, W.W., 2013. Are all trade protection policies created equal? Empirical evidence for nonequivalent market power effects of tariffs and quotas. J. Int. Econ. 89 (2), 369–378.

Bohara, A.K., Kaempfer, W.H., 1991. A test of tariff endogeneity in the United States. Am. Econ. Rev. 81 (4), 952–960.

Bond, E.W., Trachtman, J.P., 2016. China-Rare earths: export restrictions and the limits of textual interpretation. World Trade Rev. 15 (2), 189–209.

Bown, C.P., 2002a. The economics of trade disputes, the GATT's Article XXIII and the WTO's Dispute Settlement Understanding. Econ. Polit. 14 (3), 283–323.

Bown, C.P., 2002b. Why are safeguards under the WTO so unpopular? World Trade Rev. 1 (1), 47–62.

Bown, C.P., 2004. Trade disputes and the implementation of protection under the GATT: an empirical assessment. J. Int. Econ. 62 (2), 263–294.

Bown, C.P., 2009. Self-Enforcing Trade: Developing Countries and WTO Dispute Settlement. Brookings Institution Press, Washington, DC.

Bown, C.P., 2010. China's WTO entry: antidumping, safeguards, and dispute settlement. In: Feenstra, R. C., Wei, S.J. (Eds.), China's Growing Role in World Trade. University of Chicago Press for the NBER, Chicago, IL, pp. 281–337.

Bown, C.P., 2011a. Introduction. In: Bown, C.P. (Ed.), The Great Recession and Import Protection: The Role of Temporary Trade Barriers. CEPR and World Bank, London, UK, pp. 1–51.

Bown, C.P., 2011b. Taking stock of antidumping, safeguards and countervailing duties, 1990-2009. World Econ. 34 (12), 1955–1998.

Bown, C.P., 2013a. Emerging economies and the emergence of south-south protectionism. J. World Trade 47 (1), 1–44.

Bown, C.P., 2013b. How different are safeguards from antidumping? Evidence from U.S. trade policies toward steel. Rev. Ind. Organ. 42 (4), 449–481.

Bown, C.P., 2014a. Temporary trade barriers database. The World Bank. Available from: http://econ. worldbank.org/ttbd/ (accessed 25.07.14).

Bown, C.P., 2014b. Trade policy flexibilities and Turkey: tariffs, antidumping, safeguards, and WTO dispute settlement. World Econ. 37 (2), 193–218.

Bown, C.P., 2015. What's left for the WTO? CEPR Discussion Paper No. 11003.

Bown, C.P., Crowley, M.A., 2010. China's export growth and the China safeguard: threats to the world trading system? Can. J. Econ. 43 (4), 1353–1388.

Bown, C.P., Crowley, M.A., 2013a. Import protection, business cycles, and exchange rates: evidence from the Great Recession. J. Int. Econ. 90 (1), 50–64.

Bown, C.P., Crowley, M.A., 2013b. Self-enforcing trade agreements: evidence from time-varying trade policy. Am. Econ. Rev. 103 (2), 1071–1090.

Bown, C.P., Crowley, M.A., 2014. Emerging economies, trade policy, and macroeconomic shocks. J. Dev. Econ. 111, 261–273.

Bown, C.P., Hillman, J.A., 2016. Bird flu, the OIE, and national regulation: a legal-economic assessment of India–Agricultural products. World Trade Rev. 15 (2), 235–257.

Bown, C.P., Irwin, D.A., 2015. The GATT's starting point: tariff levels circa 1947. NBER Working Paper No. 21782.

Bown, C.P., McCulloch, R., 2003. Nondiscrimination and the WTO Agreement on Safeguards. World Trade Rev. 2 (3), 327–348.

Bown, C.P., McCulloch, R., 2009. U.S.-Japan and U.S.-China trade conflict: export growth, reciprocity, and the international trading system. J. Asian Econ. 20 (6), 669–687.

Bown, C.P., Pauwelyn, J., (Eds.) 2010. The Law, Economics and Politics of Retaliation in WTO Dispute Settlement. Cambridge University Press, Cambridge, UK.

Bown, C.P., Reynolds, K.M., 2015. Trade flows and trade disputes. Rev. Int. Organ. 10 (2), 145–177.

Bown, C.P., Tovar, P., 2011. Trade liberalization, antidumping, and safeguards: evidence from India's tariff reform. J. Dev. Econ. 96 (1), 115–125.

Bown, C.P., Trachtman, J.P., 2009. Brazil–Measures affecting imports of retreaded tyres: a balancing act. World Trade Rev. 8 (1), 85–135.

Bown, C.P., Karacaovali, B., Tovar, P., 2015. What do we know about preferential trade agreements and temporary trade barriers? In: Dür, A., Elsig, M. (Eds.), Trade Cooperation: The Purpose, Design and Effects of Preferential Trade Agreements. Cambridge University Press, Cambridge, UK, pp. 433–462.

Brambilla, I., Khandelwal, A.K., Schott, P.K., 2010. China's experience under the multi-fiber arrangement (MFA) and the agreement on textiles and clothing (ATC). In: Feenstra, R.C., Wei, S.J. (Eds.), China's Growing Role in World Trade. University of Chicago Press for the NBER, Chicago, IL, pp. 345–387.

Brander, J., 1995. Strategic trade policy. In: Grossman, G.M., Rogoff, K. (Eds.), Handbook of International Economics. North Holland, Amsterdam.

Brandt, L., Morrow, P.M., 2015. Tariffs and the Organization of Trade in China. University of Toronto, Mimeogr.

Brewster, R., Brunel, C., Mayda, A.M., 2016. Trade in environmental goods: a review of the WTO appellate bodys ruling in US–Countervailing measures (China). World Trade Rev. 15 (2), 327–349.

Broda, C., Limão, N., Weinstein, D.E., 2008. Optimal tariffs and market power: the evidence. Am. Econ. Rev. 98 (5), 2032–2065.

Bronckers, M., Maskus, K.E., 2014. China–Raw materials: a controversial step towards evenhanded exploitation of natural resources. World Trade Rev. 13 (2), 393–408.

Broude, T., Levy, P.I., 2014. Do you mind if I don't smoke? Products, purpose and indeterminacy in US–Measures affecting the production and sale of clove cigarettes. World Trade Rev. 13 (2), 357–392.

Burger, B., 2014. Electricity production from solar and wind in Germany in 2014. Mimeogr.

Butler, R.A., 1952. The balance of payments situation. Chancellor of the exchequer, cabinet memo c(52) 10 (top secret), 19th January. Available from: http://www.nationalarchives.gov.uk.

Calvo-Pardo, H., Freund, C., Ornelas, E., 2011. The ASEAN free trade agreement: impact on trade flows and external trade barriers. In: Barro, R.J., Lee, J.W. (Eds.), Costs and Benefits of Economic Integration in Asia. Oxford University Press, Oxford, UK, pp. 157–186.

Cassing, J., McKeown, T.J., Ochs, J., 1986. The political economy of the tariff cycle. Am. Polit. Sci. Rev. 80 (3), 843–862.

Charnovitz, S., Fischer, C., 2015. Canada–Renewable energy: implications for WTO law on green and not-so-green subsidies. World Trade Rev. 14 (2), 177–210.

Charnovitz, S., Hoekman, B.M., 2013. US-Tyres: upholding a WTO accession contract–imposing pain for little gain. World Trade Rev. 12 (2), 273–296.

Conconi, P., Pauwelyn, J., 2011. Trading cultures: appellate body report on China–Audiovisuals (WT/DS363/AB/R, adopted 19 January 2010). World Trade Rev. 10 (1), 95–118.

Conconi, P., Voon, T., 2016. EC–Seal products: the tension between public morals and international trade agreements. World Trade Rev. 15 (2), 211–234.

Cosar, A.K., Grieco, P.L.E., Tintelnot, F., 2015. Borders, geography, and oligopoly: evidence from the wind turbine industry. Rev. Econ. Stat. 97 (3), 623–637.

Crowley, M.A., Howse, R., 2014. Tuna-Dolphin II: a legal and economic analysis of the Appellate Body report. World Trade Rev. 13 (2), 321–355.

Crowley, M.A., Palmeter, D., 2009. Japan–Countervailing duties on dynamic random access memories from Korea. World Trade Rev. 8 (1), 259–272.

Crowley, M.A., Song, H., 2015. Policy Shocks and Stock Market Returns: Evidence from Chinese Solar Panels. University of Cambridge, Mimeogr.

Crowley, M.A., Song, H., Meng, N., 2016. Tariff Scares: Trade Policy Information and the Extensive Margin of Chinese Exporting Firms. University of Cambridge, Mimeogr.

Crucini, M.J., 1994. Sources of variation in real tariff rates: the United States, 1900-1940. Am. Econ. Rev. 84 (3), 732–743.

Curzon, G., 1965. Multilateral Commercial Diplomacy: The General Agreement on Tariffs and Trade and Its Impact on National Commercial Policies and Techniques. Michael Joseph, London.

Dean, J., 1995. Market disruption and the incidence of VERs under the MFA. Rev. Econ. Stat. 77 (2), 383–388.

Delipalla, S., Keen, M., 1992. The comparison between ad valorem and specific taxation under imperfect competition. J. Public Econ. 49 (3), 351–367.

Djankov, S., Freund, C., Pham, C.S., 2010. Trading on time. Rev. Econ. Stat. 92 (1), 166–173.

Eaton, J., Kortum, S., Kramarz, F., 2011. An anatomy of international trade: evidence from French firms. Econometrica 79 (5), 1453–1498.

Ederington, J., Ruta, M., 2016. Nontariff measures and the world trading system. In: Bagwell, K., Staiger, R.W. (Eds.), The Handbook of Commercial Policy, vol. 1B. Elsevier, Netherlands, pp. 211–277.

Edmonds, E.V., Pavcnik, N., Topalova, P., 2010. Trade adjustment and human capital investments: evidence from Indian tariff reform. Am. Econ. J.: Appl. Econ. 2 (4), 42–75.

Edwards, L., 2011. South Africa: from proliferation to moderation. In: Bown, C.P. (Ed.), The Great Recession and Import Protection: The Role of Temporary Trade Barriers. CEPR and World Bank, London, UK, pp. 429–469.

Estevadordal, A., Freund, C., Ornelas, E., 2008. Does regionalism affect trade liberalization toward nonmembers? Q. J. Econ. 123 (4), 1531–1575.

Feenstra, R.C., 1988. Quality change under trade restraints in Japanese autos. Q. J. Econ. 103 (1), 131–146.

Feenstra, R.C., 1995. Estimating the effects of trade policy. In: Grossman, G.M., Rogoff, K. (Eds.), Handbook of International Economics, vol. 3. North Holland, Amterdam, pp. 1553–1595.

Foletti, L., Fugazza, M., Nicita, A., Olarreaga, M., 2011. Smoke in the (tariff) water. World Econ. 34 (2), 248–264.

Fontagné, L., Orefice, G., Piermartini, R., Rocha, N., 2015. Product standards and margins of trade: firm-level evidence. J. Int. Econ. 97 (1), 29–44.

Francois, J., Palmeter, D., 2008. US-countervailing duty investigation of DRAMS. World Trade Rev. 7 (1), 219–229.

Gawande, K., Bandyopadhyay, U., 2000. Is protection for sale? Evidence on the Grossman-Helpman theory of endogenous protection. Rev. Econ. Stat. 82 (1), 139–215.

Gawande, K., Krishna, P., Robbins, M.J., 2006. Foreign lobbies and U.S. trade policy. Rev. Econ. Stat. 88 (3), 563–571.

Gawande, K., Krishna, P., Olarreaga, M., 2009. What governments maximize and why: the view from trade. Int. Organ. 63 (3), 491–532.

Gawande, K., Hoekman, B.M., Cui, Y., 2015. Global supply chains and trade policy responses to the 2008 crisis. World Bank Econ. Rev. 29 (1), 102–128.

Goldberg, P.K., 1995. Product differentiation and oligopoly in international markets: the case of the U.S. automobile industry. Econometrica 63 (4), 891–951.

Goldberg, P.K., Maggi, G., 1999. Protection for sale: an empirical investigation. Am. Econ. Rev. 89 (5), 1135–1155.

Goldberg, P.K., Pavcnik, N., 2016. The effects of trade policy. In: Bagwell, K., Staiger, R.W. (Eds.), The Handbook of Commercial Policy, vol. 1A. Elsevier, Netherlands, pp. 161–206.

Goldberg, P.K., Khandelwal, A.K., Pavcnik, N., Topalova, P., 2010a. Imported intermediate inputs and domestic product growth: evidence from India. Q. J. Econ. 125 (4), 1727–1767.

Goldberg, P.K., Khandelwal, A.K., Pavcnik, N., Topalova, P., 2010b. Multiproduct firms and product turnover in the developing world: evidence from India. Rev. Econ. Stat. 92 (4), 1042–1049.

Grossman, G.M., Helpman, E., 1994. Protection for sale. Am. Econ. Rev. 84 (4), 833–850.

Hahn, M., Mehta, K., 2013. Its a bird, its a plane: some remarks on the Airbus Appellate Body Report (EC and Certain Member States–Large Civil Aircraft, WT/DS316/AB/R). World Trade Rev. 12 (2), 139–161.

Hakobyan, S., 2015. Accounting for underutilization of trade preference programs: the US Generalized System of Preferences. Can. J. Econ. 48 (2), 408–436.

Handley, K., 2014. Exporting under trade policy uncertainty: theory and evidence. J. Int. Econ. 94 (1), 50–66.

Handley, K., Limão, N., 2014. Policy Uncertainty, Trade and Welfare: Theory and Evidence for China and the U.S. University of Maryland, Mimeogr.

Handley, K., Limão, N., 2015. Trade and investment under policy uncertainty: theory and firm evidence. Am. Econ. J.: Econ. Policy 7 (4), 189–222.

Harrigan, J., Barrows, G., 2009. Testing the theory of trade policy: evidence from the abrupt end of the multifiber arrangement. Rev. Econ. Stat. 91 (2), 282–294.

Harris, R., 1985. Why voluntary export restraints are 'voluntary'. Can. J. Econ. 18 (4), 799–809.

Hoekman, B., Howse, R., 2008. EC–Sugar. World Trade Rev. 7 (1), 149–178.

Hoekman, B., Trachtman, J.P., 2008. Canada–Wheat: discrimination, non-commercial considerations, and the right to regulate through state trading enterprises. World Trade Rev. 7 (1), 45–66.

Hoekman, B.M., Kostecki, M.M., 2009. The Political Economy of the World Trading System: The WTO and Beyond. Oxford University Press, Oxford, UK.

Hoekman, B., Ng, F., Olarreaga, M., 2002. Eliminating excessive tariffs on exports of least developed countries. World Bank Econ. Rev. 16 (1), 1–21.

Hoekman, B., Ng, F., Olarreaga, M., 2004. Agricultural tariffs or subsidies: which are more important for developing economies? World Bank Econ. Rev. 18 (2), 175–204.

Horn, H., 2006. National treatment in the GATT. Am. Econ. Rev. 96 (1), 394–404.

Horn, H., Weiler, J.H.H., 2003. EC–Asbestos: European communities measures affecting asbestos and asbestos-containing products. In: Horn, H., Mavroidis, P.C. (Eds.), The WTO Case Law of 2001. Cambridge University Press, Cambridge, UK.

Howse, R., Levy, P.I., 2013. The TBT panels: US–Cloves, US–Tuna, US–COOL. World Trade Rev. 12 (2), 327–375.

Howse, R., Neven, D.J., 2003. US–Shrimp: United States–import prohibition of certain shrimp and shrimp products, recourse to article 21.5 of the DSU by Malaysia. In: Horn, H., Mavroidis, P.C. (Eds.), The WTO Case Law of 2001. Cambridge University Press, Cambridge, UK.

Howse, R., Neven, D.J., 2005a. Canada–Export credits and loan guarantees for regional aircraft (WT/DS222/R): a comment. In: Horn, H., Mavroidis, P.C. (Eds.), The WTO Case Law of 2002. Cambridge University Press, Cambridge, UK.

Howse, R., Neven, D.J., 2005b. United States–Tax treatment for 'Foreign Sales Corporations' recourse to arbitration by the United States under article 22.6 of the DSU and article 4.11 of the SCM agreement (WT/DS106/ARB): a comment. In: Horn, H., Mavroidis, P.C. (Eds.), The WTO Case Law of 2002. Cambridge University Press, Cambridge, UK.

Howse, R.L., Horn, H., 2009. European Communities—Measures affecting the approval and marketing of biotech products. World Trade Rev. 8 (1), 49–83.

Hudec, R.E., 1993. Enforcing International Trade Law: The Evolution of the Modern GATT Legal System. Butterworth Legal Publishers, New Hampshire.

Hummels, D., 2007. Transportation costs and international trade in the second era of globalization. J. Econ. Perspect. 21 (3), 131–154.

Irwin, D.A., 1998a. Change in U.S. tariffs: the role of import prices and commercial policies. Am. Econ. Rev. 88 (4), 1015–1026.

Irwin, D.A., 1998b. The Smoot-Hawley tariff: a quantitative assessment. Rev. Econ. Stat. 80 (2), 326–334.

Irwin, D.A., 2005. The rise of US anti-dumping activity in historical perspective. World Econ. 28 (5), 651–668.

Irwin, D.A., 2011. Peddling Protectionsim: Smoot-Hawley and the Great Depression. Princeton University Press, Princeton and Oxford.

Irwin, D.A., 2012. Trade Policy Disaster: Lessons from the 1930s. The MIT Press, Cambridge, MA.

Irwin, D.A., 2013. The Nixon Shock after 40 years: the import surcharge revisited. World Trade Rev. 12 (1), 29–66.

Irwin, D.A., Klenow, P.J., 1994. Learning-by-doing spillovers in the semiconductor industry. J. Polit. Econ. 102 (6), 1200–1227.

Irwin, D.A., Pavcnik, N., 2004. Airbus versus Boeing revisited: international competition in the aircraft market. J. Int. Econ. 64 (2), 223–245.

Irwin, D.A., Weiler, J., 2008. Measures affecting the cross-border supply of gambling and betting services (DS 285). World Trade Rev. 7 (1), 71–113.

Irwin, D.A., Mavroidis, P.C., Sykes, A.O., 2008. The Genesis of the GATT. Cambridge University Press, Cambridge, UK.

ITC, 2009. Export Promotion and the WTO: A Brief Guide. International Trade Centre, Geneva.

Javorcik, B., Narciso, G., 2008. Differentiated products and evasion of import tariffs. J. Int. Econ. 76 (2), 208–222.

Karacaovali, B., Limão, N., 2008. The clash of liberalizations: preferential vs. multilateral trade liberalization in the European Union. J. Int. Econ. 74 (2), 299–327.

Keck, A., Lendle, A., 2014. New Evidence on Preference Utilization. WTO, Mimeogr.

Kee, H.L., Neagu, C., Nicita, A., 2013. Is protectionism on the rise? Assessing national trade policies during the crisis of 2008. Rev. Econ. Stat. 95 (1), 342–346.

Kee, H.L., Nicita, A., Olarreaga, M., 2009. Estimating trade restrictiveness indices. Econ. J. 119 (534), 172–199.

Keen, M., 1998. The balance between specific and ad valorem taxation. Fisc. Stud. 19 (1), 1–37.

Keen, M., 2008. Vat, tariffs, and withholding: border taxes and informality in developing countries. J. Public Econ. 92 (2), 1892–1906.

Khandelwal, A.K., Schott, P.K., Wei, S.J., 2013. Trade liberalization and embedded institutional reform: evidence from Chinese exporters. Am. Econ. Rev. 103 (6), 2169–2195.

Knetter, M.M., Prusa, T.J., 2003. Macroeconomic factors and antidumping filings: evidence from four countries. J. Int. Econ. 61 (1), 1–17.

Krishna, K., 1989. Trade restrictions as facilitating practices. J. Int. Econ. 26 (3-4), 251–270.

Krishna, P., Mitra, D., 1998. Trade liberalization, market discipline and productivity growth: new evidence from India. J. Dev. Econ. 56 (2), 447–462.

Krueger, A.O., 1974. The political economy of the rent-seeking society. Am. Econ. Rev. 64 (3), 291–303.

Lee, G.M., 2016. Subsidies and countervailing duties. In: Bagwell, K., Staiger, R.W. (Eds.), The Handbook of Commercial Policy, vol. 1B. Elsevier, Netherlands, pp. 161–210.

Levy, P.I., Regan, D.H., 2015. EC–Seal products: seals and sensibilities (TBT aspects of the panel and appellate body reports). World Trade Rev. 14 (2), 337–339.

Limão, N., 2006. Preferential trade agreements as stumbling blocks for multilateral trade liberalization: evidence for the U.S. Am. Econ. Rev. 96 (3), 896–914.

Limão, N., 2007. Are preferential trade agreements with non-trade objectives a stumbling block for multilateral liberalization? Rev. Econ. Stud. 74 (3), 821–855.

Limão, N., 2016. Preferential trade agreements. In: Bagwell, K., Staiger, R.W. (Eds.), The Handbook of Commercial Policy, vol. 1B. Elsevier, Netherlands, pp. 279–367.

Limão, N., Tovar, P., 2011. Policy choice: theory and evidence from commitment via international trade agreements. J. Int. Econ. 85 (2), 186–205.

Ludema, R.D., Mayda, A.M., 2013. Do terms-of trade effects matter for trade agreements? Theory and evidence from WTO countries. Q. J. Econ. 128 (4), 1837–1893.

Madani, D., 1999. A review of the role and impact of export processing zones. World Bank Policy Research Working Paper No. 2238.

Maggi, G., 2014. International trade agreements. In: Gopinath, G., Helpman, E., Rogoff, K. (Eds.), Handbook of International Economics, vol. 4. Elevier, Amsterdam, NL, pp. 317–390.

Maggi, G., Rodriguez-Clare, A., 1998. The value of trade agreements in the presence of political pressures. J. Polit. Econ. 106 (3), 574–601.

Mattoo, A., Subramanian, A., 2009. From Doha to the next Bretton Woods: a new multilateral trade agenda. Foreign Aff. 88 (1), 15–26.

Mavroidis, P.C., 2016. Dispute settlement in the WTO: mind over matter. In: Bagwell, K., Staiger, R.W. (Eds.), Handbook of Commercial Policy, vol. 1A. Elsevier, Netherlands, pp. 333–377.

Mavroidis, P.C., Saggi, K., 2014. What is not so cool about US-COOL regulations? A critical analysis of the Appellate Body's ruling on US-COOL. World Trade Rev. 13 (2), 299–320.

McCulloch, R., Pinera, J., 1976. Trade as aid: the political economy of tariff preferences. Am. Econ. Rev. 67 (5), 959–967.

McLaren, J., 2016. The political economy of commercial policy. In: Bagwell, K., Staiger, R.W. (Eds.), The Handbook of Commercial Policy, vol. 1A. Elsevier, Netherlands, pp. 109–159.

Mishra, P., Subramanian, A., Topalova, P., 2008. Tariffs, enforcement, and customs evasion: evidence from India. J. Public Econ. 92 (10-11), 1907–1925.

Mitra, D., Thomakos, D.D., Ulubasoglu, M.A., 2002. 'Protection for sale' in a developing country: democracy vs. dictatorship. Rev. Econ. Stat. 84 (3), 497–508.

Neven, D., Sykes, A.O., 2014. United States–Measures affecting trade in large civil aircraft (second complaint): some comments. World Trade Rev. 13 (2), 281–298.

Neven, D., Trachtman, J.P., 2013. Philippines–Taxes on distilled spirits: like products and market definition. World Trade Rev. 12 (2), 297–326.

Neven, D., Weiler, J.H.H., 2006. Japan–Measures affecting the importation of apples (AB-2003-4): one bad apple? In: Horn, H., Mavroidis, P.C. (Eds.), The WTO Case Law of 2003. Cambridge University Press, Cambridge, UK.

Nicita, A., Olarreaga, M., Silva, P., 2014. Cooperation in WTO's Tariff Waters. University of Geneva, Mimeogr.

Ornelas, E., 2016. Special and differential treatment for developing countries. In: Bagwell, K., Staiger, R.W. (Eds.), The Handbook of Commercial Policy, vol. 1B. Elsevier, Netherlands, pp. 369–432.

Ossa, R., 2014. Trade wars and trade talks with data. Am. Econ. Rev. 104 (12), 4104–4146.

Palgrave Macmillan, 2013. International Historical Statistics. Available from: http://www.palgraveconnect.com/pc/doifinder/10.1057/9781137305688.0216 (accessed 17.09.15).

Panagariya, A., 1981. Quantitative restrictions in international trade under monopoly. J. Int. Econ. 11 (1), 15–31.

Panagariya, A., 1982. Tariff policy under monopoly in general equilibrium. Int. Econ. Rev. 23 (1), 143–156.

Prusa, T.J., 2008. Comment: US–Countervailing duty investigation of DRAMS. World Trade Rev. 7 (1), 231–234.

Ries, J.C., 1993. Windfall profits and vertical relationships: who gained in the Japanese auto industry from VERs? J. Ind. Econ. 41 (3), 259–276.

Rodrik, D., 1995. Political economy of trade policy. In: Grossman, G.M., Rogoff, K. (Eds.), Handbook of International Economics, vol. 3. North Holland, Amterdam, pp. 1457–1494.

Rose, A.K., 2013. The March of an economic idea? Protectionism isn't counter-cyclic (anymore). Econ. Policy 28 (76), 569–612.

Rubini, L., 2015. 'The wide and the narrow gate': benchmarking in the SCM agreement after the Canada–Renewable energy/FIT ruling. World Trade Rev. 14 (2), 211–237.

Saggi, K., Mark, W., 2016. Understanding agricultural price range systems as trade restraints: Peru–Agricultural products. World Trade Rev. 15 (2), 259–286.

Sapir, A., Trachtman, J.P., 2008. Subsidization, price suppression, and expertise: causation and precision in Upland Cotton. World Trade Rev. 7 (1), 183–209.

Schott, P.K., 2004. Across-product versus within-product specialization in international trade. Q. J. Econ. 119 (2), 646–677.

Staiger, R.W., 1995. International rules and institutions for trade policy. In: Grossman, G.M., Rogoff, K. (Eds.), Handbook of International Economics, vol. 3. North Holland, Amterdam, pp. 1495–1551.

Staiger, R.W., 2006. What can developing countries achieve in the WTO? J. Econ. Lit. 44 (2), 779–795.

Staiger, R.W., Sykes, A.O., 2010. 'Currency manipulation' and world trade. World Trade Rev. 9 (4), 583–627.

Staiger, R.W., Sykes, A.O., 2011. International trade, national treatment, and domestic regulation. J. Legal Stud. 40 (1), 149–203.

Subramanian, A., Wei, S.J., 2007. The WTO promotes trade, strongly but unevenly. J. Int. Econ. 72 (1), 151–175.

Topalova, P., Khandelwal, A., 2011. Trade liberalization and firm productivity: the case of India. Rev. Econ. Stat. 93 (3), 995–1009.

Tovar, P., 2012. Preferential trade agreements and unilateral liberalization: evidence from CAFTA. World Trade Rev. 11 (4), 591–619.

Trefler, D., 1993. Trade liberalization and the theory of endogenous protection: an econometric study of U.S. import policy. J. Polit. Econ. 101 (1), 138–160.

UK, 1952. Further (March 1952) reductions in United Kingdom external expenditure: memorandum by the government of the United Kingdom. GATT Digital Archive, L/2 20 March 1952.

USTR, 2012. U.S. Trade Representative Ron Kirk comments on presidential actions related to the Generalized System of Preferences. Available from: http://www.ustr.gov/about-us/press-office/press-releases/2012/march/us-trade-representative-ron-kirk-comments-presidenti (accessed 25.09.14).

Vandenbussche, H., Zanardi, M., 2008. What explains the proliferation of antidumping laws? Econ. Policy 23 (1), 93–138.

Viner, J., 1950. The Customs Union Issue. Carnegie Endowment for International Peace, New York.

Volpe, C.M., Carballo, J., Graziano, A., 2015. Customs. J. Int. Econ. 96 (1), 119–137.

Wauters, J.M., Vandenbussche, H., 2010. China-Measures affecting imports of automobile parts. World Trade Rev. 9 (1), 201–238.

WTO, 1995. Analytical Index: Guide to GATT Law and Practice, vols. 1 and 2. WTO, Geneva.

WTO, 2007. World Trade Report 2007: Six Decades of Multilateral Trade Cooperation: What Have We Learnt? WTO, Geneva.

WTO, 2011. World Trade Report 2011: The WTO and Preferential Trade Agreements: From Co-Existence to Coherence. WTO, Geneva.

WTO, 2012. World Trade Report 2012: Trade and Public Policies: A Closer Look at Non-Tariff Measures in the 21st Century. WTO, Geneva.

WTO, 2014. World Tariff Profiles 2014. Geneva, WTO, UNCTAD, and ITC.

WTO, 2015a. Database on preferential trade arrangements. Available from: http://ptadb.wto.org/default.aspx (accessed 30 December).

WTO, 2015b. Disputes by agreement. Available from: https://www.wto.org/english/tratop_e/dispu_e/dispu_agreements_index_e.htm (accessed 30 December).

WTO, 2015c. Regional trade agreements information system. Available from: http://rtais.wto.org/UI/PublicMaintainRTAHome.aspx (accessed 30 December).

Yu, M., 2015. Processing trade, tariff reductions and firm productivity: evidence from Chinese firms. Econ. J. 125, 943–988, 585.

CHAPTER 2

The Political Economy of Commercial Policy

J. McLaren
University of Virginia, Charlottesville, VA, United States

Contents

Abstract

This chapter surveys research on the demand for protectionism as well as theoretical and empirical work on the (i) electoral mechanisms, the (ii) lobbying institutions, and the (iii) legislative bargaining that affect its supply. A recent trend is mutual feedbacks between commercial policy on the one hand

and economic conditions and political institutions on the other. Areas ripe for more exploration include informational lobbying, the role of the media, firm-level analysis of lobbying and more realistic approaches to labor markets.

Keywords

Lobbying, Voting, Political economy, Tariffs, Nontariff Barriers

JEL Classification Codes

F13, F21, F22, D72, D78

This chapter surveys the political determinants of commercial policy. The term "political" is broad, and encompasses any mechanism by which commercial policy is forged, but we will be especially interested in any motivation in setting policy that is different from pure social welfare maximization.[a] Analyzing this question requires knowledge of what different political agents' demands and preferences are regarding commercial policy, and also how political institutions and political conditions convey those demands and preferences into realized policy. This requires an understanding of electoral rules, lobbying, and legislative bargaining. We will examine these questions in turn, and lastly point out that political institutions and conditions can in turn be shaped by commercial policy, leading to feedback effects that can at times be of great importance.[b]

Although our main interest is with cases in which policy outcomes depart from the socially optimal, it will be helpful to review as a starting point what optimal policies are in a range of models, which may be used as a benchmark as we study political outcomes down the road.

1. SOCIALLY OPTIMAL POLICY: A CURSORY REVIEW

1.1 Neoclassical Models

Because we will lean so heavily on it in discussing political models, it is worth rehearsing for 3 minutes the standard neoclassical partial-equilibrium trade model. Consider an economy, Home, that produces shoelaces under conditions of perfect competition. A large number of investors own capital specific to production of shoelaces (in other words, it is not useful in producing anything else), which they combine with labor to produce the output. The capital is in fixed and exogenous supply, and the industry is small

---

[a] In most of what follows, we will treat this term as synonymous with maximization of aggregate real income, as with most of the literature. Where a broader concept of social welfare comes into play, encompassing distributional considerations, it will be noted.

[b] This chapter builds on the earlier surveys by Rodrik (1995) and Gawande and Krishna (2004). I am indebted to Paula Conconi and Anna Maria Mayda for extremely constructive comments, as well as to the editors of this volume.

enough in the Home economy that wages can be taken as fixed and unaffected by the shoelace industry. For any given price, profit-maximizing shoelace producers will choose a quantity to maximize profit, yielding a supply curve; aggregating these up to the industry level yields the industry supply relation $y(p)$, where p denotes the domestic price of shoelaces and y the quantity produced by the domestic industry, and $y'(p) > 0$. Producer surplus, $\pi(p)$, is then the area between the supply curve and the price, with $\pi'(p) = y(p) > 0$. Shoelaces are a small part of each consumer's budget set, so we can derive a demand curve for each consumer, aggregate them up to a Home demand curve $d(p)$ with $d'(p) < 0$, and compute consumer surplus as the area between the price and the demand curve $s(p) > 0$, with $s'(p) = -d(p) < 0$. Export supply from the rest of the world is given by $XS(p^*)$, where p^* is the world price and $XS'(p^*) \geq 0$. If this export-supply curve is flat, Home is "small."

If Home is a net importer of shoelaces, then a specific import tariff[c] of t per unit creates a wedge between the world price and the domestic price so that $p = p^* + t$, and equilibrium satisfies $m(p^* + t) \equiv d(p^* + t) - y(p^* + t) = XS(p^*)$, where $m(p)$ denotes Home's imports of shoelaces. An increase in t pushes the world price down and the domestic price up.[d] If Home's social welfare derived from the shoelace industry is $SW(t) = \pi(p(t)) + s(p(t)) + tm(p(t)) = \pi(p(t)) + s(p(t)) + tXS(p^*(t))$, where the last term represents tariff revenue to be rebated to Home consumers, then:

$$
\begin{aligned}
SW'(t) &= [y(p) - d(p)]\frac{dp}{dt} + m(p) + tXS'(p^*)\frac{dp^*}{dt} \\
&= [y(p) - d(p) + m(p)] + [tXS'(p^*) - XS(p^*)]\frac{dp^*}{dt}
\end{aligned}
\tag{1}
$$

since $XS(p^*) = m(p)$ and $\dfrac{dp}{dt} = 1 + \dfrac{dp^*}{dt}$. The first expression in square brackets in (1) is equal to zero. The reason is that it represents a simple transfer to domestic producers of shoelaces $(y(p))$ and to taxpayers $(m(p))$ from consumers of shoelaces $(d(p))$ in Home, and all three groups have equal weight. This is crucial; much of the later work in political models will be driven by this term's deviation from zero when these groups have *unequal* weight. The remaining two terms are the distortion caused by the rise in the tariff and the terms–of–trade benefit to Home. Setting (1) equal to zero and rearranging readily yields:

$$
\tau = \frac{1}{\epsilon^*},
\tag{2}
$$

---

[c] A specific tariff is assessed as a fixed charge per unit of goods imported.

[d] In a partial-equilibrium model such as this, it is easy to confirm that the world price falls by less than the tariff, so that the domestic price rises. In general equilibrium, some additional conditions are required to guarantee this; failure is known as the "Metzler paradox."

where $\tau \equiv \dfrac{t}{p^*}$ is the *ad valorem* tariff[e] and $\epsilon^* \equiv \dfrac{p^* XS'(p^*)}{XS(p^*)}$ is the elasticity of export supply. This is the "inverse elasticity formula."[f] In the case of an exported good, the analogue equates the export tax with the inverse foreign import demand elasticity.

This sometimes generalizes to general-equilibrium models. A general n-good competitive model requires a choice of a vector of tariffs/subsidies, say, $\mathbf{t}$, where a positive i^{th} element indicates a positive import tariff if the ith good is imported and an export subsidy if the ith good is exported. Thus, the domestic price vector, $\mathbf{p}$, will be equal to $\mathbf{p}^* + \mathbf{t}$, where $\mathbf{p}^*$ is the world price vector. Denote by $\mathbf{XS}(p^*)$ the foreign export supply, a function mapping n-dimensional price vectors to n-dimensional traded quantities. Then, the general first-order condition for the optimal tariff vector is $\mathbf{p}\nabla\mathbf{XS} = \mathbf{0}$, or the condition that the domestic price vector be orthogonal to the gradient of the export supply function for each product (see Dixit and Norman, 1980, ch. 6).

This does not yield anything that can be described as an "inverse elasticity formula" except under very special circumstances, for two reasons. The more technical reason is that in general equilibrium there is always a continuum of trade vectors that yield the same equilibrium.[g] The more substantive reason is that cross-price effects in the foreign export supply need to be taken into account. However, in the event that $n = 2$, an analogue of the "formula" holds. In addition, if utility is additively separable with one good whose marginal utility is constant, then the tools of partial equilibrium apply in general equilibrium, and the "formula" follows by the same logic as used above. This is used by Broda et al. (2008) to derive testable implications of optimal tariff theory, for which they find considerable empirical support. They estimate inverse export-supply elasticities specific to each country and group of industries, and because the theory applies to unilateral optimal tariffs rather than negotiated tariffs, they focus on tariffs set by countries that have not joined the World Trade Organization (WTO), and for US tariffs against non-WTO members and US nontariff barriers (NTB's). They find a quite robust tendency for tariffs to be lower against foreign export supply that is more elastic, as the "formula" predicts.

On the other hand, Costinot et al. (2015) study optimal tariffs in a two-country, many-good Ricardian model with Constant Elasticity of Substitution preferences. In that model, *if* Home had no influence on Foreign's wage, then the inverse-elasticity formula would apply in each industry. The result for optimal trade policy would have three parts: (i) There would be zero tariff on all imports (since their world prices are pinned down by

---

[e] An *ad valorem* tariff is assessed as a fraction of value.

[f] Of course it is not a formula. The right hand side is a function of the tariff, so it is a recursive equation in τ which generally requires a recursive procedure to solve. If it were a formula, we could plug known values into the right-hand side to compute the value of the left-hand side.

[g] For any trade policy $\mathbf{t}^0$ yielding domestic price vector $\mathbf{p}^0$ and for any positive scalar α, a tariff vector $(\alpha - 1)$ $\mathbf{p}^* + \alpha\, \mathbf{t}^0$ will yield domestic prices equal to $\alpha\, \mathbf{p}^0$, giving the same outcomes. A corollary is the Lerner symmetry theorem.

production costs in Foreign). (ii) On exports with a strong comparative advantage, the inverse elasticity "formula" would hold, and since the Foreign import demand for each could would be the same because of the CES structure, this would imply a common export tax for each strong-comparative-advantage exported good. (iii) For exported goods with a weaker comparative advantage, the inverse-elasticity export tax would not be feasible because it would push the price of the good in Foreign high enough that Foreign producers would begin to produce it. For these goods, the optimal export tax would be the highest tax such that Foreign does not produce the good. However, this three-part description is not the optimal trade-tax regime, because the Foreign wage is *not* fixed, and so it is optimal to tighten trade restrictions in order to reduce it, thus reducing the world price of each good imported from Foreign. As a result, the export taxes will be higher than the level that satisfies the inverse-elasticity "formula." A further complication is that, as noted above, the optimum can be realized with a continuum of different policies. The Home government could equivalently set the export tax on the strongest comparative-advantage goods equal to zero, set positive import tariffs, and set a *subsidy* on weak-comparative-advantage exports, just big enough in each industry to keep Foreign from producing the good.

All of this suggests that the inverse-elasticity approach is only a timid first step, not at all a general optimum. How to apply analysis of a full optimum in a rich model would be a significant challenge for empirical work.

1.2 Imperfect Competition

It is well known that the presence of imperfect competition complicates social welfare maximizing trade policy. Brander and Spencer (1985) showed that in an international Cournot oligopoly, the government of each exporting firm could have an incentive to subsidize the firm's exports (or R&D) in order to transfer rents from competing firms in other countries to its own firm, a conclusion at odds with what perfectly-competitive models prescribe. This conclusion changes when the oligopoly is of the Bertrand variety, in which case optimal policy tends to be an export tax, and is sensitive to other assumptions such as the possibility of entry (Eaton and Grossman, 1986). Maggi (1996) formulated a model that absorbs both Cournot and Bertrand as special cases, so that whether an export subsidy or tax is optimal depends on parameters, but found that in all cases a subsidy to *ex ante* investment that lowers marginal cost raises national welfare. In the case of monopolistic competition, Demidova and Rodriguez-Clare (2009) study a small-open economy with an industry that produces differentiated tradeable goods by firms with heterogeneous productivities. The economy also imports differentiated products from the rest of the world; it is small in the sense that foreign wages and the scope of foreign products produced are unaffected by anything the Home government does, but foreign producers need to incur a fixed cost to export to Home, so the range of foreign products actually available to Home consumers will be affected. It turns out that the optimal policy is an import tariff; the gap between price and marginal cost means that each domestically produced product is underconsumed, and the tariff addresses that.

1.3 Foreign Asset Issues

Computation of social welfare maximizing trade policy can be complicated if some of the domestic productive assets are foreign owned, or if some foreign-owned assets are domestically owned. Blanchard (2007) shows how the optimal tariff on imports tends to be lower if the exporting sector in the foreign country is partly owned by domestic citizens, and Blanchard and Matschke (2015) shows that these effects have an important effect on trade policy in practice. Blanchard et al. (2014) show that optimal tariffs on a given imported product are in general affected by the amount of domestically produced content incorporated in the product, and show that these considerations appear to matter empirically.

1.4 Social Welfare Maximizing Policy Without Lump-Sum Transfers

Most models of optimal trade policy are conditioned on an assumption that lump-sum transfers are available to government, so domestic income distribution concerns are irrelevant to optimal policy. Of course, this is a grotesque oversimplification, and if government does care about inequality in its calculation of social welfare, the absence of lump-sum transfers can have a large effect on optimal policy. Limão and Panagariya (2007) study a class of general-equilibrium models in which, absent domestic lump-sum transfers, inequality aversion creates an antitrade bias in optimal policy.

2. WHAT WE KNOW ABOUT THE DEMAND FOR PROTECTION

Turning now to the *politics* of trade policy, we first consider the demand for protection. The classic theories of political demand for protection were based on an assumption that each political/economic agent would seek trade policies that would maximize his/her real income, and thus politics would be based on the structure of the factor market; thus, for example, a Heckscher–Ohlin (HO) theory of trade would yield a different prediction for trade politics than would a specific-factors (SF) model. Most of the studies that assess voter demand for protectionism, indeed, are cast very narrowly as a "horse race" (to use Mayda and Rodrik's (2005, p. 1,413) term) between HO—in which industry of employment does not matter for one's stand on trade policy, only which factor of production one owns—and SF, where industry of employment is all that matters. More recently, new approaches beyond the factor-market approach have been explored, in which the importance of learning and information in voters' trade-policy preferences have been emphasized. We will review studies based on the behavior of politicians; based on election results; and based on survey data and then try to draw some general lessons.

It may be worth clarifying first what is meant by "HO" and "SF" in this discussion. Most authors have in mind a very primitive version of HO, with two factors, usually unskilled labor and skilled labor, in fixed and exogenous endowments. Each factor can move from one industry to another costlessly, so the skilled and unskilled wages are the same throughout the economy. Skill-abundant countries—that is, high-income countries —export skill-intensive goods, and so trade raises the real incomes of skilled workers, while protection reduces those incomes. The effects are opposite for unskilled workers in those economies, and the roles of the two factors are reversed in a skill-scarce country, which is also a low-income country. On the other hand, the SF model that authors usually have in mind is what Magee (1989) called a "Cairns-Ricardo-Viner" model, in which *every* factor of production is specific to its industry.[h] This is best thought of as a metaphor for a model in which workers face high costs of switching industries, such as Artuc et al. (2010), but for simplicity the standard assumption is that industry-switching costs are infinite. In such a model, all workers in an import-competing industry will benefit from trade protection, while workers in exporting industries will be harmed by it.

2.1 Studies Based on Behavior of Politicians

Examining the behavior of a politician in order to identify what his or her constituents want is indirect, and has the disadvantage that politicians may be moved by other factors as well, such as their own policy views or by interest groups (about which much more later). On the other hand, this approach has the advantage that it can focus on very specific policy measures, such as a trade bill or free trade agreement, instead of a vague survey question that may have different meanings for different respondents.

Conconi et al. (2012a) examine all final votes in the US House of Representatives on bills related to trade and immigration policy between 1970 and 2006, and find quite similar behavior on both issues: The most robust determinant of the representative's vote is the skill ratio, or the ratio of skilled to unskilled workers, of the population in that House district. A higher skill ratio leads to more votes for liberalization of both trade and immigration. This can easily be rationalized in HO terms as maximization of district-level welfare. However, for trade policy, the ratio of export industries to import-competing industries in the district seems to be much more important,[i] while the latter does not

---

[h] The language is sometimes confusing, because outside of the political-economy literature, a "specific factors" model usually means a model in which labor is perfectly mobile across industries, thus receiving the same wage in each industry.

[i] From table 8 and table 4, the marginal effect of a one-standard-deviation increase in the trade-exposure variable is $0.009 \times 95.04 = 0.855$, while the marginal effect of a one-standard-deviation in the skill-ratio variable is $1.961 \times 0.09 = 0.176$.

matter at all for immigration votes. This suggests a point for SF. At the same time, unlike trade votes, a vote for immigration liberalization is less likely in a district with more inequality or fewer foreign-born constituents, and overall votes for freer immigration are far less common than votes for freer trade.

Two provocative studies of politician behavior raise questions that cannot be addressed within conventional political-economy models within the economics literature. The first, Blonigen and Figlio (1998), studies how the trade stance of US Senators is affected by FDI inflows to their state. One could write down models that predict either a protrade or a proprotection effect of an FDI inflow; perhaps once a new foreign-owned plant is in place, citizens of the state would want it to be protected and would desire a tariff, leading to a proprotection effect; or perhaps the new plant managers would make it clear that they need open trade to import needed inputs, and the Senator would respect that, leading to a protrade effect. The authors find that in Senate votes on trade policy from 1985 to 1994, if a senator had tended to make protrade votes in the past, and if the state received a big influx of FDI, that same Senator's protrade tendency increased; but if the senator had tended to vote antitrade, the FDI influx increases the antitrade tendency. Either way, an influx of FDI went along with an *intensification* of whatever stand the Senator had. This is a panel regression with Senator fixed effects, and in the data there are states where the two Senators have opposite positions on trade. It is possible that some kind of learning story might be told, in which voters unsure of how FDI can be attracted update their beliefs in favor of the approach local leaders have been promoting in light of recent success. But explanation of these findings is an open question.

The second, Conconi et al. (2014), studies the effect of a politician's *time horizon* on trade-policy votes. The authors collect every major vote on trade policy in the US Congress from 1973 to 2005 to examine the effect of time remaining until the next election. Systematically, members of the House, who serve 2-year terms, vote for open trade less often than members of the Senate, who serve 6-year terms. The authors show that this difference disappears when a Senator is in the last 2 years of her term, and thus faces the same time horizon before reelection as a House member. This is true after controlling for a wide range of factors, and true when the sample is restricted to Senators who voted on two or more bills and Senator fixed-effects are included. The implication appears to be that in most states most voters are antitrade on balance, but that they have imperfect memories: A member of Congress feels the latitude to place a protrade liberalization vote if the next election is more than 2 years in the future, but it is risky to do so if the election is sooner than that. Again, voters' information seems to be crucial.

2.2 Studies Based on Elections

Given the assumption that politicians' behavior is a signal of voters' wishes because the politician is largely motivated by winning the next election, the natural next step is to look directly at actual voters' behavior by studying election outcomes. For our purpose, the main difficulty with this approach is that elections are affected by many factors beyond trade policy, but occasionally an election is fought almost purely on issues of trade policy and thus can serve as a kind of natural experiment.

One such example is the 1923 election in the United Kingdom, studied in Irwin (1996). Since the repeal of the Corn Laws in 1846, the United Kingdom had long had a low-tariff policy, but in the lingering unemployment following the First World War the Conservative party had been pushing "tariff reform" (that is, dramatic increases in tariffs) under the argument that it would improve the labor market. The Conservatives gained a majority in parliament in 1922 and began pushing toward new legislation, but decided to dissolve parliament and run an election on the issue in order to be able to claim a mandate. As a result, the 1923 election was explicitly run as a referendum on increases in import tariffs. Irwin examines the vote share for the antitariff (Liberal and Labor) parties by county as a function of the occupational breakdown and the skill class of the local population, taken from the 1921 census, in various specifications, controlling for the vote share in the previous election to focus on the vote share deviation in the free-trade election. The overall finding is that skill shares do not have any appreciable explanatory power, but occupational shares do. In particular, counties with a large share of workers in the agricultural, textile and mining sectors were the ones most likely to swing toward the Conservatives, indicating a demand for protectionism among those groups. This seems like a point for SF. Incidentally, the Conservatives were resoundingly defeated in the election, postponing the next wave of protectionist policy until the Great Depression.

A similar example arose in Canada in 1988, studied by Beaulieu (2002). The Progressive Conservative government, led by Brian Mulroney, had just negotiated a free trade agreement with the United States (Canada–US Free Trade Agreement, or CUFTA), which prove to be extremely controversial. The prime minister called an election, which was fought almost entirely on the issue of the agreement, with the opposition Liberals pledging to rip up the agreement if they came to power. Beaulieu (2002) uses the 1988 Canadian National Election Survey (CNES) to analyze individual Canadian voters' stands on the agreement (the survey provides 2797 observations). Classifying industries into those that were expected to benefit from CUFTA and those that were expected to be hurt, the results show that both education level and industry of employment have predictive power for support for CUFTA, but education is much more robust. More educated Canadians supported CUFTA and less educated workers tended to oppose it. The paper argues that this is consistent with HO theory even though Canada is not skill abundant relative to the United States, because Canadian tariffs tended to be higher on less skill-intensive industries.

2.3 Studies Based on Survey Data

The most direct way to find out what voters want in trade policy is to conduct a survey and ask them, and a number of surveys have become available for this purpose over the years. A pioneering study of this type is Scheve and Slaughter (2001), which uses the US 1992 National Election Survey (NES), with a sample of 1736 individuals. The survey collected a wide variety of information about respondents' personal situation, such as education, industry of employment, county of residence and political views on a range of topics. One of the questions asked about whether or not "new limits" should be placed on "foreign imports in order to protect American jobs." They find that respondents with more education are significantly less likely to support trade restrictions, but that workers in industries with higher tariffs or in net exporting industries do not have significantly different views than others. They take this as a win for HO. Interestingly, they find that living in a county with a concentration of industries with high trade exposure (either industries with high tariffs or net-importing industries) increases one's support of trade restrictions, but only for homeowners. The implication appears to be that the effect of trade competition on house prices through its effect on the local economy is a significant concern for those who own a house. This is a channel for distributive effects of trade that does not seem to have been recognized in the theory literature, and seems worth confirmation and more exploration.

Blonigen (2011) offers a critique of the factor-market interpretation of the findings in Scheve and Slaughter (2001), showing that the only robust determinant of voter preferences in the NES data is education, which matters even for retirees who have no obvious state in the factor market. He suggests that education may matter for the voters' trade preferences far beyond its role as a proxy for skilled labor.

Perhaps the most useful of all survey studies is Mayda and Rodrik (2005), which uses two separate international surveys, the 1995 survey of the International Social Survey Programme (ISSP), which polled 28,000 individuals in 23 countries, and the 1995–7 World Values Survey (WVS), with respondents in 47 countries. The ISSP has information on respondents' industry of employment along with education level, whereas the WVS has much better country coverage including a good variety of developing countries, but no occupational data. A dummy variable for a respondent's general support for trade is regressed on a range of controls including the individual's education level and the education level interacted with the country's GDP per capita. This allows for the possibility that, per HO, in skill scarce countries support for trade will be negatively correlated with an individual's skill, while in skill abundant countries the correlation will be positive (since in HO models, trade is good for the abundant factor in each country, and in low-income countries skill is the scarce factor). This prediction comes out strongly in both data sets and in all specifications: In the lowest-income countries, the higher-income individuals are more likely to oppose trade, while in higher-income countries the reverse is true. The ISSP results do show an effect of industry of occupation as well, namely that employees in import-competing industries are less likely to support trade, but the HO effects are generally stronger than the SF effects.

Some survey studies provide some extra insight by comparing attitudes toward trade policy with those toward immigration policy. Economically, the two policy areas present many of the same issues, but they are far from identical. Mayda (2008) examines the ISSP data to examine a striking stylized fact: in every country vastly more respondents favor increased restrictions on immigration compared to restrictions on trade. Indeed, in each country, the correlation between protrade and proimmigration attitudes is positive but very weak, running from 37% for East Germany down to 4% for the Philippines. Running parallel regressions on trade and immigration attitudes similar to the regressions in Mayda and Rodrik (2005), she finds that the one major difference in the responses is the effect of employment in the nontraded sector. Nontraded workers are strongly more likely to favor trade openness, across countries, than traded-sector workers, but nontraded employment has barely any effect on immigration attitudes. Mayda has no quick and ready theoretical explanation for these features, which should be considered an intriguing puzzle, but it should be underlined that these findings are very inconsistent with an HO model (since in that model a factor's returns would be the same in the nontraded sector as in any other).

In a similar vein, Hanson et al. (2007) study NES data to examine the differences that fiscal effects may have on attitudes towards immigration and trade. They find that a major difference between the two is that more-educated voters in states where the fiscal burden of immigrants is higher are less likely to support immigration, compared to less-educated workers in the same state as well as similarly educated workers in states with either fewer immigrants or less generous welfare programs. Hanson et al interpret this is as a response to progressive taxation; where immigrants will require more payments out of state finances, the burden is more likely to be borne by higher-income residents of that state. These fiscal effects are completely absent for trade policy opinions.

An important innovation in the use of survey data for trade-policy preferences is developed in Jäkel and Smolka (2015), who break away from the two-factor HO prison by deriving a "correlation" result similar to those developed by Deardorff (2000). Within a multifactor, many-good framework with perfect competition and comparing free trade with a tariff-affected equilibrium, Jäkel et al use the equilibrium zero-profit conditions for each industry to derive the proposition that within each country, the change in income affecting a factor of production is negatively correlated with the net export of that factor embodied in the country's trade. Then, using the ISSP data, they interpret each occupation as a different factor of production, compute quantities of each occupation embodied in each country's trade (normalized by the size of the economy),[j] and use that as an

---

[j] In practice, they use the relative abundance of each factor, $V_{f,c} - s_c V_{f,w}$, where $V_{f,c}$ is country c's endowment of factor f, $V_{f,w}$ is the world's endowment, and s_c is country c's share of world GDP. In equilibrium, in theory, this must be equal to the net embodied exports of factor f according to the Heckscher–Ohlin–Vanek equation.

explanatory variable to explain attitudes toward trade. The results show that factors with larger embodied exports strongly support more open trade than factors with smaller net embodied exports or embodied net imports. A caveat is that in this study a "factor of production" is identified as an "occupation" in the data. This is somewhat troublesome, since the distribution of occupations in a given country is more easily thought of as endogenous compared with more traditional factors. But the approach seems promising.

2.4 General Observations

Contrary to Mayda and Rodrik (2005)'s "horse race" metaphor, perhaps the competition between HO and SF implied by many of these studies is better compared to a preschool soccer tournament, in which everyone is a winner. Both factor ownership as indicated by higher income and education, and the import-vulnerability of industry of employment matter in a range of studies for a voter's attitude toward trade, although the former is more robust than the latter.

We seemed to have learned that in lower-income countries support for more open trade is negatively correlated with income, while in higher-income countries the opposite is true. This is broadly consistent with a global HO story. However, it is past time for this literature to graduate from the most primitive neoclassical models. Moving past a two-factor HO model is crucial, and explorations along the lines of Jäkel and Smolka (2015) may be helpful. In addition, instead of using as a benchmark a pair of static models where factor mobility in all directions is either perfectly costless or infinitely costly, one could adopt a benchmark of costly mobility (such as Dix-Carneiro, 2014, for example). In such a model, depending on parameters, both industry of employment and human capital status along with age and other factors can determine one's stand on trade policy together. Rather than asking which of the extreme assumptions of HO or SF is consistent with the political-economy data, one could ask what pattern of factor mobility costs fits the data the best, and see how consistent that is with the costs that are measured directly from data on mobility.

More broadly, there are paradoxes that do not seem to fit with conventional political-economy models that may require thinking about voters' information more seriously. Hall and Nelson (2004) point out that between 1991 and 1995, voters' views on the North American Free Trade Agreement (NAFTA), which was negotiated and ratified during that period, changed radically. Particularly between 1991 and 1993, popular support for NAFTA dropped from 70% to the mid-30s, and opposition rose from 15% to the mid-30s. During those 2 years the material interest of voters surely had not changed drastically; mobility costs or skill endowments had not undergone a radical overhaul. What did happen is that public debate started up, and information about the prospective agreement and its possible effects began to be much more available. The media, and perhaps the efforts of lobbyists or public-interest groups to sway the opinions of the public, likely had a large role. Hall and Nelson suggest that a rational-herding model might help understand the rapid change in opinion; at any rate, the effect of voters' *information* has no place in the standard models all though this literature. The curious results in Blonigen and Figlio (1998) seem to imply a learning process, and Blonigen (2011)'s findings seem to indicate a role for education as more than a marker for skilled labor. Another paradoxical result that raises the same sort of questions is Conconi et al. (2014), which seem to imply a depreciation rate for voters' information about trade policy, and one of which politicians are acutely aware and which greatly affects their voting decisions. It would be good to have this built into our theory, as well.

These observations suggest, at the very least, the desirability of a serious look at the role of the media (and perhaps education) in the political economy of commercial policy. In other topic areas, television has been shown to have a statistically measurable and quantitatively important influence on partisan voting behavior in the United States (DellaVigna and Kaplan, 2007), attitudes toward women's status in India (Jensen and Oster, 2009), and many other issues. In light of these findings and the anomalies just noted, it seems a glaring lack that the literature on the demand for trade policy has barely addressed the effect of the media at all.

On this issue, two pioneering papers deserve mention. Ponzetto (2011) (which will be discussed as a theoretical contribution in Section 3.1) studies the effect of media coverage of an industry's trade policy on the level of protection that the industry receives. He searches US news sources from 1980 to 1983 for news stories on industries whose names match industries in the data and that pertain to trade policy. This provides an index of how much the news media tended to inform voters about trade policy in each industry. Under the assumption that all voters know about trade policy in their own industries but few know much about trade policy in other industries, Ponzetto argues that more news coverage of trade policy in a given industry should increase the demand for liberalization of imports in that industry, as consumers become more aware of the issue. This seems to be confirmed by empirical evidence that nontariff barriers are used less, *ceteris paribus*, in industries that have more media coverage (this is dubbed the "Dracula" effect—the weakening effect of sunlight on pressure for protection).

Facchini et al. (2013) use roll-call votes in the US Congress on trade and immigration bills from 1986 to 2004 to explore how news media affect the responsiveness of a representative to her constituents' wishes. The paper uses a variable designed by Snyder and Strömberg (2010) to be an exogenous source of variation in media scrutiny—the "congruence" of a congressional district with the local news media market. Essentially, if the natural boundaries of local newspapers' market areas match up with the congressional district boundaries, the representative faces the maximum possible media coverage. Using NES data on voter preferences regarding trade and immigration policy, Facchini et al. (2013) find that a representative is more likely to vote along the lines preferred by her constituents if she faces more media scrutiny—but only for immigration policy, not for trade. A plausible reason is that trade policy is the most important issue for far fewer voters than immigration is.

Both of these papers show that media coverage can have an important effect on the politics of international policy, and there is much scope to explore these ideas further.

Aside from information and media issues, the literature has been slow to incorporate *firm-level* analysis of the demand for protection. Gulotty (2016) and Osgood (2012) both study theoretical models of differentiated-goods industries with heterogeneous firms and intra-industry trade, and point out that the effects of trade policy are likely to be very heterogeneous within each industry, implying challenges to effective coalition formation. Gulotty (2016) shows that the more productive firms in each industry can benefit from stricter product standards that raise fixed costs of production and exporting, because these can shake out smaller competitors. This suggests that technical barriers to trade can be a matter of intense intra-industry disagreement. Osgood (2012) shows that while the more productive firms in an industry will tend to benefit from bilateral trade opening, the most productive firms will generally prefer higher tariffs than medium-productivity firms, for similar reasons: Higher bilateral tariffs can reduce entry and thus competition. These raise intriguing questions about the pattern of demand for protection *within* an industry, which could be the subject of very fruitful empirical study.

3. POLITICAL CONDITIONS SHAPE COMMERCIAL POLICY

To this point, we have grappled with measuring the demand for trade policy. Given the demand for protection, political institutions determine how those demands are channeled into actual trade policies. In a democracy, politicians campaign to win an election and thereby gain power; once they have gained power, they bargain with each other while being influenced by lobbyists, and the result is a realized policy. A full model would involve all three of these mechanisms, (i) electoral competition, (ii) legislative bargaining, and (iii) lobbying; but in practice these three have tended to be studied separately, and so we will do that here as well. First we turn to electoral competition.

3.1 Electoral Competition: Theory

To isolate electoral effects, let us consider a "pure" model of electoral competition as one in which two parties vie for control of government by publicly committing to a policy before voters place their votes, and after the election, the winning party cannot renege on its policy commitment. Further, let us assume that each party cares only about winning, and has no interest in policy other than as an instrument for winning the election.

Naturally, the electoral rules matter for the nature of electoral competition, and perhaps the most important distinction along these lines is between models of proportional representation and majoritarian systems; see Persson and Tabellini (2002, ch. 8), for an introduction. If the country is divided into districts, then a majoritarian system is one in which one representative is elected from each district, and then control of the government goes to the party that wins the largest number of districts.[k] A proportional system in one in which each district has multiple representatives, who are chosen from each party in proportion to the party vote in that district. A special case is the case in which the whole country is a single district; either way, if there are enough representatives, the nationwide share of each party in total representatives is equal to its nationwide share of votes. Both systems are common; The United States, the United Kingdom, and Canada are examples of countries with majoritarian systems; Germany, Brazil and Turkey are examples with proportional systems.

The seminal model of trade policy determination through electoral competition is Mayer (1984), whose main argument is built on a straight HO model injected into the proportional representation paradigm.[l] Home is a small open economy that produces two goods, the imported good 1 and the exported numeraire 2, using labor and capital. Both factors are homogeneous and mobile across industries. There are a continuum of citizens in Home, and each citizen i has a unit endowment of labor and an exogenous endowment k^i of capital. The government must choose a level for the tariff t on imports of good 1. The production income of citizen i is $w + rk^i$, where w is the wage and r is the price of capital services, and so i's production income relative to the average is $\phi^i = (w + rk^i)/(wL + rK)$, where L and K are the aggregate Home endowments of the two factors. All Home citizens have identical and homothetic preferences represented by the indirect utility function $U(p,y)$ for a good-1 price p and income of y.

Tariff revenue is redistributed to Home citizens lump sum; to clear away nuisances in the algebra, it is assumed that citizen i's tariff revenue rebate is proportional to her share of production income, so that her total income will be given by $y^i = w + rk^i + \phi^i T$, where T is the aggregate tariff revenue. Consequently, the utility achieved by i can be written as $U^i(t) = \phi^i(t)U(\pi(1 + t), Y(t))$, where π is the world price of good 1 and $Y(t)$ is aggregate income in Home evaluated at domestic prices, including tariff revenue. The first factor is i's share in total welfare, and the second is total welfare. Total welfare is maximized at $t = 0$ because Home is a small open economy, so if $d\phi^i(t)/dt > 0$ at $t = 0$, then citizen i would prefer a positive tariff to free trade, and if $d\phi^i(t)/dt < 0$ at $t = 0$ she would prefer a negative tariff, an import subsidy, to free trade.

---

[k] The definition is generally extended to a presidential system such as in the United States, where each state has a certain number of electoral votes, and the candidate who wins the most votes in a state receives all of the electoral votes for that state. The winning candidate is the one with the most electoral votes.

[l] Strictly speaking, Mayer does not use a model of inter-party competition, but rather makes an argument about equilibrium from cooperative game theory. However, the equilibrium of his model is exactly what would be obtained by a noncooperative electoral game of the sort described here, which is the standard approach in the literature at this point, and the structure of the model is exactly that of proportional representation, so we slot his model into that category.

The sign of $d\phi^i(t)/dt$ is determined by i's position in the asset distribution as well as by Home's factor endowment. A change in tariffs affects the factor prices by Stolper–Samuelson logic, since it changes the domestic price of good 1, and this is how it affects ϕ^i. In particular:

$$\frac{d\phi^i}{dt} = \frac{wL}{(wL + rK)^2(1+t)} \frac{r(k - k^i)(\hat{w} - \hat{r})}{\hat{p}}, \tag{3}$$

where $k \equiv K/L$ and a hat indicates a proportional rate of change (so for example $\hat{w} = \frac{1}{w}dw/dt$). Thus, $d\phi^i(t)/dt > 0$ if $\hat{w} > \hat{r}$ and $k > k^i$, or if both inequalities are reversed; otherwise, $d\phi^i(t)/dt < 0$. Since the tariff raises the domestic price of good 1, by Stolper–Samuelson, $\hat{w} > \hat{r}$ iff good 1 is labor-intensive, and since good 1 is imported, that would mean that Home is capital abundant. Thus, *citizen i's share of national income is increasing in the tariff*, and so i will want a positive tariff, *if the country is capital-abundant and i has below-average capital, or if the country is capital scarce and i has above-average capital.* Otherwise, citizen i's share is decreasing in the tariff and she will prefer a negative tariff.

Now, consider the "pure electoral" game sketched above. Party A and B must each choose a value of t, simultaneously; these choices then become public, as an irrevocable policy commitment; the voters see these choices, and each votes for the party that offers the tariff value that voter prefers; the party with the most votes wins, and implements the tariff to which it had committed. The winning party receives a positive rent from power, while the losing party receives a payoff of zero. It is easy to see that, provided the utility relation $U^i(t)$ is a single-peaked function of t, there is a unique equilibrium in pure strategies: Both parties commit to the most preferred tariff level t^m of the median voter, the voter whose capital endowment is greater than that of exactly one half of the population.[m] Couple this observation with the assumption that in each country the median voter has less capital than the average voter (a safe assumption, borne out in every data set on income and asset ownership), and the model yields two crisp predictions. First, *in high-income countries, tariffs will be positive* because the median voter is a worker who wants to raise the price of labor-intensive imports, while *in low-income countries, tariffs will be negative* because the median voter is a worker who wants to lower the price of capital-intensive imports. Second, this will occur only in countries with a skewed income distribution; if the median voter has the average capital endowment, the outcome will be free trade. As a result, *in high-income countries, a rise in the gap between mean and median income*

---

[m] First, note that in any equilibrium in pure strategies, each party must have at least a 50% chance of winning, since it can always pick the tariff that the other party picks and enjoy a 50% chance. But then in equilibrium each party must win with exactly a 50% probability. Next, suppose that party A chooses a tariff value $t^A > t^m$. In this case, party B will win with certainty, since it can do so with any value $t^B \in [t^m, t^A]$. This yields a contradiction, as does any other deviation.

will increase the tariff, but in low-income economies it will have the opposite effect. These predictions are testable, as we will discuss in the next section.

It is worth pausing to reflect the fragility of these conclusions, however. First, the political-economy game really does require the 2×2 structure of the economy. With more than two goods, there is no meaningful sense in which there is a median voter, and generically no equilibrium (Plott, 1967). Indeed, even in the two-good model the equilibrium makes sense only if the election is held as a referendum on trade policy, with no other issues relevant.

Second, the equilibrium is not robust to adding tiny amounts of noise to voters' preferences. To see this, consider a variant based on Lindbeck and Weibull (1993). This is a model of pure electoral competition in the meaning suggested above, but has the added feature that each voter votes for the party that offers her the highest utility, where utility has two components: (i) a real-income component that is derived from general equilibrium given the policy and the voter's utility function, as above, and (ii) a second component that is an exogenous preference for one party or the other. It could be based on ethnic affinity, the charisma of the party leader, or some element of the party's history. Regardless of the source, suppose that each voter has an exogenous preference for party A given by an idiosyncratic value $\mu \in \mathfrak{R}$. For voters of each economic type, Lindbeck and Weibull (1993) allow for μ to be drawn from a mean-zero distribution. In the Mayer model, the only way voters differ is by capital ownership, so suppose that for each group of voters who share the same value $\tilde{k}$ of capital endowment, the values of μ are distributed by a probability density function $f(\mu; \tilde{k})$ with mean zero. If we restrict attention to densities that imply a very small variance to the μ values, then the model is the same as the Mayer model but with a tiny amount of noise added to voters' preferences. In other words, one can think of letting $f(0, \tilde{k})$ become arbitrarily large for each value of $\tilde{k}$, so that voters barely care at all about anything other than policy.

Lindbeck and Weibull (1993) show that equilibrium of the electoral competition in this case results in both parties choosing the same policy, and the policy maximizes the weighted sum of utilities for Home voters, where the weight on voters with endowment $\tilde{k}$ is given by $f(0; \tilde{k})$.[n] Now, if the density does not depend on $\tilde{k}$ (so that $f(\mu; \tilde{k}) = f(\mu; K/L) \forall \tilde{k}$), this clearly indicates social welfare maximization, which is a stark departure from the median-voter model. Further, by varying the densities to make $f(0; \tilde{k})$ greater for some values of $\tilde{k}$ than for others, the most-preferred tariff corresponding to any $\tilde{k}$ value can be arbitrarily closely approached in equilibrium. The fact that this can be done for an arbitrarily small amount of noise means that the median voter equilibrium fails a basic stability test.

---

[n] If $f(0; \tilde{k})$ is very large for some $\tilde{k}$, then the partisan preferences for individuals in that group are tightly clustered around 0, and so a large fraction of those voters can be won over with a small change in trade policy. As a result, those voters tend to be favored in equilibrium.

The solution is most plausibly to build idiosyncratic partisan preference shocks into the model from the beginning, as is standard in the rest of the literature (for example, Persson and Tabellini, 2002, ch. 8 and Strömberg, 2008), rather than trying to preserve the median-voter result for its own sake.

An important extension of the pure electoral model is explored by Ponzetto (2011), who focusses on the effect of voters' incomplete information on trade policy. A small open economy has several industries, each using a specific factor and labor; all consumers have identical additively separable utility functions so that partial-equilibrium analysis can be applied (the model is the same as is used by Grossman and Helpman, 1994; see Section 3.3.2). Two parties compete for votes by choice of trade policy vector. Each voter who owns a specific factor wants trade protection for her own industry, but prefers free trade in all other industries. Voters also have partisan preferences in the Lindbeck and Weibull (1993) mold. The trick is that it is difficult for each voter to learn what each policy proposal is; each proposed tariff by each party is learned with a probability less than one by any given voter, with a higher probability for the voter's own industry (this is given a microfoundation based on information networks). Since a voter cannot be swayed by a tariff proposal of which she is unaware, and since each voter is more likely to be aware of tariff proposals for her own industry, each party knows that by offering a tariff to industry i it will win more votes from voters in i than it will lose from other industries. Consequently, all tariffs are positive in equilibrium. Further, if information about an industry becomes more evenly distributed (so that the difference between the rate at which people in that industry and people outside that industry become informed about it declines), then the equilibrium tariff in that industry falls. This effect, dubbed the "Dracula" effect (meaning the influence of sunlight on protectionism), is interpreted as reflecting the influence of the media on trade policy; as noted in Section 2.4, the evidence suggests that this interpretation holds water in the real world.

We now turn to majoritarian systems, and to discuss these we need a model with at least three districts. The simplest example can be constructed by dividing up the voters in the Mayer model into multiple districts, a majority of which must be won by a party in order to control the government. Karabay and McLaren (2004) point out that in such a model, the equilibrium tariff rate is the most preferred rate of the median voter in the median district (when the districts are ranked by the most-preferred tariff of their median voters). As a result, depending on how voters are allocated to districts, the equilibrium tariff can be anywhere from the national 25th percentile voter's to the 75th percentile voter's most preferred tariff. This, of course, suffers from the problems of the original Mayer model.

Grossman and Helpman (2005) present a three-district majoritarian model with legislative bargaining after the election, which becomes a pure electoral competition model as a special case.° There are three industries that produce with specific capital together with labor, plus a numeraire sector that produces only with labor. Each district has some of each industry's capital, and the districts are symmetric in that each district has the largest share of one industry's capital and smaller shares of the other two; the pattern of shares is the same for all three districts, with the identities of the three industries permuted. The outcome of the political game will be a vector of tariffs for these three industries. Voters have idiosyncratic partisan preference shocks, and each district has an aggregate partisan preference shock revealed after the campaigning is over, but the *ex ante* distributions of these shocks is the same for each district. In that setting, the equilibrium of the pure electoral competition is free trade, which is a stark contrast with the same model when post-election legislative bargaining is allowed, as we shall see.

Clearly, in the pure electoral-competition version of Grossman and Helpman (2005), the majoritarian electoral system has no effect on policy. This is because of the symmetry of the setup. However, a large part of the interest in majoritarian systems stems from effects that arise when the districts are not *ex ante* identical in their partisan tendencies. The basic model of fiscal and redistributive policy in a majoritarian democracy in Persson and Tabellini (2002, ch. 8) has two districts with partisan biases, each biassed toward one of the two parties, plus a third that is biassed toward neither, which we might call a "swing" district. Since the swing district is more likely to be pivotal (in other words, to be the district that determines the outcome of the election), both parties commit to redistribution toward that district. In addition, since neither party derives much electoral benefit from public good provision for the partisan districts, only the benefit from public goods to the swing district matters, and consequently less public good is provided than under proportional representation (and less than optimal). Because districts differ in their partisan bias *ex ante*, majoritarian elections make a big difference to the policy in equilibrium. A rich model of the US electoral contest in Strömberg (2008) allows for probabilistic voting and uncertain outcomes but states with different levels of *ex ante* partisan bias. The analysis shows that a state with a higher probability of being pivotal receives more campaign resources, a prediction confirmed in the empirical portion of the paper.

These differences between partisan states and swing states in a majoritarian system can of course matter for trade policy as well. Muûls and Petropoulou (2013) present a stylized model of the electoral college with four types of voter: those who always vote for

---

° The way it works is that two national parties compete for votes by committing to policy platforms before the election. After the election, the representatives from the winning party control the legislature and will be able to deviate from their party's platform, but if they do they will be "fined" by their party in proportion to the size of the deviation, with a parameter δ as the parameter of proportionality. The model becomes a pure electoral competition model with no postelection deviation as δ becomes large. We will discuss the postelection bargaining and the model more fully in Section 3.5.

Democrats (type D); those who always vote for Republicans (type R); those who vote for the candidate most likely to provide tariff protection (type P); and those who vote for the candidate most likely to provide free trade (type F). The allocation of these voters can differ across states. In particular, $\omega_p^s \in [0,1]$ is the difference between D voters' share of state s and R voters' share. If $|\omega_p^s|$ is close to 1, then trade policy will not have much effect on the outcome of state s's electoral vote, because the state has a strong partisan leaning in one direction or the other, but if $|\omega_p^s|$ is close to 0, trade policy can possibly swing the state's election. (Although each voter's choice is deterministic, the aggregate outcome is still random because the number of voters that turn out to vote can vary randomly.) The model has an unusual feature in that it assumes away any commitment by politicians. A newly-elected president can choose free trade or protectionism in her first term, which can then signal her true trade-policy preferences to voters who must choose whether or not to support her for a second and constitutionally final term. In an incumbent's second term she will simply implement her most preferred trade policy.

If there are enough P-type voters crammed into enough low-$|\omega_p^s|$ states, then in equilibrium a free-trade-preferring president will, with positive probability, choose trade protection in her first term in order to dupe those protectionist voters into supporting reelection. Note that this can be an outcome even if there are more F-type, free-trade-loving voters than the P-type, provided that the F-type voters are concentrated in states that are sufficiently partisan.

Ma and McLaren (2015) study a pure-electoral-competition version that works out more simply. Two parties compete for electoral votes by committing to policy positions; each voter has an idiosyncratic partisan bias, and each state has an aggregate partisan bias, except for one state, the "swing state," whose bias is zero. In the baseline model with no aggregate uncertainty, in any equilibrium in pure strategies, both parties commit to the policy vector that maximizes swing-state welfare, placing a weight of zero on nonswing-state welfare. Adding a probabalistic element to the voting so that the bias of the swing state is not exactly zero and is not known precisely before the election creates a swing-state bias that converges to the extreme of the baseline model as the aggregate uncertainty becomes small, so that the effective weight on nonswing-state welfare converges to zero in the limit. Fitting the model to data on tariffs suggest that US politicians put a weight on nonswing-state welfare about 0.7 as large as on swing-state welfare.

3.2 Electoral Competition: Empirics

The basic prediction of Mayer (1984) is brought to data by Dutt and Mitra (2002). The regression idea is simple: On the left-hand side, a measure of country i's overall level of trade restrictions. On the right-hand side, along with other controls, the variables of interest are a measure of inequality in country i and the interaction of that variable with a measure of i's capital abundance. As discussed above, the model predicts that a rise in the gap between mean and median capital ownership should raise tariffs if i is capital rich, but lower it if i is capital poor. Dutt and Mitra measure these effects in a range of ways on a sample of between 49 and 64 countries depending on the specification (there is no time-series component to the data). The main measure of trade restrictions is tariff revenue as a fraction of imports, but a variety of others are used for robustness. Consistently, the authors find that the main prediction is borne out. For each regression, they report the implied capital/labor "turning point," or the level of capital abundance above which tariffs are increasing in inequality. The value varies, but in most cases it is close to the capital-labor ratio of South Korea. A related paper, Tavares (2008), relates tariff rates to an index of political rights. On the theory that improved political rights will allow poorer people to participate more in elections, thereby making the median voter a poorer person (without changing anyone's income), a Mayer-type model would imply that increased political rights would raise tariffs in rich countries and lower them in poor ones. This is indeed what the data show.

So, despite the theoretical problems with the model discussed above, the Mayer (1984) formulation seems to hold up to the data quite well on first blush. However, we should note two crucial problems. First, the model not only predicts the sign of *comparative statics* for the tariff, but also the sign of tariff *level*, and for labor-abundant countries that sign must be negative. Of course there are no countries for which the average tariff, however measured, is negative. This problem is addressed by Dhingra (2014), who notes that in the original model every country was assumed to be small for simplicity. Once that assumption is relaxed, there is a terms-of-trade motive that can in principle push tariffs above zero for all countries, while preserving the original comparative statics prediction. Dhingra derives an estimating equation for the model with large countries, and it indeed resembles the Dutt and Mitra (2002) estimating equation with the addition of a new term, the inverse elasticity of foreign export supply, just as in (2). She has the benefit of a comprehensive set of measures of trade restrictiveness produced by Kee et al. (2009) and estimates of trade elasticities from Kee et al. (2008), and constructs a data set of 35 countries from 1993 to 2004. There are a number of minor changes compared to the earlier study; instead of the physical capital/labor ratio, she proxies "capital abundance" with a human capital index, the average number of years of schooling in the adult population. However, the spirit of the exercise is the same, and over a wide range of specifications and robustness checks the Dutt and Mitra (2002) results hold up. As a bonus, the coefficient on the inverse-elasticity term is positive, so the Broda et al. (2008) results referred to in Section 1.1 receive some additional support as well.[P]

[P] A natural concern is that under the WTO, the inverse elasticity term should no longer matter. Dhingra does the estimation with an extra dummy for WTO membership and finds that it matters a lot more for non-members. The fact that it does have influence for members as well may be explained by Ludema and Mayda (2013), who show that the free-rider problem that goes with Most-Favored-Nation (MFN) rules in the WTO can lead to exactly this sort of phenomenon.

The other crucial problem with the model is that it is unavoidably a one-dimensional model. Introducing a third factor of production generically means that there is no meaningful median voter and no clear prediction of the model. A reminder of this problem is offered by the historical study of O'Rourke and Taylor (2007). They investigate the relationship between democracy and trade policy in a set of 35 countries from 1870 to 1914. They use the index of democracy from the Polity database, and ask the question: As democratic reforms spread and each country's democracy index improves over time, does that tend to increase or reduce trade restrictions? Taking their inspiration, again, from Mayer (1984), they first regress a country's average tariff on the country's land/labor ratio, its index of democracy, and the interaction between the two. Reasoning that democratic reform will tend to increase participation in the electoral process, making the median voter a poorer citizen than would have been the case before the reform (as in Tavares, 2008), they suggest that this should lower tariffs in a land-scarce country and raise them in a land-rich country, as would be indicated by a negative coefficient on the democracy index and a positive one on the interaction term. They find an insignificant coefficient on democracy but a positive one on the interaction, once again providing at least partial support for the Mayer model. (Country fixed effects are present, so the driving force is indeed changes over time within a country.) But then they add capital-labor ratios to the equation, since after all both capital and land are important parts of the economy, and find that the coefficient on the capital-labor term is strongly *negative*. O'Rourke and Taylor suggest that the explanation may have to do with the dynamics of domestic coalition formation in the 19th century, which likely does not generalize to the present, but the broader point is that the Mayer model simply cannot handle these findings. One cannot simply squeeze capital and labor plus human capital into a lump called "assets" and pretend that we are living in a two-factor model (and it is fair to ask how the results of Dutt and Mitra (2002) and Dhingra (2014) would hold up to the addition of, for example, land/labor ratios to the equation). The literature awaits a serious theoretical treatment that can accommodate an arbitrary number of factors; the approach of Jäkel and Smolka (2015) may hold some promise in this regard.

Turning to the differences between proportional and majoritarian electoral systems, Evans (2009) looks at a sample of 147 countries to test for the effect of electoral system on average tariffs. Including controls for colonial origins and legal system, she finds a robust and substantial positive effect of majoritarian systems on average tariffs. Controlling for the selection of countries into electoral systems with a two-step procedure, using date of adoption of constitution and distance from equator as instruments, only strengthens the effect, leading to a conclusion that majoritarian systems produce significantly higher tariffs. However, these results are qualified by Hatfield and Hauk (2014), who find that much of the effect is due to the fact that countries with proportional representation tend to be smaller than majoritarian countries, and smaller countries tend to have low tariffs.

More broadly, a number of authors have found strong correlations between commercial policy and the spread of democracy. Pandya (2014, ch. 4) finds a strong effect of a country's transition to democracy on its propensity to liberalize FDI inflows, after controlling for country fixed effect and also after using number of years since independence as an instrument for democratization. Milner and Kubota (2005) find a strong tariff-lowering effect of democratization, and Mansfield et al. (2002) find that democracies are more likely than autocracies to form trade agreements with each other. Eichengreen and Leblang (2008), looking at data from 1870 to 2000, find a strong effect of democracy on trade openness and capital-account openness. (A related exploration of trade policy and democracy, Liu and Ornelas (2014), will be discussed in Section 4.)

3.3 Lobbying: Theory

Once a government has taken power there are many ways for private citizens to try to affect its decisions. We will call any attempt to do so "lobbying," a term that can encompass many motives including public interest and humanitarian concerns, but we will focus on the efforts of commercial interests to influence policy to increase their own incomes.

One might not realize it from reading the trade literature, but there are a wide variety of approaches to modeling lobbying. One of the earliest attempts to treat lobbying as an equilibrium phenomenon is the introduction to Krueger (1974), which suggests that lobbying should be treated as a competitive industry that uses potentially productive resources (such as the skilled labor of the lobbyists) to transfer rents from one business to another, so that the size of the rents should be treated as a measure of the deadweight loss from the lobbying sector. Findlay and Wellisz (1983) posit a "tariff production function," which is an increasing function of lobbyists employed by the import-competing sector requesting a higher tariff, and a decreasing function of lobbyists employed by the export sector requesting a lower tariff. The outcome is a Nash equilibrium in opposing lobbying efforts by the two sectors, and of course it is a pure deadweight loss.

These early attempts treat what lobbyists actually do as a black box. Since then, considerable effort has been expended on deriving lobbying behavior from first principles,[q]

---

[q] An interesting use of the black-box approach is Pecorino (1998), which investigates the problem of self-enforcement of collusion in lobbying. If we postulate that lobbyists can obtain a tariff t for their industry through spending S according to an exogenous tariff production function $t(S)$, then any one firm can secure a tariff by lobbying on its own, and in an uncoordinated Nash equilibrium each firm will spend a positive amount on lobbying; but this spending will be less than the optimum because the tariff is a public good for members of the industry. The collusive optimum could be supported in an infinitely-repeated game with the punishment of reversion to the Nash equilibrium if anyone defects, but the discount factor must be high enough for this to work. Pecorino shows that the value of this discount factor does not necessarily rise with the number of firms in the industry, which may help explain the empirical finding that lobbying does not seem to be systematically more effective in more concentrated industries *ceteris paribus*.

which have mostly followed two strands: Informational lobbying and influence peddling, or protection for sale.

3.3.1 Informational Lobbying

The idea of informational lobbying is that lobbyists affect policymakers' decisions by affecting their beliefs or information. This can take the form of directly informative lobbying, in which the lobbyist provides precise information about a policy issue (for example, statistical research to show what the likely economic effect of a change in tariff would be), or signaling about how important the issue is to the lobbyists' clients (and thus, for example, how many votes are likely to be gained in the next election from a given change in policy). This type of interpretation of lobbying has been studied in political science but has not been used much in the area of trade policy.

Austen-Smith (1993) pioneered the area with a model of a lobbyist who knows the state of the world (which could take an infinite number of values) and wishes to convey information about it to a politician who does not know the state of the world but would like to know it to set social welfare maximizing policy. The lobbyist must first undertake costly signaling in order to convey to the policy-maker that she has valuable information (the policy-maker's time is costly), and then once achieving an audience, she names the state of the world. The policy maker understands that he does not have the same interests as the lobbyist, so the lobbyist may have an incentive to mislead. As a result, the information that can be revealed in this "cheap talk" equilibrium is coarse: The lobbyist can convey that the state of the world is on one of several discrete partitions of the state space, but not exactly which state has been realized. A sequence of much simpler and much more transparent models conveying a similar story is found in Grossman and Helpman (2002, ch. 4). Potters et al. (1997) show how campaign contributions made in public by an entity with a known public-policy agenda can have an effect on elections if the voters are less well informed about candidates' policy preferences than the donor is.

However, these ideas have barely made an appearance in the trade literature. One exception is Karabay (2009), who studies a Brander and Spencer (1985) style model in which a Home firm and a Foreign firm compete as a Cournot oligopoly in a third market. The export market has a demand curve with an intercept that is known to the firms but not to the Home government. Social welfare maximization calls for a subsidy, and the optimal size of the subsidy depends positively on the height of the export-market demand curve. The Home firm can make a payment to the government in order to signal that the demand-curve intercept is high, so as to persuade the government to provide a high subsidy; but of course, regardless of the height of the demand curve, the firm would like a higher subsidy, so a separating equilibrium requires that the cost of the transfer be enough that only a firm that knows the intercept is actually high would be willing to incur the cost. It can be in the interest both of the firm and the government for the government to impose a fixed cost to lobbying; Karabay shows (proposition 1) that there is a range for this cost such that it makes a separating equilibrium possible, and in this case, provided there is not too much deadweight loss in the transfer to the government (λ not too far below $\frac{1}{2}$, in the notation of the paper), the lobbying equilibrium is welfare enhancing.

The idea of informational lobbying has had very little empirical attention in international economics, but Ludema et al. (2010) provide a very compelling piece of evidence for its importance. They study tariff suspensions in the US Congress. Any firm can request temporary suspension of a tariff, and such requests are routinely made by a firm located in a given congressional district to the representative for that district, to reduce the costs of the firm's inputs. However, Congress provides opportunities for comment by firms opposed to the suspension. Ludema et al. (2010) show that a requested tariff suspension is more likely to pass, the more firms that express support for it, and less likely to pass, the more firms that object to it; and controlling for statements of support or opposition, it is more likely to pass, the more is spent on trade-policy lobbying by supporting firms, and the less is spent by opposing firms. All of this is consistent with a pure informational theory of lobbying. The firms are not *purchasing* the trade policy in question, and in particular are not providing campaign contributions, but are revealing information to the politicians about how much the value (or oppose) the change in question. This intriguing piece of evidence suggests that the informational role of lobbying in trade policy needs to be explored further.

3.3.2 Influence Peddling

By contrast with informational lobbying, influence peddling models are models in which members of an interest group pay the decision maker for a policy favor. They have become the dominant paradigm for studying lobbying in international trade policy, led by the seminal Protection-for-Sale model of Grossman and Helpman (1994). We will review this in detail before discussing applications.

This is a model in which owners of specific factors organize themselves to lobby the government over trade policy, by a process of competitive bidding. The economy is extremely simple: There are $n + 1$ goods, of which good 0 is a numeraire, produced with labor only; the marginal product of labor in producing good 0 is equal to 1, due to which the wage is fixed in equilibrium. Each of the remaining n goods is produced with labor together with a specific factor that can be used only for that good and which is available in a fixed and exogenous supply. As a result, we can write an upward-sloping supply function for good i, say $y_i(p_i)$, $i = 1,\ldots,n$, where p_i is the domestic price of good i and y_i is the quantity supplied, and we can write the income to specific factor owners in industry i, which is the same thing as producer surplus, as $\pi_i(p_i)$. On the demand side, the utility of a typical citizen is additively separable: $U = x_0 + \sum_{i=1}^{n} u_i(x_i)$, where x_i denotes consumption of good i and u_i is an increasing, strictly concave and differentiable function. As a result, we can derive a downward-sloping demand curve, $d_i(p_i)$, $i = 1,\ldots,n$, and the utility of a given consumer can be written in terms of consumer surplus $s_i(p_i)$ from each good i, so that total utility of any consumer is equal to $E + s(\mathbf{p})$, where $\mathbf{p}$ is the vector of domestic goods prices, E is the consumer's expenditure, and $s(\mathbf{p}) = \sum_{i=1}^{n} s_i(p_i)$ is the consumer's total surplus.

The country is small on world markets, so it takes the world prices, p_i^*, of all goods as given. Trade policy is a specific import tariff/subsidy or export tax/subsidy t_i for each nonnumeraire good, so that $p_i = p_i^* + t_i$. If i is an imported good, $t_i > 0$ indicates an import tariff that raises the domestic price; if i is an exported good, $t_i > 0$ indicates an export subsidy that raises the domestic price, and so forth. Given that each good has an easily-derived domestic demand and supply curve, we can write the *import* demand curve $m_i(p_i)$ as the difference between the two, and the revenue (perhaps negative) from the ith trade tax as $r_i(p_i) = (p_i - p_i^*)m_i(p_i)$. The sum across goods is total trade-tax revenue per capital, $r(\mathbf{p})$.

Now, to discuss the actual influence peddling. Tariffs are set by a politician who has full discretion. A subset of the industries have their specific-factor owners exogenously organized into an interest group. Interest group i writes a contribution schedule, $C_i(\mathbf{p})$, that specifies how much the politician will be paid as a function of the domestic tariff vector $\mathbf{p}$ (which of course implies a trade tax vector $\mathbf{t} = \mathbf{p} - \mathbf{p}^*$). These payments are financed by the specific factor owners in industry i, who have somehow solved their internal public good problem and do not suffer from free riding. Each organized interest group chooses its contribution schedule simultaneously, writes it down, puts it into an envelope and drops it into the politician's mailbox, who then opens them, examines them, and chooses his optimal policy, taking the combined contribution schedules into account. The interest groups are required to honor their contribution schedules *ex post*. For each organized interest group i, the payoff is $W_i(\mathbf{p}) - C_i(\mathbf{p})$, where $W_i(\mathbf{p})$ is welfare gross of the contribution:

$$W_i(\mathbf{p}) = l_i + \pi_i(\mathbf{p}) + \alpha_i N[r(\mathbf{p}) + s(\mathbf{p})], \qquad (4)$$

and where l_i is the combined labor supply of the owners of specific factors in the ith interest group, α_i is their share of the population, and N is the total population. Expression (4) is just labor income plus income from the specific factor plus the interest group's share of national tariff revenue and consumer surplus. The politician's payoff is $aW(\mathbf{p}) + \sum_{i=1}^{n} C_i(\mathbf{p})$, where $a > 0$ is a parameter and $W(\mathbf{p})$ is simply total social welfare:

$$W(\mathbf{p}) = l + \sum_{i=1}^{n} \pi_i(\mathbf{p}) + N[r(\mathbf{p}) + s(\mathbf{p})]. \qquad (5)$$

That sets up the game. Now, this game has a vast number of subgame-perfect equilibria. Much of the original paper is devoted to choice of equilibrium, and the authors argue for a Truthful Equilibrium, meaning an equilibrium in which $\nabla C_i(\mathbf{p}) = \nabla W_i(\mathbf{p})$

everywhere, on the grounds that such an equilibrium is coalition proof. Such an equilibrium produces a trade policy vector that maximizes:

$$aW(\mathbf{p}) + \sum_{i \in L} W_i(\mathbf{p}), \tag{6}$$

where L is the set of organized industries. However, those details of equilibrium selection are not crucial; as Goldberg and Maggi (1999) pointed out later, for example, (6) is just the sum of the payoffs of all interest groups and the politician, so it is the optimand that would be maximized by any efficient bargaining mechanism between those parties. In effect, the bargaining between lobbyists and the politician maximizes weighted welfare, where every citizen's welfare receives a weight a except for the members of organized lobbies, whose welfare receives a weight $a + 1$.

The outcome of this maximization is a tariff vector that satisfies:

$$\frac{\tau_i}{1 + \tau_i} = \frac{I_i - \alpha_L}{a + \alpha_L} \left(\frac{z_i}{e_i} \right), \tag{7}$$

where τ_i is the *ad valorem* equivalent tariff for industry i; α_L is the fraction of the population that belongs to an organized interest group; I_i is a dummy variable that takes a value of 1 if industry i has an organized interest group; $z_i \equiv y_i / m_i$ is the inverse import penetration ratio for industry i; and e_i is the absolute value of the import-demand elasticity for industry i.

Note that (7) implies that (i) Organized industries will receive a positive import tariff or export subsidy as the case may be; (ii) Unorganized industries will suffer a *negative* tariff or a tax on their exports, as the case may be; and (iii) All of these effects are moot, and the equilibrium is free trade, if everyone is part of an organized industry (so that $I_i \equiv 1$ and $\alpha_L = 1$). Further, the more the politician values social welfare, so the higher is the parameter a, the smaller will be the deviations from free trade. Condition (7) has been the basis of a large empirical literature; indeed, one could say that this one equation has been the main driver of empirical research in the political economy of trade policy for the last 20 years. It seems to be routinely misunderstood, however, so it is worth taking a moment to walk through it.

Consider raising the specific tariff on i, an imported good, by 1 dollar, and suppose that i is an organized industry. The income to specific factor owners in i goes up by y_i. The benefit, from the point of view of weighted welfare, is $(1 + a)y_i$.

At the same time, consumer surplus for all citizens goes down by the initial level of consumption of good i, also equal to domestic production plus imports: $d_i = y_i + m_i$. The tariff revenue changes by $m_i + t_i m_i'$ (recall that t_i is the *specific* tariff on good i). Therefore, the net drop in utility for each citizen not in the interest group is $[y_i + m_i] - [m_i + t_i m_i'] = y_i - t_i m_i'$. This lowers the weighted welfare function by

$(a + \alpha_L)(y_i - t_i m_i')$ (remember that the α_L people in organized interest groups each have a weight equal to a plus 1).

The optimal tariff will set this marginal increase in weighted welfare equal to this marginal decrease, or:

$$(1 + a)y_i = (a + \alpha_L)(y_i - t_i m_i'); \tag{8}$$

rewriting slightly:

$$(1 - \alpha_L)y_i = (a + \alpha_L)(-t_i m_i'). \tag{9}$$

The left-hand side of this equation is the benefit from redistribution. A 1-dollar increase in the tariff transfers y_i dollars of real income to organized persons from everyone else. Since organized persons have extra weight in the welfare function, this raises the value of the maximand. Note that this is exactly the term in square brackets at the beginning of (1), where it took a value of zero as a pure transfer; here the value of the redistribution is positive because the recipients have higher weight than the donors. The right-hand side is the distortion cost of the tariff increase. Solving for the tariff, we obtain:

$$t_i^* = \frac{(1 - \alpha_L)}{(a + \alpha_L)}\left(\frac{y_i}{-m_i'}\right). \tag{10}$$

The last term on the right-hand side is the only part that differs from industry to industry, the ratio of output to the derivative of import demand. In light of the cost-benefit analysis discussed above, we can usefully call this the *redistribution-distortion ratio*. The bigger is this ratio for a given industry, the more politically useful redistribution a politician can achieve with a tariff per unit of costly distortion, and so the more aggressively will the tariff be used. Now, if we divide numerator and denominator by m_i, and then divide the whole equation by p_i to convert to *ad valorem* tariff and elasticity, we obtain the famed condition (7), but now we understand the term z_i/e_i as a measure of the ratio of redistribution to distortion.

This helps understand the primary empirical prediction of the protection-for-sale model: If the industry is organized so that it receives positive protection, it receives more protection, the larger is its redistribution–distortion ratio. On the other hand, if it is unorganized so that it suffers negative protection, it suffers larger negative protection the large is its redistribution–distortion ratio. This will be crucial in discussing the empirical work in the next section.

The literature has mostly developed on empirical lines, but there are some theoretical variations that are worth noting. Mitra (1999) endogenies the number of organized industries in a protection-for-sale model with symmetric industries. Each industry's specific-factors owners must incur a fixed cost to organize, and the benefit to doing so decreases as more of the industries become organized. As a result, there is an equilibrium number of industries that become organized, and this changes when the economic environment changes. Some striking insights emerge. As the economy becomes larger, the number of industries that become organized increases; in the limit, they will all be organized. As a result, free trade emerges in the limit either for very small countries (where there is no industry that finds it worthwhile to organize) or for very large ones (where everyone is organized). A similar U-shaped result follows from varying the parameter a. These predictions do not seem to have been exploited at all in empirical work.

Two papers show how protection for sale might help explain the persistence of NTB's. Limão and Tovar (2011) show how the choice of an inefficient policy instrument (such as quantitative restrictions in the presence of rent seeking) can arise because of strategic bargaining between a politician and an interest group. If lump-sum transfers are not possible (for example, the only feasible payment is a campaign contribution, and there are diminishing marginal returns to campaign spending), then the utility-possibility frontier between the politician and the lobbyist is curved. A politician can use a tariff ceiling from a trade agreement to tie the politician's own hands in bargaining with a domestic lobbyist, bending that UPF and thereby improving the politician's bargaining power. If it bends enough, use of a strictly less efficient instrument such as an NTB becomes a possible equilibrium choice. A very different story is told by Anderson and Zanardi (2009), who interpret NTB's as a form of "political deflection" because of their bureaucratic procedures that allow a politician to wash hands of the decision making. In their model, a lobbyist offers to pay for protection. The politician is aware that providing protection may induce antiprotection interest groups to fund a challenger in the next election, but refusing the favor outright can reveal the politician to be antiprotection by ideological preference, which will generate a proprotection challenger. Delegating to a bureaucratic process may therefore save the politician from being challenged.

3.3.3 General Observations

The importance of Grossman and Helpman (1994) is obvious, but it is worth pausing to note its limitations, particularly its unsuitability to be an all-purpose workhorse theory of lobbying. Note, first, that the model requires all participants to engage in felonious activity. The contribution schedules that are the heart of the model might be called a "reverse Cunningham,"[r] and are surely a very poor representation of what actual lobbyists do day after day. Further, it is essential for the model that the lobbyists make not only offers of bribery contingent on policy, but that these take the form of *enforceable contracts*, despite begin nakedly illegal.

---

[r] Randy "Duke" Cunningham, Republican Congressman, served as representative of California's 50th Congressional District from 1991 to 2005. To help facilitate the transactions that made him famous, he wrote out a schedule of legislative favors he could offer, and the bribe required for each, on US Congressional stationary, thus providing a rare example of "contribution schedules" in practice. He served 7 years in federal prison.

It is also worth pointing out that the structure of the economy is not merely simple, but very special. In particular, any positive import tariffs in this model are guaranteed to raise income inequality. They will raise specific-factor incomes relative to the numeraire, but leave the wage unchanged. This forces, *by construction*, a particular answer to one of the most important questions about trade policy, and it forces an answer that is very much at odds with the way most voters think about the question, based on a great deal of survey data reviewed in Section 2.3. Further, in a model constructed in this way, it is not possible that a blue-collar worker in Detroit could be harmed by the rise of low-cost automotive imports from overseas; the workers' wage would remain equal to 1, and cars would now be cheaper, so the worker would clearly be better off. There are reasons that this structure has been adopted, and much insight comes out of it, but it should be underlined that much and perhaps most of the interest in the politics of trade policy and income-distribution effects of trade policy that can be observed in the discourse outside of academia has been excised from the discussion before starting.

A last general point about this approach is that by construction, in this model lobbyists are a pernicious influence. With lobbying banned and the ban enforced, the decision maker in this model would be resigned to mere social welfare maximization. Lobbyists can only distort the policy outcome away from that optimum. This is a major contrast with informational models such as Grossman and Helpman (2002, ch. 4) and Karabay (2009), where lobbying can, depending on parameters, raise social welfare by providing a better-informed policy-maker. (This leads to an interesting paradox studied by Gawande et al. (2006) and discussed in Section 3.4.3 below.)

3.4 Lobbying: Empirics
3.4.1 The First Wave
The two pioneering papers that first took the equilibrium condition (7) to the data were Goldberg and Maggi (1999) and Gawande and Bandyopadhyay (2000). Their approaches were quite similar in most ways. They both avoided applying the model to tariff data, since for any WTO member tariffs are determined by a process of multilateral negotiation rather than through unilateral action. Both focussed on US Non-Tariff-Barrier (NTB) coverage ratios from 1983, meaning for each four-digit SIC industry the fraction of disaggregated industries that are affected by some sort of NTB. They both construct z_i from trade data and use e_i from Shiells et al. (1986). Both use contributions by firms in each industry to Political Action Committees (PAC's) to break the sample into organized and unorganized industries.

Both then run a regression with the NTB coverage ratio on the left-hand side and on the right-hand side z_i/e_i as well as z_i/e_i interacted with I_i, the dummy for an "organized" industry. Following (7), in both papers the hypothesis of interest is that the coefficient on z_i/e_i is negative, the coefficient on $I_i z_i/e_i$ should be positive, and the sum of the two coefficients should be positive, so that the effect of a higher z_i/e_i for an organized industry will be an increase in protection.

Many of the details differ between the two studies. Goldberg and Maggi (1999) actually take the e_i from the denominator of the right-hand side variables and multiply it with the NTB coverage ratio on the left-hand side, since it is an estimated variable. Gawande and Bandyopadhyay (2000), instead, deal with that issue by using the standard error of the regression reported in Shiells et al. (1986) to weight their regression. Further, they augment the protection-for-sale model with traded intermediate inputs, carefully develop instrumental variables for all right-hand side variables, and add an equation to determine the size of contributions as well as the degree of protection. Goldberg and Maggi (1999) call an industry organized if its recorded PAC donations are greater than a specified threshold, while Gawande and Bandyopadhyay (2000) regress PAC contributions on imports from various countries and classify an industry as organized if its contributions are positively correlated with imports from at least one source country.

The results of the two studies are broadly similar: The NTB coverage ratios are strongly increasing in z_i/e_i for organized industries and strongly decreasing in z_i/e_i for unorganized ones. Further, they are able to estimate the a parameter, and both find it to be huge (an implied value of 61.5 for Grossman–Maggi; 3175 for Gawande–Bandyopadhyay).[5]

The verdict seemed to be that the protection for sale model works, and a tsunami of studies followed using this method and adding to it. However, many observers expressed surprise at the size of the estimated values of a; even with a value of $a = 61.5$, citizens outside of any organized interest group get a weight in the implied social welfare function (6) that is $\dfrac{61.5}{61.5 + 1} = 98.5\%$ as much as the weight on those who are inside an organized interest group—hardly any bias at all. Gawande and Krishna (2004) point out that these estimates call into question the usefulness of political-economy models in explaining trade policy.

3.4.2 The Ederington–Minier Calamity and Other Critiques

An important paper criticizing this approach, Ederington and Minier (2008), should give further pause to readers of the protection-for-sale empirical literature. This paper looks at some of the gaps between theory and econometric practice.

Two main points are worth focus. First, as the pioneering papers pointed out, the model requires dividing up the industries into a politically unorganized subset and a

---

[5] A related contribution is Eicher and Osang (2002), who derive equilibrium first-order conditions from a model of tariff-production-function Nash equilibrium between import-competing-industry lobbies and export-industry lobbies, as in Findlay and Wellisz (1983). They derive a structure similar to (7), which allows a test of Findlay and Wellisz (1983) and Grossman and Helpman (1994) as non-nested alternatives. Both models do reasonably well, but the data provide stronger support for protection for sale.

politically organized subset, but in practice there are PAC's for each industry in the data with positive contributions from firms, so there appears to be no unorganized industry in the data. The argument that these papers make is that some industries are likely to be organized for other lobbying purposes, not trade, and thus can be treated as unorganized for the purpose of analyzing trade policy. Now, that argument is difficult to begin with, since it is difficult to imagine how one could have incurred the fixed cost of staffing a lobbying operation and then be simply unable to have its members raise the issue of tariffs while talking to politicians. But Ederington and Minier suggest that we take the suggestion seriously: Insert into the model some other policy over which the industry owners may wish to lobby. An easy and natural example is an output subsidy. But if one adds the possibility of an output subsidy to the model, *trade taxes vanish* in equilibrium. The reason is that output subsidies are a more efficient way of transferring income to specific-factor owners in a given industry than tariffs; tariffs distort both production and consumption, while an output subsidy distorts only production. If one argues that this argument is too optimistic about the efficiency of subsidies in practice, one can add to the model some administrative costs that subsidies incur but tariffs do not, and assume that these costs are increasing in the level of subsidy provided. This returns tariffs to the equilibrium, as the policymaker trades off the consumption inefficiency of tariffs against the administrative inefficiency of subsidies in redistribution. But now the equilibrium condition looks very different from (7): The optimal tariff for industry i is proportional to the marginal administrative cost of the subsidy for industry i relative to the slope of the demand curve for i. Both instruments create a production distortion; the tariff will be used to equate the marginal "extra cost" of the subsidy (administration) to the marginal "extra" cost of the tariff (consumption distortion). *Imports and the import-demand elasticity are irrelevant.*

Second, all papers on the protection-for-sale model face the problem that the model predicts negative tariffs for unorganized sectors, a feature never discovered in the data. The standard argument in the literature is to suggest that the theory is not about the *level* of tariffs as much as the *variation* in tariffs; one can add to the model, for example, a political motive for giving some positive tariff to the unorganized sectors, and shift the intercept up, but the slopes of the protection as a function of z_i/e_i will not be affected. Once again, Ederington and Minier suggest that we stop waving our hands and actually add such a factor to the model. Suppose that there are a number of sectors that are not organized but the politician feels a need to keep them happy; perhaps their voters have high turnout rates in elections; perhaps they care less about partisanship than other voters (so that, in Lindbeck and Weibull, 1993 terms, they have a high value of $f(0, \tilde{k})$; recall Section 3.1.). In this case (simplifying their argument somewhat), once could have a politician who puts a weight of a on social welfare from other sectors, but a higher weight, say $a' > a$, on the set of sectors that are unorganized. (Indeed, perhaps that is why they are not organized—they do not need to be.) Maximize weighted welfare with a weight of a on workers, a weight of $a + 1$ on specific-factor owners in the organized industries, and a weight of d' on specific-factor owners in the unorganized industries, derive the first-order condition, and rearrange it to yield the analogue of (7).

$$\frac{\tau_i}{1+\tau_i} = \frac{(I_i - \alpha_L) + (d' - A)}{A + \alpha_L}\left(\frac{z_i}{e_i}\right), \tag{11}$$

where A is the average value of a and d', weighted by the proportion of the population who own specific factors in the organized and unorganized industries, respectively. Condition (11) looks very much like (7), and it has the feature that if d' is bigger than a by enough, all tariffs will be positive. However, a devastating problem has emerged: *When the tariffs for unorganized industries are positive*, they will be *increasing*, not decreasing, in z_i/e_i. This is readily understood if we recall the interpretation of z_i/e_i as the redistribution/distortion ratio. When it is optimal to redistribute income *away* from owners of unorganized industries with a negative tariff, it is optimal to do so most aggressively in industries with big values of z_i/e_i, since the redistribution can be done at low cost. That is where the original model provided a negative effect of z_i/e_i on unorganized tariffs: Low-cost redistribution implies a big negative tariff for those industries. However, if there are additional political considerations that make it optimal to distribute income *toward* the owners of unorganized industries with a *positive* tariff, then it is optimal to do so most aggressively in industries with big values of z_i/e_i. That provides a *positive* effect of z_i/e_i on unorganized tariffs.

In other words, once one adds elements to the model to rationalize the positive unorganized tariffs, the sign of the coefficient flips from the sign actually observed in the data to the opposite sign. It appears that these various empirical studies that are held up as verifying the protection-for-sale model have actually been rejecting it. Now, this is not to criticize the theory model, because without it we would not even know what to look for. One possible interpretation is that the protection-for-sale regressions have helped identify a robust empirical puzzle, to which theorists can now usefully apply themselves—somewhat in the spirit of the equity-premium puzzle or the statistical rejection of Euler-equation models in macroeconomics, which have generated very rich research literatures.[t]

A related critique is offered by Imai et al. (2013), who point out a number of problems with the way existing studies have divided up industries into "organized" and

---

[t] Another way of thinking about the absence of negative tariffs is to recall, as discussed in footnote g, that there is a continuum of different tariff vectors that yield the same equilibrium, and for any trade policy it is easy to formulate an equivalent policy with no negative tariffs. However, for that interpretation to work, one must identify the numeraire industry (which must exist in order for the model to work, and must be unorganized), and verify that it also has a positive tariff, which is below the tariffs of the industries with predicted positive tariffs but above the tariffs of the industries with predicted negative tariffs. Further, if that interpretation is correct, (7) can not longer be used as an estimating equation. I am grateful to Arnaud Costinot for suggesting this question.

"unorganized"—which always requires some arbitrary decisions, since as discussed above in practice all industries are usually politically organized. Imai et al. (2013) suggest an alternative derived from the theory: In the protection-for-sale model, conditional on the level of z_i/e_i, all organized industries will receive higher protection than any unorganized industry, so the conditional upper quantiles of the tariff distribution should represent organized industries and the lower ones unorganized industries. As a result, a quantile regression of the x-percentile tariff on z_i/e_i should yield a positive coefficient if x is close enough to 1 and a negative coefficient if x is close enough to zero. In fact, the estimation demonstrates the opposite—suggesting both that previous studies had seriously misclassified industries and that the data are inconsistent with the protection-for-sale model.

Apart from these issues of theoretical interpretation, many authors have become skeptical of the empirical formulation based on NTB coverage ratios. In effect, the first wave of empirical work pretended that the coverage ratios could be plugged into the first-order condition for choice of tariffs to maximize weighted welfare, and the condition be interpreted as a first-order condition for the coverage ratio instead. But this is a fiction; Matschke (2008), for example, points out that an important feature of the analysis is the effect on tariff revenues, but many NTB's generate no revenues at all. Gawande and Krishna (2004) point out broader logical problems with interpreting the coverage ratios as measures of the intensity of protection. More recent work has tended to use Most-Favored-Nation (MFN) tariffs (Matschke, 2008, which offers a detailed rationalization for the use of MFN tariffs; Fredriksson et al., 2011), or preferential tariffs where multilateral rules allow national discretion, such under as the Generalized System of Preferences (Blanchard and Matschke, 2015; Blanchard et al., 2014).

3.4.3 Other Contributions
Leaving these critiques to one side, a number of interesting and useful wrinkles have been added to the basic model. Here we review a few noteworthy examples.

1. *Dictatorship and lobbying.* Mitra et al. (2002) estimate a protection-for-sale model for Turkey for four separate years of data, beginning in 1983. Of course, extending the model to ever more countries is of interest in itself, but what makes the choice of location and years here highly significant is that 1983 was the last year of a military dictatorship. This allows the authors to ask, for example, whether the dictatorship appears to be more or less susceptible to influence-peddling than the subsequent democracy—a question with great relevance to understanding policy formation in the developing world, and one to which no obviously compelling answer springs out of theory. The model qualitatively follows the features estimated on US data, but the estimate of the parameter a turns out to be 76.3 during the dictatorship year and on average 87 during the democratic years, suggesting that—at least in this example—the dictatorship was somewhat *less* concerned about social welfare and

somewhat *more* susceptible to the influence of the lobbyists than the democracy that followed.

2. *Labor-market institutions and lobbying.* Matschke and Sherlund (2006) augment the basic protection-for-sale model with important features of the labor market: A portion of the industries have workers who are not mobile across industries, and a number of industries are unionized, and so have wages that are determined by bargaining between the employers and the union. This corrects, in a stylized way, one of the most glaring weaknesses of the classic protection-for-sale model: The fact that nothing that happens in trade policy has any effect on wages. In the Matschke and Sherlund (2006) model, a rise in a tariff to an industry raises not only profits but also wages, if the industry either has immobile labor or is unionized. Further, in each unionized industry, not only the employers but also the union has the option of lobbying the government. Not surprisingly, this adds an enormous amount of complication to the model, but in the end the authors derive a variant of the original protection-for-sale estimating equation, with an added term to take account of how labor-market conditions vary from industry to industry. The empirical results show that this term is highly significant, and helpful in explaining the pattern of trade barriers. For example, in industries that the authors classify as having immobile labor, industry lobbies on their own seem to be unable to obtain protection; they need the assistance of union lobbying.[u]

3. *Firm-level approaches to lobbying.* Bombardini (2008) presents a protection-for-sale model in which *individual firms* make the contributions as a Nash equilibrium. Any firm can pay a fixed cost and present a contribution schedule to the government. Firms differ in their size (because of exogenously heterogenous ownership of industry-specific human capital), and, conditional on an equilibrium selection assumption elaborated in the paper, only the larger firms choose to make contributions. Further, more heterogeneous industries, other things equal, receive more trade protection. In the extreme case, if the industry has one giant firm and a fringe of tiny competitors, the large firm will internalize more of the benefits of the tariff, and the public-goods under-provision problem will be minimized.[v] The paper uses industry data as in Gawande and Bandyopadhyay (2000) to test the hypothesis that more heterogeneous industries receive more protection, after controlling for the usual protection-for-sale variables, and finds a strong affirmative answer, as well as the finding that the heterogeneity helps the explanatory power of the standard

---

[u] This result can be seen in table 2, in the case $m_i = 0$ (immobile industry), with $k_i = 1$ (employers are lobbying) and $n_i = 0$ (union is not lobbying). The dramatic negative value indicates a much lower rate of protection compared to other, otherwise similar industries.

[v] The model raises the question of why the firms do not try to collude as in Pecorino (1998). This might be a worthwhile extension.

protection-for-sale regression quite a bit. It then uses firm-level data on political contributions from COMPUSTAT to confirm the hypothesis that larger firms participate with higher probability.

This is closely related to Gawande and Magee (2012), who specify a model with only the largest firm contributing as a contrast to the perfect-cooperation model. They derive the protection-for-sale estimating equation in this model and show that it depends on the *share* of the largest firm in total industry output. In the preferred econometric specifications, they find that this coefficient comes out as positive and significant, and they can robustly reject the hypothesis of perfect industry cooperation. Thus, both this paper and Bombardini (2008) provide strong evidence for the existence of a free-riding problem.

Bombardini and Trebbi (2012) observe that under US law, firms that lobby the government must file public reports that specify what the broad subject area of the lobbying effort is. This, unlike PAC contributions, allows a researcher to identify trade-policy-related influence activities directly. They examine firm-level data on lobbying reports and find that many firms lobby government over trade policy unilaterally, while many also join forces with other firms to lobby as a team. A simple model of an industry with multiple firms producing related products that are imperfect substitutes is solved, and predicts that industries with less differentiated products will tend to lobby jointly (since a tariff to firm i will tend to send customers to rival firm j; they team up to internalize the positive externality). On the other hand, firms with highly differentiated products will tend to lobby individually (to avoid the free-riding problem). These predictions are supported by the data.

4. *Interactions with public finance.* Matschke (2008) augments the original protection-for-sale model with government revenue needs. Much of policy analysis in the public-finance field is motivated by the lack of nondistortionary revenue sources for government, so that the value of \$1 in the government's hands is typically greater at the margin than the value of that same \$1 in private hands. If we take this into account, then the revenue that results from tariffs should be valued with a premium, often called the "cost of funds," and this needs to be taken into account in tariff setting. Matschke derives the equilibrium condition with this feature added to the model, and recovers a version of (7) with an extra term proportional to the imported quantity of good i divided by the derivative of import demand, where the constant of proportionality is a function of the premium to public funds.[w] Applied to US data, the results for the standard protection-for-sale terms are similar to what other authors have obtained, including estimates of a, but the revenue-cost term is also significant, and yields an estimate of the cost of funds equal to 1.06. This figure is quite close to

---

[w] This is Matschke's equation (8). A different version, equivalent but somewhat less intuitive, is used as the estimating equation.

what public-finance researchers have tended to find. A significant feature of this study is that (along with Fredriksson et al., 2011 and scattered others) it uses tariff data instead of NTB coverage ratios. Obviously, most NTB's do not generate revenue, so the model would not make much sense with them, and strikingly the results that emerge are quite similar to findings in other papers despite this difference in dependent variable.

5. *Foreign lobbyists.* Gawande et al. (2006) is a lovely wrinkle on the protection-for-sale literature: It points out that not only domestic industries but foreign ones as well might try to influence a country's trade policy, to reduce barriers to its own exports into the country. The paper uses the US registry of foreign agents to identify foreign lobbyists and finds strong evidence that they do indeed lower trade barriers on their own country's products. The authors point out that it implies a kind of paradox: The influence of foreign lobbyists working on behalf of foreign clients can raise domestic social welfare, by counteracting the pernicious influence of *domestic* lobbyists. In a somewhat similar spirit, Gawande et al. (2012) expands the protection-for-sale model to account for lobbying by (i) final-goods producers for higher tariffs on their own products and low tariffs on the imported inputs that they use, and (ii) input producers, for *high* tariffs on those same products. The authors show that this tug of war between lobbyists may help explain the high values of the social welfare weight *a* estimated by other authors: Many tariffs are low not because the government cares about social welfare, but because it is being bribed to keep them low.

6. *Surging industries and declining industries.* Observers of trade policy in practice will notice a paradox in the protection-for-sale theory: It tends to reward more productive industries, and industries whose products are more in demand, with higher tariffs. Recalling (7), if the world price of industry i goods or the productivity of the domestic industry i rises with no change in the elasticity of import demand, then domestic output will rise and imports will fall, so that the tariff on industry-i goods will increase. Of course, in general the import elasticity will generally change; Karacaovali (2011) rigourously derives a condition under which an industry's tariff will be an increasing function of its productivity. However, in practice it is often *declining* industries that receive protection. Both Freund and Özden (2008) and Tovar (2009) show that incorporating loss aversion into the preferences of interest groups can help explain this. Under loss aversion, an economic agent experiences disutility from income falling below a target income, in addition to utility from consumption. If the target income is based in part on past income, owners of specific factors in a declining industry will be willing to pay more for protection at the margin than those in other industries. The standard formulation of loss aversion includes an assumption of a diminishing sensitivity to loss; if the realized income is slightly below the target, the marginal disutility is large, but if it falls far below the target, the marginal effect tapers off to zero. As a result, the declining industry receives enhanced protection up

to a point, but when its output or world prices fall sufficiently far, the effect disappears. Both Freund and Özden (2008) and Tovar (2009) provide empirical support for these propositions, so loss aversion may be helpful in explaining trade protection patterns.[x] At the same time, there is a serious tension between these findings and the evidence presented by Karacaovali (2011) that, in Colombian data, industries with surging productivity tend to have tariffs that decline more slowly than stagnant or declining industries.[y]

3.4.4 General Observations

The literature on lobbying has become obviously very rich, but at the same time is still strikingly narrow. In World War I thousands of lives would be spilled over a few feet of land, and in this literature thousands of pages are written to examine and debate a single equation.

It is striking how little empirical work there is on lobbying expenditures *per se* as opposed to PAC contributions, since as Bombardini and Trebbi (2012) point out, the former exceed the latter by an order of magnitude. It is puzzling how little there is either theoretically or empirically in the trade literature on informational theories of lobbying, which are important in political science and appear to represent a large portion of what lobbying does in practice. For example, one option open to lobbyists is to use the media to provide information or persuasion directed at voters (recall the discussion in Section 2.4), to change the electoral incentives of politicians. At the time of this writing, for example, the US Chamber of Commerce is running radio ads on the importance of continued Congressional support of the Ex-Im bank. But these channels do not seem to be explored in the trade literature.

Even within the realm of PAC contributions, the literature is focussed entirely on a model in which the only purpose of a contribution is to influence an incumbent politician's trade-policy decisions, while a second major purpose of PAC contributions is likely to be to influence *which politicians compose the government*. The latter is explored and shown to be important by Magee (2007) in a nontrade-policy context, but this motive is ripe for exploration within trade as well (and it was already noted in Section 3.3 that this is a well-known motive in the general political-economy theory literature; see Potters et al., 1997).

---

[x] An alternative interpretation is that surging industries attract entry, and so any rents from protection for those industries would be dissipated by entry. Baldwin and Robert-Nicoud (2007) formalize this argument, in a closed-economy model in which each industry is subject to demand shocks over time, and each industry can lobby for a subsidy in each period. In equilibrium, only industries hit with an adverse demand shock lobby for a subsidy.

[y] His main point is that this endogeneity of tariffs implies a downward bias in estimates of the productivity effect of trade liberalization, but it is important in and of itself for the present discussion.

An additional avenue that could be promising is to take government revenue effects more seriously. An approach similar to Matschke (2008) might profitably be applied in a range of medium- and low-income economies, where often trade taxes are a large fraction of central government finances and tax levers are limited. It would be of interest to see if the effect of revenue constraints on the pattern of trade policy would be even more acute than it appears to be in the United States.

Finally, as noted above, some studies have indicated that free-rider problems are important in this area in practice (see comments above on Bombardini, 2008 and Gawande and Magee, 2012). It seems that much more could be done to identify the conditions under which such *organizational* barriers to successful influence can be overcome. Intriguing results by Busch and Reinhardt (1999) show that industries that are more geographically concentrated—in a very specific sense—tend to have more trade protection, *ceteris paribus*. Specifically, for each industry in the United States, one can identify the point on the map that is the center of gravity of the industry, and then calculate the average square distance of that industry's employment from that center. (This is very different from the Herfindahl index of geographic concentration, which is much easier to compute.) The fact that this measure shows up so strongly suggests that more concentrated industries have an advantage in organizing in order to achieve influence, but exactly why is unclear. Notice that protection-for-sale models typically assume that the industry can either coordinate perfectly or not at all, but evidently there is much more to the story.

3.5 Legislative Bargaining

In the event that commercial policy is determined by a legislative assembly, once the legislators have been seated, the realized policy can be determined by coalition-formation within the legislature.

The seminal paper is Grossman and Helpman (2005), previously discussed in Section 3.1, since it has an *ex ante* electoral component as well as an *ex post* legislative bargaining component. In that model, two national parties compete for votes by committing to policy platforms before the election. After the election, the representatives from the winning party control the legislature and will be able to deviate from their party's platform, but if they do they will be "fined" by their party in proportion to the size of the deviation, with a parameter δ as the parameter of proportionality. The model becomes a pure electoral competition model with no postelection deviation as δ becomes large, and a model of pure postelection legislative bargaining (with representatives randomly determined) as $\delta \to 0$. In Section 3.1 we focussed on the case with δ large, and here we will focus on the case with δ close to 0.

There are three legislative districts. The party that wins two or more of them controls the legislature. There are also three industries, each of which produces tradeable output by combining a specific factor with labor, plus a fourth numeraire industry that produces with labor only, with a constant marginal product. As in Grossman and Helpman (1994), utility is additively separable in all goods and linear in the numeraire good, so that utility can be evaluated in terms of consumer surplus. The model is symmetric: Each nonnumeraire industry has an identical supply and demand curve. Further, crucially, each legislative district has a portion of the specific factor owners of all three industries, but they are not evenly distributed: Each district has a fraction α_1 of one industry, α_2 of another and α_3 of the third, with $\alpha_1 > \alpha_2 > \alpha_3$. Of course, $\alpha_1 + \alpha_2 + \alpha_3$ must equal 1 (so α_1 must be bigger than $\frac{1}{3}$ and α_3 must be smaller than $\frac{1}{3}$). Number the industries so that district 1 has the biggest piece of industry 1, and so on: Each industry has a disproportionate amount of its capital in the district with the same number.

This is a small open economy, with a world price p^* for each of the nonnumeraire goods. Government can set tariffs (assuming for concreteness that the three nonnumeraire goods are imported), so that the domestic price of good i will be $p_i = p^* + t_i$, where t_i is the tariff on good i.

The legislator representing each district wishes to pursue policy that will maximize the welfare of the residents of that district. If party A wins all three districts, its members negotiate among themselves and choose a tariff vector to maximize total social welfare. Since this is a small open economy, this amounts to free trade. The same outcome occurs if party B wins all districts. The interesting possibility occurs if one party (say A) wins two districts (say 1 and 2) but not the third. In this case, party A controls the assembly, and can pass whatever bill it wants without help from party B. Now, the two legislators from party A conspire to maximize the welfare of districts 1 plus 2, without regard for welfare of the enemy territory held by party B. This leads to a positive tariff for industries 1 and 2 and a negative tariff for industry 3, for reasons analogous to the tariff setting in Grossman and Helpman (1994). The welfare function being maximized has $\frac{2}{3}$ of the consumers and taxpayers of the economy, but more than $\frac{2}{3}$ of the capital of industries 1 and 2, and less than $\frac{2}{3}$ of the capital for industry 3.

But Grossman and Helpman take us one step further: One might expect that the sign of the *average* tariff is undetermined, with two positive values and one negative value, but it turns out that in the special case of linear supply and demand curves, with the assumed symmetry of the model, *the average tariff is strictly positive* as long as the supply curves slope upward. Given that there is an equal probability of either party capturing either legislative district *ex ante*, this implies that *the expected value of each of the three tariffs is strictly positive*.

It is worth taking a moment to unpack where this result comes from. Take the special case in which $\alpha_2 = \alpha_3 = 0$, so each industry's specific factor is located in only one district. Consider raising the specific tariff on good 1 by 1 dollar. The income to specific factor owners in 1 goes up by the output of industry 1, y_1. This is the benefit to party A.

Consumer surplus to all citizens goes down by: $d_1 = y_1 + m_1$, where d_i is the domestic consumption of good 1 and m_i is the quantity of i that is imported, and tariff revenue goes up by: $m_1 + t_1 m_1'$. Therefore, the net drop in utility for each citizen who is not a good-1 producer is $y_1 - t_1 m_1'$. Since a fraction $\frac{2}{3}$ of consumers and taxpayers live in the territory controlled by Party A, the cost to party A is then $\frac{2}{3}(y_1 - t_1 m_1')$.

The optimal tariff then sets this marginal benefit equal to the marginal cost, so:

$$y_1 = \frac{2}{3}(y_1 - t_1 m_1').$$

$$y_1 = 2(-t_i m_i').$$

The left-hand side is the benefit from redistribution, analogous to the left-hand side of (9), and the right-hand side is the cost from distortion, analogous to the right-hand side of (9), with different weights as appropriate. This yields the optimal tariff on good 1:

$$t_1^* = \left(\frac{1}{2}\right)\left(\frac{y_1}{-m_1'}\right) > 0. \tag{12}$$

Of course, good 2 is exactly analogous. Now, for the disfavored good, if party A members consider raising the specific tariff on good 3 by 1 dollar, the income to specific factor owners in 3 goes up by y_3 but that is not relevant to the interests of Party A so we ignore it. On the other hand, the consumer surplus of all citizens goes down by $d_3 = y_3 + m_3$ and tariff revenue goes up by $m_3 + t_3 m_3'$. The net drop in utility for each citizen not a good-3 producer is then:

$$y_3 - t_1 m_3'$$

Given that two-thirds of these citizens are included in the Party A welfare function, the cost to party A is:

$$\frac{2}{3}(y_3 - t_3 m_3'). \tag{13}$$

The first term in parentheses is once again the redistributive benefit, but this time the benefit of transferring income *from* producers of good 3 *to* consumers and taxpayers in Party-A territory. The optimal tariff sets this equal to zero:

$$t_3 = \left(\frac{y_3}{m_3'}\right) < 0, \text{ so the equilibrium tariffs satisfy:}$$

$$t_1 = \left(\frac{1}{2}\right)\left(\frac{y_1}{-m_1'}\right) > 0.$$

$$t_2 = \left(\frac{1}{2}\right)\left(\frac{y_2}{-m_2'}\right) > 0.$$

$$t_3 = \left(\frac{y_3}{m_3'}\right) < 0.$$

In the special case of linear supply and demand: $m'_1 \equiv m'_2 \equiv m'_3$. If the output levels in the three industries had been equal, we would have $(t_1 + t_2 + t_3)/3 = 0$, but given the symmetry in the model and the fact that the domestic price of goods 1 and 2 are raised above the world price but the domestic price of good 3 is pushed down below the world price, we have $y_1 = y_2 > y_3$. Therefore *the average tariff is positive.*

Note that this results hangs on both the linear supply and demand curves and on the symmetry. It would not be difficult to construct an example with varying slopes or asymmetries across industries such that the average tariff would be negative. However, the observation that the authors make that the positive effect is due to "the convexity of the profit function" does seem to be a very general one: This is simply the point that supply curves slope up. As a result, when one raises the domestic price of a favored good with a tariff, the redistributive benefit—which as in (12) is proportional to the industry's output—rises, and when one lowers the domestic price of a disfavored good, the redistributive benefit—as in (13)—falls. This tends to raise the magnitude of the positive tariffs and lower the magnitude of the negative tariffs, yielding the protectionist bias.

Two more recent contributions to this area combine lobbying with legislative bargaining: Hauk (2011) and Fredriksson et al. (2011). Both feature lobbyists in the Grossman and Helpman (1994) mold who present contribution schedules to members of the legislature before the legislative bargaining occurs, with the result that the legislators' objective function becomes a weighted welfare of the constituents' welfare, with extra weight on the organized industries. Fredriksson et al. (2011) is closest to Grossman and Helpman (2005) in that the legislators belong to distinct parties, and members of the majority party collude to maximize their joint welfare, excluding the minority. They derive an estimating equation that resembles the original protection-for-sale Eq. (7) but with an extra term indicating that industries concentrated in districts represented by the majority party[z] receive extra protection. Applying this to data on US tariffs (along with Matschke, 2008, they use tariff data instead of NTB data) and partisan control of the US House of Representatives, they find that this term has a consistently significant coefficient, but with interesting variation over time. In data for 1993 and 1995, it is positive as expected, but in 1997 it is *negative*. The authors point out that 1995 was the year in which the Republican party took over Congress after a long reign by the Democrats, and so the values of the "majority" variable flipped dramatically, but tariffs change infrequently. Thus, in the 1997 data, tariffs enacted by a prior Democratic majority are regressed on political measures that come from a new Republican majority.[aa] The authors have done a great service by introducing time variation into a literature that is based almost

---

[z]   Precisely, if the districts controlled by the majority party contain a larger share of an industry's capital than of the nation's population, that industry receives extra protection.

[aa]   This explanation does not seem to explain why the 1995 regression has a positive coefficient for the majority variable, since the Republican congress was seated in January 1995.

entirely on cross-sectional data, but the inertia in tariff data also shows the difficulty in doing so.

On the other hand, Hauk (2011) has a model with no partisan politics. In his model, a proposer is chosen randomly from among the seated legislators; following this, lobbyists present their contribution schedules; and then the proposer must propose a tariff bill. If a majority of legislators vote for the bill, it becomes law. If not, the bill fails and free-trade prevails. As a result, the agenda-setter must choose a minimum winning coalition, a bare majority of fellow legislators, and choose a tariff vector combined with other redistributive policies that will maximize her own weighted constituent welfare,[ab] taking into account the organized industry if any, subject to the constraint that enough other legislators are willing to vote for the bill to pass it, meaning that those legislators receive at a least as high a payoff from the proposed tariff as from free trade. (In the three-person legislature of the theory model, this of course means that one other legislator must be persuaded to support the bill.) The main focus of this study is on the effects of "malproportionment," namely, disproportionate allocation of voters across legislative districts. In the United States, this is an issue with the Senate, since each state is represented by two Senators, regardless of the population of the state (districts comprising the House, on the other hand, are quite similar in size). Equilibrium tariffs for industries in the winning coalition are affected by malproportionment in two ways. First, holding industry size constant, the larger is a state's share in an industry's capital relative to its share of national population, the more likely is its Senator to prefer protection for that industry. Second, and more subtly, holding all other variables constant, an industry concentrated in a *smaller state* will tend to receive more protection. This is because the Senator will value consumer surplus and tax revenue much less in a state with few consumers and taxpayers, and so will support aggressive protection for the local industry. More subtly still, a smaller state is more likely to be chosen as a coalition partner by a proposer. Support for these propositions is found in data on Senate votes between 1880 and 1930, and on modern NTB data.

Despite their similarities, the assumption of pure partisan unity in Fredriksson et al. (2011) and purely opportunistic legislative coalition formation in Hauk (2011) give them extremely different predictions. Both papers provide good empirical support for their approaches, but it would be desirable to be able to determine if one of them fits the data better than the other, if perhaps one approach can be rejected if the two are incorporated in the same estimation procedure. (Of course, that would require focussing both on Senate data, unlike the empirical work in Fredriksson et al., 2011).

[ab] It is assumed that lobbyists lobby only the legislator representing the district in which their client's capital is located. The consequences of relaxing this assumption seem worth exploring. By contrast, in Fredriksson et al. (2011), any industry in the country, wherever located, can lobby the majority coalition.

A final legislative bargaining approach is the dynamic bargaining approach pioneered in public finance by Baron and Ferejohn (1989), who study the allocation of public funds by a legislature. Applied to trade policy, it allows for the possibility that if a tariff bill is not accepted at any date, a new bill can be introduced down the road, a small detail that can be seen to make a large difference in how the model works. An example of this approach is Celik et al. (2013). Here, once again, there are three members of a legislature, each representing a district that is home to the specific capital for one industry. In each period, a proposer is chosen by Nature and has the ability to propose a tariff vector. If a majority of representatives vote for the proposal, it becomes law and the game ends. Otherwise, the status-quo tariff vector remains in place and a new proposer is chosen randomly (which could turn out to be the same one again). As in the static models discussed above, the proposer's optimal strategy is to choose one other member and offer a tariff vector that makes that other member just willing to support the proposal,[ac] disregarding the welfare of the excluded member. However, the dynamic nature of the game results in very different equilibria. First, the equilibrium is typically in mixed strategies, in the sense that each member randomizes between coalition partners when she has a chance to propose.[ad] As a result, the set of favored, high-tariff industries within the coalition cannot be predicted from industry and district characteristics alone; there is an irreducible random element to it. Further, the proposer at times may rationally propose a tariff vector that makes even the proposer's district worse off than the status quo tariff, and it will be passed and become law. The reason is that the proposer may be terrified of what will happen if her bill is not passed and with $\frac{2}{3}$ probability another proposer will have a chance to propose. The danger of being left out of the coalition and facing high tariffs on other industries but a negative tariff on one's one may make the proposer eager enough to pass a bill that, to avoid disaster tomorrow, she will accept a worsening compared to the status quo today. This outcome is impossible in a static bargaining model such as those discussed above. It is not clear how to bring these possibilities to data for econometric tests, but the model does seem to fit some anecdotal evidence from late-nineteenth century US tariff setting. Further, the inefficiency of the equilibrium can provide a motivation for Congress to try to delegate its tariff setting through institutions such as "Fast Track Authority" (Celik et al., 2015; see Conconi et al., 2012b for an alternative interpretation). A richer model in the same general framework is explored by Bowen (2011), who shows that tariff ceilings imposed through the WTO and floors that result from administered protection can have surprising effects on the legislated tariff outcomes.

[ac]   Unlike in Hauk (2011), the model allows no redistributive policy aside from tariffs.
[ad]   To cut down on the number of equilibria under consideration, the paper focusses on stationary subgame perfect equilibrium, in which a player will always take the same (random) action when faced with the same circumstances.

4. FEEDBACK EFFECTS: POLITICAL CONDITIONS ARE ALSO ENDOGENOUS

All of the above discussion takes the political and economic environment and institutions as exogenous, but of course commercial policy also *shapes* these conditions. This feedback can result in inefficiencies and multiple equilibria that cannot even be contemplated when the political and economic environment are taken as exogenous. Here we will discuss some suggestive examples.

1. For example, in all work cited so far (take Grossman and Helpman, 1994 as a quintessential case), the existing pattern of industry-specific capital has been taken as given, and is a key driver of the demand for protection. However, this pattern of capital can be endogenous to the political game; if a given industry has political clout and can gain protectionism as a political favor, the *expectation* of that favor can encourage investment in that industry, which increases its political clout and the resulting protectionism even more. Both the investment in the industry and the protectionism wind up greater than optimal, even taking into account the government's preferences with its built-in bias toward the industry in question (Staiger and Tabellini, 1987). This type of time-inconsistency problem can help rationalize the use of devices to reduce the government's discretion, and has been shown to be a possible motivation for free-trade agreements as a way a government can lock in a low tariff and thus tie its own hands (Maggi and Rodriguez-Clare, 1998).

2. The *international* pattern of capital can also be endogenous to the political game, creating feedback effects that can result in surprising insights unimaginable in a static model. For example, multinational firms deciding whether or not to commit to foreign direct investment (FDI) in a given economy need to take into account what future commercial policy in that economy and in their home economy will be; but FDI also affects the political conditions so that commercial policy will be affected by FDI in the aggregate. Grossman and Helpman (1996) focus on the case of imperfectly competitive firms in Home, which consider horizontal FDI in an import-competing sector in Foreign. Foreign's import tariff on the industry, which protects both Foreign firms and subsidiaries of Home multinationals, will be affected by the number of Home firms who have invested in Foreign; the more firms that have invested, the smaller will be the imports to which the tariff applies. However, each Home firm takes the Foreign tariff as given. In a benchmark case, the Foreign tariff is decreasing in the amount of FDI, and FDI is increasing in the expected Foreign tariff, so there is a unique equilibrium. The more political weight the Foreign government puts on its own firms, the higher will be the equilibrium tariff, and the more crowded will the local industry be with subsidiaries from Home.

   On the other hand, Blanchard (2007) focusses on Home capital moving to the *export* sector in Foreign, and the effect this has on the Home tariff. Under standard assumptions, the more Home capital has moved into Foreign, the lower will be the optimal tariff for Home to impose on its imports from Foreign since the tariff lowers income on Home's own capital abroad. Equilibrium FDI thus lowers tariffs, and can even eliminate them entirely; further, Foreign has an incentive to *subsidize* inward FDI to manipulate Home's tariff setting. Empirical support for these effects is provided by Blanchard and Matschke (2015), who show that the US tends to give more of a tariff preference on imports from a given industry in a given country if subsidiaries of US firms there produce a large fraction of those imports. Further, Blanchard et al. (2014) shows that in a panel of 14 countries, country *i*'s tariffs tend to be lower on products of a given industry from country *j*, the larger is *i*'s share of value added in that industry in *j*, and the smaller is *j*'s share of value added in that industry in *i*.

3. As another example, the pattern of *human* capital, taken as given in most analyses of the demand for protection (see Section 2.3), can very much be endogenous to the political-economy game. In Blanchard and Willmann (2011), an overlapping-generations model of voting over commercial policy can lead to a low-tariff steady state or a high-tariff "protectionist rut," due to the fact that expectations of future high tariffs can discourage the current young from investing in human capital needed for the export sector. Over time, this pattern of human capital creates political conditions that are not favorable to trade liberalization, so protectionism becomes a self-fulfilling prophecy. An implication is that a short-term political push for liberalization can also be self-sustaining in the long run.

4. Beyond these examples, there is accumulating evidence of possible important feedbacks between commercial policy and democratic institutions that could turn out to be quite important in developing countries—far beyond the Harberger-triangle losses from protectionism that are the bread and butter of traditional commercial-policy welfare analysis. Liu and Ornelas (2014) shows that politicians in a country with a new and fragile democracy can use a trade agreement to eliminate rents that could be a motivation for a military coup, thus raising the probability that democracy will survive. Without the trade agreement to tie its hands, a future government could offer protection for sale, which makes political power a profitable business and therefore provides a motivation for an armed clique to try to gain power by force. The authors present empirical evidence that suggests that in many cases free-trade agreements signed by governments of developing economies have such a role. At the same time, with a long-span historical panel, Eichengreen and Leblang (2008) show that democracy tends to be followed by increased trade openness, and increased trade openness tends to be followed by more democracy, suggesting a virtuous spiral.

It may be that these feedback effects from protection back to political and economic conditions will be regarded as the really important features of the political economy of commercial policy, involving welfare effects that dwarf the distortions that are the subject of models where the causation runs in one direction only.

5. CONCLUSION

Perhaps the most useful concluding comment is to sum up the directions that have been noted along the way as the most promising for future work.

1. *Informational lobbying.* Ludema et al. (2010) showed that in one particular form of trade policy adjustment, informational lobbying is crucial, and effective. This is very likely to be the tip of the iceberg. Informational approaches may wind up more important for understanding lobbying than protection for sale.

2. *The role of the media.* Facchini et al. (2013) and Ponzetto (2011) are two pioneering approaches that merge media data with data on trade and trade policy. The role of the media as a way of shaping the demand for protectionism as well as commercial policy outcomes, and perhaps as a tool of lobbying, is a very under-researched topic.

3. *A richer treatment of labor markets.* Matschke and Sherlund (2006) is a start in incorporating labor frictions and labor unions into lobbying analysis, working from the Grossman and Helpman (1994) model, which makes labor issues difficult to tease out. It would be desirable to begin with a much richer model of the labor market to begin with, so that issues such as unemployment and job-creation, so much a part of the public discourse, can be a central part of the political-economy analysis.

4. *Firm-level analysis of lobbying.* Bombardini (2008), Bombardini and Trebbi (2012), and Ludema et al. (2010), for example, have shown that firm-level empirical work can be fruitful. Given the likelihood that incentives for lobbying are heterogeneous even within each industry, this direction needs to be pursued.

5. *Feedback effects.* More generally, the two-way feedbacks between underlying economic and political conditions on the one hand and commercial policy on the other are likely to become more central over time.

REFERENCES

Anderson, J.E., Zanardi, M., 2009. Political pressure deflection. Public Choice 141 (1–2), 129–150.

Artuc, E., Chaudhuri, S., McLaren, J., 2010. Trade shocks and labor adjustment: a structural empirical approach. Am. Econ. Rev. 100 (3), 1008–1045.

Austen-Smith, D., 1993. Information and influence: lobbying for agendas and votes. Am. J. Polit. Sci., 37 (3), 799–833.

Baldwin, R.E., Robert-Nicoud, F., 2007. Entry and asymmetric lobbying: why governments pick losers. J. Eur. Econ. Assoc. 5 (5), 1064–1093.

Baron, D.P., Ferejohn, J.A., 1989. Bargaining in legislatures. Am. Polit. Sci. Rev. 83 (4), 1181–1206.

Beaulieu, E., 2002. Factor or industry cleavages in trade policy? An empirical analysis of the Stolper-Samuelson theorem. Econ. Polit. 14 (2), 99–131.

Blanchard, E.J., 2007. Foreign direct investment, endogenous tariffs, and preferential trade agreements. BE J. Econ. Anal. Policy 7 (1), 1–52.

Blanchard, E., Matschke, X., 2015. US multinationals and preferential market access. Rev. Econ. Stat. 97 (4), 839–854.

Blanchard, E., Willmann, G., 2011. Escaping a protectionist rut: policy mechanisms for trade reform in a democracy. J. Int. Econ. 85 (1), 72–85.

Blanchard, E., Bown, C., Johnson, R., 2014. Global supply chains and trade policy. Working paper, Dartmouth.

Blonigen, B.A., 2011. Revisiting the evidence on trade policy preferences. J. Int. Econ. 85 (1), 129–135.

Blonigen, B.A., Figlio, D.N., 1998. Voting for protection: does direct foreign investment influence legislator behavior? Am. Econ. Rev. 88, 1002–1014.

Bombardini, M., 2008. Firm heterogeneity and lobby participation. J. Int. Econ. 75 (2), 329–348.

Bombardini, M., Trebbi, F., 2012. Competition and political organization: together or alone in lobbying for trade policy? J. Int. Econ. 87 (1), 18–26.

Bowen, T.R., 2011. Legislated protection and the WTO. Int. Econ. Rev. 56 (4), 1349–1384.

Brander, J.A., Spencer, B.J., 1985. Export subsidies and international market share rivalry. J. Int. Econ. 18 (1), 83–100.

Broda, C., Limao, N., Weinstein, D.E., 2008. Optimal tariffs and market power: the evidence. Am. Econ. Rev. 98 (5), 2032–2065.

Busch, M.L., Reinhardt, E., 1999. Industrial location and protection: the political and economic geography of U.S. nontariff barriers. Am. J. Polit. Sci. 43 (4), 1028–1050.

Celik, L., Karabay, B., McLaren, J., 2013. Trade policy-making in a model of legislative bargaining. J. Int. Econ. 91 (2), 179–190.

Celik, L., Karabay, B., McLaren, J., 2015. When is it optimal to delegate: the theory of fast-track authority. Am. Econ. J.: Microecon. 73, 347–389.

Conconi, P., Facchini, G., Steinhardt, M.F., Zanardi, M., 2012a. The political economy of trade and migration: evidence from the US congress. Discussion Paper.

Conconi, P., Facchini, G., Zanardi, M., 2012b. Fast-track authority and international trade negotiations. Am. Econ. J.: Econ. Policy 4, 146–189.

Conconi, P., Facchini, G., Zanardi, M., 2014. Policymakers' horizon and trade reforms. J. Int. Econ. 94, 102–118.

Costinot, A., Donaldson, D., Vogel, J., Werning, I., 2015. Comparative advantage and optimal trade policy. Q. J. Econ. 130 (2), 659–702.

Deardorff, A.V., 2000. Factor prices and the factor content of trade revisited: what's the use? J. Int. Econ. 50 (1), 73–90.

DellaVigna, S., Kaplan, E.D., 2007. The fox news effect: media bias and voting. Q. J. Econ. 122 (3), 1187–1234.

Demidova, S., Rodriguez-Clare, A., 2009. Trade policy under firm-level heterogeneity in a small economy. J. Int. Econ. 78 (1), 100–112.

Dhingra, S., 2014. Reconciling observed tariffs and the median voter model. Econ. Polit. 26 (3), 483–504.

Dix-Carneiro, R., 2014. Trade liberalization and labor market dynamics. Econometrica 82 (3), 825–885.

Dixit, A., Norman, V., 1980. Theory of International Trade: A Dual, General Equilibrium Approach. Cambridge University Press, Cambridge, UK.

Dutt, P., Mitra, D., 2002. Endogenous trade policy through majority voting: an empirical investigation. J. Int. Econ. 58 (1), 107–133.

Eaton, J., Grossman, G.M., 1986. Optimal trade and industrial policy under oligopoly. Q. J. Econ. 101, 383–406.

Ederington, J., Minier, J., 2008. Reconsidering the empirical evidence on the Grossman-Helpman model of endogenous protection. Can. J. Econ./Rev. Can. Econ. 41 (2), 501–516.

Eichengreen, B., Leblang, D., 2008. Democracy and globalization. Econ. Polit. 20 (3), 289–334.

Eicher, T., Osang, T., 2002. Protection for sale: an empirical investigation: comment. Am. Econ. Rev. 92 (5), 1702–1710.

Evans, C.L., 2009. A protectionist bias in majoritarian politics: an empirical investigation. Econ. Polit. 21 (2), 278–307.

Facchini, G., Frattini, T., Signorotto, C., 2013. Mind what your voters read: media exposure and international economic policy making. Centro Studi Luca d'Agliano Development Studies Working Paper No. 358.

Findlay, R., Wellisz, S., 1983. Some aspects of the political economy of trade restrictions. Kyklos 36 (3), 469–481.

Fredriksson, P.G., Matschke, X., Minier, J., 2011. Trade policy in majoritarian systems: the case of the US. Can. J. Econ./Rev. Can. Econ. 44 (2), 607–626.

Freund, C., Özden, Ç., 2008. Trade policy and loss aversion. Am. Econ. Rev. 98 (4), 1675–1691.

Gawande, K., Bandyopadhyay, U., 2000. Is protection for sale? Evidence on the Grossman-Helpman theory of endogenous protection. Rev. Econ. Stat. 82 (1), 139–152.

Gawande, K., Krishna, P., 2004. The political economy of trade policy: empirical approaches. In: Choi, E. K., Harrigan, J. (Eds.), Handbook of International Trade. Wiley-Blackwell, Hoboken, NJ, pp. 139–152.

Gawande, K., Magee, C., 2012. Free riding and protection for sale. Int. Stud. Q. 56 (4), 735–747.

Gawande, B.K., Krishna, P., Olarreaga, M., 2012. Lobbying competition over trade policy. Int. Econ. Rev. 53 (1), 115–132.

Gawande, K., Krishna, P., Robbins, M.J., 2006. Foreign lobbies and US trade policy. Rev. Econ. Stat. 88 (3), 563–571.

Goldberg, P.K., Maggi, G., 1999. Protection for sale: an empirical investigation. Am. Econ. Rev. 89, 1135–1155.

Grossman, G.M., Helpman, E., 1994. Protection for sale. Am. Econ. Rev. 84 (4), 833–850.

Grossman, G.M., Helpman, E., 1996. Foreign investment with endogenous protection. In: Feenstra, R.C., Grossman, G.M. (Eds.), The Political Economy of Trade Policy: Papers in Honor of Jagdish Bhagwati. MIT Press, Cambridge, MA, pp. 199–224.

Grossman, G.M., Helpman, E., 2002. Special Interest Politics. MIT Press, Cambridge, MA.

Grossman, G.M., Helpman, E., 2005. A protectionist bias in majoritarian politics. Q. J. Econ. 120 (4), 11239–11282.

Gulotty, R., 2016. Firm profits in the presence of regulatory barriers. Mimeo, University of Chicago.

Hall, H.K., Nelson, D., 2004. The peculiar political economy of NAFTA: complexity, uncertainty and footloose policy preferences. In: Mitra, D., Panagariya, A. (Eds.), The Political Economy of Trade and Foreign Investment Policies. Elsevier, Amsterdam, pp. 91–109.

Hanson, G.H., Scheve, K., Slaughter, M.J., 2007. Public finance and individual preferences over globalization strategies. Econ. Polit. 19 (1), 1–33.

Hatfield, J.W., Hauk, W.R., 2014. Electoral regime and trade policy. J. Comp. Econ. 42 (3), 518–534.

Hauk, W.R., 2011. Protection with many sellers: an application to legislatures with malapportionment. Econ. Polit. 23 (3), 313–344.

Imai, S., Katayama, H., Krishna, K., 2013. A quantile-based test of protection for sale model. J. Int. Econ. 91 (1), 40–52.

Irwin, D.A., 1996. Industry or class cleavages over trade policy? Evidence from the British general election of 1923. In: Feenstra, R.C., Grossman, G.M. (Eds.), The Political Economy of Trade Policy: Papers in Honor of Jagdish Bhagwati. MIT Press, Cambridge, MA, pp. 53–76.

Jäkel, I.C., Smolka, M., 2015. Trade policy preferences and the factor content of trade. Working Paper.

Jensen, R., Oster, E., 2009. The power of TV: cable television and women's status in India. Q. J. Econ. 124 (3), 1057–1094.

Karabay, B., 2009. Lobbying under asymmetric information. Econ. Polit. 21 (1), 1–41.

Karabay, B., McLaren, J., 2004. Trade policy making by an assembly. In: Mitra, D., Panagariya, A. (Eds.), The Political Economy of Trade and Foreign Investment Policies. Elsevier, Amsterdam, pp. 91–109.

Karacaovali, B., 2011. Productivity matters for trade policy: theory and evidence. Int. Econ. Rev. 52 (1), 33–62.

Kee, H.L., Nicita, A., Olarreaga, M., 2008. Import demand elasticities and trade distortions. Rev. Econ. Stat. 90 (4), 666–682.

Kee, H.L., Nicita, A., Olarreaga, M., 2009. Estimating trade restrictiveness indices. Econ. J. 119 (534), 172–199.

Krueger, A.O., 1974. The political economy of the rent-seeking society. Am. Econ. Rev., 64 (3), 291–303.

Limão, N., Panagariya, A., 2007. Inequality and endogenous trade policy outcomes. J. Int. Econ. 72 (2), 292–309.

Limão, N., Tovar, P., 2011. Policy choice: theory and evidence from commitment via international trade agreements. J. Int. Econ. 85 (2), 186–205.

Lindbeck, A., Weibull, J.W., 1993. A model of political equilibrium in a representative democracy. J. Public Econ. 51 (2), 195–209.

Liu, X., Ornelas, E., 2014. Free trade agreements and the consolidation of democracy. Am. Econ. J.: Macroecon. 6 (2), 29–70.

Ludema, R.D., Mayda, A.M., 2013. Do terms-of-trade effects matter for trade agreements? Theory and evidence from WTO countries. Q. J. Econ. 128 (4), 1837–1893.

Ludema, R.D., Mayda, A.M., Mishra, P., 2010. Protection for free? The political economy of US tariff suspensions. CEPR Discussion Paper No. DP7926.

Ma, X., McLaren, J., 2015. A swing-state theorem, with evidence. Mimeo, University of Virginia.

Magee, C.S., 2007. Influence, elections, and the value of a vote in the US house of representatives. Econ. Polit. 19 (3), 289–315.

Magee, S.P., 1989. Three simple tests of the Stolper-Samuelson theorem. In: Magee, S.P. (Ed.), Black Hole Tariffs. Cambridge University Press, Cambridge, UK.

Maggi, G., 1996. Strategic trade policies with endogenous mode of competition. Am. Econ. Rev. 86, 237–258.

Maggi, G., Rodriguez-Clare, A., 1998. The value of trade agreements in the presence of political pressures. J. Polit. Econ. 106 (3), 574–601.

Mansfield, E.D., Milner, H.V., Rosendorff, B.P., 2002. Why democracies cooperate more: electoral control and international trade agreements. Int. Organ. 56 (3), 477–513.

Matschke, X., 2008. Costly revenue-raising and the case for favoring import-competing industries. J. Int. Econ. 74 (1), 143–157.

Matschke, X., Sherlund, S.M., 2006. Do labor issues matter in the determination of US trade policy? An empirical reevaluation. Am. Econ. Rev. 96, 405–421.

Mayda, A.M., 2008. Why are people more pro-trade than pro-migration? Econ. Lett. 101 (3), 160–163.

Mayda, A.M., Rodrik, D., 2005. Why are some people (and countries) more protectionist than others? Eur. Econ. Rev. 49 (6), 1393–1430.

Mayer, W., 1984. Endogenous tariff formation. Am. Econ. Rev. 74, 970–985.

Milner, H.V., Kubota, K., 2005. Why the move to free trade? Democracy and trade policy in the developing countries. Int. Organ. 59 (1), 107–143.

Mitra, D., 1999. Endogenous lobby formation and endogenous protection: a long-run model of trade policy determination. Am. Econ. Rev. 89, 1116–1134.

Mitra, D., Thomakos, D.D., Ulubaşoğlu, M.A., 2002. Protection for sale? In a developing country: democracy vs. dictatorship. Rev. Econ. Stat. 84 (3), 497–508.

Muûls, M., Petropoulou, D., 2013. A swing state theory of trade protection in the Electoral College. Can. J. Econ./Rev. Can. Econ. 46 (2), 705–724.

O'Rourke, K.H., Taylor, A.M., 2007. Democracy and protectionism. In: Hatton, T.J., O'Rourke, K.H. (Eds.), The New Comparative Economic History: Essays in Honor of Jeffrey G. Williamson, MIT Press, Cambridge, MA, p. 193.

Osgood, I., 2012. Differentiated products, divided industries: a theory of firm preferences over trade liberalization. Mimeo, Harvard University.

Pandya, S., 2014. Trading Spaces: Foreign Direct Investment Regulation, 1970–2000. Cambridge University Press, New York, NY.

Pecorino, P., 1998. Is there a free-rider problem in lobbying? Endogenous tariffs, trigger strategies, and the number of firms. Am. Econ. Rev. 88 (3), 652–660.

Persson, T., Tabellini, G.E., 2002. Political Economics: Explaining Economic Policy. MIT Press, Cambridge, MA.

Plott, C.R., 1967. A notion of equilibrium and its possibility under majority rule. Am. Econ. Rev. 57, 787–806.

Ponzetto, G.A., 2011. Heterogeneous information and trade policy. CEPR Discussion Paper DP8726.

Potters, J., Sloof, R., Van Winden, F., 1997. Campaign expenditures, contributions and direct endorsements: the strategic use of information and money to influence voter behavior. Eur. J. Polit. Econ. 13 (1), 1–31.

Rodrik, D., 1995. Political economy of trade policy. In: Grossman, G., Rogoff, K. (Eds.), Handbook of International Economics. vol. 3. North Holland, Amsterdam, pp. 1457–1494.

Scheve, K.F., Slaughter, M.J., 2001. What determines individual trade-policy preferences? J. Int. Econ. 54 (2), 267–292.

Shiells, C.R., Stern, R.M., Deardorff, A.V., 1986. Estimates of the elasticities of substitution between imports and home goods for the united states. Weltwirtschaftliches Arch. 122 (3), 497–519.

Snyder, J.M., Strömberg, D., 2010. Press coverage and political accountability. J. Polit. Econ. 118 (2), 355–408.

Staiger, R.W., Tabellini, G., 1987. Discretionary trade policy and excessive protection. Am. Econ. Rev. 77, 823–837.

Strömberg, D., 2008. How the Electoral College influences campaigns and policy: the probability of being Florida. Am. Econ. Rev. 98 (3), 769–807.

Tavares, J., 2008. Trade, factor proportions, and political rights. Rev. Econ. Stat. 90 (1), 163–168.

Tovar, P., 2009. The effects of loss aversion on trade policy: theory and evidence. J. Int. Econ. 78 (1), 154–167.

CHAPTER 3

The Effects of Trade Policy

P.K. Goldberg*, N. Pavcnik†
*Yale University, New Haven, CT, United States
†Dartmouth College, Hanover, NH, United States

Contents

Abstract

The last two decades have witnessed a shift in the focus of international trade research from trade policy to other forms of trade frictions (eg, transportation, information and communication costs). Implicit in this development is the widespread view that trade policy no longer matters. We confront this view by critically examining a large body of evidence on the effects of trade policy on economically important outcomes. We focus on *actual* as opposed to *hypothetical* policy changes. We begin with a discussion of the methodological challenges one faces in the measurement of trade policy and identification of its causal effects. We then discuss the evidence on the effects of trade policy on a series of outcomes that include: (1) aggregate outcomes, such as trade volumes (and their price and quantity subcomponents), the extensive margin of trade, and static, aggregate gains from trade; (2) firm and industry performance, ie, productivity, costs, and markups; (3) labor markets, ie, wages, employment, and wage inequality; (4) long-run aggregate growth and poverty, secondary distortions, and misallocation, uncertainty. We conclude that the perception that trade policy is no longer relevant arises to a large extent from the inability to precisely measure the various forms of nontariff barriers that have replaced tariffs as the primary tools of trade policy. Better measurement is thus an essential prerequisite of policy-relevant research in the future. Despite measurement challenges and scant evidence on the impact of actual policy changes, existing evidence when properly interpreted points to large effects of trade policy on economically relevant outcomes, especially when trade policy interacts with other developments, eg, technological change. We point to areas and opportunities for further research and draw lessons from the past to apply to future studies.

Keywords

Trade policy, International trade, Firms and trade, Labor markets, Growth

JEL Classification Codes

F10, F13, F14, L11, F63, F66

1. INTRODUCTION

1.1 Does *Trade Policy* Matter?

In an influential study of the factors driving the growth of world trade, Baier and Bergstrand (2001) cite an equally influential quote by Krugman (1995):

> *Most journalistic discussion of the growth of world trade seems to view growing integration as driven by a technological imperative—to believe that improvements in transportation and communication technology constitute an irresistible force dissolving national boundaries. International economists, however, tend to view much, though not all, of the growth of trade as having essentially political causes, seeing its great expansion after World War II largely as a result of the removal of the protectionist measures that had constricted world markets since 1913 (p. 328).*

Twenty years later, the view that trade policy plays only a secondary role in the growing importance of international trade remains pervasive, with one difference: the view is no longer confined to journalistic circles but has now become dominant in academic research. Though most frequently expressed informally, during seminar and conference presentations, it is also reflected in the academic trade literature.

The main focus in recent academic work, both theoretical and empirical/quantitative, has been on "trade costs," which are often measured as iceberg costs. Such costs are typically backed out from empirical specifications that are informed by specific theoretical models without any attempt to relate them to actual trade policy measures. Of course, trade costs capture much more than trade policy. In fact a frequent claim is that the "backed out" trade costs appear to be much larger than the costs that observable trade policy restrictions alone would justify. However, without actually measuring the restrictiveness of trade policy measures, it is hard to determine what exactly is captured in trade costs. Part of the problem lies with the difficulties in the measurement of trade policy—an issue to which we will repeatedly come back to in the course of this chapter. These measurement challenges are compounded by the belief that "other trade costs," such as transportation, search, and communication costs that are not unique to cross-country trade, as well as productivity growth in less developed countries (most importantly, China), have been more important than trade policy in the last few decades. If this belief is true, any effort to carefully measure and study trade policy barriers would be a waste of time. The field is slowly moving toward the analysis of the spatial allocation of economic activity, which is akin more to economic geography than *international* trade. Even in studies that exploit specific trade policy changes, trade policy is more often an afterthought than the primary focus of analysis. Recent work on trade liberalization episodes in developing countries, for example, has used trade policy as an identification device—the interest has been less on the trade policy per se and more on the effects of increased trade (for which trade policy serves as an instrument). Similarly, in theoretical and quantitative work, trade policy changes are often used in counterfactual exercises in order to demonstrate the workings of a model, but there is little interest in the policy itself. Perhaps the most indicative sign of this attitude is the absence of any rigorous academic study of the recent "Buy American" clause of the Recovery Act. This dearth of policy-oriented research in international trade is to be contrasted with the plethora of academic papers in the fields of labor, public finance, health, education, and industrial organization that have studied specific policy changes (eg, "No-Child-Left-Behind" Act, Affordable Care Act, mergers, etc.). The only exception to this pattern is studies of trade agreements, which are by nature closely linked to trade policy and its institutions.

The view that commercial policy has become unimportant for world trade seems like an oxymoron in a field that would not exist without the existence of frictions to cross-border trade induced by policy (tariffs, nontariff barriers, different currencies, etc.). It begs the question of why this perspective has gained support among academics over the last two decades. Is it indeed the case that trade policy has become irrelevant, or is the shift of academic research away from trade policy simply the result of the difficulties and complexities associated with its measurement?

To a large extent, the postulated irrelevance of trade policy arises from the observation that, especially in the developed world, international trade has been already significantly liberalized. Lant Pritchett succinctly summarized this viewpoint in a recent interview with the magazine Reason (2008):

Relative to when I started working as a trade economist in the early 1980s, the world is completely liberalized. So the incremental gains from anything that could happen as a result of WTO negotiations are just infinitesimal.[a]

Taken at face value, Pritchett's claim suggests that commercial policy has in fact had significant effects in the past, and that its own success has rendered it irrelevant. However, early studies of the effects of trade policies and agreements from the 1970s and 1980s tend to report small effects of these policies (see Deardorff and Stern, 1986 for a review of this early evidence). Several later studies have employed gravity-equation-based approaches in order to identify the relative contributions of trade policies, reduction in transportation and other trade costs, and income growth or convergence of trading partners to the growth of trade, yielding mixed results. Among these studies, perhaps the best-known and most controversial is a study by Rose (2004) that claimed that GATT or WTO membership had no discernible effects on trade volumes. Though the results of this study were subsequently questioned and challenged in several follow-up papers,[b] the debate they inspired pointed to a concern that is distinct from the standard measurement problems faced in the evaluation of trade policy: its fundamental endogeneity. In the extreme, this concern implies that trade policy is the result rather than the cause of changes in the trade environment; hence, it may not be surprising that some studies find that trade policy has no bite—by the time it comes into effect, trade changes may already be in motion.

Claims of the diminishing relevance of trade policy, which are based partly on the undisputed observation that significant liberalization has already taken place and partly on studies of the aggregate effects of trade agreements employing gravity-equation-type approaches, are to be contrasted with the evidence from occasional detailed studies of the effects of trade restrictions (or their removal) on specific industries: Voluntary Export Restraints on autos, antidumping suits, and the Multi-Fibre Agreement in apparel and textiles. Although narrower in scope, such studies have the benefit of careful measurement of trade policy and attention to institutional features of the economic environment that broader aggregate studies of trade policies may not permit. Several of these industry case studies have documented significant adjustments to trade policy changes along several margins, suggesting that the world may not be as liberalized as it seems and that failure to document significant effects of trade policies may instead be due to measurement and identification challenges rather than the absence of such effects.

Against this background, the question that this chapter poses and seeks to address is: "What is the evidence on the actual effects of trade policy, as opposed to other causes of changes in trade?" Does trade *policy* matter?

---

[a] This quote was originally used in Levy (2008).

[b] See Tomz et al. (2007) comment on Rose's paper or Subramanian and Wei (2007).

1.2 Conceptual Issues and Focus of This Chapter

Before we proceed, it is useful to delineate the focus of this chapter and clarify some conceptual issues.

We start this chapter by discussing the main methodological challenges one faces in the evaluation of trade policy and by describing the ways the literature has addressed them. Our discussion covers general methodological issues that arise in the evaluation of *any* type of trade policy, including specific policies that are the focus of other chapters in this Handbook. These methodological issues are addressed in Section 2. The most significant of them are briefly summarized below:

(a) *Measurement*: Measurement of trade policy is perhaps one of the toughest issues faced in the evaluation of trade policy, especially in cases where nontariff barriers are the primary trade policy instrument. The challenges in the measurement of trade policy raise the question of whether the world is truly liberalized, as many believe, or if this impression is misguided and due to our inability to measure the restrictions that really matter.

(b) *Aggregation and heterogeneity*: Even when trade restriction measures are available, as is the case with import tariffs, the available information comes at a highly disaggregate level. Economic analysis of these restrictions' effects often requires the researcher to aggregate the information to a higher level (eg, industry, region, or country). Given that there are many different ways to aggregate the information, aggregation would ideally be guided by a clear theoretical or conceptual framework. But this in turn raises the question of whether the results are not merely consistent with but also dictated by the framework. In addition, the conceptual framework underlying the analysis may imply homogenous or heterogeneous (across types of workers, firms, sectors of the economy, etc.) effects. Any analysis of heterogeneous effects needs to be consistent with the underlying framework.

(c) *Endogeneity of trade policy*: The endogeneity of policy is not an issue unique to trade policy. However, in contrast to the case of domestic policies, randomized experiments, the gold standard for identification in empirical work, are substantially harder, if not impossible, to carry out in the context of trade policy. Despite this disadvantage, trade policy has at times the advantage of plausibly economically exogenous, quasi-experimental variation induced by events that are outside the control of specific industries or lobbies within a specific country (eg, IMF interventions that dictated the pace and scope of trade liberalization, WTO accession, etc.). Nevertheless, even when trade policy is plausibly economically exogenous, in the sense that it was not set deliberately in response to certain economic developments, the concern about econometric endogeneity (ie, omitted variable bias, effect of preexisting trends, etc.) remains and must be adequately addressed.

(d) *Anticipation and uncertainty about trade policy*: If a trade policy change is unanticipated, firms and consumers cannot change their behavior prior to the policy implementation. However, trade policy changes and agreements are often preannounced, so that firms and consumers may adjust their behavior in anticipation of the announced policy change. In addition, trade reforms and agreements are presumed to reduce the uncertainty about the trading environment. An agreement that leads to small changes in the levels of trade restrictions, but large declines in uncertainty about trade policy, could in principle have large effects on trade flows and other outcomes. Inference about the trade policy effects therefore needs to take into account behavioral responses due to anticipation or uncertainty about trade policy changes.

The second issue that arises in an assessment of the effects of trade policy is: effects on what? In Section 3, we begin by reviewing the evidence regarding the effects of trade policy on trade volumes. Such effects can be further decomposed to: (a) effects on traded quantities; (b) effects on prices; and (c) effects on the imports of new goods and varieties, ie, the extensive margin of trade. We then consider the evidence on the effects of trade policy on the static, aggregate gains from trade. The aforementioned analysis refers to aggregate outcomes. Next, we consider the impact of trade policy on specific parts of the economy. We discuss the effects of trade policy on firms (namely their productivity, costs, and markups) in Section 4 and on labor markets (namely wages, employment, and wage inequality) in Section 5.

Much of the literature on the above outcomes captures the static and short-run effects of trade policy. The long-run effects of trade policy are substantially harder to pin down empirically. As a result, arguments about dynamic long-run effects are often made based solely on principles and theoretical models, with little formal empirical support. In Section 6, we consider the (scant) evidence on long-run dynamic effects of trade policy on aggregate growth and poverty. Finally, in Section 7, we examine the impact of trade policy on outcomes that have traditionally not received much attention in the literature, yet, might play an important role. These include the effects of trade policy on secondary distortions and misallocation of resources as well as its effects of reducing uncertainty.

One of the main challenges of this chapter is determining how to pick and organize material from studies on the effects of trade policies across space and time. The focus of this chapter is primarily on *actual* (as opposed to hypothetical) policy changes; counterfactual analysis of hypothetical policy scenarios carried out within the framework of quantitative models of trade is covered in another chapter of this Handbook (see Ossa, 2016). Second, we focus on the time period following the creation of GATT and WTO. While a historical analysis of the effects of trade policy extending to earlier periods would be fascinating, it is only recently that the relevance of trade policy has been questioned. Examining the current relevance of trade policy to world trade requires a focus on more recent time periods and data. Third, we provide evidence on both developed and developing countries. Developing countries are still substantially less liberalized than developed countries, and the role of international trade in their growth and development remains one of the most interesting and policy-relevant questions. Finally, we primarily discuss evidence based on studies of broad, large-scale trade liberalizations. We focus on these reforms because we aim to minimize the overlap with other chapters in this Handbook, which concentrate on specific trade policy instruments, including preferential trade agreements, antidumping duties, WTO rules and clauses, and other nontariff barriers to trade. We occasionally draw on lessons from industry case studies of trade policy as such studies offer the advantages of deeper institutional understanding and better measurement.

Overall, the main message of our chapter is that for international trade to remain a policy-relevant field, it needs to focus on better measurement. If the main message of the Leamer and Levinsohn (1995) in the 1995 Handbook of International Economics Chapter was "Estimate, don't test!" Our message 20 years later is: "Measure before you estimate!"

2. METHODOLOGY

2.1 Overview of Methodology

The empirical literature on the consequences of trade policy has embraced a variety of research methods to evaluate the effects of trade policy on outcomes of interest to international economists and policy makers. These research methods provide complementary ways to evaluate the consequences of trade policy. The ultimate choice of the research approach depends on the specific research question and the available data. One set of studies evaluates the consequences of trade policy through the lens of a structural model of behavior of consumers and producers and estimates key economic parameters that influence the responsiveness of consumers and firms to trade policy in this setting. Studies in this category include industry-specific studies of trade policy that use the approach pioneered in the industrial organization literature (Feenstra, 1995; Nevo and Whinston, 2010) and economy-wide quantitative studies of trade policy (Costinot and Rodríguez-Clare, 2014; Ossa, 2016). This approach is particularly useful to ex-ante evaluate a proposed trade policy change. Another advantage of this approach is that it can be used to evaluate the overall effects of an actual (or counterfactual) trade policy—operating through the mechanisms specified in the underlying model, as well as the policy's welfare consequences. The estimated effects from this approach depend on the assumptions of the underlying structural model and the consistency of the estimated behavioral parameters of demand, supply, and implied trade elasticities.

Trade policy could, in principle, also be evaluated through randomized control trials (RCTs), which are increasingly used to study the consequences of domestic policy. RCTs appear difficult, if not impossible, to implement in the context of trade policy, especially in the context of economy-wide trade policy liberalizations. That said, recent work has used randomized experiments to evaluate the effectiveness of export promotion programs (Atkin et al., 2014) and this approach could be more broadly applied to evaluate the effectiveness of export promotion programs of the World Bank and export promotion agencies or aid for trade schemes (Cadot et al., 2011). We do not focus on this method in the survey given its nascent state in the trade literature.

A third research approach estimates the consequences of actual trade policies by exploiting quasi-experimental research design (see Angrist and Krueger, 1999; Angrist and Pischke, 2010). The exact research design is guided by theory, but the identification of the causal effects of trade policy in these studies depends less on specific functional-form assumptions about the underlying demand, production, or market structure. Instead, the studies estimate the direct causal effect of actual trade policy on the outcomes of interest. This flexibility, however, comes at a cost. The quasi-experimental approach is not suited to evaluate welfare implications of actual trade policy changes or the overall effects of trade policy change, both of which require fully specified structural or quantitative models of trade.

Quasi-experimental studies of actual policy changes illuminate the causal effects of the particular policy in question. More generally, these studies provide evidence on the relevance of various mechanisms through which trade policy (and trade more broadly) affects consumer and producer welfare, without ex ante imposing such relationships on the data. These studies also provide evidence on the importance of mechanisms that are difficult to capture in quantitative studies of trade policy, including the effects of trade policy on firm-level productivity, innovation, markups, and elimination of institutional distortions. The evidence can in turn influence development of theoretical models that embed these features, which subsequently yield more informative counterfactual evaluations of future trade policy changes. Importantly, the empirical studies of the effects of trade policy on firms and workers has provided an important input for the development of trade models that examine the consequences of trade with firm heterogeneity (Bernard et al., 2003; Melitz, 2003; Yeaple, 2005) as well as models of labor market adjustment to trade costs that feature labor market frictions and/or heterogeneous firms (Artuc et al., 2010; Cosar, 2013; Dix-Carneiro, 2014; Goldberg, 2015; Harrison et al., 2011; Helpman et al., 2010; Kambourov, 2009).

We now briefly illustrate key ingredients of this research approach. These studies estimate the effect of trade policy using information from repeated cross-sectional or panel data on outcomes of interest (eg, firm-level performance measures, wages of individuals, firm-employee match, etc.) that spans the period before, during, and after a policy implementation.[c] The outcomes of interest are related to cross-sectional and time-series variation in trade policy because of the exposure of the relevant economic agents to policy

---

[c] To this end, studies have taken advantage of increased availability of data sets with detailed information about the outcomes and characteristics of firms, individuals, households, and, most recently, administrative employer–employee matches.

through industry affiliation, produced or consumed products, or spatial location. The causal effect of trade policy is hence identified based on differential exposure of economic agents to implemented trade policy.

The variation in trade policy across cross-sectional units and time is only helpful for identifying the effects of trade policy in the presence of some type of friction and/or heterogeneity in exposure to policy change. Consider empirical studies that aim to identify the effects of trade policy on labor markets in a frictionless world, as in a Heckscher-Ohlin model of trade. With a perfectly integrated national labor market, the effects of trade policy on workers operate at the country level, yielding one observation per trade liberalization episode (see Goldberg and Pavcnik, 2007). In principle, the effects of trade policy could then be identified by exploiting cross-country variation in trade exposure, or by using time-series variation in a country's exposure to trade. In practice, such approaches rarely yield credible results, as there are many unobserved factors that vary across countries or over time (eg, other aggregate trends or reforms) that could contaminate causal inference. In such a setting, the effects of trade policy can only be evaluated in a fully specified structural model of trade via counterfactual simulations (see Porto, 2006 as an example). Alternatively, if the mobility of workers is restricted across industries (as in Ricardo-Viner model) or across regions of a country (see Kovak, 2013; Topalova, 2010), some workers will be more exposed to trade policy changes than others due to their industry affiliation or location. This is akin to assuming industry or region-specific labor markets, with the degrees of freedom in the estimation corresponding to the number of industries or local markets per trade liberalization episode. In this setting, the effects of trade policy can be identified through differential exposure of workers in different industries (or regions) to trade policy changes.

Frictions and heterogeneity in responses to policy are not simply a convenient modeling assumption, but realistic (see the evidence surveyed in Autor et al., 2013; Goldberg and Pavcnik, 2007; Kovak, 2013; Pierce and Schott, 2015; Topalova, 2010 for different labor market frictions). The exact specification of how the variation in trade policy is related to outcomes of interest across industries, products, and space depends on the question at hand and the underlying theoretical model (see Goldberg and Pavcnik, 2005; Kovak, 2013; Topalova, 2010) for three alternative approaches in the literature on trade policy and labor markets. Furthermore, there is no harm in relying on assumptions about frictions for identification. If the assumptions about the frictions or heterogeneity are not valid (meaning workers can easily move across industries and locations or that firms' industry affiliation or underlying heterogeneity in productivity is irrelevant), the estimates based on this approach will show no systematic relationship between trade policy changes and the outcomes of interest. Thus, the main limitation of relying on differential exposure of economic agents to trade policy to identify its causal effects is not that the approach is not valid if the assumptions regarding the differential exposure are not valid, but that this approach by its nature will generally reveal only the relative and not absolute effects of a policy change. The latter require a theoretical framework within which the relative effects can be interpreted.

Irrespective of the particular approach used, the evaluation of the causal effects of trade policy faces several methodological challenges, including the measurement of trade policy, aggregation issues, endogeneity of trade policy, and other identification concerns. These are discussed in Section 2.2.1.

2.2 Methodological Challenges

2.2.1 Measurement of Trade Policy

Measurement of trade policy is one of the toughest issues in the evaluation of trade policy, especially in cases where nontariff barriers are the primary trade policy instrument. Domestic regulations and standards, which act as barriers to international trade, also affect our ability to assess the extent to which international trade is free. Consider the automobile market within the European Union. Imports of automobiles within the European Union are not subject to import tariffs. However, until very recently, country-specific requirements on car specifications, national car registration rules, and a selective and exclusive distribution system restricted international trade in automobiles within the single market.[d] The challenges in the measurement of trade policy raise the question of whether the world is truly liberalized, or whether this impression is misguided and due to our inability to measure restrictions to trade that really matter. Multicountry, multiindustry studies are particularly prone to measurement issues. Because of the scope of their analyses, these studies are more affected by data limitations regarding the measurement of trade policy as measures of trade policy restrictiveness are often not comparable across industries, countries, and time.

The measurement of trade policy is challenging even when the definition of trade policy is confined to traditional tariff and nontariff barriers to international trade. In part, the measurement is affected by the lack of detailed comprehensive information on trade barriers for a large set of countries prior to 1980s (Anderson and van Wincoop, 2004). The United Nations' TRAINS database or the World Bank's WITS database is systematically available only from 1989 onward. In general, measures of tariffs are more readily available than measures of nontariff barriers to trade. In addition, for many countries, these databases do not provide comprehensive information on trade policy measures. For example, fewer than 20% of countries report tariffs, nontariff barriers to trade, and trade flows in any given year (Anderson and van Wincoop, 2004).

---

[d] See Goldberg and Verboven (2001, 2005) for a discussion of these restrictions in the European car market. More recently, Miravete et al. (2015) report that the greenhouse emissions policy enacted by European regulators gave a competitive advantage to European auto makers over foreign imports by enabling the adoption of diesel cars, and that this non-tariff policy was equivalent to a 20% import tariff; effectively cutting imports in half.

In situations in which trade policy measures exist, systematic measurement of their restrictiveness across products, industries, countries, and time is difficult, especially when policies curtail international trade through nonprice-based instruments. As price-based measures, ad-valorem tariffs are easiest to measure and most comparable across industries and time, because they restrict international trade by imposing a tax on imported products that varies proportionally to the product's price. On the other hand, policy instruments such as specific tariffs, which are imposed as a per-unit surcharge on an import, or quantitative restrictions on imports, vary with underlying market conditions.[e] The comparability of measured trade policy across countries, industries, and time can therefore affect inference about the effects of trade policy in cross-country and multiindustry studies. This is less of an issue in studies that examine the effects of a particular nontariff barrier in an industry, for example, the literature on the effects of the Multi-Fibre Agreement (Brambilla et al., 2010; Harrigan and Barrows, 2009; Khandelwal et al., 2013), studies of antidumping (Blonigen and Prusa, 2003, 2016), and studies of VERs in the automobile industry (Berry et al., 1999; Goldberg, 1995; Verboven, 1996). These studies incorporate the relevant industry-specific institutional and regulatory details, and can appropriately capture variations in industry-specific market conditions that affect the restrictiveness of implemented policy.

Data availability and measurement issues, combined with the timing and nature of large-scale trade liberalizations, help explain why most of the recent empirical studies that examine the effects of trade policy changes from large-scale, economy-wide trade liberalizations focus on trade liberalization episodes in less-developed countries rather than in developed economies. Import tariffs in many developed countries, which the WTO estimates averaged between 20% and 30% in ad-valorem terms prior to the first WTO negotiation round, were reduced in early rounds of the GATT/WTO negotiations. The bound tariffs averaged 8.9% by the end of the Dillon negotiation round in 1962, and 4.1% by the conclusion of the Tokyo Round in 1978 (WTO, 2007).[f] These liberalizations preceded the collection of readily available data on detailed trade flows and surveys of firms and workers, both of which are needed for the analysis of the effects of trade policy.[g] In addition, tariffs were often replaced by NTBs, including import quotas (such as the Multi-Fibre Agreement in the apparel and textiles and the VERs in the US automobile industry in the 1980s), and antidumping duties. Many studies have found that these nontariff barriers to trade have severely restricted trade, sometimes even prior to

[e] For example, industry-level coverage ratios, a commonly used measure of prevalence of nontariff barriers, may overstate restrictiveness of these measures in industries in which import quotas might not be binding.
[f] See tables 6 and 7 in WTO (2007). The countries include the United States, Japan, the United Kingdom, and the members of the European Economic Community at the time.
[g] For example, the analysis in Rose (2004) is based on a data set that does not contain information on periods prior to the initial 1947 WTO round and that covers very few countries in the 1950s and 1960s.

the imposition of the barriers.[h] To the extent that one cannot comprehensively control for these NTBs, the identification of trade policy effects, especially in multisector and multicountry studies that include developed countries, is challenging. With a few notable exceptions, most empirical studies on developed countries have focused on the effects of import competition or exporting rather than the effects of trade policy on outcomes of interest. A handful of studies have examined the effects of recent trade agreements, such as NAFTA and CUFTA, in developed countries.[i]

In studies that focus on developing countries, which encompass most of the recent studies on consequences of trade policy, these measurement issues present less of a problem. Most developing countries did not actively participate in earlier GATT/WTO negotiation rounds. As a result, import tariffs remained high in many of these countries at the onset of their large-scale trade liberalizations since the 1980s. For example, ad-valorem tariffs averaged over 50% in Colombia and over 80% in India prior to their trade liberalizations. Trade liberalizations in these countries, therefore, are characterized by large declines in import tariffs. In many cases, nontariff barriers were also reduced, and declines in tariffs were highly correlated with declines in NTBs (see Goldberg and Pavcnik, 2005 for Colombia's trade liberalization). These characteristics of the trade liberalization episodes in less-developed countries facilitate the measurement and identification of the effects of trade policy.

2.2.2 Aggregation and Heterogeneity

A related issue is the issue of aggregation and heterogeneity. National governments apply trade policy to products at a disaggregated level, dictated by national, or international trade product classification schemes (such as the now commonly used harmonized system). However, economic analysis of the effect of these restrictions often requires the researcher to aggregate the information to a higher level (eg, industry, region, bilateral trade flow, or country) to map it to the level at which economic outcomes of interest is measured.

Given that there are many different ways to aggregate the information, aggregation would ideally be guided by a clear theoretical or conceptual framework. But this in turn raises the question of whether the results are not merely consistent with but also dictated by the framework. Kovak (2013), for example, uses a specific factors model to construct a measure of a region's exposure to trade liberalization and shows that this theoretically founded measure differs from the measures used in prior work (Topalova, 2007, 2010). However, his measure is formally correct only within the specific-factors model

---

[h] See Staiger and Wolak (1994) for such effects of antidumping duties, Blonigen and Prusa (2003) and Blonigen and Prusa (2016) for surveys on antidumping and antidumping duties. See Harrigan and Barrows (2009) and Brambilla et al. (2010) on Multi-Fibre Agreement; Goldberg (1995) and Berry et al. (1999) for VERs. Feenstra (1995) reviews several of these earlier studies.

[i] See Trefler (2004), Lileeva and Trefler (2010), and Bernard et al. (2006).

he assumes. This raises the question of whether the conclusions of his analysis would be robust to other theoretical frameworks. In addition, the conceptual framework underlying the analysis of trade policy may imply homogenous or heterogeneous (across types of workers, firms, sectors of the economy, etc.) effects. Any analysis of heterogeneous effects needs to be consistent with the underlying framework (see Dix-Carneiro and Kovak, 2015a; Kovak, 2013).

In practice, aggregation choices are often dictated by available industry or product concordances and the level of aggregation at which variables of interest are collected. Imperfect concordance mappings across classifications introduce measurement error in the variables of interest. This is particularly problematic in studies covering many countries from different data sources. In addition, product and industry-level classifications in firm-level, worker-level, or household-level data sets tend to be substantially more aggregated than the categories to which trade policy is applied. Even with a perfect mapping across categories, aggregation of the relevant data to the industry level will lead one to ignore variation in trade policy within an industry. Both of these measurement issues may attenuate the estimated effects of trade policy.

2.2.3 Endogeneity of Trade Policy

A key challenge in examining the causal effects of trade policy is that trade policy may itself be the outcome of economic conditions. Economic theory suggests that economic conditions affect the timing of trade liberalizations and their reversals (Bagwell and Staiger, 2003) as well as cross-sectional patterns of protection across industries (Grossman and Helpman, 1994). These predictions are supported by abundant empirical evidence (Rodrik, 1995). More recent studies also suggest that global fragmentation of production provides additional incentives for firms and industries to influence trade policy (Blanchard, 2007, 2010; Blanchard and Matschke, 2015; Blanchard et al., 2016).

The economic endogeneity of trade policy provides one potential explanation for the profession's perception that trade policy does not matter, particularly in cases where trade reforms are enacted ex post, in order to ratify developments in trade that were already in motion. To illustrate the problem, consider first a case where trade barriers are imposed in order to halt a rise in imports. As a result, imports drop. In this case, trade policy has a clear effect on imports, though the enactment of the policy was endogenous to the increase in imports. The policy endogeneity in this instance would not lead one to conclude that the policy was ineffective. But now consider an alternative scenario, in which the domestic industry is doing well and does not feel threatened by imports. As a result, no one objects to trade liberalization and trade barriers fall. Suppose that imports were unaffected by this liberalization. The economic endogeneity of trade policy would pose a big problem for inference in this case. The lack of relationship between trade policy and imports would be due to the endogeneity of trade policy: the policy was only enacted because it was expected to have no effects. Trade policy in this case ratifies changes in trade that were already happening for other reasons.

The above example does not imply that a truly random decrease in trade barriers would have no effect on imports. But it does suggest that in practice, the enacted trade policies may have no observable impact because of their economic endogeneity. In a systematic study of the effects of endogeneity of trade policy on import penetration for the United States, Trefler (1993) finds that the absolute magnitude of the effect of nontariff barriers to trade on import penetration substantially increases once the empirical framework accounts for the endogeneity of trade policy. Of course, the effect could also go the other way: the economic endogeneity of trade policy could bias estimates of the effects of trade policy upward, overstating the true effects of trade policy. Consider countries that foresee future increases in mutual trade and as a result form a preferential regional trade agreement. In this instance, empirical estimates of the effect of policy that do not account for endogeneity of agreement's formation, overstate the effects of trade agreements on trade flows.

This discussion suggests that it is informative to study both types of effects of trade policy: the effects of observed trade policy (without corrections for endogeneity) and the effects of exogenous variation in trade policy. The former tells us what actually happened. Did trade policy matter, or did it come too late to have effects? The latter is useful for normative implications and for assessing the effects of counterfactual scenarios, including potential further liberalization and liberalization in other settings.

With this latter goal in mind, studies of the causal effects of actual trade policies rely on institutional details of trade policy changes to determine whether such changes were plausibly economically exogenous. The arguments for economic exogeneity are carefully established on a case-by-case basis. In many instances, researchers have taken advantage of plausibly economically exogenous, quasi-experimental variation in trade policy induced by events that are outside the control of specific industries or lobbies within a specific country. Because less-developed countries did not actively participate in early GATT/WTO negotiation rounds, many of these liberalizations have been implemented in less-developed countries. They include unilateral liberalizations that occurred as a result of IMF interventions that dictated the pace and scope of the reforms (India's trade liberalization in 1991), WTO accessions (Mexico in 1985), unilateral liberalizations where the government's goal was to reduce dispersion of tariffs across industries to a more uniform level (Colombia in late 1980s and early 1990s), and the signing of a broad trade agreement that did not involve negotiations over particular tariff lines (the US–Vietnam Bilateral Trade Agreement in 2001).

Importantly, these liberalizations not only lowered the levels of tariffs but also led to plausibly economically exogenous differential changes in trade policy changes across industries. It is this variation in trade policy across industries that empirical studies exploit to identify the causal effects of trade policy on outcomes of interest. Take for example, the case of India's trade liberalization. Declines in India's tariffs varied widely across industries and were largely set as part of the IMF conditions in 1991, rather than set to reflect the underlying industry-specific conditions across India's industries (see Khandelwal and Topalova, 2011). So, while the timing of India's trade liberalization was clearly a function of existing economic conditions (after all, it was induced by India's balance of payments crisis in the aftermath of the US–Iraq war), the magnitudes of the industry-specific tariff changes were not influenced by economic conditions in India's industries at the time of trade reform.[j]

So far, we have discussed the economic endogeneity of trade policy arising from the political economy of trade protection (ie, trade policy is enacted in response to economic conditions and lobbying). Equally important is the issue of econometric endogeneity. Even when trade policy is plausibly economically exogenous in the sense that it was not set deliberately in response to certain economic developments, the concern about econometric endogeneity remains and needs to be adequately addressed. Econometric endogeneity may arise from omitted variable bias when there are other concurrent policy reforms or demand and supply shocks on the world markets. General equilibrium considerations further complicate the analysis. Bagwell and Staiger (2005, 2014) show that two countries could receive the same MFN tariff cut and yet experience different changes in their export volumes, depending on whether they also cut their own import tariffs. So a careful empirical analysis needs to control for changes in the trade policies of a country's trading partners that may have occurred as part of a reciprocal exchange for a tariff cut. Another concern is preexisting trends in the outcomes of interest that might be spuriously correlated with trade policy changes. To this end, studies of trade policy have used a wide range of falsification or placebo tests to check the validity of assumptions needed to identify the effects of trade policy. For example, if data on outcomes of interest are available prior to the implementation of trade policy, one can rule out spurious preexisting trends by showing that trade policy does not have a significant impact on outcomes of interest prior to its implementation (see Edmonds et al., 2010; Topalova, 2010).[k] Likewise, one can show that the implemented trade policy had effects only on economic agents who were affected by the policy, but not on unaffected agents (for example, see Edmonds et al., 2010; McCaig and Pavcnik, 2014; Pierce and Schott, 2015).

---

[j] Khandelwal and Topalova (2011) formally show lack of correlation between industry-specific tariff changes and preform industry characteristics and conditions. This lack of correlation is also consistent with the institutional details of India's trade policy. Gang and Pandey (1996) suggest that India's trade policy prior to liberalization was largely set as part of India's Second Economic Plan after the Independence. Subsequently, trade policy levels were not adjusted to reflect particular economic conditions across industries. It is therefore not surprising that industry-specific changes are not correlated with industry's conditions in 1991.

[k] Time-invariant spurious correlation between the outcome of interest and preexisting patterns in the levels of trade protection across industries or products can be controlled for with the inclusion of industry (or product) fixed effects if the data has an industry (or product)-level panel dimension.

The above discussion emphasizes the causality of trade policy in studies that evaluate the effects of actual trade policy changes. The issues of causality and endogeneity are just as important in the studies that evaluate counterfactual effects of trade policy within a structural or quantitative model of trade. The estimated counterfactual effects of trade policy depend crucially on the consistent estimates of key parameters of the model (such as the trade elasticity) and the plausibility of the underlying assumptions of the structural model.

Industry-specific studies of trade policy directly model trade policy within the context of the particular industry under study and evaluate the effects of actual and counterfactual trade policies through simulations. In recent quantitative models of trade however, the effects of trade policy, especially on welfare, are typically evaluated by considering a counterfactual in which the economy moves from autarky to a frictionless world. The question then is whether such a counterfactual is informative about the consequences of declines in trade costs associated with actual policies. Would a counterfactual in which trade costs decline from a more to less restrictive trade regime yield similar conclusions about the effects of trade on welfare or income distribution? In addition, counterfactual simulations in the above models abstract from political economy concerns that may be key in understanding the patterns of trade protection and the effects of reducing it. Consider for example the following scenario. A counterfactual simulation of the move from autarky to free trade in a simple $2 \times 2 \times 2$ Heckscher-Ohlin model would predict a decline in income inequality between educated and less-educated workers in unskilled labor-abundant countries. This is based on the premise that the protected sectors in an unskilled labor-abundant country would be those that use unskilled labor relatively more intensively. However, the *actual* structure of protection in several less-developed countries, such as Colombia and Mexico, was such that tariffs were higher in more unskilled-labor-intensive industries. The actual trade liberalizations implemented in these countries in the past three decades led to bigger declines in tariffs in more unskilled-labor-intensive industries (see Goldberg and Pavcnik, 2007; Hanson and Harrison, 1999). In this setting, the simple counterfactual considered above that relies on a comparison of autarky to the free trade equilibrium, without taking into account the political economy of protection, would fail to capture the effects of the actual trade policy that was implemented.

2.2.4 Anticipation of Trade Reform and Reduction in Uncertainty About Trading Environment

The estimates of the effects of implemented trade policies are also affected by the anticipation of trade policy. The effects of trade policy are estimated by examining how outcomes of interest change after the policy is implemented relative to the period before policy implementation. The implicit assumption in this research design is that trade policy only has an effect on the outcome of interest after its implementation.

If a trade policy is unanticipated (as it was the case in India's 1991 trade liberalization), the quasi-experimental research design will fully capture its effects because firms and consumers cannot change their behavior prior to implementation. If a trade policy is anticipated (and its implementation credible), firms and consumers might react to it before its implementation. For example, in anticipation of trade liberalization, firms might change their investment decisions, either delaying them or expediting them. Likewise, consumers might delay purchases of durable products until after the trade liberalization is implemented. Anticipation is a greater concern in studies that use higher frequency data. Depending on the situation in question, it could lead to either overestimates or underestimates of the policy effects. However, as long as the data include observations that cover a long enough period prior to the announcement and implementation of a particular policy, one can directly examine whether the policy affected behavior prior to its implementation, and accordingly adjust the estimated effects.

A related issue is trade policy uncertainty (see Handley, 2014; Handley and Limão, 2015; Pierce and Schott, 2015). Uncertainty may arise among other reasons because the actual tariffs that are applied in any particular period are distinct from the tariff bounds that represent the highest possible tariffs a country can apply according to a specific trade agreement or the WTO. Even if the actual applied tariffs are low in a specific setting, firms, and consumers may fear tariff hikes in the future. Trade agreements can reduce the uncertainty about trade policy by committing countries to a specific trade policy regime more permanently. To the extent that uncertainty about trade policy affects firms' and consumers' decisions on market entry, investment, and purchases of durable products, the effects of trade policy changes on trade flows and other outcomes of interest may be larger than suggested by the magnitudes of the trade barrier reductions. Consider for example recent trade agreements such as NAFTA, CUFTA, and the Chinese entry into the WTO. The associated trade reforms did not lead to large declines in tariff levels. But despite the small tariff changes, these trade agreements may have had significant effects through the elimination (or reduction) of uncertainty.

These methodological challenges notwithstanding, recent research has found creative ways to address them and make significant progress toward assessing the effects of trade policies. This evidence is discussed in the next sections.

3. THE EFFECTS OF TRADE POLICY: TRADE VOLUME, PRICES, EXTENSIVE MARGIN, AND GAINS FROM TRADE

3.1 Effects on Trade Volume

3.1.1 Evidence on Effects on Trade Volume

We start by revisiting an old question on the topic of trade policy: To what extent can the growth of world trade since World War II be attributed to trade liberalization? Baier and Bergstrand (2001) used a gravity-equation-framework to run a horserace between several factors contributing to world trade growth: income, tariff reductions, transport costs, and income convergence. Baier and Bergstrand examined data for 16 OECD countries between the late 1950s and late 1980s and concluded that trade policy played a critical role in the growth of trade. According to their results, real GDP growth explains approximately 67–69% of the trade growth, tariff reductions and preferential trade agreements explain 23–26%, transport cost reductions explain 8–9%, and real GDP convergence is found to have no effect at all. Baier and Bergstrand highlight in their discussion the fact that tariff reductions are found to have approximately three times the effect of reductions in transport costs; hence, lending support to the view that trade policy is more important than changes in transport costs. However, they acknowledge that the explanatory factors they include in the gravity equation explain only 40% of the variation in trade flow growth, which leaves the possibility open that other factors, including technological advances (which may have reduced communication and search costs in international markets), played an important role in trade growth. Finally, due to data constraints, their results cover only 16 highly developed OECD countries that experienced dramatic tariff reductions post-World War II. In addition, the study has little to say about the role of nontariff barriers or the impact of trade policy in less developed countries that did not experience the same degree of tariff liberalization. Despite these limitations of sample coverage, the main message of Baier and Bergstrand's work is that trade policy (ie, tariff reductions) matters.

Yi's (2003) study of the determinants of world trade growth reached a very different conclusion. Yi considers a more extended sample than Baier and Bergstrand, but more importantly, he extends his empirical analysis to more recent years that cover the period between the mid-1980s and 2000s. He points out two facts that are hard to reconcile with the view that tariff reductions were instrumental in the growth of world trade: (1) First, tariff rates declined by only 11% after the mid-1960s, yet trade grew rapidly in subsequent decades. In order to explain this rapid trade growth, one would have to appeal to implausibly large trade elasticities. (2) Second, and perhaps more importantly, the tariff reductions were larger before than after the mid-1980s; yet, trade growth was much smaller in the earlier than in the later period. In order to explain these trade patterns, one would have to assume a trade elasticity (elasticity of exports with respect to tariffs) of seven for the 1962–1985 period and an elasticity of 50 for the 1986–1999 period. Traditional trade models have a hard time generating such nonlinearity in trade elasticities, and in general, it is hard to come up with an explanation that would justify such nonlinear effects. The main take away from this evidence is that there must have been something else than tariff reductions alone driving the growth in trade.

Yi proceeds to show, both theoretically and quantitatively (through calibration), that these patterns can be explained through vertical specialization: vertical trading chains spanning many countries where each country specializes in a particular stage of a good's production sequence. Importantly, he shows that vertical specialization and multiple border crossing can generate a magnified and nonlinear response to tariff reductions.

Consider, for example, a product that has five stages of production, each produced in a different country. When tariffs fall by 1%, the cost of producing this good will fall by 5%, in contrast to the 1% decrease of a standard traded good produced in a single country. This magnified cost decline will lead to a magnified response of trade. This magnification is solely related to the intensive margin. In addition, there is an extensive margin: as tariffs fall, vertical specialization will start occurring in cases where it was previously not profitable due to high trade costs. This will lead to an additional magnification effect and generate a nonlinear response of trade flows to tariffs.

Yi's argument is not that trade policy does not matter, but rather than it matters most *in interaction* with vertical specialization. Vertical specialization may be to a large extent technologically driven, but as Yi shows, it responds to trade liberalization. Hence, the main takeaway from Yi's work is twofold. First, empirical work that tries to assess the importance of trade policy by relating trade growth to tariff reductions may seriously understate the true effect of trade policy, as trade policy may affect trade flows in interaction with other factors, including vertical specialization. The significance of these interactions has likely increased over time. Second, the increasing importance of vertical specialization in world trade suggests that the focus on export or import flows as measures of trade may be misguided and understate the true extent of trade. Measures based on value added are thus more appropriate and realistic as they do justice to the sequential and fragmented nature of the production process.

The latter point is made most explicitly in a recent paper by Johnson and Noguera (2014), which examines both value-added and gross exports over the last four decades (1970–2009) and seeks to identify the driving forces behind the changing patterns in cross-border trade. The authors use the ratio of value added to gross exports as a measure of international vertical specialization and document that this ratio has fallen significantly (in the range of 10 percentage points) over the last four decades. This aggregate number masks significant heterogeneity across countries and sectors. The decline in the valued-added ratio implies that double counting in gross trade data (due to multiple border crossing of traded goods) is more pervasive in recent years than in the past. When the authors relate the value added to gross export ratio to regional trade agreements, they find that trade agreements have a substantial impact on the decline of this ratio. By simulating a gravity model with input–output linkages, the authors further show that changes in trade frictions following trade agreements do not only explain changes in the bilateral trade patterns but also account for approximately 20% of the global decline in the ratio of value added to gross exports. They conclude that trade frictions and regional trade agreements play a first-order role in explaining changes in bilateral and global trade patterns and suggest revisiting many classic questions regarding the role of trade frictions and policy from a value-added perspective.

To conclude, the message of recent work that has taken the international fragmentation of production seriously is not that trade policy is second order in explaining the explosion of global trade in recent decades. On the contrary, the message of this work is that trade policy has played a critical role, but only in interaction with other (possibly technologically driven) developments that have contributed to the rise of vertical specialization in the production process. The implication for empirical work is that trade policy measures should enter empirical specifications in interaction with other measures capturing vertical specialization and that—depending on the particular research question—it might be more appropriate to measure trade flows in valued added rather than gross terms.

3.1.2 Trade Growth vs Trade Elasticity and Gains from Trade

Independent of the question of how large the effects of tariffs or other trade policy frictions on trade flows are, Yi's analysis raises another interesting question: Even if trade policy matters for trade volume, does it matter for the gains from trade? In addition, are "trade flows" what we should be focusing on if we want to demonstrate the relevance of trade policy?

The reason Yi's work brings up this question is that his analysis was motivated by the observation that the growth of trade in the last three decades implied implausibly large trade elasticities if one were to explain the trade growth by tariff reductions alone. But large elasticities imply (conditional on trade volume) small gains from trade. One cannot have it both ways: if trade policy generates large increases in trade, then it also generates small (static) gains from trade. We will revisit this issue when we examine the evidence on the impact of trade policy on the aggregate gains from trade. For now, we simply point out that showing that trade policy played an important role in the increase of world trade does not imply that trade policy matters from a welfare point of view. And vice versa, a finding of small effects of trade policy changes on trade volume does not imply that the gains associated with these trade policy changes are small.

3.1.3 Trade Elasticity and Trade Policy

As we conclude the topic of the effects of trade policy on trade flows and gradually move toward an analysis of its effects on the gains from trade, one more observation is necessary. Recent work on the gains from trade (Arkolakis et al., 2010) has highlighted the importance of the reduced-form trade elasticity in computing the aggregate gains from trade. Given that the trade elasticity relates—by its very definition—changes in trade flows to changes in trade costs, exploiting observable changes in trade policy (ie, tariff reductions) seems an obvious way to credibly estimate it. What trade elasticity estimates do changes in trade policy imply?

Perhaps surprisingly, estimates of the trade elasticity based on *actual* trade policy changes are scarce, and the few that exist are all over the place. As discussed in Hillberry and Hummels (2013) in their review of the trade elasticity parameters used in the literature, the "trade elasticity" is usually estimated either based on cross-sectional (cross-country and cross-industry) variation of trade costs other than trade policy barriers or based on time series variation stemming from exchange rate fluctuations. Studies that rely on cross-sectional variation are often labeled "micro" studies and yield high values for the trade elasticity (around five or higher). Studies that rely on time-series variation are often identified as "macro" studies and yield low estimates for the trade elasticity, around one or lower. A standard explanation for these divergent results is that cross-sectional studies identify long-run effects corresponding to different steady states associated with different trade costs, while studies based on time-series variation capture only the short-run effects of changing trade costs. Economic agents have time to adjust in the long run so the long-run trade elasticity is larger than the short-run elasticity. While this explanation is appealing, it abstracts from the fact that the two types of studies rely on very different sources of variation, so that the different estimates could instead be due to these different sources of variation. Indicatively, Shapiro (2014) relies on panel data in order to estimate the trade elasticity. The use of panel data implies that his elasticity estimate should be best thought of as a short-run one; yet, his results are closer to the ones obtained by cross-sectional studies because he relies on similar sources of variation.

This review does not examine work on estimation of the trade elasticity, but given the central role that trade elasticity plays in a number of trade models and in welfare analysis, it is surprising that trade policy has not been exploited to a larger extent to identify this crucial parameter. To our knowledge, the only exceptions to this pattern are the work by Yi (2003)—who however calculated the trade elasticity implied by tariff reductions only to subsequently denounce it as implausible—and the estimates provided in recent work by Caliendo and Parro (2015). Caliendo and Parro estimate sectoral trade elasticities based on the import tariff reductions associated with NAFTA. The estimates displayed in table 1 of their paper display substantial heterogeneity, with trade elasticities ranging from 0.37 to 51.8! The authors reject the null hypothesis of a common elasticity across sectors. The heterogeneity of the estimates suggests that trade elasticity estimates may vary by sector, time, and country. This makes careful empirical work that exploits trade policy variation in order to identify the trade elasticity/ies more important. The fact that a key parameter in the trade literature is so rarely estimated based on trade policy variation speaks to the secondary role assigned to trade policy.

3.2 Effects on Prices

While studies on the effects of trade policy on trade flows abound, evidence on its effects on prices is rare. Traditional trade models feature either perfect competition or monopolistic competition with CES demand implying perfect pass-through of tariffs or other trade barrier changes to prices. Accordingly, there has been relatively little interest in examining the response of prices to trade reforms in the past. The standard premise has been that tariff or NTB reductions led to a proportional decrease in the prices of imported products.

This premise has been called into question in more recent work that has highlighted the relevance of variable markups. Before we examine the implications of variable markups for price adjustment, it is important to note that, absent a Metzler paradox,[1] a reduction of trade policy barriers would be expected to lead to lower prices in the importing country independent of the particular theoretical model underlying the analysis. This price reduction seems unambiguous in *qualitative* terms and is realized through several channels.

First, trade policy changes will directly impact the prices of imported goods. A reduction of tariffs, for example, will generally lead to a decline in the price of imports, though the exact magnitude of the decline will depend on market conditions. Second, a reduction of trade barriers exerts competitive pressure on the domestic producers of final products. Producers face a downward shift in the residual demand for their products accompanied by an increase in the price elasticity of the residual demand curve given the intensified import competition. With variable markups, these changes in the residual demand facing domestic producers imply lower markups and lower prices. This is the procompetitive effect of trade liberalization. In addition, one would expect a trade liberalization to also have a cost reduction effect. To the extent that the reduction of trade barriers affects products that are used as intermediate inputs in domestic production, one would expect a decline in the prices of these intermediate inputs. Further, trade liberalization may lead to improved firm efficiency (for example, through the elimination of X-inefficiencies, or the introduction of new products that contribute to lower costs), which will further lower costs. These cost reductions should also contribute to lower prices. In sum, the above considerations lead to the *qualitatively* unambiguous conclusion that a reduction of trade barriers should lead to lower prices in the importing country. The *quantitative* effect however is less clear and will depend on many factors regarding the demand, market structure, and competitive conditions.

A recent quantitative study of the effects of trade liberalization (Edmond et al., 2015) uses counterfactual simulations to quantify the procompetitive effect of trade policy and concludes that trade liberalization leads to lower markups and lower prices. But evidence on actual, as opposed to counterfactual, trade policy changes is scant. This is partly due to the fact that reliable data on prices are difficult to find and partly due to the aforementioned assumption that prices move one to one with trade policy changes, so that an examination of the price response is not necessary or particularly interesting. To our knowledge, only two recent studies have directly examined the price response to trade

---

[1] The Metzler paradox refers to the theoretical possibility that the domestic price of an imported good declines (rises) as a result of a tariff increase (decline). There is a theoretical literature that examines the conditions under which such a paradox can arise, but to our knowledge, there has been no empirical evidence of the Metzler paradox. Even if the Metzler paradox does not arise, so that the prices of imported products decline as a result of tariff reductions, the effects of the tariff cuts on the prices of domestically produced goods are less clear cut for the reasons discussed in this section.

liberalization: Topalova (2010) and De Loecker, Goldberg, Khandelwal, and Pavcnik (2016), henceforth DLGKP, both on India. Both studies found that domestic prices decline approximately 10% as a result of India's trade liberalization. However, this reduction is small relative to the cost reductions implied by the trade liberalization, which are substantial. The reason for the attenuated response of prices is that the pass-through of cost reductions to final goods prices is incomplete. This incomplete pass-through in turn implies rising markups. This result may seem counterintuitive at first, but it can be easily generated in many models featuring imperfect competition and demand with variable markups. The authors also report that once they condition on changes in marginal costs arising from trade liberalization, they can identify the procompetitive effect of trade liberalization: a decline in markups arising from the exposure of domestic producers to intensified competition. Hence, the results do not imply that this procompetitive effect does not exist, but rather that in their setting, the procompetitive effect is dominated by the incomplete pass-through effect associated with variable markups.

The possibility that prices respond only partially to trade policy changes is important for trade policy evaluation. Many key results in the literature have been derived under the assumption of complete price adjustment and need to be revisited once the possibility of incomplete adjustment is considered. As microdata on prices are becoming more widely available, this is an important question for future research. While it is too early to say whether the results of DLGKP generalize to other settings, it is instructive to draw a parallel to the macroliterature on price rigidities and incomplete exchange rate pass-through. This literature has repeatedly documented incomplete pass-through of exchange rate changes to prices, not only in the short, but also in the long-run, resulting in persistent deviations from the Law of One Price. Despite this evidence, the microoriented trade literature has for years proceeded under the assumption that price rigidities do not exist and that prices fully respond to trade policy changes.[m] The insights from these two literatures should be merged in order to assess the actual effects of trade policy changes. Examining the actual response of prices to trade policy changes is a first step in this direction.

3.3 Effects on the Extensive Margin

If trade policy has attenuated effects on prices, how can it have large effects on trade quantities and volumes? One possibility is that trade policy changes lead to the trade of new products and varieties. Following the convention in the trade literature, we will use the

---

[m] An important exception to this pattern is a recent paper by Atkin and Donaldson (2015) that examines the implications of incomplete pass-through for intranational prices in Ethiopia and Nigeria. We do not discuss this paper here since it does not consider any actual trade policy changes, but it should be noted that its results do have implications for the effects of trade policy, and in particular, for how trade barrier reductions would affect prices in ports vs inland locations, especially in developing countries.

term "product" to describe genuinely new products, and the term "variety" to refer to a product/source country pair. For example, if a policy change leads to the import of bananas, and bananas were previously not imported, bananas will be considered a new product. If bananas were already imported, but a trade policy change leads to imports from a new country, such as Ecuador, Ecuadorian bananas will be referred to as a new variety. In addition to the introduction of new imported products and varieties, trade policy may also indirectly lead to the introduction of new domestic products. This could occur if the technology and imported inputs for producing certain products domestically were unavailable or too expensive prior to trade liberalization and the reduction of trade barriers made their production economically viable. And vice versa, trade policy could lead to the discontinuation of production of certain domestic products or varieties, if these could no longer compete with imports following a reduction in import barriers.[n]

The empirical trade literature has extensively investigated the effects of trade on the extensive margin (see Broda and Weinstein, 2006; Feenstra, 1994). However, the majority of the work has focused on the impact of *trade*, not *trade policy*. Both Feenstra and Broda and Weinstein rely on an identification strategy that does not use any information on trade policy. They find very large effects of trade on the extensive margin, but given that trade policy is completely absent from their work, it is not clear that these effects can be interpreted as the outcome of trade policy.

In contrast, two studies that explicitly focus on trade policy, Klenow and Rodriguez-Clare (1997) and Arkolakis et al. (2008), find miniscule effects. Both studies focus on the tariff reductions associated with the Costa Rican trade liberalization. The authors' interpretation for the small effects of trade policy on the extensive margin is that the liberalization led to the import of marginal, or relatively unimportant, products and varieties, as reflected in the relative low shares of these products/varieties in total expenditure. The products/varieties that were important for Costa Rica were already being imported prior to the liberalization. Along the same lines, it seems that the reason that Feenstra and Broda and Weinstein find an important role of trade for the extensive margin in the United States is that in the United States the new imported products/varieties were important for the economy. In this setting, however, these new imports were not necessarily the result of trade policy changes. Though never explicitly stated, the sentiment underlying the Costa Rican papers is that trade policy may again not "matter." By the time a trade liberalization comes into effect, the products that were important for the economy were already imported.

In a different study on India, that also examines the effects of trade policy changes on the extensive margin, Goldberg et al. (2010) find results that are strongly at odds with those reported in the previous two papers on Costa Rica. In the case of India, the effects

---

[n] See Melitz and Redding (2014) for a survey of recent related theoretical work on this topic.

of the tariff reductions on the introduction of new imported products and varieties are large and result in significant welfare gains for the economy, as measured by the decline in the exact price index. Moreover, the authors document that the tariff reductions also led to the introduction of new domestic products. The intuition behind these results is straightforward: Indian businesses and policy makers had complained for years that restrictions on the imports of important inputs held back domestic production and low-ered the quality of the domestically produced products. The trade liberalization relaxed these constraints. Hence, in contrast to the case of Costa Rica, the Indian trade liberal-ization resulted in the import of new products and varieties that were important.

The contrast between the two studies on Costa Rica and India makes clear that there is nothing inherent in the nature of trade policy that implies it would have small effects on the extensive margin. Rather, the results depend on the setting, preexisting conditions, and in particular the severity of the trade restrictions facing the economy prior to the onset of the trade liberalization. As with prices, much more work in this area is needed before a general assessment of the extensive margin effects of trade policy is possible.

A recent working paper by Caliendo et al. (2015) examines the effects of trade policy (ie, tariff reductions) on a different type of extensive margin: the decisions of firms to enter new markets. The evidence presented in the paper suggests that tariff reductions over the period 1990–2010 had a large impact on firm entry and selection into markets and that this effect was more pronounced in developed than in developing countries. Interpreting their estimates within a quantitative model of trade, the authors attribute more than 90% of the gains from trade to the reductions in MFN tariffs.

3.4 Effects on Aggregate (Static) Gains from Trade

Ultimately, what is most relevant is not how trade flows or prices or the extensive margin respond to commercial policy, but how the economy as a whole is affected by policy. What gains are associated with trade liberalization and what losses are associated with trade protection?

In principle, this seems like a question that should have been addressed in the liter-ature. Although estimates of the gains from "trade" abound, there is relatively little work on estimating the gains associated with particular trade liberalization episodes. There are few exceptions, and these consist of either older studies that employed CGE models or case studies of particular industries (eg, welfare effects of VERs on autos; Berry et al., 1999). A general challenge for these studies is that they need to assume a particular the-oretical structure in order to derive the welfare implications of trade policy. Thus, the conclusions are as credible as the underlying model.

Arkolakis et al. (2010), ACR henceforth, in an influential paper, provide a simple formula that can be easily applied ex post to trade liberalization episodes to assess the gains associated with the policy changes: the welfare gains are related to the reduced form "trade elasticity" and to the change in the share of domestic expenditure. The advantage of this approach is that it is consistent with a large class of models, in fact with all workhorse models of trade. Hence, while the formula is theoretically informed, it does not depend on the validity of one specific model. Moreover, at first sight, it seems easy to implement: one needs information on the change in domestic expenditure attributable to the trade policy change (which, subject to identification challenges, can be obtained from widely available data) and the trade elasticity (which, again subject to the same identification challenges, should be estimable from publicly available data). To our knowledge, the ACR formula has been applied only to assess the gains from trade relative to autarky, not the gains or losses associated with particular policies.

This observation is surprising because trade policy is not only interesting by itself, but it also provides a natural way for identifying the change in the domestic expenditure that arises from changes in trade costs. In the process of assigning changes in the domestic expenditure to changes in trade policy, one also identifies the "trade elasticity" which plays a key role in welfare analysis. In short, implementation of an ex post welfare analysis as suggested by the ACR formula is tantamount to estimating the "trade elasticity." This brings us back to the topic discussed earlier, of why variation induced by trade policy has not been used more extensively in order to identify the "trade elasticity." This is a hole in the literature that future research will hopefully address.

The more challenging question is whether estimates of the trade elasticity and the ACR formula can also be applied ex-ante, in lieu of counterfactual simulations conducted within the framework of a specific theoretical model, to predict the gains or losses from a trade policy intervention that has not yet occurred. From a theoretical point of view, such ex-ante application is justified within models that predict that the trade elasticity should be invariant to the policy change. From an empirical point of view, we would like to have substantially richer evidence on the magnitude of the trade elasticity based on trade policy variation, and most importantly, on the question of whether the trade elasticity appears to be invariant across time and space, or is dependent on the particular setting. The divergent results regarding Costa Rica and India mentioned earlier, suggest that the latter may be the case.

4. THE EFFECTS OF TRADE POLICY ON FIRMS: PRODUCTIVITY, COSTS, AND MARKUPS

A repeated observation we have made up to this point is that while there is a large literature that has focused on various forms of trade costs other than trade policy barriers, empirical work on trade *policy* is surprisingly scarce. The one exception to this pattern is the literature focusing on firms, specifically relating to how productivity, costs and markups are affected by trade liberalization. This is the one part of the trade literature that has been policy oriented from the outset.

Because this literature is mature and voluminous, it has been reviewed extensively in previous surveys (De Loecker and Goldberg, 2014; Harrison and Rodríguez-Clare, 2010; Melitz and Redding, 2014). Therefore, we will abstain from providing another detailed review of existing findings. Instead, we will highlight the main messages from this literature.

The main and robust finding of research in this area is that a reduction of trade policy barriers leads to an unambiguous increase in industry revenue productivity. The evidence on the exact channels through which the productivity improvements are realized is, however, more mixed and depends on the particular setting and trade liberalization episode. In general, the literature has found support for the hypothesis that industry productivity increases through reallocation of market shares toward more productive firms and the hypothesis that within-firm revenue productivity increases in response to trade liberalization. Within-firm revenue improvements can in turn be attributed either to the increase of productive efficiency (ie, physical productivity) or the increase of markups.

A main challenge for the interpretation of the results of this literature is that until recently, most studies had access to revenue data only, so that a distinction between revenue and physical productivity was not possible. While in both cases firms benefit as a result of trade liberalization, increases in revenue vs physical productivity may have different welfare implications and distributional consequences. It is only recently that the literature has started taking this distinction seriously by examining separately the effects of trade liberalization on physical productivity, costs, and markups.

Changes in within-firm physical efficiency and costs can be attributed either to the reduction of X-inefficiencies and adoption of better management practices, or to the import of new and higher quality inputs that generate an increase in measured productivity. In addition, declines in the prices of existing imported inputs will show up as a direct cost decrease for importing firms. In general, one would expect reductions of tariffs on imported final products (output tariffs) that compete with those offered by domestic firms to affect management and X-inefficiencies through the additional competitive pressure they exert on domestic firms. On the other hand, declines in the tariffs of imported intermediate products that are used as inputs (input tariffs) in the production of domestic firms should have a direct cost reduction effect and an indirect effect on measured productivity through the introduction of new imported products (see Halpern et al., 2015). A second robust finding of the literature on firm productivity is that input tariffs have large effects on firm productivity, often much larger than the ones found for output tariffs (Amiti and Konings, 2007; De Loecker et al., 2016; Khandelwal and Topalova, 2011).

An additional channel through which trade barrier reductions may contribute to within-firm productivity enhancements is by encouraging investment in new technology and R&D, which will also lead to productivity improvements. This point is exemplified in Bustos (2011) who is among the few who have studied actual trade liberalization episodes. Bustos shows that firms in Argentina increased their innovative activity as a result of Mercosur, though the effects were heterogeneous across firms of different size.

We already referred to some recent results regarding the effects of trade liberalization on markups, when we reviewed the evidence on prices. In addition to De Loecker et al. (2016), two earlier papers examined the effects of actual trade liberalization episodes on markups, though in these cases without exploiting information on prices: Levinsohn (1993) in his study of the trade reforms of Turkey, and Harrison (1994) in her study of the trade liberalization in the Cote d'Ivoire. Even though the authors did not have firm or product-specific data on prices, they managed to estimate price-cost margins for the pre and postreform periods by using a method proposed by Hall (1986). Both studies found that markups decreased as a result of the respective trade liberalization episodes, lending support to the view that trade policy has procompetitive effects. At first, these results may seem at odds with DLGKP's recent findings on India, which indicate an increase in markups. However, both Levinsohn and Harrison focus on trade liberalizations that affected final goods, and hence their work captures only the procompetitive effect of tariff reductions. They do not consider the potential cost reduction effect of trade reforms on intermediate inputs which drive—via the incomplete pass-through mechanism—the increase in markups in DLGKP. Ideally, we would like to have more evidence from many different settings in order to assess whether and how trade policy affects firms' market power. Moreover, all studies mentioned above focus on unilateral trade liberalizations. Arkolakis et al. (2015) point out that in the case of a bilateral trade liberalization the general equilibrium effects on prices and markups would be more complicated as exporters, in addition to importers, adjust their prices. This is an interesting possibility that future work could investigate. Price data are becoming more widely available, and by combining them with information on actual trade liberalization episodes, one can shed light on how actual markups respond to trade policy and examine whether the mechanisms postulated in theoretical papers and counterfactual simulations are indeed borne out in the data.

The message from the existing literature on the effects of trade policy on firm performance (ie, firm productivity and markups) is very different from the one that is implicit in examinations of aggregate outcomes. Trade policy seems to truly matter here for firm performance and deliver large, economically significant effects.[°] It seems clear that initially better performing firms benefit from trade liberalization while less profitable firms are forced to exit, which translates to improvements in aggregate industry performance. What is less clear is whether improvements in firm profitability are due to higher efficiency or increased market power. The trade literature to date seems to have operated predominantly under the premise that exposure to more international competition inevitably leads to a containment of firms' market power and benefits consumers. Recent findings on firms' markups posttrade policy changes challenge this conventional wisdom.

[°] Industry-specific studies of trade policy reviewed by Feenstra (1995) also conclude that trade policy matters for firm performance.

One notable exception to the policy-oriented focus of the empirical studies of firms and trade is the literature on multinational firms. Multinational firms account for a large share of international trade transactions and a vast literature in international economics examines the impact of such firms on the structure of international trade, host-country firm performance, and labor markets (see Antras and Yeaple, 2014; Harrison and Rodríguez-Clare, 2010 for recent surveys).[P] However, very few studies provide a detailed examination of the effects of trade policy on the performance of multinationals and their organization and expansion across space.[q] An exception is the literature that examines the tariff-jumping argument for foreign direct investment in the context of US antidumping duties (see, for example, Blonigen, 2002). The lack of studies is in part data driven: data sets on multinationals rarely include detailed information about their activities in multiple countries. Given the growing interest in understanding the global production chains and improvements in data availability, this remains a promising area for future research.

5. THE EFFECTS OF TRADE POLICY ON LABOR MARKETS

As is the case with literature on the effects of trade policy on firm performance, the literature on trade and labor markets is extensive and has been reviewed in several previous surveys (Goldberg, 2015; Goldberg and Pavcnik, 2007; Harrison et al., 2011; Pavcnik, 2012; Wood, 1999). With a few notable exceptions, studies on trade and labor markets in developed countries focus on the effects of import competition or exporting on labor market outcomes. This is in stark contrast to the literature in developing countries, which has, from the onset, focused on the effects of trade policy. The difference in the emphasis of trade policy in the two settings in part stems from the methodological issues discussed in Section 2. In this section, we highlight the main messages from the studies that focus explicitly on the effect of trade policy, with emphasis on the more recent literature.

One of the main findings is that the effects of trade policy on labor market outcomes depend on relevant labor market frictions within a country. Because of these frictions, observationally equivalent workers earn different wages, depending on the workers' industry affiliation and local labor market conditions. Correspondingly, the effect of trade policy on workers' earnings and employment vary with industry affiliation and local labor market conditions. However, the importance of the extent of these frictions appears to differ across settings.

The literature on the effects of trade policy on industry employment and earnings in developing countries finds small industry employment responses to trade policy changes,

---

[P] Harrison and Rodríguez-Clare (2010) also discuss the implications for industrial and trade policy.
[q] Blonigen and Figlio (1998) and Blanchard and Matschke (2015) show that the presence of multinational firms influences trade policy.

with wage adjustment playing a more important role. However, trade liberalization decreases the industry wage premiums of workers in industries that experienced the largest tariff reductions, relative to workers in industries with lower tariff declines. When wage responses to trade liberalization are more pronounced than quantity (ie, employment) responses, labor market rigidities are plausible. That said, the evidence so far suggests that changes in industry wage premia induced by trade policy can explain only a small share of the observed increase in wage inequality in developing countries.[r]

In contrast, studies of the effect of trade policy in developed countries find larger employment responses than industry wage responses to declines in industry tariff protection (Grossman, 1986).[s] More recently, Trefler (2004) documents contractions in employment in Canadian industries subject to larger declines in tariffs induced by the CUFTA, and notes that earlier studies failed to find adjustments in industry wages. Pierce and Schott (2015) examine the effects of the elimination of trade policy uncertainty vis-à-vis China with the China's WTO entry on the employment in the US manufacturing industries. Instead of examining the direct effect of trade policy on industry employment through lower levels of protection, as emphasized in earlier studies, Pierce and Schott (2015) focus on the effects of the elimination of trade policy uncertainty.[t] They measure trade policy uncertainty prior to China's WTO entry with the gap between the non-MFN tariff and the MNF tariff imposed on the Chinese exporters. The results suggest that the US manufacturing industries that experience the largest decline in tariff uncertainty experienced the biggest employment contraction. This interpretation of results is further supported by the lack of corresponding losses in employment in the manufacturing industries in the European Union after China's entry into the WTO. Unlike the United States, the European Union granted China permanent MFN status prior to China joining the WTO, so that China's entry into the WTO did not change trade policy uncertainty vis-à-vis the EU.

Other studies have emphasized the importance of the effects of trade policy on worker earnings that operate through local labor markets and thus location-specific component of wages. The definition of a geographic unit that corresponds to a local labor market is country specific, depending on the commuting and mobility patters of workers within and across geographic areas in a country. To the extent that workers are not mobile across

---

[r] For example, while trade liberalization in Colombia lead to large and statistically significant declines on industry wage premia in Colombian apparel, industry wage premia account for less than 5% of the variation in worker earnings, so that the effects of trade policy on worker earnings through this channel do not make an economically significant contribution to the observed increase in wage inequality (or skill premium). See Attanasio et al. (2004) and Goldberg and Pavcnik (2005).

[s] A negative cross-sectional relationship between industry tariffs and industry wage premia of US workers in Trefler and Gaston (1994, 1995) are also consistent with this view. Trefler and Gaston (1994, 1995) argue that lower industry wages in industries with higher trade protection might reflect that unions trade off employment security for lower wages.

[t] Section 7.2 discusses the literature on the effects of trade policy uncertainty more generally.

local labor markets, trade policy implemented at the national level can have differential effects on worker earnings across these geographic regions. Local labor markets differ in composition of industry employment prior to trade policy reforms: areas that have higher concentration of industries affected by large trade policy changes are more exposed to trade policy reform than others.[u] Consistent with the frictions in labor mobility across these geographic regions, the literature finds no or weak effects of trade policy on regional population or migration patterns in less-developed countries (Kovak, 2013; McCaig, 2011; Topalova, 2007, 2010). Workers mobility is also constrained across geographic areas within developed countries such as the United States (Autor et al., 2013). However, to our knowledge, only McLaren and Hakobyan (2012) have examined the effects of trade policy on local labor markets in a developed country setting.

A second finding of these studies is that the effects of trade policy on worker earnings vary systematically across geographic regions, depending on the region's exposure to a particular trade policy reform, and their magnitudes are also economically significant. The sign of the effect depends on the nature of trade policy change. Studies that examine the effects of large-scale unilateral tariff liberalizations in developing countries find that relative poverty declined by less in areas that had higher concentration of industries that lost protection as a result of import tariff declines (Kovak, 2013; Topalova, 2010). Topalova (2010), for example, ties her results to lower industry and agricultural wages in more affected areas after trade reform, which disproportionally harmed living standards of the poor households. Along the same lines, McLaren and Hakobyan (2012) find declines in location-specific wages of US workers due to tariff reductions implemented as part of NAFTA.

McCaig (2011), on the other hand, focuses on the local labor market effects of a trade liberalization, which mainly lowered import tariffs by a major trade partner on exports from a low-wage country. He focuses on the consequences of the US–Vietnam Bilateral Trade Agreement on Vietnamese households. McCaig finds that declines in US import tariffs on Vietnamese exports led to bigger poverty reductions in provinces in Vietnam that had a higher prereform concentration of industries that ultimately experienced larger tariff cuts. Lower poverty rates reflect increased wages of workers in provinces better positioned to gain from the trade agreement, especially the less educated workers.[v]

The above studies highlight the importance geographic frictions to mobility of workers in assessing the effects of trade policy on labor market outcomes through the location-specific earnings of workers and increased wage inequality across regions. Trade policy exhibits persistent longer term effects in this setting as well. For example, by affecting the living standards of families, local labor market effects of trade policy influences

---

[u] See Kovak (2013) for theory on how to measure exposure of local labor markets to trade policy.

[v] McCaig and Pavcnik (2014) show that the agreement induced reallocation of workers from the informal sector to employers in the formal sector, which were most pronounced in internationally integrated provinces.

household decisions on schooling of children (Edmonds et al., 2009, 2010). In addition, regional wage gaps that emerge after trade policy reforms appear to widen, rather than decrease, over time, pointing to persistence of frictions in geographic mobility over longer time horizons (Dix-Carneiro and Kovak, 2015b).

Overall, as is the case for the literature on trade policy and firm performance, the message from the literature on the effects of trade policy on labor markets is very different from the one that is implicit in examinations of aggregate outcomes. Trade policy seems to matter for worker outcomes, although the magnitude of the contribution of trade policy to changes in aggregate income distribution varies across settings. Another message that emerges from this literature is that labor frictions across geographic regions (and across industries in developing country settings) are important channels through which trade policy plays a role.

The literature is lacking in analysis of how the effects of trade policy on worker outcomes are related and interact with the effect of trade policy on firm performance. With a few exceptions (Amiti and Davis, 2012; Dix-Carneiro and Kovak, 2015b; Menezes-Filho and Muendler, 2011; Pierce and Schott, 2015), the studies of labor market adjustment to actual external policy and shocks at the firm level are confined to exchange rate shocks (Brambilla et al., 2012; Verhoogen, 2008).[w] The increased availability of detailed employee–employer data in developed and developing countries, which can be linked to data on a firms' domestic activities and a firms' exposure to trade through exporting and importing, provides a fruitful setting to continue to explore the channels through which trade policy affects labor market outcomes.

6. THE EFFECTS OF TRADE POLICY ON AGGREGATE GROWTH AND POVERTY

Much of the literature on the effects of trade policy on the outcomes discussed in Sections 3 and 4 focuses on its short-run and static effects. The distinction between short- and long-run effects is not unique to trade policy. But in the case of trade policy, there are good reasons to believe that the long-run effects are orders of magnitude larger than the short-run effects. While the latter can be potentially identified through careful empirical work, the long-run effects are substantially harder to pin down empirically. As a result, arguments about dynamic long-run effects are often made based solely on principles and theoretical models, with little formal empirical support. In this section, we consider the (scant) evidence on long-run effects of trade policy on aggregate growth and poverty.

---

[w] For example, Pierce and Schott (2015) suggest that the reduced trade policy uncertainty lead to employment losses in the US manufacturing through several channels. These include increased sourcing of inputs by US firms from China, expansion of Chinese export to the United States (which includes foreign-owned firms located China), the shift in structure within US industries away from labor-intensive plants, increased capital-deepening among the surviving US plants, and increased offshoring by US firms.

The relationship between a country's trade policy and aggregate economic growth is of key policy interest, and the empirical literature on the topic is one of the oldest areas of empirical inquiry in international economics. Although many economists believe, based on economic theory, that reductions in trade barriers promote economic growth, robust evidence on this relationship at the aggregate level has been elusive. Rodrik and Rodriguez (2001) and Hanson and Harrison (1999) review the issues that affect the estimation of the effect of trade policy on aggregate growth and conclude that the estimates of the effect are not robust. Most of the literature on the topic has examined the relationship between trade policy and growth in a cross section of countries. The issues that influence the inference include weak links between the empirical work to the underlying predictions from the theoretical literature, selective samples of countries with available data, measurement of trade policy at the aggregate level, consistency of measurement of key variables across countries and time, and endogeneity of trade liberalizations. To the extent that there is a positive relationship between trade policy and economic growth, it is not clear whether trade policy leads or lags. Does trade policy lead to higher economic growth or do countries at a certain level of development choose to implement more liberalized trade policy? Alternatively, do countries with less restrictive trade policy in general have economic institutions in these economies that are associated with higher growth?

While the robustness of findings in this area of research continues to be debated, researchers have recently used microlevel data on trade policy from trade liberalizations during the 1980s and 1990s and empirical frameworks guided by economic theory to make progress on the effects of trade policy on aggregate growth. Estevadeordal and Taylor (2013) find that countries that liberalized trade policy during the 1980s and 1990s (in part driven by the Uruguay round of the WTO negotiations) observed higher growth rates in GDP per capita over this period relative to countries that did not liberalize. According to a version of Solow model they develop, decline in import tariffs on capital goods increases incentives for firms to invest, which in turn increases steady state growth. Lower tariffs on intermediate inputs increase productivity, and subsequently steady state growth. Further analysis, which distinguishes between liberalized trade in production inputs and final consumption goods, finds that the positive relationship between trade liberalization and economic growth is driven by declines in tariffs on intermediate inputs and capital goods. Consistent with these channels, they show that countries that lowered tariffs on intermediate inputs and capital goods observed increased imports of intermediate and capital goods. On the other hand, there is no relationship between lower tariffs on consumer goods and economic growth. These findings provide country-level support for the effects of liberalized trade on improved efficiency of production through imported inputs and technology, channels that have been emphasized in studies of firm performance (Amiti and Konings, 2007; Goldberg et al., 2010; Khandelwal and Topalova, 2011).

The effects of trade policy (via economic growth) on poverty are even more difficult to quantify empirically than the relationship between trade policy and growth. In addition to establishing that trade policy affects growth, one needs to determine both whether and how trade policy-induced growth affects the poor. This is a challenging task to accomplish with aggregate data. Lack of availability of household survey data with information on consumption and income from many low-income countries affects measurement of poverty and average incomes of the poor (Deaton, 2005; Ravallion, 2001). In the absence of reliable survey data, average incomes of the poor, which are often measured by the average income of the households in the bottom fifth of income distribution, are imputed from very noisy measures of income distribution within a country. With noisy measures of income inequality, this imputation makes is likely that measures of income of the poor simply follow changes in average incomes (Banerjee et al., 2006). This biases the results in favor of pro-poor effects of growth.[x] In recent years, household surveys are increasingly available and the World Bank Research Department has made substantial progress on measurement of poverty across time and space. Nonetheless, the poverty measures do not span periods of trade liberalization for a large share of countries, so the relationship between trade policy and poverty across countries remains empirically elusive.

In summary, the literature on the effects of trade policy on aggregate growth does not provide much robust evidence that trade policy affects growth. This is a very different conclusion from the message in the studies of the effects of trade on firm performance. This leaves one wondering whether the lack of robust aggregate evidence in part reflects the methodological challenges highlighted in Section 2, which are amplified in aggregate studies. Recent work by Estevadeordal and Taylor (2013) makes headway on overcoming some of these issues, while focusing on one particular channel of the link between trade policy and growth. Its findings are consistent with the evidence from firm-level studies that emphasize the role of trade policy in promoting efficiency and innovation through access to imported inputs and capital goods in less developed countries. However, more work is needed is this area.

7. THE EFFECTS OF TRADE POLICY: SECONDARY DISTORTIONS, MISALLOCATION, THE ROLE OF POLICY UNCERTAINTY, AND DYNAMICS

7.1 Effects of Secondary Distortions and Misallocation

Most studies evaluate the effects of trade policy under the assumption that the resources are optimally allocated given the level of trade policy and market structure, without considering the role of secondary distortions. If resources are misallocated, the effects of trade policy that operate through secondary distortions might be just as important as the

---

[x] Banerjee et al. (2006) discuss how measurement of average incomes of the poor affected several key policy debates within the World Bank, including the relationship between trade policy and poverty.

primary effects. In an early study, Leibenstein (1966) argues that welfare gains from trade through reduction of secondary distortions might be an order of magnitude more important than the welfare gains from primary effects of trade on allocative efficiency that are emphasized in traditional trade models.[y]

With a few exceptions, secondary distortions have not received much attention in the studies of the effects of trade policy.[z] An important exception is the literature on the rent-seeking activities associated with import quotas (Krueger, 1974). More recently, Khandelwal et al. (2013) argue that distortions in institutions that manage trade policy impose welfare costs of trade restrictions in addition to those emphasized in standard trade models and rent-seeking literature. If the institutions that allocate trading rights award them to politically connect rather than the most productive firms, the misallocation of trading rights generates productivity losses in addition to the productivity losses due to the actual trade restriction.

Khandelwal et al. (2013) examine distortions in trade institutions in China in the context of the elimination of the Multi-Fibre Agreement in 2005. If the Chinese government would allocate quota licenses efficiently across firms through a competitive auction, these licenses would be allocated to the most productive firms because they are sufficiently profitable to pay the per-unit license fee.[aa] Under this scenario, the theory predicts that the removal of quotas would expand exports of the most productive incumbent exporters and encourage export market entry of less productive firms. In addition, the prices of products exported by the most efficient incumbents would be expected to fall, while new entrants into exporting would be expected to increase the prices of exported goods. These predictions are not borne out in the data. After the quotas are eliminated, firms that newly enter the export markets, rather than the incumbent exporters, account for most of the expansion of export volumes and decline in export prices. This implies that quota licenses were misallocated. The new entrants are mostly comprised of foreign-owned firms and domestic privately owned firms, both of which tend to be more productive than the incumbent state-owned enterprises. In this study, liberalized trade policy generates bigger productivity gains through the elimination of secondary distortions than the primary ones. The elimination of the MFA leads to a 21% increase in revenue productivity, with counterfactual analysis attributing two-thirds of the productivity gains to the elimination of misallocated quota licenses.

Overall, Khandelwal et al. (2013) illustrate that the effect of trade policy is potentially substantially underestimated if one does not consider the effects of trade policy on secondary distortions. The relative magnitude of the effects of trade policy through primary

---

[y] Leibenstein (1966) focuses on X-inefficiencies and managerial performance within a firm.

[z] Krueger (1984) provides an early discussion of this issue.

[aa] See Khandelwal et al. (2013) for detailed discussion of the underlying model of quota license allocation across heterogeneous firms, where quotas licenses are auctioned in a competitive process for a per-unit license fee.

vs secondary effects is consistent with the predictions made previously by Leibenstein (1966). An interesting question for future work is whether the relatively greater magnitudes of the effects of trade policy through secondary distortions hold more generally.

Another setting where trade policy could have effects through secondary distortions is the allocation of resources between informal and formal sector in low-income countries. One unique feature of firm distribution in low-income countries is prevalence of small, unproductive, informal firms, which account for a large portion of aggregate employment, and scarcity of productive establishments (see Hsieh and Olken, 2014; La Porta and Shleifer, 2014). To the extent that distortions generate a wedge in the marginal productivity of workers between the informal and formal sector, the reallocation of workers from household businesses to firms in the enterprise sector could be associated with improved aggregate labor productivity. McCaig and Pavcnik (2014) show that reductions in trade barriers to exporting—a product market policy change that disproportionately lowers the profitability of more productive establishments—lead to reallocation of workers from the informal to the formal sector. The estimated effects of the associated aggregate productivity gains depend on the size of the marginal productivity wedge.

The focus on the effects of trade policy through the secondary distortions might be a fruitful area of future research given that the distortions due to misallocation of resources appear to matter in other settings. Recent literature has emphasized that misallocation of resources across firms has large implications for aggregate income differences across countries (Banerjee and Duflo, 2005; Hsieh and Klenow, 2009; Restuccia and Rogerson, 2008). Hsieh and Klenow (2009) show that the elimination of such distortions would raise the aggregate productivity in China and India by 30–60%. In addition, distortions in sectors that are key inputs in the production process of other sectors have multiplier-like effects, amplifying aggregate income differences across countries (Jones, 2011, 2013). Surprisingly, most of this literature has not linked the degree of misallocation (as measured by dispersion in revenue TFP) to a particular policy. Taking the Hsieh and Klenow (2009) framework as a starting point, it would be natural for the future work to examine whether trade reforms affect misallocation as measured by the metric in their framework, namely the dispersion in revenue TFP.

7.2 The Role of Trade Policy Uncertainty

The literature usually examines the effects of trade policy that operate through changes in the levels of trade barriers rather than through changes in the uncertainty regarding future policies. Trade agreements can reduce the uncertainty about trade policy by more permanently committing countries to a specific trade policy regime. To the extent that uncertainty about trade policy affects firms' decisions on investment, reduced uncertainty about trade policy could have large effects on trade flows and other outcomes.

Handley (2014) and Handley and Limão (2015) formally model this channel in a framework that incorporates the effect of trade policy uncertainty on a firm's exporting and technology upgrading decisions. Their framework further suggests that trade policy uncertainty provides an explanation as to why trade agreements that yield relatively small changes in trade policy levels, but large declines in uncertainty, could have large effects on trade flows and other outcomes. Consider trade liberalizations such as NAFTA, CUFTA, and China's entry into the WTO with respect to the US import tariffs on Chinese exports. These liberalization episodes are all characterized by small changes in tariff levels. Even though the actual tariff changes were small, these trade agreements might have eliminated uncertainty about trade policy and could potentially have large effects through this channel. This is especially the case for China's entry into the WTO given that the loss of China's MFN status in the United States would increase an average tariff facing Chinese export to the United States from 4% to 31% and that Chinese MFN status has to be renewed by the US Congress on an annual basis (Handley and Limão, 2014).[bb]

The empirical literature on the effects of trade policy has largely abstracted from estimating the effects of trade policy uncertainty. One issue facing the literature is measurement of trade policy uncertainty. Handley and Limão (2014) argue that, relative to other sources of uncertainty, measurement of trade policy uncertainty is in many situations aided by observed information about the applied trade policy and the maximum allowed level of trade policy. To this end, all studies measure trade policy uncertainty as a function of the gap between the largest possible import tariff and the applied tariff facing a product (or an industry). A product (or an industry) faces less uncertainty when this gap is reduced.

Recent studies suggest that this channel plays an important role. One set of studies examines the effect of trade policy uncertainty on trade volumes and export market participation (Handley, 2014; Handley and Limão, 2014). Handley (2014) examines the effects of trade policy uncertainty that occurs through the imposition of tariff bounds on applied tariffs within the WTO for the case of Australia. The study finds that the reduction in tariff bounds is associated with increased entry of products from new import destinations to Australia. This effect occurs even though the Australian tariff bounds exceed the applied tariffs, highlighting the role of trade policy uncertainty (as opposed to changes in applied tariffs). Handley and Limão (2014) find that the reductions in trade policy uncertainty, associated with Portugal's entry into the European Community, increased export participation of Portuguese firms in the European Community. Handley and Limão (2014) examine the effects of China's entry into the WTO, which eliminated the uncertainty about China's tariff levels vis-à-vis the United States on China's exports to the United States. Elimination of trade policy uncertainty is associated with increased export volumes of Chinese products to the United States. Furthermore,

---

[bb] Handley and Limão (2014) and Pierce and Schott (2015) document several anecdotes on the importance of uncertainty about US–China trade policy in this context.

higher export volumes are driven by increased exports among the incumbent products rather than by the new entry, as emphasized in the Handley studies.

Pierce and Schott (2015) examine the effects of the elimination of trade policy uncertainty vis-à-vis China on the employment in the US manufacturing industries. They measure trade policy uncertainty prior to China's WTO entry with the gap between the non-MFN tariff and the MNF tariff imposed on the Chinese exporters. The study finds that the US manufacturing industries that experience the largest decline in tariff uncertainty experienced the biggest employment contraction. This trade-policy uncertainty-based interpretation of results is further supported by the lack of corresponding losses in employment in the manufacturing industries in the European Union after China's entry into the WTO. Unlike the United States, the European Union granted China permanent MFN status prior to China joining the WTO, so that China's entry into the WTO did not change trade policy uncertainty vis-à-vis the EU.

Overall, these studies suggest that the effects of trade policy uncertainty matter. However, the size of the effects will likely vary, depending on the setting. A related issue is identifying the settings in which the effects of trade policy uncertainty are most relevant. The concern about the trade policy uncertainty likely depends on the identity of the trading partners. To this end, most of the work has been done on the effects of uncertainty in trade policy between China and the United States. This is not surprising given that the uncertainty surrounding a trade war between two large trading partners such as the United States and China (or the United States and the European Community) would exert a large influence. The uncertainty about trade policy might also be important from the perspective of a small country vis-à-vis a large trading partner (as shown in Handley and Limão, 2014). Interestingly, to date, there is no study that examines the effects of the uncertainty trade policy uncertainty in the context of small, less-developed economy vis-à-vis large trading partners. The case study later provides an informative illustration that uncertainty about trade policy, coupled with weak institutions that link producers to exporters, could play an important role.

In less-developed countries, small-holder farmers often do not produce cash crops for export markets even though these appear more profitable than the crops produced for local or personal consumption. Uncertainty about conditions on the export markets, including trade policy and associated regulations, could play a role. A randomized control trial by Ashraf et al. (2009) examined the effects of a marketing scheme that provided some Kenyan farmers with the incentives to switch to cash crops for export markets in the European Community. These incentives were administered by a local organization, which facilitated interactions between small-scale farmers and exporters. The study finds that the incentives initially increased production of cash crops by farmers in the treatment group relative to the control group, but over the longer time frame the farmers abandoned cash crop production. After the implementation of the field experiment, the European Community increased sanitary and health standards on food imports by the European Community in 2005 (the EurepGap). Ashraf et al. (2009) argue that the drop in cash crop production was related to the change in this policy. Because small-holder farmers did not become certified for exporting as required by the EurepGap, the Kenyan exporters stopped purchasing the crops from small-holder farmers, inducing the farmers to abandon the cash crops.

The case study illustrates that the uncertainty about the regulatory regime, coupled with the inability of the local organization to foresee and adequately prepare small-scale producers to the changing regulatory environment, can lead to the collapse in cash crop production. Low participation in cash crops for export markets observed in low-income countries might reflect such considerations. In future work, it would be interesting to examine the role of trade policy and regulation uncertainty, coupled with lack of institutions to effectively deal with uncertainty, in explaining low participation in export markets in low-income settings.

Overall, the existing studies suggest that the magnitudes of the effects of trade policy uncertainty are potentially large. Because the studies so far have focused on situations where one would ex ante expect the effect of trade policy uncertainty to potentially matter the most (for example, the US–China trade) further research is needed to determine the role of trade policy uncertainty in other contexts. Trade liberalization episodes and trade agreements implemented at the regional and multilateral levels provide rich settings for further investigation of this topic.

8. CONCLUDING THOUGHTS

We started this chapter by posing the question: Does trade policy still matter? The view that it does not seems surprising given the evidence we reviewed. Even when one focuses on import tariffs, which have been reduced to historically low levels in developed countries post World War II, the evidence suggests large, nonlinear effects of tariff liberalization on trade volumes—in fact such effects are so large that they were initially deemed implausible. However, as we discussed, both their magnitudes and time patterns can be rationalized by the interaction of tariff liberalization with increasing vertical specialization that created a magnification effect. Accordingly, the conclusion is not that tariffs do not matter: they do matter but only in interaction with technology, specifically increasing vertical specialization. A perhaps more difficult question to answer is whether trade volumes is the relevant outcome one should focus on when debating the relevance of trade policy. A more appropriate metric would be welfare. But assessing the impact of trade policy on the welfare gains from trade presumes knowledge of the "elasticity of trade." Surprisingly, while estimates of this elasticity abound in the literature, estimates based on variation in *trade policy* are rare, and the ones that exist point to substantial heterogeneity across sectors. Obtaining credible elasticity estimates that can be directly linked to policy is a fruitful area of future research and a prerequisite for assessing the relevance of policy to welfare.

The evidence on the relevance of trade policy is even stronger for outcomes that concern specific parts of the economy rather than aggregate outcomes. This is especially the case when assessing the impact of trade policy on firm and industry productivity where the literature has consistently documented large effects of trade reforms on revenue productivity. Increased availability of data on product prices has revived the debate on whether trade policy affects firm performance through its effects on markups or through its effects on cost/productivity. The strength of the evidence is partly due to the fact that the focus on specific firms and industries allows the researcher to more accurately measure the actual trade barriers, assess their impact through particular channels, and take into account the specific institutional setting. The recent literature on the effects of trade policy on labor markets also finds statistically significant (and at times economically large) effects of trade policy on the wage distribution, albeit the magnitude of the effects depends on the particular setting.

In general, proper measurement and identification of causal impacts are first-order issues in the evaluation of trade policy. The recent literature has made progress on both issues. Empirical studies of the actual effects of trade policy increasingly focus on the nature of the policy changes and the institutional settings in which trade policy takes place. This new focus, combined with the increased availability of detailed microdata on trade flows, firms, and workers, has enabled researchers to identify several mechanisms through which trade policy affects outcomes of interest and assess the economic significance of these effects. The empirical evidence has in turn influenced the development of richer theoretical models that embed features that have been shown to be important empirically (eg, labor market frictions, firm heterogeneity, and incomplete pass-through). Such models can be used to yield a more informative counterfactual evaluation of future trade policy changes.

Nonetheless, several open questions pertaining to measurement remain. Most of the existing work still focuses on trade policy as measured by import tariffs. In order to answer the question of whether the world is as liberalized as the profession believes, and to more accurately evaluate the effects of trade policy, we need better and more comprehensive measures of trade policy instruments beyond import tariffs. Some of these measures are (or could be) systematically collected by international organizations. Recent data-collection efforts by the World Bank and measurement of Temporary Trade Barriers are a productive step forward and draw on the Bank's institutional capacity to implement such large-scale measurement projects. In some cases, especially for nonprice based barriers, the focus on the effects of nontariff barriers to trade requires a move away from assessing the effects of trade policy at the economy-wide level and towards industry-specific studies. The later approach ensures that the impact of nontariff barriers is assessed in the context of an industry's market structure (and industry-specific demand and supply conditions) to appropriately capture the institutional details, restrictiveness, and consequences of these regulations.

While better measurement of trade policy should be the number one priority of future research, the measurement of trade volumes can also be improved. The increasing importance of vertical specialization suggests that it would be more appropriate to measure trade flows in valued-added rather than gross terms. In general, the main message of our chapter is that for international trade to remain a policy-relevant field, it needs to focus on better measurement. If the main message of the Leamer and Levinsohn (1995) chapter in the 1995 Handbook of International Economics Chapter was "Estimate, don't test!" Our message 20 years later is: "Measure before you estimate!"

Our survey also identifies several promising new areas for future work. These focus on the more "dynamic" aspects of trade policy. They include the role of price adjustments to trade policy changes, the impact of trade policy on the performance and organization of multinational firms, the effects of trade policy through reductions in secondary distortions/misallocation, and the effects of trade policy through a decline of uncertainty. Initial studies on these topics suggest that the effects of trade policy through these channels might play an important role and thus warrant further examination.

ACKNOWLEDGMENTS

We thank the editors and seminar participants at the Dartmouth-SNU Conference and the Handbook Conference at Dartmouth, especially Bruce Blonigen, Woan Foong Wong, and Peter Schott, for comments. We thank Carla Larin and Konrad von Moltke for research assistance.

REFERENCES

Amiti, M., Davis, D., 2012. Trade, firms, and wages: theory and evidence. Rev. Econ. Stud. 79 (1), 1–36.
Amiti, M., Konings, J., 2007. Trade liberalization, intermediate inputs, and productivity: evidence from Indonesia. Am. Econ. Rev. 97 (5), 1611–1638.
Anderson, J.E., Van Wincoop, E., 2004. Trade costs. J. Econ. Lit. 42 (3), 691–751.
Angrist, J.D., Krueger, A.B., 1999. Empirical strategies in labor economics. In: Ashenfelter, O., Card, D. (Eds.), Handbook of Labor Economics, vol. 3. Elsevier, Amsterdam, The Netherlands, pp. 1277–1366.
Angrist, J., Pischke, J.S., 2010. The credibility revolution in empirical economics: how better research design is taking the con out of econometrics. J. Econ. Perspect. 24 (2), 3–30.
Antras, P., Yeaple, S., 2014. Multinational forms and the structure of international trade. In: Gopinath, G., Helpman, E., Rogoff, K. (Eds.), Handbook of International Economics, vol. 4. Elsevier, Amsterdam, The Netherlands, pp. 55–130.
Arkolakis, C., Demidova, S., Klenow, P., Rodriguez-Clare, A., 2008. Endogenous variety and the gains from trade. Am. Econ. Rev. Pap. Proc. 98, 444–450.
Arkolakis, C., Costinot, A., Rodriguez-Clare, A., 2010. New trade models, same old gains? Am. Econ. Rev. 102 (1), 94–130.
Arkolakis, C., Costinot, A., Donaldson, D., Rodriguez-Clare, A., 2015. The Elusive Pro-Competitive Effects of Trade. National Bureau of Economic Research Working Paper No. 21370.
Artuc, E., Chaudhuri, S., McLaren, J., 2010. Trade shocks and labor adjustments: a structural empirical approach. Am. Econ. Rev. 100 (3), 1008–1045.
Ashraf, N., Gine, X., Karlan, D., 2009. Findings missing markets (and a disturbing epilogue): evidence from an export crop adoption and marketing intervention in Kenya. Am. J. Agric. Econ. 91 (4), 973–990.

Atkin, D., Donaldson, D., 2015. Who's Getting Globalized? The Size and Implications of Intranational Trade Costs. NBER Working Paper No. 21439.

Atkin, D., Khandelwal, A.K., Osman, A., 2014. Exporting and Firm Performance: Evidence from a Randomized Trial. National Bureau of Economic Research Working Paper No. 20690.

Attanasio, O., Goldberg, P., Pavcnik, P., 2004. Trade reforms and wage inequality in Colombia. J. Dev. Econ. 74 (4), 331–366.

Autor, D., Dorn, D., Hanson, G., 2013. The China Syndrome: local labor market effects of import competition in the United States. Am. Econ. Rev. 103 (6), 2121–2168.

Bagwell, K., Staiger, R.W., 2003. Protection and the business cycle. Adv. Econ. Anal. Policy 3 (1), 1–43.

Bagwell, K., Staiger, R.W., 2005. Multilateral trade negotiations, bilateral opportunism and the rules of GATT/WTO. J. Int. Econ. 67 (2), 268–294.

Bagwell, K., Staiger, R.W., 2014. Can the Doha round be a development round? Setting a place at the table. In: Feenstra, R.C., Taylor, A.M. (Eds.), Globalization in an Age of Crisis: Multilateral Economic Cooperation in the Twenty-First Century. University of Chicago Press, NBER, Chicago, pp. 91–124.

Baier, S., Bergstrand, J., 2001. The growth of world trade: tariffs, transport costs, and income similarity. J. Int. Econ. 53, 1–27.

Banerjee, A., Duflo, E., 2005. Growth theory through the lens of development economics. In: Aghion, P., Durlauf, S. (Eds.), Handbook of Economic Growth, vol. 1A. Elsevier, Amsterdam, The Netherlands, pp. 473–554.

Banerjee, A., Deaton, A., Lustig, N., Rogoff, K., Hsu, E., 2006. An Evaluation of World Bank Research 1998–2005. World Bank, Washington, DC. Available at https://openknowledge.worldbank.org/handle/10986/17896.

Bernard, A., Eaton, J., Jensen, J.B., Kortum, S., 2003. Plants and productivity in international trade. Am. Econ. Rev. 93 (4), 1268–1290.

Bernard, A., Jensen, J.B., Schott, P.K., 2006. Trade costs, firms, and productivity. J. Monet. Econ. 53 (5), 917–937.

Berry, S., Levinsohn, J., Pakes, A., 1999. Voluntary export restraints on automobiles: evaluating a strategic trade policy. Am. Econ. Rev. 89 (3), 400–430.

Blanchard, E.J., 2007. Foreign direct investment, endogenous tariffs, and preferential trade agreements. B.E. J. Econ. Anal. Policy 7 (1), 1–52.

Blanchard, E.J., 2010. Reevaluating the role of trade agreements: does investment globalization make the WTO obsolete? J. Int. Econ. 82 (1), 63–72.

Blanchard, E., Matschke, X., 2015. U.S. multinationals and preferential market access. Rev. Econ. Stat. 97 (4), 839–854.

Blanchard, E.J., Bown, C.P., Johnson, R.C., 2016. Global Supply Chains and Trade Policy. NBER Working Paper No. 21883.

Blonigen, B., 2002. Tariff-jumping antidumping duties. J. Int. Econ. 57, 31–50.

Blonigen, B., Figlio, D., 1998. Voting for protection: does direct foreign investment influence legislator behavior? Am. Econ. Rev. 88 (4), 1002–1014.

Blonigen, B., Prusa, T., 2003. Antidumping. In: Choi, E.K., Harrigan, J. (Eds.), Handbook of International Trade. Blackwell Publishers, Oxford, UK and Cambridge, MA, pp. 251–284.

Blonigen, B., Prusa, T., 2016. Dumping and antidumping duties. In: Bagwell, K., Staiger, R. (Eds.), Handbook of Commercial Policy, vol. 1B. Elsevier, Amsterdam, The Netherlands, Chapter 12, pp. 107–159.

Brambilla, I., Khandelwal, A.K., Schott, P.K., 2010. China's experience under the multi-fiber arrangement (MFA) and the agreement on textiles and clothing (ATC). In: Feenstra, R., Wei, S.J. (Eds.), China's Growing Role in World Trade. University of Chicago Press, Chicago, IL, pp. 345–387.

Brambilla, I., Lederman, D., Porto, G., 2012. Exports, export destinations, and skills. Am. Econ. Rev. 102 (7), 3406–3438.

Broda, C., Weinstein, D., 2006. Globalization and the gains from variety. Q. J. Econ. 121 (2), 541–585.

Bustos, P., 2011. Trade liberalization, exports, and technology upgrading: evidence on the impact of MERCOSUR on Argentinian firms. Am. Econ. Rev. 101 (1), 304–340.

Cadot, O., Fernandes, A.M., Gourdon, J., Mattoo, A. (Eds.), 2011. Where to Spend the Next Million? Applying Impact Evaluation to Trade Assistance. Centre for Economic Policy Research and the World Bank, Washington, DC.

Caliendo, L., Parro, F., 2015. Estimates of the trade and welfare effects of NAFTA. Rev. Econ. Stud. 82 (1), 1–44.

Caliendo, L., Feenstra, R., Romalis, J., Taylor, A., 2015. Tariff Reductions, Entry, and Welfare: Theory and Evidence for the Last Two Decades. Working Paper.

Cosar, K., 2013. Adjusting to Trade Liberalization: Reallocation and Labor Market Policies. Working Paper.

Costinot, A., Rodríguez-Clare, A., 2014. Trade theory with numbers: quantifying the consequences of globalization. In: Gopinath, G., Helpman, E., Rogoff, K. (Eds.), Handbook of International Economics, vol. 4. Elsevier, Amsterdam, pp. 197–261.

De Loecker, J., Goldberg, P., 2014. Firm performance in a global market. Annu. Rev. Econ. 6, 201–227.

De Loecker, J., Goldberg, P., Khandelwal, A., Pavcnik, N., 2016. Prices, markups and trade reform. Econometrica 84 (2), 445–510.

Deardorff, A.V., Stern, R.M., 1986. The Michigan Model of World Production and Trade. MIT Press, London and Cambridge, MA.

Deaton, A., 2005. Measuring poverty in a growing world (or measuring growth in a poor world). Rev. Econ. Stat. 87 (1), 1–19.

Dix-Carneiro, R., 2014. Trade liberalization and labor market dynamics. Econometrica 82 (3), 825–885.

Dix-Carneiro, R., Kovak, B., 2015a. Trade liberalization and the skill premium: a local labor markets approach. Am. Econ. Rev. 105 (5), 551–557.

Dix-Carneiro, R., Kovak, B., 2015b. Trade Reform and Regional Dynamics: Evidence from 25 Years of Brazilian Matched Employer-Employee Data. Working Paper.

Edmond, C., Midrigan, V., Xu, D., 2015. Competition, markups, and the gains from international trade. Am. Econ. Rev. 105 (10), 3183–3221.

Edmonds, E., Pavcnik, N., Topalova, P., 2009. Child labor and schooling in a globalizing economy: some evidence from urban India. J. Eur. Econ. Assoc. Pap. Proc. 7 (2–3), 498–507.

Edmonds, E., Pavcnik, N., Topalova, P., 2010. Trade adjustment and human capital investment: evidence from Indian tariff reforms. Am. Econ. J. Appl. Econ. 2 (4), 42–75.

Estevadeordal, A., Taylor, A., 2013. Is the Washington consensus dead? Growth, openness, and the great liberalization, 1970s–2000s. Rev. Econ. Stat. 95, 1669–1690.

Feenstra, R., 1994. New product varieties and the measurement of international prices. Am. Econ. Rev. 84 (1), 157–177.

Feenstra, R., 1995. Estimating the effects of trade policy. In: Grossman, G.M., Rogoff, K. (Eds.), Handbook of International Economics, vol. 3. Elsevier, Amsterdam, The Netherlands, pp. 1553–1595.

Gang, I.N., Pandey, M., 1996. Trade Protection in India: Economics vs. Politics? Available online at http://ssrn.com/abstract=5069. Working Paper 9616.

Goldberg, P., 1995. Product differentiation and oligopoly in international markets: the case of the U.S. automobile industry. Econometrica 63 (4), 891–951.

Goldberg, P. (Ed.), 2015. Introduction to Book on Trade and Inequality. Edward Elgar Research Collections, Gloucester, United Kingdom.

Goldberg, P., Pavcnik, N., 2005. Trade, wages, and the political economy of trade protection: evidence from the Colombian trade reforms. J. Int. Econ. 66 (1), 75–105.

Goldberg, P., Pavcnik, N., 2007. Distributional effects of globalization in developing countries. J. Econ. Lit. 45 (1), 39–82.

Goldberg, P., Verboven, F., 2001. The evolution of price dispersion in European car markets. Rev. Econ. Stud. 2001, 811–848.

Goldberg, P., Verboven, F., 2005. Market integration and convergence to the law of one price: evidence from the European car market. J. Int. Econ. 65, 49–73.

Goldberg, P., Khandelwal, A., Pavcnik, N., Topalova, P., 2010. Imported intermediate inputs and domestic product growth: evidence from India. Q. J. Econ. 125 (4), 1727–1767.

Grossman, G.M., 1986. Imports as a cause of injury: the case of the U.S. steel industry. J. Int. Econ. 20 (3–4), 201–223.

Grossman, G.M., Helpman, E., 1994. Protection for sale. Am. Econ. Rev. 84 (4), 833–850.

Hall, R., 1986. The relation between price and marginal cost in US industry. J. Polit. Econ. 96 (5), 921–947.

Halpern, L., Koren, M., Szeidl, A., 2015. Imported inputs and productivity. Am. Econ. Rev. 105 (12), 3660–3703.

Handley, K., 2014. Exporting under trade policy uncertainty: theory and evidence. J. Int. Econ. 94 (1), 50–66.

Handley, K., Limão, N., 2014. Policy Uncertainty, Trade and Welfare: Theory and Evidence for China and the U.S. NBER Working Papers No. 19376.

Handley, K., Limão, N., 2015. Trade and investment under policy uncertainty: theory and firm evidence. Am. Econ. J. Econ. Pol. 7 (4), 189–222.

Hanson, G., Harrison, A., 1999. Who gains from trade reform? Some remaining puzzles. J. Dev. Econ. 59 (1), 125–154.

Harrigan, J., Barrows, G., 2009. Testing the theory of trade policy: evidence from the abrupt end of the multifiber arrangement. Rev. Econ. Stat. 91 (2), 282–294.

Harrison, A.E., 1994. Productivity, imperfect competition and trade reform: theory and evidence. J. Int. Econ. 36 (1), 53–73.

Harrison, A., Rodríguez-Clare, A., 2010. Trade, foreign investment, and industrial policy for developing countries. In: Rodrik, D., Rosenzweig, M.R. (Eds.), Handbook of Development Economics, vol. 5. Elsevier, Amsterdam, The Netherlands, pp. 4039–4214.

Harrison, A., McLaren, J., McMillan, M., 2011. Recent perspectives on trade and inequality. Annu. Rev. Econ. 3, 261–289.

Helpman, E., Itskhoki, O., Redding, S., 2010. Inequality and unemployment in a global economy. Econometrica 78 (4), 1239–1283.

Hillberry, R., Hummels, D., 2013. Trade elasticity parameters for a computable general equilibrium model. In: Dixon, P.B., Jorgenson, D.W. (Eds.), Handbook of Computable General Equilibrium Modeling, vol. 1. Amsterdam, The Netherlands, pp. 1213–1269.

Hsieh, C., Klenow, P.J., 2009. Misallocation and manufacturing TFP in China and India. Q. J. Econ. 124 (4), 1403–1448.

Hsieh, C., Olken, B., 2014. The missing 'missing middle'. J. Econ. Perspect. 28 (3), 89–108.

Johnson, R., Noguera, G., 2014. A Portrait of Trade in Value Added over Four Decades. Mimeo, Dartmouth College, Hanover, NH.

Jones, C., 2011. Intermediate goods and weak links in the theory of economic development. Am. Econ. J. Macroecon. 3 (2), 1–28.

Jones, C., 2013. Misallocation, input-output economics, and economic growth. In: Acemoglu, D., Arellano, M., Dekel, E. (Eds.), Advances in Economics and Econometrics: Tenth World Congress, vol. 2. Cambridge University Press, Cambridge, UK, pp. 419–458.

Kambourov, G., 2009. Labor market regulations and the sectoral reallocation of workers: the case of trade reforms. Rev. Econ. Stud. 76 (4), 1321–1358.

Khandelwal, A., Topalova, P., 2011. Trade liberalization and firm productivity: the case of India. Rev. Econ. Stat. 93 (3), 995–1009.

Khandelwal, A., Schott, P., Wei, S., 2013. Trade liberalization and embedded institutional reform: evidence from Chinese exporters. Am. Econ. Rev. 103 (6), 2169–2195.

Klenow, P., Rodriguez-Clare, A., 1997. Quantifying Variety Gains from Trade Liberalization. Mimeo, University of Chicgao, Chicago, IL.

Kovak, B., 2013. Regional effects of trade reform: what is the correct measure of liberalization? Am. Econ. Rev. 103 (5), 1960–1976.

Krueger, A., 1974. Political economy of the rent-seeking society. Am. Econ. Rev. 64 (3), 291–303.

Krueger, A., 1984. Trade policies in developing countries. In: Jones, R., Kenen, P. (Eds.), Handbook of International Economics, vol. 1. Elsevier, Amsterdam, The Netherlands, pp. 519–569.

Krugman, P., 1995. Growing world trade: causes and consequences. Brook. Pap. Econ. Act 1 (25), 327–377.

La Porta, R., Shleifer, A., 2014. Informality and development. J. Econ. Perspect. 28 (3), 109–126.

Leamer, E., Levinsohn, J., 1995. International trade theory: the evidence. In: Grossman, G., Rogoff, K. (Eds.), Handbook of International Economics, vol. 3. Elsevier, Amsterdam, The Netherlands, pp. 1339–1394.

Leibenstein, H., 1966. Allocative efficiency vs. X-efficiency. Am. Econ. Rev. 56 (3), 392–415.

Levinsohn, J., 1993. Testing the imports-as-market-discipline hypothesis. J. Int. Econ. 35 (1), 1–22.

Levy, P., 2008. Does Trade Policy Matter? American Enterprise Institute Online, available at https://www.aei.org/publication/does-trade-policy-matter/accessed. April 19, 2014.

Lileeva, A., Trefler, D., 2010. Improved access to foreign markets raises plant-level productivity... for some plants. Q. J. Econ. 125 (3), 1051–1099.

McCaig, B., 2011. Exporting out of poverty: provincial poverty in Vietnam and U.S. market access. J. Int. Econ. 85 (1), 102–113.

McCaig, B., Pavcnik, N., 2014. Export Markets and Labor Reallocation in a Low-Income Country. NBER Working Paper No. 20455.

McLaren, J., Hakobyan, S., 2012. Looking for Local Labor-Market Effects of the NAFTA. NBER Working Paper No. 16535.

Melitz, M., 2003. The impact of trade on intra-industry reallocations and aggregate industry productivity. Econometrica 71 (6), 1696–1725.

Melitz, M.J., Redding, S.J., 2014. Heterogeneous firms and trade. In: Gopinath, G., Helpman, E., Rogoff, K. (Eds.), Handbook of International Economics, vol. 4. Elsevier, Amsterdam, pp. 1–54.

Menezes-Filho, N., Muendler, M., 2011. Labor Reallocation in Response to Trade Reform. NBER Working Paper 17372.

Miravete, E., Moral, M.J., Thurk, J., 2015. Innovation, Emissions Policy, and Competitive Advantage in the Diffusion of European Diesel Automobiles. CEPR DP No. 10783.

Nevo, A., Whinston, M., 2010. Taking the dogma out of econometrics: structural modeling and credible inference. J. Econ. Perspect. 24 (2), 69–81.

Ossa, R., 2016. Quantitative models of commercial policy. In: Bagwell, K., Staiger, R. (Eds.), Handbook of Commercial Policy, vol. 1A. Elsevier, Amsterdam, The Netherlands, Chapter 4, pp. 207–259.

Pavcnik, N., 2012. Globalization and within-country inequality. In: Bacchetta, M., Jansen, M. (Eds.), Making Globalization Socially Sustainable. WTO/ILO, Geneva, Switzerland, pp. 233–259.

Pierce, J., Schott, P., 2015. The Surprisingly Swift Decline of U.S. Manufacturing Employment. NBER Working Paper 18655.

Porto, G., 2006. Using survey data to assess the distributional effects of trade policy. J. Int. Econ. 70 (1), 140–160.

Ravallion, M., 2001. Growth, inequality, and poverty: looking beyond averages. World Dev. 29 (1), 1803–1815.

Reason, 2008. Ending Global Apartheid. Available at https://reason.com/archives/2008/01/24/ending-global-apartheid/print. accessed April 19, 2014.

Restuccia, D., Rogerson, R., 2008. Policy distortions and aggregate productivity with heterogeneous establishments. Rev. Econ. Dyn. 11, 707–720.

Rodrik, D., 1995. The political economy of trade policy. In: Grossman, G., Rogoff, K. (Eds.), Handbook of International Economics, vol. 3. Elsevier, Amsterdam, The Netherlands, pp. 1457–1494.

Rodrik, D., Rodriguez, F., 2001. Trade policy and economic growth: a skeptic's guide to cross-national evidence. In: Bernanke, B., Rogoff, K. (Eds.), In: NBER Macro Annual 2000, vol. 15. MIT Press, Cambridge, MA, pp. 261–338.

Rose, A., 2004. Do we really know that the WTO increases trade? Am. Econ. Rev., 94–98.

Shapiro, J., 2014. Trade, CO_2, and the Environment. Yale University Mimeo, New Haven, CT.

Staiger, R., Wolak, F., 1994. Measuring industry specific protection: antidumping in the United States. Brook. Pap. Econ. Act Microecon. 1, 51–118.

Subramanian, A., Wei, S., 2007. The WTO promotes trade, strongly but unevenly. J. Int. Econ. 72 (1), 151–175. Elsevier.

Tomz, M., Goldstein, J.L., Rivers, D., 2007. Do we really know that the WTO increases trade? Comment. Am. Econ. Rev. 97 (5), 2005–2018.

Topalova, P., 2007. Trade liberalization, poverty and inequality: evidence from Indian districts. In: Harrison, A. (Ed.), Globalization and Poverty. University of Chicago Press, Chicago, IL, pp. 291–336.

Topalova, P., 2010. Factor immobility and regional impacts of trade liberalization: evidence on poverty from India. Am. Econ. J. Appl. Econ. 2 (4), 1–41.

Trefler, D., 1993. Trade liberalization and the theory of endogenous protection: an econometric study of US import policy. J. Polit. Econ. 101 (1), 138–160.

Trefler, D., 2004. The long and short of the Canada–U.S. free trade agreement. Am. Econ. Rev. 94 (4), 870–895.

Trefler, D., Gaston, N., 1994. Protection, trade, and wages: evidence from U.S. manufacturing. Ind. Labour Relat. Rev. 47, 574–593.

Trefler, D., Gaston, N., 1995. Union wage sensitivity to trade and protection: theory and evidence. J. Int. Econ. 39 (1–2), 1–25.

Verboven, F., 1996. International price discrimination in the European market. RAND J. Econ. 27 (2), 240–268.

Verhoogen, E., 2008. Trade, quality upgrading, and wage inequality in the Mexican manufacturing sector. Q. J. Econ. 123 (2), 489–530.

Wood, A., 1999. Openness and wage inequality in developing countries: the Latin American challenge to East Asian conventional wisdom. In: Baldwin, R., et al., (Eds.), Market Integration, Regionalism and the Global Economy. Cambridge University Press, Cambridge, pp. 153–181.

World Trade Organization, 2007. World Trade Report. World Trade Organization, Geneva, Switzerland.

Yeaple, S., 2005. A simple model of firm heterogeneity, international trade, and wages. J. Int. Econ. 65 (1), 1–20.

Yi, K., 2003. Can vertical specialization explain the growth of world trade? J. Polit. Econ. 111 (1), 52–102.

CHAPTER 4

Quantitative Models of Commercial Policy

R. Ossa

University of Chicago, Booth School of Business, Chicago, IL, United States
NBER, Cambridge, MA, United States

Contents

Abstract

What tariffs would countries impose if they did not have to fear any retaliation? What would occur if there was a complete breakdown of trade policy cooperation? What would be the outcome if countries engaged in fully efficient trade negotiations? And what would happen to trade policy cooperation if the world trading system had a different institutional design? While such questions feature prominently in the theoretical trade policy literature, they have proven difficult to address empirically, because they

Handbook of Commercial Policy, Volume 1A
ISSN 2214-3122, http://dx.doi.org/10.1016/bs.hescop.2016.04.003

refer to what-if scenarios for which direct empirical counterparts are hard to find. In this chapter, I introduce research which suggests overcoming this difficulty by applying quantitative models of commercial policy.

Keywords

Optimal tariffs, Trade wars, Trade talks

JEL Classification Codes:

F12, F13, O19

1. INTRODUCTION

At least since Johnson's 1953-1954 pioneering analysis of optimal tariffs and retaliation, what-if questions regarding potential policy scenarios have dominated the theoretical trade policy literature: What tariffs would countries impose if they did not have to fear any retaliation? What would occur if there was a complete breakdown of trade policy cooperation? What would be the outcome if countries engaged in fully efficient trade negotiations? And what would happen to trade policy cooperation if the world trading system had a different institutional design?

In this chapter, I introduce research which takes this theoretical literature to the data using quantitative models of commercial policy. Quantitative models are a natural tool for empirical work in this area because they are designed for counterfactual analyses. As a result, they can shed light on the what-if scenarios emphasized in the theoretical literature without necessarily requiring historical precedents. This is especially useful for key benchmark scenarios such as fully escalated trade wars or fully efficient trade talks for which direct empirical counterparts are hard to find.

My particular focus is on quantitative research which assumes that trade policy choices are made by optimizing governments. While this is a standard assumption in the theoretical literature, it has long been avoided in quantitative applications because of the unique methodological challenges it brings about. As a result, little was known about the magnitudes of optimal tariffs, the potential welfare costs of a breakdown of trade policy cooperation, or the potential welfare gains which can be achieved in future trade negotiations. Instead, quantitative analyses mainly focused on comparative statics exercises such as predicting the effects of particular trade agreements.

While this is still very much an emerging literature, I believe a separate introduction is valuable to have since the required tools go beyond what is commonly used in the quantitative trade literature. Moreover, excellent accounts of the broader quantitative trade literature are already easy to obtain. In particular, a thorough introduction to traditional Quantitative General Equilibrium (CGE) models is provided in the Handbook of Computable General Equilibrium Modeling edited by Dixon and Jorgenson (2013). Moreover, a comprehensive review of the more recent quantitative gravity literature building on the work of Eaton and Kortum (2002) is available from the Handbook of International Economics chapter by Costinot and Rodriguez-Clare (2014).[a]

My goal is to equip readers who are interested in this area with the knowledge required to expand its frontier. Assuming no background in quantitative modeling, I provide an in-depth discussion of the key tools, the key findings, and the key limitations of the literature so far. An integral part of this chapter is a programming toolkit which is available from the accompanying website (http://dx.doi.org/10.1016/bs.hescop.2016.04.003). It contains a set of fully documented MATLAB programs which can be used to efficiently compute counterfactuals, optimal tariffs, Nash tariffs, and cooperative tariffs. While they are tailored to the workhorse model used in this chapter, they can be easily modified to apply to other environments.

I structure my explanations around my analysis in Ossa (2014) which is the most comprehensive one available to date. However, I go beyond it by elaborating more extensively on the underlying methods, including the "exact hat algebra" technique of Dekle et al. (2007), the elasticity estimations of Feenstra (1994), Broda and Weinstein (2006), and Caliendo and Parro (2015), and the mathematical programming with equilibrium constraints (MPEC) algorithm of Su and Judd (2012). The central theme throughout this chapter is numerical optimization which differentiates it from the abovementioned contribution of Costinot and Rodriguez-Clare (2014). As will become clear shortly, this is a critical theme for this literature as challenges associated with it have forced earlier studies to confine attention to low dimensional setups with only a few countries and industries.

To the best of my knowledge, there are only five papers other than Ossa (2014) which have seriously attempted to quantify trade policy equilibria featuring optimizing governments. Hamilton and Whalley (1983) were the first to attempt a serious calibration of optimal trade policy. Employing simple CES specifications on the demand and the supply side of the economy, they explore optimal tariffs with and without retaliation in a range of simple two regions, one import good models. They conclude that optimal tariffs are far away from the tariffs observed in the data and that the margin for tariff retaliation in a worldwide tariff war is potentially large.

Markusen and Wigle (1989) explore Nash equilibrium tariffs and their welfare effects in a much richer numerical general equilibrium framework featuring scale economies and capital mobility. While their framework allows for eight regions and six industries, they only consider a tariff war between the United States and Canada further constraining the tariffs to vary proportionately across all industries. They find that the Nash equilibrium tariffs are much lower than the ones computed by Hamilton and Whalley (1983) and conjecture that this is due to scale economies and capital mobility.

---

[a] See also Spearot (2016) and Caliendo et al. (2015) for two more recent quantitative analyses of trade policy counterfactuals.

Perroni and Whalley (2000), Ossa (2011), and Ossa (2012) calculate optimal tariffs with and without retaliation in a quantitative Armington model, a quantitative Krugman (1980) model with free entry, and a quantitative Krugman (1980) model without free entry, respectively. They now allow for seven instead of two regions but still assume that each country imposes a single tariff against all imports from a given trading partner. While Perroni and Whalley (2000) are particularly interested in the potential effect of regional trade agreements on Nash tariffs, Ossa's (2011, 2012) calculations are part of a broader attempt to explore optimal trade policy in "new trade" environments.[b]

The quantitative approach discussed in this chapter is more closely related to the quantitative gravity literature pioneered by Eaton and Kortum (2002) than the traditional Computable General Equilibrium (CGE) literature. As argued by Costinot and Rodriguez-Clare (2014), this newer literature distinguishes itself by having more appealing micro-theoretical foundations, offering a tighter connection between theory and data, and prioritizing transparency over realism.

While this is true, it is also important to recognize that the differences between newer and older quantitative trade models are often overemphasized. For example, Eaton and Kortum (2002) indeed develop a full-fledged Ricardian model which has more appealing micro-theoretical foundations than the ad-hoc Armington (1969) model the CGE literature typically relies on. Yet, we now know from the work of Arkolakis et al. (2012) that these models are actually isomorphic in terms of their quantitative predictions so that these micro-theoretical differences matter much less than it originally seemed.

Also, some of the new techniques of connecting theory to data have close counterparts in the earlier CGE literature. For example, the "exact hat algebra" approach of Dekle et al. (2007) closely resembles a standard method in the CGE literature of expressing equilibrium conditions in "calibrated share form." In light of this, the main difference between newer and older quantitative trade models seems to be that important model parameters such as trade elasticities are now usually estimated using the same model relationships that are then also used for counterfactual analyses instead of just taken from existing studies in the literature.

---

[b] Rudimentary quantitative analyses can already be found in the early formal trade policy literature. Johnson (1953-1954) numerically calculated demand elasticity combinations for which a country gains or loses in a tariff war. His analysis was subsequently extended by Gorman (1958) to a broader class of models, by Kuga (1973) to many countries and industries, and by Kennan and Riezman (1990) to allow for customs unions. While numerical calculations feature prominently in all of these papers, they were clearly meant to be numerical illustrations rather than serious calibration exercises. For completeness, let me also mention that Baldwin and Clarke (1987) calculate various equilibria of a simple two-country tariff game which is meant to capture some of the salient features of the Tokyo Round and that Alvarez and Lucas (2007) provide a short discussion of optimal tariffs in small open economies.

In that sense, the newer quantitative trade literature comes somewhat closer to full-fledged structural estimation than the earlier CGE literature did even though it is still best described as "theory with numbers" in my view. This means that its quantitative findings so far should not be taken at face value but rather as offering a sense of the magnitudes. Of course, this is not only interesting in its own right but can also provide valuable insights into the plausibility of the underlying theory. For example, we will see that the trade war equilibrium predicted by the benchmark model of this chapter seems broadly consistent with the observed trade war following the Great Depression which is an encouraging result.

The remainder of this chapter is divided into three sections. Section 2 introduces the main methods, including the theoretical framework of Ossa (2014), the "exact hat algebra" technique of Dekle et al. (2007), the elasticity estimations of Feenstra (1994), Broda and Weinstein (2006), and Caliendo and Parro (2015), ways to deal with aggregate trade imbalances, and the MPEC algorithm of Su and Judd (2012). Section 3 illustrates these methods in an application to 10 countries and 33 industries calculating optimal tariffs, Nash tariffs, and efficient tariffs. Section 4 considers a number of extensions which have been analyzed in the literature and discusses ideas for future work.

2. METHODS

2.1 Theory

In this section, I introduce the model of Ossa (2014) which I use as a workhorse model throughout. As will become clear shortly, it nests many of the forces emphasized in the theoretical literature, which makes it a natural starting point for quantitative trade policy work. Having said this, none of the methods discussed in this chapter are specific to this model and could be applied readily to any of the other gravity models surveyed in Costinot and Rodriguez-Clare (2014). I will further elaborate on this in the following and also point to some specific alternative models which seem particularly interesting to me.

2.1.1 Setup

There are N countries indexed mainly by i or j and S industries indexed mainly by s. Households have access to a continuum of differentiated varieties and make their consumption decisions according to the following nested Cobb–Douglas–CES utility functions:

$$C_j = \prod_{s=1}^{S} \left(\sum_{i=1}^{N} \int_0^{M_{is}} c_{ijs}(\omega_{is})^{\frac{\sigma_s-1}{\sigma_s}} d\omega_{is} \right)^{\frac{\sigma_s}{\sigma_s-1}\mu_{js}} \tag{1}$$

where c_{ijs} denotes consumption of an industry s variety from country i in country j, M_{is} is the mass of industry s varieties produced in country i, $\sigma_s > 1$ is the elasticity of substitution between industry s varieties, and μ_{js} is the share of expenditure country j households spend on industry s varieties. Households collect all labor income, profits, and tariff revenue generated in the economy and there are a total of L_i workers residing in country i.

Each consumption variety is produced by a single monopolistic firm. Firms hire labor only, produce output using constant returns to scale technologies, and incur iceberg shipping costs. Their technologies are summarized by the following inverse production functions:

$$l_{is} = \sum_{j=1}^{N} \frac{\theta_{ijs}c_{ijs}}{\varphi_{is}} \tag{2}$$

where l_{is} is the amount of labor hired by an industry s firm in country i, φ_{is} is the productivity of industry s firms in country i, and $\theta_{ijs} > 1$ is an iceberg trade barrier in the sense that θ_{ijs} units of an industry s variety have to be shipped out of country i for one unit to arrive in country j. There are no fixed costs of production and the mass of firms is exogenous everywhere.

Governments impose import tariffs but do not have access to other policy instruments. I denote the ad valorem tariff imposed by country j against industry s imports from country i by t_{ijs}, where $t_{ijs} \geq 0$ for all $i \neq j$ and $t_{ijs} = 0$ for all $i = j$, and define the shorthand $\tau_{ijs} \equiv 1 + t_{ijs}$ for future use. Government preferences are given by:

$$G_j = \sum_{s=1}^{S} \lambda_{js} W_{js} \tag{3}$$

where W_{js} is the welfare of industry s in country j and λ_{js} is a political economy weight. I will elaborate on the details of this specification in the application section and for now only consider the special case of welfare maximizing governments which arises if $\lambda_{js} = 1$ for all j and s which then implies $G_j = C_j$.[c]

Notice that this model is a hybrid between a multisector Krugman (1980) model and a multisector Armington (1969) model. Unlike a standard Krugman (1980) model, it abstracts from fixed costs of production and does not allow for free entry. Unlike a standard Armington (1969) model, it features imperfect competition and products which are differentiated at the level of firms. These modifications ensure that there are no corner solutions and that there is more to trade policy than just terms-of-trade effects. While this is useful in practice, it is in no way critical for

---

[c] As will become clear in the application section, industry welfare is simply defined as nominal industry income deflated by the ideal aggregate price index which then sums to total real income or total welfare if $\lambda_{js} = 1$ for all j and s.

the applicability of the methods discussed in this chapter which can be used for any gravity model as indicated before.[d]

2.1.2 Equilibrium in Levels

Utility maximization implies that firms in industry s of country i face demands:

$$c_{ijs} = \frac{\left(p_{is}\theta_{ijs}\tau_{ijs}\right)^{-\sigma_s}}{P_{js}^{1-\sigma_s}}\mu_{js}E_j \tag{4}$$

where p_{is} is the ex-factory price set by industry s firms in country i, P_{js} is the ideal price index of industry s varieties in country j, and E_j is the total expenditure of consumers in country j.

Profit maximization requires that firms charge a constant markup over marginal costs:

$$p_{is} = \frac{\sigma_s}{\sigma_s - 1}\frac{w_i}{\varphi_{is}} \tag{5}$$

where w_i is the wage rate in country i. This also implies that profits account for a fraction $\frac{1}{\sigma_s}$ of industry s revenues, as is easy to verify by substituting Eqs. (2), (4), and (5) into the definition of industry profits $\pi_{is} = M_{is}\left(\sum_{j=1}^{N} p_{is}\theta_{ijs}c_{ijs} - w_i l_{is}\right)$.

The ideal industry price indices are given by $P_{js} = \left(\sum_{i=1}^{N}\left(p_{is}\theta_{ijs}\tau_{ijs}\right)^{1-\sigma_s}\right)^{\frac{1}{1-\sigma_s}}$ so that:

$$P_{js} = \left(\sum_{i=1}^{N}M_{is}\left(\frac{\sigma_s}{\sigma_s - 1}\frac{w_i}{\varphi_{is}}\theta_{ijs}\tau_{ijs}\right)^{1-\sigma_s}\right)^{\frac{1}{1-\sigma_s}} \tag{6}$$

together with Eq. (5). They combine to the ideal aggregate price indices in a Cobb–Douglas fashion implying $P_j = \prod_{s=1}^{S}\left(\frac{P_{js}}{\mu_{js}}\right)^{\mu_{js}}$. For future reference, recall that the ideal aggregate price indices are unit expenditure functions so that $C_j = \frac{E_j}{P_j}$.

Defining $X_{ijs} = M_{is}p_{is}\theta_{ijs}c_{ijs}$ as the value of trade flowing from country i to country j in industry s evaluated at ex-factory prices, Eqs. (4) and (5) imply:

---

[d] Readers familiar with the work of Arkolakis et al. (2012) will know that these models anyway all have the same predictions in the special case of one industry. However, as soon as there is more than one industry, differences between these models emerge in the sense that "new trade" production relocation or profit shifting effects appear in addition to traditional terms-of-trade effects in imperfectly competitive environments.

$$X_{ijs} = M_{is}\left(\tau_{ijs}\right)^{-\sigma_s}\left(\frac{\sigma_s}{\sigma_s - 1}\frac{w_i}{\varphi_{is}}\theta_{ijs}\right)^{1-\sigma_s}\left(P_{js}\right)^{\sigma_s-1}\mu_{js}E_j \qquad (7)$$

This is, of course, just a standard gravity equation decomposing bilateral trade flows into bilateral trade costs as well as origin and destination effects. Notice that the elasticity of trade with respect to tariffs is different from the elasticity of trade with respect to iceberg trade costs. This is simply because the considered trade flows are evaluated at ex-factory prices which are net of tariffs but gross of iceberg trade costs.

Recall that all labor incomes, profits, and tariff revenues ultimately accrue to households which can be captured by the budget constraint:

$$E_i = \sum_{n=1}^{N}\sum_{s=1}^{S}X_{ins} + \sum_{m=1}^{N}\sum_{s=1}^{S}t_{mis}X_{mis} - \Omega_i \qquad (8)$$

Notice that $\sum_{n=1}^{N}\sum_{s=1}^{S}X_{ins}$ is the sum of labor incomes and profits and $\sum_{m=1}^{N}\sum_{s=1}^{S}t_{mis}X_{mis}$ are tariff revenues. Ω_i are exogenous international transfers satisfying $\sum_{i=1}^{N}\Omega_i = 0$ which will prove useful later on.

Since a fraction $\dfrac{1}{\sigma_s}$ of revenues is distributed as profits, the remaining fraction $1 - \dfrac{1}{\sigma_s}$ is distributed as labor income. As a result:

$$w_iL_i = \sum_{n=1}^{N}\sum_{s=1}^{S}\left(1 - \frac{1}{\sigma_s}\right)X_{ins} \qquad (9)$$

This can also be interpreted as a labor market clearing condition since it reduces to $L_i = \sum_{s=1}^{S}M_{is}l_{is}$ after substituting Eqs. (2), (4), (5), and (7).

For given tariffs, conditions (7)–(9) jointly determine the equilibrium of the model. For future reference, it is useful to summarize this in Definition 1:

Definition 1 For given tariffs, an equilibrium can be defined as a set of $\{E_i, w_i\}$ such that

$$E_i = \sum_{n=1}^{N}\sum_{s=1}^{S}X_{ins} + \sum_{m=1}^{N}\sum_{s=1}^{S}t_{mis}X_{mis} - \Omega_i$$

$$w_iL_i = \sum_{n=1}^{N}\sum_{s=1}^{S}\left(1 - \frac{1}{\sigma_s}\right)X_{ins}$$

where

$$X_{ijs} = M_{is}\left(\tau_{ijs}\right)^{-\sigma_s}\left(\frac{\sigma_s}{\sigma_s - 1}\frac{w_i}{\varphi_{is}}\theta_{ijs}\right)^{1-\sigma_s}\left(P_{js}\right)^{\sigma_s-1}\mu_{js}E_j$$

$$P_{is} = \left(\sum_{m=1}^{N} M_{ms} \left(\frac{\sigma_s}{\sigma_s - 1} \frac{w_m}{\varphi_{ms}} \theta_{mis} \tau_{mis} \right)^{1-\sigma_s} \right)^{\frac{1}{1-\sigma_s}}$$

Notice that the equilibrium for given tariffs could be summarized in a very similar fashion in other gravity models. For example, a multisector Armington (1969) model would feature the same conditions with the exceptions that there would be no markups and profits so that the respective terms would be dropped from the second, third, and fourth equation of Definition 1. Similar arguments can be made for other well-known frameworks including Eaton and Kortum (2002), Krugman (1980) with free entry, and Melitz (2003) with Pareto distributed productivity draws.

2.1.3 Equilibrium in Changes

In principle, it would be possible to take the equilibrium as summarized in Definition 1 to the data by calibrating the structural parameters $\{L_i, M_{is}, \varphi_{is}, \theta_{ijs}\}$ as well as the elasticities σ_s. However, these structural parameters are hard to recover in practice which makes Definition 1 a challenging starting point for quantitative work. Notice that calibrating μ_{js} would not be a problem since it is just an expenditure share: $\mu_{js} = \frac{\sum_{i=1}^{N} \tau_{ijs} X_{ijs}}{\sum_{m=1}^{N} \sum_{t=1}^{S} \tau_{mjt} X_{mjt}}$. As will become clear later, Ω_i would also be easy to recover since it corresponds to aggregate trade surpluses here: $\Omega_i = \sum_{j=1}^{N} \sum_{s=1}^{S} (X_{ijs} - X_{jis})$.

A technique which has come to be known as "exact hat algebra" in the literature circumvents this identification problem in an elegant way. It is usually attributed to Dekle et al. (2007) but a version of it is also frequently applied in the traditional computable general equilibrium literature where researchers refer to it as expressing equations in "calibrated share form."[e] I will illustrate this technique step-by-step in the following using the equilibrium conditions from Definition 1.

The basic idea is to perform a quantitative comparative statics exercise taking some observed equilibrium of the world economy as a starting point. In the application, I will later focus on a case with 10 regions and 33 industries in the year 2007 but any equilibrium for which sufficient data is available will do. The comparative statics exercise can, in principle, be conducted with respect to any exogenous variable but I will focus on changes in tariffs and international side payments and assume that all other exogenous variables from Definition 1 remain unchanged.

Denote the factual (ie, observed) values of tariffs and side payments by $\{t_{ijs}, \tau_{ijs}, \Omega_i\}$ and consider the effects of changing them to some counterfactual (ie, different from observed) values $\{t'_{ijs}, \tau'_{ijs}, \Omega'_i\}$ holding all other exogenous variables from Definition 1

[e] See, for example, the note prepared by Rutherford (1995) which can be viewed under http://www.gams.com/solvers/mpsge/cesfun.htm.

unchanged. Clearly, changing tariffs and side payments also changes all endogenous variables from Definition 1 to some counterfactual values $\{E_i', w_i', P_{is}', X_{ijs}'\}$ but all equilibrium conditions from Definition 1 must continue to hold.

Applying this logic to the gravity equation means that it comes in a factual and counterfactual version. Denoting proportional changes of variables with a "hat," $\hat{x} = \dfrac{x'}{x}$, the trick is now to simply divide one by the other yielding:

$$X_{ijs} = M_{is}\left(\tau_{ijs}\right)^{-\sigma_s}\left(\frac{\sigma_s}{\sigma_s - 1}\frac{w_i}{\varphi_{is}}\theta_{ijs}\right)^{1-\sigma_s}\left(P_{js}\right)^{\sigma_s-1}\mu_{js}E_j$$

$$X_{ijs}' = M_{is}\left(\tau_{ijs}'\right)^{-\sigma_s}\left(\frac{\sigma_s}{\sigma_s - 1}\frac{w_i'}{\varphi_{is}}\theta_{ijs}\right)^{1-\sigma_s}\left(P_{js}'\right)^{\sigma_s-1}\mu_{js}E_j'$$

$$\Rightarrow \hat{X}_{ijs} = \left(\hat{\tau}_{ijs}\right)^{-\sigma_s}\left(\hat{w}_i\right)^{1-\sigma_s}\left(\hat{P}_{js}\right)^{\sigma_s-1}\hat{E}_j \qquad (10)$$

Notice that all parameters that enter multiplicatively simply cancel because they take on the same values before and after the change. This eliminates much of the original complication because it is then no longer necessary to estimate them.

A slightly extended version of this approach needs to be taken when transforming the other equations because they also include additive terms. The basic idea is to express these terms as a weighted sum of proportional changes, where the weights have some factual empirical counterpart. For example, if the factual and counterfactual equations were $x = y + z$ and $x' = y' + z'$, one would divide one by the other generating $\hat{x} = \dfrac{y}{x}\hat{y} + \dfrac{z}{x}\hat{z}$ and transform the weights $\dfrac{y}{x}$ and $\dfrac{z}{x}$ until they can be measured somehow.

This basic idea can be applied directly to the budget constraint from Definition 1. Defining $\beta_{ijs} = \dfrac{X_{ijs}}{E_i}$ as the sales of country i to country j in industry s as a share of the total expenditure of country i and $\gamma_{ijs} = \dfrac{X_{ijs}}{E_j}$ as the sales of country i to country j in industry s as a share of the total expenditure of country j, it should be straightforward to verify that it can be written in changes as follows:

$$E_i = \sum_{n=1}^{N}\sum_{s=1}^{S}X_{ins} + \sum_{m=1}^{N}\sum_{s=1}^{S}t_{mis}X_{mis} - \Omega_i$$

$$E_i' = \sum_{n=1}^{N}\sum_{s=1}^{S}X_{ins}' + \sum_{m=1}^{N}\sum_{s=1}^{S}t_{mis}'X_{mis}' - \Omega_i'$$

$$\Rightarrow \hat{E}_i = \sum_{n=1}^{N}\sum_{s=1}^{S}\beta_{ins}\hat{X}_{ins} + \sum_{m=1}^{N}\sum_{s=1}^{S}t_{mis}'\gamma_{mis}\hat{X}_{mis} - \frac{\Omega_i'}{E_i} \qquad (11)$$

$E_j = \sum_i \tau_{ijs} X_{ijs}$ by definition so that β_{ijs} and γ_{ijs} can be easily computed with factual data on bilateral tariffs and trade. I have avoided expressing t_{ijs} and Ω_i in changes to allow for special cases featuring zero factual tariffs or transfers.

An equally simple transformation can be applied to the labor income equation from

Definition 1. Defining $\delta_{ijs} = \dfrac{\left(1 - \dfrac{1}{\sigma_s}\right) X_{ijs}}{w_i L_i}$, one obtains:

$$w_i L_i = \sum_{n=1}^{N} \sum_{s=1}^{S} \left(1 - \frac{1}{\sigma_s}\right) X_{ins}$$

$$w_i' L_i = \sum_{n=1}^{N} \sum_{s=1}^{S} \left(1 - \frac{1}{\sigma_s}\right) X_{ins}'$$

$$\Rightarrow \hat{w}_i = \sum_{n=1}^{N} \sum_{s=1}^{S} \delta_{ins} \hat{X}_{ins} \tag{12}$$

δ_{ijs} is also straightforward to recover from trade data given some elasticity estimates since a share $1 - \dfrac{1}{\sigma_s}$ of revenues accrue to workers so that $w_i L_i = \sum_n \sum_s \left(1 - \dfrac{1}{\sigma_s}\right) X_{ins}$.

Defining $\alpha_{ijs} = \dfrac{\tau_{ijs} X_{ijs}}{\sum_m \tau_{mjs} X_{mjs}}$ as the expenditure of country j consumers on industry s varieties from country i as a share of the expenditure of country j consumers on industry s varieties overall, the price index equation from Definition 1 can be manipulated as follows:

$$P_{is} = \left(\sum_{m=1}^{N} M_{ms} \left(\frac{\sigma_s}{\sigma_s - 1} \frac{w_m}{\varphi_{ms}} \theta_{mis} \tau_{mis}\right)^{1-\sigma_s}\right)^{\frac{1}{1-\sigma_s}}$$

$$P_{is}' = \left(\sum_{m=1}^{N} M_{ms} \left(\frac{\sigma_s}{\sigma_s - 1} \frac{w_m'}{\varphi_{ms}} \theta_{mis} \tau_{mis}'\right)^{1-\sigma_s}\right)^{\frac{1}{1-\sigma_s}}$$

$$\Rightarrow \frac{P_{is}'}{P_{is}} = \left(\sum_{m=1}^{N} \frac{M_{ms} \left(\dfrac{\sigma_s}{\sigma_s - 1} \dfrac{w_m}{\varphi_{ms}} \theta_{mis} \tau_{mis}\right)^{1-\sigma_s}}{\sum_{k=1}^{N} M_{ks} \left(\dfrac{\sigma_s}{\sigma_s - 1} \dfrac{w_k}{\varphi_{ks}} \theta_{kis} \tau_{kis}\right)^{1-\sigma_s}} \frac{M_{ms} \left(\dfrac{\sigma_s}{\sigma_s - 1} \dfrac{w_m'}{\varphi_{ms}} \theta_{mis} \tau_{mis}'\right)^{1-\sigma_s}}{M_{ms} \left(\dfrac{\sigma_s}{\sigma_s - 1} \dfrac{w_m}{\varphi_{ms}} \theta_{mis} \tau_{mis}\right)^{1-\sigma_s}}\right)^{\frac{1}{1-\sigma_s}} \tag{13}$$

$$\Leftrightarrow \hat{P}_{is} = \left(\sum_{m=1}^{N} \alpha_{mis} (\hat{w}_m \hat{\tau}_{mis})^{1-\sigma_s}\right)^{\frac{1}{1-\sigma_s}}$$

The last step follows from substituting the gravity equation into the above definition of α_{ijs}, as should be straightforward to verify. Intuitively, this says that price index changes are expenditure share weighted averages of changes in prices, which in turn are driven by changes in wages and tariffs in this environment.

Just like Eqs. (6)–(9) can be used to solve for the equilibrium in levels, Eqs. (10)–(13) can be used to solve for the equilibrium in changes, which is useful to summarize in Definition 2:

Definition 2 For given tariff changes, an equilibrium is a set of $\left\{\hat{E}_i, \hat{w}_i\right\}$ such that

$$\hat{E}_i = \sum_{n=1}^{N}\sum_{s=1}^{S}\beta_{ins}\hat{X}_{ins} + \sum_{m=1}^{N}\sum_{s=1}^{S}\gamma_{mis}t'_{mis}\hat{X}_{mis} - \frac{\Omega'_i}{E_i}$$

$$\hat{w}_i = \sum_{n=1}^{N}\sum_{s=1}^{S}\delta_{ins}\hat{X}_{ins}$$

where

$$\hat{X}_{ijs} = \left(\hat{\tau}_{ijs}\right)^{-\sigma_s}\left(\hat{w}_i\right)^{1-\sigma_s}\left(\hat{P}_{js}\right)^{\sigma_s-1}\hat{E}_j$$

$$\hat{P}_{is} = \left(\sum_{m=1}^{N}\alpha_{mis}\left(\hat{w}_m\hat{\tau}_{mis}\right)^{1-\sigma_s}\right)^{\frac{1}{1-\sigma_s}}$$

and

$$\alpha_{ijs} = \frac{\tau_{ijs}X_{ijs}}{\sum_{m=1}^{N}\tau_{mjs}X_{mjs}}$$

$$\beta_{ijs} = \frac{X_{ijs}}{E_i}$$

$$\gamma_{ijs} = \frac{X_{ijs}}{E_j}$$

$$\delta_{ijs} = \frac{\left(1-\frac{1}{\sigma_s}\right)X_{ijs}}{w_iL_i}$$

While the equilibrium formulation in Definition 2 therefore circumvents the need to explicitly estimate $\left\{L_i, M_{is}, \varphi_{is}, \theta_{ijs}\right\}$, it also ensures that the counterfactual effects of changes in tariffs and international transfers can be computed from a reference point which perfectly matches industry-level trade flows and tariffs. Essentially, it imposes a restriction on the set of unknown parameters $\left\{L_i, M_{is}, \varphi_{is}, \theta_{ijs}\right\}$ such that the predicted

X_{ijs} perfectly match the observed X_{ijs} for given τ_{ijs} and σ_s. Recall that $\left\{\alpha_{ijs}, \beta_{ijs}, \gamma_{ijs}, \delta_{ijs}\right\}$ can all be expressed as simple functions of X_{ijs}, τ_{ijs}, and σ_s.

Notice that this procedure does not deliver any estimates of $\left\{L_i, M_{is}, \varphi_{is}, \theta_{ijs}\right\}$ simply because there are too many degrees of freedom. For example, the iceberg trade costs alone could be adjusted to perfectly match any pattern of industry-level trade. Of course, this also means that many different gravity models could be perfectly matched to the same trade data using "exact hat algebra" techniques. As a result, there is a real issue of how to discriminate between different gravity models, which I discuss more extensively below.[f]

As should now almost go without saying, the equilibrium for given tariff changes could be summarized in very similar ways in other gravity models. For example, removing the term $\left(1 - \dfrac{1}{\sigma_s}\right)$ from the definition of δ_{ijs} is all it takes to instead implement a multisector Armington (1969) model since the markups cancel from the third and fourth equations of Definition 1 as a result of applying the "exact hat algebra" technique. Of course, small differences in the equations can cause large differences in the outcomes so that this does not mean that those differences have to be economically irrelevant.

2.1.4 First-Order Conditions

The "exact hat algebra" approach is not only a useful tool to calculate counterfactual tariff changes but can also be used to go one step further and characterize which of those tariff changes is chosen by optimizing governments. I now illustrate this point using optimal tariffs as an example but the analysis can be readily extended to Nash tariffs and cooperative tariffs. The idea is to express optimal tariffs as functions of endogenous elasticities and then use the structure of the model to solve for them. A special case of this is Gros' (1987) well-known version of the classic optimal tariff formula that a country's optimal tariff equals the inverse of its trading partner's export supply elasticity.

As mentioned above, I abstract from political economy considerations for now and simply assume that tariffs are set by welfare maximizing governments. As a result, country l chooses its tariffs against its trading partners $k \neq l$ in all industries t, τ_{klt}, to maximize its real income $G_l = \dfrac{E_l}{\prod_s \left(\dfrac{P_{ls}}{\mu_{ls}}\right)^{\mu_{ls}}}$. To be able to leverage the "exact hat algebra" approach, it is useful to think of the equivalent formulation in changes, where country l chooses its tariff changes $\hat{\tau}_{klt}$ to maximize its real income change $\hat{G}_l = \dfrac{\hat{E}_l}{\prod_s \left(\hat{P}_{ls}\right)^{\mu_{ls}}}$, all relative to the factual equilibrium. Using this formulation, it should be easy to verify that the associated first-order conditions can be written as:

---

[f] Costinot and Rodriguez-Clare (2014) discuss in more detail for which trade models this "exact hat algebra" approach works.

$$\frac{\partial \hat{E}_l/\hat{E}_l}{\partial \hat{\tau}_{klt}} = \sum_{s=1}^{S} \mu_{ls} \frac{\partial \hat{P}_{ls}/\hat{P}_{ls}}{\partial \hat{\tau}_{klt}} \tag{14}$$

The semielasticities $\dfrac{\partial \hat{E}_l/\hat{E}_l}{\partial \hat{\tau}_{klt}}$ and $\dfrac{\partial \hat{P}_{ls}/\hat{P}_{ls}}{\partial \hat{\tau}_{klt}}$ are equilibrium objects which can be character-ized by differentiating the equilibrium conditions in changes from Definition 2. How-ever, these equilibrium conditions first have to be evaluated at the optimal tariffs because this is where the first-order conditions have to hold. As a result, optimal tariff changes can be defined as a set of $\hat{\tau}_{klt}$ such that the equilibrium conditions in changes from Definition 2 predict a set of counterfactual parameters $\left\{\alpha'_{ijs}, \beta'_{ijs}, \gamma'_{ijs}, \delta'_{ijs}\right\}$ for which the derivatives of the equilibrium conditions in changes from Definition 2 are consistent with the first-order conditions (14).[g] Differentiating the equilibrium conditions in changes from Definition 2, this logic is summarized as Definition 3:

Definition 3 Country l's optimal tariff changes are characterized by a set of $\left\{\dfrac{\partial \hat{E}_i/\hat{E}_i}{\partial \hat{\tau}_{klt}}, \dfrac{\partial \hat{w}_i/\hat{w}_i}{\partial \hat{\tau}_{klt}}, \hat{\tau}_{klt}\right\}$ such that

$$\frac{\partial \hat{E}_l/\hat{E}_l}{\partial \hat{\tau}_{klt}} = \sum_{s=1}^{S} \mu_{ls} \frac{\partial \hat{P}_{ls}/\hat{P}_{ls}}{\partial \hat{\tau}_{klt}}$$

$$\frac{\partial \hat{E}_i/\hat{E}_i}{\partial \hat{\tau}_{klt}} = \sum_{n=1}^{N}\sum_{s=1}^{S} \beta'_{ins} \frac{\partial \hat{X}_{ins}/\hat{X}_{ins}}{\partial \hat{\tau}_{klt}} + \sum_{m=1}^{N}\sum_{s=1}^{S} \gamma'_{mis}\tau'_{mis}\left(\frac{\partial \hat{\tau}_{mis}/\hat{\tau}_{mis}}{\partial \hat{\tau}_{klt}} + \frac{t'_{mis}}{\tau'_{mis}}\frac{\partial \hat{X}_{mis}/\hat{X}_{mis}}{\partial \hat{\tau}_{klt}}\right)$$

$$\frac{\partial \hat{w}_i/\hat{w}_i}{\partial \hat{\tau}_{klt}} = \sum_{n=1}^{N}\sum_{s=1}^{S} \delta'_{ins} \frac{\partial \hat{X}_{ins}/\hat{X}_{ins}}{\partial \hat{\tau}_{klt}}$$

where

$$\frac{\partial \hat{X}_{ijs}/\hat{X}_{ijs}}{\partial \hat{\tau}_{klt}} = -\sigma_s \frac{\partial \hat{\tau}_{ijs}/\hat{\tau}_{ijs}}{\partial \hat{\tau}_{klt}} - (\sigma_s - 1)\frac{\partial \hat{w}_i/\hat{w}_i}{\partial \hat{\tau}_{klt}} + (\sigma_s - 1)\frac{\partial \hat{P}_{js}/\hat{P}_{js}}{\partial \hat{\tau}_{klt}} + \frac{\partial \hat{E}_j/\hat{E}_j}{\partial \hat{\tau}_{klt}}$$

$$\frac{\partial \hat{P}_{is}/\hat{P}_{is}}{\partial \hat{\tau}_{klt}} = \sum_{m=1}^{N} \alpha'_{mis}\left(\frac{\partial \hat{w}_m/\hat{w}_m}{\partial \hat{\tau}_{klt}} + \frac{\partial \hat{\tau}_{mis}/\hat{\tau}_{mis}}{\partial \hat{\tau}_{klt}}\right)$$

and $\left\{\alpha'_{ijs}, \beta'_{ijs}, \gamma'_{ijs}, \delta'_{ijs}\right\}$ are calculated using the equilibrium conditions from Definition 2.

---

[g] To be clear, $\alpha'_{ijs} = \dfrac{\tau'_{ijs}X'_{ijs}}{\sum_{m=1}^{N}\tau'_{mjs}X'_{mjs}}$, $\beta'_{ijs} = \dfrac{X'_{ijs}}{E'_i}$, $\gamma'_{ijs} = \dfrac{X'_{ijs}}{E'_j}$, and $\delta'_{ijs} = \dfrac{\left(1 - \frac{1}{\sigma_s}\right)X'_{ijs}}{w'_i L_i}$, where τ'_{ijs} are the optimal tariffs in levels and $\left\{E'_i, w'_i, X'_{ijs}\right\}$ can be calculated from the equations in Definition 2. Notice that coun-terfactual levels and changes can always be linked using the identity $x' = x\hat{x}$.

Optimal tariffs can therefore be calculated as the solution to a system of linear and non-linear equations. While I explain below that this approach is not the most efficient to actually calculate optimal tariffs, I suspect that it could prove useful to study the properties of optimal tariffs, Nash tariffs, and cooperative tariffs theoretically. For example, it might be possible to formally establish conditions for existence and uniqueness in the spirit of Allen and Arkolakis (2014) by leveraging existing knowledge about the properties of systems of equations with these particular functional forms.

Moreover, this formulation might help shed light on the qualitative and quantitative determinants of optimal trade policy. An encouraging start is that it can be reduced to Gros' (1987) well-known version of the classic optimal tariff formula in the special case $N = 2$, $S = 1$, and $\Omega_1 = \Omega_2 = 0$:[h] $t'_{21} = \dfrac{1}{\alpha'_{22}(\sigma - 1)}$. This is a version of the classic optimal tariff formula because $\alpha'_{22}(\sigma - 1)$ can be shown to correspond to country 2's export supply elasticity. It depends on the trade elasticity $\sigma - 1$ and the own trade share α'_{22}, where the apostrophe indicates that it is evaluated at the optimal tariff.

2.2 Calibration

2.2.1 Elasticity Estimation

I now discuss two complementary approaches that are widely used to estimate the elasticities σ_s. I begin with the traditional approach due to Feenstra (1994) which requires panel data on values and quantities of trade flows. I then turn to the alternative approach suggested by Caliendo and Parro (2015) which can be implemented in principle using cross-sectional data on tariffs and values of trade flows alone. While I illustrate these approaches in the context a model in which the σ_s correspond to substitution elasticities, the methods really focus on estimating trade elasticities, that is the partial elasticities of trade flows with respect to trade costs. As is well known, trade elasticities are associated with different structural parameters in different gravity models which should be kept in mind when exploring variations of the workhorse model emphasized here.

2.2.1.1 Feenstra (1994)

The approach of Feenstra (1994) is based on an earlier insight of Leamer (1981) which I now briefly summarize: Suppose you have time-series data on prices and quantities and ask which supply and demand elasticities maximize the likelihood of this data given that the supply and demand curves have constant elasticity forms. While it is impossible to uniquely identify these elasticities for standard endogeneity reasons, Leamer (1981) shows that one can still narrow them down to combinations described by a hyperbolic curve

---

[h] A detailed derivation of this is available from me upon request. It is straightforward but tedious so I will not reproduce it here.

whose precise shape depends on the variances and covariances of the supply and demand shocks generating the data.

Feenstra's (1994) basic idea is to exploit cross-country variation in the variances and covariances of these supply and demand shocks to obtain unique estimates of the supply and demand elasticities. Loosely speaking, a different Leamer hyperbola can be constructed for each country and the estimation approach simply determines which elasticity combination is the best fit for all. The key identifying assumptions are that the supply and demand elasticities are constant and do not vary across countries and that the supply and demand shocks are all drawn independently.

This idea is surprisingly easy to implement using a panel of import values and quantities. The first step is to use the import data to construct a panel of unit values p_{ist} and expenditure shares α_{ijst} for a particular importer j and a particular industry s in which there is variation across exporters i and time t. The definitions of p_{ist} and α_{ijst} are the same as the ones used before with the exception that the subscript t is now added to indicate the time dimension which was absent before. Feenstra (1994) shows that a consistent estimate of σ_s can then be obtained by applying the following simple procedure assuming that the above identifying assumptions hold:[i]

1. Define $Y_{ist} \equiv \left(\Delta \ln p_{ist} - \Delta \ln p_{kst}\right)^2$, $Z_{1ijst} \equiv \left(\Delta \ln \alpha_{ijst} - \Delta \ln \alpha_{kjst}\right)^2$, and $Z_{2ijst} \equiv \left(\Delta \ln p_{ist} - \Delta \ln p_{kst}\right)\left(\Delta \ln \alpha_{ijst} - \Delta \ln \alpha_{kjst}\right)$, where Δ denotes time differences and k is an arbitrary reference country, and use ordinary least-squares to estimate the following linear regression:[j]

$$Y_{ist} = \theta_{1s} Z_{1ijst} + \theta_{2s} Z_{2ijst} + u_{ijst} \tag{15}$$

2. Take the estimated coefficients $\tilde{\theta}_{1s}$ and $\tilde{\theta}_{2s}$ from the above regression and back out the estimated supply elasticities $\tilde{\rho}_s$ using the formulas:

$$\tilde{\rho}_s = 0.5 + \left(0.25 - \left(4 + \tilde{\theta}_{2s}^2/\tilde{\theta}_{1s}\right)^{-1}\right)^{\frac{1}{2}}, \text{ if } \tilde{\theta}_{2s} > 0$$

$$\tilde{\rho}_s = 0.5 - \left(0.25 - \left(4 + \tilde{\theta}_{2s}^2/\tilde{\theta}_{1s}\right)^{-1}\right)^{\frac{1}{2}}, \text{ if } \tilde{\theta}_{2s} < 0 \tag{16}$$

---

[i] This is based on the explanations in Feenstra (2010), in which the Feenstra (1994) procedure is particularly clearly explained.

[j] To obtain efficient estimates of the elasticities, this regression needs to be run a second time using weighted least squares, where the weights are computed from the inverse of the standard deviation of the residuals from the unweighted regression. This is done in the STATA code I use to estimate the elasticities for this chapter which follows the STATA code from Feenstra (2010).

3. Use the estimated supply elasticities $\tilde{\rho}_s$ from the above formulas and calculate the estimated demand elasticities $\tilde{\sigma}_s$ from the relationship:

$$\tilde{\sigma}_s = 1 + \left(\frac{2\tilde{\rho}_s - 1}{1 - \tilde{\rho}_s}\right)\frac{1}{\tilde{\theta}_{2s}} \tag{17}$$

Notice that this procedure cannot be applied if $0.25 < \left(4 + \tilde{\theta}_{2s}^2/\tilde{\theta}_{1s}\right)^{-1}$ because then the elasticity formulas would have imaginary values as results. However, Broda and Weinstein (2006) suggest a grid search approach for this case with which one can still recover estimates of ρ_s and σ_s. The idea is to simply find the values of ρ_s and σ_s which minimize the residual sum of squares of regression (15) subject to the constraints that $0 \leq \rho_s < 1$ and $\sigma_s > 1$. It makes use of the theoretical restrictions derived in Feenstra (1994) that $\theta_{1s} = \dfrac{\rho_s}{(\sigma_s - 1)^2(1 - \rho_s)}$ and $\theta_{2s} = \dfrac{2\rho_s - 1}{(\sigma_s - 1)(1 - \rho_s)}$.

As is the case with any estimation procedure, the Feenstra (1994) method is not without flaws. One major drawback is that the assumption of independent supply and demand shocks is likely to be violated in practice leading to inconsistent estimates. For example, one might think that productivity and spending simultaneously fall in recessions in which case both the supply and the demand curves shift in. Another issue is that Feenstra's (1994) assumption of constant export supply elasticities does not apply in standard gravity models such as the one discussed in this chapter. Strictly speaking, the Feenstra (1994) method is therefore not correctly specified to estimate demand elasticities in such settings but it is frequently applied to them anyway.

Despite these caveats, the Feenstra (1994) method can deliver plausible estimates of σ_s. In particular, Table 1 reports elasticity estimates calculated by applying the STATA code provided in Feenstra (2010) to Comtrade data for the years 1994–2008.[k] In anticipation of the below application section, they are provided for the 33 industries with which I work later on. My only departure from the standard procedure is that I pool the data

---

[k] The Comtrade data is originally at the SITC-Rev2 four-digit level and I convert it, first, to the SITC-Rev3 four-digit level using a concordance from the Center for International Data at UC Davis and, second, to the GTAP sector level using a concordance which I manually constructed with the help of various concordances available from the GTAP website. This involved combining the original GTAP sectors "raw milk" and "dairy products" into a new GTAP sector "raw and processed dairy", the original GTAP sectors "paddy rice" and "processed rice" into a new GTAP sector "raw and processed rice," and the original GTAP sectors "raw and processed sugar" and "sugar cane, sugar beet" into a new GTAP sector "sugar." This is exactly the same procedure I follow in Ossa (2014).

Table 1 Elasticity estimates

Wheat	12.37	Oil seeds	2.89
Dairy	5.60	Metal products	2.79
Wearing apparel	5.31	Other food products	2.78
Vegetable oils, etc.	4.98	Paper products, etc.	2.73
Rice	4.87	Bovine cattle, etc.	2.58
Bovine meat products	4.39	Other crops	2.54
Other metals	4.38	Sugar	2.52
Leather products	4.11	Electronic equipment	2.49
Other manufactures	3.52	Other mineral products	2.47
Other cereal grains	3.29	Chemical products, etc.	2.37
Other meat products	3.14	Other machinery, etc.	2.37
Motor vehicles, etc.	3.13	Plant-based fibers	2.33
Ferrous metals	3.01	Forestry	2.33
Other transport equipment	2.99	Wood products	2.29
Beverages, etc.	2.93	Vegetables, etc.	2.19
Textiles	2.90	Other animal products	2.12
Wool, etc.	2.89	Mean	3.44

Notes: These are the elasticities of substitution estimated following the Feenstra (1994) method for the 33 GTAP industries included in the analysis.

over a number of major importers.[1] This is consistent with my earlier assumption that σ_s does not vary across countries and allows me to use a larger dataset leading to more precise estimates. As can be seen, homogeneous goods such as wheat are estimated to have the highest elasticities. Also, the mean elasticity is found to be 3.44 which is within the range of estimates from the literature.

While the Feenstra (1994) method is mostly applied to estimate import demand elasticities, Broda et al. (2008) also make use of the associated export supply elasticities in an interesting trade policy application. Focusing on a number of non-WTO member countries, they show that tariffs are increasing in the export supply elasticities faced by importing countries just as the classic optimal tariff formula predicts. The focus on non-WTO member countries is necessary because the export supply elasticities themselves depend on tariffs under all but the most restrictive assumptions. As a result, one has to assume that

[1] In particular, I pool over the importers with which I work later on, namely Canada, China, India, Japan, Korea, Russia, and the United States as well as the EU-25 countries Austria, Belgium, Cyprus, Czech Republic, Denmark, Estonia, Finland, France, Germany, Greece, Hungary, Ireland, Italy, Latvia, Lithuania, Luxembourg, Malta, The Netherlands, Poland, Portugal, Slovakia, Slovenia, Sweden, Spain, and the United Kingdom and the Mercosur countries Argentina, Brazil, Paraguay, and Uruguay. Soderbery (2015) has recently suggested an interesting extension to the Feenstra (1994) method which deals with a small sample bias found to be present in the original methodology. While I have not yet applied this methodology myself, I know that my elasticity estimates look much less plausible if I do not pool across importers which I suspect is exactly due to the fact that the sample size used for each elasticity estimation is then much reduced.

factual tariffs are equal to optimal tariffs for the exercise to make sense, which is more plausible for non-WTO member countries.

2.2.1.2 Caliendo and Parro (2015)

Caliendo and Parro (2015) suggest an alternative method which identifies σ_s from the effect tariff changes have on trade flows. It exploits the particular structure of gravity equations and can be applied directly to Eq. (7). In particular, consider industry s trade flows from country i to country j, from country j to country k, and from country k to country i and multiply them together as $X_{ijs}X_{jks}X_{kis}$. Now divide this by the same term just with trade flows of the reverse direction and substitute the gravity Eq. (7) to obtain:

$$\frac{X_{ijs}X_{jks}X_{kis}}{X_{jis}X_{kjs}X_{iks}} = \left(\frac{\tau_{ijs}\tau_{jks}\tau_{kis}}{\tau_{jis}\tau_{kjs}\tau_{iks}}\right)^{-\sigma_s}\left(\frac{\theta_{ijs}\theta_{jks}\theta_{kis}}{\theta_{jis}\theta_{kjs}\theta_{iks}}\right)^{1-\sigma_s} \tag{18}$$

Notice that all terms which are specific to a particular origin or destination have been cancelled by taking this ratio so that only pair-specific tariffs and iceberg trade costs remain. The next step is to assume that iceberg trade costs can be decomposed into an origin-specific, a destination-specific, and a pair-specific component, where the pair-specific component has a deterministic and a stochastic part: $\theta_{ijs} = \vartheta_{ijs}\vartheta_{is}\vartheta_{js}\varepsilon_{ijs}$. Under the plausible restriction that the pair-specific component is symmetric in the sense that $\vartheta_{ijs} = \vartheta_{jis}$, the above equation simplifies to:

$$\frac{X_{ijs}X_{jks}X_{kis}}{X_{jis}X_{kjs}X_{iks}} = \left(\frac{\tau_{ijs}\tau_{jks}\tau_{kis}}{\tau_{jis}\tau_{kjs}\tau_{iks}}\right)^{-\sigma_s}\left(\frac{\varepsilon_{ijs}\varepsilon_{jks}\varepsilon_{kis}}{\varepsilon_{jis}\varepsilon_{kjs}\varepsilon_{iks}}\right)^{1-\sigma_s} \tag{19}$$

Taking logs and defining the error term $\nu_{ijks} \equiv \dfrac{\varepsilon_{ijs}\varepsilon_{jks}\varepsilon_{kis}}{\varepsilon_{jis}\varepsilon_{kjs}\varepsilon_{iks}}$ to simplify the notation, this

yields Caliendo and Parro's 2015 estimating equation which can be written in levels or changes, where a "hat" denotes a proportional change just as above:

$$\ln\left(\frac{X_{ijs}X_{jks}X_{kis}}{X_{jis}X_{kjs}X_{iks}}\right) = -\sigma_s\ln\left(\frac{\tau_{ijs}\tau_{jks}\tau_{kis}}{\tau_{jis}\tau_{kjs}\tau_{iks}}\right) + \nu_{ijks}$$

$$\ln\left(\frac{\hat{X}_{ijs}\hat{X}_{jks}\hat{X}_{kis}}{\hat{X}_{jis}\hat{X}_{kjs}\hat{X}_{iks}}\right) = -\sigma_s\ln\left(\frac{\hat{\tau}_{ijs}\hat{\tau}_{jks}\hat{\tau}_{kis}}{\hat{\tau}_{jis}\hat{\tau}_{kjs}\hat{\tau}_{iks}}\right) + \hat{\nu}_{ijks} \tag{20}$$

Just like the Feenstra (1994) method, the Caliendo and Parro (2015) approach is based on a strong identifying assumption. In particular, $\dfrac{\tau_{ijs}\tau_{jks}\tau_{kis}}{\tau_{jis}\tau_{kjs}\tau_{iks}}$ has to be independent of ν_{ijks} (or its equivalent in changes) for regression (20) to yield consistent estimates. This is violated, for example, if pair-specific tariff and nontariff barriers are correlated which is likely to be the case. An additional problem is that all identification comes from discriminatory tariff barriers because all MFN tariff barriers cancel out. While this does not invalidate the method in any manner, it is still likely to limit its power in many applications because it eliminates much of the variation the tariff data contain.[m]

While Caliendo and Parro (2015) have shown that their methodology can be successfully applied using trade and tariff data from the North American Free Trade Agreement (NAFTA), I was unable to obtain meaningful estimates using a cross-section of trade and tariff data from the Global Trade Analysis Project (GTAP) for the year 2007. This is the data I use in the below application section and it features the tariffs and trade flows of 10 regions in 33 agricultural and manufacturing industries. Less than half of the estimates were significant and some even had negative signs. Presumably, this is because the included regions comprise mainly WTO member countries so that there is not enough variation in discriminatory tariff barriers.

2.2.1.3 Discussion
In many ways, the elasticity estimation is the Achilles' heel of quantitative trade policy analyses. Not only is it plagued by serious identification problems, but also do most results critically depend on the elasticity estimates. This will become clear in the below application section where the elasticity estimates are shown to be important drivers of optimal tariffs, Nash tariffs, and cooperative tariffs as well as their associated welfare effects. Unfortunately, it seems difficult to overcome the identification problem since convincing instruments are hard to come by for many countries and industries. The natural alternative is to present all results for a range of elasticity estimates and then interpret them with the level of caution they need.

Moreover, the elasticity estimation is often the only time when the model is seriously confronted with the data because all gravity models can be trivially made to match bilateral trade flows in levels by choosing appropriate iceberg trade costs. The analysis of Caliendo and Parro (2015) represents a commendable exception to this rule because the authors actually try to match the trade growth following NAFTA given the tariff cuts NAFTA implied. In my view, much more work is needed along these lines because different gravity models have different predictions even though they can all match the levels perfectly fine. For example, multisector Krugman (1980) models feature home-market effects whereas multisector Eaton and Kortum (2002) models don't and the quantitative literature so far has little to say about which one works best.

A more general concern in the same spirit is that most gravity models so far impose very strong assumptions on the nature of demand elasticities. In particular, demand

---

[m] A subtle point that is developed more fully in Costinot and Rodriguez-Clare (2014) is that it matters whether tariffs are assumed to be imposed before markups or after markups (thereby acting as cost shifters or demand shifters) in gravity models featuring monopolistic competition and selection effects such as Melitz (2003). This implies that care must be taken when interpreting the elasticity of trade flows with respect to tariffs obtained from Caliendo and Parro (2015) type estimations in such environments. See also Felbermayr et al. (2013) and Felbermayr et al. (2015).

elasticities are usually assumed not to vary across countries which amounts to saying that preferences are the same everywhere. Also, demand elasticities are assumed to be constant which seems more plausible as a local approximation than as a global property holding along the entire demand curve. While the first concern seems to apply to all quantitative trade analyses, the second one could be particularly important for optimal tariff calculations such as the ones performed here. As will become clear in the below application section, the estimated optimal tariffs are rather high in constant elasticity models so that the extrapolation is taken quite far.[n]

2.2.2 Trade Deficits

Static models like the one used in this chapter really have no compelling way of rationalizing aggregate trade deficits. As a result, they are usually accounted for in an ad hoc manner by introducing international transfers such as the ones labeled Ω_i above.[o] Effectively, the assumption is that countries running trade surpluses finance the trade deficits of the other ones. The mechanics of this can be seen by combining the budget constraint (8) with the requirement that $E_i = \sum_{m=1}^{N} \sum_{s=1}^{S} \tau_{mis} X_{mis}$ by definition. Recalling the shorthand $\tau_{ijs} = 1 + t_{ijs}$ from above, this yields

$$\Omega_i = \sum_{n=1}^{N} \sum_{s=1}^{S} X_{ins} - \sum_{m=1}^{N} \sum_{s=1}^{S} X_{mis} \tag{21}$$

A common assumption is now to leave the trade deficits unchanged when performing counterfactuals by imposing $\Omega_i' = \Omega_i$ for all i. However, this assumption is problematic for two reasons. First, it implies extreme general equilibrium adjustments for high tariffs as the model then tries to reconcile falling trade volumes with constant aggregate trade deficits and cannot hold at all in the limit as tariffs approach infinity. Second, it requires a decision in which units the aggregate trade deficits are to be measured which often seems to be made unconsciously in the literature by choosing a particular numeraire. To see this, notice that the budget constraint (8) implies that real income includes a term $\dfrac{\Omega_i}{P_i}$ so that it matters in what units Ω_i is held fixed.

In Ossa (2014), I suggest one possible solution to this problem which is to simply eliminate all aggregate trade deficits before performing any trade policy counterfactuals. In particular, the idea is to set $\Omega_i' = 0$ for all i and use the equations summarized in

---

[n] While the methods of Feenstra (1994) and Caliendo and Parro (2015) are commonly used to estimate trade elasticities, they are by no means the only approaches offered in the literature. For example, Eaton and Kortum (2002) develop an alternative procedure based on price data which has recently been extended by Simonovska and Waugh (2014).

[o] Instead of modeling Ω_i as an exogenous transfer of country i, one could also model it as the endogenous portion of country i's income accruing to foreign shareholders who own part of country i's economy. This idea is developed more fully by Caliendo et al. (2014) in an economic geography environment.

Table 2 Effects of eliminating aggregate trade deficits

	Net exports (in %)	Δ exports (in %)	Δ imports (in %)
Canada	−2	−7	−11
China	21	−17	28
EU	8	−10	5
India	−4	1	−8
Japan	28	−17	46
Korea	20	−11	34
Mercosur	18	−17	21
RoW	−11	9	−13
Russia	−29	24	−32
United States	−22	16	−26

Notes: "Net exports" refers to (exports − imports)/(exports + imports) in the raw data, "Δ exports" refers to the change in exports resulting from setting aggregate trade deficits equal to zero, and "Δ imports" refers to the change in imports resulting from setting aggregate trade deficits equal to zero.

Definition 2 above to calculate a counterfactual matrix of bilateral trade flows X'_{ijs} which is free of trade deficits. This is essentially a replication of the exercise performed by Dekle et al. (2007) which popularized the "exact hat algebra" approach introduced above. Notice that the abovementioned measurement problem does not arise in this particular application because all transfers are set equal to zero anyway.

Table 2 summarizes the effects of this procedure using the 10 region, 33 industry, GTAP data used in the below application section. The first column lists the aggregate trade deficits in the raw data calculated as aggregate exports minus aggregate imports as a share of aggregate export plus aggregate imports. The second and third columns summarize the percentage changes in the values of exports and imports the model predicts as a result of setting $\Omega'_i = 0$ for all i. As one would expect, aggregate trade imbalances are large in the raw data so that exports and imports have to change substantially to eliminate them.

While I work with this purged dataset in the below application section, it seems clear to me that a better solution to the aggregate trade deficit problem needs to be found. The ideal, of course, would be to set up a dynamic model which can rationalize aggregate trade deficits by appealing to intertemporal trade. Such a model would also allow for the possibility to study how trade policy and aggregate trade imbalances interact. So far, the literature largely treats aggregate trade imbalances as orthogonal to trade policy and investigating this further seems like a great opportunity for future work.

2.2.3 Optimization
While solving for optimal tariffs, Nash tariffs, or cooperative tariffs is not a hard problem in principle, making it feasible in practice has been the main challenge faced by this literature. To see this, consider the problem of calculating optimal tariffs in a model with 10 regions and 33 industries such as the one considered in the below application section.

Since each country can choose a different tariff against each trading partner, solving for one country's optimal tariffs already involves solving an optimization problem with $9 \times 33 = 297$ arguments. This becomes even more complex when cooperative tariffs are considered because countries then have to jointly set $10 \times 9 \times 33 = 2970$ tariffs efficiently.

In light of this, it is important to carefully choose the numerical approach. In my experience, three strategies have proven particularly effective. First, formulating the problem in such a way that the number of variables which have to be solved for numerically is minimized. Second, using an algorithm in the mathematical programming with equilibrium constraints (MPEC) tradition such as the one recently suggested by Su and Judd (2012). And third, providing the solver with analytical first-derivatives of the objective functions and the constraints so that they do not have to be repeatedly approximated numerically.

While the second and third point require a more extensive elaboration, the first point is much more easily explained. As will become clear shortly, calculating optimal tariffs, Nash tariffs, and cooperative tariffs is best done using the equations summarized in Definition 2. In this context, minimizing the number of numerically solved variables just means writing everything as a system of nonlinear equations in the $2N$ unknowns $\{\hat{E}_i, \hat{w}_i\}$. While this is already made explicit in the statement of Definition 2, the problem could have been formulated alternatively as one which includes $\hat{P}_{is}$ or $\hat{X}_{ijs}$ in the list of unknowns which would have drastically increased the number of numerically solved variables.

2.2.3.1 Optimal Tariffs

To understand the idea behind the MPEC approach, it is useful to begin by considering a more naive way of formulating the optimal tariff problem using the equations summarized in Definition 2:

Problem 1 Solve

$$\min_{\{\hat{\tau}_{klt}\}} -\hat{C}_l(\hat{\tau}_{klt})$$

where $\hat{C}_l(\hat{\tau}_{klt})$ is calculated as

$$\hat{C}_l = \frac{\hat{E}_l}{\prod_{s=1}^{S}(\hat{P}_{ls})^{\mu_{ls}}}$$

after solving for $\hat{E}_i$ and $\hat{w}_i$ from

$$0 = \hat{E}_i - \sum_{n=1}^{N}\sum_{s=1}^{S}\beta_{ins}\hat{X}_{ins} - \sum_{m=1}^{N}\sum_{s=1}^{S}\gamma_{mis}t'_{mis}\hat{X}_{mis}$$

$$0 = \hat{w}_i - \sum_{n=1}^{N}\sum_{s=1}^{S}\delta_{ins}\hat{X}_{ins}$$

where $\hat{X}_{ijs}$ and $\hat{P}_{is}$ are given by

$$\hat{X}_{ijs} = \left(\hat{\tau}_{ijs}\right)^{-\sigma_s} \left(\hat{w}_i\right)^{1-\sigma_s} \left(\hat{P}_{js}\right)^{\sigma_s-1} \hat{E}_j$$

$$\hat{P}_{is} = \left(\sum_{m=1}^{N} \alpha_{mis} \left(\hat{w}_m \hat{\tau}_{mis}\right)^{1-\sigma_s}\right)^{\frac{1}{1-\sigma_s}}$$

and $\left\{\alpha_{ijs}, \beta_{ijs}, \gamma_{ijs}, \delta_{ijs}\right\}$ are defined as above.

This formulation would be implemented in MATLAB following a two-stage approach. First, one would define a function which computes welfare changes as a function of tariff changes by solving a system of nonlinear equations, for example using "fsolve." Second, one would apply an optimization routine to this function calculating the tariff changes which maximize the welfare change for the country in question, for example "fminunc." While this would work fine in applications with few countries and industries, it would quickly become inefficient for larger scale problems simply because the "fsolve" algorithm would solve the function with high accuracy for each iteration of the "fminunc" routine.

The MPEC approach circumvents this problem by treating the equilibrium conditions as constraints. It has recently received much attention in the context of structural estimation following the work of Su and Judd (2012). Using their logic, it is useful to restate Problem 2 as follows:

Problem 2 Solve

$$\min_{\left\{\hat{C}_i, \hat{w}_i, \hat{E}_i, \hat{\tau}_{ils}\right\}} -\hat{C}_l$$

subject to

$$0 = \hat{E}_i - \sum_{n=1}^{N}\sum_{s=1}^{S} \beta_{ins}\hat{X}_{ins} - \sum_{m=1}^{N}\sum_{s=1}^{S} \gamma_{mis}t'_{mis}\hat{X}_{mis}$$

$$0 = \hat{w}_i - \sum_{n=1}^{N}\sum_{s=1}^{S} \delta_{ins}\hat{X}_{ins}$$

$$0 = \hat{C}_i - \frac{\hat{E}_i}{\prod_{s=1}^{S}\left(\hat{P}_{is}\right)^{\mu_{is}}}$$

where $\hat{X}_{ijs}$ and $\hat{P}_{is}$ are given by

$$\hat{X}_{ijs} = \left(\hat{\tau}_{ijs}\right)^{-\sigma_s} \left(\hat{w}_i\right)^{1-\sigma_s} \left(\hat{P}_{js}\right)^{\sigma_s-1} \hat{E}_j$$

$$\hat{P}_{is} = \left(\sum_{m=1}^{N} \alpha_{mis} \left(\hat{w}_m \hat{\tau}_{mis}\right)^{1-\sigma_s}\right)^{\frac{1}{1-\sigma_s}}$$

and $\left\{ \alpha_{ijs}, \beta_{ijs}, \gamma_{ijs}, \delta_{ijs} \right\}$ are defined as above.[P]

This formulation can be implemented in MATLAB using a constrained optimization solver such as "fmincon." While Problem 1 and Problem 2 are formally identical, Problem 2 can be solved much more quickly numerically. This is simply because most solvers do not enforce constraints to be satisfied until the final iteration which eliminates much of the abovementioned redundant accuracy.

Most solvers allow the user to manually supply the first-derivatives of the objective function and the constraints improving speed and accuracy. While this is a relatively tedious endeavor, it is well worth the effort in my experience because it improves the algorithm's performance in large-scale problems significantly. The derivative of the objective function from Problem 2 is simply a $3N + (N-1)S$-by-1 vector with a -1 as its lth element and zeros everywhere else. Denoting the constraints from Problem 2 by the functions $F_i(.)$, $G_i(.)$, and $H_i(.)$, the derivative of the constraints is a $3N + (N-1)S$-by-$3N$ matrix:

$$D = \begin{bmatrix} \frac{\partial F_1}{\partial \hat{C}_1} & \cdots & \frac{\partial F_N}{\partial \hat{C}_1} & \frac{\partial G_1}{\partial \hat{C}_1} & \cdots & \frac{\partial G_N}{\partial \hat{C}_1} & \frac{\partial H_1}{\partial \hat{C}_1} & \cdots & \frac{\partial H_N}{\partial \hat{C}_1} \\ \vdots & \ddots & \vdots & \vdots & \ddots & \vdots & \vdots & \ddots & \vdots \\ \frac{\partial F_1}{\partial \hat{C}_N} & \cdots & \frac{\partial F_N}{\partial \hat{C}_N} & \frac{\partial G_1}{\partial \hat{C}_N} & \cdots & \frac{\partial G_N}{\partial \hat{C}_N} & \frac{\partial H_1}{\partial \hat{C}_N} & \cdots & \frac{\partial H_N}{\partial \hat{C}_N} \\ \frac{\partial F_1}{\partial \hat{E}_1} & \cdots & \frac{\partial F_N}{\partial \hat{E}_1} & \frac{\partial G_1}{\partial \hat{E}_1} & \cdots & \frac{\partial G_N}{\partial \hat{E}_1} & \frac{\partial H_1}{\partial \hat{E}_1} & \cdots & \frac{\partial H_N}{\partial \hat{E}_1} \\ \vdots & \ddots & \vdots & \vdots & \ddots & \vdots & \vdots & \ddots & \vdots \\ \frac{\partial F_1}{\partial \hat{E}_N} & \cdots & \frac{\partial F_N}{\partial \hat{E}_N} & \frac{\partial G_1}{\partial \hat{E}_N} & \cdots & \frac{\partial G_N}{\partial \hat{E}_N} & \frac{\partial H_1}{\partial \hat{E}_N} & \cdots & \frac{\partial H_N}{\partial \hat{E}_N} \\ \frac{\partial F_1}{\partial \hat{w}_1} & \cdots & \frac{\partial F_N}{\partial \hat{w}_1} & \frac{\partial G_1}{\partial \hat{w}_1} & \cdots & \frac{\partial G_N}{\partial \hat{w}_1} & \frac{\partial H_1}{\partial \hat{w}_1} & \cdots & \frac{\partial H_N}{\partial \hat{w}_1} \\ \vdots & \ddots & \vdots & \vdots & \ddots & \vdots & \vdots & \ddots & \vdots \\ \frac{\partial F_1}{\partial \hat{w}_N} & \cdots & \frac{\partial F_N}{\partial \hat{w}_N} & \frac{\partial G_1}{\partial \hat{w}_N} & \cdots & \frac{\partial G_N}{\partial \hat{w}_N} & \frac{\partial H_1}{\partial \hat{w}_N} & \cdots & \frac{\partial H_N}{\partial \hat{w}_N} \\ \frac{\partial F_1}{\partial \hat{\tau}_{beg}} & \cdots & \frac{\partial F_N}{\partial \hat{\tau}_{beg}} & \frac{\partial G_1}{\partial \hat{\tau}_{beg}} & \cdots & \frac{\partial G_N}{\partial \hat{\tau}_{beg}} & \frac{\partial H_1}{\partial \hat{\tau}_{beg}} & \cdots & \frac{\partial H_N}{\partial \hat{\tau}_{beg}} \\ \vdots & \ddots & \vdots & \vdots & \ddots & \vdots & \vdots & \ddots & \vdots \\ \frac{\partial F_1}{\partial \hat{\tau}_{end}} & \cdots & \frac{\partial F_N}{\partial \hat{\tau}_{end}} & \frac{\partial G_1}{\partial \hat{\tau}_{end}} & \cdots & \frac{\partial G_N}{\partial \hat{\tau}_{end}} & \frac{\partial H_1}{\partial \hat{\tau}_{end}} & \cdots & \frac{\partial H_N}{\partial \hat{\tau}_{end}} \end{bmatrix} \tag{22}$$

[P] Notice that it is actually not necessary to include all $\hat{C}_i$ in the list of arguments as well as all $0 = \hat{C}_i - \dfrac{\hat{E}_i}{\prod_{s=1}^{S} \left(\hat{P}_{is} \right)^{\mu_{is}}}$ in the list of constraints (instead only the one for $i = l$). However, this is how I implement it in the MATLAB code available on the website accompanying this chapter to also calculate the welfare effects on all other countries right away.

where $\left\{\hat{\tau}_{beg}, \ldots, \hat{\tau}_{end}\right\}$ abbreviates the $(N-1)S$ tariffs imposed by country l, the partial derivatives of the first set of constraints from Problem 2 are:

$$\frac{\partial F_i}{\partial \hat{C}_k} = 0$$

$$\frac{\partial F_i}{\partial \hat{E}_k} = \frac{\partial \hat{E}_i}{\partial \hat{E}_k} - \sum_{n=1}^{N}\sum_{s=1}^{S}\beta_{ins}\frac{\partial \hat{X}_{ins}}{\partial \hat{E}_k} - \sum_{m=1}^{N}\sum_{s=1}^{S}\gamma_{mis}t'_{mis}\frac{\partial \hat{X}_{mis}}{\partial \hat{E}_k}$$

$$\frac{\partial F_i}{\partial \hat{w}_k} = -\sum_{n=1}^{N}\sum_{s=1}^{S}\beta_{ins}\frac{\partial \hat{X}_{ins}}{\partial \hat{w}_k} - \sum_{m=1}^{N}\sum_{s=1}^{S}\gamma_{mis}t'_{mis}\frac{\partial \hat{X}_{mis}}{\partial \hat{w}_k} \qquad (23)$$

$$\frac{\partial F_i}{\partial \hat{\tau}_{klt}} = -\sum_{n=1}^{N}\sum_{s=1}^{S}\beta_{ins}\frac{\partial \hat{X}_{ins}}{\partial \hat{\tau}_{klt}} - \sum_{m=1}^{N}\sum_{s=1}^{S}\gamma_{mis}t'_{mis}\hat{X}_{mis}\left(\frac{1}{\hat{X}_{mis}}\frac{\partial \hat{X}_{mis}}{\partial \hat{\tau}_{klt}} + \frac{\tau_{mis}}{t'_{mis}}\frac{\partial \hat{\tau}_{mis}}{\partial \hat{\tau}_{klt}}\right)$$

the partial derivatives of the second set of constraints from Problem 2 are:

$$\frac{\partial G_i}{\partial \hat{C}_k} = 0$$

$$\frac{\partial G_i}{\partial \hat{E}_k} = -\sum_{n=1}^{N}\sum_{s=1}^{S}\delta_{ins}\frac{\partial \hat{X}_{ins}}{\partial \hat{E}_k}$$

$$\frac{\partial G_i}{\partial \hat{w}_k} = \frac{\partial \hat{w}_i}{\partial \hat{w}_k} - \sum_{n=1}^{N}\sum_{s=1}^{S}\delta_{ins}\frac{\partial \hat{X}_{ins}}{\partial \hat{w}_k} \qquad (24)$$

$$\frac{\partial G_i}{\partial \hat{\tau}_{klt}} = -\sum_{n=1}^{N}\sum_{s=1}^{S}\delta_{ins}\frac{\partial \hat{X}_{ins}}{\partial \hat{\tau}_{klt}}$$

the partial derivatives of the third set of constraints from Problem 2 are:

$$\frac{\partial H_i}{\partial \hat{C}_k} = \frac{\partial \hat{C}_i}{\partial \hat{C}_k}$$

$$\frac{\partial H_i}{\partial \hat{E}_k} = -\frac{\hat{E}_i}{\prod_{s=1}^{S}\left(\hat{P}_{is}\right)^{\mu_{is}}}\frac{1}{\hat{E}_i}\frac{\partial \hat{E}_i}{\partial \hat{E}_k}$$

$$\frac{\partial H_i}{\partial \hat{w}_k} = \frac{\hat{E}_i}{\prod_{s=1}^{S}\left(\hat{P}_{is}\right)^{\mu_{is}}}\sum_{s=1}^{S}\mu_{is}\alpha'_{kis}\frac{1}{\hat{w}_k} \qquad (25)$$

$$\frac{\partial H_i}{\partial \hat{\tau}_{klt}} = \frac{\hat{E}_i}{\prod_{s=1}^{S}\left(\hat{P}_{is}\right)^{\mu_{is}}}\mu_{it}\alpha'_{kit}\frac{1}{\hat{\tau}_{kit}}\frac{\partial \hat{\tau}_{kit}}{\partial \hat{\tau}_{klt}}$$

the partial derivatives of the equations describing $\hat{X}_{ijs}$ in Problem 2 are:

$$\frac{\partial \hat{X}_{ijs}}{\partial \hat{C}_k} = 0$$

$$\frac{\partial \hat{X}_{ijs}}{\partial \hat{E}_k} = \frac{\hat{X}_{ijs}}{\hat{E}_j} \frac{\partial \hat{E}_j}{\partial \hat{E}_k}$$

$$\frac{\partial \hat{X}_{ijs}}{\partial \hat{w}_k} = (1 - \sigma_s)\hat{X}_{ijs} \left(\frac{1}{\hat{w}_i} \frac{\partial \hat{w}_i}{\partial \hat{w}_k} - \alpha'_{kjs} \frac{1}{\hat{w}_k} \right)$$

$$\frac{\partial \hat{X}_{ijs}}{\partial \hat{\tau}_{klt}} = \hat{X}_{ijs} \left(-\sigma_s \frac{1}{\hat{\tau}_{ijs}} \frac{\partial \hat{\tau}_{ijs}}{\partial \hat{\tau}_{klt}} + (\sigma_s - 1)\alpha'_{kjs} \frac{1}{\hat{\tau}_{kjs}} \frac{\partial \hat{\tau}_{kjs}}{\partial \hat{\tau}_{klt}} \right)$$

(26)

and the partial derivatives of the equations describing $\hat{P}_{is}$ in Problem 2 are:

$$\frac{\partial \hat{P}_{is}}{\partial \hat{C}_k} = 0$$

$$\frac{\partial \hat{P}_{is}}{\partial \hat{E}_k} = 0$$

$$\frac{\partial \hat{P}_{is}}{\partial \hat{w}_k} = \alpha'_{kis} \frac{\hat{P}_{is}}{\hat{w}_k}$$

$$\frac{\partial \hat{P}_{is}}{\partial \hat{\tau}_{klt}} = \alpha'_{kis} \frac{\hat{P}_{is}}{\hat{\tau}_{kis}} \frac{\partial \hat{\tau}_{kis}}{\partial \hat{\tau}_{klt}}$$

(27)

To be clear, $\dfrac{\partial \hat{C}_i}{\partial \hat{C}_k}$ represents an N-by-1 vector which has a value of 1 at position $i = k$ and zeros everywhere else with a similar logic applying to similar expressions above. Also, α'_{ijs} refers to the value of α_{ijs} at the counterfactual tariffs with a similar logic applying to similar expressions above. All expressions are simply partial derivatives and should be relatively easy to derive. Of course, it is easy to make mistakes when implementing this in practice especially since all derivatives also have to be stacked in exactly the right way. However, most solvers can check user-supplied derivatives numerically so that those mistakes are usually relatively easy to find.

Fig. 1A and B displays the results of testing the above procedure for calculating optimal tariffs in a simple two-country one-industry example. The example uses the same data I use in the below application section but aggregates it to two countries and one industry with the two countries being Canada and the United States. As will become clear later, countries set tariffs purely for terms-of-trade motives in the one industry special case of this model so that the classic optimal tariff argument applies. In particular, the

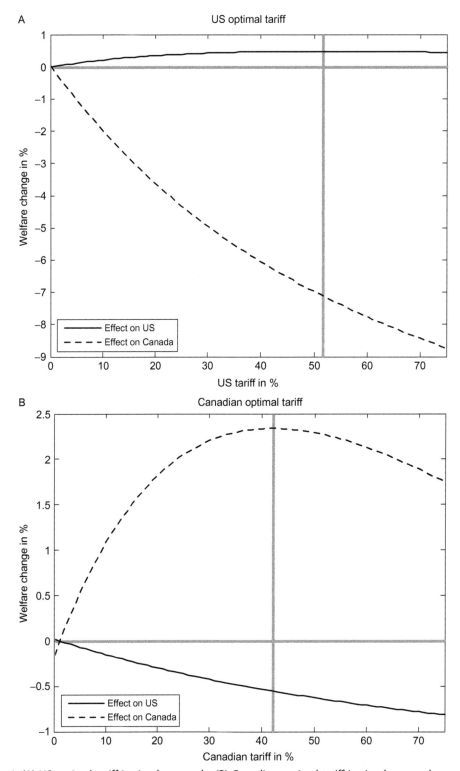

Fig. 1 (A) US optimal tariff in simple example. (B) Canadian optimal tariff in simple example.

terms-of-trade gain outweighs the distortion loss for small enough tariffs so that the optimal tariff is positive.

Fig. 1A plots the welfare effects of unilateral changes in the US tariff against Canada using the equations summarized in Definition 2. It also shows the optimal US tariff calculated using the above MPEC procedure as a grey vertical line. As can be seen, the welfare maximizing US tariff indeed coincides with the shown optimal US tariff so that the applied optimization procedure seems to work. Fig. 1B repeats this for the optimal Canadian tariff yielding the same basic results. Besides providing simple verification checks, Fig. 1A and B also reveals interesting economic points which I discuss in more detail later on. In particular, notice that the US optimal tariff is larger than the Canadian optimal tariff and that the welfare effects on Canada are always larger than the welfare effects on the United States.

2.2.3.2 Nash Tariffs

Given an efficient algorithm to calculate optimal tariffs, Nash tariffs can be computed relatively straightforwardly. Recall that Nash tariffs are optimal tariffs with retaliation, that is the best-response tariffs one would expect to prevail in a full-blown tariff war. Perroni and Whalley (2000) already report that iteration over optimal tariffs typically yields fast convergence to a seemingly unique result. The procedure is to simply impose optimal tariffs given factual tariffs and then reoptimize repeatedly until the best-response equilibrium is found. Fig. 2 illustrates why this works in the simple Canada–US example by plotting the best-response functions of both countries. As can be seen, the best response functions are relatively flat and have a unique intersection which explains why an iterative algorithm quickly converges.

While it is obvious that there is a unique Nash equilibrium in Fig. 2, this of course does not necessarily have to extend to cases with many countries and industries. However, I have been unable to find multiple Nash equilibria even in more complicated applications when exploring the implications of choosing different starting points. A trivial exception to this is autarky which is a Nash equilibrium in all tariff games simply because any country's unilateral trade liberalization would not trigger any trade in general equilibrium if all other countries keep their tariffs at infinity. Trying to formally prove the conjecture that there is a unique interior Nash equilibrium would be an interesting objective for future work. One possible approach would be to explore the formal properties of the first-order conditions summarized in Definition 3.

2.2.3.3 Cooperative Tariffs

Calculating cooperative tariffs is far more challenging than calculating optimal tariffs and Nash tariffs because all countries' tariffs have to be chosen at the same time. It is

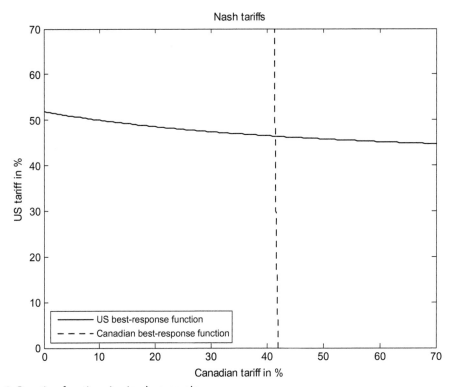

Fig. 2 Reaction functions in simple example.

also best done by using an MPEC algorithm and supplying analytical first derivatives. As I discuss more extensively in the below application section, cooperative tariffs are not just zero for three reasons. First, there is an entire efficiency frontier even in perfectly competitive models of which free trade is only one point. Second, governments might use cooperative tariffs as a second-best policy to correct existing distortions in imperfectly competitive environments. And third, political economy pressures might imply that free trade is not efficient from the point of view of governments even though it might be efficient from the point of view of the population as a whole.

Cooperative tariffs can be calculated by applying a bargaining protocol in the spirit of symmetric Nash bargaining assuming that countries equally split all efficiency gains. This can be implemented by extending the MPEC formulation of the optimal tariff problem summarized in Problem 2 above. In particular, allowing the optimization to be over all tariff changes and not just the tariff changes of country l, assuming that the objective is to maximize the welfare change of country 1 and not country l, and imposing a fourth set of constraints ensuring that all countries' welfare changes are the same, the bargaining problem can be formulated as follows:[q]

Problem 3 Solve

$$\min_{\left\{\hat{C}_i, \hat{w}_i, \hat{E}_i, \hat{\tau}_{ijs}\right\}} -\hat{C}_1$$

subject to

$$0 = \hat{E}_i - \sum_{n=1}^{N}\sum_{s=1}^{S} \beta_{ins}\hat{X}_{ins} - \sum_{m=1}^{N}\sum_{s=1}^{S} \gamma_{mis} t'_{mis}\hat{X}_{mis}$$

$$0 = \hat{w}_i - \sum_{n=1}^{N}\sum_{s=1}^{S} \delta_{ins}\hat{X}_{ins}$$

$$0 = \hat{C}_i - \frac{\hat{E}_i}{\prod_{s=1}^{S}\left(\hat{P}_{is}\right)^{\mu_{is}}}$$

$$0 = \hat{C}_i - \hat{C}_1$$

where $\hat{X}_{ijs}$ and $\hat{P}_{is}$ are given by

$$\hat{X}_{ijs} = \left(\hat{\tau}_{ijs}\right)^{-\sigma_s}\left(\hat{w}_i\right)^{1-\sigma_s}\left(\hat{P}_{js}\right)^{\sigma_s-1}\hat{E}_j$$

$$\hat{P}_{is} = \left(\sum_{m=1}^{N}\alpha_{mis}\left(\hat{w}_m\hat{\tau}_{mis}\right)^{1-\sigma_s}\right)^{\frac{1}{1-\sigma_s}}$$

and $\left\{\alpha_{ijs}, \beta_{ijs}, \gamma_{ijs}, \delta_{ijs}\right\}$ are defined as above.

Given that Problem 3 is just an extension of Problem 2, the derivatives associated with Problem 3 also build on the derivatives associated with Problem 2. The derivative of the objective function from Problem 3 is now a $3N + N(N-1)S$-by-1 vector with a -1 as its first element and zeros everywhere else. Denoting the constraints from Problem 3 by the functions $F_i(.), G_i(.), H_i(.),$ and $I(.)$ the derivative of the constraints is a $3N + N(N-1)$ S-by-$4N$ matrix:

---

[q] As will become clear shortly in the discussion surrounding Fig. 3, there is no unique efficient tariff vector but instead an entire efficiency frontier. While the suggested algorithm identifies the point on the efficiency frontier which ensures that all countries' welfare changes are the same, one could alternatively try to identify the point on the efficiency frontier which maximizes the sum of all countries' welfares as is often done in the theoretical literature. In practice, this would involve maximizing the sum of all countries' welfares in changes, ie, $\sum_i \frac{C_i}{\sum_n C_n}\hat{C}_i$, which would require data on $\frac{C_i}{\sum_n C_n}$.

$$D = \begin{bmatrix} \dfrac{\partial F_1}{\partial \hat{C}_1} & \cdots & \dfrac{\partial F_N}{\partial \hat{C}_1} & \dfrac{\partial G_1}{\partial \hat{C}_1} & \cdots & \dfrac{\partial G_N}{\partial \hat{C}_1} & \dfrac{\partial H_1}{\partial \hat{C}_1} & \cdots & \dfrac{\partial H_N}{\partial \hat{C}_1} & \dfrac{\partial I_1}{\partial \hat{C}_1} & \cdots & \dfrac{\partial I_N}{\partial \hat{C}_1} \\[2ex] \vdots & \ddots & \vdots & \vdots & \ddots & \vdots & \vdots & \ddots & \vdots & \vdots & \ddots & \vdots \\[2ex] \dfrac{\partial F_1}{\partial \hat{C}_N} & \cdots & \dfrac{\partial F_N}{\partial \hat{C}_N} & \dfrac{\partial G_1}{\partial \hat{C}_N} & \cdots & \dfrac{\partial G_N}{\partial \hat{C}_N} & \dfrac{\partial H_1}{\partial \hat{C}_N} & \cdots & \dfrac{\partial H_N}{\partial \hat{C}_N} & \dfrac{\partial I_1}{\partial \hat{C}_N} & \cdots & \dfrac{\partial I_N}{\partial \hat{C}_N} \\[2ex] \dfrac{\partial F_1}{\partial \hat{E}_1} & \cdots & \dfrac{\partial F_N}{\partial \hat{E}_1} & \dfrac{\partial G_1}{\partial \hat{E}_1} & \cdots & \dfrac{\partial G_N}{\partial \hat{E}_1} & \dfrac{\partial H_1}{\partial \hat{E}_1} & \cdots & \dfrac{\partial H_N}{\partial \hat{E}_1} & \dfrac{\partial I_1}{\partial \hat{E}_1} & \cdots & \dfrac{\partial I_N}{\partial \hat{E}_1} \\[2ex] \vdots & \ddots & \vdots & \vdots & \ddots & \vdots & \vdots & \ddots & \vdots & \vdots & \ddots & \vdots \\[2ex] \dfrac{\partial F_1}{\partial \hat{E}_N} & \cdots & \dfrac{\partial F_N}{\partial \hat{E}_N} & \dfrac{\partial G_1}{\partial \hat{E}_N} & \cdots & \dfrac{\partial G_N}{\partial \hat{E}_N} & \dfrac{\partial H_1}{\partial \hat{E}_N} & \cdots & \dfrac{\partial H_N}{\partial \hat{E}_N} & \dfrac{\partial I_1}{\partial \hat{E}_N} & \cdots & \dfrac{\partial I_N}{\partial \hat{E}_N} \\[2ex] \dfrac{\partial F_1}{\partial \hat{w}_1} & \cdots & \dfrac{\partial F_N}{\partial \hat{w}_1} & \dfrac{\partial G_1}{\partial \hat{w}_1} & \cdots & \dfrac{\partial G_N}{\partial \hat{w}_1} & \dfrac{\partial H_1}{\partial \hat{w}_1} & \cdots & \dfrac{\partial H_N}{\partial \hat{w}_1} & \dfrac{\partial I_1}{\partial \hat{w}_1} & \cdots & \dfrac{\partial I_N}{\partial \hat{w}_1} \\[2ex] \vdots & \ddots & \vdots & \vdots & \ddots & \vdots & \vdots & \ddots & \vdots & \vdots & \ddots & \vdots \\[2ex] \dfrac{\partial F_1}{\partial \hat{w}_N} & \cdots & \dfrac{\partial F_N}{\partial \hat{w}_N} & \dfrac{\partial G_1}{\partial \hat{w}_N} & \cdots & \dfrac{\partial G_N}{\partial \hat{w}_N} & \dfrac{\partial H_1}{\partial \hat{w}_N} & \cdots & \dfrac{\partial H_N}{\partial \hat{w}_N} & \dfrac{\partial I_1}{\partial \hat{w}_N} & \cdots & \dfrac{\partial I_N}{\partial \hat{w}_N} \\[2ex] \dfrac{\partial F_1}{\partial \hat{\tau}_{beg}} & \cdots & \dfrac{\partial F_N}{\partial \hat{\tau}_{beg}} & \dfrac{\partial G_1}{\partial \hat{\tau}_{beg}} & \cdots & \dfrac{\partial G_N}{\partial \hat{\tau}_{beg}} & \dfrac{\partial H_1}{\partial \hat{\tau}_{beg}} & \cdots & \dfrac{\partial H_N}{\partial \hat{\tau}_{beg}} & \dfrac{\partial I_1}{\partial \hat{\tau}_{beg}} & \cdots & \dfrac{\partial I_N}{\partial \hat{\tau}_{beg}} \\[2ex] \vdots & \ddots & \vdots & \vdots & \ddots & \vdots & \vdots & \ddots & \vdots & \vdots & \ddots & \vdots \\[2ex] \dfrac{\partial F_1}{\partial \hat{\tau}_{end}} & \cdots & \dfrac{\partial F_N}{\partial \hat{\tau}_{end}} & \dfrac{\partial G_1}{\partial \hat{\tau}_{end}} & \cdots & \dfrac{\partial G_N}{\partial \hat{\tau}_{end}} & \dfrac{\partial H_1}{\partial \hat{\tau}_{end}} & \cdots & \dfrac{\partial H_N}{\partial \hat{\tau}_{end}} & \dfrac{\partial I_1}{\partial \hat{\tau}_{end}} & \cdots & \dfrac{\partial I_N}{\partial \hat{\tau}_{end}} \end{bmatrix} \quad (28)$$

where $\{\hat{\tau}_{beg}, \ldots, \hat{\tau}_{end}\}$ abbreviates the $N(N-1)S$ tariffs jointly imposed by all countries. The partial derivatives of $F_i(.)$, $G_i(.)$, $H_i(.)$, $\hat{X}_{ijs}$, and $\hat{P}_{is}$ are exactly the same as the ones shown above for Problem 2 with the important exception that the derivatives with respect to tariffs now have to be taken with respect to all $l = \{1, \ldots, N\}$ and not just one particular l. Other than $\dfrac{\partial I_i}{\partial \hat{C}_k} = \dfrac{\partial \hat{C}_1}{\partial \hat{C}_k} - \dfrac{\partial \hat{C}_i}{\partial \hat{C}_k}$, the partial derivatives of $I(.)$ are all zero, namely $\dfrac{\partial I_i}{\partial \hat{E}_k} = 0$, $\dfrac{\partial I_i}{\partial \hat{w}_k} = 0$, and $\dfrac{\partial I_i}{\partial \hat{\tau}_{klt}} = 0$.

Fig. 3 illustrates the cooperative tariffs using the simple US–Canada example from above and compares them to the Nash tariffs calculated previously. While cooperative tariffs are calculated using the MPEC approach summarized in Problem 3, I have allowed for asymmetric bargaining weights just for this example to be able to trace out a whole segment of the efficiency frontier. Readers familiar with the theoretical trade policy literature will recognize Fig. 3 as a quantitative example of a familiar illustration of

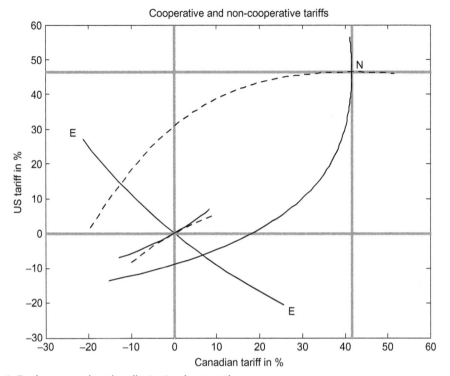

Fig. 3 Trade wars and trade talks in simple example.

cooperative and noncooperative tariffs which can be found, for example, in Bagwell and Staiger (2002).

The curve labeled E is simply the efficiency frontier tracing out combinations of Pareto efficient tariffs obtained by solving a version of Problem 3 with varying bargaining weights. As can be seen, free trade is on the efficiency frontier in the one sector special case of our model which I discuss in more detail later on. The other curves are iso-welfare loci of the United States and Canada which are solid and dashed, respectively. I have drawn one small pair passing through free trade and another larger pair passing through the Nash equilibrium tariffs which I have labeled N. As one would expect, the smaller ones are tangent to one another at zero tariffs whereas the larger ones intersect perpendicularly at Nash tariffs.

3. APPLICATION

I now put the above tools to work in a more serious application, calculating the optimal tariffs, Nash tariffs, and cooperative tariffs for the 10 largest trading blocks of the world. This is essentially an extension of my analysis in Ossa (2014) from 7 to 10 regions and is supposed to highlight some of the main results which have been obtained so far. In the interest of minimizing replication, I limit my discussion to some key points in this section and refer the reader to Ossa (2014) for a more comprehensive analysis.

3.1 Data

Obtaining the necessary data on trade flows and tariffs is not as easy as one might think. The main complication regarding the trade data is to obtain the diagonal elements of the trade matrix capturing within-country flows especially at the industry level. The main difficulty regarding the tariff data is to get accurate ad valorem equivalents of specific tariffs which are hard to compute because converting per-unit tariffs into per-value equivalents requires price data. In my experience, a particularly convenient source is the Global Trade Analysis Project (GTAP) database which is available from the Department of Agricultural Economics at Purdue University. While commonly used for a quantitative general equilibrium model called the GTAP model, the database can also be downloaded for alternative uses which is what I did for my application here.

In particular, I work with a 10 region and 33 industry aggregation of the GTAP 8 database for the year 2007. I include the world's 9 largest trading blocks and a residual Rest of the World as well as all available agricultural and manufacturing industries. The GTAP 8 database is itself based on a number of data sources which are carefully cleaned by a large team of researchers to ensure global consistency. Specifically, the international trade data is mainly drawn from the UN's Comtrade database, its domestic trade data is mainly constructed from national input–output accounts, and the tariff data is mainly taken from the International Trade Centre's Market Access Map database. The database is documented in Narayanan et al. (2012) which can be accessed directly from the GTAP website under https://www.gtap.agecon.purdue.edu.[r]

While the most recent editions of the GTAP data have to be purchased, earlier versions are available free of charge. To use the data outside of the GTAP model, one has to follow a number of steps. First, one has to aggregate the data as needed using a GTAP-supplied software called "GTAPAgg" which saves the aggregated data as ".har" files. Second, these ".har" files have to be converted into ".csv" files using a GEMPACK program called "har2csv" which can be executed with a simple batch file. These ".csv" files can then be imported into MATLAB and used normally. The original GTAP data spans all sectors of the economy. I simply drop all industries which do not belong to the

---

[r] While the GTAP data is particularly useful in my experience, there are a number of other excellent data sources such as CEPII databases which can be accessed under http://www.cepii.fr/cepii/en/bdd_modele/bdd.asp and the World Input Output Database which can be accessed under http://www.wiod.org/new_site/home.htm. Many researchers also make use of the World Bank's Word Integrated Trade Solution available under http://wits.worldbank.org/ and the NBER-UN data available under http://cid.econ.ucdavis.edu/data/undata/undata.html.

agricultural or manufacturing sector and further aggregate a few agricultural sectors to match the Comtrade data used in the elasticity estimation above.

3.2 Welfare Effects

Before considering optimal tariffs, Nash tariffs, and efficient tariffs, it is useful to illustrate the welfare effects of tariff changes in this environment. This can be done most clearly by totally differentiating the budget constraint and the price index from Definition 1. Assuming $d\Omega_i = 0$ for simplicity and recalling that industry revenues are split between industry labor income and industry profits, $\sum_{n=1}^{N} X_{ins} = w_i L_{is} + \pi_{is}$, this yields:

$$\frac{dE_i}{E_i} = \frac{w_i L_i}{E_i} \frac{dw_i}{w_i} + \sum_{s=1}^{S} \frac{\pi_{is}}{E_i} \frac{d\pi_{is}}{\pi_{is}} + \sum_{m=1}^{N} \sum_{s=1}^{S} \frac{t_{mis} X_{mis}}{E_i} \left(\frac{dX_{mis}}{X_{mis}} + \frac{dt_{mis}}{t_{mis}} \right) \tag{29}$$

$$\frac{dP_{is}}{P_{is}} = \sum_{m=1}^{N} \frac{\tau_{mis} X_{mis}}{\mu_{is} E_i} \left(\frac{dw_m}{w_m} + \frac{d\tau_{mis}}{\tau_{mis}} \right) \tag{30}$$

These two derivatives can now be combined to an informative decomposition of the welfare change $\frac{dC_i}{C_i} = \frac{dE_i}{E_i} - \frac{dP_i}{P_i}$. In particular, recalling that $P_i = \prod_{s=1}^{S} \left(\frac{P_{is}}{\mu_{is}} \right)^{\mu_{is}}$ so that $\frac{dP_i}{P_i} = \sum_{s=1}^{S} \mu_{is} \frac{dP_{is}}{P_{is}}$, that $\tau_{ijs} = 1 + t_{ijs}$ so that $d\tau_{ijs} = dt_{ijs}$, that $p_{is} = \frac{\sigma_s}{\sigma_s - 1} \frac{w_i}{\varphi_{is}}$ so that $\frac{dp_{is}}{p_{is}} = \frac{dw_i}{w_i}$, and that $\sum_{n=1}^{N} \sum_{s=1}^{S} X_{ins} = E_i - \sum_{m=1}^{N} \sum_{s=1}^{S} t_{mis} X_{mis}$, it should be easy to verify that around zero tariffs:[s]

$$\frac{dC_i}{C_i} = \underbrace{\sum_{m=1}^{N} \sum_{s=1}^{S} \frac{X_{mis}}{E_i} \left(\frac{dp_{is}}{p_{is}} - \frac{dp_{ms}}{p_{ms}} \right)}_{\text{terms-of-trade effect}} + \underbrace{\sum_{s=1}^{S} \frac{\pi_{is}}{E_i} \left(\frac{d\pi_{is}}{\pi_{is}} - \frac{dp_{is}}{p_{is}} \right)}_{\text{profit shifting effect}} \tag{31}$$

The first term of this decomposition is a traditional terms-of-trade effect. It captures that a country benefits if the value of its export bundle increases relative to the value of its import bundle. Here, the terms-of-trade effect can also be interpreted as a relative wage effect because a country's export bundle only becomes more expensive relative to its import bundle if its wage goes up relative to the wages of its trading partners. Notice that this close link between relative prices and relative wages implies that tariffs always change the terms-of-trade in all industries at the same time. It would be interesting to explore setups in which this would no longer be true for example by allowing for variable markups, changing marginal costs, multiple mobile factors of production, or input–output linkages.

The second term of this decomposition is a "new trade" profit shifting effect. It captures that a country benefits if its profits increase on aggregate because of a reallocation of resources towards more profitable industries. To see this, notice that $\dfrac{d\pi_{is}}{\pi_{is}} - \dfrac{dp_{is}}{p_{is}} = \dfrac{dL_{is}}{L_{is}}$ so that the profit shifting effect can be rewritten as $\sum_{s=1}^{S} \dfrac{\pi_{is}}{E_i}\dfrac{dL_{is}}{L_{is}}$, which follows straightforwardly from the fact that industry profits equal a share $\dfrac{1}{\sigma_s}$ of industry revenues, $\pi_{is} = \dfrac{1}{\sigma_s}\sum_{j=1}^{N} M_{is}p_{is}\theta_{ijs}c_{ijs}$, technology (2), and the identity $L_{is} = M_{is}l_{is}$. It can be shown that the profit shifting effect is equal to zero if $\sigma_s = \sigma$ for all s which makes sense since there is no variation in profitability across industries if markups are the same everywhere.

To illustrate this, the upper panel of Table 3 shows the general equilibrium adjustments following a unilateral increase in the tariffs protecting the US chemicals or apparel industry by 50 percentage points. As can be seen, this intervention increases the US wage relative to other countries and allows the United States to expand its protected industry at the expense of its other industries. Intuitively, a unilateral increase in protection makes imports more expensive for domestic consumers so that they switch expenditure towards the protected domestic industry. This then allows the protected US industry to expand which bids up wages and forces the other industries in the United States to contract. These general equilibrium effects are computed using the equilibrium conditions in changes summarized in Definition 2.

Table 3 Effect of a 50 percentage point increase in US tariff

	Δ US wage (in %)	Δ US production in protected (in %)	Δ US production in other (in %)
Chemicals	1.52	5.85	−1.41
Apparel	0.69	33.23	−0.99

	Δ US welfare (in %)	Terms-of-trade effect (in %)	Profit shifting effect (in %)
Chemicals	0.17	0.35	0.12
Apparel	−0.13	0.16	−0.14

Notes: The entries in the upper panel are the wage change of the United States normalized such that the average wage change across all countries equals zero, the change in the quantity of output in the US chemicals or apparel industry, and the average change in the quantity of output in all other US industries. The entries in the lower panel list the associated welfare effects decomposed into terms-of-trade and profit shifting effects according to the formula in the main text. The terms-of-trade and profit shifting effects do not add up to the overall welfare effects because they are computed using a linear approximation.

The lower panel of table 3 then turns to the associated welfare effects. As can be seen, the US benefits from the unilateral intervention in the chemicals industry but loses from the unilateral intervention in the apparel industry. While the terms-of-trade effects are positive in both cases as a result of the increase in the US relative wage, the profit shifting effect is positive if the US protects the chemicals industry but negative if the United States protect the apparel industry. The explanation for this is simply that the chemicals industry is a relatively high profitability industry because its products have a relatively low elasticity of substitution whereas the apparel industry is a relatively low profitability industry because its products have a relatively low elasticity of substitution, as can be seen from the elasticity estimates in Table 1.

Notice that the profit shifting effect disappears from decomposition (31) in the special case of only one industry because then $\pi_i = \dfrac{1}{\sigma - 1} w_i L_i$ so that $\dfrac{d\pi_i}{\pi_i} - \dfrac{dp_i}{p_i} = 0$. In this case, the model is actually isomorphic to an Armington (1969) model (and indeed many other gravity models) which is just an example of the point made by Arkolakis et al. (2012). However, different versions of decomposition (31) apply in different multisector gravity models because the strict isomorphism then breaks down. For example, it can be shown that only the terms-of-trade effect remains in a multisector Armington (1969) model. Also, it can be shown that the profit shifting effect is replaced by the production reloca-tion effect $\sum_{m=1}^{N} \sum_{s=1}^{S} \dfrac{1}{\sigma_s - 1} \dfrac{X_{mis}}{E_i} \dfrac{dM_{ms}}{M_{ms}}$ in a multisector Krugman (1980) model with free entry.[t]

3.3 Optimal Tariffs

Fig. 4 illustrates the optimal tariffs of all countries calculated using the methods intro-duced above. Recall that optimal tariffs are defined as welfare-maximizing tariffs without retaliation so that this figure contains 10 separate policy experiments. In particular, each panel focuses on one country and shows its optimal tariffs for all trading partners and all industries assuming that all other countries continue to impose their factual tariffs. Each dot represents the optimal tariff in one industry against one trading partner and industries are ranked along the horizontal axis in increasing order of their elasticities. I was able to calculate these optimal tariffs in around 15 min using a high-end desktop which suggests that the analysis could be easily extended beyond 10 regions and 33 industries.

As one would expect from the above examples, the optimal tariffs are positive for all countries, industries, and trading partners and tend to be lower in higher elasticity

---

[t] In this case, countries would still benefit from a reallocation of resources towards low σ_s industries but now because this decreases the aggregate price index. In particular, consumers prefer local varieties to imported varieties because they are delivered without trade costs. Moreover, this preference is more pronounced for more differentiated varieties so that consumers would rather have low σ_s varieties produced nearby.

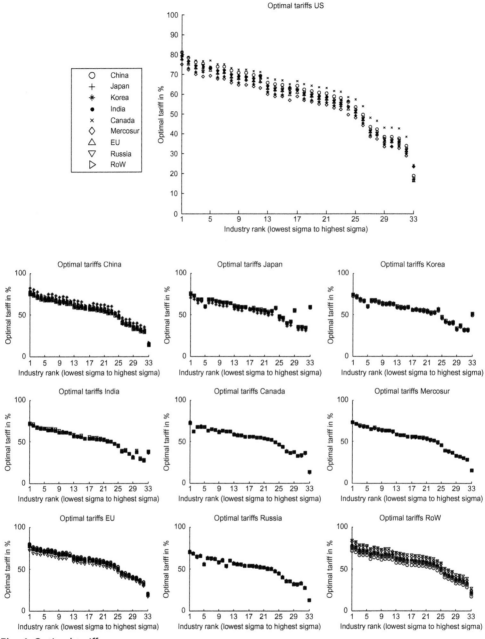

Fig. 4 Optimal tariffs.

Table 4A Optimal tariffs

	Δ welfare (in %)		Δ wage (in %)		Δ profits (in %)		Tariff (in %)
	Own	Other	Own	Other	Own	Other	Median
China	1.6	−0.9	23.3	−2.6	0.7	−0.2	58.8
Japan	3.4	−0.4	19.4	−2.2	1.1	−0.1	58.3
Korea	2.5	−0.2	19.8	−2.2	0.0	0.0	56.5
India	2.0	−0.1	8.9	−1.0	3.2	−0.2	54.0
Canada	4.5	−0.1	14.8	−1.6	3.8	−0.1	55.6
United States	2.4	−1.6	26.0	−2.9	0.6	−0.3	61.0
Mercosur	1.1	−0.1	17.6	−2.0	1.3	−0.1	55.2
EU	1.9	−1.3	24.0	−2.7	0.2	−0.3	60.6
Russia	1.9	−0.1	13.9	−1.5	2.6	0.0	52.9
RoW	2.7	−1.2	19.6	−2.2	1.1	−0.5	60.3
Mean	2.4	−0.6	18.7	−2.1	1.5	−0.2	57.3

industries. By imposing positive tariffs, countries improve their relative wages generating positive terms-of-trade effects. By tilting tariffs towards low elasticity industries, they further shift resources towards more profitable industries generating positive profit shifting effects. While optimal tariffs tend to be lower in higher elasticity industries, the figure also makes clear that this is not always the case. This simply reflects the fact that optimal tariffs also depend on other factors such as the industry's trade exposure as the simple two-country one-industry optimal tariff formula discussed earlier already made clear.

Table 4A turns to the welfare effects of these optimal tariffs always listing the effects on the tariff imposing country as well as the averages of the effects on all other countries. As can be seen, real income increases by an average 2.4% for the tariff imposing country and decreases by an average −0.6% elsewhere. Countries can benefit at the expense of other countries because the terms-of-trade and profit shifting effects have a beggar-thy-neighbor character. As can be seen, wages go up in the tariff imposing country relative to all other countries and profits go up in the tariff imposing country at the other countries' expense. Table 4A also lists the median optimal tariffs which reveal that the optimal tariffs tend to be higher for economically larger countries as one would expect.

Table 4B illustrates that the optimal tariffs as well as their welfare effects are strongly decreasing in the average elasticity. In particular, I take the original elasticity estimates from table 1 and scale them proportionately to have a mean of 3.5, 5.0, or 6.5. I then redo all calculations required to construct table 4A for these scaled values and report the last row of table 4A in table 4B. As can be seen, the average optimal tariffs more than halves when using elasticity estimates with mean 6.5 instead of mean 3.5 which simply reflects the fact that countries then have less monopoly power to exploit in world markets. Recall that the elasticity estimates average to 3.44 in the original calculations which is why the last row of table 4A differs slightly from the first row of table 4B.

Table 4B Sensitivity of optimal tariffs w.r.t. σ

σ	Δ welfare (in %)		Δ wage (in %)		Δ profits (in %)		Tariff (in %)
Mean	Own	Other	Own	Other	Own	Other	Median
3.5	2.4	−0.6	18.2	−2.0	1.5	−0.2	55.9
5.0	1.7	−0.3	9.7	−1.1	1.5	−0.2	33.8
6.5	1.5	−0.2	6.1	−0.7	1.5	−0.2	24.2

Notes: The entries under "welfare" are the changes in real income, the entries under "wage" are the changes in wages normalized such that the average wage change across all countries equals zero, the entries under "profits" are the changes in profits due to changes in industry output, and the entries under "tariff" are the optimal tariffs. The columns labeled "own" refer to effects on the tariff imposing country while the changes labeled "other" refer to the average of the effects on all other countries. The last row of Table 4A reports averages. Table 4B reports only such averages.

In Ossa (2014), I also explore the case in which governments are politically motivated so that the welfare weights in the government preferences (3) deviate from 1. W_{js} is then defined as the welfare of industry s in country j which is just the nominal income accruing to the associated workers and firms deflated by the ideal aggregate price index. The welfare weights λ_{js} are normalized to satisfy $\frac{1}{S}\sum_{s=1}^{S}\lambda_{js}=1$ so that one dollar of income accruing to industry s in country j matters λ_{js} as much to the government as one dollar of income accruing to an industry which receives average political support. This is meant to capture political economy motives such as the ones emphasized by Grossman and Helpman (1994) in a reduced form way.

I show that the political economy weights can be calibrated such that the distribution of optimal tariffs matches the distribution of noncooperative tariffs from the data. These noncooperative tariffs include tariffs such as the so-called column-two tariffs of the United States which are applied to countries with which the United States does not have normal trade relations. With the exception of China, the predicted optimal tariffs are substantially higher than the measured noncooperative tariffs given the baseline elasticity estimates. However, the levels can also be brought in line much more closely if the higher elasticities from the sensitivity checks are used. The bottom line is that the average optimal tariffs and their average welfare effects are quite similar with and without political economy pressures. This is because political economy pressures are more about the intranational rather than the international redistribution of rents.

While the calibrated political economy weights appear highly plausible with the most favored sectors being wearing apparel, dairy, textiles, beverages and tobacco products, and wheat, they could also just capture other determinants of trade policy that the underlying model fails to account for. In order to investigate this possibility further, it would be interesting to relate the calibrated political economy weights to observables such as campaign contributions which the earlier empirical literature has emphasized (see, for example, Gawande and Krishna (2003) for an excellent overview).

3.4 Trade Wars

Fig. 5 illustrates the Nash tariffs of all countries using the same template as Fig. 4. Recall that Nash tariffs capture the best-response tariffs that would prevail in a full-blown tariff war so that Fig. 5 now summarizes a single policy experiment. As can be seen from comparing Figs. 4 and 5, the Nash tariffs are very similar to the optimal tariffs suggesting that the best response functions are again relatively flat just like in the simple US–Canada example discussed earlier. Using the optimal tariffs as a starting point, the iterative algorithm calculating Nash tariffs discussed above converges in around 20 min on my desktop so that the analysis could again easily be extended beyond 10 regions and 33 industries.

Table 5A summarizes the welfare effects of moving from factual tariffs to Nash tariffs. The real-world analog to this is a breakdown of trade policy cooperation escalating in a full-blown tariff war. As can be seen, all countries lose from the tariff war with the average welfare loss equaling −3.5%. The losses are most severe for Canada which is explained by the fact that Canada is the most open economy in the sample followed by the Rest of the World, Korea, and Russia who also lose a lot. The losses are least severe for Japan which is due to Japan's inefficient factual trade policy. In particular, Japan imposes extreme tariffs on agricultural products such as a 237% tariff on rice so that a move to Nash tariffs actually reduces its self-inflicted distortions significantly.

Table 5B again reports sensitivity checks for proportionately scaled versions of the elasticities. Just like optimal tariffs, Nash tariffs and their welfare effects are also strongly decreasing in the elasticities, as one would expect from the similarity between the two. I consider mean elasticities between 3.5 and 6.5 because this corresponds to the range of aggregate trade elasticities suggested by Simonovska and Waugh (2014). This range also captures what most empirical trade economists would regard as reasonable today so that the average Nash tariffs consistent with the model are somewhere between 25% and 57%. This is broadly consistent with the tariffs imposed during the trade war following the Great Depression which are typically reported to average around 50%.

3.5 Trade Talks

Fig. 6A–C illustrates the outcomes of efficient trade negotiations starting at Nash tariffs, factual tariffs, and free trade, respectively. They are computed by implementing a bargaining protocol in the spirit of symmetric Nash bargaining just as discussed above. In particular, I first simulate the equilibria given Nash tariffs, factual tariffs, and free trade and then solve for the tariff change which maximizes country 1's welfare subject to the condition that all countries gain the same. This is supposed to simulate the outcome of perfect trade negotiations, that is the best-case scenario of what can be achieved under the WTO. Calculating these cooperative tariffs is very demanding computationally and takes approximately one full day per case on my desktop computer.

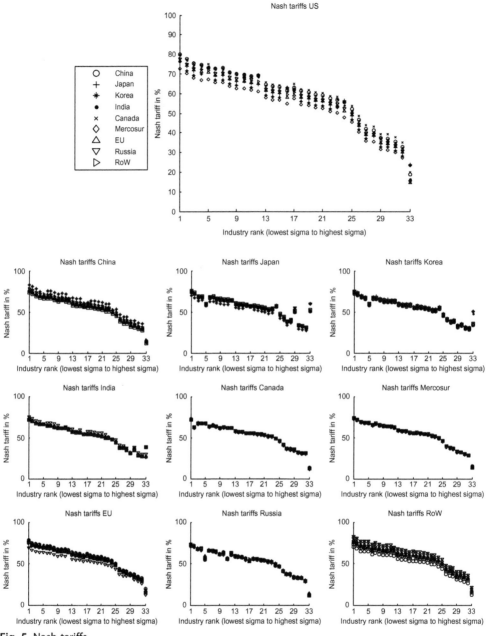

Fig. 5 Nash tariffs.

Table 5A Nash tariffs

	Δ welfare (in %)	Δ wage (in %)	Δ profits (in %)	Tariff (in %)
China	−2.1	4.4	0.1	58.2
Japan	−1.5	0.0	0.1	57.5
Korea	−4.6	−0.1	−1.2	56.2
India	−1.9	−9.4	2.4	54.1
Canada	−7.8	−5.1	0.5	54.9
United States	−2.4	6.1	−0.5	60.1
Mercosur	−1.9	1.6	1.0	55.3
EU	−2.5	4.2	−1.0	59.0
Russia	−4.7	−1.2	−0.2	55.2
RoW	−5.5	−0.4	−0.9	59.6
Mean	−3.5	0.0	0.0	57.0

Table 5B Sensitivity of Nash tariffs w.r.t. σ

σ	Δ welfare (in %)	Δ wage (in %)	Δ profits (in %)	Tariff (in %)
3.5	−3.4	0.0	0.0	55.6
5.0	−1.8	0.0	0.2	33.9
6.5	−1.1	0.0	0.2	24.6

Notes: The entries under "welfare" are the changes in real income, the entries under "wage" are the changes in wages normalized such that the average wage change across all countries equals zero, the entries under "profits" are the changes in profits due to changes in industry output, and the entries under "tariff" are the Nash tariffs. The last row of Table 5A reports averages. Table 5B reports only such averages.

As can be seen from these figures, cooperative tariffs have very similar cross-industry distributions across all three cases but vary with respect to the average levels with which they apply. The cross-industry distributions reflect countries' attempts to correct a distortion originating from the fact that prices are too high in low elasticity industries. The cross-country distribution reflects countries' attempt to make implicit side payments ensuring that the bargaining protocol is satisfied and all countries gain the same. For that reason, the tariff levels vary across the three cases because the three different benchmarks require three different sets of side payments for all efficiency gains to be equally spread.

For example, we have seen above that Canada loses most as a result of the tariff war which is why all countries impose high tariffs against Canada in the case of trade negotiations starting at Nash tariffs summarized in Fig. 6A. Essentially, Canada's terms-of-trade have to be sufficiently bad in equilibrium to ensure that Canada does not gain more than anyone else. Similarly, Japan faces the highest tariffs following the trade negotiations starting at factual tariffs summarized in Fig. 6B because Japan would otherwise gain too much from dismantling its inefficient factual tariff regime. Of course, this would

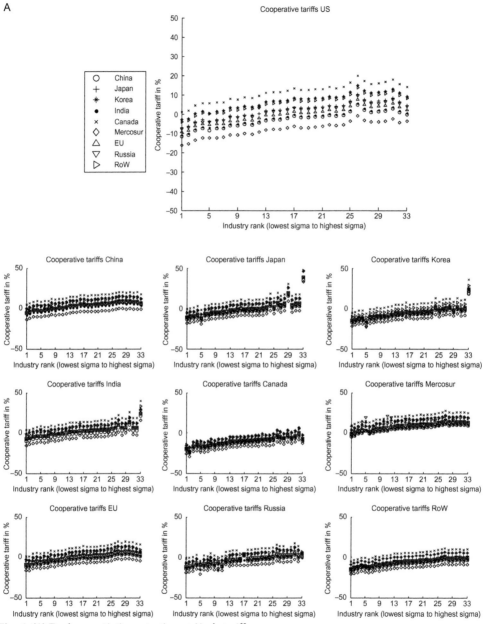

Fig. 6 (A) Trade negotiations starting at Nash tariffs.

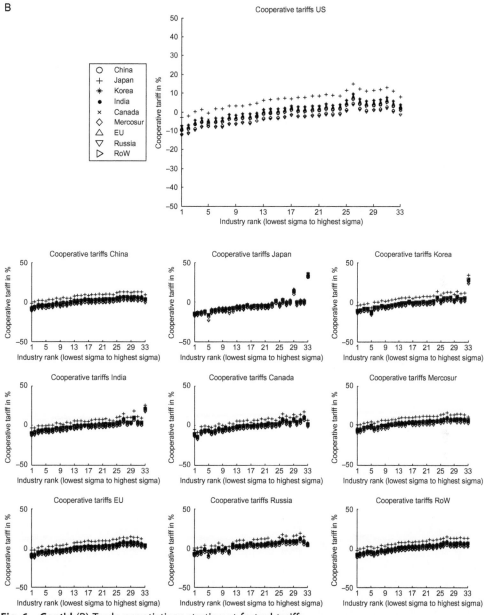

Fig. 6—Cont'd (B) Trade negotiations starting at factual tariffs.

C

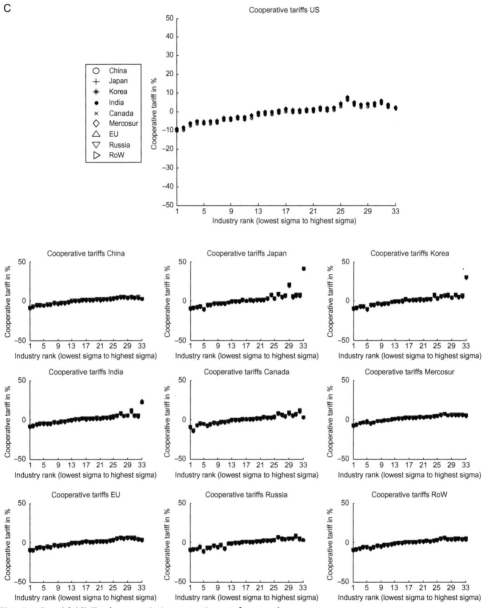

Fig. 6—Cont'd (C) Trade negotiations starting at free trade.

look different if one explicitly allowed for side payments, which might be more realistic since import subsidies are rarely seen.

Table 6A lists the welfare benefits associated with these trade negotiations. As can be seen, moving from Nash tariffs to cooperative tariffs improves each country's welfare by 3.5% so that this number can be seen as the maximum possible value of the WTO. In contrast, moving from factual tariffs to efficient tariffs only improves welfare by 0.4% suggesting that almost 90% of all possible welfare gains have already been realized in past trade negotiations. The finding that trade negotiations starting at free trade would only increase welfare by 0.1% confirms that tariffs are a poor instrument to address distortions. This should have been expected from the targeting principle which implies that distortions are best addressed with the appropriate direct policy instruments.

In Ossa (2014), I also explore the implications of the most-favored nation (MFN) clause of the WTO which generally prohibits countries from applying discriminatory tariffs against other countries. I start by recalculating optimal tariffs and Nash tariffs under the

Table 6A Cooperative tariffs

	Δ welfare (in %)			Δ wage (in %)			Δ profits (in %)		
	Nash	Fact.	Free	Nash	Fact.	Free	Nash	Fact.	Free
China	3.5	0.4	0.1	1.8	2.1	−0.1	−0.2	−0.2	0.3
Japan	3.5	0.4	0.1	−0.6	−6.7	0.7	1.4	1.4	0.0
Korea	3.5	0.4	0.1	−4.9	−0.6	0.4	1.6	0.3	0.0
India	3.5	0.4	0.1	7.1	−6.8	0.1	−0.8	1.4	0.3
Canada	3.5	0.4	0.1	−5.4	−0.9	−0.4	0.7	1.6	1.1
United States	3.5	0.4	0.1	−2.8	2.1	−0.1	0.5	0.0	0.3
Mercosur	3.5	0.4	0.1	10.0	3.9	0.0	−1.5	−0.6	0.3
EU	3.5	0.4	0.1	−0.7	2.0	0.2	1.2	0.2	0.1
Russia	3.5	0.4	0.1	−0.2	3.8	−0.7	−2.0	−2.0	1.1
RoW	3.5	0.4	0.1	−4.5	1.1	−0.2	1.4	0.5	0.7
Mean	3.5	0.4	0.1	0.0	0.0	0.0	0.2	0.3	0.4

Table 6B Sensitivity of cooperative tariffs w.r.t. σ

σ	Δ welfare (in %)			Δ wage (in %)			Δ profits (in %)		
Mean	Nash	Fact.	Free	Nash	Fact.	Free	Nash	Fact.	Free
3.5	3.4	0.4	0.1	0.0	0.0	0.0	0.2	0.3	0.4
5.0	2.1	0.4	0.0	0.0	0.0	0.0	−0.2	0.0	0.2
6.5	1.6	0.5	0.0	0.0	0.0	0.0	−0.3	−0.2	0.2

Notes: The entries under "welfare" are the changes in real income, the entries under "wage" are the changes in wages normalized such that the average wage change across all countries equals zero, the entries under "profits" are the changes in profits due to changes in industry output, and the entries under "tariff" are the cooperative tariffs. The columns labeled "Nash," "Fact.," and "Free" refer to trade negotiations stating at Nash tariffs, factual tariffs, and zero tariffs, respectively. The last row of Table 6A reports averages. Table 6B reports only such averages.

restriction of MFN to see if this clause by itself has any bite. I find that the welfare results are almost identical to the unrestricted case which also makes sense given the small amount of discrimination shown in Figs. 4 and 5. I then consider if trade liberalizations of a group of insider countries affect nonparticipating outsider countries if the insider countries extend their concessions to the outsider countries in an MFN fashion. I find that these MFN tariffs cuts would actually overcompensate the outsiders for the trade diversion they experience which qualifies earlier results from Bagwell and Staiger (2005).

3.6 Discussion

If one is willing to take the model as a maintained hypothesis, the above results can be viewed as providing answers to questions of immediate policy relevance. For example, they illustrate what would happen if there was a complete breakdown of trade policy cooperation and quantify how much there is to gain from future tariff negotiations. If one instead takes a more cautious approach, they can be interpreted as a plausibility check on some of the leading models of trade policy making. For example, they show that the Nash tariffs are of the same order of magnitude as the tariffs observed during the trade war following the Great Depression and highlight that there is enough to gain from trade policy cooperation to plausibly justify the ordeal of real-world trade negotiations organized by the WTO.

While I believe that the model captures many important forces, I lean towards taking a cautious interpretation for now, simply because much more can be done to explore the model's validity. One obvious task seems to be to assess how sensitive the results are to alternative assumptions about the economic environment. For example, it would be interesting to explore what happens if one introduces intermediate goods and nontraded goods into the analysis which clearly feature prominently in the real world. Also, it would be fascinating to carefully confront the quantitative predictions of the model with the trade war following the Great Depression to see if the highlighted forces are consistent with what has been observed.

With that in mind, it is still insightful to elaborate on what the numbers suggest so far. In particular, if one combines the welfare effects from tables 5A and 6A with data on manufacturing and agricultural value added from 2007, it is straightforward to calculate that a complete breakdown of trade policy cooperation would cost the world approximately $300 billion per year while further tariff negotiations could bring about gains of approximately $40 billion per year. So, to the extent that one credits the WTO for preventing the outbreak of trade wars and blames the WTO for failing to promote further trade talks, one has to conclude that the WTO's track record is quite impressive so far.[u]

---

[u] These calculations refer to 2005 US dollars and are analogous to the ones I performed in a VOX column which can be accessed under http://www.voxeu.org/article/wto-success-no-trade-agreement-no-trade-war.

4. EXTENSIONS

In this section, I discuss a number of promising directions in which this literature could be taken in future work. Overall, the trade policy literature so far is long on theory and short on quantification so that there is an abundance of opportunities for interesting research. I organize my discussion into three main categories, namely alternative models, other trade policy applications, and applications in other fields. As will become clear shortly, the applications in other fields I envision also have a trade policy character but answer questions which are normally associated with other literatures.

4.1 Alternative Models

Perhaps the most obvious direction for future work in this area is to analyze optimal tariffs, Nash tariffs, and cooperative tariffs in a range of alternative gravity models applying the techniques introduced above. The Handbook of International Economics chapter of Costinot and Rodriguez-Clare (2014) is a great resource for researchers interested in this area because it provides a comprehensive overview of how the many different gravity models relate. In fact, their chapter already includes a short section on the effects of tariffs in various gravity models which can serve as an excellent starting point.

An important contribution of such analyses would be to assess the robustness of the results provided so far. As mentioned earlier, introducing intermediate goods should be a high priority in my opinion given how central they are to international trade. In the process of writing this chapter, I have actually experimented with this already but ultimately concluded that it requires a more thorough treatment than I can offer here. One complication is that intermediate goods introduce a factor market distortion into the Ossa (2014) model giving rise to a new margin for optimal tariffs to manipulate. In particular, firms then buy labor on perfectly competitive markets but intermediate goods on imperfectly competitive markets so that relative intermediate goods prices are too high. While this could turn out to be an interesting mechanism, it might make more sense to first characterize optimal tariffs with intermediate goods in a perfectly competitive model such as Caliendo and Parro's 2015 extension of Eaton and Kortum (2002).

Another interesting extension would be to relax the exclusive focus on tariffs and allow for alternative policy instruments. In my assessment, it would be particularly useful to disentangle the questions of optimal allocation and implementation by following the primal approach of the public finance literature. An interesting example of this is the recent analysis by Costinot et al. (2015) who solve for optimal trade policy in a Ricardian trade model. They first assume that governments can directly control the resource allocation as social planners and then ask how their preferred allocations can be implemented with a particular set of policy instruments. While their paper is predominantly theoretical, they also provide some quantifications which would be interesting to expand upon.

4.2 Other Trade Policy Applications

While a quantification of optimal tariffs, Nash tariffs, and cooperative tariffs is probably a natural first application of the above techniques, they could really be used to connect most branches of the theoretical trade policy literature to the data. As an illustration, let me focus on the part of the theoretical literature which emphasizes the world trading system's institutional design. In a nutshell, WTO members are supposed to concentrate all protective measures into tariffs, apply these tariffs on a nondiscriminatory basis, and change these tariffs in a reciprocal fashion. Influenced by Bagwell and Staiger (1999), an extensive literature has studied the implications of these and other WTO principles and their exceptions for the efficiency of trade negotiations.

Consider first the principle of nondiscrimination which has the important exception that WTO members are allowed to enter into preferential trade agreements under some conditions. This exception is controversial in the theoretical literature for three main reasons. First, there is a concern that joining preferential trade agreements causes trade diversion which can even make the parties to the preferential trade agreement worse off (Viner, 1950). Second, there is a discussion whether preferential trade agreements encourage or discourage further liberalizations and are therefore building blocks or stumbling blocks on the way to free trade (Bhagwati, 1991). And third, there is an argument that MFN tariffs protect outsiders to reciprocal trade liberalizations from any externalities and work in conjunction with the principle of reciprocity to guide countries to the efficiency frontier (Bagwell and Staiger, 1999).

A quantitative analysis could shed some new light on this debate. First of all, the equilibrium conditions in changes summarized in Definition 2 could be used to quantify the extent of trade diversion real-world trade agreements bring about. My conjecture is that these effects are negligible when focusing on tariff changes alone but that they might become more important when changes in nontariff barriers are also taken into account. Nowadays, many preferential trade agreements also reduce nontariff barriers as part of some deep integration process and measuring such reductions convincingly would be the key challenge to overcome.

Moreover, a modified version of the optimization procedure summarized in Problem 2 could be used to assess which preferential trade agreements countries would optimally sign. Besides speaking to the building blocks vs stumbling blocks debate, this could readdress the influential question asked by Baier and Bergstrand (2002) whether the observed proliferation of preferential trade agreements is consistent with welfare maximization. In this context, it could also be explored how members of preferential trade agreements would optimally adjust their external tariffs thereby assessing the above-mentioned Bagwell and Staiger (1999) argument.

Consider now the principle of reciprocity which is only a norm during phases of trade liberalization but binds more strictly when retaliatory actions are concerned. In particular, WTO member countries are authorized to withdraw substantially equivalent concessions if one of their trading partners reneges on previously made tariff commitments. In practice, this institutionalized threat of retaliation tends to prevent trading partners from reneging in the first place and can thus be interpreted as an explicit tit-for-tat rule aimed at ensuring that trade agreements are self-enforcing.

A quantitative analysis could help determine how much bite this interpretation has. In particular, the welfare effects associated with optimal tariffs summarized in table 4A quantify the value of unilateral deviations from the status quo. Also, the welfare effects associated with Nash tariffs summarized in table 4B quantify the costs of a breakdown of trade policy cooperation which a unilateral deviation would likely entail. Given a discount factor, one could now calculate the most cooperative tariffs which can be sustained in a repeated game in the spirit of Bagwell and Staiger (1990). In doing so, one could also distinguish between bilateral and multilateral enforcement mechanisms along the lines of Maggi (1999).

Moreover, it would be interesting to quantify how important it is for the success of trade negotiations that the principle of reciprocity applies multilaterally instead of bilaterally. As is discussed more extensively in Bagwell et al. (2015) as well as chapter "The Design of Trade Agreements" by Bagwell and Staiger of this Handbook, one of the key innovations of the General Agreement on Tariffs and Trade (GATT) relative to the earlier US Reciprocal Trade Agreements Act was to relax the bilateral reciprocity constraint and replace it with a multilateral one. The basic idea is that it is easier to find an overall balance of concessions if it does not have to apply individually for each country pair.

4.3 Applications in Other Fields

While these examples should suffice to illustrate that there are many interesting opportunities for quantitative work within the traditional trade policy literature, it is also easy to think of closely related applications in other fields. For example, I use similar tools in Ossa (2015) to study subsidy competition among US states in a quantitative economic geography model. US states spend substantial resources to subsidize the relocation of firms from other states. I show that this is consistent with welfare maximization because firm relocations allow states to benefit at the expense of other states. I also show that observed subsidies are much closer to cooperative than to noncooperative levels but that the potential costs of an escalation of subsidy competition are large.

It would be interesting to extend this analysis beyond the domestic US economy and analyze subsidies offered to attract foreign firms. This could then be tied in again with the traditional trade policy literature because WTO rules also limit the foreign direct investment (FDI) policies governments can apply. For example, the Trade Related Investment Measures (TRIMS) agreement limits the local content requirements which can be imposed on foreign-owned firms. Also, FDI flows are increasingly subject to bilateral investment treaties which would be fascinating to analyze.

Another promising area is climate policy. For example, Nordhaus (2015) argued in his 2015 Presidential Address to the American Economic Association that small tariff penalties could be a powerful tool to entice countries to join climate clubs which impose stricter policies fighting climate change. His argument is based on the so-called Coalition Dynamic Integrated Model of Climate and the Economy (C-DICE) which is a quantitative model developed by Nordhaus and his team. It uses the results from Ossa (2014) to construct a reduced-form trade benefit function which is needed to quantify the effectiveness of tariff penalties.

ACKNOWLEDGMENTS

I would like to thank the editors Kyle Bagwell and Bob Staiger, my discussants Lorenzo Caliendo and Penny Goldberg, as well as my student reviewers Ohyun Kwon and Wisarut Suwanprasert for very helpful comments and discussions. I am indebted to Yuxing Peng for streamlining the code published on the website accompanying this chapter and to Yuan Mei for proofreading the draft. All remaining errors are mine.

REFERENCES

Allen, T., Arkolakis, C., 2014. Trade and the topography of the spatial economy. Q. J. Econ. 129 (3), 1085–1140.
Alvarez, F., Lucas, R., 2007. General equilibrium analysis of the Eaton-Kortum model of international trade. J. Monet. Econ. 54 (6), 1726–1768.
Arkolakis, K., Costinot, A., Rodriguez-Clare, A., 2012. New trade models, same old gains? Am. Econ. Rev. 102 (1), 94–130.
Armington, P., 1969. A theory of demand for products distinguished by place of production. IMF Staff. Pap. 16, 159–176.
Bagwell, K., Staiger, R., 1990. A theory of managed trade. Am. Econ. Rev. 80 (4), 779–795.
Bagwell, K., Staiger, R., 1999. An economic theory of GATT. Am. Econ. Rev. 89 (1), 215–248.
Bagwell, K., Staiger, R., 2002. The Economics of the World Trading System. MIT Press, Cambridge, MA.
Bagwell, K., Staiger, R., 2005. Multilateral trade negotiations, bilateral opportunism and the rules of the GATT/WTO. J. Int. Econ. 67, 268–294.
Bagwell, K., Staiger, R., Yurukoglu, A., 2015. Multilateral Trade Bargaining: A First Peak at the GATT Bargaining Records. Stanford University.
Baier, S., Bergstrand, J., 2002. Economic determinants of free trade agreements. J. Int. Econ. 64 (1), 29–63.
Baldwin, R., Clarke, R., 1987. Game-modeling multilateral trade negotiations. J. Policy Model 9 (2), 257–284.
Bhagwati, J., 1991. The World Trading System at Risk. Princeton University Press.
Broda, C., Weinstein, D., 2006. Globalization and the gains from variety. Q. J. Econ. 121 (2), 541–585.
Broda, C., Limao, N., Weinstein, D., 2008. Optimal tariffs and market power: the evidence. Am. Econ. Rev. 98 (5), 2032–2065.
Caliendo, L., Parro, F., 2015. Estimates of the trade and welfare effects of NAFTA. Rev. Econ. Stud. 82 (1), 1–44.
Caliendo, L., Parro, F., Rossi-Hansberg, E., Sarte, P., 2014. The impact of regional and sectoral productivity changes on the U.S. economy. NBER Working Paper 20168.
Caliendo, L., Feenstra, R., Romalis, J., Taylor, A., 2015. Tariff reductions, entry, and welfare: theory and evidence for the last two decades. NBER Working Paper 21768.
Costinot, A., Rodriguez-Clare, A., 2014. Trade theory with numbers. In: Helpman, E., Rogoff, K., Gopinath, G. (Eds.), Handbook of International Economics, vol. 4. North Holland, Amsterdam, The Netherlands.
Costinot, A., Donaldson, D., Vogel, J., Werning, I., 2015. Comparative advantage and optimal trade policy. Q. J. Econ. 130 (2), 659–702.

Dekle, R., Eaton, J., Kortum, S., 2007. Unbalanced trade. Am. Econ. Rev. 97 (2), 351–355.

Dixon, P., Jorgenson, D., 2013. Handbook of Computable General Equilibrium Modeling. North Holland, Amsterdam, The Netherlands.

Eaton, J., Kortum, S., 2002. Technology, geography, and trade. Econometrica 70 (5), 1741–1779.

Feenstra, R., 1994. New product varieties and the measurement of international prices. Am. Econ. Rev. 84 (1), 157–177.

Feenstra, R., 2010. Product Variety and the Gains from International Trade. MIT Press, Cambridge, MA.

Felbermayr, G., Jung, B., Larch, M., 2013. Optimal tariffs, retaliation, and the welfare loss from tariff wars in the Melitz model. J. Int. Econ. 89 (1), 13–25.

Felbermayr, G., Jung, B., Larch, M., 2015. The welfare consequences of import tariffs: a quantitative perspective. J. Int. Econ. 97 (2), 295–309.

Gawande, K., Krishna, P., 2003. The political economy of trade policy: empirical approaches. In: Choi, E., Harrigan, J. (Eds.), Handbook of International Trade. Blackwell, Oxford, UK.

Gorman, W., 1958. Tariffs, retaliation, and the elasticity of demand for imports. Rev. Econ. Stud. 25 (3), 133–162.

Gros, D., 1987. A note on the optimal tariff, retaliation and the welfare loss from tariff wars in a framework with intra-industry trade. J. Int. Econ. 23 (3-4), 357–367.

Grossman, G., Helpman, E., 1994. Protection for sale. Am. Econ. Rev. 84 (4), 833–850.

Hamilton, B., Whalley, J., 1983. Optimal tariff calculations in alternative trade models and some possible implications for current world trading arrangements. J. Int. Econ. 15 (3-4), 323–348.

Johnson, H., 1953-1954. Optimum tariffs and retaliation. Rev. Econ. Stud. 21 (2), 142–153.

Kennan, J., Riezman, R., 1990. Optimal tariff equilibria with customs unions. Can. J. Econ. 23 (1), 70–83.

Krugman, P., 1980. Scale economies, product differentiation, and the pattern of trade. Am. Econ. Rev. 70 (5), 950–959.

Kuga, K., 1973. Tariff retaliation and policy equilibrium. J. Int. Econ. 3, 351–366.

Leamer, E., 1981. Is it a demand curve, or is it a supply curve? Partial identification through inequality constraints. Rev. Econ. Stat. 63 (3), 319–327.

Maggi, G., 1999. On the role of multilateral institutions in international trade cooperation. Am. Econ. Rev. 89 (1), 190–214.

Markusen, J., Wigle, R., 1989. Nash equilibrium tariffs for the United States and Canada: the roles of country size, scale economies, and capital mobility. J. Polit. Econ. 97 (2), 368–386.

Melitz, M., 2003. The impact of trade on intra-industry reallocations and aggregate industry productivity. Econometrica 71 (6), 1695–1725.

Narayanan, B., Aguiar, A., McDougall, R., (Eds.) 2012. Global Trade, Assistance, and Production: The GTAP 8 Data Base. Center for Global Trade Analysis, Purdue University, West Lafayette, IN.

Nordhaus, W., 2015. Climate clubs: overcoming free-riding in international climate policy. Am. Econ. Rev. 105 (4), 1339–1370.

Ossa, R., 2011. A "new trade" theory of GATT/WTO negotiations. J. Polit. Econ. 119 (1), 122–152.

Ossa, R., 2012. Profits in the "new trade" approach to trade negotiations. Am. Econ. Rev. 102 (3), 466–469.

Ossa, R., 2014. Trade wars and trade talks with data. Am. Econ. Rev. 104 (2), 4104–4146.

Ossa, R., 2015. A quantitative analysis of subsidy competition in the U.S. NBER Working Paper 20975.

Perroni, C., Whalley, J., 2000. The new regionalism: trade liberalization or insurance? Can. J. Econ. 33 (1), 1–24.

Rutherford, T., 1995. Constant Elasticity of Substitution Functions: Some Hints and Useful Formulae. University of Colorado.

Simonovska, I., Waugh, M., 2014. The elasticity of trade: estimates and evidence. J. Int. Econ. 92 (1), 34–50.

Soderbery, A., 2015. Estimating import supply and demand elasticities: analysis and implications. J. Int. Econ. 96 (1), 1–17.

Spearot, A., 2016. Unpacking the long-run effects of tariff shocks: new structural implications from firm heterogeneity models. Am. Econ. J. Microecon. 8 (2), 128–167.

Su, C., Judd, K., 2012. Constrained optimization approaches to estimation of structural models. Econometrica 80 (5), 2213–2230.

Viner, J., 1950. The Customs Union Issue. Anderson Kramer Associates, Washington, DC.

PART II

Trade Agreements: Legal Background, Purpose and Design

CHAPTER 5

Legal Aspects of Commercial Policy Rules

A.O. Sykes
Stanford University, Stanford, CA, United States

Contents

Handbook of Commercial Policy, Volume 1A
ISSN 2214-3122, http://dx.doi.org/10.1016/bs.hescop.2016.04.014

Abstract

This chapter provides an overview of the legal obligations of the WTO/GATT system and certain related national, bilateral, and plurilateral arrangements. It is intended for economists and other social scientists who seek a concise and accessible introduction to the core legal obligations of the international trading system. Topics include the relationship between international and national law, the constraints on border instruments, the most-favored-nation obligation and its exceptions such as those for regional and preferential trading arrangements, the national treatment obligation, the general exceptions to GATT, technical barriers to trade, safeguard measures, subsidies and countervailing measures, antidumping measures, and trade in services.

Keywords

WTO, GATT, Tariffs, Quotas, Subsidies, Antidumping, Safeguards, National treatment, Most-favored-nation, GATS

JEL Classification Code

F1, F5, K3

This chapter provides a selective survey of the legal rules and policies governing international trade in goods. The sources of law in this area are numerous. At the global level, the World Trade Organization (WTO) and its constituent treaties supply a legal framework governing the relationship among its 162 member nations (as of January 2016). Additional international rules are to be found in the hundreds of bilateral and multilateral "regional trade agreements[a]" (RTAs) that have proliferated in recent years, such as the European Union, NAFTA, and MERCOSUR.[b] Finally, trading nations have numerous domestic laws governing international trade. In the United States, for example, tariffs are applied in accordance with the US Tariff Schedules, along with antidumping duties, countervailing duties, safeguard measures, and so on. Exports are regulated for national security and other purposes.

Given the enormous legal landscape, a narrower focus is necessary for this limited contribution, and the law of the WTO will be emphasized. The core rules of most RTAs are broadly similar in their content,[c] however, while national laws and regulations exist in the shadow of WTO law and at least in principle conform to governing WTO principles. A survey of WTO rules, therefore, is sufficient to convey most of the important legal concepts, although the discussion will note a few issues of prominence with respect to RTAs. Along the way, the chapter will also note some prominent WTO legal decisions, but it cannot provide a thorough survey of the case law, which now encompasses hundreds of cases.[d]

Other chapters in this collection address economic issues pertaining to particular aspects of the legal system, and I will leave most of the economic discussion to those chapters. The discussion later will nevertheless touch briefly on some of the law and economics literature published in legal journals that might not otherwise come to the attention of international economists, as well as note a few areas where economic research has not yet made major contributions.

1. THE HIERARCHY OF RULES

As noted, international trade law exists at the global, regional, and national levels. The relationship among these three sources of law is complex.

One must first distinguish between *international law* and *national law*. WTO commitments and commitments in RTAs are international law. When a state violates international law, it triggers certain rights and remedies of counterparties that are defined by that

---

[a] The WTO defines an RTA as a reciprocal trading arrangement among two or more member nations, wherein all parties offer concessions to the others. A "preferential trade arrangement" (PTA) is an arrangement in which concessions are offered unilaterally (such as the under the Generalized System of Preferences, GSP). I adopt the WTO terminology herein.

[b] The WTO reports that nearly 400 such arrangements are in force as of January 2016.

[c] A thorough survey of the features of the United States and EU RTAs may be found in Horn et al. (2010), with an updated dataset on the provisions of RTAs at https://www.wto.org/english/res_e/publications_e/wtr11_dataset_e.htm.

[d] Readers interested in greater legal detail on particular topics may wish to consult Mavroidis (2012, 2016) or Trebilcock et al. (2013).

body of international law. A violation of WTO law, for example, entitles an aggrieved member state to pursue a legal claim under the WTO Dispute Settlement Understanding (DSU) discussed in chapter "Dispute Settlement in the WTO" by Mavroidis in this volume. A violation of NAFTA entitles an aggrieved counterparty to invoke the NAFTA dispute process. In some instances, an action may violate both the law of the WTO and the law of an RTA, possibly giving the aggrieved party a choice of dispute fora. Whatever the forum, however, only member governments have standing to invoke the dispute process in modern trade agreements—private actors lack "standing" to bring cases.[e]

With some exceptions noted later, *international* trade law is not enforceable in domestic courts. The legal principle is that international trade law does not have "direct effect" in the national legal system (European phrasing) or that international trade law is not "self-executing" (American phrasing). Rather, international law gains domestic force in most countries only when (and if) it is enacted into domestic law by the competent domestic legislature.

National laws, by contrast, have domestic legal force. This dichotomy affords the principal explanation of how a trading nation may violate international trade rules—a nation may take an action under domestic law that is inconsistent with international law. A WTO member may adopt a domestic statute that conflicts with a WTO rule, for example, or interpret and apply a domestic statute (or agency regulation) in a manner that conflicts. And because international law generally does not apply directly in domestic courts, an aggrieved party usually cannot challenge such acts in a domestic court on the grounds that it conflicts with international law, and must instead look to international legal remedies. Likewise, if the international dispute process rules in favor of an aggrieved party, that ruling does not in itself change the domestic law that produced the violation in most situations.

An exception arises for states that legal scholars term "monist." A monist state incorporates international law directly into domestic law, and it becomes enforceable in domestic courts. In Costa Rica, for example, international trade treaties take precedence over any inconsistent domestic law once they are ratified by the legislature and the executive.[f] Major trading nations are more likely to be "dualist," however, and thus to require domestic legislation before an international legal commitment (or legal decision) becomes legally enforceable domestically.

The choice between monist and dualist approaches raises interesting issues that have not been explored much from an economic perspective. On the one hand, dualism

---

[e] An important exception arises in trade agreements that also contain investor rights provisions, such as NAFTA. Private investors have standing to pursue money damages claims under the NAFTA investor rights provisions and those of certain other trade agreements. For a discussion of why private rights of action are present in investment but not trade agreements, see Sykes (2005).

[f] A collection of papers on the domestic status of international trade law in 10 WTO member countries plus the EU may be found in Jackson and Sykes (1997).

seemingly creates greater opportunity for nations to cheat on their commitments, and monism would seem to reduce the transaction costs of fidelity to international commitments. On the other hand, dualism may enable central governments to exercise greater control over domestic adjudicators that might interpret international obligations incorrectly, and may also allow nations to engage in modest deviation from commitments that other nations do not care about, thereby yielding a Pareto improvement.

2. BORDER INSTRUMENTS

The modern WTO legal system began in 1947 with the negotiation of the General Agreement on Tariffs and Trade (GATT), a legal arrangement that is now incorporated into the constituent treaties of the WTO. It applies to trade in goods and does not cover services. As its name suggests, the focus of GATT was the negotiated reduction of tariffs, which had risen sharply during the 1930s. To be sure, other types of trade barriers existed at the time as well, such as various quantitative restrictions (QRs) on imports. Tariffs and QRs constitute the "border instruments" that were a primary focus of GATT. Speaking roughly, the strategy of GATT was to facilitate negotiated limits on tariffs, while prohibiting QRs, subject to some enumerated exceptions. That approach remains the basic architecture today.

2.1 Tariffs

Under GATT Article II, WTO members can divide their tariffs into two categories—"bound" and "unbound." Bound tariffs consist of the tariffs on particular categories of goods as to which a member has made a commitment during GATT or WTO negotiations over the years. Unbound tariffs, which have become less common over time, consist of tariffs with respect to which the member in question has not made any negotiated commitments [beyond a most-favored-nation (MFN) obligation].

2.1.1 GATT Article II and the Tariff Bindings

Unbound tariffs are unconstrained, and members may raise them on an MFN basis. Bound tariffs, by contrast, must respect the negotiated binding, which amounts to a ceiling on the permissible tariff rate [which may be expressed as a percentage of the value of a good (ad valorem tariff) or a specific amount per unit of the good (specific tariff)]. Members are free to charge any tariff below the negotiated binding, and often do. Tariffs that are set below their bound rate are said to generate "binding overhang."

The commitment to respect tariff bindings is contained in Article II of GATT, which obliges members to charge tariffs "no less favorable" than the bound rates recorded in each member's tariff schedule. The schedules for each member are auxiliary documents that memorialize the negotiated tariff commitments by each member from the inception of GATT to date. Article II makes reference to Parts I and II of the schedules.

Part I contains the basic tariff bindings that must be respected for imports from all WTO members. Part II contains certain preferential rates that were allowed to persist at the founding of GATT, largely at the insistence of the British Commonwealth members. Preferential tariff rates in the modern era are often the product of RTAs noted earlier. RTA preferences are not reflected in Article II schedules, but instead in national tariff schedules and in legal instruments associated with particular RTAs.

2.1.2 National Tariff Schedules

The WTO schedules differ from the applied tariffs under national law, which are reflected in domestic legal documents. Thus, for example, the Tariff Schedules of the United States (a Federal statute) contain three classes of tariffs. Column 1—General tariff rates are the rates that are *applied* to imports from WTO members that receive no special preference. These rates will be less than or equal to the negotiated bindings in the WTO schedules of the United States if the tariff at issue is bound. Column 1—Special rates are those applied under US RTAs such as NAFTA and various bilateral free trade agreements. Column 2 rates apply to imports from countries that are not entitled to the benefits of the WTO member rate, and typically represent the applied rate under the Smoot–Hawley Tariff of 1930.

To apply tariffs at the border, customs officials must undertake three tasks. First, they must "classify" the good in question. If the tariff on widgets is 10% and that on gadgets is 15%, one must know whether the import is a widget or a gadget. Many disputes arise over classification issues, a few of which find their way into the WTO, but most of which are adjudicated in domestic courts because they involve interpretations of domestic law. Disputes have been reduced, though not eliminated, by the creation of the Harmonized Commodity Description and Coding System, developed by the International Customs Cooperation Council, which classifies goods at the two-, four-, and six-digit levels. The goal is to ensure that goods are classified under the same heading in all countries, but customs officials can disagree over their interpretation. Furthermore, members are free to adopt a more fine-grained classification (eg, eight digit) for their own purposes, which will not be the same for all members, and such classification measures have become more and more common.

A second task for customs officials, in instances where tariffs are expressed in ad valorem terms, is to value the goods in question. Valuation is usually straightforward if importation occurs in connection with an arms length transaction (with the caveat that fraud can occur), but often imports come from related parties (foreign subsidiaries and so forth), and so the stated "price" may not be deemed trustworthy. Article VII of GATT, and a WTO "Valuation Agreement" elaborating Article VII, concern the use of various proxies for valuation that look to such things as the price in an arms length sale between the seller and an unrelated buyer for the same or sufficiently similar merchandise, and in the worst case scenario to a cost of production calculation [see WTO Valuation Agreement, Articles 1–6].

Finally, to the degree that different tariffs apply according to the origin of the good (recall the three columns in the US Tariff Schedules noted earlier), it is necessary for customs officials to identify the nation in which the import was "produced." When all stages of production occur in one country, the process is easy, but many products today contain components manufactured in various countries, which are then assembled in still other countries. Trading nations thus require "rules of origin" to resolve the matter.

The WTO Agreement on Rules of Origin encourages transparency in the rules used by members and established an ongoing work program to establish harmonized rules of origin. The guiding principle of the program is the establishment of rules that focus on the locus of the last "substantial transformation" of the article in question (see Article 3). The concept of substantial transformation is itself ambiguous, however, and the work program hopes to produce some clarification. Factors that may bear on the occurrence of substantial transformation include a transformation that results in a change in tariff classification, and the amount of value added at each stage of production.

Further complicating the rules of origin issue is the fact that WTO rules apply only to the classification of goods for purposes of applying WTO law (eg, is this good from a WTO member or not? Is this good from a WTO member covered by a WTO legal antidumping order?) Many origination decisions, however, are taken pursuant to RTAs, which have their own body of law and potentially their own rules of origin. The decision whether to afford a certain good Mexican origin for NAFTA purposes, for example, is governed by NAFTA law, which has a number of rules of origin that focus on value-added criteria rather than the broader "substantial transformation" concept.

2.1.3 Plugging Loopholes in GATT Article II

The drafters of GATT recognized that tariff bindings would be of little utility if members could simply substitute other protectionist barriers. Thus, much of GATT can be understood as plugging loopholes that would exist if the tariff bindings were the sole legal obligation, and Article II does some of this work. For example, members cannot impose "other duties or charges of any kind imposed on or in connection with importation" (for example, an import license fee) in excess of those in existence when the tariff binding was negotiated [Article II(1)(b)]. These "other" charges are now recorded for transparency. Exceptions exist for antidumping and countervailing duties, for charges that are equivalent to GATT-legal internal taxes that are imposed on like domestic goods, and for fees to cover the "costs of services rendered" (such as customs processing) [Article II(2)]. In addition, if a WTO member establishes an "import monopoly," its pricing policies must respect the terms of any applicable binding on the goods that it imports. [Article II(4)]. For example, when a member gives an alcoholic beverage control authority the exclusive right to import distilled spirits, its markup over costs cannot be used to afford more protection to domestic competitors than the tariff binding allows.

2.1.4 Renegotiation of Tariff Bindings

GATT drafters recognized that tariff commitments might prove politically regrettable after the fact and included mechanisms to adjust them. One such mechanism—a safeguard measure—is discussed in Section 9. But GATT also included a general authorization for tariff renegotiation and modification in Article XXVIII. The procedures are complex and turn on the timing of the negotiations (known as "in season" and "out of season" negotiations, the latter subject to greater central oversight). The procedures also specify which members have the right to participate in renegotiations and to complain or to retaliate if the negotiations do not reach a successful outcome (the parties with "initial negotiating rights," a "principal supplying interest," or a "substantial interest.").[g]

A key feature of the system is its use of a "liability rule" approach if negotiations are unsuccessful. The preamble to GATT refers to the desirability of "reciprocal and mutually advantageous" negotiations to reduce tariffs. Reciprocity is nowhere defined, and it is not a meaningful legal obligation, but it connotes an arrangement whereby all parties make concessions to benefit others. The withdrawal of a concession undermines this balance of concessions and entitles others to some rebalancing of the bargain through compensating concessions. Accordingly, if a member wishes to raise a tariff above an existing binding, it must negotiate for the right to do so in good faith. If it is unable to secure the consent of the other members with standing to demand compensation under the rules, the member is nevertheless free to raise its tariff. Aggrieved members in one of the three categories noted earlier may then withdraw "substantially equivalent concessions." The evident design is to insulate members desiring to raise bound tariffs from the holdup problem that might arise under a "property rule" system that required the permission of all affected members before any tariff increase could take effect.[h] Among the outstanding legal issues is the question whether a withdrawal of equivalent concessions is bilateral (applied only to the nation that raised its tariff), or applied to all trading partners. Disputes over the "equivalence" of concessions can presumably be resolved by arbitration under the Dispute Settlement Understanding (DSU).

2.1.5 Progressive Tariff Liberalization

Historically, most tariff liberalization under WTO/GATT auspices has occurred during periodic negotiating "rounds." The last successful round was the Uruguay Round, which created the WTO, and it has been over 20 years since its conclusion. The current Doha Round remains stalled and moribund at this writing.

---

[g] See Mavroidis (2012), section 2.9 for a thorough survey of the detailed rules in this regard.
[h] See Schwartz and Sykes (2002).

WTO members occasionally pursue additional multilateral tariff liberalization in other settings. The most prominent modern example is the 2015 expansion of the Information Technology Agreement, pursuant to which approximately 50 members representing 90% of all trade in certain information technology products committed to eliminate tariffs on 201 high-tech items, with all tariff reductions to be implemented on an MFN basis.

2.2 QRs

A key strategy of GATT is "tariffication," a channeling of protectionist policies into tariffs and away from QRs and other nontariff barriers. Tariffs have a number of advantages that explain this preference. Any buyer willing to pay the tariff can always obtain the imported good, whereas quotas may be filled unexpectedly, and in this sense the trade effects of tariffs are more transparent and predictable. Related, quotas may result in discriminatory treatment of trading partners, either because of the way that quota rights are allocated or because some trading partners lose out when quotas are filled on a first come first served basis. Tariffs also allow trade to grow as economies expand. And tariffs systematically raise revenue for importing governments.

Accordingly, GATT Article XI requires the "general elimination" of various other border measures. It obliges members to avoid "prohibitions or restrictions other than duties, taxes, or other charges, whether made effective through quotas, import or export licenses, or other measures." The obligation applies to both import and export restrictions. The latter principle has been at issue in a number of disputes involving restrictions on the exportation of input products for downstream industries, a practice that can drive the local price of the input below the world price and advantage domestic downstream firms.

Occasional disputes arise as to whether some government policy amounts to a "measure" within the coverage of Article XI. One example from the GATT years involved steps taken by the Japanese government to ward off antidumping cases in the United States against its semiconductor exporters. The government undertook a number of efforts to monitor conditions in the market and urged its exporters not to engage in "dumping" but did not formally prohibit it. The EU, fearful that the measures would divert cheap exports to Europe, complained that the policies violated Article XI, and a GATT panel agreed.[i]

The prohibition on QRs is subject to a number of exceptions.[j] Article XI allows export restrictions to relieve critical shortages of foodstuffs and "other products essential

---

[i] Japan – Trade in Semiconductors, GATT Panel Report adopted May 4, 1988, 35th Supp. BISD 116 (1989).

[j] In addition to those noted in the text, safeguard measures, the General Exceptions and the National Security Exception of GATT Articles XIX–XXI can justify quotas.

to the exporting contracting party," a phrase that is not defined and has received only limited clarification in litigation.[k] Article XI also allows QRs for purposes of implementing schemes for the classification or grading of commodities and import restrictions to prevent imports from undermining price support schemes for agricultural and fisheries products (including imports at an earlier stage of processing than the product subject to the domestic scheme) and related efforts to dispose of temporary surpluses of such products. Restrictions in connection with price support schemes, however, should not reduce the market share of imports below the level that would prevail absent the price support scheme.

Another group of exceptions applies to balance of payments measures. GATT Article XII permits import restrictions necessary to "forestall the imminent threat of, or to stop, a serious decline in its monetary reserves," or for a party with "very low" reserves "to achieve a reasonable rate of increase in its reserves." It also affords members the flexibility to use import restrictions selectively "to give priority to the importation of those products which are more essential." Article XVIII(B) contains similar language and offers some additional flexibility for developing countries to restrict imports for balance of payments purposes.

The perception exists that the balance of payments exceptions have been subject to some abuse, and used as an excuse for protectionist measures that had little connection to bona fide balance of payments concerns. An important ruling against India in 1999, in response to a complaint by the United States, held that India had maintained a wide range of measures that could not be justified under Article XVIII[l] and resulted in the eventual dismantling of those restrictions.

3. MFN OBLIGATIONS AND EXCEPTIONS

The impetus for the creation of GATT had two components—a desire to reduce the *level* of tariffs following the tariff wars of the 1930s and a desire to eliminate *discrimination* in tariffs, which had proliferated and become more important as tariff levels rose. The United States, in particular, sought the dismantling of the many colonial preferences that existed after World War II (see Irwin et al., 2008).

3.1 Article I(1)

The negotiations regarding tariff discrimination culminated with GATT Article I, concerning "General Most-Favored-Nation Treatment." We begin with the core obligations contained in paragraph one and consider various exceptions in a moment.

---

[k] See, eg, China – Measures Related to the Exportation of Various Raw Materials, WTO/DS394, 395 and 398/AB/R, adopted February 22, 2012.

[l] India – Quantitative Restrictions on Imports of Agricultural, Textile, and Industrial Products WT/DS90/AB/R, adopted September 22, 1999.

The coverage of Article I(1) is broad indeed, applying to "customs duties and charges of any kind imposed on or in connection with importation or exportation" or international payments transfers, "the method of levying" these charges, all "rules or formalities" in connection with imports and exports, all domestic product taxes, and all "laws, regulations, and requirements" affecting the internal sale of products. With respect to all such measures, "any advantage, favor, privilege, or immunity" granted by a member to any product originating in or destined for any other country must be accorded "immediately and unconditionally" to a "like product" originating in or destined to the territories of other members. Note the coverage of exports as well as imports, and the fact that this obligation applies regardless of whether the tariffs at issue are bound.

A key aspect of the MFN obligation is the requirement that advantages be extended "unconditionally" to all WTO members. Thus, members cannot condition MFN treatment on any quid pro quo. An obvious advantage of this system is that members negotiating a tariff concession are protected against the possibility that their counterparty may subsequently offer a "better deal" to their competitors, which enhances the security of negotiated concessions and makes them more valuable. The downside of unconditional MFN, of course, is that it can create free rider problems as nations withhold concessions on imports into their own market, hoping to gain access to foreign markets for "free." This set of issues has spawned a rich literature on the effects of the MFN obligation.

Perhaps, the thorniest interpretive issue raised by the language of Article I(1) concerns the term "like product," a term that appears in a number of WTO treaty provisions. If members are free to define "like products" as narrowly as they wish, the MFN obligation can often be circumvented. The classic example is found in the Swiss-German Treaty of 1904, which reduced tariffs on "large dopple mountain cattle or brown cattle reared at a spot at least 300 m above sea level and having at least one month's grazing each year at a spot at least 800 m above sea level." The MFN obligation does nothing to extend such a tariff concession to most other cattle producers if this category offers an acceptable conception of "likeness."

The WTO Appellate Body has held that the term "like product" does not necessarily mean the same thing each time it is used in WTO treaty text, a holding that complicates the jurisprudence and limits the value of past precedents. WTO jurisprudence on the meaning of the term in Article I is particularly sparse, tipping a hat to the analysis of the term in other contexts[m] but offering little in the way of definitive analysis.

The issue was addressed in the GATT years by several decisions. At one time, it was suggested that "likeness" might depend on the expectations of the parties to a tariff negotiation about likeness, an idea that has shown little vitality in the WTO where the

---

[m] See the United States – Certain Measures Affecting Imports of Poultry from China, WT/DS392/R, adopted October 25, 2010.

emphasis is on textual standards. The other factors that surfaced during the GATT years concerned the degree of consumer substitutability between products, and their tariff classification—closer substitutes are more likely to be found "like," and goods that fall under the same tariff heading are more likely to be found "like."[n] These factors are plainly relevant today, but leave much room for uncertainty in particular cases.

Some legal commentators have urged that antitrust principles should be applied to the determination of "like products," deploying the same methods as those used to define a "relevant market" for antitrust purposes. It is hardly obvious that such proposals are wise, however, as the policy objectives at issue here are quite different. A broader scope of likeness for purposes of the MFN obligation plainly diminishes the degree of tariff discrimination, with its potential to cause trade diversion and distortion of consumer choice. But a broader scope of likeness also complicates tariff negotiations, seemingly exacerbating the free rider problem, and creating greater uncertainty for negotiators regarding the impact of tariff concessions that they offer. The ideal balance is by no means clear and, concomitantly, a wooden application of antitrust principles might do little to advance members' mutual interests. The general question of "likeness," and the virtues of broader vs narrower conceptions of likeness, has not received much attention from economists.

Another set of issues arises in cases where a trading advantage is made conditional on some factor that does not directly implicate the origin of goods. Suppose, for example, that a WTO member offers duty free treatment on automobile imports from any foreign manufacturer that also produces a significant quantity of automobiles domestically. In principle, any foreign manufacturer can establish a domestic production facility and thereby qualify for duty free treatment of its imports. Many foreign manufacturers do not have such facilities, however, and complain that their automobile imports are subject to a positive rate of duty while "like" imports from other manufacturers (located in other countries) are imported duty free. Is the importing nation's policy nondiscriminatory, on the theory that any foreign manufacturer can take advantage of it? Or does the disparate treatment of imports from various sources constitute de facto discrimination condemned by Article I? The tendency in WTO jurisprudence so far has been to find de facto discrimination in such circumstances.[o]

3.2 Quota MFN

As noted in the previous section on border measures, the GATT prohibition on QRs is subject to a number of exceptions, such as those for agricultural price support schemes

---

[n] See Spain – Tariff Treatment of Unroasted Coffee, GATT Panel Report, adopted June 11, 1981, 28th Supp. BISD 102 (1982); Japan – Tariff on Import of Spruce-Pine-Fir (SPGF) Dimension Lumber, GATT Panel Report, adopted July 19, 1989, 36th Supp. BISD 167 (1990).

[o] See Canada – Certain Measures Affecting the Automotive Industry, WT/DS139&142/AB/R, adopted June 19, 2000.

and balance of payments measures. GATT Article XIII creates the "quota MFN" obligation to be applied in such circumstances. It states that prohibitions on importation and exportation cannot be applied on goods from or destined to another member unless the "like products" of third countries are "similarly prohibited or restricted."

This provision became an issue in the long-running "bananas" dispute. Among other things, Europe allocated tariff quota shares to certain African, Caribbean, and Pacific (ACP) countries but not to other WTO members, a practice that was deemed to violate Article XIII. The EC's defense—that it treated all ACP countries alike, and treated all non-ACP countries alike, was rejected.[P]

Article XIII further provides that quota regimes should endeavor to provide members with market shares to approximate "as closely as possible" the shares that each member would have in the absence of the quota regime. If market shares are to be set for each member, they may be set by agreement among the members with a "substantial interest" in the product at issue, or based on the market shares of those members during a "previous representative period."

3.3 MFN Exceptions

The MFN obligation is subject to an array of exceptions. At the outset of GATT, the US objective of putting an end to colonial preferences was thwarted by the refusal of Great Britain to give them up, and many of the preferences were accordingly preserved as exceptions to the obligation in Article I(1)—see Articles I(2)–(4). The importance of colonial preferences has diminished over time, but other exceptions to the MFN obligation have grown dramatically in significance.

3.3.1 Customs Unions and Free Trade Areas (RTAs)

Since the concept of trade diversion was isolated by Jacob Viner, economists have eyed RTAs with some skepticism. The drafters of GATT, by contrast, assumed from the outset that a customs union exception to the MFN obligation was desirable, with the proviso that its effect should be primarily to liberalize trade among its members and not to diminish trade with outsiders. During the course of GATT negotiations, the parties agreed to add an exception for free trade areas, and for definitive "interim agreements" to establish such entities (see Jackson, 1969).

3.3.1.1 GATT Rules

The relevant GATT provisions are contained in Article XXIV. Paragraph 4 contains hortatory language about liberalizing trade within the entity rather than raising barriers to outsiders. Paragraph 5 then states that "the provisions of [GATT] shall not prevent ... the formation of a customs union or of a free trade area or the adoption of an interim

[P] EC – Bananas III, WT/DS27/AB/R, adopted September 25, 1997.

agreement" to create one, thus ensuring that customs unions and free trade areas are not prohibited by the Article I MFN obligation.

Paragraph 8 defines customs unions and free trade areas. Customs unions are organizations in which "duties and other restrictive regulations of commerce (with a few exceptions such as GATT-legal quotas, other balance of payments measures, and measures falling within the general exceptions of Article XX) are eliminated with respect to substantially all the trade between the constituent territories," and in which "substantially the same duties and other regulations of commerce" are applied by the members to trade from nonmembers. Among other things, therefore, customs unions should have a common external tariff. Free trade areas are defined similarly with respect to the elimination of barriers to internal trade, but their members retain the right to treat nonmembers differently (and thus, for example, do not have a common external tariff). The term "substantially all the trade" is not defined.

With these definitions in mind, paragraph 5 conditions the exception to GATT obligations for these arrangements on an important proviso. In the case of a customs union (or interim agreement to form one), the duties and other regulations applied to nonmembers "shall not on the whole be higher or more restrictive" than those in place prior to the formation of the customs union. The WTO understanding on Article XXIV elaborates (in paragraph 2) that in evaluating the overall restrictiveness of the measures applied to nonmembers, one looks to the weighted average tariff rates and to the total value of customs duties collected before and after. And because the creation of a common external tariff will generally involve raising some of the tariffs applied by members (while others are lowered), paragraph 6 provides that members must negotiate with adversely affected members pursuant to the procedures already noted under Article XXVIII. It is understood that increases in bound tariffs require compensation.

The proviso for free trade areas is more straightforward. It simply states that the duties and other regulations of commerce shall not be higher or more restrictive on nonmembers than before the formation of the free trade area (or interim agreement). Because a common external tariff is not required, there is no need to negotiate or compensate for any tariff increases.

The final proviso applies to "interim agreements," and states that they must result in the completion of the free trade area or customs union within a "reasonable time." The WTO understanding on Article XXIV now provides that the reasonable time should not exceed 10 years except in "exceptional cases" (paragraph 3).

The difference between customs unions and free trade areas raises a number of interesting issues. With respect to customs unions, the proviso respecting trade with nonmembers might in theory be used to require customs unions to implement an external tariff which, drawing on the well-known Kemp–Wan result, preserves trade with nonmembers and ensures that the customs union is welfare enhancing from a global perspective. Were the proviso implemented in this fashion, it might be possible to argue that customs unions are normatively superior to free trade areas, where no similar mechanism to prevent trade diversion is in place.

In fact, however, supervision of customs unions and free trade areas by the GATT/WTO membership is feeble indeed, with little serious effort made to ensure that the provisos in Article XXIV are respected. Customs unions and free trade areas have proliferated enormously,[q] and although they are notified to the WTO, what happens thereafter is little more than a rubber stamp process (see Mavroidis, 2011). Part of the explanation may be that challenges to customs unions or FTAs on the grounds that they do not do enough to liberalize trade internally might result in more discrimination against the outsiders that might bring the challenge.

Accordingly, the provisions of Article XXIV do little to ensure that customs unions and free trade areas are welfare enhancing from a global perspective, or to channel new agreements into arrangements that do little damage to outsiders. The modern tendency is clearly toward the choice of free trade agreements over customs unions,[r] perhaps because they avoid the need for Article XXVIII negotiations over increases in bound tariffs.

Likewise, litigation regarding Article XXIV has been sparse, with one notable exception. Turkey—Textiles[s] involved the following scenario. Turkey was joining the EU, and at that time imposed QRs on 19 categories of textile products from India. Turkey argued that this policy, which otherwise violated Article GATT XI, was permissible under Article XXIV. Turkey reasoned that without the QRs, the other members of the EU would not be willing to open their markets to textile exports from Turkey, fearing transshipment of products made in countries such as India. Noting that textile exports were a substantial portion of its total exports, Turkey claimed that if the EU did not open up to textile exports from Turkey, the customs union would not qualify under Article XXIV because it would not have eliminated barriers to "substantially all the trade" between Turkey and the EU. Thus, the QRS were "necessary" to the formation of the customs union, and allowable under the language of Article XXIV(5): "the provisions of [GATT] shall not prevent the formation of a customs union."

Neither the panel nor the Appellate Body directly assessed Turkey's claim that opening up EU markets to Turkish textile exports was necessary (or sufficient) for the customs union to meet the requirements of Article XXIV. Instead, Turkey's defense of its QR regime failed because other means might have been used to address the EU's concerns about transshipment, such as rules of origin or certificates of origin, which would not have violated any provisions of GATT. Thus, requiring Turkey to obey Article XI would

[q] As of January 2016, 419 RTAs have been notified to the WTO and are in force.
[r] See http://rtais.wto.org/UI/PublicAllRTAList.aspx, listing all agreements in force and showing the overwhelming predominance of free trade agreements over customs unions.
[s] Turkey – Restrictions on Imports of Textile and Clothing Products, WT/DS34/AB/R, adopted November 19, 1999.

not "prevent" the formation of the customs union. The decision leaves open the possibility, however, that Article XXIV can justify violations of GATT in other circumstances where the measures are introduced at the formation of the customs union, and they are genuinely necessary to facilitate it.

3.3.1.2 Special Legal Features of RTAs

With approximately 500 RTAs in force, a meaningful survey of their legal content is far beyond this essay. As noted in the introduction, however, typical RTAs have obligations that are conceptually similar to those of the WTO. They constrain tariffs (below the MFN tariff bindings of the WTO), they tend to follow WTO rules on QRs, they require nondiscrimination (MFN and national treatment), they address technical barriers, safeguards, antidumping, and countervailing duties and so on. Many include provisions on services and intellectual property.

Nevertheless, many differences exist between WTO obligations and RTA obligations.[t] A common difference lies in dispute resolution, as few RTAs have the compulsory arbitral arrangement that characterizes the WTO DSU. NAFTA, for example, resembles the old GATT, under which a party to a dispute on trade issues can block most disputes from being adjudicated. It also contains a special provision for an international panel to hear appeals from agency determinations in antidumping and countervailing duty cases.

A significant number of RTAs contain investor rights provisions, akin to those typically found in bilateral investment treaties. NAFTA is again a good example, as it allows private investors from one member to bring actions for money damages before international arbitrators to redress violations of investment obligations by a host member. Such obligations include, among other things, a prohibition on expropriation or measures "tantamount" to it without fair compensation, MFN and national treatment, and the minimum standard of treatment owed to aliens under customary international law (fair and equitable treatment).

Labor and environmental standards are also a common subject of provisions in RTAs, as is competition policy (particularly in RTAs with the EU). The enforceability of such obligations is quite variable, however, as some of these issues are exempted from ordinary dispute resolution (if meaningful dispute resolution exists at all), and others are vaguely worded.

3.3.2 Special and Differential Treatment

From the outset of GATT, developing countries have sought and received certain special allowances. It is well known that developing countries have not been asked to make tariff concessions to the same degree as developed nations, an unsurprising fact given the

---

[t] Horn et al. (2010) study the RTAs to which the United States and the EU are a party, and catalog their features.

smaller size of developing country markets. Additional flexibilities were provided in GATT Article XVIII. It affords somewhat relaxed rules for tariff renegotiations for the purpose of promoting a "particular industry," for balance of payments measures (already noted in connection with the case against India), and for measures that violate other GATT provisions after notification and consultation with other members. Part IV of GATT, which was added in response to developments in the 1950s and early 1960s, contains mostly hortatory language urging GATT members to take account of the interests of developing countries in their commercial policies. Two provisions in Article XXVII are arguably binding, however, concerning an obligation on the part of developed members to refrain from raising tariffs and nontariff barriers on goods of export interest to less-developed members, and to refrain from new fiscal measures that would hamper the exports of primary products from less-developed members. There has not been any enforcement litigation under these provisions, however, despite numerous occasions on which developed members have taken measures that affect exports from less-developed members.

In addition to these provisions of GATT, many other WTO treaties afford some form of special and differential treatment. Examples include longer phase-in and transition periods for developing country members under the Agriculture Agreement, the SPS and TBT Agreements, the Subsidies Agreement, and TRIPs, as well as exemptions from certain obligations for least-developed countries under several agreements.

One the most significant instances of special and differential treatment in practice has been the development of the Generalized System of Preferences (GSP), pursuant to which (mostly developed) members afford duty exemptions and other preferences to developing country exports. GSP was authorized by a 10-year waiver under GATT in 1971, and made permanent by the 1979 "Enabling Clause," which refers back to the 1971 waiver and its "generalized, nonreciprocal, and nondiscriminatory preferences beneficial to the developing countries" (footnote 6). Developed countries are not obligated to extend GSP benefits, but are authorized to do so subject to certain constraints. Major GSP schemes include those of the EU, the United States, Japan, and Australia.

In practice, GSP schemes are quite selective in their coverage, often excluding politically sensitive imports, excluding imports of particular goods from countries that are deemed to be already competitive, and "graduating" certain countries altogether from the scheme based on their level of development. GSP benefits may also be conditioned on the willingness of beneficiary countries to afford adequate intellectual property protections, to afford internationally recognized worker rights, and to assist in efforts to combat international terrorism, among other things.[u] Thus, GSP benefits have been used to encourage beneficiaries to cooperate in a variety of economic and political initiatives.

---

[u] See, eg, Title V of the US Trade Act of 1974, as amended.

It is questionable, therefore, whether existing GSP schemes meet the standards of "generalized, nonreciprocal, and nondiscriminatory preferences" set forth in the Enabling Clause. India brought a case against the EU's GSP scheme on this basis, challenging in particular some special preferences given to 12 nations, ostensibly granted because of the special needs of those countries to combat drug production and trafficking. These special preferences, which did not apply to India, did apply to Pakistan. The Appellate Body ultimately held that the EU scheme was discriminatory and inconsistent with the Enabling Clause because the EU had not justified in any careful way the selection of the 12 beneficiaries. Ultimately, the EU rejiggered its criteria for granting special preferences in a manner that excluded Pakistan, and the issue has been quiescent since then.[v] There is little doubt that other features of various national schemes involving limitations on coverage, implicit reciprocity, and discrimination among countries could be challenged under the Enabling Clause, but such challenges have not been brought to date, probably because the respondent might respond by abolishing its GSP scheme altogether.

4. DOMESTIC TAX AND REGULATORY POLICIES: NATIONAL TREATMENT

Many of the most controversial and high-visibility WTO disputes have involved domestic tax and especially various domestic regulatory policies. Such policies were constrained in the original GATT by Article III, the "national treatment" article.

Article III applies to three broad classes of internal measures: taxes; "laws, regulations, and requirements affecting internal sale"; and "internal quantitative regulations requiring the mixture, processing, or use of products in specified amounts of proportions". Paragraph 1 is a hortatory statement of general principle, stating that these measures "should not be applied ... so as to afford protection to domestic production." The remainder of Article III consists of nine paragraphs elaborating substantive rules in accordance with this principle, and a handful of exceptions. Paragraphs 3 and 6 involve transition or grandfathering rules, which will not be discussed. Paragraph 9 contains some hortatory language on maximum price controls, and paragraph 10 is an exception for cinematograph films. A footnote to Article III adds that an internal tax or regulation that applies to an imported product and a "like domestic product" can be enforced at the border in the case of the imported good, and still be regarded as an internal tax or regulation subject to Article III (rather than, for example, a tariff or QR subject to Article II or XI). The remaining paragraphs of Article III are discussed later.

[v] European Communities – Conditions for the Granting of Tariff Preferences to Developing Countries, WT/DS246/AB/R, adopted April 20, 2004.

4.1 Internal Taxes

The core obligation with respect to internal taxes is contained in paragraph 2 and has two parts. The first sentence provides that imported products from GATT members "shall not be subject, directly or indirectly, to internal taxes or other internal charges of any kind in excess of those applied, directly or indirectly, to like domestic products." The second sentence provides that members may not "otherwise apply internal taxes or other internal charges ... in a manner contrary to the principles set forth in paragraph 1"—that is, in a manner "so as to afford protection." A footnote explains that a tax conforming to the first sentence will not violate the second sentence unless it involves "directly competitive or substitutable" products, and the products are not "similarly taxed."

This somewhat convoluted structure has been interpreted through the years to create one obligation regarding the taxation of "like products," and another regarding the taxation of "directly competitive or substitutable products." With respect to the former group of products, any tax on imports "in excess of" the tax on domestic products, "directly or indirectly," violates Art. III(2) first sentence. If the products involved are not "like" but are nevertheless directly competitive or substitutable, sentence two requires that taxation be "similar" and not "so as to afford protection." In practice, this means that small differences in taxation may be acceptable, a "de minimis" test. The decisions make clear that "so as to afford protection" is not a test regarding the *intent* of the tax difference, but pertains to its *effect*—the way that it is "applied." Adjudicators must determine whether the impact of a non-de minimis tax differential is protective, and typically the answer will be yes.[w]

This body of rules raises a variety of interpretive questions. Once again, one must confront the issue of what constitutes a "like product," and how to distinguish "like" products from those that are "directly competitive or substitutable." With respect to "likeness," the Appellate Body suggests, rather unhelpfully, that the issue must be considered "case-by-case." It has also endorsed the approach embodied in a 1970 GATT working party report on border tax adjustments (the question of when an imported good can be taxed at the border in an amount designed to be equivalent to an internal tax of domestic products). The *Border Tax* working party[x] remarked:

> Some criteria were suggested for determining, on a case-by-case basis, whether a product is "similar": the product's end uses in a given market; consumer's tastes and habits, which change from country to country; the product's properties, nature and quality.

These factors all capture indicators of substitutability in consumption, and hence the degree of substitutability is clearly a core part of the analysis. The Appellate Body adds

[w] A key decision on these standards is Japan – Taxes on Alcoholic Beverages, WT/DS10&11/AB/R, adopted November 1, 1996.
[x] Report of the Working Party on Border Tax Adjustments, BISD 18S/97.

that tariff classification is a further element of the inquiry.[y] But there is assuredly no bright line test, and the Appellate Body has emphasized that "likeness" is contextual and varies across different WTO treaty provisions. Because of the presence of Article III(2), sentence two, in particular, the notion of likeness is to be applied "narrowly" for purposes of sentence one, although it does not require that products be identical.[z]

The concept of "directly competitive or substitutable" is to be assessed using much the same border tax factors and simply captures a lesser degree of competitive relationship between products than "likeness." The Appellate Body expressly notes that the "elasticity of substitution" or the "cross elasticity of demand" is an appropriate consideration,[aa] seemingly opening the door to econometric estimates of such parameters. Once again, however, there is clearly no bright line test. And the drafting history of Article III suggests that the concept may be applied to reasonably disparate products, giving the example of a country that produces apples but not oranges, and that uses an internal tax on oranges to afford protection to the domestic apple industry.[bb]

The footnote to Article III allowing taxation at the border when it is equivalent to an internal tax on like products—in effect, a border tax to "level the playing field"—also raises a variety of intriguing issues. What constitutes an "internal tax" on a product? The Border Tax working party distinguished between taxes levied directly on products (such as sales or excise taxes) and taxes that only "indirectly" affect products (such as payroll taxes). Even though the latter types of taxes can surely affect the marginal costs of production for domestic firms, and thereby their competitiveness, it is now accepted that they cannot be the subject of a border tax adjustment.

A related body of WTO rules concerns the permissibility of *rebating* product taxes upon exportation, an option available to an exporting country that raises revenue through product taxes (including value-added taxes). These rules will be discussed later in the materials on subsidies.

A further issue arises with respect to a tax imposed directly on a product, but motivated by a domestic distortion. For example, suppose that a Pigouvian tax is imposed on domestic polluters to internalize a local pollution externality, and that it is structured as a tax per unit of output. Can imported like goods be subjected to the same tax at the border, even if their production is not a source of domestic pollution? One GATT panel answered this question in the affirmative, refusing to consider the purpose behind the tax as relevant to the availability of a border tax adjustment.[cc] Following this body of case law, it would be permissible to impose at the border a tax on imported products equal to a

---

[y] See Japan – Alcoholic beverages, supra.
[z] Philippines – Taxes on Distilled Spirits, WT/DS396&403/AB/R, adopted January 20, 2012.
[aa] Japan – Alcoholic beverages, supra.
[bb] See Jackson et al. (2013), p. 604.
[cc] The United States – Taxes on Petroleum and Certain Imported Substances, 34th Supp. BISD 136 (1988) (panel report adopted June 17, 1987).

carbon tax imposed directly on "like" domestic products. If the domestic carbon tax was imposed on, say, energy consumption, however, and thus only indirectly affected the prices of end products, a border tax adjustment would raise much more complex practical and legal issues.[dd]

Note as well the reference to differential taxation that occurs "directly or indirectly." As an illustration, consider an old dispute known as the "wine gallon–proof gallon" controversy (decided under a bilateral treaty rather than GATT). The United States imposed a specific tax per gallon on distilled spirits when they entered the stream of US commerce. Imported spirits entered the country already bottled for retail sale and were thus taxed at their retail alcohol strength (wine gallons). Domestic spirits were taxed upon withdrawal from a bonded warehouse, usually in a concentrated form with high alcohol content (proof gallons) and were thereafter diluted for retail bottling. The "indirect" tax on the domestic spirits was accordingly lower per unit of retail volume than the direct tax on imported spirits. [ee]

A final set of thorny issues concerns the concept of discrimination, and the standards for determining whether products are differently taxed. Consider, for example, a uniform specific tax on distilled spirits of x per gallon. Or consider a uniformly applied tax on the alcohol content of spirits, equal to x per unit of alcohol contained therein. Or consider a tax on all distilled spirits equal to 10% ad valorem. Are all of these taxation systems nondiscriminatory because they treat all distilled spirits "alike?" Note that a uniform specific tax could be said to favor high-valued distilled spirits, in that the implicit ad valorem tax can be much lower on higher valued products. A uniform tax on alcohol content likewise might be said to favor lower alcohol spirits.

Putting it differently, what is the appropriate benchmark for determining whether tax "discrimination" arises? The cases do not address this issue squarely, but instead judge tax systems on their own terms—if the tax system is specific, then it must not discriminate in the level of specific taxation, and so on.[ff] The result is that a "nondiscriminatory" tax system based on volume or alcohol content is permissible even if it results in a wide disparity among implicit ad valorem taxes, and vice versa. Artful selection of the "tax base" may then be used by taxing authorities to favor domestic products without violating Article III.[gg]

[dd] See Pauwelyn (2013).

[ee] Schieffelin v. the United States, 424 F.2d 1396 (CCPA, 1970) (holding that wine gallons and proof gallons did not present a "like situation" and accordingly the tax difference did not violate the Friendship, Commerce, and Navigation Treaty with Ireland).

[ff] See Japan – Alcoholic beverages, supra, in which the Japanese system had differential specific taxes for categories of spirits based on both volume and alcohol content.

[gg] For a lengthy treatment of the concept of discrimination in WTO law, see Qin (2005).

4.2 Internal Regulations

Among the most difficult challenges facing the GATT system through the years has been the task of distinguishing socially constructive domestic regulation from regulatory policies that are deliberately or unnecessarily protectionist. The stakes are considerable, as regulatory protectionism is particularly destructive of social surplus, with the potential to transform the tariff revenue that exists with a tariff, or the quota rent that exists with a quota, into deadweight loss. The initial GATT strategy in this respect was a simple non-discrimination obligation, the subject of this section. When that alone proved inadequate, the membership developed additional disciplines, culminating in the technical barriers agreements to be discussed in a later section.

GATT Article III(4) addresses all "laws, regulations, and requirements" affecting "internal sale, offering for sale, purchase, transportation, distribution, or use." It requires that goods imported from another member receive "treatment no less favorable" than that accorded to *like products* of national origin. As its language suggests, the scope of the measures addressed by paragraph 4 is exceedingly broad. Examples include legal procedures that make it easier to bring successful lawsuits against imported goods that infringe patent rights than against domestic goods,[hh] an unnecessary requirement that tax stamps be affixed to imported goods after importation rather than before,[ii] a "dual retail" system ostensibly designed to ensure that lower grade imported meats are not fraudulently commingled with higher grade domestic meats,[jj] and a labeling regulation requiring sellers of imported goods to display a placard describing their wares as "foreign.[kk]" Any mandatory rule applicable to the sale or distribution of products is potentially subject to coverage.

In contrast to Article III(2), paragraph 4 contains no second sentence regarding directly competitive or substitutable products. Because the Appellate Body views "likeness" as an elastic concept that varies with context' however, the scope of "likeness" is broader here,[ll] and one can doubt whether the set of competitive imported goods protected by paragraph 4 is really any smaller than that protected by paragraph 2.

But there is still much room for debate over the question whether imported goods are "like" the domestic goods that receive more favorable treatment. That issue was a central point of disagreement in EC—Asbestos. The case involved a Canadian challenge to a

---

[hh] The United States – Section 337 of the Tariff Act of 1930, 36th Supp. BISD 345 (1990), GATT panel report adopted November 7, 1989.

[ii] Dominican Republic – Measures Affecting the Importation and Internal Sale of Cigarettes, WT/DS302/AB/R, adopted May 19, 2005.

[jj] Korea – Measures Affecting Imports of Fresh, Chilled, and Frozen Beef, WT/DS161&169/AB/R, adopted January 10, 2001.

[kk] Hawaii v. Ho, 41 Hawaii 565 (1957).

[ll] See European Communities – Measures Affecting Asbestos and Asbestos-Containing Products, WT/DS135/AB/R, adopted April 5, 2001.

French regulation that prohibited the manufacture, sale, or importation of any type of asbestos product, including products into which asbestos has been incorporated, with a limited exception for products that have no commercial substitutes. The panel determined that prohibited asbestos fibers were "like" substitute fibers of polyvinyl alcohol, cellulose, and glass because they are used for many of the same purposes and have many of the same end uses. Likewise, products incorporating these different fibers, such as cement products with fiber reinforcement, were "like" products. Accordingly, the French regulation had the effect of prohibiting the sale of imported products that are "like" domestic products, and violated Article III(4), albeit subject to a possible public health defense under GATT Article XX (discussed later).

The Appellate Body reversed the panel. It once again endorsed the border tax factors (discussed earlier) as a basis for assessing likeness, and emphasized that the panel had not given sufficient attention to the question whether the different health risks associated with the different types of fibers might be important enough to consumers to render the various fibers "unlike" from a consumer perspective. A rare concurring opinion went so far as to argue that the various fibers were plainly not "like" given the difference in health risks.[mm]

The Asbestos case raises a broader question—of the various product dimensions that underlie differences in regulatory treatment, which can support a finding that two products are not "like?" The decision clearly suggests that physical differences among products of possible importance to consumer choice, and that may lead consumers to prefer one product over another (such as differential health risks due to different product components), may be a proper basis for distinction. But what about a difference in the carbon emissions from the production processes of two products, when the products are otherwise interchangeable from the consumer perspective? Or suppose that one product is produced in a setting that threatens an endangered species, and one is not (such as otherwise substitutable shrimp, only one of which is caught in waters where sea turtles are endangered by shrimping)? The latter two examples raise the "processes and production methods" issue: can products be considered "unlike" because of the different societal implications of how they are produced, rather than because of physical differences in the end products?

This issue remains somewhat murky. The decisions regarding likeness under GATT provisions do not yet offer much basis for distinguishing products based on process and production methods, although one can argue by extension from the Asbestos case that if consumers "care" about underlying process and production methods to the point that they prefer some products over others on that basis, then these consumer preferences

---

[mm] The complainants in Asbestos also lodged a nonviolation claim, suggesting that the change in the French regulation of asbestos upset reasonable expectations of negotiated market access. The nonviolation claim also proved unsuccessful.

can be taken into account in assessing likeness. No case to date, however, has allowed likeness to turn solely on the notion that consumers "care" about differences in the production processes of otherwise identical products.

A related question concerns the interpretation of "less favorable treatment." If a regulatory distinction is applied uniformly to imported and domestic goods, and has sound rationale, might it be said that imports receive no less favorable treatment, even if some imported goods subject to tougher standards are deemed "like" the domestic goods subject to lesser standards? Under GATT, the answer so far has tended to be no—less favorable treatment arises whenever like imported goods suffer competitive detriment, even if a regulatory justification exists for the disparate treatment of imports. Instead, the existence of a regulatory justification for disparate treatment of like products is adjudicated under the "affirmative defenses" of GATT Article XX. As shall be seen, however, the jurisprudence has evolved differently under the technical barriers agreements.

4.3 Mixing Regulations/Local Content Requirements

Article III(5) prohibits "internal quantitative regulations" relating to the "mixture, processing, or use of products in specified amounts or proportions" which require that "any specified amount or proportion" of the product subject to the regulation be supplied from "domestic sources." Originally termed "mixing regulations," such regulations are now more commonly termed "local content requirements." They are also addressed by the WTO Agreement on Trade-Related Investment Measures (TRIMs), which makes clear that any requirement that producers (such as firms owned by foreign investors) use domestic products in their production operations (whether in fixed proportions or not) is a violation of the national treatment obligation. The violation arises not because of the adverse effect on foreign investors, but because such local content requirements encourage the purchase of domestic goods over substitutable imported goods. Note that the scope of this obligation is limited to instances in which the regulation requires the use of domestic products—a requirement to use domestically supplied services, for example, would not be included (but services commitments may exist under GATS, discussed later).

4.4 Exceptions: Government Procurement and Subsidies

Article III(8) contains two important exceptions to the national treatment obligation. The first concerns "laws, regulations, and requirements" relating to government procurement. Members are free to favor domestic suppliers in this regard, subject to any commitments that they may have made under the plurilateral WTO Agreement on Government Procurement. That agreement allows its members to schedule commitments for certain types of procurement (eg, by certain of their government agencies). For procurement covered by a schedule above certain monetary thresholds, members are obligated to extend national treatment and MFN treatment to suppliers of other signatories, and to obey certain transparency obligations. As one might expect, certain more sensitive forms of procurement (as for national defense) are typically excluded from commitments.

The second exception in Article III(8) is for "the payment of subsidies exclusively to domestic producers," including payments "from the proceeds of internal taxes" applied consistently with Article III. This exception raises a host of problems, many of which will be discussed later with reference to the Agreement on Subsidies and Countervailing Measures (SCMs). A few preliminary issues warrant attention here.

First, the exception applies to "producer" subsidies and not purchaser subsidies. Thus, for example, a subsidy to domestic agricultural machinery manufacturers can fall within the exemption. But a subsidy to purchasers of domestically produced agricultural machinery is a law adversely affecting the internal sale of imported agricultural machinery, and thus violates Article III(4).[nn] This asymmetry in the treatment of producer and purchaser subsidies is a bit puzzling. If the domestic producers do not export, then a producer subsidy and a purchaser subsidy of a given magnitude can have an identical effect on the market opportunities for the sale of imported substitutes.

Second, the opportunity to subsidize domestic producers seemingly opens the door to opportunism following the negotiation of tariff bindings. Imagine that a WTO member negotiates a tariff binding on some product, and then immediately begins subsidizing the domestic producers of substitutes. The value of the tariff binding to the recipient may be entirely undermined. Recognizing this danger, GATT members evolved the principle that a new and unanticipated subsidy to the domestic producers of a product subject to a negotiated tariff binding would support a "nonviolation" complaint under GATT Article XXIII.[oo]

Finally, a more subtle form of opportunism might entail the use of the subsidy exemption to circumvent the national treatment obligation on domestic taxation. Imagine a nondiscriminatory excise tax imposed on some type of imported and domestic product. The proceeds of the tax are then used to subsidize the domestic producers of the product, thus replicating the effect of a discriminatory excise tax that would violate GATT Article III(2). To date, no dispute has raised this issue, but the language of Article III(8) seems to facilitate this type of policy. The discussion of the SCMs Agreement below will suggest some additional disciplines that might apply.

[nn] See Italian Discrimination Against Imported Agricultural Machinery, 7th Supp. BISD 60 (1959), GATT panel report adopted October 23, 1958.

[oo] EEC – Payments and Subsidies Paid to Processors and Producers of Oilseeds and Related Animal Feed Proteins, 37th Supp. BISD 86, GATT panel report adopted January 25, 1990. This principle is now found in the SCMs Agreement.

5. THE GENERAL EXCEPTIONS TO GATT: ARTICLES XX AND XXI

GATT Article XX contains a list of exceptions to GATT obligations. It is invoked most commonly to justify measures that might otherwise violate Article III or Article XI, but applies without limitation to all obligations in the original GATT.

It is structured as list of particular sorts of measures that are permissible, providing that they satisfy the conditions in the introductory paragraph of Article XX, known as the "chapeau." The categories of permissible measures are those:

(a) necessary to protect public morals;

(b) necessary to protect human, animal, or plant life or health;

(c) relating to the importations or exportations of gold or silver;

(d) necessary to secure compliance with laws or regulations which are not inconsistent with the provisions of this agreement, including those relating to customs enforcement, the enforcement of monopolies operated under paragraph 4 of Article II and Article XVII, the protection of patents, trademarks, copyrights, and the prevention of deceptive practices;

(e) relating to the products of prison labor;

(f) imposed for the protection of national treasures of artistic, historic, or archeological value;

(g) relating to the conservation of exhaustible natural resources if such measures are made effective in conjunction with restrictions on domestic production or consumption;

(h) undertaken in pursuance of obligations under any intergovernmental commodity agreement which conforms to criteria submitted to the [membership], …

(i) involving restrictions on exports of domestic materials necessary to ensure essential quantities of such materials to a domestic processing industry during periods when the domestic price of such materials is held below the world price as part of a governmental stabilization plan, …

(j) essential to the acquisition or distribution of products in general or local short supply, …

Items (a), (b), (d), and (g) have been at issue in important disputes. The others have proven less important.

Measures falling into one of the enumerated categories are permissible as long as they do not offend the chapeau, which provides that acceptable measures under Article XX are "[s]ubject to the requirement that such measures are not applied in a manner which would constitute a means of arbitrary or unjustifiable discrimination between countries where the same conditions prevail, or a disguised restriction on international trade." The chapeau has been held to create three distinct limitations—arbitrary discrimination, unjustifiable discrimination, and disguised restriction on trade. Analytically, a member proposing to invoke Article XX must first establish that its measures fall within one of the categories (a)–(j), and then establish compliance with the chapeau.

An important general principle concerns the burden of proof in such cases. In general, a member complaining about the policies of another member has the burden of proof to establish that those policies violate some WYO/GATT treaty provision. Once that burden has been carried, the responding member seeking to invoke an exception bears the burden of proof to establish the applicability of the exception. One caveat is that the complainant has the burden of showing that an alternative, less-trade restrictive measure exists when the complainant asserts that the measure at issue is unnecessarily trade restrictive (pursuant to the "necessity test" in items (a), (b), and (d) to be discussed later).

A review of several leading cases under Article XX will give a flavor of how the general exceptions operate in practice. The "public morals" exception of item (a) was at issue in the recent EC—Seal Products dispute.[pp] Europe had imposed a prohibition on the importation and sale of seal products, based on a judgment that the killing of seals is inhumane. Among other things, it allowed an exception for the production of indigenous peoples (Inuit), which in practice seemed to benefit only the Greenlandic Inuit and not the Canadian Inuit. The exception was found to violate GATT Article I, by treating imports from Canada and Norway less favorably than imports from Greenland. Europe defended the measure as "necessary to protect public morals" regarding the inhumane treatment of seals. Both the panel and the Appellate Body ultimately accepted this proposition and accepted the limited evidence regarding the effectiveness of the measure (one contrary argument, for example, was that the EU demand for seal products could be filled entirely from Greenland, and hence the measure simply redirected business to Greenland with negligible impact on the number of seals killed). Both the panel and the Appellate Body also rejected any suggestion that Europe was obliged to regulate other aspects of animal welfare in a consistent fashion (such as slaughterhouse practices and terrestrial hunting), or that evidence of weaker regulation in those areas undermined the claim that serious "public morals" were at issue. Finally, both rejected the notion that Europe could employ a less-restrictive measure requiring seal product imports to be certified as deriving from animals that are humanely killed. The latter issue was central to the discussion of whether the European measure was "necessary" to protect public morals. This so-called necessity test is found in items (a), (b), and (d) of Article XX. The European measure was ultimately found lacking in relation to the Article XX chapeau, however, because Inuit communities in Canada were not equally able to take advantage of the exception granted to Greenland, resulting in "arbitrary and unjustifiable discrimination."

Under item (b), two of the more prominent decisions are EC—Asbestos, noted earlier, and Brazil—Tyres.[qq] In the latter case, Brazil enacted a ban on the importation of retreaded tires to reduce the accumulation of waste tires in landfills, which were a

[pp] European Communities – Measures Prohibiting the Importation and Marketing of Seal Products, WT/DS400&401/AB/R, adopted June 28, 2014.

[qq] Brazil – Measures Affecting Imports of Retreaded Tires, WT/DS332/AB/R, adopted December 17, 2007.

breeding ground for mosquitoes and mosquito-borne disease. Both Asbestos and Tyres presented colorable public health claims, and the harder issue concerned the "necessity" of the measures. "Controlled use" presented a possible alternative to the ban on asbestos-containing products, whereby workers would wear masks whenever exposed to airborne asbestos particles. In Tyres, incineration of waste tires offered an alternative way to prevent their accumulation. In both cases, however, the Appellate Body accepted that the importing nation's measure was "necessary" given the costs or risks of the proposed alternatives.[rr] To be necessary, according to the Appellate Body, measures need not be indispensible, but must make a material contribution to the objective. Likewise, there must not be a less-trade restrictive measure that is "reasonably available." An alternative measure is not reasonably available if such measures do not achieve the regulatory goal satisfactorily or if the alternatives impose an "undue burden" on the regulating member.

The leading case under item (d) is Korea—Beef, noted earlier. Korea's dual retail system for beef was ostensibly aimed at preventing the commingling of low quality imported beef with high quality domestic beef, allowing the former to be passed off as the latter to unsuspecting consumers. Regulations to prevent consumer deception are among the "laws or regulations not inconsistent" with GATT, and thus measures to secure compliance with them can fall under Article XX(d). Korea's efforts to invoke Article XX nevertheless foundered on the "necessity" test, because Korea might have used other means to prevent fraudulent commingling. It was observed that Korea relied on conventional antifraud sanctions in other areas of potential consumer deception, such as the commingling of low quality and high quality domestic beef and the danger of consumer deception in restaurants. Careful monitoring of violations short of a dual retail system thus supplied a reasonably available alternative. The decision also emphasized that Korea had chosen an approach to enforcement that shifted "all, or the great bulk of … potential enforcement costs to imported goods and retailers of imported goods.[ss]"

The Article XX jurisprudence on necessity raises some intriguing issues. Plainly, crude considerations of cost effectiveness are pertinent to the issue of necessity, as alternative measures that are ineffective or quite costly are unlikely to supply "reasonably available" alternatives. But as Korea—Beef highlights, cost effectiveness can be assessed from a national or global perspective, and the two need not coincide. Furthermore, adjudicators seem to accord more deference to national regulators in certain issue areas (such as public health) than in others (such as prevention of consumer deception in the beef market). One hypothesis is that the costs of error associated with second-guessing national regulatory choices may be greater with matters that implicate human health and certain other particularly important concerns.[tt]

[rr]   In the Tires case, however, the measure once again failed the test of the chapeau because of an exception allowed for imports from MERCOSUR partners.

[ss]   Korea – Beef, ¶172.

[tt]   On the relationship between "necessity" and notions of cost effectiveness, see Sykes (2003).

Regarding exception (g), measures "relating to the conservation of exhaustible natural resources," two important decisions are United States—Reformulated Gasoline[uu] and United States—Shrimp Products[vv] (popularly known as the shrimp–turtle case). Reformulated Gasoline involved US rules regarding the production of gasoline for urban areas, and collateral efforts to ensure that pollutants removed from such gasoline were not shifted into gasoline produced for other areas. Without going into detail, the standards for US refineries were based on the historical pollution data for individual US refineries, but the standards for foreign refineries were based on average data for foreign refineries, thus disadvantaging refineries abroad that produced more pollution than average. A critical ruling in the case was that "clean air" is an exhaustible natural resource, and that the US measures "related to" its conservation because they were "primarily aimed at" conservation. Nonetheless, the US measures failed the test of the chapeau by discriminating against foreign refiners in a manner that was not necessary—the United States had not made efforts to obtain the refinery-specific data to regulate foreign refiners in the same manner as domestic refiners.

Shrimp–Turtle played out in similar fashion. The United States prohibited shrimp imports from certain Southeast Asian countries that had not been certified as engaged in shrimping methods that provided appropriate protection to endangered sea turtles. The adjudicators had no difficulty in determining that endangered sea turtles were an exhaustible natural resource, or that the US measures "related to" their conservation.[ww] But the United States had treated the Southeast Asian complainants less favorably than shrimpers in nearby Caribbean countries, with whom a negotiation had been held on the process of providing their shrimpers with certification, who had been given a 3-year phase-in period to comply with US requirements, and for whom the United States had engaged in some helpful technology transfer for shrimpers. Likewise, the US rules did not take account of different circumstances in different shrimping areas (such as a possible dearth of sea turtles). The disparate treatment was said to constitute "unjustifiable" discrimination. Furthermore, the lack of transparency in the US certification process and failure to provide a sort of due process to applicants, was held to constitute "arbitrary" discrimination. A subsequent dispute report, however, found that the United States had corrected these deficiencies through its later efforts to reach an accommodation with the complainants.

A central issue lurking in the background of the Shrimp–Turtle dispute was the capacity of a country such as the United States to impose its regulatory preferences on activities

---

[uu] The United States – Standards for Reformulated and Conventional Gasoline, WT/DS2?AB/R, adopted May 20, 1996.

[vv] The United States – Restrictions on Importation of Certain Shrimp and Shrimp Products, WT/DS58/AB/R, adopted November 6, 1998.

[ww] The reader might wonder why the United States focused its argument on the conservation exception XX(g) rather than the animal health exception XX(b). One consideration is the absence of a "necessity" test under (g), with the weaker "relating to" requirement instead.

outside of US jurisdiction. Is it permissible for the United States to declare its concern for sea turtles, and then force all other nations to protect them to a similar degree? Of course, a similar issue arose in EC—Seal Products, in which the animal welfare concerns of Europe were used as a basis to constrain imports from countries outside. Another famous example from the GATT years was the so-called Tuna Dolphin case, in which the United States banned imports of tuna caught with fishing methods that endangered dolphins excessively (in the view of the United States). The (unadopted) GATT panel report in that case held that the Untied States overstepped its bounds by undertaking to regulate fishing methods outside of US waters.

The more recent WTO jurisprudence has retreated considerably from that position. In Shrimp–Turtle, the issue was finessed with the observation that the endangered sea turtles were migratory, and perhaps entered US waters at times. Also in play were various international agreements on the protection of endangered species that afforded the United States some international authority for its position. In Seal Products, however, the issue was not in serious contention between the parties and the Appellate Body expressly ducked it in its opinion, suggesting that much of the WTO community has implicitly accepted the right of importing nations to deny their national markets to products manufactured abroad in a manner that offends public sensibilities. With regard to the process and production methods issue noted earlier in the discussion of "like products" under Article III, it seems that the Article XX exceptions now in practice extend to regulation based on process and production methods, at least in certain classes of cases, even if the products produced by an objectionable process or method are "like" those produced in a more acceptable fashion.

One final feature of the Article XX jurisprudence warrants mention. WTO adjudicators have generally been quite deferential to claims by a member that its measures fall within one of the enumerated categories under Article XX (animal welfare as a matter of "public morals," waste tires as a "human health" issue, clean air as an "exhaustible natural resource," the absence of implicit limitation on extraterritorial regulation). Adjudicators engage in more searching inquiry, however, when the issue concerns the "necessity" of the measures, or the justification for any apparent discrimination in their application or administration. The cases exhibit a clear preference for resolving disputes on these narrower technical points, and for avoiding broader rulings that might threaten the capacity of members to regulate at all on politically delicate subjects.

GATT Article XXI, on national security exceptions, requires a brief note. It provides that GATT shall not require any information or disclosure that jeopardizes national security, or interfere with any action to maintain peace under the UN charter. The more important part is a "self-judging" provision, permitting a member to take action which "it considers necessary" relating to fissionable materials, arms trafficking, or taken in time of war or other "emergency" in international relations. Formal disputes under Article XXI have been few, although a handful arose during the GATT years concerning matters relating to the Falklands crisis and the US conflict with Nicaragua. The lack of significant disputes no doubt relates in part to the fact that the grounds for invoking the exception are quite narrow, and its use is accordingly limited.

6. THE TECHNICAL BARRIERS CODES

During the waning years of GATT, a handful of prominent disputes came to impasse over the applicability of national treatment disciplines. A notable example was the "Beef Hormones" dispute. The EU enacted a prohibition on the sale and importation of beef from animals raised with growth hormones, ostensibly because of public health concerns about hormone ingestion by consumers of beef. The United States and others, where the administration of hormones was legal subject to residue standards, contended that the prohibition was essentially a protectionist ruse for keeping out imported beef, and further argued that there was no scientific basis for the EU's purported health concerns. The United States tried to obtain satisfaction under the Tokyo Round "Standards Code," but the GATT dispute process was stalled and the United States ultimately undertook unilateral retaliation.

Such intransigent disputes provided the impetus for more comprehensive disciplines regarding domestic regulatory measures, which culminated in the WTO Agreement on Technical Barriers to Trade (TBT) (successor to the Standards Code) and the Agreement on Sanitary and Phytosanitary Measures (SPS). The separate agreements resulted from the fact that two different negotiating groups were involved, the latter agreement emerging as part of the broader agriculture negotiations.

Both agreements are lengthy, and a thorough survey is far beyond the scope of this chapter.[xx] Instead, this section simply underscores some of the important obligations that overlap with, and especially those that extend, the commitments found in GATT Articles III and XX.

6.1 Coverage

The TBT Agreement distinguishes "technical regulations," "standards," and "conformity assessment" procedures. Technical regulations are defined as a "document which lays down product characteristics or their related processes and production methods ... with which compliance is mandatory." Standards provide "rules, guidelines, or characteristics ... with which compliance is not mandatory." "Conformity assessment procedures" include "any procedure used ... to determine that relevant requirements in technical regulations or standards are fulfilled" (see TBT Annex I). Although

---

[xx] Sykes (1995) provides more detail on the legal details. The economic logic of the technical barriers agreements is discussed in Sykes (1999).

commitments exist for each category, the clear focus is on mandatory measures and the procedures for assessing compliance with them.

Disputes can arise over whether certain types of measures constitute a "technical regulation." The Appellate Body has ruled, for example, that a labeling requirement for imported species of sardines is a technical regulation,[yy] while a ban on seal products does not "lay down product characteristics" and may not be a technical regulation.[zz]

The SPS Agreement does not use the three categories of measures found in TBT, but simply refers to SPS "measures." Clearly, however, the focus again is mainly on mandatory measures. These are defined in the Annex as measures to protect animal or plant life or health within the territory of the member from the spread of pests and disease, measures to protect human or animal life or health within the territory of the member from additives, contaminants, toxins, or diseases-causing organisms in foodstuffs, measures to protect human life or health within the territory of the member from diseases carried by animals or plants and from the entry of pests, and measures to protect against other damage in the territory of the member from the spread of pests. Note the limitation to issues "within the territory of the member," making clear that extraterritorial regulation is impermissible. Note also that pursuant to the TBT Agreement 1.5, SPS measures are *not* covered by TBT, thus establishing a clean separation between the measures covered by each.

6.2 MFN, National Treatment, and Exceptions

Both the TBT and SPS Agreements contain MFN and national treatment obligations, albeit phrased slightly differently. TBT Art. 2.1, SPS Art. 2.3. Because SPS measures are by definition aimed at human, animal, or plant life or health, no litany of exceptions comparable to GATT Article XX is included in the SPS Agreement. But the principles of the Article XX chapeau, prohibiting "arbitrary or unjustifiable discrimination" among members where similar conditions prevail, and prohibiting "disguised restrictions on international trade," are incorporated. SPS Art. 2.3. In the TBT Agreement, by contrast, the obligation is to avoid "unnecessary obstacles to international trade," which includes the idea that technical regulations should not be "more trade restrictive than necessary to fulfill a legitimate objective" such as national security, the prevention of deceptive practices, the protection of health and safety, and the environment. TBT Art. 2.2.

Both Agreements are thus structured in a rather different fashion than GATT. Instead of an affirmative obligation (such as MFN or national treatment) qualified by a list of exceptions (as in GATT Article XX), the "exceptions" and attendant qualifiers are

---

[yy] European Communities – Trade Description of Sardines, WT/DS231/AB/R. adopted October 23, 2002.

[zz] EC – Seal Products, supra. The Appellate Body left open to the possibility that the ban may be a technical regulation because it lays down process and production methods.

effectively folded into the affirmative obligations. The inevitable result is some distinctions in jurisprudence that may seem puzzling to anyone who does not appreciate the structural differences. For example, it was noted earlier that in the recent EC—Seal Products dispute, the Appellate Body rejected an argument by Europe that the exception to the seal products ban for indigenous peoples did not violate the GATT Article I MFN obligation even if it stemmed from a legitimate regulatory distinction, with the Appellate Body insisting that the issue be resolved under the exceptions jurisprudence of GATT Article XX. By contrast, under the TBT Agreement, the Appellate Body has interpreted the concept of "treatment no less favorable" in TBT 2.1 to allow for the possibility that no violation of the nondiscrimination obligation arises if imported products are disadvantaged because of legitimate regulatory distinctions.[aaa] This difference is seemingly due to the absence of an exception list in the TBT Agreement comparable to GATT Article XX.

The United States—Clove Cigarettes[bbb] illustrates the basic approach. The United States banned the sale of flavored cigarettes, ostensibly because of their special attraction for young smokers. But it included a gaping exception for menthol cigarettes, arguing that many Americans were addicted to them, and that a ban on menthol products would result in withdrawal issues as well as a black market. Indonesia, a producer of clove-flavored cigarettes, brought a complaint. Menthol and clove cigarettes were found to be like, and the case turned on the soundness of the US argument that imports did not receive "less favorable treatment" because the ban and its exception were applied in origin-neutral fashion, and the disparate treatment of menthol and other flavored cigarettes rested on a legitimate regulatory distinction. The United States lost because its regulatory rationale proved unpersuasive—addicts could turn to unflavored cigarettes to avoid withdrawal, and the likelihood of black market activity was likewise reduced by the availability of unflavored cigarettes.

A similar outcome resulted in the United States—Tuna Labeling.[ccc] The United States prohibited tuna caught by a method known as "setting on dolphins" from being marketed with a dolphin safe label. Mexico's fleet used that technique in the Eastern Tropical Pacific (ETP), although it had been abandoned by the US fleet. All of the tuna products at issue were deemed "like," and the United States was found to afford less favorable treatment to Mexico despite the fact that the rules for setting on dolphins were

---

[aaa] See the United States – Measures Affecting the Production and Sale of Clove Cigarettes, WT/DS406/AB/R, adopted April 23, 2012 (paragraph 175); the United States – Measures Concerning the Importation, Marketing, and Sale of Tuna and Tuna Products, WT/DS381/AB/R, adopted June 13, 2012 (paragraph 297).

[bbb] The United States – Measures Affecting the Production and Sale of Clove Cigarettes, WT/DS406/AB/R, adopted April 23, 2012.

[ccc] The United States – Measures Concerning the Importation, Marketing, and Sale of Tuna and Tuna Products, WT/DS381/AB/R, adopted June 13, 2012.

applied uniformly to imported and domestic goods. Among other things, the United States allowed tuna caught outside the ETP to be marketed as dolphin safe even if the associated dolphin kill may have been just as great as that associated with setting on dolphins.

The concept of "necessity" also appears in both Agreements. TBT Art. 2.2; SPS Art. 2.2. In both contexts, regulations are subject to an inquiry as to whether a less-trade restrictive alternative exists to achieve relevant objectives. The TBT Agreement adds an important corollary, with its preference for performance rather than design regulations (TBT 2.8). Thus, for example, if a regulation is designed to ensure that fire doors in public buildings resist burn-through for an adequate period of time, the regulation should be written in terms of a required burn-through time rather than in terms of required thickness or materials.

6.3 Scientific Evidence Requirements

Driven in part by the dispute over the scientific basis for the hormone-raised beef ban, the SPS Agreement requires that SPS measures be "based on scientific principles" and not maintained "without sufficient scientific evidence," subject to an exception for cases of scientific uncertainty in the face of ongoing research (a variant of the precautionary principle). SPS Art. 2.2. Likewise, SPS measures must be "based on" a "risk assessment," taking into account, among other things, "available scientific evidence." SPS Art. 5.2. The corresponding TBT obligation appears in the paragraph on measures necessary to achieve a "legitimate objective," stating that in assessing "risks" the elements of consideration include "available scientific and technical information." TBT Art. 2.2.

The evident goal of these provisions is to afford some opportunity for the dispute process to scrutinize the scientific underpinning of regulatory measures that impede trade. Their application in practice has been less than fully successful, however, as the Beef Hormones dispute again illustrates. It is well settled that members are free to select their own levels of risk tolerance—the WTO agreements do not require members to tolerate dangers that they wish to avoid in the name of promoting liberal trade. Rather, the obligation is to avoid unnecessary obstacles to trade while pursuing sovereign choices about acceptable risk levels. In the hormone beef dispute, there was no question that certain chemicals akin to the growth hormones used in cattle are associated with health risks, including carcinogenesis. Instead, the United States and other complainants argued that the risk is miniscule or even nonexistent at the low residue levels found in properly raised animals. The EC insisted that it was entitled to choose a zero-risk policy and trotted out some weak scientific support for the view that low residues create some modest risk. The WTO ruled, however, that the available evidence supporting the EU's position did not meet the requirements of a "risk assessment" under the SPS Agreement. Likewise, it ruled that the available studies that qualified as "risk assessments" supported the proposition that hormone use is "safe." The "based on" requirement was said to require a rational relationship between the risk assessment and the associated measure—it is not enough that regulators have taken account of the studies in their policy deliberations.

The EC responded to the ruling by undertaking more studies, and over time generated additional material that it claimed was sufficient to meet the standards for a supportive "risk assessment." The complainants disagreed. The dispute remained intransigent despite the new SPS disciplines, and was eventually settled (for now) by an agreement to admit more hormone-free beef from the complaining nations. The settlement became possible as consumer demand for hormone-free beef grew in the complainants' domestic markets to the point that it became economical for ranchers to maintain hormone-free herds. The dispute highlights a fundamental tension between the principle that sovereignty allows members choose their own risk tolerance on the one hand, and the principle that WTO adjudicators may adjudicate the scientific soundness of regulation on the other hand.

6.4 Harmonization and Reference to International Standards

The nontariff barriers to trade that result from heterogeneous product regulations result primarily from the fact that different countries have different regulations. Accordingly, both the TBT and SPS Agreements encourage members to harmonize regulations to the extent possible. The principal mechanism for attaining harmonization is to encourage members to employ international standards in their regulatory policies, such as those promulgated by the International Organization for Standardization and the Codex Alimentarius Commission.

The TBT Agreement provides that "where technical regulations are required and relevant international standards exist ... Members shall use them ... as a basis for their technical regulations ... except when such international standards ... would be an ineffective or inappropriate means for the fulfillment of the legitimate objectives pursued." TBT Art. 2.4. The SPS Agreement likewise states that "Members shall base their [SPS measures] on international standards ... where they exist," provided that they may introduce or maintain "a higher level of [SPS] protection if there is a scientific justification ... or as a consequence of [an appropriate risk assessment]." SPS Art. 3.1. Thus, the core obligation is to use international standards as a "basis" for domestic regulation unless those standards are inadequate to achieve the regulatory objective.

A central issue in the administration of these commitments concerns the degree of deference afforded to national regulators who determine that international standards are not adequate to achieve the relevant objectives. In EC—Sardines, the panel determined (in a finding undisturbed by the Appellate Body) that a Codex standard for the labeling of sardines, which allowed the label "sardines" to be used for different species from different geographical regions, had not been shown inadequate to achieve the EU's objective of avoiding consumer confusion.

A further issue concerns international standards that have not been supported by the member asked to rely on them. The Codex has a hormone-residue standard for beef, for example, which the EU did not support. Likewise, the Codex standard for the labeling of sardines was not adopted by consensus. In the latter case, the Appellate Body held that the Codex standard was nevertheless a relevant international standard and that the EU had an obligation to use it as a "basis" for its own regulatory standard.

6.5 Mutual Recognition

Another important strategy for eliminating barriers to trade resulting from heterogeneous regulations is "mutual recognition," whereby importing nations agree that despite their differences in approach to an issue, each approach achieves the relevant objective. For example, one country might test live animals for excessive drug residues, while another country conducts spot tests on meat. Yet, both approaches might be deemed sufficient to ensure safe levels of drug residue in meat for human consumption.

To this end, the TBT Agreement states that "Members shall give positive consideration to accepting as equivalent technical regulations of other Members ... provided they are satisfied that these regulations adequately fulfill the objectives of their own regulations." TBT Art. 2.7. The SPS Agreement in turn provides that members "shall accept the ... measures of other members as equivalent ... if the exporting Member objectively demonstrates ... that its measures achieve the importing Member's appropriate level of [SPS] protection." SPS Art. 4.1. These mutual recognition requirements are phrased somewhat weakly, however, with the issue arguably being self-judging under the TBT Agreement. Perhaps unsurprisingly, therefore, dispute settlement has yet to insist on mutual recognition in a case where a member has declined to afford it.

6.6 Consistency Requirements

Among the more intriguing principles in the SPS Agreement is the "consistency requirement" in SPS 5.5. It provides that Members "shall avoid arbitrary or unjustifiable distinctions in the [SPS protection] levels it considers to be appropriate in different situations, if such distinctions result in discrimination or a disguised restriction on international trade." The TBT Agreement does not contain a comparable provision.

In the initial panel decision in the Beef Hormones dispute, the panel held that the EC had violated the consistency requirement because it insisted on a zero-risk policy with respect to hormone residues in beef, yet did nothing about the naturally occurring and far more substantial residues of comparable hormones in natural foodstuffs such as eggs. The Appellate Body reversed this finding, however, concluding that an important distinction arises between naturally occurring hormones and hormones artificially introduced into foodstuffs. The decision to leave naturally occurring hormones unregulated, therefore, was not "arbitrary." The panel also found inconsistency in the treatment of pigs, because the EU allowed certain drugs to be used for growth promotion in piglets that have greater potential for carcinogenesis than the growth hormones used in beef cattle. The Appellate Body also reversed this finding on the grounds that it did not constitute a "disguised restriction" on trade.

In addition, as EC—Seal Products illustrates (where the Appellate Body rejected any requirement that the EU exhibit comparable concern for animal welfare in slaughterhouses and terrestrial hunts), great hesitation exists to extend consistency requirements outside the SPS Agreement. Nonetheless, the variation in regulatory tolerance for risk across issue areas seems enormous within the domestic policies of WTO members. In this context, a fundamental question arises as to the meaning of the concept of "consistency," and its desirability. Among other things, an exclusive focus on the level of risk tolerated in different issue areas is surely too narrow, as it ignores the costs of regulation as well as the benefits of refraining from regulation.

Consistency requirements thus raise intriguing economic issues that have not received much attention. At some level, discrimination that violates national treatment or MFN principles is an "inconsistency" in the treatment of similar (or identical) situations. The harder question is whether consistency requirements can play a useful role across more disparate regulatory problems. Among other things, a question arises as to how to draw the line between cases in which inconsistency reflects an international externality that is the appropriate subject of discipline under a trade agreement or is simply a product of imperfections in the domestic political system that trade agreements should not disturb.

6.7 Notice, Comment, and Transparency Requirements

Regulatory measures can impede trade not only because of the challenges of complying with them, but because domestic producers of regulated products may learn about prospective regulations sooner and have a lead time to retool. Likewise, domestic firms may have greater opportunity to participate in the process of formulating regulations, and in encouraging regulators to shade them toward policies that favor domestic firms. Finally, exporters may be disadvantaged relative to domestic firms because they are unclear about the content of regulatory requirements and incur sizeable costs to learn about them.

Both the TBT and SPS Agreements address these issues. Notice requirements oblige members to provide advance notice of proposed regulations through accessible publications and through the WTO Secretariat, and to provide other Members with advance copies of proposed regulations, unless exigent circumstances make such steps unrealistic. TBT Arts. 2.9–2.10; SPS Annex B. Other Members should also be given an opportunity to comment on proposed regulations, and the regulating Member must take those comments into account. TBT Art. 2.9.4; SPS Annex B 5(d). Finally, regulations must be published promptly and in a manner that is accessible to other Members, Members must establish an enquiry point for other Members to obtain information about regulations, and absent exigent circumstances must allow other Members a reasonable time to adapt their products to comply with new regulations. TBT Arts. 2.11–2.12, 10; SPS Annex B (1)–(3).

7. SUBSIDIES

The treatment of subsidies in the WTO/GATT system has evolved greatly over time. I begin with the limited rules of GATT and proceed to the more detailed provisions of the Agreement on Subsidies and Countervailing Measures (SCMs).

7.1 GATT Rules

A subsidy to domestic producers that compete with imported goods can lead to lower prices and a competitive advantage over imports just as can a protective tariff. Accordingly, such subsidies are "laws … affecting … internal sale" of like product imports that would seem to violate GATT Article III(4). The drafters did not wish to outlaw all subsidies, however, and so included an exception in GATT Art. III(8)(b) for "the payment of subsidies exclusively to domestic producers, including payments to domestic producers derived from the proceeds of internal taxes or charges applied consistently with the provisions of this Article."

This provision creates the possibility of mischief in a trade agreement with negotiated market access commitments. For example, an importing nation might negotiate a tariff binding with a trading partner, and subsequently introduce a producer subsidy to import-competing firms, thereby nullifying the benefits of the tariff binding. The GATT thus evolved the principle that a *new and unanticipated* subsidy to import-competing firms producing goods that compete with imports subject to a tariff binding constitutes a "nonviolation" nullification or impairment under GATT.

A similar form of mischief arises if an importing nation imposes a nondiscriminatory tax on imports and domestic products alike, and then uses the revenue to subsidize domestic producers. Such actions can replicate the effects of a tariff, and also presumably justifies a claim of nullification or impairment in cases where a binding has been negotiated, although no case posing exactly this scenario has arisen.

Early in the GATT, the scope of Article III(8)(b) was tested in a case where the importing nation gave subsidies to domestic *purchasers* of domestically produced products. This was found to be a violation of GATT Art. III(4), on the premise that III(8)(b) only permits *producer* subsidies.[ddd] Thus, "import substitution subsidies" violate GATT. The logic of this distinction between producer and purchaser subsidies can be questioned, as they potentially have the same economic impact, and the explanation for the inconsistent treatment is perhaps political.

[ddd] Italian Discrimination Against Imported Agricultural Machinery, GATT panel report adopted October 23, 1958, 7th BISD 60 (1959).

As for subsidies on the export side, the original GATT contained nothing more than a reporting requirement in Article XVI. That Article was subsequently amended to introduce some additional disciplines on export subsidies for "primary" and "other than … primary" products, but those rules have been supplanted by the SCMs Agreement and will not be discussed further.

One other principle is to be found in GATT Article XVI and Ad Article VI, which provide that the exemption of exports "from duties or taxes borne by the like product when destined for consumption in the country of origin or exportation," or the "refund of such duties or taxes," shall not constitute a subsidy. Accordingly, product taxes that would apply to exports if sold in the home market, and product taxes and import duties on input products used to make such products, can be exempted or refunded on exports under specified conditions. This principle explains why, for example, products exported from Europe can be exempted from the value-added tax without triggering any subsidy disciplines.

A question arises as to exactly what types of taxes are "borne by the like product" in the home market. A 1970 working party on border tax adjustments concluded that taxes "directly levied on products," such as excise taxes and value-added taxes, are subject to adjustment. By contrast, taxes "not directly levied on products" were not subject to adjustment, such as social security and payroll taxes.[eee]

Aside from this provision precluding a finding of subsidization for a proper export exemption or rebate, the GATT made no attempt to define the concept of "subsidy" or the related term "bounty or grant" in Article VI. The thorny task of distinguishing legitimate government activity from troublesome "subsidies" was left open.

Finally, GATT Article VI addresses the unilateral use of countervailing measures (duties) by GATT members. Countervailing duties evolved as unilateral actions to counter purportedly unfair subsidization of imported goods. GATT Article II permits countervailing duties as an exception to negotiated tariff bindings, but only if they are imposed consistently with Article VI. Most importantly, countervailing duties cannot be imposed in an amount in excess of the estimated subsidy per unit on imported goods, cannot be duplicative of antidumping duties imposed on the same goods, and cannot be imposed unless subsidized imports are causing or threatening material injury to competing domestic producers.

7.2 The SCMs Agreement

The newer WTO rules on subsidies are to be found in the SCMs Agreement and in separate provisions of the Agreement on Agriculture. Given space limitations I focus here only on SCMs.[fff]

[eee] Report of the Working Party on Border Tax Adjustments, BISD 18S/97 (1970).

[fff] A nice summary of the Agriculture Agreement, including important features of its rules on subsidies, can be found at https://www.wto.org/english/tratop_e/agric_e/ag_intro00_contents_e.htm.

The SCMs Agreement has five basic components. The first is a section that seeks to define the concept of "subsidy." The second concerns the limited types of "prohibited" subsidies. The third concerns "actionable" subsidies, which are not prohibited but may be the subject of a WTO complaint if they cause certain types of harm to other members. The fourth is a now expired set of "safe harbor" provisions, permitting certain subsidies for research and development, environmental improvement, and assistance to disadvantaged regions. Because of their expiration I do not address them. The fifth category contains a number of constraints on the use of countervailing duties by importing countries.

7.2.1 "Subsidy" and "Specificity"

SCMs Article I defines subsidy as a "financial contribution" by a government, such as a "direct transfer of funds" (eg, grants, loans, equity infusions, loan guarantees), a tax policy whereby "government revenue that is otherwise due is foregone or not collected," or the "government provides goods or services other than general infrastructure, or purchases goods." In addition to a financial contribution, the existence of a "subsidy" requires that "a benefit is thereby conferred." With regard to the latter requirement, no subsidy would arise if, for example, a government were to sell goods at market prices. Finally, Article I provides that no "subsidy" shall be deemed prohibited or actionable, or be subjected to countervailing duties, unless it is "specific" as defined in Article 2.

The concept of subsidy under Article 1 raises some interesting issues. In many cases, the test for the existence of a "benefit" will look to market benchmarks. But suppose the government borrows at 5%, and lends at 6%, to a company that must ordinarily borrow at 7% in the capital markets. It is well settled that the requirement of a "benefit" demands an assessment from the perspective of the recipient,[ggg] and so a subsidy exists on these facts even if the government is "making a profit."[hhh] This principle seems uncontroversial.

Other issues are more controversial. Suppose that the government restricts the exportation of some input product, such as logs, reducing their local price and affording a competitive advantage to domestic lumber mills. The lumber producers benefit just as surely as they would from a direct cash payment, but is there a subsidy? The tentative answer in WTO litigation is no, because the government has not made a "financial contribution,"[iii] although the log export restrictions might well violate GATT Article XI.

Now imagine that the government builds a steel mill in an industry already suffering from considerable overcapacity. Assume that no rational private investor would build such a mill given the condition of the industry. Once the mill is constructed, the

---

[ggg] Canada – Measure Affecting the Export of Civilian Aircraft, WT/DS&)/AB/R, adopted August 20, 1999.

[hhh] Of course, there is no real "profit" if the government's lending rate does not properly compensate for risk.

[iii] The United States – Measures Treating Export Restraints as Subsidies, WT/DS194/R, adopted August 23, 2001.

government "privatizes" the mill by auctioning it off to the highest bidder in a fair and transparent auction. Is the mill "subsidized?" The answer thus far is no, on the premise that the private owner of the mill paid fair market value and did not receive any "benefit," as long as the auction was transparent and open.[jjj] The economic soundness of this proposition may certainly be questioned.

A further issue arises when a subsidy is conferred on input products. Suppose, for example, that standing timber is "subsidized," but the exported good is lumber. Does the subsidy conferred on timber "pass through" to the downstream product? The general view of WTO law is that subsidies cannot be presumed to "pass through" if the upstream product is sold at arm's length to the downstream producer, and that an empirical analysis is required to determine the amount of "pass through." If the upstream and downstream producers are vertically integrated, by contrast, a pass through analysis may not be required, a questionable principle given that the vertically integrated firm faces an opportunity cost to the use of in-house inputs equal to their fair market value.[kkk]

Tax subsidies raise particular puzzles. Consider two hypothetical WTO members. One has a tax policy of exempting corporations from tax on all income earned abroad, on the premise that the foreign jurisdiction in which the income is earned will tax it. The second has a policy of taxing foreign income, but exempts income earned from certain export-related operations abroad. Which member, if either, is conferring a "subsidy?" The current answer is the second member only, because the exemption for certain export-related operations reduces the taxes "otherwise due" under its tax system, whereas the first member has simply chosen not to tax at all.[lll] Such examples raise the suspicion that the concept of a tax subsidy is arbitrary and to a great degree exalts form over substance.

As a final example, consider a member that owns all the timberland within its jurisdiction. It allows private loggers to harvest the timber at a price far below what the timber could bring in a public auction. Does it confer a "subsidy?" Article I suggests that the answer depends on a comparison between the price charged by the government and the fair market price. But if all timber is government-owned and no local private market exists, how does one resolve that question? Or suppose that the local private market is quite small and that its sales must compete with government sales—is the price thereby distorted and unreliable? Or is the price of standing timber just a division of the economic rent between the timber owner and the harvester, such that no downstream effect on prices arises? The jurisprudence seems to accept the notion that government participation

[jjj] See the United States – Imposition of Countervailing Duties on Certain Hot-Rolled Lead and Bismuth Carbon Steel Products Originating in the United Kingdom, WT/DS138/AB/R, adopted June 7, 2000.
[kkk] See the Untied States – Final Countervailing Duty Determination with Respect to Certain Softwood Lumber from Canada, WT/DS257/AB/R, adopted February 17, 2004.
[lll] The United States – Tax Treatment for Foreign Sales Corporations, WT/DS108/AB/R, adopted March 20, 2000.

in the market can distort market benchmarks for subsidization, but has not suggested any clear solution to the problem.[mmm]

This last example raises a broader question. Theory suggests that a "subsidy" will not harm unsubsidized competitors unless it results in more output in the short- or long-run, through its effects on short- or long-run marginal costs. Nothing in the SCMs Agreement requires such an effect, however—a onetime "lump sum" tax credit to a domestic firm is still a "subsidy." Various proposals have been advanced by commentators through the years to require an assessment of whether and how "subsidies" affect marginal costs, but none have gained political traction.[nnn]

Finally, the concept of "subsidy" is deeply myopic in an important sense. Each government program is evaluated in isolation. No attempt is made to ascertain, for example, whether a subsidy might be offset by extra regulatory burdens imposed on the recipient, or by the fact that taxes on the recipient are otherwise higher than taxes on competitors. In other words, a "subsidy" can be found regardless of the *net* impact of government taxation and regulation on the international competitive position of the recipients. No other approach seems administrable, but as a result one can question whether the antisubsidy rules under WTO law meaningfully address government distortions of competitiveness.

Consider now the concept of "specificity," a precondition for any action to be taken in the WTO or by an importing member against a "subsidy." Two types of subsidies are automatically deemed "specific"—export subsidies and import substitution subsidies, the subject of the next section (SCMs Article 2.3).

For other, ordinary "domestic" subsidies given to producers, the specificity test is rather vague. The first test is whether "the granting authority, or the legislation pursuant to which the granting authority operates, explicitly limits access to a subsidy to certain enterprises." SCMs Art. 2.1(a). No definition of "certain enterprises" is given. Specificity under this test is known as de jure specificity.

Under Art. 2.1(b), the concept is de jure specificity is qualified. If "the granting authority … establishes objective criteria or conditions governing the eligibility for, and the amount of, a subsidy, specificity shall not exist, provided that the eligibility is automatic and that such criteria and conditions are strictly adhered to." A footnote explains that "[o]bjective criteria or conditions, as used herein, mean criteria or conditions which are neutral, which do not favor certain enterprises over others, and which are economic in nature and horizontal in application, such as number of employees or size of enterprise."

Next, Art. 2.1(c) introduces a notion of de facto specificity: "If, notwithstanding any appearance of nonspecificity resulting from the application of the principles laid down in

---

[mmm] See the Untied States – Final Countervailing Duty Determination with Respect to Certain Softwood Lumber from Canada, WT/DS257/AB/R, adopted February 17, 2004.

[nnn] See Goetz et al. (1986).

subparagraphs (a) and (b), there are reasons to believe that the subsidy may in fact be specific, other factors may be considered. Such factors are: use of a subsidy program by a limited number of certain enterprises, predominant use by certain enterprises, the granting of disproportionately large amounts of subsidy to certain enterprises, and the manner in which discretion has been exercised by the granting authority in the decision to grant a subsidy." As an example, a government might offer crude oil for sale to all domestic comers at a price below the world market price. Nominally, any enterprise could purchase it, but in fact, only oil refiners and petrochemical producers have any use for it.

Finally, Art. 2.2 concerns geographic specificity. "A subsidy which is limited to certain enterprises located within a designated geographical region within the jurisdiction of the granting authority shall be specific."

Like the concept of "subsidy," the so-called specificity test raises a number of issues. Most fundamentally, what is meant by "certain enterprises?" The evident objective is to associate specificity with a degree of industrial targeting, while insulating the ordinary activities of most governments (roads, utility infrastructure, public education) from any suggestion that they constitute an unfair subsidy. But how much "targeting" is required? No definitive answer exists in the text or cases to date. Possible anomalies include the following. Member A has a farm program that provides income support to farmers of all plant products. Member B has a program that provides the identical level of support only to potato farmers. In all likelihood, member B is the only one providing a specific subsidy.

Related, Member A wishes to subsidize 10 different industries, and enacts a separate statute to provide the funds for each. Member B wishes to subsidize the same 10 industries, but enacts a single statute providing comparable benefits to each (such as a 10% tax credit on all capital investment). A strong argument exists that only member A is conferring specific subsidies.

The notion of geographic specificity is similarly peculiar. If the US Federal government enacts a program benefiting a substantial number of industries in California, geographic specificity can be found. But if the government of California enacts an identical program, no specificity exists as long as the set of industries subject to the program comprise more than "certain enterprises."

The specificity test is also peculiar in its implicit premise that there is something inherently objectionable about industrial targeting. Economic theory counsels in favor of policy instruments that target distorted behavioral margins directly, and there is no reason to assume that distorted margins in particular settings are never limited to "certain enterprises." Targeted subsidies, in some circumstances, may be the optimal instrument to address market failures.

In light of these various issues regarding the conceptualization of "subsidy" and "specificity," one can at least wonder whether the SCMs Agreement is at all satisfactory in its efforts to distinguish permissible subsidies from those that are potentially "unfair," and whether the effort to draw the line between subsidies that are subject to legal action and those that are not is worth the bother. Especially given the fact that subsidies often confer positive externalities, and the most obvious case of subsidies with negative externalities—those that impair negotiated tariff bindings—are policed by the longstanding nonviolation doctrine now enshrined in the SCMs Agreement, it may be argued that a laissez faire approach to other forms of subsidies is a plausible legal approach. Such an approach predominates in the US Federal system.[ooo]

7.2.2 Prohibited Subsidies

The SCMs Agreement prohibits two types of subsidies. One is familiar from the days of GATT—import substitution subsidies, or "subsidies contingent … upon the use of domestic over imported goods." Recall that such subsidies to *purchasers* of domestic goods were long ago found to violate GATT Article III(4), and to be outside the exception in Article III(8)(b) for domestic *producer* subsidies.

The second type of prohibited subsidy is an "export subsidy," defined as "subsidies contingent in law or in fact … upon export performance." The notion of contingency "in fact" applies when a subsidy is not formally contingent on export performance but is in fact administered in such a fashion. Annex I to the SCMs Agreement contains an "illustrative" (and thus nonexclusive) list of export subsidies.[ppp] It also reflects the principles contained in GATT Article VI regarding the exemption of exports from taxes and import duties borne by like products sold for domestic consumption, elaborating those principles in some detail and making clear that tax rebates or exemptions, duty drawbacks and the like in conformity with those principles are not considered export subsidies.

Item (k) in the Annex also contains an interesting exception to the general export subsidy rules, applicable to government export credits. The basic principle is that an export credit (such as those offered by the US Export Import Bank) is judged to be a prohibited export subsidy only if it is offered at a rate that is below the cost of borrowing for the government that confers the credit (even if it is well below the borrowing costs of the beneficiary exporter, the usual benchmark). Moreover, a further safe harbor exists for credits that comply with the OECD interest rate guidelines on export credits.

It is also well settled that a subsidy to a company that engages in exportation is not an export subsidy for that reason alone. Rather, the subsidy must distort the relative incentive to export vs to sell in the domestic market.[qqq]

The logic of the prohibition on these two categories of subsidies is unclear. Import substitution subsidies, as noted, can have effects that are identical to permissible producer

[ooo] Sykes (2010) includes a lengthy survey of the different approaches to subsidies issues in the WTO, EU State Aid law, and the US constitutional law.

[ppp] See SCMs Annex I.

[qqq] See European Communities and Certain Member States – Measures Affecting Trade in Large Civil Aircraft, WT/DS316/AB/R, adopted June 1, 2011.

subsidies. Export subsidies can expand trade toward its efficient levels in the presence of trade barriers, and can be comparable in their global welfare effects to tariff liberalization.

7.2.3 Actionable Subsidies

Part III of the SCMs Agreement pertains to actionable subsidies. It authorizes complaints against subsidies that, although not prohibited, nevertheless cause certain "adverse effects" for other members. Article 5 lists three types of adverse effects. The first is "injury to the domestic industry of another Member." An injury requirement was present under GATT Article VI as a precondition for the use of countervailing duties. The inclusion of this concept here allows an importing member to challenge the subsidy before the WTO as an alternative to unilaterally imposed countervailing duties. Given the advantage to the importing nation's treasury of the countervailing duty option, however, it is unclear whether this provision will have much impact.

The second type of adverse effect is "nullification or impairment of benefits" under GATT, such as the benefits of tariff bindings. This provision in essence codifies the notion that new and unanticipated subsidies may impair the benefits of market access negotiations, which was a basis for a nonviolation claim under GATT, and thus converts such claims into violation claims under the SCMs Agreement.

The third type of adverse effect is by far the most important relative to preexisting GATT rules—the concept of "serious prejudice." Article 6.3 provides that serious prejudice exists if[rrr]:

(a) the effect of the subsidy is to displace or impede the imports of a like product of another Member into the market of the subsidizing Member;

(b) the effect of the subsidy is to displace or impede the exports of a like product of another Member from a third country market;

(c) the effect of the subsidy is a significant price undercutting by the subsidized product as compared with the price of a like product of another Member in the same market or significant price suppression, price depression, or lost sales in the same market;

(d) the effect of the subsidy is an increase in the world market share of the subsidizing Member in a particular subsidized primary product or commodity as compared to the average share it had during the previous period of 3 years and this increase follows a consistent trend over a period when subsidies have been granted.

The important innovation here is recognition that subsidies can have adverse effects on the *exports* of other members, either to the market of the subsidizing member or to third country markets. These effects were commonly insulated from any challenge under GATT, as they may not have impaired any negotiated tariff bindings or the limited rules on export subsidies, and aggrieved members could not address them through their own countervailing duties (which they can impose only on imports into their own markets).

[rrr] Note that Articles 6.1 and 6.2 expired and are no longer in force (see Art. 31).

These provisions have been central in several high-visibility disputes thus far, perhaps most notably the Boeing–Airbus litigation, where serious prejudice has been found. The analysis of serious prejudice embroils panels in elaborate and challenging fact-finding analyses whereby they must assess how a complaining member's exports would have performed in counterfactual scenarios without the actionable subsidies.[sss]

7.2.4 Countervailing Duties

Part V of the SCMs Agreement is its lengthiest section, containing extensive rules regarding the imposition of countervailing measures by importing nations. The details are beyond the scope of this survey, and I simply note a few core points.

Members must limit countervailing measures to circumstances in which specific subsidies, as defined in Part I of the SCMs Agreement, have been shown to exist. Countervailing duties cannot exceed the per unit value of the subsidy on imported goods, creating a measurement problem that is often complex (as, for example, when subsidies for capital equipment purchases must be allocated over time). Transparent proceedings must be followed, allowing affecting parties a chance to participate and to have their views considered. Members must provide opportunities for judicial review of proceedings that result in countervailing duties, and members must periodically review whether the conditions warranting countervailing measures have changed.

Furthermore, as required by GATT Article VI, countervailing duties may not be imposed unless "the effect of the subsidization ... is to cause or threaten material injury" to a domestic industry. This so-called "injury test" requires first that the "industry" be defined, and it will typically consist of "the domestic producers as a whole of the like products" to the imported products under investigation. The Agreement contains a number of requirements for the injury analysis, including lists of factors that must be "considered" as part of the analysis.

8. ANTIDUMPING MEASURES

Like countervailing duties, antidumping measures evolved as unilateral policies to counter the "unfairness" of dumped imports. Some measures, such as the US Antidumping Act of 1916, established judicial proceedings with civil damages as a possible response to dumping. But the predominant approach quickly came to involve the use of antidumping duties to offset the amount or "margin" of dumping, calculated as described later.

[sss] See, eg, EU – Large Civil Aircraft, supra, and the United States – Measures Affecting Trade in Large Civil Aircraft (Second Complaint), WT/DS353/AB/R, adopted March 23, 2012. See also the United States – Subsidies on Upland Cotton, WT/DS267/AB/R, adopted March 21, 2005.

8.1 Basic Principles

With the advent of GATT, the primary concern was that antidumping duties not be employed in a manner that would undercut negotiated tariff bindings. GATT Article II provided that antidumping duties were an exception to the tariff bindings, but only if imposed in accordance with GATT Article VI.

Under Article VI, "dumping, by which products of one country are introduced into the commerce of another country at less than the normal value of the products, is to be condemned if it causes or threatens material injury to an established industry ..." Dumping is not prohibited, however, and indeed GATT cannot directly prohibit it because it results from the pricing decisions of private firms rather than from the policies of GATT member states.

In addition to the requirement of injury, the key to the imposition of antidumping duties is a determination that imports are priced below their "normal value." Under Article VI, a price below normal value arises:

if the price of the product exported from one country to another

(a) is less than the comparable price, in the ordinary course of trade, for the like product when destined for consumption in the exporting country, or,

(b) in the absence of such domestic price, is less than either

  (i) the highest comparable price for the like product for export to any third country in the ordinary course of trade, or

  (ii) the cost of production of the product in the country of origin plus a reasonable addition for selling cost and profit.

Article VI further provides, as in the case of subsidies, that the exemption of a product from duties or taxes borne by the like product when destined for consumption in the home market shall not be a basis for a finding of dumping. Accordingly, to the extent that these tax exemptions, rebates, duty drawbacks, and the like result in export prices that would otherwise be found to be below "normal value," importing nations must adjust their dumping calculations to avoid such a finding.

These principles have been carried forward, elaborated, and somewhat modified in the WTO Agreement on Antidumping Measures (AD Agreement). Like Part V of the SCMs Agreement, the AD Agreement contains an extensive set of rules regarding the use of antidumping duties by WTO members. These rules concern, among other things, the measurement and calculation of dumping margins, the administration of the injury test, a wide range of transparency and procedural requirements designed to ensure that members have a right to participate in the proceedings, requirements of judicial review, and for periodic review of the continued need for dumping duties (often termed "sunset reviews"). The details of the AD Agreement are for the most part beyond the scope of this survey, and I will note just a few points.

Regarding the determination of the dumping margin, the preferred option is a comparison of the price of the imports under investigation with their home market price. This seemingly simple comparison can be complicated by an enormous number of considerations. Transactions need to be more or less contemporaneous to be comparable, a notion that is not entirely clear and allows for judgment and manipulation. The products sold in the home market may be quite different from the products exported, which will necessitate a number of adjustments based on differences in production cost to enable an "apples to apples" comparison. In some cases, the dissimilarities may be so great that the home market price does not seem a viable comparator. Likewise, the number of sales in the home market may be very small, to the point that importing nations may fear that their prices are manipulated to avoid findings of dumping, and again they may not be a good comparator. Still further, many transactions may occur between related parties, such as parent corporations and subsidiaries, again raising the possibility that the "prices" are manipulated to avoid findings of dumping. Arm's length transactions, which are generally presumed to yield reliable prices, may occur at quite different stages in the chain of distribution, necessitating further adjustments to make them "comparable." Finally, the AD Agreement recognizes that sales below "cost of production" may be disregarded for purposes of computing normal value, as normal value is intended to reflect a price that covers costs.

Accordingly, the typical antidumping calculation involves a careful search for arm's length prices to begin the price comparison, followed often by a myriad of adjustments to facilitate apples to apples comparison, relating to differences in the merchandise, the level of trade at which the price is observed, differences in selling and warranty terms, differences in freight, insurance and packing costs, and so on. Even then, a normal value based on the home market price will not be used if the home merchandise is too dissimilar, if the number of sales is too small, or if too many of the sales are below "cost." "Cost" here is understood to include not only variable costs but also an allocation of fixed costs and general selling and administrative expense (but not "profit"). It is thus quite imperfectly akin to an accounting estimate of long-run average cost in economic terms.

When the home market price is not a viable comparator, the price of sales to a third country may be used. These prices too may require a wide range of adjustments to make them comparable, and may be deemed inadequate for the same reasons as home market prices. Furthermore, the importing nation has discretion to choose an "appropriate" third country for comparison, and of course this choice may be made strategically to maximize the apparent amount of dumping.

Finally, the importing nation may determine that price comparisons are not viable for the reasons noted earlier, and may then use "cost of production" as the basis for normal value. This will typically represent "cost" as described earlier plus a normal profit allowance.

The reader can no doubt appreciate the complexity of these calculations, the amount of data required, the number of judgments that must be made along the way (such as for cost allocation purposes), and the potential expense involved. Note further that dumping is an activity of firms, so that if the exporting nation under investigation has many exporters, in principle a dumping calculation must be done for each of them. To reduce the burden on investigating authorities, sampling is allowed in cases involving large numbers of exporters. The largest exporters are typically investigated individually, with smaller numbers subject to duties based on a weighted average of the firms individually investigated.

The reliability of the data gathered in these investigations is also a concern. Not surprisingly, importing nations do not simply trust exporters to provide accurate information for price and cost calculations. Investigating authorities will instead typically conduct audits of the information provided, adding to the complexity and expense.

Given the burden on exporters of antidumping investigations, it is no surprise that the cases are "settled" with some regularity by agreements between exporting firms and the importing government. Settlement agreements may be based on a commitment to raise prices to eliminate dumping or to eliminate its injurious effect if a lesser price increase would suffice. In practice, the former undertakings are more likely. Even after settlement, however, investigating authorities usually continue to monitor import prices to ensure compliance with the agreement.

Antidumping cases are quite arcane and technical, and the disputes that arise often involve detailed issues that are far beyond the scope of this survey. Because of the extensive litigation and publicity regarding the subject, however, I include a brief note on the "zeroing issue."

Consider a simple example to demonstrate the use of zeroing: An exporter from some country is accused of dumping. It has one home market sale in January at a price of 50, and one in February at a price of 30. Likewise, it has one sale to the importing nation in January at 50, and one in February at 30. Is the exporter dumping? Under a "transaction to transaction" comparison, the January sales are both at the same price, and the February sales are at the same price, so there is no dumping. Under an "average to average" comparison, the average home market price is 40 and the average export price is 40, so again there is no dumping. Under the "average to transaction" comparison method, however, the normal value is 40—the average of the home market prices. The export prices are each compared to the normal value. The January sale at 50 is above normal value, and so the dumping margin is zero (hence the term "zeroing"). The February sale at 30 is below normal value and the margin of dumping is 10. The average margin of dumping is $(10+0)/2=5$, resulting in an average percentage of dumping equal to 5/40 (the denominator being the average price of imported sales) $= 12.5\%$. Zeroing will thus produce an antidumping duty in that amount.

This type of calculation was routinely employed by the United States for many years. This technique was challenged in a number of cases at the WTO, all of which to date have resulted in rulings that the zeroing calculation inflates antidumping duties in violation of the AD Agreement.[ttt] The Agreement clearly allows for the use of the average to trans-action method of calculation, however, "if the authorities find a pattern of export prices which differ significantly among different purchasers, regions or time periods, and if an explanation is provided as to why such differences cannot be taken into account appropriately by the use of a weighted average-to-weighted average or transaction-to-transaction comparison." AD Agreement Art. 2.4.2. These cases of so-called "targeted dumping," a concept that is not well-defined, afford a potential new frontier in the battle over zeroing, and allegations of targeted dumping are now common is the US antidump-ing petitions.

Another highly controversial area of antidumping practice concerns the investigation of imports from nonmarket economy countries (of particular interest regarding China). The AD Agreement does not address the matter, but a footnote to GATT Article VI states that "in the case of imports from a country which has a complete or substantially complete monopoly of its trade and where all domestic prices are fixed by the State, spe-cial difficulties may exist in determining price comparability … [and] importing contract-ing parties may find it necessary to take into account the possibility that a strict comparison with domestic prices in such a country may not always be appropriate." Relying on this footnote, WTO members have developed special procedures for dump-ing investigations involving nonmarket-economies. In the United States, the preferred procedure under Section 773(c) of the Tariff Act of 1930 is to establish normal value by taking the input *quantities* used to produce the good by the nonmarket exporter, and to value those inputs using *prices* obtained from market economy countries "considered to be appropriate" by the investigating authorities. In other words, normal value is based on a cost of production estimate obtained using input prices from some third country.

Alternatively in the United States (and routinely in the EU), normal value is deter-mined based on the sales prices of merchandise produce in a market economy country. The US statute simply requires that the merchandise be "comparable" and that the cho-sen comparator country(ies) be at a comparable "level of economic development."

In general, the comparator countries used to establish input prices or merchandise value are chosen during the course of antidumping investigations based on data availabil-ity, as well as potential strategic considerations that affect the computed dumping margin. As a consequence, nonmarket economy exporters often have no way to determine what normal value their products will be deemed to have until after antidumping investigations are completed, and may anticipate that comparators will be chosen to maximize apparent dumping.

To conclude this section, it is perhaps useful to ask why firms potentially subject to dumping investigations find it rational to engage in dumping. One response is that dump-ing may often go undetected or unchallenged. A second answer is that given the

---

[ttt] Zeroing has also been the subject of much critical commentary. See, eg, Boltuck and Litan (1991).

complexities of the dumping calculation, even a firm determined not to dump may have great difficulty in forecasting its "normal value," and may engage in dumping by accident. And once a firm becomes subject to antidumping duties, it can avoid future findings of dumping, roughly speaking, only by raising its prices to eliminate the margin of dumping, while its customers nonetheless continue to pay the antidumping duty as well for some possibly considerable period of time. A superior strategy may be to take a chance of dumping and, if subject to an antidumping investigation down the road, to raise prices to settle the case.

8.2 Antidumping Law vs Antitrust Law

Antidumping law was first introduced in Canada in 1904, and spread to the United States via Federal statutes in 1916 and 1921. Throughout this period, many of its proponents touted it as a necessary supplement to antitrust law, aimed at methods of unfair competition and monopolization.[uuu] Popular understanding of the function of antidumping law today also commonly links antidumping with antitrust policy. It is thus useful to contrast antidumping law briefly with modern antitrust law.[vvv]

The closest analog to a concern for "dumping" in antitrust law is the concept of predatory pricing. Under US law, for example, a firm that lowers its prices to drive out its competitors, and thereafter to secure a "monopoly," violates Section 2 of the Sherman Act, which prohibits "monopolization." Beyond predation in this classic sense, a firm that uses discriminatory low prices to discipline an aggressive oligopolistic competitor, and thereby to restore the oligopolistic pricing umbrella, does not "monopolize" but may nevertheless violate the Robinson–Patman Act if "the effect of such discrimination may be substantially to lessen competition." The Robinson–Patman Act more broadly concerns price discrimination that may "injure, destroy, or prevent competition with any person who either grants or knowingly receives the benefit of such discrimination, or with customers of either of them."

Much has been written about the merits of these doctrines. Many early decisions were roundly criticized as overaggressive and inefficient, protecting "competitors" rather than "competition." A variety of academic contributions suggested more refined tests for anticompetitive behavior, most prominently the suggestion that only prices below marginal cost offered reliable evidence of predation, while prices above marginal costs were most likely procompetitive (the rare exceptions being impossible to distinguish reliably). The well-known Areeda–Turner rule declares that prices above the best available proxy for marginal cost, such as average variable cost, are presumptively nonpredatory. The US Supreme Court ultimately embraced an "appropriate" cost-based test for cases alleging that low prices are driving out competitors in an anticompetitive fashion, applying it both

---

[uuu] See Sykes (1998) for a detailed history.
[vvv] See also Barcelo (1979).

to claims under the Sherman Act and under the Robinson–Patman Act, in a decision that also required a plaintiff to show that the defendant was likely to recoup the losses from lower prices through an ability to increase prices later.[www]

Accordingly, although modern antitrust law allows for the possibility that low prices may be anticompetitive, the standards for proving such a case are quite different from the standards for the imposition of antidumping duties. The differences may be summarized as follows:

(i) No presumption exists under antitrust law that discriminatory prices are harmful to competition, although the Robinson–Patman Act does provide greater discipline for discriminatory prices than nondiscriminatory prices. The mere fact that a company sells in one market at a price below its home market price, or its price in some third market, is of no significance per se, and is understood to result from rational pricing decisions by firms with no anticompetitive ambitions facing different demand conditions in different markets.

(ii) Antidumping law finds dumping when prices are below an accounting measure of fully allocated costs, including fixed costs, GS&A expense, and so on. The precise cost benchmark in antitrust is somewhat uncertain, but it is undoubtedly lower, based on some proxy for short-run average or marginal costs, and fashioned with a recognition of the fact that prices above marginal cost are rational for firms with no anticompetitive ambitions.

(iii) Antitrust requires that losses due to below cost prices be offset by a likely period of recoupment later through higher prices, a requirement that is altogether absent in antidumping law.

(iv) Although antidumping law requires "material injury or threat" to a domestic industry as a precondition for antidumping duties, this standard merely requires a determination that dumped imports are causing a material reduction in prices, profits, output, employment, or some other indicator(s) of domestic industry performance. The focus of antitrust, by contrast, is on the emergence (or restoration) of an environment in which firms have the ability to raise prices to anticompetitive levels. An examination of this issue considers much more than the issue of "injury," and looks for an industrial structure in which a dominant firm with monopoly power or an oligopoly exists or may emerge as a result of the pricing practices at issue.

Many other differences exist as well, such as differences in remedies (duties vs damages). But the key point is that antidumping law routinely addresses pricing behavior that bears no plausible relation to anything that raises bona fide competition policy concerns.

8.3 The Puzzling Persistence of Antidumping Law

Economic commentary is by-and-large critical of antidumping policy for the reasons suggested earlier. It is not a useful supplement to antitrust policy, and instead punishes

[www] Brooke Group Ltd. v. Brown & Williamson Tobacco Corp., 509 US 209 (1993).

discriminatory prices and prices below long-run average costs that represent perfectly normal business practices in response to differing demand elasticities across markets, business cycles, learning by doing economies, and so on. The question then arises as to why the WTO community does not eliminate antidumping measures. Indeed, during the Uruguay Round, Canadian negotiators proposed eliminating antidumping law and replacing it with a sensible competition policy agreement, but the proposal went nowhere.

To be sure, antidumping law has been eliminated in some smaller trading arrangements. It has never been possible to "dump" within the US Federal System. Antidumping measures are eliminated within the European Union. A few RTAs, such as the Canada-Chile Free Trade Agreement, also eliminate antidumping measures. What explains the disappearance of antidumping law in these contexts? And why does the same political dynamic not emerge within the WTO?

This issue has received rather little attention to my knowledge. One conjecture is that within the WTO, the political constituency for antidumping measures may overlap closely with the political constituency for safeguard measures. As the next section will suggest, legal obstacles to safeguard measures have become substantial. At the same time, antidumping actions have faced fewer obstacles before the Appellate Body and are subject to weaker legal prerequisites in certain respects (such as a "material injury" test rather than a "serious injury" test). The technique of "cumulation," whereby all imports from countries under investigation for dumping are "cumulated" for purposes of establishing injury, is another feature that allows the injury test to be satisfied more easily and encourages investigations of many countries simultaneously. See Antidumping Agreement, Art. 3.5. It is thus possible in principle to impose antidumping duties across a broad range of trading partners, much like a safeguard measure. And antidumping measures, although subject to periodic "sunset reviews," are not strictly time limited and phased out in the same manner as safeguard measures. Antidumping measures may thus afford a form of protection akin to safeguard measures that faces fewer legal obstacles and is more durable over time.

9. SAFEGUARD MEASURES

The safeguards provisions of WTO law authorize members to respond to increased import competition that causes serious problems for import-competing industries with temporary periods of import protection that would otherwise violated WTO commitments. The authority for safeguard measures is contained in GATT Article XIX, as elaborated by the WTO Agreement on Safeguards (SA).

9.1 Textual Prerequisites for Safeguard Measures

The basic prerequisites for the use of safeguard measures are contained GATT Art. XIX(1)(a):

If, as a result of unforeseen developments and of the effect of the obligations incurred by a contracting party under this Agreement, including tariff concessions, any product is being imported into the territory of that contracting party in such increased quantities and under such conditions as to cause or threaten serious injury to domestic producers in that territory of like or directly competitive products, the contracting party shall be free, in respect of such product, and to the extent and for such time as may be necessary to prevent or remedy such injury, to suspend the obligation in whole or in part or to withdraw or modify the concession.

These prerequisites are established during the course of an investigation conducted by national authorities under domestic law (in the United States, for example, the relevant statute is Section 201 et. seq. of the Trade Act of 1974).

Analytically, the domestic authorities must proceed through several steps:

  (i) demonstrate "increased quantities" of imports relative to some appropriate baseline period;
 (ii) determine that they result from "unforeseen developments" and GATT "obligations incurred";
(iii) define the domestic industry producing "like or directly competitive products";
 (iv) determine whether that industry is "seriously injured" or threatened with such injury; and
  (v) ascertain whether such injury or threat is "caused" by "increased quantities" of imports.

The SA elaborates these requirements to some degree. The basic prerequisites are set out in SA Art. 2, which tracks the language of GATT Art. XIX closely, except for the omission of any reference to "unforeseen developments" and the effects of GATT "obligations."

Additional provisions in the SA concern the definition of "serious injury," defined as "a significant overall impairment in the position of a domestic industry," and threat of serious injury, defined as "serious injury that is clearly imminent … based on facts and not merely on allegation, conjecture, or remote possibility." SA Art. 4.1(a) and (b). With regard to the causal connection between increased imports and serious injury, "the competent authorities shall evaluate all relevant factors of an objective and quantifiable nature having a bearing on the situation of that industry, in particular, the rate and amount of the increase in imports of the product concerned in absolute and relative terms, the share of the domestic market taken by increased imports, changes in the level of sales, production, productivity, capacity utilization, profits and losses, and employment." Art. 4.2(a). The investigation must demonstrate "on the basis of objective evidence, the existence of the causal link between increased imports of the product concerned and serious injury or threat thereof. When factors other than increased imports are causing injury to the domestic industry at the same time, such injury shall not be attributed to increased imports." Art. 4.2(b). The latter principle is known as the "nonattribution requirement."

9.2 Issues in Application and Developments in WTO Jurisprudence

The prerequisites for safeguard measures raise a number of interpretive issues and conceptual conundra. Many of these issues are unresolved or have been addressed in confusing and even incoherent fashion in WTO dispute resolution.

9.2.1 Increased Quantities

The test for increased quantities of imports requires that a baseline be selected against which to establish the increase. What is the proper baseline?

A natural baseline at the outset of GATT was the date of the initial tariff bindings. But this baseline became problematic over time. The initial concessions might have been decades earlier, and imports may have grown dramatically along with the economy generally. Likewise, a given product may have been the subject of a sequence of concessions over time.

Cases through the years under national law illustrate how the choice of baseline can readily be manipulated to satisfy or defeat the increased imports requirement.[xxx] The US authorities eventually converged on a 5-year rule of thumb to establish the baseline in preference to constant wrangling over the issue, and some other countries followed suit. In reviewing a challenge to an Argentinian measure based on an increase over a 5-year period, however, the Appellate Body concluded that the phrase "is being imported" in Article XIX requires "the competent authorities to examine recent imports, and not simply trends in imports during the past 5 years—or, for that matter, during any other period of several years.[yyy]" "[N]ot just *any* increased quantities of imports will suffice. There must be '*such* increased quantities' as to cause or threaten to cause serious injury to the domestic industry in order to fulfill this requirement for applying a safeguard measure … [T]he increase in imports must have been recent enough, sudden enough, sharp enough, and significant enough, both quantitatively and qualitatively, to cause or threaten to cause 'serious injury'.[zzz]"

Thus, the Appellate Body insists that imports must have increased "recently." But how recently, and in what amount? The phrase "recent enough, sudden enough, sharp enough, and significant enough" offers no useful guidance, nor does the insistence on "not just any increase" but "such increased quantities" as to cause injury.

9.2.2 Unforeseen Developments and Obligations Incurred

Article XIX was part of the original 1947 GATT, when members negotiated initial tariff bindings. The negotiators could surely anticipate that reduced tariffs would result in increased imports of various goods, and wished to foreclose the possibility that safeguard

---

[xxx] See the collection of cases on the issue under US law in Jackson et al. (2013).
[yyy] Argentina – Safeguard Measures on Imports of Footwear, WT/DS121/AB/R (1999).
[zzz] Id. ¶131.

measures might be used to retract these initial concessions because of their readily fore-seeable consequences. Accordingly, safeguard measures were limited to unforeseeable developments yielding unexpectedly high import surges.

Over time, however, the role of this provision became fuzzy. Ten or 20 or 50 years into GATT, were all developments unforeseeable vis-à-vis the drafters of Article XIX? If not, what differentiates the foreseeable from the unforeseeable? Unforeseeable by whom, at what point in time? The absence of any clear answers to these questions led GATT members to disregard this prerequisite for safeguard measures by the time that the SA was drafted. It is altogether omitted from modern US statutes concerning safeguards, for example. Its omission from Article 2 of the SA is arguably an acknowledgment of this evolution in GATT practice, and a recognition of the fact that the unforeseen develop-ments requirement became highly problematic with the passage of time.

In its first important ruling in a safeguards dispute, however, the Appellate Body held Article XIX and the Safeguards Agreement are to be read cumulatively, and that all of the original requirements of Article XIX remain binding, including the unforeseen develop-ments requirement.[aaaa] The Appellate Body went on to state: "'unforeseen develop-ments' should be interpreted to mean developments occurring after the negotiation of the relevant tariff concession which it would not be reasonable to expect that the nego-tiators of the country making the concession could and should have foreseen at the time when the concession was negotiated."

This ruling, confirmed in a number of later cases, leaves open many questions. What is the "relevant tariff concession" if there have been many over time? How does one dem-onstrate that recent developments were unforeseen at the relevant time? Once the unforeseen developments are identified, how does one demonstrate that "increased quantities" of imports result from them? Must the unforeseen developments concern events abroad, or can events in the importing country (such as a domestic supply shock) be considered? In a number of cases, safeguard measures have been ruled to violate Article XIX because of inadequate attention to these issues, but little guidance has been provided on how to proceed.

As for the linkage between increased quantities of imports and obligations incurred under GATT, it appears that the mere existence of a tariff binding suffices to meet this requirement. An importing nation can argue that, but for the binding, it would raise its tariffs to eliminate the import surge. And if the relevant tariff is unbound, safeguard mea-sures are obviously unnecessary.

9.2.3 Industry Definition

The industry in a safeguards investigation includes domestic producers of both "like" and "directly competitive" products. To a degree, these terms raise the same definitional issues discussed earlier in sections on the MFN and national treatment obligations.

[aaaa] Korea – Definitive Safeguard Measure on Imports of Certain Dairy Products, WT/DS98/AB/R (1999).

An issue of particular importance in injury investigations, however, concerns the effects of import competition on upstream firms. If inexpensive imports of processed fish lead to price reductions for domestically produced processed fish, for example, the economic impact may be felt as much or more by commercial fishermen as by fish processors. In one important case, however, the Appellate Body held that domestic producers of the raw product could not be included in the "industry" for purposes of injury analysis because the raw and processed products are not "like.[bbbb]" The question whether imports of processed products might be "directly competitive" with the domestic raw product has not been adjudicated.

9.2.4 Serious Injury

The SA defines serious injury as significant overall impairment and provides a list of factors that must be considered in the evaluation of the industry. It is clear that members must "consider" all of these factors to comply with the SA. Beyond this requirement, the Appellate Body characterizes the serious injury standard as "high" and "exacting.[cccc]" It is not necessary that every "relevant factor" reflect industrial decline, however, for serious injury to be present—"a certain factor may not be declining, but the overall picture may nevertheless demonstrate 'significant overall impairment.'" The reference to a high and exacting standard is of limited value in providing guidance, and simply indicates that national authorities cannot expect a deferential review of their findings at the WTO level.

9.2.5 Causation and Nonattribution

Difficult issues also arise in applying the causation and nonattribution requirements for safeguard measures. Recall that the text requires a causal connection between "increased quantities" of imports and serious injury. From an economic standpoint, of course, import quantities are an endogenous variable. In a competitive market, they are determined by the interaction among domestic supply, domestic demand and import supply (assuming no exports). Likewise, domestic price and output, and their implications for other indicators of domestic industrial health such as employment and profits, are endogenous. The causal requirement under GATT and the SA thus requires national authorities to assess the causal relationship between quanta that are in fact endogenously and simultaneously determined.

This problem has been recognized for some time, and three general approaches have been advanced to deal with it. The first may be described as "pretending the problem does not exist," substituting an analysis of correlation for an analysis of causation. National authorities look to see whether a time series of import quantities (or market

---

[bbbb] The United States – Safeguard Measures on Imports of Fresh, Chilled, or Frozen Lamb Meat from New Zealand and Australia, WT/DS178/AB/R (2001).
[cccc] Id. ¶124.

share) is correlated (perhaps with a lag) to various indicators of domestic industrial decline. If sufficient correlation is evident, causation will be found.

An alternative approach suggested by several economic commentators and briefly embraced by two Commissioners at the US International Trade Commission in the 1980s, is to redefine the causal inquiry to focus on the causal effects of shifts of the import supply curve (assuming competition). If such shifts yield "serious injury" causation may be found; if any "serious injury" is instead attributable to domestic supply or demand shocks, causation is not present.[dddd]

A third approach was suggested by respondents in a US proceeding involving imports of unwrought copper, but was not embraced by US adjudicators. The effect of increased imports on the domestic industry was assessed by positing a hypothetical quota, limiting imports to their baseline level. A counterfactual simulation then determined how much better off the domestic industry would have been if imports had not been permitted to increase, and next asked whether the detriment due to the absence of the quota amounted to "serious injury."

Comparable issues arise with respect to the nonattribution requirement. National authorities must first determine what causes of injury are distinct from imports. This task is reasonably straightforward in a framework that focuses on import supply, domestic demand, and domestic supply as the three relevant sources of variation over time in industrial condition,[eeee] but less straightforward under the other approaches to the analysis. Once the alternative causes are identified, it is necessary to determine what contribution they have made to injury, and to ensure that this contribution is not "attributed" to imports.

The Appellate Body has repeatedly stated that it will not specify how all of this analysis is to be done, and will leave it to national authorities to devise their own methods. The limited guidance provided by the Appellate Body on how to proceed, however, is open to serious criticism.

On the question of how to conceptualize increased import quantities as a causal variable, the Appellate Body has largely endorsed the "pretending the problem does not exist" approach. It endorsed a statement by a dispute panel to the effect that "if causation is present, an increase in imports normally should coincide with a decline in the relevant injury factors," going on to say that "in an analysis of causation, 'it is the *relationship* between the *movements* in imports (volume and market share) and the *movements* in injury factors that must be central to a causation analysis and determination.' Furthermore, with respect to a 'coincidence' between an increase in imports and a decline in the relevant

---

[dddd] This approach and the alternative discussed in the next paragraph are explored at greater length in Jackson et al. (2013), chapter 15.

[eeee] Even then ambiguities arise. If the domestic industry is harmed by an adverse shift in exchange rates, is that a cause "distinct" from imports?

injury factors, we note that the Panel simply said that this should 'normally' occur if causation is present.[ffff]"

Aside from the lack of intellectual rigor, such analysis creates a logical conundrum for "nonattribution" analysis. Consider a scenario raised in the United States—Lamb.[gggg] The United States ends certain subsidy payments to lamb growers. Their costs rise, domestic lamb prices rise, and imports of imported lamb increase. A "coincidence" exists between increased import quantities and a decline in the domestic industry, suggesting "causation." But if the cessation of subsidies is a distinct cause of injury, its effects must not be attributed to imports. How does one avoid "attributing" the cessation of subsidy payments to increased imports when they are the cause of the increased imports[hhhh]? Indeed, since increased quantities of imports are always the *result* of something else, how can they ever be a distinct cause of injury?

Perhaps these issues will be resolved over time through further developments in member government practice and WTO jurisprudence. At this point, however, the issues remain confused, and it is quite unclear what approaches can pass muster if challenged. Every complaint to date brought against a safeguard measure taken under GATT Article XIX has resulted in a ruling that the measure in question violated WTO law.[iiii]

9.3 Remedial Issues and the Balance of Concessions

Although most of the safeguard disputes in the WTO have been focused on the prerequisites for safeguard measures, Article XIX and the SA contain important provisions regarding the nature of the measures that may be employed once the prerequisites have been satisfied. They also address the extent to which WTO members must afford compensation for the effects of safeguards.

SA Art. 7 requires that measures be limited "to such period of time as may be necessary to prevent or remedy serious injury and to facilitate adjustment." This period is not to exceed 4 years, although it may be extended after an additional investigation for a total of no more than 8 years. Members are also obliged to liberalize their safeguard measures over time at "regular intervals." Once a safeguard measure has been terminated, it cannot be reapplied in the same industry for a period of time equal to its prior duration.

SA Art. 2.1 also provides that safeguard measures "shall be applied to a product being imported irrespective of its source." This variant of the MFN obligation was intended to

---

[ffff] Argentina – Safeguard Measures on Imports of Footwear, WT/DS121/AB/R (1999) ¶¶141,144. Support for an emphasis on "correlation" without regard to "causation" is also found in the United States – Measures Affecting Imports of Certain Passenger Vehicle and Light Truck Tyres from China, WT/DS399/AB/R, ¶¶238–241.

[gggg] Supra.

[hhhh] Precisely this issue arose in the United States – Lamb, supra, and the nonattribution analysis of the United States was deemed inadequate.

[iiii] Sykes (2006) contains a more extensive discussion of the problems with WTO jurisprudence.

put an end to so-called "selective" safeguard measures that discriminate against particular sources of imports. An exception exists under SA Art. 5(2)(b) for situations in which "imports from certain Members have increased in disproportionate percentage," subject to several additional qualifications.

An unsettled question is whether selective safeguards may be justified if they exempt imports from other members of a customs union or free trade area, an issue seemingly left open by a footnote to SA Art. 2. The Appellate Body has not ruled on the issue directly, but has determined that it is impermissible to include such imports in the "increased quantities" that satisfy the prerequisites for safeguards, and then to exempt them from the coverage of the resulting safeguard measures, a requirement known as "parallelism.[iiii]"

SA Art. 11 concerns the prohibition of "certain measures" colloquially known as "gray area measures," such as "voluntary export restraints, orderly marketing agreements or any other similar measures on the export or import side." These arrangements, often bilateral, proliferated in the waning years of GATT. They were typically negotiated outside the ambit of any formal reliance on GATT Article XIX, under circumstances that often did not meet the prerequisites for safeguard measures. For example, a US safeguard investigation during the 1970s involving the auto industry determined that the requirements for a safeguard measure had not been met, but President Carter proceeded to negotiate auto export restraints with Japan anyway. A political backlash against such arrangements offered much of the impetus for the Safeguards Agreement,[kkkk] and the prohibition of gray area measures in Article 11 was a central focus of the negotiators.

A related, final issue concerns the balance of concessions after a safeguard measure has been undertaken. Under GATT Article XIX, a member employing safeguards was obliged to afford compensation acceptable to adversely affected GATT members. Failing an agreement on compensation, those members were permitted to withdraw "substantially equivalent concessions." This "liability rule" structure was similar to the rules on tariff renegotiation under GATT Article XXVIII.

SA Art. 8 softened this requirement. It requires members employing safeguards to "endeavor to maintain a substantially equivalent level of concessions." Failing an agreement on trade compensation, however, other members are not permitted to withdraw their own concessions for the first 3 years of a safeguard measure, provided that it responds to an absolute increase in imports (not just a market share increase) and that it conforms to the other requirements of the SA. The logic of this change was to make safeguard measures more attractive relative to extra-legal gray area measures, and thereby

---

[iiii]   The United States – Definitive Safeguard Measures on Imports of Wheat Gluten from the European Communities, WT/DS166/AB/R, adopted January 19, 2001.

[kkkk] The reasons for this backlash are a bit murky. Measures such as voluntary export restraints regularly transferred quota rents to exporters, potentially compensating them for a loss of volume.

to reinforce the movement away from gray area measures toward measures in compliance with the SA. A potentially thorny issue lurks in this structure, however—suppose a member complains that some safeguard measure is not in response to an absolute import increase, or violates some other SA provision? May it unilaterally adjudicate such issues, or must it wait for a WTO dispute process to rule? Under the former approach, safeguard measures may beget an inappropriate retaliatory suspension of concessions. But under the latter approach, a member with a right to suspend concessions may be prevented from doing so for the period that it takes WTO adjudication to resolve the matter, which could easily exhaust the 3-year safe harbor for compliant safeguard measures under Article 8.

10. MISCELLANEOUS LEGAL ISSUES

This section considers a few additional legal issues of importance in the WTO that do not fit neatly under the prior headings. They include the effect of obligations on subsidiary governments, the process of accession and the legal significance of accession protocols, the possibility of waivers, and the relation among the various WTO treaty instruments.

10.1 Subsidiary Governments

Central governments accede to WTO membership. Their subsidiary governments (states, provinces, municipalities) are not "members" in a formal sense. Are WTO obligations nevertheless binding on subsidiary governments? What if the central government lacks the constitutional or other legal authority to force subsidiary governments to comply?

The original GATT was rather unclear. Article XXIV(12) required GATT members to take "such reasonable measures as may be available" to ensure compliance by regional and local governments. What does this mean—all "politically reasonable" measures? All legally feasible measures? Something else?

A subsequent WTO Understanding on Article XXIV clarifies to a great extent. It retains the "reasonable measures" language, but adds that the provisions of the DSU apply when subsidiary governments violate obligations. If the central government is unable to secure compliance by a subsidiary government, the requirement of compensation, or suspension of concessions applies. Thus, a central government that lacks the legal authority to secure compliance with GATT is not in violation of its obligations per se, but adversely affected trading partners are entitled to the full array of remedies for a violation that is not corrected within a reasonable time. Some of the more recent WTO treaties contain additional and broadly similar language. See, eg, TBT Agreement Article 3; SPS Agreement Article 13.

10.2 Accession and Accession Protocols

Most major trading nations are presently members of the WTO. Nonmembers include a number of smaller countries as well as many Middle Eastern nations, many of which are now "observers." Observers ordinarily begin negotiations to join the WTO within 5 years.[llll]

The process of joining the WTO is termed "accession." It involves a negotiation between the would-be member and other WTO members, which produces an "accession protocol" laying out the obligations of the new member. As with other decisions in the WTO, the organization strives for consensus on matters of accession. But if consensus is lacking, accession can be approved by two-thirds of the membership, although objectors may opt out of the relationship with the new member. See Agreement Establishing the WTO, Arts. XII–XIII.

Accession can be a complicated process, particularly for an important trading nation, because it has not participated in the many previous rounds of WTO/GATT tariff negotiations. An aspiring member will accordingly be asked to make rather dramatic trade concessions to "make up" for the absence of any concessions in the past. The negotiations may also seek commitments on matters other than tariffs that may go beyond the general commitments of the WTO/GATT system that all members assume. As an example, nothing in WTO law prohibits export taxes, although they may become subject to negotiated bindings much like import tariffs. As part of its accession process, however, China agreed not to employ export taxes on many products, a commitment embodied in the Chinese Accession Protocol. Its export taxes on various raw material products were then found to violate the terms of that protocol, even though they would not have violated ordinary GATT rules.[mmmm]

10.3 Waiver, Amendment, and Plurilaterals

The WTO was implemented as a "single undertaking." Formally, the members of GATT withdrew from the GATT and immediately entered into the WTO, incorporating the old GATT as GATT 1994. The additional treaties negotiated during the Uruguay Round along with GATT 1994 were then accepted by all WTO members (with the exception of four "plurilaterals" concerning civil aircraft, government procurement, dairy, and bovine meat: the latter two expired in 1997). This structure put an end to much of the patchwork that had emerged over the course of GATT, whereby many subsequent agreements (eg, the Tokyo Round Subsidies Code and Standards Code) were negotiated and accepted by only a subset of the GATT membership.

[llll]   See https://www.wto.org/english/thewto_e/whatis_e/tif_e/org6_e.htm#observer.
[mmmm]   China – Measures Relating to the Export of Various Raw Materials, WT/DS394,395&398/AB/R, adopted February 22, 2012.

That degree of unanimity in the acceptance of obligations has proven elusive since the end of the Uruguay Round, and this section briefly notes some of the options for modification of WTO obligations through actions that do not require unanimous consent.

One option is waiver, whereby (pursuant to Article IX of the Agreement Establishing the WTO) the membership may by a three-fourths vote agree to waive an obligation at the request of a member. Waivers are generally limited in time, applied only to "exceptional circumstances," and are to be narrowly construed. Waivers have been used with some regularity historically.[nnnn]

Another option is amendment (Article X). Amendments are adopted by consensus, although in the absence of consensus the membership may by two-thirds vote choose to submit the amendment to the members anyway. With a few exceptions requiring unanimous acceptance, amendments take effect after two-thirds approval, but only bind the members that accept them.

A further option is a return to greater use of plurilateral agreements, pursuant to which like-minded members reach agreement and other members opt out with an option to join later. The Information Technology Agreement, noted earlier, is an important example. Other ongoing plurilateral negotiations pertain to services trade, government procurement, and environmental goods.

10.4 The Relationship Among WTO Agreements

The WTO/GATT system now has many somewhat overlapping components. Regulatory measures, as seen earlier, are addressed by the original GATT as well as the technical barriers agreements. Export restrictions are addressed by the original GATT and certain accession protocols. Antidumping and subsidies are addressed by the original GATT and the freestanding Antidumping and SCMs Agreements, and so on. The general exceptions of GATT Article XX, and the national security exception of Article XXI, pertain to matters that might seem important with respect to obligations covered by other WTO agreements. What is the relationship among these various treaty components of the system? Suppose some part of the original GATT seems in tension with a newer WTO agreement? Does GATT Article XX afford an exception to the SCMs Agreement, for example, or only to the original GATT?

On the possibility of a conflict between GATT and another of the WTO Agreements that are part of the single undertaking, an Interpretative Note to the Agreement Establishing the WTO provides that the newer agreement shall prevail over conflicting GATT language. Generally speaking, however, adjudicators have preferred to avoid findings of conflict, and tend to find that GATT obligations and obligations under other agreements are cumulative (recall the treatment of the "unforeseen developments" issue in the safeguards context).

[nnnn] See Feichtner (2014).

Regarding the defenses of GATT Article XX, a few developments warrant mention. The limited jurisprudence on the applicability of GATT Article XX to other agreements suggests that the Article XX defenses do not in general apply to agreements other than GATT. Those agreements often have their own exceptions, and the text of Article XX, with its reference to "this Agreement" (GATT) does not support broader application.[oooo]

Similarly, Article XX defenses are not in general available to justify deviations from commitments in an accession protocol. If the protocol contains language suggesting that it is to be applied consistently with WTO law as a whole, however, that language may support the availability of an Article XX defense.[pppp]

11. TRADE IN SERVICES (GATS)

GATT has nothing to say about trade in services, and with the rapid growth of services trade in the last decades the absence of international legal discipline became more and more significant. An initial and important foray into services trade liberalization was undertaken in chapter 12 of NAFTA, which in some ways served as a template for the WTO General Agreement on Trade in Services (GATS). The legal obligations in GATS are extensive and broadly comparable in scope to those of GATT. This section provides only a brief introduction, with a focus on the features of GATS that are distinctive.

Unlike goods, which can be taxed as they physically cross the border, services trade rarely presents a taxable event at the border. Accordingly, tariffs play little role in services trade, and tariff liberalization does not lie at the heart of services trade liberalization. The absence of tariffs, and the fact that services trade protectionism takes a variety of other forms, is the key to understanding many of the differences between GATT and GATS.

GATS begins by classifying services trade into four "modes." Mode 1 involves the supply of a service from the territory of an exporting member into the territory of an importing member. An American company might hire a Japanese law firm to provide it with an opinion on Japanese law over the internet, for example, or a Canadian company might purchase casualty insurance by mail from Lloyd's of London. Such transactions are difficult for importing nations to observe in most instances, and interference with them for protectionist purposes is fairly rare even if domestic interest groups might want protection from the foreign competition.

[oooo] See China – Measures Related to the Exportation of Various Raw Materials, WT/DS394/R, adopted February 22, 2012.
[pppp] China – Measures Affecting Trading Rights and Distribution Services for Certain Publications and Audiovisual Entertainment Products, WT/DS363/AB/R, adopted January 19, 2010.

Mode 2 trade involves the supply of a service in the territory of a member to a consumer of another member. An American tourist stays at a hotel in Paris, for example, or a Mexican national traveling in the United States consults a US stockbroker. These transactions too are difficult for governments to observe, and there is no political impetus to interfere with them in any event. Mode 2 trade thus involves no protectionism to speak of, and requires little by way of liberalization.

Mode 3 trade entails the supply of a service by a supplier of one member via a commercial presence in the territory of the services purchaser. An American consumer establishes a bank account at a branch of the Royal Bank of Scotland in New York, for example, or a European company purchases auditing services from Price Waterhouse in Brussels. Here, the opportunities for government interference with the transaction are much greater, as the importing nation may employ its branch banking laws or its licensing rules concerning the supply of accounting services to exclude foreign competitors. Likewise, regulatory policies that ostensibly have nothing to do with protection but instead address prudential concerns, consumer protection issues, and the like may be designed or implemented in ways that deliberately or unnecessarily burden foreign suppliers. The role for negotiated liberalization is thus much greater than in the case of Modes 1 and 2.

Mode 4 trade is similar to mode 3, except that it also involves the presence of natural persons (as opposed to firms) from the exporting member in the territory of the importing member. In the prior examples, perhaps the New York branch of the Royal Bank of Scotland has a Scottish management team, or Price Waterhouse in Brussels is staffed by US nationals. Mode 4 thus adds another layer of government regulation to the mix—immigration and visa policies—all of which may be used deliberately or inadvertently to protect domestic competitors.

Accordingly, most (though not all) of the action in services trade liberalization involves modes 3 and 4, and virtually none of it involves anything resembling tariffs. Instead, trade barriers take the form of quantitative constraints and more often a wide variety of regulatory measures that impede the supply of services by foreign suppliers. And while GATT pursues a policy of "tariffication" as noted earlier, channeling protection into the relatively transparent (and efficient) instrument of a nondiscriminatory tariff, there is no comparable instrument that serves as the obvious candidate for protection in services sectors. As a corollary, it is not obvious that domestic tax or regulatory discrimination against foreign service suppliers is an inefficient form of protection in some services sectors. Assuming that trading nations do not wish to proceed immediately to "free trade," therefore, a general national treatment obligation such as that of GATT Article III may not be desirable.

The basic structure of GATS has two pillars. First, GATS Article II imposes (after a transition period that has largely passed, see the Annex on Article II exceptions) a general most-favored nation obligation, prohibiting discrimination among foreign service suppliers. Second, GATS requires members to determine whether or not to make additional "commitments" (beyond MFN) in specific service sectors. The analogy is to the bound and unbound tariffs of GATT. In the sectors in which members make additional commitments, members must schedule the impediments to trade that they wish to retain. These schedules are divided by mode of trade for each sector covered by a commitment. GATS Article XVI requires members to schedule, by mode, the "market access" limitations that they wish to retain. These limitations are:

(a) limitations on the number of service suppliers whether in the form of numerical quotas, monopolies, exclusive service suppliers, or the requirements of an economic needs test;

(b) limitations on the total value of service transactions or assets in the form of numerical quotas or the requirement of an economic needs test;

(c) limitations on the total number of service operations or on the total quantity of service output expressed in terms of designated numerical units in the form of quotas or the requirement of an economic needs test;

(d) limitations on the total number of natural persons that may be employed in a particular service sector or that a service supplier may employ and who are necessary for, and directly related to, the supply of a specific service in the form of numerical quotas or the requirement of an economic needs test;

(e) measures which restrict or require specific types of legal entity or joint venture through which a service supplier may supply a service; and

(f) limitations on the participation of foreign capital in terms of maximum percentage limit on foreign shareholding or the total value of individual or aggregate foreign investment.

GATS Article XVII imposes an additional scheduling requirement:

> In the sectors inscribed in its Schedule, and subject to any conditions and qualifications set out therein, each Member shall accord to services and service suppliers of any other Member, in respect of all measures affecting the supply of services, treatment no less favorable than that it accords to its own like services and service suppliers.

Thus, in sectors where commitments are made, national treatment is the default rule, and any deviations from national treatment beyond those already scheduled under Article XVI must be set forth in each member's schedule.

This structure gives GATS members a great deal of flexibility. They may choose to make no commitments in particular sectors, in which case they need only obey the MFN principle. Where they are willing to make commitments, they are still able to retain a variety of market access limitations and deviations from national treatment, as long as they are scheduled. The approach of GATS thus enhances transparency in scheduled sectors, but does not force liberalization. Members are free, of course, to negotiate greater commitments over time. They may also negotiate commitments on matters that do not fit the definition of market access restrictions and national treatment exceptions, such as commitments on across-the-board licensing practices, and embody these further commitments in their schedules (see Article XVIII).

One other aspect of GATS differs importantly from the general approach of GATT and other agreements pertaining to trade in goods. Most of the treaty commitments regarding trade in goods apply across the board to all goods sectors. GATS members recognize, however, that different service sectors have regulatory issues that are unique. Accordingly, some of the GATS framework, and many of the further negotiations since its formation, involve sector-specific disciplines. GATS includes annexes pertaining to air transport services, financial services, maritime transport services, and telecommunications. Later negotiations produced an important agreement on Disciplines on Domestic Regulation in the Accountancy Sector.[qqqq]

Other features of GATS are more analogous to GATT obligations. Rounds of liberalization in the future are envisioned (Article XIX), and commitments may be renegotiated or withdrawn subject to a compensation requirement (Article XXI). Obligations are subject to general exceptions and a national security exception (Articles XIV and XIV bis). RTAs may be negotiated in service sectors pursuant to Article V, subject to requirements loosely analogous to those of GATT Article XXIV. Nascent obligations akin to those of the technical barriers agreements may be found in Articles VI and VII. The creation of rules respecting subsidies and safeguards are deferred to the future (Articles X and XV).

Litigation under GATS has been limited thus far, but some important issues have arisen. A common thread in several cases is that measures restricting trade in goods may also burden service suppliers. Restrictions on goods imports may burden foreign-owned companies engaged in wholesaling or retailing, and trigger GATS violations if commitments have been made in those sectors.[rrrr] Similarly, restrictions on advertising services may affect trade in the physical medium containing the advertising (imported periodicals).[ssss]

Perhaps the most notable services case to date is the United States—Gambling,[tttt] a case brought by Antigua. The United States made commitments on "recreational, cultural and sporting services," and did not schedule any market access restrictions or national treatment exceptions. These commitments were deemed to cover internet gambling, which was largely prohibited in the United States except for off-track betting on horse races, and the US policies were found to be "market access restrictions" that should

---

[qqqq] S/WPPS/W/21, adopted December 14, 2000.

[rrrr] See European Communities – Regime for the Importation, Sale, and Distribution of Bananas, WT/DS27/AB/R, adopted September 25, 1997.

[ssss] Canada – Certain Measures Concerning Periodicals, WT/DS31/AB/R, adopted July 30, 1997.

[tttt] The United States – Measures Affecting the Cross-Border Supply of Gambling and Betting Services, WT/DS285/AB/R, adopted April 20, 2005.

have been scheduled under GATS Article XVI. The United States then invoked the "public morals" exception of GATS Article XIV(a). The defense was successful save for the fact that the United States permitted domestic entities to supply internet betting on horse races, which led to a finding that the Article XVI chapeau was not satisfied.

Economic analysis of GATS is much more embryonic than the study of trade in goods. GATS is similar to GATT in that it needs to preserve policy space for sensible domestic regulatory measures, but the "tariffication" approach of GATT, whereby protection is channeled into tariffs and other instruments are to apply uniformly to domestic and imported sellers for the most part, will not work for GATS. Moreover, many of the issues that arise under GATS appear on the surface to be sector specific—the optimal instruments for regulating foreign entry into the legal profession, for example, are surely different from the optimal instruments for regulating foreign entry into banking or insurance. Careful analysis of these issues is certainly among the frontiers for further research.

12. TRIPs

Prior to the creation of the WTO, the United States pursued a policy of imposing unilateral trade sanctions on countries that, in the judgment of the United States, failed to afford adequate protection to US intellectual property rights, usually developing countries. This "issue linkage" between IP rights and trade policy carried over into the Uruguay Round negotiations. Politically influential US industries, especially sound recording, film, and pharmaceuticals, were reluctant to give up the ability to use trade sanctions to coerce changes in foreign intellectual property laws. The US trading partners, at the same time, wanted to rein in US unilateralism. The eventual bargain included the Agreement on Trade-Related Aspects of Intellectual Property Rights (TRIPs). In exchange for a greatly diminished threat of unilateralism, the WTO membership agreed to minimal standards for intellectual property protection, enforceable under the WTO DSU. From the developing country perspective, the deal was sweetened somewhat by concessions on other trade issues (such as textiles).

TRIPs is a complex agreement touching on a wide range of issues that go beyond traditional trade policy. It prescribes minimum standards of protection for patents, copyrights, trademarks, geographical indications, industrial designs, integrated circuits, and trade secrets. It also addresses the enforcement obligations of WTO members under domestic law, and their rights to engage in compulsory licensing and control of anticompetitive licensing practices. A brief summary of its basic structure and core obligations may be found in chapter "Trade, Intellectual Property Rights, and the WTO" by Saggi in this volume. A more detailed treatment can be found in Jackson et al. (2013, chapter 20). Correa (2007, 2010) provides comprehensive analyses.

13. CONCLUSION

This chapter provided an overview of the legal obligations of the WTO system and certain related national, bilateral, and plurilateral arrangements. Each of the topics considered earlier has been the subject of book-length treatments elsewhere, and of necessity many details of the legal system have been omitted. The chapter nevertheless highlights most of the important areas of interest to economists, and along the way offers some thoughts about issues for further research. As the other chapters in this Handbook make clear, the application of economic analysis to these issue areas is enormously fruitful and contributes greatly to our understanding of the legal system.

ACKNOWLEDGMENTS

I have received thoughtful comments from Petros Mavroidis, Joel Watson, the editors, and the participants in the June 2015 Dartmouth conference on the Handbook of Commercial Policy.

REFERENCES

Barcelo, J.J., 1979. The antidumping law: repeal it or revise it. In: Jackson, J.H. (Ed.), Antidumping Law: Policy and Implementation. University of Michigan, Ann Arbor, pp. 41–97.

Boltuck, R., Litan, R.E. (Eds.), 1991. Down in the Dumps. Brookings Institution, Washington.

Correa, C.M., 2007. Trade Related Aspects of Intellectual Property Rights: A Commentary on the TRIPS Agreement. Oxford University Press, Oxford, UK.

Correa, C.M. (Ed.), 2010. Research Handbook on the Interpretation and Enforcement of Intellectual Property Under WTO Rules: Intellectual Property in the WTO. Edward Elgar, Cheltenham, UK.

Feichtner, I., 2014. The Law and Politics of WTO Waivers. Cambridge University Press, Cambridge, UK.

Goetz, C., Granet, L., Schwartz, W.F., 1986. A search for economic and financial principles in the administration of U.S. countervailing duty law. Int. Rev. Law Econ. 6, 17–32.

Horn, H., Mavroidis, P., Sapir, A., 2010. Beyond the WTO? An anatomy of EU and US preferential trade agreements. World Econ. 33, 1565–1588.

Irwin, D.A., Mavroidis, P.C., Sykes, A.O., 2008. The Genesis of the GATT. Cambridge Press, Cambridge, UK.

Jackson, J.H., 1969. World Trade and the Law of GATT. Bobbs Merrill, Indianapolis.

Jackson, J.H., Davey, W.J., Sykes, A.O., 2013. Legal Problems of International Economic Relations, sixth ed. West Academic Publishing, St. Paul, MN.

Jackson, J.H., Sykes, A.O. (Eds.), 1997. Implementing the Uruguay Round. Clarendon Press, Oxford.

Mavroidis, P.C., 2011. Always look at the bright side of non-delivery: WTO and preferential trade agreements, yesterday and today. World Trade Rev. 10, 375–387.

Mavroidis, P.C., 2012. Trade in Goods, second ed. Oxford University Press, Oxford, UK.

Mavroidis, P.C., 2016. The Regulation of International Trade, vol. 1. MIT Press, Cambridge, MA.

Pauwelyn, J., 2013. Carbon leakage measures and border tax adjustments under WTO law. In: van Calster, G., Prevost, D. (Eds.), Research Handbook in Environment, Health and the WTO. Edward Elgar, Cheltenham, UK, pp. 448–506.

Qin, J.Y., 2005. Defining nondiscrimination under the law of the World Trade Organization. Boston Univ. Int. Law J. 23, 215–297.

Schwartz, W.F., Sykes, A.O., 2002. The economic structure of renegotiation and dispute settlement in the World Trade Organization. J. Legal Stud. 31, S179–S204.

Sykes, A.O., 1995. Product Standards for Internationally Integrated Goods Markets. Brookings, Washington, DC.

Sykes, A.O., 1998. Antidumping and antitrust: what problems does each address? In: Lawrence, R.Z. (Ed.), Brookings Trade Forum 1998. Brookings Institution, Washington, pp. 1–43.

Sykes, A.O., 1999. Regulatory protectionism and the law of international trade. Univ. Chic. Law Rev. 66, 1–46.

Sykes, A.O., 2003. The least restrictive means. Univ. Chic. Law Rev. 70, 403–419.

Sykes, A.O., 2005. Public versus private enforcement of international economic law: standing and remedy. J. Legal Stud. 34, 631–666.

Sykes, A.O., 2006. The WTO Agreement on Safeguards: A Commentary. Oxford University Press, Cambridge.

Sykes, A.O., 2010. The questionable case for subsidies regulation: a comparative perspective. J. Legal Anal. 2, 473–523.

Trebilcock, M., Howse, R., Eliason, A., 2013. The Regulation of International Trade, fourth ed. Routledge, New York.

CHAPTER 6

Dispute Settlement in the WTO: Mind Over Matter

P.C. Mavroidis

Edwin B. Parker Professor of Law at Columbia Law School, New York City, NY, United States

Contents

Handbook of Commercial Policy, Volume 1A
ISSN 2214-3122, http://dx.doi.org/10.1016/bs.hescop.2016.04.004

Abstract

The basic point I advocate in this chapter is that the WTO dispute settlement system aims to curb unilateral punishment. Sanctions can be imposed only in accordance with the outcome of a multilateral process that has been established in order to decide on the (il)legality of actions by WTO members, and the legal consequences thereof. The purpose of this process is to ensure that reciprocal commitments entered should not be unilaterally undone through the commission of illegal acts. There are good reasons though, to doubt whether reciprocity, its statutory underpinnings notwithstanding has also been observed in practice. The insistence on calculating remedies prospectively, and not as of the date when an illegality has been committed, and the ensuing losses for everybody that could or could not be symmetric lend support to the claim that the WTO regime serves "diffuse" as opposed to "specific" reciprocity. Still, WTO members continue to routinely submit their disputes to the WTO adjudicating fora, showing through their behavior that, if necessary, they would rather live in a world where punishment is curbed, than in a world where punishment acts as deterrent.

Keywords

WTO, Dispute settlement, Diffuse reciprocity, Specific reciprocity, Section 301

JEL Classification Code

K40

1. THE ARGUMENT

The question that this paper asks is how does the WTO dispute settlement system, the DSU,[a] preserve the balance of rights and obligations assumed by the trading partners,

---

[a] DSU stands for "Dispute Settlement Understanding," the WTO Agreement administering the dispute settlement system (DSS) of the WTO. In this paper, I look into the WTO in "self-contained" manner. WTO Members might use "sticks" and "carrots" from other areas of international relations in order to enforcement of WTO obligations. They have little (if any) incentive to publicly reveal similar information, and, as a result, it is impossible to (dis)prove similar claims. Analytically, everything becomes very complicated (if not quixotic) if we were to view trade disputes within the (highly realistic) wider realm of interstate relations.

members of the WTO? The WTO, the successor to the GATT, administers liberaliza-tion of international trade.[b] The agreed rights and obligations represent the outcome of reciprocal commitments entered by the trading nations during trade rounds. Reciprocity does not mean mathematical equivalence across commitments. The Director General of the GATT put it very eloquently, when stating:

> *reciprocity cannot be determined exactly, it can only be agreed upon.[c]*

The final product of negotiations will be included in the final package of each negotiating round and will represent the balance of rights and obligations of WTO members. Article 3.2 of the DSU understands the role of the DSU in the following manner:

> *the Members recognize that it serves to preserve the rights and obligations of Members under the covered agreements.*

This provision implicitly accepts that no WTO member should be better off through violation of the WTO. The role of the dispute settlement system is to restore the balance, the intuition being that WTO members might (will) be disincentivized to breach the agreement if they have nothing to gain from it.

To this effect, two features of the WTO dispute settlement system matter: first, disputes will always be resolved through adjudication, and it suffices that a complainant submits a complaint to this effect; second, the breaching WTO member will face retaliation equivalent to the damage done. This is the "DSU-think" so to speak, the quintessential feature of WTO adjudication.[d]

---

[b] WTO stands for the World Trade Organization, and GATT for the General Agreement on Tariffs and Trade. The WTO is an international organization and counts 162 members. The GATT was an agreement that would come under the ITO (International Trade Organization), the institution that would liberalize trade in goods. The ITO never saw the light of day, but the GATT, that had a narrower focus than the ITO since it only dealt with state practices inhibiting the freedom to trade, entered into force on Jan. 1, 1948, and gradually developed into an international institution. Because it was conceived originally as an agree-ment, it did not count "members," but "contracting parties." The GATT CONTRACTING PARTIES (in bloc letters) were the highest organ and would decide on consensus (see Jackson, 1969; Irwin et al., 2008).

[c] GATT Press Release 1312, Mar. 5, 1982.

[d] The DSU aims at removing disputes from the docket, if possible. If bilateral resolution fails, then the only way to resolve disputes would be through submission to an independent adjudicator. Losing parties will be called to comply with adverse rulings, or face retaliation equaling the damage inflicted through the illegal act. The framers nonetheless did not manage to agree on a clear method to calculate the amount of retal-iation. They used the term "substantially equivalent concessions" that would serve as the legal benchmark for calculating retaliation. Enforcement depends on various other factors, of course. The ability to detect illegal trade barriers matters, as does the ability to process information and decide on their (in)consistency. Private enforcement as well affects the amount of litigation, since governments might be willing to avoid litigation if this serves their overall interests, when private agents would opt for the opposite course of action.

There is no need for a trade-off between the two features mentioned earlier. "A" DSU could include both compulsory third-party adjudication, as well as a remedy that would disincentivize potential violators from committing illegalities. "The" DSU, as it emerges following 20 years of practice, comports a trade-off. Under the circumstances, we can distinguish between "specific-" and "diffuse reciprocity," two notions on which I will base the main conclusion of this paper. "Specific reciprocity" would correspond to a situation where deviations from obligations assumed would be punished so as to ensure that the violating party would pay the damage that bridges the gap between the current situation (where violation has occurred) and a counterfactual where no violation at all had occurred. Specific reciprocity would call for implementation of retroactive remedies. "Diffuse reciprocity" is a reduction from this benchmark. The amount of reduction is not specified. Reduction is warranted since there is "trust" between players that deviation will be addressed anyway, and today's culprit will be tomorrow's generous player who will accept similar deviation from other players, safe in the knowledge that they will be addressed in time as well. Diffuse reciprocity would call for implementation of prospective remedies, some sort of "reciprocal balance going forward."[e] The DSU as it now stands, promotes diffuse-, as opposed to specific reciprocity.

How did we end up here? Whereas negotiators left the issue open, practice has sided with the more "conservative" approach, that is, WTO judges have consistently recommended prospective remedies. The DSU negotiators aimed at constraining punishment and, in the altar of this objective, they were prepared to forego the negotiating cost of an additional agreement that would include precise calculations of damages. They included language, that is, akin to "specific reciprocity." Indeed, the term "substantially equivalent concessions" comes close to this term, although the adjective "substantially" leaves some room for manoeuver. This is a remedy of last resort though, eg, a remedy that comes into play against recalcitrant WTO members only. The DSU does not specify what exactly WTO judges should recommend in the first place. On the other hand, negotiators attached high value to evaluations of damages by impartial judges, even if they comported the risk of under-evaluation, an outcome that could not be discarded in the absence of statutory language preempting it.[f] Article 23.2 of DSU makes it plain that any dispute arising from the operation of the WTO contract can be resolved exclusively through recourse to the WTO dispute settlement system. It is not, in other words, for WTO members to decide on whether a certain measure is or is not WTO-consistent. Both, authors of the measure, as well as affected WTO members might have the wrong

---

[e] I borrow this term from private conversations with Robert W. Staiger.

[f] Legally, the risk of overevaluation is less of an issue for various reasons. First, the judge cannot accord the complainant more than what it has requested by virtue of the maxim *nonultra petita* (loosely translated as "the judge cannot go beyond what has been requested to adjudicate"). Second, when facing overevaluation of damages by the complainant, the defendant will most likely propose another, lower estimation of damage. In practice, WTO adjudicators have tried to come up with a number between the two evaluations.

incentives, and their judgment to this effect could be biased. It is the exclusive privilege of WTO judges to decide on the legal consistency of measures that have been challenged for being WTO-inconsistent. All WTO members can do is submit a dispute to this effect. To understand the negotiators' urge to shut the door to any other form of enforcement (unilateral or multilateral), we will delve into the historical context of the negotiation and the influence the US Section 301 exerted on the process.[g]

WTO courts, 20 years following their advent, continue to be the busiest courts litigating state-to-state disputes. This leads me to conclude that what seems to have mattered, and still matters, most to WTO members was the spirit of cooperation in adjudication, the establishment of a multilateral process to curb unilateralism. WTO members were thus prepared to sacrifice some of their belongings in order to keep the system in place as is.

The rest of the paper is organized as follows. In Section 2, I discuss the negotiating record, not the full record of course, but the parts relating to the quintessential elements of the process established, as well as the discussion on remedies in case of breach of obligations. It is here that I aim to establish that the DSU framers were unanimous in their quest to curb unilateralism, but not so unanimous when it came to providing a methodology for quantification of damages in case of contractual breach. The main point here is that, in name at least, the agreement calls for respect of reciprocity, without however, providing for a mechanism to ensure that this will always be the case. Section 3 describes in a matter of factual manner the outcome of the negotiation, the DSU. It is in this section that I will provide the procedural framework that will entertain requests for dispute adjudication. Section 4 is where I discuss case law to make the point that panels, in light of the divergence of views between various WTO Members regarding the quantification of damages, opted for a very "conservative" approach that, de facto, sides with the views of those opposed to full compensation of damages. Section 5 is the "plat de resistance" where I explain why, in my view, the current regime for remedies as practiced in WTO does not guarantee respect of specific reciprocity, and why it comes closer to what political scientists call "diffuse reciprocity." The idea here is that, while the balance of commitments is not fully redressed, WTO members expect that deviations will be addressed through the same process in comparable terms. It is more of a process obligation aiming to curb unilateral responses to (perceived) illegalities, rather than a means for removing the incentive to commit illegalities because of the ensuing competence to pay back all proceeds of the illegal act. Section 6 contains the main conclusions of this paper.

---

[g] The US Section 301 is a legal instrument allowing the US government to represent private claims before the GATT/WTO. In that, it is necessary, since private parties have no standing before the GATT/WTO. The United States nevertheless used it in order to decide itself on the illegality of foreign practices, that is, bypassing the GATT adjudication process. This is what provoked not only the wrath of their trading partners but also their resolve to curtail unilateralism, as we explain in more detail in what follows.

2. THE URUGUAY ROUND AND THE BIRTH OF THE DSU

Articles 1, 22.4, and 23.2 DSU capture the essence of the WTO dispute settlement, the quintessential elements of which have been described earlier. These provisions reflect the extent of agreement, but not how we ended up with it. To do this, we have to delve into the negotiating record.

2.1 Uruguay to Geneva: The Makings of the DSU

Three basic conclusions emerge from the study of the negotiating record. First, there was widespread agreement to design a system that would eliminate the threat of unilateral action à la "Section 301," the legal instrument through which United States would unilaterally prosecute illegal (in its view) behavior by its trading partners. Second, to address legitimate US concerns, negotiators managed to design a system of compulsory third-party adjudication, and thus, avoid "system failure" if defendant refused to consent to establishment of a panel, the GATT/WTO "court." In this vein, they agreed that WTO judges would be exclusively competent to decide on whether an illegality had been committed. This was the price to pay for obliging the United States to accept that it would use Section 301 not as instrument for self-help, but as instrument for representing "private" complaints before WTO where private parties have no standing. Third, negotiators could not bridge their differences regarding the remedies that would be appropriate to address illegalities. While they stated clearly that, if need be, countermeasures could not supersede the damage inflicted, they did not provide for a specific mechanism that would "quantify" damage. This issue as well was left to WTO judges.

2.1.1 Background of the Negotiation

The negotiation of the DSU did not take place on a vacuum, but against a background of 40 years of GATT litigation. Hudec (1993) provides a comprehensive account of dispute settlement during the GATT years. The main conclusions of his study could be described as follows. The GATT became de facto compulsory third-party adjudication, since with one exception all requests for establishment of a panel were met affirmatively, and over 80% of all reports issued were adopted. Hudec has made a very persuasive case of how it is GATT "pragmatism," in the sense of consensus-based decisions to adopt (and thus provide them with legal value) reports by experts on legal challenges raised, that helped evolve the system to de facto compulsory third-party adjudication.[h]

The one request for establishment of a panel that was rejected, involved the United States, the instigator of "Section 301." It had requested from the EU to submit their 1980s dispute regarding trade in hormone-treated beef to a panel. The EU and the

---

[h] In Hudec (1972), he discusses in most succinct terms the intellectual debate between "legalists" and "pragmatists," represented by Jackson (1969) and Dam (1970).

United States had disagreed about the composition of the panel (that is, the identity of panelists) and, as a result, the EU refused to accept the US request.[i]

Is one case one case too many? Not so, one is tempted to say, by any reasonable benchmark. Even more so when compared with other international fora: the paradigmatic adjudication in international relations involved the acceptance of a request by the defendant. Defendants routinely rejected similar requests.

We do not know of course, how many times potential complainants, for fear of seeing their request rejected, shirked requests for establishment.[j] There is no reliable record of compliance with adverse rulings but, with few exceptions (like the notorious "Chicken War" in the 1960s), spiraling of countermeasures was constrained for the best part of the GATT-era. The same people, who were adjudicating disputes, were the people deciding how to confront persistent illegalities. They all belonged to the same "club," since the GATT had been negotiated by a nucleus of 23 like-minded countries,[k] and membership did not increase in numbers dramatically until the Tokyo round, that is, over 30 years after its advent. It is easier of course to set aside trigger-happy attitude among repeat like-minded players, of course.

The custom developed to view GATT dispute adjudication as a mechanism aimed to help implicated parties to reach amicable solutions. It was thought more as input to final resolution, rather than the final resolution itself. In this view, the dispute process:

> did not provide for judicial settlement of international trade disputes, … was primarily of concil-
> iatory nature … a rule-oriented approach enabling legally binding interpretations should not be
> viewed as a hindrance to conciliatory settlement … main objective … the avoidance or speedy
> resolution of disputes.[l]

A GATT Secretariat document issued early on during the Uruguay round confirms that this was the "acceptable" view, to which all GATT members more or less could subscribe.[m]

The GATT dispute settlement system functioned surprisingly well, especially if we were to take into account its highly imperfect institutional infrastructure. In fact, only two provisions in GATT dealt with dispute settlement, and none of them discussed the institutional design of dispute adjudication. After all, it was the ITO that was supposed to include elaborate provisions on this score.[n]

---

[i] Meng (1990) discusses this dispute in considerable detail.
[j] Point picked up by negotiators MTN.GNG/NG13/16 of Nov. 13, 1989.
[k] Irwin et al. (2008).
[l] GATT Doc. MTN.GNG/NG13/1 of Apr. 10, 1987. Hudec's (1993) study provides further support to this view.
[m] GATT Doc. MTN.GNG/NG13/W/14 of Nov. 3, 1987.
[n] See the relevant discussion in Hudec (1993), Irwin et al. (2008), and Jackson (1969).

This "idyllic" view of GATT dispute adjudication was disturbed in GATT's last years by the emergence and reinvigoration through successive statutes of Section 301. Following the end of the Tokyo round (1979) the picture changed. A number of panel reports remained unadopted, and a few times recourse to unauthorized countermeasures took place as well. The change is due to many factors.

Around that time, the United States had decided that it was high time it challenged the consistency of the EU CAP (common agricultural policy) with the GATT rules. For fear that it might be questioning the quintessence of the EU integration process, the United States had refrained from attacking the CAP, privileging a negotiating solution. When this did not happen during the Tokyo round, and/or in order to force similar solution during the Uruguay round, the United States initiated a number of challenges against the CAP, and the EU refused to "legitimize" the Panel reports (and thus, weaken its negotiating position during the round) by adopting them.

The United States also initiated a number of "Section 301" actions against a host of GATT members. Some of them in an effort to affect the negotiating agenda of the Uruguay round (the so-called Super 301 in the area of intellectual property), and some in order to show its displeasure with the long delays in attributing justice in the GATT, and the possibility to block hostile reports.[o]

Finally, a series of panels in the 1980s dealt specifically with the remedies issue in the context of contingent protection. They all faced claims to the effect that antidumping (countervailing) duties had been illegally imposed. Echoing the standard in customary international law, panels recommended that orders imposing duties be revoked and all illegally perceived duties be reimbursed.[p] The defendant was either the EU or the United States, and all but one report remain unadopted. The EU and the United States expressed their disagreement with panels' findings to the effect that retroactive remedies were appropriate, an issue that was very much under discussion during the Uruguay round, which had already been initiated by that time (1986).

2.1.2 Section 301, and the Turn to Unilateralism

It is largely because the United States felt frustrated with its inability to reform through negotiations the EU CAP, and to enlarge the coverage of the GATT, that it turned toward unilateral enforcement using Section 301 to this effect. It felt that it had been quite generous trying to accommodate the EU integration process within the GATT. The US farm lobby was knocking with increasing intensity and frequency on the door of the US administration. It was not alone. US administration was also under pressure by

---

[o] Various contributions in Bhagwati and Patrick (1990) as well, underscore this point.

[p] A Secretariat document, GATT Doc. MTN.GNG/NG13/W/32 of Jul. 14, 1989, discusses all reports. See also, Mavroidis (1993) and Petersmann (1993).

its domestic lobbies to add trade in services and protection of intellectual property rights to the GATT-mandate. Expansion of disciplines to "new" areas was politically the holy grail for the US government that saw there the potential to balance the high trade deficits that the United States was experiencing in the 1980s. What it could not obtain at the negotiating table, the United States tried to obtain through adjudication under the threat of retaliation. This is the story of "Section 301" and its many variances,[q] that occupied centre stage in the international trade discourse in the period between the end of the Tokyo- and the eventual agreements during the Uruguay round.

2.2 Curbing Unilateralism

Section 301 was part of the US Trade Act of 1974. De facto it came to prominence in the 1980s, the decade that coincides with the preparation and initiation of the Uruguay round proceedings. United States used unilateral enforcement during that era as complement to its negotiation tactics. What it could not obtain through carrots (reciprocal concessions at the negotiating table), it attempted to obtain through stick (enforcement). This attitude did not go down well with its trading partners.

There is not one single account offered by those who participated in the Uruguay round that does not acknowledge that curbing unilateralism was the overarching objective that trade delegates set for themselves when negotiating the DSU.[r] It is no exaggeration to state that the bulk of the negotiation concerned the "price to pay" for unilateralism to be curbed. Deadlines were worked around the US statutory deadlines, and procedural improvements of all sorts were agreed. Above all, the power of defendant to block the road to adjudication was eliminated. This is how this story unravels.

2.2.1 Section 301: Loved in DC, Hated Everywhere Else

Recourse to "Section 301" was considered a welcome change by lobbies in the United States, but was met with skepticism, if not plain hostility by the GATT membership. A GATT Secretariat document leaves no doubt as to the "reception" of Section 301 beyond the US border:

> no contracting party should resort to counter-measures without the authorization of the CON-TRACTING PARTIES.[s]

Those with lesser bargaining power that had paid the price of US unilateralism were particularly vocal in expressing their opposition to "Section 301," and the need to put an end

---

[q] Various contributions in Bhagwati and Patrick (1990) deal with the political economy, the legality, and the impact of this instrument.

[r] Paemen and Bentsch (1995), Stewart and Callahan (1998), and especially Sykes (2012) who provides a lot of information on this score.

[s] GATT Doc. MTN.GNG/NG13/W/14 of Nov. 3, 1987.

to it and to similar practices as well. The submissions by Nicaragua[t] and Argentina[u] offer good illustrations to this effect.

As if "Section 301" was already not enough, the United States amended it in 1988 so as to increase its scope. The new statute included provisions on challenges against inadequate (in the eyes of the United States) protection of intellectual property rights, even though some of the actions were addressed against countries that did not incur international obligations to this effect. This is the famous "Super 301." This provoked renewed hostile reactions by various trading nations, a chorus of reactions indeed. The delegate of the EU, for example:

> *expressed grave concerns on behalf of the Community and its member States about the US Omnibus Trade and Competitiveness Act, the gestation of which had for a long time burdened GATT's work, particularly during the delicate period leading up to the Uruguay Round.[v]*

The delegate of Japan:

> *... deeply regretted that this Act, which contained a number of problematic provisions, had come into effect.[w]*

Arthur Dunkel has been quoted stating that the 1988 amendments constituted:

> *... the single trade policy initiative which had most galvanized the attention of the international trading community.[x]*

The delegates of Australia, Brazil, Canada, Hong Kong, India, Sweden, Switzerland, and Uruguay expressed similar criticism.[y] The US delegate explained why "Section 301" had been expanded:

> *a major US objective in the Uruguay Round was to strengthen the GATT as an institution and to extend its jurisdiction, so that it could address more disputes. Until that occurred, the United States had to handle bilaterally unfair trade practices, in areas not covered by GATT rules.[z]*

---

[t] GATT Doc. MTN.GNG/NG13/W/15 of Nov. 6, 1987.

[u] GATT Doc. MTN.GNG/NG13/W/17 of Nov. 12, 1987.

[v] GATT Doc. C/M/224 of Oct. 17, 1988 at p. 28.

[w] Idem at p. 30.

[x] Quoted by Stewart and Callahan (1998) at p. 2762.

[y] Idem at p. 31ff.

[z] Idem at p. 34. The problem with unilateral initiatives of the sort (when one becomes the judge of its own cause) is that judgment risks of course being biased. This is a well-known issue for a long long time, and initiatives to address it and move to third-party adjudication have been around since ancient times. Tellingly, the medieval city of Sienna adopted an initiative like this, and Bowsky (1981) explains how the city wanted to separate officials from local ties. Sienna opted for foreign judges, and Bowsky explains in p. 109ff the rationale for this decision: "the prestige, ambition, family connections, and in some cases wealth of these men impelled the oligarchy to keep them out of the Sienese courts and to staff these courts with foreigners, whose lack of local family connections, brief residence in the city, and dependence upon the commune for income would keep them relatively honest." Wills (2002) argues that this type of thinking inspired Madison, one of the architects of the US Constitution.

2.2.2 The Price to Stop Section 301

Following a series of discussions, and a trial and error period ("Montreal rules," 1989), where compulsory third-party adjudication was practiced on probationary terms, Art. 23.2 DSU was eventually agreed. It reads:

> members shall:
>
>   (a) not make a determination to the effect that a violation has occurred, that benefits have been nullified or impaired or that the attainment of any objective of the covered agreements has been impeded, except through recourse to dispute settlement in accordance with the rules and procedures of this Understanding, and shall make any such determination consistent with the findings contained in the panel or Appellate Body report adopted by the DSB or an arbitration award rendered under this Understanding.

This is the quintessential provision in the current DSU and has been interpreted in various reports consistently as a ban on unilateral self-help. In EC-Commercial Vessels, the panel put it eloquently when it stated in §7.190:

> if Members were free to attempt to seek the redress of a violation by trying to achieve unilaterally what could be obtained through the DSU, it is difficult to see how the obligation to have recourse to the DSU could contribute to the "strengthening of the multilateral trading system."

The United States thus agreed to stop unilaterally deciding on the illegality of its trading partners' practices, and, most importantly, to stop recourse to self-help. What would the United States get an exchange? Everything it wanted is the short answer. The disciplines of the GATT would enlarge so as to include services and intellectual property rights in the post-Uruguay round era. Disputes would be adjudicated fast. Statutory deadlines, and negative consensus, that is, the institutionalized impossibility for defendant to block request for consultations, establishment of panel, adoption of its report, recourse to retaliation when warranted (Arts. 6, 16, 17, 22 DSU reflect this institution), would ensure that this would be the case.[aa]

Still, the possibility that defendants refuse to comply with adverse rulings at the end of the day could not be eliminated. Negotiations on this issue to which we now turn reveal discussions both about the form of remedies, as well as about their level.

2.3 Remedies in Case of Noncompliance

The GATT (Article XXIII.2) contained a brief sentence on this issue. Assuming the totality of the GATT membership considered that the circumstances were serious enough to justify similar action, they could by consensus authorize the complainant to suspend tariff concessions of a value equivalent to the damage suffered vis-à-vis the recalcitrant defendant. Recourse to this remedy happened only once in the GATT-era, when the Netherlands requested and obtained authorization to this effect

---

[aa] Sykes (2012) concludes in similar manner.

in 1956. It never implemented its intent, and did not impose countermeasures against the United States.[bb]

Negotiators of the DSU managed to agree on a process that could be followed in order to sensitize recalcitrant WTO members about their obligations. It was clear though to everyone, that this should be last resort. Some were, initially at least, unwilling to allow for "automaticity" when it comes to retaliating against recalcitrant states. They wanted to avoid that decisions about recourse to countermeasures be agreed on "negative consensus," that is, based solely on the willingness of injured WTO members to proceed in this way. Negative consensus would apply to every step of the procedure, except for this. Eventually, they gave up, since they were totally isolated on this issue.[cc]

There was unanimity that the preferred option should remain the removal of the illegality. There was further unanimity that compensation and/or suspension of concessions should be temporary measures until removal of the illegality occurred, if removal had not taken place immediately. There was finally, unanimity regarding the level of response to illegalities. It should not be higher than the damage done. And they all agreed that, in the absence of agreement between the parties, it should be an Arbitrator that should decide on the level of permissible retaliation.

There was no agreement as to the calculation of damages, an issue that was addressed neither in Article 19, nor in Article 22 of DSU. Nothing in these provisions, for example, explicitly discusses how damages should be calculated, what should serve as the counterfactual, or whether damages should be calculated from the moment when the illegality has been committed, or from a different point in time. Adjudicators would have to eventually decide this issue.

Capping responses to illegalities committed to the level of damage done is akin to stating that reciprocal commitments should not be affected as a result of unilateral (illegal) behavior. This is of course, not the type of remedy one would seek for if the prime objective was deterrence. Indeed, in some antitrust statutes, where deterrence is the objective sought, violators are called to pay treble damages. The underlying assumption in the GATT/WTO world is that, by preserving reciprocity (in the sense that violators will not be better off by committing an illegality), the incentive to violate in the first place will be undermined.[dd]

[bb] Pauwelyn (2003) discusses how international law here, but in more general terms as well, can help fill the gaps of the GATT contract. Trachtman (2007) has taken a more nuanced view, arguing against similar constructions. We will return to this issue later in this paper.

[cc] They wanted to limit negative consensus to establishment of panels and adoption of reports.

[dd] Maybe there are grains of truth in this assumption. Whether true, depends on various factors: governments' incentives to start with, since they might in equilibrium prefer support from the lobby whose illegal practices they support, over the lobbies that might pay the price of retaliation through exclusion from international markets. The two are not necessarily the same, but WTO members retaliating, assuming knowledge about what matters to the government committing the illegality, might strategically pick those sectors that hurt the government committing the illegality most. Transparency could be an issue as well, as WTO retaliation does not make the headlines everywhere around the world and is linked to the manner in which specific regimes function. Other factors could, of course, be relevant as well.

2.3.1 Transatlantic Harmony

EU was in favor of speedy resolution of disputes during the negotiation of the DSU but silent as to the retroactivity of damages.[ee] Canada wanted fast implementation, within 6 months from circulation of the report, and was in favor of quantifying the damage from the date of circulation of panel/AB report. It did not pronounce on retroactive damages.[ff] United States as well wanted fast relief, and binding deadlines, and, like the EU, did not offer specific opinions on the calculation of damages.[gg] Switzerland was in the same wavelength. It wanted to avoid lengthy processes and went so far as to state that speedy resolution of disputes removed the necessity for retroactive remedies that it did not want to entertain.[hh]

2.3.2 Latins Like Retro

Developing countries as well favored speedy resolution, and some proposed that all disputes should be resolved within 15 months when developing countries complained.[ii] In contrast to developed countries though, a number of them favored retroactive remedial action, even if the process could be completed fast. There could be no guarantee that commission of illegality, and detection of it would coincide time-wise. Damages should be calculated from the moment an illegal measure had entered into force, and both Argentina[jj] and Peru[kk] tabled proposals to this effect. Mexico was a bit more nuanced, as it supported remedial action from the date of adoption of measures only if compliance had not occurred within the RPT.[ll] Retroactive remedies, in this view, would act as incentive to remove illegalities within the RPT.

Mexico also supported the introduction of interim measures, eg, remedial action between the moment when the final award would be issued, and the moment when implementation would occur. Similar action should take the form of compensation as opposed to suspension of concessions, since compensation, unlike suspension of concessions, increases trade.[mm] Compensation could, in principle, take the form of payment in the sense of tariff reductions, or even lump sump payments of monetary funds. Suspension of concessions on the other hand amounted to increases in tariff duties.

[ee] GATT Doc. MTN.GNG/NG13/W/44 of Jul. 19, 1990.

[ff] GATT Doc. MTN.GNG/NG13/W/41 of Jun. 28, 1990. AB stands for the Appellate Body (AB), the second and final instance "court" at the WTO, an innovation of the Uruguay round. Prior to that, all dispute would be resolved by panels at first and last instance.

[gg] GATT Doc. MTN.GNG/NG13/W/6 of Jun. 25, 1987.

[hh] GATT Doc. MTN.GNG/NG13/W/8 of Sep. 18, 1987.

[ii] GATT Doc. MTN.GNG/NG13/10 of Oct. 10, 1988.

[jj] GATT Doc. MTN.GNG/NG13/W/17 of Nov. 12, 1987.

[kk] GATT Doc. MTN.GNG/NG13/W/23 of Mar. 3, 1988.

[ll] RPT refers to the reasonable period of time within which compliance should occur. RPT is necessary since, for various reasons, immediate compliance might not be on the cards, see GATT Doc. MTN. GNG/NG13/W/42 of Jul. 12, 1990.

[mm] GATT Doc. MTN.GNG/NG13/W/26 of Jun. 23, 1988.

The gap between Latins and Transatlantic partners regarding retroactivity of damages could not be overcome. Eventually, the Chairman of the negotiating group issued a document that reflected the extent of disagreements on the issue of retroactivity of remedial action.[nn]

2.3.3 Some Preferred Persuasion

Recourse to retaliation was originally met with a lot of skepticism. Only one negotiator favored automatic authorization to retaliation during the early stages of the negotiation,[oo] as most speakers conditioned similar action on prior approval by the membership.[pp] Japan[qq] and Korea[rr] were particularly vocal on this score. Japan issued a separate document explaining why in its view similar action should never take place absent consensus.[ss] This is an area where developed countries did not speak with one voice, as United States wanted endorsement of an automatic right to retaliate after a specified period of time in case of course defendant had not complied therein.[tt]

Article 22 of DSU was a victory for the United States in this respect, since it conditions recourse to retaliation on the will of the injured party that has prevailed before litigation. There are some conditions regarding the level of retaliation that have to be of course, respected, and we will return to this issue infra.

2.3.4 The Compromise

The impossibility to agree on the precise level of retaliation led negotiators to the formulation of Article 22.4 of DSU. According to this provision, retaliation should be substantially equivalent to the damage suffered. The manner in which equivalence will be established was left to the discretion of arbitrators, in case the parties could not agree to it. There was not much urgency during the negotiations to propose methods for quantifying damages, as they all agreed that the removal of illegalities should remain as prime objective of the whole endeavor.[uu] The EU,[vv] and the United States as well, issued documents to this effect,[ww] and many others endorsed this view.[xx]

[nn] GATT Doc. MTN.GNG/NG13/W/43 of Jul. 18, 1990.
[oo] GATT Doc. MTN.GNG/NG13/17 of Dec. 15, 1989.
[pp] GATT Doc. MTN.GNG/NG13/19 of May 28, 1990.
[qq] GATT Doc. MTN.GNG/NG13/6 of Mar. 31, 1988.
[rr] GATT Doc. MTN.GNG/NG13/W/19 of Nov. 20, 1987.
[ss] GATT Doc. MTN.GNG/NG13/W/21 of Mar. 1, 1988.
[tt] GATT Doc. MTN.GNG/NG13/W/40 of Apr. 6, 1990.
[uu] GATT Doc. MTN.GNG/NG13/16 of Nov. 13, 1989.
[vv] GATT Doc. MTN.GNG/NG13/W/12 of Sep. 12, 1987.
[ww] GATT Doc. MTN.GNG/NG13/W/3 of Apr. 22, 1987.
[xx] GATT Doc. MTN.GNG/NG13/8 of Jul. 5, 1988.

Article 22.4 of DSU reads:

the level of suspension of concessions or other obligations authorized by the DSB shall be equivalent to the level of the nullification or impairment.

So, negotiators managed to agree that only the DSB (Dispute Settlement Body) could recommend retaliation and that recalcitrant states refusing to implement adverse rulings could face retaliation up to the damage inflicted. The mechanics of establishing equivalence between damage and retaliation was not spelled out.[yy] We now turn to the other, procedural features that would "contextualize" this basic understanding.

3. DISPUTE ADJUDICATION IN WTO

Article 3.2 of DSU states that the objective of dispute adjudication is to preserve the rights and obligations of WTO Members. Article 3.7 of DSU states an ordering of preferences so to speak. A mutually agreed solution (MAS) between the parties to a dispute is always preferable. WTO members should thus exercise judgment and aim to resolve their disputes in diplomatic manner before submitting them to a panel. If it proves untenable, submission to a panel comes next. Panels, if they agree with the complainant, will recommend that the losing party brings its measures into compliance with its obligations and may also suggest ways to do so (Article 19 of DSU). Usually in practice, removal of the illegal act is considered adequate compliance, without the defendant incurring the obligation to also compensate the complainant for damages suffered during the period when the illegality persisted. In case defendant refuses to remove the challenged measure, then two interim measures are at the disposal of WTO members, namely, compensation and/or suspension of concession. Compensation is voluntary and has happened twice. Suspension of concessions requires the respect of certain procedural steps. The injured party will deposit a list with retaliatory measures. In case the defendant does not agree with the proposed list, it can request an Arbitrator (if possible, the original panel) to decide on the level of retaliation.[zz] Whereas panel decisions are appealable, this one is not. Arbitrators' reports are first and last resort. Suspension of concessions (and/or compensation) should be withdrawn when compliance has occurred. On paper thus, property rules (compliance) are preferred over liability rules (compensation/suspension of

---

[yy] The formulation of this provision could be misleading. It is unclear whether it refers to past or ongoing damage. As we will see later, adjudicators will calculate damage at the moment (or near the moment) of the establishment of the arbitration panel. Based on this calculation they will authorize retaliation. If the level of damage changes over time postauthorization, a new request must be tabled.

[zz] Suspension of concessions must be "substantially equivalent" to the damage ("nullification and impairment," in WTO speak) suffered (Art. 22.4 DSU). Since the two instruments have similar function, it is expected that the amount of compensation offered will be linked to the amount of damage inflicted. Whereas it is the author of illegality that will offer compensation, it is the injured party that will draw the list of suspended concessions.

concessions). Once again, as we will see in more detail later, retaliation (and/or compensation) is prospective remedies, that is, they compensate future damages only (assuming of course that the illegality persists).

Deciding on the amount of punishment is, of course, the quintessential, but not the only feature of the regime. Logically, a decision that an illegality has been committed is the necessary step before discussing punishment. It would have been impossible for negotiators to agree on an exhaustive list of illegalities ex ante. The WTO judge "completes" the contract by interpreting open-ended terms, deciding on the legality of challenged measures, and making the resolution of future disputes (more) predictable.[aaa]

3.1 The Process

3.1.1 An "Exclusive" Forum for WTO Members Only

Forum shopping is impossible under the DSU. Furthermore, non WTO members cannot submit their disputes to the WTO, the DSU being a forum to adjudicate disputes between WTO members only (Article 23.2 of DSU).

The DSB is the WTO organ entrusted with the administration of adjudication, and all WTO members have one delegate to this body. All reports, by panels and the AB,[bbb] are submitted to it for adoption. The rules (eg, Articles 3.3, 6.1 DSU) leave no doubt that it decides by negative consensus, that is, the will of the complainant suffices to establish a panel/AB, adopt a report, authorize countermeasures.

The WTO process is open to WTO members only, although commitments under the WTO definitely affect the life of private agents. The latter have no standing before the WTO, and to advance their claims, they need to first secure the agreement of their government to represent them. The conditions under which WTO members agree to do so are not an issue as far as WTO law is concerned. WTO members can be "liberal," or "cautious" when entertaining requests by private agents to represent their interests before a panel. The WTO rules regarding adjudication kick in once a request to launch the process (request for consultation) has been formally submitted.

WTO members retain the monopoly to litigate, but why litigate in the first place? This is a very difficult issue, and there are a few only papers that discuss how disputes can arise in equilibrium.[ccc] One might be tempted to argue that there is a common understanding of what constitutes a cooperative behavior, so punishment should occur

---

[aaa] Horn et al. (2011).

[bbb] We discuss the AB in more detail later. Suffice to state for now that, contrary to the GATT-world, the WTO signals the advent of the AB, the second instance "court" that hears appeals against panels, the first instance "court" of the WTO.

[ccc] See chapter "Enforcement and Dispute Settlement" by Park. Some of the papers have persuasively argued that the frequency of recourse to WTO dispute settlement is no reliable indicator of the performance of panels/AB. Parties might be simply attempting to exploit weaknesses (see Maggi and Staiger, 2011 and also Beshkar, 2010).

even in the absence of litigation. This is not so though, in the WTO-context. Theory has explained why the GATT should be viewed as "incomplete" contract.[ddd] In principle anything can affect the trade outcome, and as a result, it is difficult to imagine what precisely the common understanding of "cooperative behavior" is. The common understanding is the agreement to ask WTO judges to define what "cooperative behavior" is based of course on information included in the WTO contract. The WTO judge thus serves as means to extract information that will help decide if the challenged measure is legitimate or not, and will thus help avoid misplaced retaliatory action. In doing that the WTO judge must respect the balance of rights and obligations (reciprocal commitments) struck between the WTO Members. The judge is an agent after all, not a principal.

The end outcome is binary. Either a violation has been established or not. There is no statutory variation of violations that would entail different remedies. If violation has been established, the road to remedial action opens. If not, this is the end of the road for the complainant.[eee]

Private parties have very limited access to WTO litigation. Under Article X.3 of GATT they can access domestic courts on customs-related matters only; under the "challenge procedures," they can litigate before domestic courts on issues coming under the aegis of the Agreement on Government Procurement.[fff] It could be that domestic law addresses this issue in a different way. It could be, for example, that private parties have standing before domestic courts where they could invoke WTO law. This is not the case, neither the case in the United States, nor in the EU.[ggg]

The bulk of litigation is between WTO members, and Article 1 of DSU acknowledges as much. Keeping it to a few players, facilitates, in principle, compromises whereby WTO members fend off disputes between them. Governments are "sums of interests" and they might find it profitable to initiate/stop litigation or avoid compliance (and thus redistribute wealth among their constituents). Private parties might object to similar deals. They cannot challenge them under WTO laws anyway, and many known domestic legal orders are hostile to similar challenges as well.[hhh]

[ddd] Horn et al. (2010a).

[eee] If violation has been established but the measure has been removed, then no remedial action is necessary. We will return to this point infra. For remedial action to be on the cards though, there is no need to establish violation. Even in case no violation has been committed, remedial action might be due if trading parties affected by an action/omission did not legitimately expect this course of action (see Bagwell et al., 2002).

[fff] Mavroidis and Wolfe (2015).

[ggg] See Jackson (1969) and Hoekman and Mavroidis (2014).

[hhh] Hoekman and Mavroidis (2014) explain why this is not the case before EU courts. Jackson (1987) explain that this is also the case in US law.

The process consists of two legs. First an attempt to resolve disputes bilaterally through consultations, followed, if need be, by a request for adjudication of the dispute by a WTO panel.

3.2 Consultations

3.2.1 Diplomacy First

By "consultations," we understand the bilateral attempt to resolve disputes behind closed doors. It is remnant of the "diplomatic" tradition of resolving disputes, and very much a feature of relational contracts. The GATT was such a contract in its early days when a group of like-minded players negotiated it, and many disputes were indeed resolved in diplomatic manner.[iii] In the DSB regime, consultations are a "necessary" first step, in the sense that no panel can be legitimately established in the absence of an attempt to solve disputes bilaterally, as per standing case law.

3.2.2 Bilateral, and yet so Multilateral

Complainant will notify the DSB of its request for consultations, which will thus become available not only to defendant but to the WTO membership at large (Article 4.4 of DSU). Complainant cannot add to the claims identified in the request for consultations at a subsequent stage, as per standard case law. Notifying the DSB is akin to preserving the umbilical cord between bilateral disputes and the multilateral system. It also helps those with less capacity to detect illegal behavior to become aware of trade barriers. There is empirical evidence to support this view.[iii] Only 35% of all G2[kkk] complaints against G2 and 39% against IND are cases where G2 joined in consultations. DEV countries, on the other hand, have a high propensity to join in when the target is the G2 (in 75% of all their complaints against G2, DEV joined in consultations). This observation could provide some ammunition to those who argue that participation is also a function of information, although additional inquiries are necessary to establish whether this is indeed the case. Bargaining power considerations could sustain similar conclusions, and to our knowledge, no one has investigated this issue any further.

[iii]   Mavroidis (2015) provides evidence of early GATT cases where blatant violations of the prohibition to impose quantitative restrictions were tolerated following a promise that they would be eliminated within a reasonable period of time.

[iii]   Horn et al. (2011) discuss this issue.

[kkk]   This classification comes from Horn et al. (2011). G2 is the EU, and the United States. IND is the remaining OECD (Organization of Economic Cooperation) members. BRICS are Brazil, Russia, India, China, and South Africa. DEV are all developing countries minus LDCs. LDCs are the poorest developing countries that the UN designates as such.

3.2.3 Diplomacy Matters

The majority of disputes are resolved at the consultations stage. Approximately 2/3 are "resolved" at this stage, as Busch and Reinhardt (2002) have first shown in a paper praising the merits of settlements at the consultations stage. Today, out of 491 requests for consultations, 165 panel reports have been issued, while 29 cases are still pending. Almost 40% of requests have been submitted to the next stage, which leaves us with 60% of all disputes "settled" at the consultations stage.[lll]

Complainant can refer the matter to a panel if 60 days after the initiation of consultations no solution has been reached. In the real world though, this rarely happens. Horn et al. (2011) calculate the average length of consultations at 164 days. Complainants might have little incentive to go through the laborious process of submitting their dispute to a Panel, and go through the motions of various procedural steps that we describe later. The absence of retroactive remedies at the end of the litigation process, if the need for remedial action has been established, adds to their incentive to consult aiming for a speedy solution rather than follow the "normal" process and submit to a panel on day 61.[mmm]

3.3 Litigation Before a Panel

A panel is the first instance WTO "court." It is composed of three panelists (judges) who are selected from a roster that comprises over 400 individuals.[nnn] Only WTO members have the right to propose individuals for inclusion to the roster. No proposal has so far been declined, since inclusion in the roster does not automatically guarantee a place in a panel. In fact, there are no recorded discussions in the DSB regarding the "quality" of individuals proposed for inclusion in the roster.

Following a request for establishment of panel, the WTO Secretariat will propose names from the roster and, if the parties agree to them, a panel will be established. Otherwise it is the Director General of the WTO that will "complete" the panel upon request.[ooo] Nonroster panelists have been chosen as well, in fact quite often so. Typically,

---

[lll] To refer to them as "settled" is probably quite optimistic. We often lack information regarding settlements at this stage. "MAS," GATT-speak for settlement must be WTO-consistent (3.5), and the DSB should be made aware of them (3.6). Horn and Mavroidis (2007) note that the record of notifications is poor, and their content quite often uninformative. Aggrieved parties can of course, initiate new litigation. For various reasons, this happens rarely. We will return to this question infra. Davey discusses the issue of inadequate notifications (2007).

[mmm] On the other hand, the unwillingness of panels to recommend retroactive remedies incentivizes parties to avoid offering as much at the consultations stage. Defendants have thus, other things equal, an incentive to procrastinate, whereas complainants to agree at this stage and avoid the laborious panel/AB process.

[nnn] The possibility to use five panelists exists (8.5 DSU), but has not been used so far in the WTO-era.

[ooo] Horn et al. (2011) report that the DG has appointed at least one Panelist in over 61% of all cases. The DG must consult not with the parties but with the Chairman of the DSB and the relevant Council before appointing (8.7 DSU).

panelists are current or former government officials stationed (or previously stationed) in Geneva.[PPP] Usually, nationals of a party to a dispute do not serve as panelists, although infrequently this has been the case.[qqq] Panels enjoy the support of the WTO Secretariat. This is almost necessary, since the majority of panelists are not experts in WTO law by any stretch of imagination. The "deference" toward expertise provided by the Secretariat depends on various factors, and it is hard to "measure" it since the process is confidential (Article 14.1 of DSU). There are good reasons to believe though, that it can be, on occasion, quite substantial.[rrr]

3.3.1 Mandate

Parties can raise various claims, even "heterogeneous" claims (eg, they can attack a measure for violating commitments both under the GATT as well as the GATS) before a panel. The ambit of the panel's review is circumscribed by the claims submitted to it (Article 6.2 of DSU).[sss] It cannot ex officio add to the claims.

Panels will accept or reject claims. They act as "triers of fact" and use WTO law as legal benchmark to assess consistency of challenged practices with WTO. It suffices that a panel adopts one of the claims advanced, and, provided that the measure has not been rescinded already, it will recommend corrective action. We will return to this question later.

Panels have unlimited investigating powers and can ask parties any question they deem appropriate (Article 13 of DSU). They can further invite experts, although they have so far limited invitations to experts in SPS[ttt] cases only, where they are routinely facing "adversarial" scientific expertise. The system is thus mixed "adversarial/inquisitorial," since parties circumscribe the ambit of dispute, but panels called to investigate the soundness of claims possess unlimited freedom to inquire into the subject matter of disputes brought before them.

[PPP] Johannesson and Mavroidis (2015) show that over 4/5 of all Panelists fall into this category.

[qqq] Johannesson and Mavroidis (2015) report all similar cases, which are very few indeed.

[rrr] Johannesson and Mavroidis (2015) mention the remuneration of Panelists, and the background of the "typical" Panelist as two grounds arguing in favor of deference. It is not a question of incentives only though, but of expertise as well. The report on US-COOL (Article 22.6-US) is a very appropriate illustration. In order to quantify the amount of retaliation, the Arbitrators have had to have recourse to elaborate econometrics, when none of them has any expertise in this area.

[sss] A "claim" is the unit of account so to speak in adjudication and refers to the identification of a subject matter (measure) and the provision of the WTO that it runs counter to. "Arguments" in support of claims are the various rationales explaining why a claim holds.

[ttt] SPS stands for the Agreement on Sanitary and Phyto-sanitary Measures. This agreement grossly covers policies aimed to address diseases or pests that are transmitted through livestock or foodstuff. Measures must in principle be adopted following a scientific risk assessment, and this is the main reason why experts are routinely invited by panels in order to assess the consistency of challenged policies.

3.3.2 Process

Once the panel has been established, it will organize two meetings with parties, where third parties (WTO members that are neither complainants nor defendants) can assist provided that they have expressed their interest to this effect in timely manner (Article 10 of DSU). Amici curiae (the "civic society") can send their briefs as well, but panels retain discretion over their eventual use in the proceedings.

The statutory duration of panel process is 180–270 days. De facto, panels take on average 445 days to complete their work.[uuu]

3.3.3 Outcome

Panels must issue reasoned reports (Article 12.7 of DSU). Panel reports reflect in the overwhelming majority of cases a unanimous opinion. There are a dozen or so reports where dissenting opinions have been issued, which have to be anonymous (Article 14.3 of DSU).

3.4 Litigation Before the AB

The AB is a WTO novelty and provides the second instance of adjudication of disputes. Unlike panels, AB members serve a term of 4 years, renewable once for an additional 4-year term. A Committee comprising the Director General of the WTO and Chairs of the most important WTO bodies selects the AB members. All WTO members can propose candidates for selection to the AB. Geographic distribution emerges as the key criterion, and the EU and United States are the only two WTO members nationals of which have always enjoyed a seat in the AB. The overwhelming majority of AB members have studied law (only a couple of AB members so far have had some economics background), and recently the majority of appointments are former government officials. They are better remunerated than panelists, since they receive a lump sum on top of ad hoc payments for work done on specific cases, and are assisted by a group of lawyers acting as clerks.[vvv]

3.4.1 The Mandate

The AB hears appeals against panel reports and has the power to accept, reject, or modify (accept the outcome albeit for different reasons) the original findings. Its review is limited to issues of law, hence the AB findings are somewhat "detached" from facts. Consequently, interpretations of provisions by the AB should, in principle, apply across cases. Although there is nothing like "binding precedent," case law (Mexico-Stainless

[uuu] Horn et al. (2011).
[vvv] Johannesson and Mavroidis (2015).

Steel)[www] has made it clear that panels are expected not to deviate from interpretations reached by the AB, unless of course they can point to "distinguishing factors." As with panels, AB cannot ex officio add to claims submitted by parties to a dispute.

3.4.2 The Process

Following a notice of appeal, a "division" of three AB members will hear a case. The formula for selecting the division is unknown. The AB will organize one meeting with the parties and enjoys investigative powers similar to those of a panel. It issues its report within 91 days on average, the statutory maximum duration of the process being 90 days.[xxx]

3.4.3 Outcome

The AB must issue reasoned reports, where dissenting, anonymous opinions might feature.[yyy]

3.5 Enforcement of Decisions

Enforcement of WTO obligations has almost monopolized the interest of the law and economics literature.[zzz] Recall that it is WTO members that can "incite" recalcitrant states to comply with their obligations through threat/adoption of countermeasures, since the WTO itself cannot impose any sanctions.

3.5.1 Compliance Process

For compliance to be an issue at all, the illegal measure must be extant at the moment when the report (panel/AB) has been issued. If the challenged measure has been removed in the meantime, then the panel/AB will issue a ruling to the effect that the illegal measure has been already removed, without recommending anything else. Case law is consistent on this point (AB, US–Certain EC Products, §81). Only if the illegality persists, will the panel/AB issue a "recommendation," and may issue a "suggestion" as well.

Suggestions reflect the panel's view on what precisely should be done in order to achieve compliance. In principle, thus, they could be seen as very helpful in the quest for compliance as they provide a concrete benchmark to evaluate implementing activities. De facto, they have been issued a handful of times only. It is true that there have not been many requests, since WTO membership has privileged an ethos in favor of

---

[www] In this paper, I use the official acronym of disputes. All reports (GATT, as well as WTO) can be found in the WTO webpage, https://www.wto.org.

[xxx] Horn et al. (2011) have calculated the average.

[yyy] Three dissenting opinions have been issued so far in US–Upland Cotton (DS267), in US–Zeroing (DS294), and in EC–Large Civil Aircraft DS316. Separate but concurring opinions have been issued in EC–Asbestos (DS135) and in US–Large Civil Aircraft (DS350, 353).

[zzz] For a survey, see Horn and Mavroidis (2007), and for a recent contribution on this score, see Wu (2015).

"nonintrusive" remedies. Very few requests for suggestions are recorded.[aaaa] Case law has heavily undermined their usefulness by consistently underscoring the nonbinding nature of suggestions. It is difficult to understand which way causality runs. Have members refrained from requesting suggestions because of case law, or is it that WTO panels tried to emulate the prevailing ethos of their principals?

At any rate, consistent case law holds that panels do not have to issue suggestions even when requested to do so (US-Antidumping Duties on OCTG, AB, §189). Suggestions are nonbinding on their addressees. Case law (EC-Bananas III, Article 21.5-Ecuador, Second Recourse, AB, §325) suggests that WTO members, even when they have implemented a nonbinding suggestion, cannot benefit from a presumption that compliance has been achieved.

We thus, de facto, live in a predominantly "recommendations" world. Panels/AB must recommend when facing a persisting illegality that defendant "brings its measure into compliance" with its obligation. This is the standard content of any recommendation by virtue of Article 19.1 of DSU. Addressees have thus, substantial discretion how to achieve this result. There are some limits of course, since they cannot at any rate continue doing what they had been practicing in the past.

Armed with a favorable outcome, the complainant will request from defendant to bring its measure into compliance. Compliance should be achieved unilaterally, or within a RPT agreed bilaterally or, in case of disagreement, by requesting from an Arbitrator, usually, a present or former AB member, to decide on its length (Article 21.3 of DSU). On 29 occasions so far, an Arbitrator has defined the "reasonable period of time" within which implementation should occur, since the parties to the dispute could not agree to it.

Agreement between the parties that implementation has occurred within the RPT, however defined, will signal the end of the dispute. Disagreement will result in renewed litigation. Complainant will have to request from a "compliance panel," the report of which can be appealed, to decide whether compliance has occurred (Article 21.5 of DSU)[bbbb] and, depending on the response, complainant might have the right to force compliance through countermeasures.

RPT when agreed bilaterally is on average 9.3 months, whereas it extends to 11.7 months when an Arbitrator has decided on its length. The statutory deadline for compliance panels to issue their report is 90 days, and the same applies to AB. In practice, the former takes 253 days to issue their report, and the latter, 88.[cccc]

[aaaa] Palmeter et al. (2016).

[bbbb] A "compliance panel" is what its name indicates. It is the original panel, if possible, that is, called to decide this time one issue only: has the defendant taken measures that are adequate for it to be deemed to be in compliance? An affirmative response (by the panel and/or the AB) will signal the end of dispute. A negative response could signal the beginning of a request to impose countermeasures. See Charnovitz (2009) and Trebilcock and Howse (2013).

[cccc] Horn et al. (2011).

3.5.2 The Last Resort

Facing noncompliance, either because defendant took no corrective action or because action taken was judged inadequate, complainant can retaliate by imposing countermeasures, "suspension of concessions" in WTO-parlance. To this effect, it will present a list of products the level of tariffs of which it will purport to raise vis-à-vis the defendant only. In case defendant agrees with the list presented, complainant can start imposing countermeasures.

If there is no agreement regarding the appropriateness of the level of proposed countermeasures, complainant can request from an Arbitrator, the original panel if possible, to decide on their level (Article 22.6 of DSU). Countermeasures can remain in place until compliance has been achieved in case there is disagreement as to whether compliance has been achieved, a new panel should be instituted to this effect, the report of which is appealable.[dddd]

Law addresses explicitly the level of countermeasures. The damage inflicted should be equal to the damage suffered (Article 22.4 of DSU). Thus, by law, countermeasures should, in principle, guarantee that reciprocal commitments will not be disturbed as a result of the commission of an illegal act.[eeee]

3.5.3 It Is a Long Way to Tipperary (or Is It?)

The process might strike lengthy (approximately 1192 days on average plus the time to request establishment of Panel before the DSB, send notice of appeal, etc.), but of course it all depends on what the benchmark is. It roughly corresponds, for example, to the length of process before the two EU courts. The length is largely function of the resolve of WTO members to ensure during the negotiating stage the advent of one key provision: Article 23.2 of DSU, that is, the provision that guarantees all decisions regarding illegality of challenged measures should be exclusively taken by WTO judges, and not by affected parties.[ffff]

4. PRACTICE

4.1 Process

The WTO is the busiest court adjudicating disputes exclusively across states. The numbers are impressive indeed. Hudec (1993) reports 250 disputes during the GATT-era. On Nov. 9, 2015 the 500th dispute was submitted to the WTO. Were we to control for the time span of the two institutions (47 years for the GATT, 20 years for the WTO), then the number of WTO disputes becomes even more impressive. Of course there are

---

[dddd] The AB established this much in US-Suspended Concession, stating that the new Panel could be a "compliance Panel," eg, a Panel with "limited mandate" as discussed supra.

[eeee] Or even a legal act that has given rise to a lawful right to compensate. This is what "nonviolation" complaints amount to the function of which has been best explained in Bagwell and Staiger (2002).

[ffff] Statutory deadlines to a large extent replicate those of US Section 301, removing thus the argument from the US delegates that the trading system does not guarantee speedy resolution of disputes.

counter-balancing factors as well. There are more members and more agreements now-adays.[gggg] The distribution of disputes across WTO Members looks like this[hhhh]:

	Complainant	Respondent	BIC	DEV	G2	IND
BIC	11.4%	12.3	2.0	9.8	74.5	3.7
DEV	22.2	18.2	5.0	36.4	47.5	11.1
G2	40.0	48.5	20.6	15.1	35.8	28.5
IND	26.2	21.0	9.4	11.1	58.1	21.4
LDC	0.2	0	0	0	0	0

The GATT is the agreement that dominates the subject matter of litigation. Claims under the GATT represent 94.2% of all claims; under GATS, 2.3%; and under TRIPs, 3.5%. G2 represents 85% of all claims under TRIPs, 50% for GATS, and 37% for GATT; BIC, 9% for TRIPs, and 9% for GATT; IND, 6% for TRIPs, 17% for GATS, 32% for GATT; DEV, 33% for GATS, 21% for GATT; LDCs, 1% for GATT.[iiii]

[gggg] Horn et al. (2005). Some authors compare the WTO to say the ICJ (International Court of Justice), which adjudicates less than two disputes/year. It is inappropriate comparison though, since the ICJ, unlike the WTO cannot adjudicate a dispute without the consent of defendant. Comparisons with investment fora are equally unwarranted. It is private parties that complain there, they do not need the governmental "green light" to litigate. The WTO would have probably been inundated with disputes had private parties been acknowledged the right to sue before it.

[hhhh] The Table is composed from information in Horn et al. (2011) G2 covers EU, and US; BIC, Brazil, India, China; DEV, developing countries; IND, OECD members; and LDCs the least developed countries. Various studies have tried to explain what explains participation. Horn et al. (2005) argue that participation represents more or less share in world trade. Analysts have focused on the cost of litigation, like Bown (2005), and the twin issue of embedded legal expertise, like Horn et al. (2011). Nordström and Shaffer (2008) argue in favor of a "small claims tribunal," a low cost mechanism that would incite developing countries to litigate more, since their claims do not typically involve payment of large sums, and might be deterred to submit to the usual procedure because of the cost of litigation.

[iiii] Horn et al. (2011). It is not the purpose of this paper to advance explanations why most of the activity is in GATT. A few words seem warranted though. If there is one area where all commentators agree about GATS is that it did not generate liberalization, it simply "crystallized" into law the preexisting regime. Under the circumstances, the number of disputes observed should come as no surprise. The TRIPs story is a bit different, since the EU and United States pushed a lot for inclusion of this agreement in WTO. The low number of disputes might come as surprise. One should not forget though, that developing countries originally benefitted from transitional periods. Furthermore, TRIPs is about enacting laws that observe "minimum standards"; it is in preferential trade agreements (PTAs) that one expects to see far-fetched disciplines. One should also be mindful of the fact that many complaints would address omissions to enforce, and the burden of proof associated with complaints against omissions should not be under-estimated. And then, one should not neglect that the provisions in TRIPs of interest to companies (like "compulsory licensing") are full of holes and loopholes. Note also that this is an area with a high number of settlements. Out of 34 requests of consultations, only 10 cases were submitted to a Panel, of which only 3 were appealed. Discussions in the TRIPs committee and the transparency regarding challenged measures provided therein are also factors contributing to settlements. Finally, WTO remedies are not attractive, as private companies might be in position to win more by litigating before domestic courts. We will return to this point infra.

4.2 Calculating the Amount of Countermeasures

Recall that the law preempts Arbitrator's discretion as to the level of permissible retaliation, since it must be substantially equivalent to the damage inflicted. Recall further, that as we have noted earlier, the text is silent as to whether the damage (level of nullification or impairment, in WTO speak) should be past or also ongoing. We have briefly stated that authorization will be issued based on calculation of the damage at the moment when the arbitration panel entrusted with the calculation of retaliation is instituted. We will now explain how exactly this happens. Before we do so, we should, for the sake of completeness, refer to the one case where the authorized retaliation overshot the amount of damage done.

In Canada-Aircraft (Article 22.6-Canada) the panel added a 20% mark up on the level of countermeasures calculated only because Canada had stated that it would maintain the contested subsidy program irrespective of the outcome of the dispute (§3.49 of the report). This is a case of "punitive damages," a one-off case, since the conclusion reached here has never been repeated in any other report. The soundness of the approach was not contested, but no other Arbitrator ever has had recourse to punitive damages.

The law does not address the method that Arbitrator must use in order to quantify damages. Case law has moved in to fill the gap. Actually, it has not just filled gaps when doing so. The argument could be raised that the case law construction of remedies has probably undone the basic understanding among principals, since arguably the manner in which damages have been calculated falls short of ensuring that reciprocal commitments are not disturbed as the result of the commission of an illegality. On the other hand, as we have already stated earlier, the argument could also be made that reciprocity is observed, but it is now understood as "reciprocity going forward".

First, case law has consistently established that retaliation shall be calculated from the end of the RPT.[iiii] Panels have not adequately explained why similar remedies are consistent with the letter and spirit of the WTO, or why the GATT-practice in this area in favor of retroactive remedies that we have cited earlier should be discontinued. They have read the terms "bring a measure into conformity with the covered agreements" appearing in Article 22.1 of DSU, the provision that discusses enforcement of obligations, as tantamount to recommending prospective action. Based on this understanding, they

---

[iiii] EC-Hormones (US) (Article 22.6-EC), §38; E-Bananas III (Ecuador) (Article 22.6-EC); Brazil-Aircraft (Article 22.6-Brazil). The best proof is the presence of consistent case law to the effect that no recommendation is due when an illegality has been brought into compliance after the process had been initiated. In this case, Panels will routinely issue a ruling to the effect that the illegality has been complied with. It follows that in the absence of recommendation, no claim can be raised regarding damages suffered between the occurrence of illegality and the date when compliance occurred.

have consistently, with one exception albeit,[kkkk] recommended prospective remedies. The terms quoted nevertheless do not necessarily lead to this conclusion. One could very well read these terms consistently with recommendations for retroactive remedies. This is by now water under the bridge though, as we now de facto live in a world of prospective remedies. Since there is no room for injunction relief in the WTO, the absence of retroactive remedies entails that WTO members violating the agreement will enjoy a few years of exit from the contract, which will remain unpunished. We will return to this issue later.

Second, damages do not cover "indirect benefits." United States lost its claim against the EU that it should be compensated for lost income resulting from reduced exports of fertilizers to Mexico, as a result of the impossibility of Mexico to export bananas to the EU (EC-Bananas III (Ecuador) (Article 22.6-EC), §§6.12–14).[llll]

Third, what matters is only value added, and nothing else. Mexico could not be compensated using the total value of exported bananas to the EU as benchmark, but only for Mexican added value to the production of bananas. Mexico had to reduce the value of imported fertilizers since, in the presence of the EU "ban" on bananas, it would not need to import fertilizers anymore (EC-Bananas III (Ecuador) (Article 22.6-EC) §6.18).

Fourth, legal costs are not recoverable (US-1916 Act (EC) (Article 22.6-US), §5.76).

Fifth, while the agreement calls for suspension of concession or "other obligations," case law seems to have closed the door to the latter possibility. This question arose during the proceedings in US AD Act 1916 (EC). Having secured a ruling to the effect that the US AD Act 1916 was WTO-inconsistent, and faced with noncompliance by the United States during the RPT, the EU submitted to the United States its proposal to adopt "mirror legislation" and be allowed to impose punitive damages against dumpers. In the absence of agreement with the United States, the EU tabled the same request before

---

[kkkk] In the WTO-era, only one Panel (Australia-Automotive Leather II) held that remedies could be applied retroactively. It did so expressing an "inconsequential" view (obiter dictum), since it did not have to decide on the level of countermeasures. A nonjurist might be tempted to argue that there is nothing prospective in counting retaliation from the end of RPT. Two parties might legitimately disagree as to the interpretation of a provision, and illegality is established only at the moment when a judge has pronounced to this effect. Consistent practice in international law suggests the opposite to be true. Judgments have "declaratory"- and not "constituent" effect. A court judgment has only a declaratory effect. It simply acknowledges that an illegality has been committed. It does not, in other words, establish the illegality for the first time when the decision is being issued. If we were to take the opposite view, not only would we be arguing against a basic tenet of international law but also of common sense. Do we need to await the judgment of a judge to decide that Home violated its obligations when imposing antidumping duties without conducting an investigation?

[llll] This ruling casts doubt on whether reciprocity can take care of cases where companies in various parts of the world are vertically linked, a rather common occurrence in today's world of global value chains. The same is true for the next point.

the Arbitrators who were asked to pronounce on whether the proposed mirror legislation satisfied the requirements of Article 22.4 of DSU. The Arbitrator responded in the negative. In their view, the EU should be permitted to suspend concessions equivalent to the amount of nullification and impairment suffered each time the US AD Act 1916 was being applied against EU economic operators. It was prohibited, however, from adopting mirror legislation since a similar measure would not be WTO-consistent because the equivalence between damage suffered and suspension of concessions could not be ex ante guaranteed and thus Article 22.4 of DSU would have been violated as a result (US AD Act 1916 (Article 22.6-US), §§7.3–9).

Finally, case law has made recourse to crossretaliation relatively onerous. Law states that concessions should be suspended within the same sector, and, "if that party considers that it is not practicable or effective, it can move to another sector and eventually to another agreement" (Article 22 of DSU). The latter option is termed "cross retaliation" and has some obvious advantages for WTO members with smaller bargaining power. By violating TRIPs, for example, the value of brand names is reduced, and as most of the brand names originate in OECD countries, the proponents of introduction of TRIPs in the WTO regime, this is a risk they could do without.

An anecdote offers appropriate illustration of the attitude of OECD countries toward crossretaliation. Robert Zoellick (ex-USTR), in a visit to Brazil, was confronted with a question regarding the possible US reaction in case Brazil were to impose lawful suspension of concessions under TRIPS (that is, crossretaliate). Zoellick quickly pointed out that Brazil might be facing countermeasures itself in that case. The United States could be removing some GSP benefits:

> there's always a danger in trade relations—these things start to slip out of control. You know, keep in mind, Brazil sells about two and a half million dollars under a special preference program to the United States, under the GSP. We have been working with Brazil because of the problems of intellectual property violations here, which could lead to their removal. It did in the case of Ukraine. So, I think it is dangerous for people to go down these paths because one retaliates, and all of the sudden you might find out that something else happens. We have felt—in the case of intellectual property rights—that Brazil is trying. We've decided to give time to work, to try. But, one decides to retaliate, well, who knows, maybe others will too. (Transcript of Joint Press Availability, Deputy Secretary of State, Robert B. Zoellick, and Brazilian Finance Minister Antonio Palocci, Ministry of Finance, Brasilia, Brazil, Oct. 6, 2005).

There is a dynamic risk as well. Counterfeiting requires the implementation of production capacities, which will be hard to shut down when there is no more valid reason for imposing countermeasures. And finally, there is a quantification issue as well.

In EC-Bananas III (Ecuador) (Article 22.6-EC), the panel faced a request by Ecuador to crossretaliate up to $261 million (the level of total damage suffered from the EU policy on bananas) in the area of TRIPs. The panel held that it had the right to review whether Ecuador had objectively reviewed the facts of the case when reaching this figure. It then revised Ecuador's calculation and authorized suspension of up to $60 million in the realm of goods, and $201million in the realm of TRIPs.[mmmm]

Finally, we mentioned that compensation is the other interim measure until compliance occurs. It can take the form of cash compensation and did so twice: in US Section 110(5) Copyright Act, and in the US–Upland Cotton dispute. In the former case,[nnnn] the United States agreed to pay a yearly installment to the EU for violating TRIPs. In the latter case, the United States paid Brazil an amount for violating the SCM Agreement.[oooo] It is a voluntary measure though and cannot be enforced against recalcitrant WTO members.

4.3 Property, or Liability Rules?

Pascal Lamy, when he was EU Commissioner for Trade (before he was appointed DG of the WTO), was quoted saying that, as long as a WTO Member is prepared to "pay" (that is, be subjected to suspension of concessions), it can lawfully continue to violate the WTO (European Union Press and Communications Service, No 3036, May 23, 2000). Is this the correct view?

The law (Article 22.1 of DSU) states that:

> …neither compensation nor the suspension of concessions or other obligations is preferred to full implementation of a recommendation to bring a measure into conformity with the covered agreements.

This has "property rules" written all over it.[pppp] And yet, assuming concessions have been suspended, they can stay in place as long as the illegality persists. There is no statutory deadline within which culprits must start respecting the contract all over again. De facto thus, by accepting to "pay," the offender can continue to violate the contract ad infinitum. It can thus "buy" its way out of the contract. This understanding is probably not in line with the "spirit" of the DSU, but there is nothing in the text that makes it legally impossible.

[mmmm] Anderson (2002) states that "practicability" is a key element here, although he would prefer cross-retaliation any time it is "ineffective" to do so in the same sector. One reason explaining the decision of Arbitrators in EC-Bananas III is probably that they observed that Ecuador had already $60million trade in goods with the EU, and it was hence "practicable" to retaliate in this area. They thus relegated "effectiveness" to a second order concern. Through their attitude, they implied that Art. 22.3 DSU is not "self-judging," a rather deplorable outcome, since Ecuador (and others) would eventually have to pay for errors committed by Panels regarding effectiveness of their retaliation.

[nnnn] Grossman and Mavroidis (2003) discuss this report. United States paid slightly over $1 million per year for the first 3 years, and as of then it has been regularly reporting its efforts to implement the report.

[oooo] WTO Doc. WT/DS267/43-46.

[pppp] Jackson (2004).

For the reasons explained later, it is doubtful whether the WTO regime can be described as "efficient breach of contract." It is unclear (doubtful at the very least) that WTO members can all equally profit from "paying" their way out. "Liability rules" nonetheless are not synonymous to "efficient breach of contract." De facto, the WTO regime amounts to accepting the liability rules as adequate remedy to address violations of WTO law.[qqqq]

4.4 Recap

The discussion so far shows that in practice the balance of rights and obligations is not restored following a decision by Arbitrators to retaliate. The time between the commission of illegality and the time when retaliation can be imposed is the reason why. In the name of securing impartial decisions, WTO members were thus prepared to accept to lose some of their entitlements. This does not necessarily mean that reciprocity is not observed. It is clear that the *original* balance of rights and obligations will not be restored. It could be though that all complainants lose symmetrically. Then, reciprocity would be reinstated. It is of course, a very challenging exercise, that is, required in order to demonstrate that, the departure from the original balance of rights and obligations notwithstanding, reciprocity is still observed. We will return to this discussion in Section 5.

The paradox in the WTO dispute settlement system is that it might be more favorable for Home to look for an adjudicated as opposed to a negotiated solution when it is facing a shock. Assume Home citizens are worried about the effects consumption of "hormones-treated beef" might have on their health, and there is no way it can justify its measures under the WTO. Home could request negotiations under Article XXVIII of GATT.[rrrr] It would be requesting an increase on its tariff duty for "hormones-treated beef" and would be willing to pay compensation by reducing its tariff protection in other areas. Two points are of importance here. First, Home will not, in principle, be in position to profit from "prospective" remedies, since it will not be in position to raise the level of duty until the moment when compensation has been paid. And even if no compensation has been agreed and it still decides to raise its duties, it will be facing immediate unilateral retaliation. Second, Home will have to pay the political price of exposing some of its lobbies to increased competition from abroad. If Home opts for "cheap exit" though and imposes a quantitative restriction on this commodity, it will have 5 years before it will be asked to comply. Moreover, it will be in position to "buy its way

[qqqq] Schwarz and Sykes (2002). The question of course arises whether this remedy is generally available, as poorer countries might find it impossible to "buy their way out of the contract."

[rrrr] This provision provides WTO members with the institutional platform, that is, necessary to renegotiate upwards the level of customs duties that they have previously bound. It calls for reciprocal adjustments, whereby the requesting state will be allowed to increase its duties if it can offer adequate compensation (in the form of reduced customs duties in other goods) to its partners. If no agreement has been reached and the requesting state still wants to increase its duties, then it might be facing retaliation.

out of the contract," if it agrees to pay compensation 5 years down the road. And it will be Foreign this time that will be deciding the areas where it will retaliate.

5. MIND OVER MATTER

The system of prospective remedies, as described earlier, does not guarantee that specific reciprocity will be observed. It does a much better job when it comes to understanding the WTO as exclusive forum for adjudicating disputes. In fact, WTO members continue to resolve their disputes before the WTO, the spectacular rise of PTAs notwithstanding. The number of disputes in WTO's second decade is lower than the corresponding number in the first decade, the ever-growing number of WTO members notwithstanding. This is probably due to the fact that the numbers of PTAs has increased dramatically since 1995, and PTA partners do not litigate between them, or rarely do so as we will show in this section. WTO members, it seems, attach a higher value to third-party adjudication and are prepared to "take one for the team" (in terms of obtaining less than specific reciprocity) to this end, the "team" being precisely compulsory third-party adjudication.

5.1 Prospective Remedies, Specific-, and Diffuse Reciprocity

The credibility of commitments entered depends of course on the enforcement of agreed obligations. Assuming an agreement between the parties that compliance[ssss] has been achieved, there is no point in inquiring any further into the question whether reciprocity has been served. This is an issue that could be left to the parties to the dispute. In the absence of agreement though, panels are entrusted with the task to ensure that authors of illegalities will not be better off following the commission of an illegality. Authors of illegal acts consistently pay back less than the damage they have inflicted, since, in the practice discussed in the previous section, remedies are prospective.[tttt]

The question whether specific reciprocity can still be respected is a different issue. The benchmark (counterfactual) to quantify the damage done should be a world where no illegality has been committed. That much is clear in standard legal theory. It is against this benchmark that the damage inflicted should be calculated (and the amount of "compensation" should be awarded) in order to ensure absolute compliance with the

---

[ssss] Inquiring into the motives for noncompliance is not within the ambit of this paper. Illustratively we state that the incentives might be lacking to always respect what has been agreed, and/or sometimes there might be legitimate disagreements as to what exactly has been committed (what does, for example, "applied so as to afford protection" mean when it comes to understanding the ambit of the obligation to not discriminate mean.

[tttt] The question whether the payment made should be linked to the profit made by breaching the contract did not even enter the mindset of the framers of the DSU. It is true of course that benefits from breaching the contract could be of "political" nature. It could help, for example, the ruling party from winning support in a "swing" state and thus win reelection.

agreement. Since damage is inflicted from the moment an illegality has been committed, it is from the moment of breach that the extent of remedial action should be calculated. Damage does not exist from the moment a court so says, but from the moment an illegality has been committed. Challenged practices do not live in the "twilight zone" of doubt and become illegal only at the moment when a judge had so stated. Court decisions *declare* that an illegality has been committed; they do not *establish* it for the first time.[uuuu] In this vein, for reciprocity to be served, remedial action must wipe out all consequences of illegality from the moment it occurred.

Retroactive remedies would definitely get us closer to specific reciprocity, since they would "travel the distance" between the world where an illegality has been committed, and the world where the contract has been observed by all. Keep in mind though, that, realistically, even a system of retroactive remedies would not necessarily de facto serve specific reciprocity, as it might turn out to be "useless" weapon in the hands of "smaller" players. Retroactive remedies serve specific reciprocity when they are implemented. Rational policies nonetheless might argue against implementation.

Keohane's (1986) distinction between "specific-" and "diffuse reciprocity" fits nicely here. "Specific reciprocity" would correspond to a situation where deviations from obligations assumed would be punished so as to ensure that the violating party would pay the damage that bridges the gap between the current situation (where violation has occurred) and a counterfactual where no violation at all had occurred. "Diffuse reciprocity" is a reduction from this benchmark. The amount of reduction is not specified. Reduction is warranted since there is "trust" between players that deviation will be addressed anyway, and today's culprit will be tomorrow's generous player who will accept similar deviation from other players, safe in the knowledge that they will be addressed in time as well. If violations are addressed imperfectly when Home has committed an illegality, they will be addressed imperfectly when Foreign violates its obligations as well. Thus, in principle, reciprocity will be observed in some rough manner even in the latter scenario, since all could profit from "cheap" exit from their contractual obligations at one point in time. Punishment would be imperfect for all.[vvvv]

Leaving bargaining power considerations aside for a moment, there is one crucial difference between prospective and retroactive remedies. The date of detection of an illegality is immaterial in the world of retroactive remedies. No matter when one discovers the commission of an illegal act (leaving aside extreme examples of course, against which

---

[uuuu] This discussion might sound odd to those not versed in legal culture. Indeed, many a time contracts are signed and yet some of their clauses are unclear. The judge called to resolve disputes even in this case is simply declaring that an illegality has been committed. Judicial errors will be borne by the contracting parties.

[vvvv] Beshkar (2010) and Maggi and Staiger (2015) have argued that less than proportional remedies are the most efficient remedies in a regime like the WTO where governments have private information about lobbies' pressure to comply or not with adverse judgments. Practice confirms his theoretical insight.

an "estoppel"/"acquiescence" defense can be mounted), it will be anyway compensated as of the date when the illegality was committed. Conversely, in the world of prospective remedies the moment of detection is quite important. The closer it is to the commission of the illegality, the likelier it is that reciprocity will be served. The question thus becomes whether WTO members have symmetric powers to detect illegalities. We will assume that they have symmetric willingness to punish violators. While bargaining power might remove the incentive from "smaller" players to prosecute "big fish," lack of trade impact will remove the incentive of "big fish" to prosecute "smaller" players. We will also assume that every WTO member violates the contract with the same frequency. This is a generous assumption, of course. It could be that for domestic law/political economy reasons, some cannot and do not deviate from WTO obligations with the same ease as others.

WTO members do not share the same capacity to detect deviations. The most powerful between them can rely on a highly diversified export portfolio and consequential presence of trade diplomacy around the globe. Weaker nations cannot rely for which information is costly and cannot rely on the WTO to supply it (the TPRM, Trade Policy Review Mechanism, or on the notification system). The former offers scattered information on periodic basis, whereas the record of notifications of national measures is good only when notifications are incentive compatible.[wwww] In the absence of centralized enforcement,[xxxx] those with the more sophisticated administrations will be in better position to detect deviations and act faster, if they deem it appropriate, reducing thus the period of impunity for deviators.

The WTO cannot of course become the "great equalizing factor" and undo asymmetries across its various members. It cannot pretend that the system in place guarantees absolute respect of reciprocal commitments either. How much of a problem is it though? As we have already explained, the WTO must be notified of all requests for consultations. Empirical evidence supports the conclusion that those with less bargaining power usually join in consultations.[yyyy] In light of this, asymmetric detection powers do not seem to be much of an issue. Those that discover illegalities later will jump on the bandwagon of consultations roughly at the same time with the original complainant. It is true that defendants can always refuse similar requests, but then, armed with information concerning illegalities, they can initiate their own dispute. Once again, the regime does not equalize absolutely identical losses, but roughly comparable. This is what diffuse reciprocity aims to capture.

[wwww] While most commentators celebrate the record before the TBT and the SPS Committee, they deplore the record before the ILC and the SCM Committees (see Collins-Williams and Wolfe, 2010).

[xxxx] Hoekman and Mavroidis (2000).

[yyyy] Horn et al. (2011).

How much of the analysis above is put into question by the asymmetric endowments of WTO members? Empirical papers, like Bown (2002) and Bown and Reynolds (2015), have shown that implementation is facilitated when the terms of trade effect are small. But there is more. Annex II reflects all cases where recourse to retaliation has been made so far. With one exception, they are cases between members of comparable bargaining power. The odd case is US-Upland Cotton, where the "big" trader agreed to "pay" the "smaller" trader when faced with a threat for countermeasures. Prima facie, one is prone to wonder why would the United States agree to compensate Brazil, and not simply face retaliation. First of all, Brazil is not a small player. It is "smaller" than the United States, but not small. It seems though that it is the US cotton lobby that forced this "solution" on the government, since it was unwilling to give up on the generous subsidies it received, and the government might have feared a backlash if "innocent bystanders" would have to pay for the US cotton industry's sins.[zzzz]

There is some additional evidence supporting the view that the end game (countermeasures) is de facto reserved for players with more or less equal bargaining power that predates US-Upland Cotton. Bagwell et al. (2005) check all cases between 1995 and 2005 and find no case where complainant has had to have recourse to countermeasures in order to secure compliance by defendants with "less" bargaining power. They divide the WTO world between OECD- and nonOECD members and then ask the question what has been the attitude of complainants when faced with noncompliance by the defendant. They identify a number of cases (less than 20) where nonOECD complainant has been faced with noncompliance (that is, cases where the WTO was not notified of a change in policy). The OECD defendant did not comply in each of these cases, and yet the complainant did not go ahead and suspend concessions. On the other hand, they find no case where an OECD complainant has had to exercise threat (by suspending concessions) in order to induce compliance by a nonOECD defendant. This observation falls squarely within Schelling's (1960) classic account that for the threat to be credible, it does not have to be exercised. This study provides some empirical proof that bargaining asymmetries might matter when it comes to discussing compliance at the WTO.[aaaaa]

Ecuador's case is quite telling to describe instances where "smaller" players attack the "big guns."[bbbbb] Having won three disputes against the EU and been authorized to impose countermeasures up to a value of $261 million ($200 of which in TRIPs), it decided against imposition of countermeasures. Although it never revealed the reasons

---

[zzzz] The EU executive did not have similar fears when implementing its bananas-policy, as Hoekman and Mavroidis (2014) explain.

[aaaaa] It is this observation that prompted the authors to analyze the introduction of tradable remedies in the WTO in Bagwell et al. (2008). It is Mexico that had tabled this proposal in the WTO negotiations, as the authors explain.

[bbbbb] A series of papers cited in this paper, both theoretical as well as empirical, and most recently Bown and Reynolds (2015), prove that bargaining power does matter.

for doing so, one can imagine that it might have realized that not only it would not be in position to recoup the damage done (so why invest in countermeasures in the first place?), but its actions, in the realm of violations of intellectual property rights (crossretaliation), could have provoked Zoellick-type reaction as previously discussed.[ccccc]

Huerta-Goldman (2009) in similar vein provides evidence to the effect that Mexico did not retaliate against the EU in the same dispute, opting for better terms in its ongoing negotiation that led to the conclusion of the free trade area between Mexico and the EU.

The EU though eventually did reach an agreement with bananas exporters, even though Ecuador never exercised its right to retaliate.[ddddd] The balance of rights and obligations was not reestablished, and Ecuador is definitely a loser in this story. But the EU also accepted a cut. When granted the right to impose countermeasures worth over $4billion in the US-FSC dispute, it suspended concessions for only a small fraction of the total sum. Once again, it is clear quantification of damages will show that the original balance of rights and obligations was not respected in any of the cases discussed here. Overall nevertheless, losses are capped and distributed (even though unequally) to the membership. The flavor here yet again is reminiscent of diffuse reciprocity. The fact that losses are not as dramatic as they could be in case retroactive remedies were routinely recommended helps. In this vein, we should include a reference to the US-Upland Cotton (Article 22.6-US) arbitration. There the Arbitrator moved away from the prior benchmark for calculating the amount of retaliation to a new, lower benchmark. Before this case, affected parties could request the right to retaliate for the whole amount of an illegal (eg, export-, local content-) subsidy paid. Indeed, this is what had happened in US-FSC. Following this case, affected parties can only retaliate up to the level of trade damage suffered. Since say export subsidies concerns goods sold worldwide, it is expected that the new, trade effects-based standard will lead to lower levels of retaliation.[eeeee]

Losers thus do not lose that much after all. The proposals submitted by developing countries regarding remedies during the Doha round suggest that they are unhappy with the current state of affairs. Some of them have reiterated their desire to see retroactive remedies introduced into the WTO system.[fffff] They have repeatedly taken the view that

---

[ccccc] Bown (2002, 2004) and Blonigen and Bown (2003) show why governments may be more likely to implement policies that violate the WTO, if they are not too worried about the retaliation capacity of the potential complainant.

[ddddd] Guth (2012).

[eeeee] There are of course also cases where nonimplementation was not necessary precisely because the threat was credible. This is essentially the argument in Bagwell et al. (2005). In similar vein, Ehring (2014) describes all instances in which the EU was authorized to impose countermeasures and shows why it did not take concrete steps in several of them. Following the condemnation of the United States in US-Steel Safeguards, the EU had targeted goods in swinging states about the time when the US general election would take place. The US administration withdrew the challenged measures in time avoiding the costly EU retaliation.

[fffff] WTO Doc. TN/DS/26 of Jan. 30, 2015.

they do not benefit equally from the current regime. They seem to imply that bigger players can certainly exercise "behind the scenes" diplomacy in order to advance their preferences. "Big" guys have anyway more "persuasive" power, in that they have more weapons to use when they decide to retaliate.[ggggg] This, however, would be the case irrespective whether the WTO had espoused retroactive remedies or not.[hhhhh]

Developing countries, their disappointment with the current regime notwithstanding, have not stopped using the system and have not used PTA dispute adjudication either. They "bite the bullet" and continue to be active, by reasonable benchmarks such as those offered in Horn et al. (2005), participants in the WTO dispute settlement system. Furthermore, by continuing to participate in the WTO, they can profit in different ways, be it aid for trade, special and differential treatment, and/or similar instruments.

5.2 Specific-, Diffuse Reciprocity, and Compliance with the WTO

The argument is routinely made that the current system works well since it has served its prime objective, that is, to achieve compliance with the rulings issued. Routinely authors refer to WTO dispute settlement as the jewel in the WTO crown, and an enviable regime that should be emulated by all. It is true that we do not hear of trade wars anymore. Is it also true that we do not hear of wars because of high rates of compliance with adverse rulings? If yes, then what is needed is prospective remedies and compulsory third-party adjudication. Why then do other regimes, like the investment regime, or the ICJ, insist on retroactive remedies? Is the WTO record so good, or is it an impressionistic account that we often encounter in literature?

Let us start by stating that it is difficult to establish the compliance record at the WTO level. Compliance can occur for many reasons, such as political economy (use GATT as an excuse), side payments (promise to vote for the complying party in another forum), reputation costs (for those who care), credibility of the threat in case of noncompliance, etc. Many of them are totally uninteresting for our discussion. The issue is whether the WTO system itself induces compliance and not whether for reasons unrelated to it compliance has occurred. If compliance occurs for reasons exogenous to the WTO contract, then one can hardly attribute compliance to the efficiency of the WTO regime.

Enter another complication. Very often the rationale for complying is a question of private information. Only the defendant itself might know what deal has been sealed behind closed doors. The incentive of the defendant should be to act opportunistically

---

[ggggg] The analysis by Bernheim and Whinston (1990) is certainly relevant here.

[hhhhh] Bagwell (2008) and Bagwell et al. (2008) have advanced "imaginative" proposals to address asymmetric bargaining power (tradable remedies), which nonetheless have not been espoused by the WTO Membership. Some developing countries have advanced proposals to adopt remedies delinked from a prior damages quantification, such as the impossibility to bring a dispute unless the complainant has first implemented all prior rulings against it. At the moment of writing, it is almost utopian to suggest that similar proposals have any chance of being endorsed by the WTO Membership.

and not reveal the truth. Does not the defendant look nicer in the eyes of the WTO membership when publicly stating "it is my duty to comply," than when it states "I could not afford the political cost of taming my domestic monopolist, thank WTO procedures for allowing me to do so," or "it is my in my public interest to accept that one producer loses money if this is necessary for me to be member of the UN Security Council?" This is classic prisoner's dilemma. Because of private information and the incentive to behave opportunistically, a comprehensive study regarding compliance in the WTO is a quixotic test. WTO Members have often little incentive to disclose information regarding details of negotiated settlements, and if they do, then they would rather substitute WTO loyalism for opportunistic behavior.[iiiii]

The compliance record looks good, if we make some assumptions. If we discard the rationale for compliance; if we assume that cases that have not been reintroduced should be accepted as cases where compliance has occurred; if we assume that panel/AB outcomes are relevant only for their addressees, in the sense that condemning zeroing in a dispute between the United States and the EU does not mean anything for the same dispute between say Japan and Korea. One might argue though, that with all the "ifs and buts" mentioned so far, we have probably thrown away the baby along with the bathwater.

Is it so though? If the system did not promote compliance, if it did not work to their satisfaction, that is, why use it in the first place? If "compensation" for complainants when addressing an illegality is suboptimal, then they must be assured that they will profit from similar suboptimal payments when they are defending their measures.[iiiii] "Reciprocal balance going forward" is the type of compliance that gets the vote of the WTO membership. The fact that we observe no forum diversion, as we discuss in what now follows is a string argument supporting this conclusion.

5.3 No Forum Diversion

The WTO has already entertained more than 500 disputes in its 20-year life. This is an impressive number by any reasonable benchmark. There is no other state-to-state court that can point to a comparable record.

For the purposes of our discussion, what matters is of course litigation behavior by WTO members only. Private parties' litigation behavior is of no concern, since private parties do not have to respect Article 23.2 of DSU, the obligation on WTO members to submit their disputes exclusively to the WTO forum. We do not care about behavior of private parties when litigating nonWTO disputes before investment fora and invoke

---

[iiiii] Collins-Williams and Wolfe (2010) make a persuasive case why incentives drive the quantity and quality of notifications.

[iiiii] An interesting question to explore would be whether the system of prospective remedies promotes the commission of illegalities, although the counterfactual would be very difficult to establish.

WTO law to support their claims either. There is ample evidence that WTO law is discussed in various investment tribunals, where private agents submit their investment claims against states. It is there that they routinely invoke WTO law.[kkkk] Private agents nonetheless do not have to observe Article 23.2 of DSU. Our inquiry here is exhausted in instances where WTO members have litigated disputes coming under the ambit of the WTO. The question we ask is whether, when doing that, they have litigated exclusively before the WTO or not.

Horn et al. (2005) mention one instance where two WTO members resolved a dispute through bilateral consultations without having had recourse to Article 4 of DSU first. They did not submit to a different forum though. There is one more known case that concerns a dispute about WTO law, where the two WTO members did not have recourse to the DSU procedures. A series of bananas exporting countries requested from the WTO DG to appoint arbitrators to decide on their dispute with the EU, noting that they did not want the process to be considered "mediation" under Article 5 of DSU.[lllll] In this case nonetheless, the "link" to the WTO remained strong.

The number of disputes litigated since 1995 is not equally distributed in the two decades. 324 Disputes were submitted the first 10 years (that is, almost 66% of all disputes submitted so far), whereas 177 only ever since.[mmmmm] There are various reasons ranging from the backlog of disputes to the will to "test" the new regime that probably explain the surge of disputes in the first 10 years.

Mavroidis and Sapir (2015) submit that the rise in the number of PTAs could be one additional reason why the number of disputes has dropped, since PTA partners tend to litigate less between them, and very often not at all. Although the number of disputes has been decreasing, the WTO continues to be a very popular state-to-state court by any reasonable benchmark, as in their view there is correlation (if not cause and effect) between reduced litigation before the WTO and the rise in the number of PTAs.

Obligations included in PTAs can be distinguished between "WTO+" and "WTOx" depending on whether they concern an issue that comes under the WTO mandate or not.[nnnnn] The latter term aims to capture trade areas that are not covered by the current WTO mandate. Arguably, litigating similar disputes before a nonWTO forum would not amount to a violation of the obligation to submit disputes before the WTO.

[kkkk]   Chevry (2015).

[lllll]   WTO Doc. WT/L/616 of Aug. 1, 2005. The DG appointed two AB members and the former Canadian ambassador to arbitrate this dispute.

[mmmmm]   Horn et al. (2011) include statistics regarding the identity of parties, the frequency of appearance, the agreements invoked, the identity of panelists, etc. Dividing the life cycle of the WTO into four 5 year periods since 1995, Mavroidis and Sapir (2015) report that 187 disputes were lodged the first 5 years, 137 then, 78, and 84 in the final 5 years (up to Dec. 2014). Fifteen more disputes have been lodged since than until now (Jan. 2016).

[nnnnn]   Horn et al. (2010b).

Consequently, we should be limiting our inquiry into WTO+ obligations. An appropriate illustration would be when, for example, Home and Foreign, WTO Members impose say a 10% tariff on widgets and agree to impose a 1% tariff when trading widgets between them. The classification between WTO+ and WTOx nonetheless can be tricky, and we propose to see how dispute adjudication in PTA fora in general looks like in order to respond to the question whether forum diversion has occurred.

There are various studies reviewing dispute adjudication at the PTA level and all point to the same result: no or little forum diversion has occurred. According to Chase et al. (2013), dispute settlement mechanisms in PTAs fall in three categories: political/diplomatic, quasi-judicial, and judicial. Political or diplomatic mechanisms are those that have no dispute settlement provisions at all that provide exclusively for negotiated settlement among the parties or that provide for referral of a dispute to a third-party adjudicator but with the PTA members having a right to veto such referral. By contrast, both quasi-judicial and judicial systems involve decisions by an adjudicating body, but only the latter implies the existence of a permanent adjudicating body such as the WTO's DSB. Two-thirds of the PTAs notified to the WTO until 2012 belonged to the quasi-judicial category. Koremenos (2007) reports similar results. These studies already establish that only a small minority of PTAs has full-fledged adjudication regimes. By construction thus of dispute settlement procedures under PTAs, forum diversion cannot be substantive.

Li and Qiu (2014) review litigation practice for a sample of over 100 PTAs. They picked randomly their sample without paying attention to the attributes of the PTA litigation regime, eg, whether it is judicial, quasi-judicial, or political/diplomatic. In fact, they do not even classify their sampled PTAs in this way. Their basic conclusion is that only a handful of disputes have been raised before PTA fora when participants are also WTO members.

Mavroidis and Sapir (2015) examine all PTAs signed by EU and United States since 1992. We have established supra that the EU and the United States are the two very active litigating parties in the WTO, the most active indeed. Their behavior thus is of utmost interest to this study. All but one of the PTAs they have signed contain a quasi-judicial dispute settlement mechanism. The outlier is the EU-Norway PTA signed on Jul. 1, 1973, which contains no dispute settlement regime at all. Norway, though, can access the EFTA (European Free Trade Association) Court, which is a "binding" regime that handles, inter alia, disputes between EEA (European Economic Area) members, which include both Norway and the EU. Their data support the view that the EU and the US litigate, in general, less with their PTA partners, and when they do so, they do not divert their litigation to a nonWTO forum. EU, for example, has litigated only on a few instances with Norway (whereas, in the WTO-era, it had litigated 22 times with all its PTA partners before it had signed a PTA with them). United States has litigated 35 times with its NAFTA partners and once with Korea. Only 9/35 cases concern new disputes though since in the remaining 26 cases the subject matter of the WTO dispute had been brought to the negotiating table of NAFTA but no solution could be reached. And even this number (9) is further reduced since some of these cases concern issues where there is no corresponding provision in the WTO contract, and/or areas where private parties have standing.

Under the circumstances it seems fair to conclude that we have not been experiencing forum diversion. The rise of PTAs coincides with (and probably causes) a reduction of intra-PTA disputes. The accounts by negotiators cited in Boskin (2014) support the view that many of the disputes that might arise will be resolved in amicable manner, without recourse to formal channels. PTAs (or at the very least, some of them) are, in essence, "relational" contracts.

The prediction of Mavroidis and Sapir (2015) for TTIP is that if past EU and US behavior serves as benchmark, we should be expecting a reduction in the number of disputes before the transatlantic partners both before the WTO, as well as before the PTA forum. In similar vein, Michael Wilson, key Canadian negotiator of NAFTA and CUSFTA, is quoted stating that one reason explaining recourse to integration of North American market was the desire to reduce trade disputes.[ooooo]

5.4 Constraining Punishment

We conclude from the discussion earlier that the WTO emerges as the exclusive forum for adjudicating disputes arising from the operation of the WTO contract, the lack of specific reciprocity notwithstanding. Was not the United States though, worrying exactly about suboptimal compensation when having recourse to Section 301? What has changed then? Why is recourse to unilateral measures unheard of in today's world?

One thing has changed. Punishment is constrained for all. Ethier (2006) has added that, in the face of uncertainty regarding the identity of culprits, the common incentive of all WTO members is to opt for weaker remedies.

By being obliged to submit exclusively to the WTO, trading nations have agreed to abandon being the judge of their own cause and to abide by whatever third-party adjudication will decide. In the altar of compulsory third-party adjudication, they were prepared to collectively sacrifice some of the trade concessions they extracted from their partners. Constraining punishment emerges as the single most important contribution of the WTO dispute settlement system. Practice is thus, in line with the negotiating intent that we discussed in Section 2.

Constraining punishment is the quintessential, but of course, not the only feature of the regime. The WTO judge, as we have argued earlier, "completes" the contract by interpreting open-ended terms, and making the resolution of future disputes (more)

[ooooo] Quoted in Boskin (2014) at p. 9. It is of course, a very demanding exercise to ask what are the causes of reduction of disputes between PTA partners. Negotiations aiming to reduce the amount of contentious issues between partners definitely go some way toward reducing friction and the ensuing disputes.

predictable. This is especially the case, because, as of the advent of the WTO, the AB has been introduced. The AB is by construction limited to interpretation of legal issues, and legal issues cut across disputes. There are reasons to doubt that this function was equally important to that of curbing unilateral punishment. The AB was not heavily negotiated, it was more of an afterthought. For some, it was a necessary counter-balance to compulsory third-party adjudication, some sort of insurance policy that judicial errors (of whatever type) will be avoided, or at least reduced. The fact that only one article of the DSU is dedicated to the highest organ of dispute adjudication is proof enough that this has indeed been the case.[PPPPP] Furthermore, it is very debatable whether it does "complete" the contract in the sense that theorists understand this function. Numerous reports prepared by the reporters of the American Law Institute (ALI), the only forum that has been scrutinizing the output of the AB, point to unjustified inconsistencies across judgments, abandoned interpretative efforts, etc. If at all, "completion" has occurred in some areas, while confusion still reigns in others.[qqqqq]

The framers of the DSU paid little time in designing the entities that would adjudicate, but precious time in putting in place a system of compulsory third-party adjudication.

6. SECTION 301: A FOE AND A FRIEND OF MULTILATERALISM

The main conclusion of this paper is what mattered most to the negotiators of the Uruguay round was to establish a spirit of cooperation and restrain trade wars. Section 301 threats were looming large, and the common effort was to introduce a regime that would put an end to unilateral enforcement. The possibility to block access to justice and/or retaliation and the statutory deadlines agreed, along with the introduction of services trade and protection of intellectual property rights, were the quid pro quo for United States to stop unilateral enforcement. In a way thus Section 301 paved the way to multilateral dispute adjudication.

Subsequent practice shows that WTO members continue to submit their disputes to the WTO and nowhere else. They live happily in a world of diffuse reciprocity, where they receive less than what they had bargained for but are not subjected anymore to unilateralism. They take some comfort in the fact that everybody more or less receives less than it has bargained for.

[PPPPP] Van den Bossche (2006) provides ample evidence to this effect.

[qqqqq] And as Maggi and Staiger (2011) explain, some litigation might be happening simply because of past failures and/or inconsistencies of panels and the AB. Compare Howse (2009), who advances a series of recommendations on how case law can lead to consistent jurisprudence.

Bagwell and Staiger (2002) and Ethier (2004) got it right when stating that the purpose of WTO dispute settlement system was to curb unilateralism. In Ethier's (2004) words:

is not to facilitate punishment, it is to constrain it.

The discussion and empirical analysis in this paper subscribes to this conclusion.

ANNEXES

Annex I Duration of Process

	Statutory (days)	Actual (days)
Consultations	60	164
Panel	180–270	445
AB	60–90	91
Compliance panel	90	253
Compliance AB	60–90	88

Annex II Recourse to Article 22 of the DSU (Jan. 1, 1995–Jan. 2, 2016)

Name of dispute	Complainant	Defendant	Retaliation level
EC-Bananas III (Ecuador)	Ecuador	EU	$201.6 mio/year
EC-Bananas III (United States)	United States	EU	$191.4 mio/year
EC-Hormones (Canada)	Canada	EU	$11.3 mio/year
EC-Hormones (United States)	United States	EU	$116.9 mio/year
Brazil-Aircraft (Canada)	Canada	Brazil	$344.2 mio/year
Canada-Aircraft (Brazil)	Brazil	Canada	$247.797 mio/year
US-FSC (EC)	EU	United States	$4.043 mio/year
US-1916 Act (EC)	EU	United States	Trade effect coefficient
US-Offset Act (Brazil et al.)	Brazil et al.	United States	Trade effect coefficient
US-Gambling (Antigua)	Antigua	United States	$21.2 mio/year

Name of dispute	Complainant	Defendant	Retaliation level
US-Upland Cotton (Brazil)	Brazil	United States	$147.3 mio/year
US-COOL (Canada)	Canada	United States	$1,054,729 mio/year
US-COOL (Mexico)	Mexico	United States	$227,758 mio/year

ACKNOWLEDGMENTS

For many helpful discussions on this issue, I am indebted to Kym Anderson, Kyle W. Bagwell, Jagdish Bhagwati, Carlo-Maria Cantore, Bill Davey, Bill Ethier, Bernard M. Hoekman, Doug Irwin, Mark Koulen, Keith Maskus, Damien J. Neven, Luca Rubini, Kamal Saggi, André Sapir, Robert W. Staiger, Hannu Wager, L. Alan Winters, Mark Wu, and participants at a conference organized at Dartmouth, Jun. 3–5, 2015. I would like to thank especially Kyle Bagwell, Chad P. Bown, and Robert W. Staiger for detailed comments and substantive guidance to improve previous drafts, as well as Henrik Horn af Rantzien, with whom I have worked in this area for a long time.

REFERENCES

Anderson, K., 2002. Peculiarities of retaliation in WTO dispute settlement system. World Trade Rev. 1, 123–134.

Bagwell, K.W., 2008. Remedies in the WTO: an economics perspective. In: Janow, M.E., Donaldson, V., Yanovich, A. (Eds.), The WTO: Governance, Dispute Settlement and Developing Countries. Juris Publishing, New York City, NY, pp. 733–770.

Bagwell, K.W., Staiger, R.W., 2002. The Economics of the World Trading System. MIT Press, Cambridge, MA.

Bagwell, K.W., Mavroidis, P.C., Staiger, R.W., 2002. It's a question of market access. Am. J. Int. Law 96, 56–76.

Bagwell, K.W., Mavroidis, P.C., Staiger, R.W., 2005. The case for tradable remedies in WTO dispute settlement system. In: Evenett, S.J., Hoekman, B.M. (Eds.), Economic Development & Multilateral Trade Cooperation. Palgrave MacMillan/The World Bank, Washington, DC, pp. 395–414.

Bagwell, K.W., Mavroidis, P.C., Staiger, R.W., 2008. Auctioning countermeasures in the WTO. J. Int. Econ. 73, 309–332.

Bernheim, D.B., Whinston, M., 1990. Multimarket contract and collusive behavior. RAND J. Econ. 21, 1–26.

Beshkar, M., 2010. Optimal remedies in international trade agreements. Eur. Econ. Rev. 54, 455–466.

Bhagwati, J., Patrick, H. (Eds.), 1990. Aggressive Unilateralism: America's 301 Trade Policy and the World Trading System. University of Michigan Press, Ann Arbor, MI.

Blonigen, B.A., Bown, C.P., 2003. Antidumping and retaliation threats. J. Int. Econ. 60, 249–273.

Boskin, M.J. (Ed.), 2014. NAFTA at 20, The North American Free Trade Agreement's Achievements and Challenges. The Hoover Institution Press, Stanford, CA.

Bown, C.P., 2002. The economics of trade disputes, the GATT's article XXIII, and the WTO's dispute settlement understanding. Econ. Polit. 14, 283–323.

Bown, C.P., 2004. On the economic success of the GATT/WTO dispute settlement. Rev. Econ. Stat. 86, 811–823.

Bown, C.P., 2005. Participation in WTO dispute settlement system: complainants, interested parties, and free riders. World Econ. Rev. 12, 287–310.

Bown, C.P., Reynolds, K.M., 2015. Trade Agreements and Enforcement: Evidence from WTO Dispute Settlement. CEPR Discussion Paper No DP10571, CEPR, London, UK.

Bowsky, W.M., 1981. A Medieval Italian Commune: Sienna Under the Nine, 1287–1355. University of California Press, Berkeley, CA.

Busch, M., Reinhardt, E., 2002. Bargaining in the shadow of law: early settlements in GATT/WTO disputes. Fordham Int. Law J. 24, 158–172.

Charnovitz, S., 2009. Enforcement of WTO judgments. Yale J. Int. Law 34, 558–566.

Chase, C., Crawford, J.-A., Ugaz, P., Yanovich, A., 2013. Mapping of Dispute Settlement Mechanisms in Regional Trade Agreements, Innovative or Variations of a Theme? WTO Discussion Paper ERSD-2013-07, The WTO, Geneva, Switzerland.

Chevry, J., 2015. Convergence in Practice: Mapping the Use of Trade Norms in Investment Arbitration. Mimeo, EUI, Florence, Italy.

Collins-Williams, T., Wolfe, R., 2010. Transparency as trade policy tool: the WTO's cloudy windows. World Trade Rev. 9, 551–581.

Dam, K.W., 1970. The General Agreement on Tariffs and Trade: Law and International Economic Organization. The University of Chicago Press, Chicago, IL.

Davey, W.J., 2007. Evaluating WTO dispute settlement: what results have been achieved through consultations and implementation of panel reports? In: Taniguchi, Y., Yanovich, A., Bohanes, J. (Eds.), The WTO in the 21st Century: Dispute Settlement, Negotiations, and Regionalism. Cambridge University Press, Cambridge, UK, pp. 98–140.

Ehring, L., 2014. The European community's experience and practice in suspending WTO obligations. In: Bown, C., Pauwelyn, J. (Eds.), The Law, Economics and Politics of Retaliation in WTO Disputes. Cambridge University Press, Cambridge, UK, pp. 244–266.

Ethier, W.J., 2004. Intellectual property and dispute settlement in the WTO. J. Int. Econ. Law 7, 449–458.

Ethier, W.J., 2006. Punishments and dispute settlement in trade agreements. The equivalent withdrawal of concessions. Keio Econ. Stud. 42, 1–23.

Grossman, G.M., Mavroidis, P.C., 2003. Would've or should've? Impaired benefits due to copyright infringement. US–Section 110 (5), In: Horn, H., Mavroidis, P.C. (Eds.), The WTO Case Law, The American Law Institute Reporters' Studies. Cambridge University Press, Cambridge, UK, pp. 294–314. 2007.

Guth, E., 2012. The end of the bananas saga. J. World Trade 46, 1–32.

Hoekman, B.M., Mavroidis, P.C., 2000. WTO dispute settlement, transparency and surveillance. World Econ. 23, 527–542.

Hoekman, B.M., Mavroidis, P.C., 2014. Trade retaliation, EU jurisprudence, and the law and economics of 'taking one for the team'. Eur. Law J. 20, 317–331.

Horn, H., Mavroidis, P.C., 2007. International trade: dispute settlement. In: Guzman, A., Sykes, A.O. (Eds.), Handbook on International Trade. Edward Elgar, Cheltenham, UK, pp. 177–210.

Horn, H., Mavroidis, P.C., Nordstrøm, H., 2005. Is the use of the WTO dispute settlement system biased? In: Mavroidis, P.C., Sykes, A.O. (Eds.), The WTO and International Trade Law Dispute Settlement. Edward Elgar, Cheltenham, UK, pp. 454–486.

Horn, H., Maggi, G., Staiger, R.W., 2010a. Trade agreements as endogenously incomplete contracts. Am. Econ. Rev. 100, 394–419.

Horn, H., Mavroidis, P.C., Sapir, A., 2010b. Beyond the WTO? An anatomy of the US and EU preferential trade agreements. World Econ. 33, 1565–1588.

Horn, H., Johannesson, L., Mavroidis, P.C., 2011. The WTO dispute settlement system (1995–2010): some descriptive statistics. J. World Trade 45, 1107–1138.

Howse, R., 2009. Moving the WTO forward—one case at a time. Cornell J. Int. Law 42, 223–251.

Hudec, R.E., 1972. GATT or GABB? The future design of the general agreement on tariffs and trade. Yale Law J. 80, 1299–1386.

Hudec, R.E., 1993. Enforcing International Trade Law. Butterworths, London, UK.

Huerta-Goldman, J., 2009. Mexico in the WTO and NAFTA, Litigating International Trade Disputes. Kluwer Publishing, Amsterdam, The Netherlands.

Irwin, D.A., Mavroidis, P.C., Sykes, A.O., 2008. The Genesis of the GATT. Cambridge University Press, Cambridge, MA.

Jackson, J.H., 1969. World Trade and the Law of the GATT. Bobbs-Merrill, Indianapolis, IN.

Jackson, J.H., 1987. United States. In: Jacobs, F.G., Roberts, S. (Eds.), The Effect of Treaties in Domestic Law. Sweet & Maxwell, London, UK, pp. 141–169.

Jackson, J.H., 2004. International law status of WTO dispute settlement reports: obligation to comply or option to "buy out"? Am. J. Int. Law 98, 109–125.

Johannesson, L., Mavroidis, P.C., 2015. Black cat, white cat: the identity of WTO judges. J. World Trade 49, 685–698.

Keohane, R., 1986. Reciprocity in international relations. Int. Org. 40, 1–27.

Koremenos, B., 2007. If only half of international agreements have dispute resolution provisions, which half needs explaining? J. Legal Stud. 36, 189–221.

Li, T., Qiu, L.D., 2014. Free Trade Agreements and Trade Disputes. Mimeo, The University of Hong Kong, Hong Kong, China.

Maggi, G., Staiger, R.W., 2011. The role of dispute settlement procedures in international trade agreements. Quart. J. Econ. 128, 1837–1893.

Maggi, G., Staiger, R.W., 2015. Optimal design of trade agreements in the presence of renegotiation. Am. Econ. J. Microecon. 7, 109–143.

Mavroidis, P.C., 1993. Government procurement agreement; the Trondheim case: the remedies issue. Aussenwirtschaft 48, 77–94.

Mavroidis, P.C., 2015. The Regulation of International Trade. MIT Press, Cambridge, MA.

Mavroidis, P.C., Sapir, A., 2015. Dial PTAs for peace: the influence of preferential trade agreements on litigation between trading partners. J. World Trade 43, 351–374.

Mavroidis, P.C., Wolfe, R., 2015. From sunshine to a common agent: the evolving understanding of transparency in the WTO. Brown J. World Affairs 21, 117–129.

Meng, W.P., 1990. The hormones conflict between the EEC and the United States within the context of GATT. Michigan J. Int. Law 11, 819–839.

Nordstrøm, H., Shaffer, G., 2008. Access to justice in the World Trade Organization: a case for a small claims procedure? World Trade Rev. 7, 587–640.

Paemen, H., Bentsch, A., 1995. From the GATT to the WTO: The European Community in the Uruguay Round. Leuven University Press, Leuven, Belgium.

Palmeter, D.N., Mavroidis, P.C., Meagher, N., 2016. Dispute Settlement in the WTO, Practice and Procedure, third ed. Cambridge University Press, Cambridge, UK.

Pauwelyn, J., 2003. Conflict of Norms in Public International Law. Cambridge University Press, Cambridge, UK.

Petersmann, E.-U., 1993. International competition rules for the GATT-MTO world trade and legal system. J. World Trade 27, 35–86.

Schelling, T., 1960. The Strategy of Conflict. Harvard University Press, Cambridge, MA.

Schwarz, W., Sykes, A.O., 2002. The economic structure of renegotiation and dispute resolution in the WTO/GATT system. J. Legal Stud. 31, 179–204.

Stewart, T.P., Callahan, C.J., 1998. Dispute settlement mechanisms. In: Stewart, T.P. (Ed.), The Uruguay Round: A Negotiating History. Kluwer, Deventer, Boston, pp. 2663–2878.

Sykes, A.O., 2012. The dispute settlement mechanism: ensuring compliance? In: Narlikar, A., Daunton, M., Stern, R.M. (Eds.), The Oxford Handbook of the WTO. Oxford University Press, Oxford, UK, pp. 560–586.

Trachtman, J.L., 2007. The WTO cathedral. Stanford J. Int. Law 43, 127–173.

Trebilcock, M., Howse, R., 2013. Regulation of Trade. Routledge, London, UK.

Van den Bossche, P.L.H., 2006. From afterthought to centrepiece: the WTO appellate body and its rise to prominence in the world trading system. In: Sacerdoti, G., Yanovic, A., Bohanes, J. (Eds.), The WTO at Ten. Cambridge University Press, Cambridge, UK, pp. 289–325.

Wills, G., 2002. James Madison. Times Books, Henry Holt and Company, New York City, NY.

Wu, M., 2015. Rethinking the temporary breach puzzle in international trade law: a window in the future of trade conflicts. Yale J. Int. Law 40, 97–146.

CHAPTER 7

The Purpose of Trade Agreements

G.M. Grossman[1]
[1]Princeton University, Princeton, NJ, United States

Contents

Abstract

In this chapter, I review the literature on governments' motivations for negotiating and joining international trade agreements. I discuss both normative explanations for trade agreements and explanations based on political-economy concerns. Most of the chapter focuses on the purpose of multilateral agreements, but I do discuss briefly the reasons we might see governments forming preferential or regional trade agreements that exclude some countries.

Keywords

Trade agreements, Trade pacts, International cooperation, Multilateralism, Regionalism

JEL Classification:

F13, F53, K33

Handbook of Commercial Policy, Volume 1A
ISSN 2214-3122, http://dx.doi.org/10.1016/bs.hescop.2016.04.016

1. INTRODUCTION

Britain and France inked the first modern trade agreement on January 23, 1860. The so-called Cobden-Chevalier Treaty promised that France would eliminate all import prohibitions on British manufactured goods while capping most duties at 30% (25% after 1865). Britain in turn agreed to remove import barriers entirely from all but 48 French commodities while reducing dramatically its tariffs on French wine and brandy (Ashley, 1904). Notably, each country promised to grant the other most-favored-nation (MFN) consideration with regard to any tariff concessions it might subsequently grant to other trading partners. There followed a veritable explosion of *bilateral* trade pacts, with an additional 56 treaties having been signed within 15 years. By 1875, virtually all of Europe was party to a low-tariff zone by dint of a web of agreements that included the linchpin MFN clause.

When the General Agreement on Tariffs and Trade (GATT) went into effect on January 1, 1948, it marked the first of a sequence of *multilateral* trade agreements. The GATT incorporated more than 45,000 tariff concessions by its original 23 signatories, while also providing a broader framework for regulating international trade. Seven subsequent "rounds" of negotiations by these and additional participants led to innumerable further tariff cuts and to the introduction of rules governing various nontariff barriers to trade. The Uruguay Round, which was signed by 123 "contracting parties" and took effect on January 1, 1995, created the World Trade Organization (WTO), while also extending trade rules to many services, harmonizing treatment of intellectual property, and establishing procedures for dispute settlement. By November 30, 2015, the WTO had grown to include 162 members that together conduct more than 96% of world trade.[a] Meanwhile, the multilateral agreement lives side-by-side with 267 different bilateral and regional trade agreements that the WTO reported to be in effect as of February 1, 2016.[b]

This chapter reviews the economics literature that poses the question, why do countries negotiate and accede to international trade agreements? The chapter focuses mostly on the motivation for multilateral agreements, in order to minimize overlap with Chapter 14 by Limão (2016) on preferential agreements. However, Section 5 does cover some literature that addresses the incentives countries have to negotiate bilateral or regional agreements alongside (or instead of) multilateral agreements in a many-country world. Also, this chapter focuses on the broad *purpose* of trade agreements, leaving discussion of their design for Chapter 8 by Bagwell and Staiger (2016).[c] I do consider both

---

[a] Current members are listed in http://www.wto.org/english/thewto_e/whatis_e/tif_e/org6_e.htm. Trade coverage of WTO members is reported in http://www.wto.org/english/thewto_e/acc_e/cbt_course_e/c1s1p1_e.htm.

[b] See http://www.wto.org/english/tratop_e/region_e/region_e.htm.

[c] This chapter covers some of the same ground as the excellent survey by Maggi (2014) in the *Handbook of International Economics*, vol. 4.

the incentives that large countries have to create trade pacts *de novo* and the incentives that small countries have to sign existing agreements.

The chapter is organized as follows. Section 2 discusses research that sees trade agreements as addressing international externalities that arise in competitive economic environments. It includes the case of both welfare-maximizing governments and politically motivated governments, both in situations with well-functioning markets and with distorted markets. One controversy in the literature concerns whether the sole motivation for trade agreements in competitive markets is to eliminate the temptation governments have to manipulate their terms of trade. I discuss this debate, concluding that it is more a matter of semantics than substance. In Section 3, I review the literature that identifies the different types of international externalities that can arise in imperfectly competitive market environments. These externalities reflect governments' incentives to influence firm location, to shift or extract profits away from foreign monopolists or oligopolists, or to affect imperfect contracting in international outsourcing relationships. I briefly discuss agreements to protect intellectual property that are motivated by externalities in the international innovation process.

In Section 4, I turn to an alternative purpose that has been suggested for trade agreements, namely to aid governments in committing not to intervene in favor of domestic special interests. The commitment motive arises when optimal policies are not time consistent; that is, when governments know they would be tempted to adjust policies *ex post* away from the levels that they prefer *ex ante*. I argue that commitment is unlikely to be the reason that two governments will sit down to negotiate a trade agreement, but that it might very well explain why some countries accede to existing agreements.

Finally, in Section 5, I turn from the purpose of multilateral agreements to that of regional and bilateral agreements. In this section I discuss only research that bears on the motivation that governments have to negotiate preferential agreements in addition to—or instead of—multilateral agreements, in a many-country world. Preferential agreements may serve to promote allocative efficiency among signatories, to improve members' terms of trade vis-à-vis nonmembers, to transfer rents to special interests via trade diversion, or to facilitate a dynamic process of multilateral trade liberalization.

2. INTERNATIONAL EXTERNALITIES FROM UNILATERAL TRADE POLICIES

Trade treaties are a formal expression of intergovernmental cooperation. Governments relinquish their sovereign rights to choose their own trade (and other) policies in exchange for similar concessions by others. Why might a government be willing to compromise its sovereignty? In a word, the answer is *interdependence*. The policies imposed by any government affect the well-being not only of its own citizens, but also of those in other countries. No matter what the objectives of the policy makers—be they benevolent, autocratic, or politically motivated—each has an interest in the choices made by its trading partners. With unilateral policy choices, governments may fail to take into account the impact of their actions on interests abroad. A trade agreement provides a means to internalize these externalities. Of course, to identify the incentives for concluding a treaty, one must begin by identifying the nature of the potential externalities, that is, by predicting the trade policies that would prevail in the absence of cooperation.

2.1 Welfare-Maximizing Policy Makers

Johnson (1953) was the first to analyze the strategic interdependence between countries' tariff-setting decisions. Johnson conceived of tariffs as being the outcome of a static game played by a pair of welfare-maximizing governments and he proceeded to provide an early application of the then-novel concept of a Nash equilibrium.

Suppose initial that there are two countries and two goods. The goods are competitively produced in each country by firms that have access to strictly convex technologies. Suppose further that aggregate welfare in each country can be represented by a strictly quasiconcave function of the country's aggregate consumption bundle. Let t be the *ad valorem* tariff rate imposed by the home country on its import good. Let t^* be the *ad valorem* rate imposed by the foreign country on its respective import good, which of course is the home country's export good. We can solve for the competitive equilibrium as a function of t and t^* and then write $W(t, t^*)$ and $W^*(t, t^*)$ as the resulting aggregate welfare levels in the home and foreign countries, respectively.

Fig. 1 depicts the best-response functions of the two welfare-maximizing policy makers, with t on the horizontal axis and t^* on the vertical axis. The inverted u-shaped curves such as the one labeled WW represent iso-welfare loci for the home country. These curves peak at the tariff rates that maximize $W(t, t^*)$, given the corresponding values of t^*. The peaks generally fall in the positive quadrant, because the

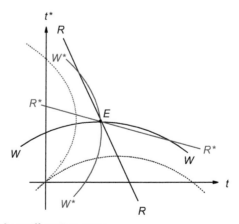

Fig. 1 Nash equilibrium of a tariff-setting game.

Mill-Bickerdike argument for an optimum tariff implies that, for any given foreign policy and economic conditions, home households can gain from a tariff that optimally exploits the country's monopoly power in trade.[d] The curve RR that connects the set of peaks is the home country's best-response function; ie, a function that gives the home country's optimal tariff in response to an arbitrary level of the foreign tariff, t^*. Among any pair of iso-welfare loci for the home country, the curve that lies above the other represents a lower level of home welfare in view of the fact that a departure from the *best* response (a horizontal move to the right or to the left of RR) must result in a welfare loss for this country.

Similarly, the right-parentheses-shaped curves such as W^*W^* represent iso-welfare loci for the foreign country. These curves "peak" in the horizontal direction at the optimal tariffs for the foreign country given the corresponding rates of the home tariff, t. The curve that connects these peaks, R^*R^*, represents the foreign country's best-response function. Among any pair of foreign iso-welfare curves, that to the right represents the lower level of foreign welfare.

As Johnson first noted, a Nash equilibrium occurs at point E, where each government's tariff choice is a best response to that of the other. At this point, neither government can raise aggregate welfare by unilaterally altering its trade policy. The pair of Nash equilibrium tariffs in the Johnson equilibrium are both nonnegative, except possibly in a perverse case such as that described in Footnote d.[e]

Fig. 2 outlines a "lens" to the southwest of point E. At any point in this lens, the aggregate welfare levels in both countries are higher than at point E. In other words, points in this set represent pairs of tariff rates that are Pareto-preferred by the two welfare-maximizing governments to the noncooperative outcome at E. A trade agreement—if one could be negotiated and enforced—that achieves any pair of tariff rates in this lens would be one that both governments prefer to the outcome that occurs without cooperation.

The basis for a trade agreement in this rather simple setting is the negative externality that each government imposes on households in the other country when it imposes its optimal tariff. At point E, a small reduction in the home tariff has virtually no effect on aggregate welfare in the home country, because the optimal tariff just balances on the

---

[d] Actually, Kemp (1967) shows that, for some values of t^*, the best response by the home country might be an import subsidy; ie, $t < 0$. This can arise only if the foreign offer curve is multi-valued, which in turn requires that the home country's import good is sufficiently inferior in the foreign country's preferences. For ease of exposition, I will neglect this rather obscure possibility.

[e] For the tariffs in the Johnson equilibrium to be nonnegative, it is sufficient that demands in each country can be derived from those of a representative agent and both goods are normal (see Bond, 1990). Dixit (1987) points out that there generally exists another Nash equilibrium, one with prohibitive tariffs in both countries. When one country chooses a prohibitive tariff, it is always a best response for the other to do likewise.

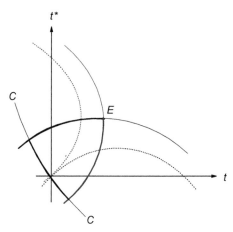

Fig. 2 Efficient agreements.

margin the positive terms-of-trade gain with the negative volume-of-trade loss (see, eg, Dixit, 1985). Any reduction in home welfare generated by a small departure from the best response is second-order small. Meanwhile, a reduction in the home tariff generates a first-order welfare gain for the foreign country inasmuch as it improves that country's terms of trade without generating any distortion of its resource allocation. In other words, each country's optimal tariff is a beggar-thy-neighbor policy that achieves gains for its own citizens (holding constant the other's policy) at the expense of citizens elsewhere and global efficiency. When governments behave unilaterally and noncooperatively, they ignore the harm that their policies impose on citizens outside their borders. This creates the opportunity for mutually beneficial exchange of tariff cuts; points to the southwest of E have approximately the same terms of trade as at E, but higher volumes of trade and a more efficient allocation of the world's resources.

The curve labeled CC in Fig. 2 connects points of tangency between iso-welfare curves of the home and foreign countries. At such points, it is not possible to raise aggregate welfare for one country without reducing it for the other; ie, CC is a locus of Pareto-efficient tariff rates. As Mayer (1981) pointed out, the tariff rates on this curve satisfy

$$(1+t)(1+t^*) = 1, \tag{1}$$

because the relative price of the home import good in the home country is $(1+t)p_w$, where p_w is the "world" relative price of this good, while the relative price of the home import good in the foreign country is $p_w/(1+t^*)$.[f] A necessary and sufficient condition

---

[f] The world price, p_w, is the relative price at a fictitious offshore port where goods are free of all trade taxes. A tariff imposed by the home country raises the internal relative price of this good by a factor $1+t$, whereas a tariff imposed by the foreign country (on the "other" good) reduces the internal relative price there by a factor $1+t^*$.

for global efficiency is that the internal relative prices in the two countries are the same, since this ensures equality worldwide of marginal rates of transformation and marginal rates of substitution.

The figure also shows a portion of this curve in bold. The northwest endpoint of this bold segment corresponds to a pair of tariff rates that yield the home country the same level of aggregate welfare as in the Nash equilibrium at E. The southeast endpoint gives the foreign country the same welfare as at E. Therefore, all points along the bold portion of CC yield a Pareto improvement for the two benevolent governments relative to the noncooperative outcome at E. Mayer (1981) concludes that, with efficient and costless bargaining, the governments should agree to some pair of tariffs along CC that leave each at least as well off as at E. The particulars of the agreement will depend on the bargaining protocol and the countries' relative negotiating proficiency. But, in all cases, both tariff rates are lower under an efficient agreement than at E; in other words, the cooperative agreement entails trade liberalization (or promotion) by both countries.[g] The noncooperative tariffs are both positive in the Nash equilibrium as each country attempts to exploit its monopoly power in beggar-thy-neighbor fashion. When the countries cooperate fully, they will choose either free trade, or else a positive tariff in one and a negative tariff in the other in order to achieve the same allocation of resources as with free trade together with a transfer of government revenue.

Some features of the Johnson (1953) and Mayer (1981) analyses are special to the two-good, two-country setting that they consider. Graaf (1949) observed that, with many goods, the vector of a country's optimal tariffs and export taxes could include negative elements, ie, some goods may be subject to import or export subsidies. This conclusion carries over to the Nash equilibrium of a tariff-setting game, and so an efficient trade agreement need not entail a reduction in all trade tax rates. But Bond (1990) shows that if the foreign offer curve is monotone—such that an increase in price reduces foreign imports on average—and if foreign excess demands can be derived from the preferences of a representative agent for whom all goods are normal, then the optimal trade policy for any country generates nonnegative tariff revenue. Under these conditions, a move to universal free trade (which is always efficient with perfect competition and no market distortions) entails an overall reduction of trade taxes and thus a liberalization of trade. Fukushima and Kim (1989) provide conditions, later relaxed by Turunen-Red and Woodland (1991), under which an equiproportionate reduction in all (specific) trade taxes and subsidies (ie, a radial movement toward zero) must raise global welfare in a world with an arbitrary number of goods and subsidies. Under these conditions,

---

[g] In the figure, the free trade point at the origin generates a Pareto improvement, and all other points of possible agreement involve a positive tariff by one country and an import subsidy by the other. It is possible, however, that one country will fare worse at the free trade point than at E. In such circumstances, a Pareto-improving agreement requires an import subsidy in the other country.

multilateral trade liberalization of this sort shifts the world's utility possibility frontier outward, but international transfers of purchasing power might still be needed to ensure Pareto gains for all countries.

2.2 Why a Formal Agreement?

Johnson assumed that, in the absence of any international treaty, policy makers would set their country's tariffs once and for all at the noncooperative levels identified by the static Nash equilibrium. In reality, of course, trade policy decisions are made repeatedly over time. This observation raises the question of whether an actual agreement is needed to achieve the gains from cooperation, or whether a cooperative outcome might be achieved as an equilibrium (without explicit cooperation) in a repeated tariff-setting game. Dixit (1987) discusses the infinitely repeated tariff game involving a pair of welfare-maximizing governments.

The "folk theorem" of repeated games (see Aumann, 1985) ensures that, if the policy makers' discount rates are sufficiently low, any point that is Pareto preferred to point E can be sustained as a subgame-perfect equilibrium in the infinitely repeated game. Each government understands that it is expected to set a given tariff rate repeatedly, such that the pair (t, t^*) is preferred by each to E. Each government further understands that any deviation by the other should invoke it to retaliate by setting its Nash-equilibrium tariff forever afterward. The anticipated punishment is credible, because if one government is expected to play its Nash equilibrium tariff in every period, the best the other can do is to respond similarly, and an indefinite repetition of the static equilibrium is itself an equilibrium of the infinitely repeated game. With this expected punishment, a government that contemplates a deviation will compare the one-period gain from behaving opportunistically against the sustained loss that results from foregoing the Pareto gains from cooperation forever afterward. With a small enough discount rate, the loss must dominate, and so any opportunistic behavior is deterred.[h]

It follows that, if discount rates are low enough, the points along the bold portion of CC in Fig. 2 can be achieved by tacit cooperation in a repeated, noncooperative game, without the need for a formal treaty. So what role does a treaty play? One might think that a formal agreement is needed to sustain high levels of cooperation (ie, points on or close to CC) in situations where the discount rates are not so low, so that governments would otherwise be tempted to behave opportunistically in order to capture short-run gains. However, this answer is not compelling, because if a given cooperative outcome

---

[h] Bond and Park (2002) show that, if cooperation via repeated play is intended to yield an asymmetric division of surplus relative to the Johnson equilibrium and if the discount rate is not too high, then achieving the Pareto frontier of national welfare levels requires a gradually declining rate of protection in the country that enjoys the lion's share of the gains from cooperation. They offer this observation as an explanation for trade agreements that involve gradual liberalization despite a stationary economic environment.

cannot be sustained by self interest in a repeated game with punishments, it is unclear how a trade agreement would solve the problem. Governments have sovereign rights under international law and there is no higher authority to which they can appeal in case their trade partners behave opportunistically. Rather, a formal international agreement or an international agency can at most threaten poor behavior with (credible) punishments. In this way of thinking, a formal agreement can only achieve those outcomes that are sustainable in an infinitely repeated game.

One role that a formal agreement might play is that of coordination. The infinitely repeated game has many equilibria involving different degrees of cooperation. Any one of them can be sustained as long as both policy makers know what is expected of them and stand ready to punish if the other deviates from its tacitly agreed behavior. How will the governments know and agree upon what behavior is expected of them and what actions constitute deviations that warrant retaliation? After all, there are many tariff rates that are consistent with *some* cooperative behavior along some equilibrium path of the repeated game. And the governments' interests diverge with respect to which of the many equilibria they would like to see played. A formal agreement can be used to achieve a mutual understanding of what is expected, so that misunderstandings do not invoke a return to noncooperative play.

Maggi (1999) explores another potential rationale for a formal institution such as the WTO. His argument explicitly takes into account that multilateral agreements have more than two participants. Maggi argues that an institution such as the WTO can play an informational role by verifying violations of the agreement and by informing third countries when they have occurred. By sharing information about deviations that take place in particular bilateral relationships, the organization can facilitate multilateral punishments for opportunistic behavior that collectively offer greater deterrence than bilateral punishments. Maggi has in mind policy deviations that can be observed directly only by the injured parties (eg, an exporter knows when its market access has been restricted) but not by uninvolved, third parties. As he notes, import tariffs are sufficiently transparent that presumably rate hikes can be observed outside the particular relationship. But other forms of nontariff barriers to trade are more subtle and more difficult for third countries to perceive.

Let us compare the cooperation that can be achieved when a country can observe only the barriers imposed on its own exports with the cooperation that can be achieved when an institution such as the WTO publicizes to all members any violation of the agreement. Consider a stylized trading environment with three countries in which each pair of countries exchanges two goods that are neither produced nor consumed in the third country. In this setting, no country is directly harmed by opportunistic behavior on the part of its trade partners in its bilateral relations with the third country. Nevertheless, in some circumstances, every country can benefit from an agreement that calls for multilateral punishment for any deviation. Such punishments would prescribe reversion to Nash equilibrium tariffs in bilateral relations with the violating country not only by the country that is directly harmed by its actions, but also by the third country.

The key consideration for whether multilateral punishments facilitate greater cooperation than do bilateral punishments alone is the existence of imbalances of power in the bilateral trading relationships. Maggi shows this point by first examining a case in which all countries are symmetric and each has balanced trade with both of its trading partners. In this case, multilateral punishments are more severe than bilateral punishments, but the temptation to behave opportunistically also is greater. The set of outcomes that can be sustained by multilateral punishments is the same as that with bilateral punishments. On the other hand, if each of the symmetric countries is a net exporter in one of its bilateral relationships and a net importer in the other and if each can apply import tariffs but not export taxes, then each country will be more powerful than its partner in the relationship in which it imports. The greater power reflects the fact that a net importer in a given bilateral relationship stands to lose less from a reversion to Nash equilibrium tariffs than does the net exporter. Then, a regime that publicizes violations and calls for punishments by third parties is more effective in deterring opportunistic behavior than one that entails punishments by only directly injured parties. As Maggi notes, the WTO rules as currently construed do not allow for explicit third-party punishments, but it is conceivable that such punishments occur implicitly by a loss of goodwill. In any case, the paper shows that a multilateral institution that monitors trade behaviors and publicizes violations *could* play a role in sustaining greater cooperation and freer trade.[i]

2.3 Trade Agreements among Politically Minded Governments

When welfare-maximizing governments can act opportunistically in an effort to improve their country's terms of trade, the resulting international externalities open the potential for mutually advantageous trade agreements. But governments' trade policies seem to be motivated as much or more by distributional concerns as by concerns about aggregate welfare. The assumption that governments maximize aggregate welfare is convenient but rather unrealistic in a world with asymmetrically informed voters and with campaign spending funded by contributions from special interest groups. Policy makers who are interested in their own political success might be tempted to choose protectionist policies not (or not only) to manipulate the terms of trade, but rather (or also) to redistribute income to swing voters in the electorate or to groups that offer campaign support. With perhaps limited interest in aggregate welfare, would these politicians be willing to

---

[i] Park (2011) illustrates another potential role of a formal organization such as the WTO in a world with imperfectly observed trade barriers. In his model, a third party can publicize private signals and thereby initiate a punishment phase after a violation of the agreement. This enhances the cooperation that can be achieved in repeated play.

negotiate with foreign counterparts? By doing so, wouldn't they curtail their own use of a valuable instrument for currying political favor?

These questions cry out for a political-economic theory of trade agreements. Hillman and Moser (1995) provided a first pass at such a theory (see also Hillman et al., 1995). They considered a model with two countries, two goods, and two sector-specific factors of production, one that derives income only from a country's import-competing industry and the other that derives income only from the country's export industry. The governments have objective functions that are expressed in reduced form; each government derives "political support" from the specific factors in its own polity, with overall support an increasing but concave function of support from each group. The support, in turn, reflects the real income of a group of specific factor owners. In short, they posit government objective functions $G(I_x, I_y)$ and $G^*\left(I_x^*, I_y^*\right)$ for the home and foreign governments, where I_j and I_j^* are the real incomes of the specific factors used to produce good j in the home and foreign countries, for $j = x, y$. The first partials of G and G^* are assumed positive while the second partials are assumed negative. Each government can set the level of a single policy variable, t or t^* respectively, which is the tariff levied on its own imports. Hillman and Moser rule out exports subsidies with casual reference to countervailing duty laws that would neutralize their effects; however, they offer no explanation for why export subsidies are subject to countervail but policy makers are free to choose import tariffs without institutional constraints.

From here, the story proceeds much as in Johnson (1953) and Mayer (1981). In the absence of an agreement, each government sets its tariff to maximize its political support taking the other government's policy choice as given. The noncooperative outcome is the Nash equilibrium pair of tariffs, much like in Fig. 1. The home tariff raises the real income of the specific factor in the home import-competing industry at the expense of the real income of the specific factor in the home export industry. Each government's choice balances the marginal effects on its own political support, but neglects entirely the adverse effect that the tariff has on the other country's export interests (and the positive effect that it has on the other country's import-competing interests). The Nash equilibrium occurs at a peak of an inverted-u shaped indifference curve for the home government drawn in the space of the two tariffs. It also occurs at the peak of a right-parenthesis shaped indifference curve for the foreign government. And, as in Fig. 2, there is a lens to the southwest of the Nash equilibrium such that, for all pairs of tariff rates in the lens, each government could achieve greater political support from its own specific factors than at the noncooperative equilibrium.

Several observations are in order. First, the motivation for a trade agreement again reflects international externalities and interdependence. Without the agreement, each government neglects the impact that its policy choices have on the *political welfare* of the opposite government. But the motivation for the agreement is not necessarily based on an improvement in social welfare, nor are the agreed-upon tariffs likely to be economically efficient, as they are in Mayer (1981). Rather, an agreement allows the governments to promote "political efficiency" by an exchange of "market access." By reducing its own tariff slightly, the home government has a negligible effect on its own political support, since the Nash tariff was chosen to balance the offsetting effects on domestic interests (including the beneficiaries of any tariff revenue). But the foreign export interests benefit from the improved market access and, although the foreign import-competing interests are harmed, their income drop is buffeted by an improvement in the foreign terms of trade. On the margin, a reduction in the home tariff improves political support for the foreign government at only negligible cost to the home government. The foreign government can reciprocate by cutting its own tariff, thereby improving market access for home exporters and raising the home government's support from its export industry.

Grossman and Helpman (1995b) attempt to provide better microfoundations for the governments' choices in a model with campaign giving by special interest groups. There are $n + 1$ industries, one of which produces the numeraire good from labor alone while the remaining n industries each produce with labor and a factor of production that is specific to the industry. Household welfare is a quasilinear function of consumption of the numeraire good and utility from consuming the various nonnumeraire goods. The home government maximizes a political objective function of the form $G(W, C) = aW + C$, where W is aggregate welfare in the home country and C is aggregate contributions from all special interest groups.[j] Meanwhile, the foreign government maximizes $G^*(W^*, C^*)$, with variables defined analogously. The politics are treated as a two-stage game in which the interest groups offer contribution schedules to their own government in the first stage and the governments choose their trade-policy vectors (import and export taxes and subsidies) in the second stage. Interest groups are assumed to represent the sector-specific factors of production in a subset of industries, namely those industries that manage to overcome free-rider problems and become politically organized. Each contribution schedule links a group's campaign contribution to the government's multidimensional policy choice. In the competition for influence that arises when the governments behave noncooperatively, the interest-group contributions are assumed to be a function of the own government's policy vector. If a cooperative trade agreement is anticipated, then an interest group can also tie its contribution to the other government's choices in the hope of influencing its own government's posture in the trade negotiations. Finally, the "trade war" outcome is taken to be the Nash equilibrium of a second-stage noncooperative game between the governments, whereas the "trade talks" outcome is the Nash bargaining solution to the second stage.

---

[j] This objective function can be derived from a two-party model of elections with impressionable and nonimpressionable voters, where the former can be influenced by campaign spending and the latter vote purely based on self-interest (see Grossman and Helpman, 1996).

The equilibrium policies in the trade war satisfy

$$t_i - 1 = -\left(\frac{I_i - \alpha_L}{a + \alpha_L}\right)\frac{x_i}{m_i}\frac{1}{e_i} + \frac{1}{e_i^*}, \tag{2}$$

$$t_i^* - 1 = -\left(\frac{I_i^* - \alpha_L^*}{a^* + \alpha_L^*}\right)\frac{x_i^*}{m_i^*}\frac{1}{e_i^*} + \frac{1}{e_i}, \tag{3}$$

where t_i is the import tax at home if good i is imported or the export subsidy if it is exported, I_j is an indicator variable that takes on the value one if industry j is politically organized or zero if it is not, α_L is the fraction of the total population that belongs to some organized interest group or another, x_i is output in home industry i, m_i is home imports (possibly negative), e_i is the elasticity of import demand (negative) or export supply (positive), as the case may be, and symbols with asterisks are analogous variables that apply to the foreign country. Grossman and Helpman interpret the first-expression on the right-hand side of each equation as the political motive for noncooperative trade policy; the competition for influence via contributions induces each government to support those local industries that are politically organized, that have a high ratio of output to trade and that are relatively immune to deadweight loss, as reflected in a small local trade elasticity. The second term in each equation is the standard terms-of-trade motive for positive tariffs and export taxes. The inverse trade elasticity in the partner country reflects a country's monopoly power in trade. Notice that, if no industry is politically organized ($I_i = 0$ and $I_i^* = 0$ for all i) or if the governments give negligible weight to campaign contributions relative to aggregate welfare ($a = a^* = \infty$) then the model predicts the vector of Nash-equilibrium optimal tariffs, as in Johnson (1953).

Starting from the trade policies indicated in (2) and (3), the two governments have an incentive to negotiate a trade agreement for much the same reason as in Hillman and Moser (1995) or, for that matter, Mayer (1981). In the Nash equilibrium, the unilateral policies chosen by each government confer externalities on the other. The pair of non-cooperative tariff vectors is economically inefficient, but that is hardly surprising, because the governments are only partly concerned with aggregate welfare. What motivates their cooperation is rather the lack of *political* efficiency. By trading policy concessions, the governments can find an agreement such that each achieves a higher weighted sum of welfare and campaign contributions as compared to the outcome at the Nash equilibrium.

When the organized interest groups design their contribution schedules in anticipation of an efficient trade negotiation (one that will yield a Pareto-efficient outcome for the two governments with respect to their objectives, G and G^*), the negotiated trade policies satisfy

$$t_i - t_{i^*} = \frac{I_i - \alpha_L}{a + \alpha_L}\frac{x_i}{m_i}\frac{1}{e_i} - \frac{I_i^* - \alpha_L^*}{a^* + \alpha_L^*}\frac{x_i^*}{m_i^*}\frac{1}{e_i^*}. \tag{4}$$

The trade talks do not determine the levels of the import and export taxes or subsidies in each country in a given industry, but only the difference between the importing country's tariff and the exporting countries export subsidy, as reflected in (4). This is so, because an equal change in the import tariff rate and the export subsidy rate would not affect internal prices in either country, and so it would not affect consumer surplus, producer surplus, or deadweight loss. An equal rate change only affects the distribution of tax revenues (positive or negative) captured by the two governments, and such a change in one industry can always be compensated by an offsetting rate change in another industry. The relative bargaining power of the two governments determines the aggregate trade tax revenue that each collects, but not the composition of that revenue by source industry.[k]

The net effect of the negotiated trade policies applied on any good reflects the difference in the political strength of the industry's special interests in the two countries. This difference reflects whether or not the specific factors in the industry are politically organized, whether price distortions in the industry cause a great or small amount of deadweight loss, and how willing the industry's own government is to sacrifice aggregate welfare in exchange for campaign contributions. The negotiated policies preserve the political motive that each government has to cater to its local interests, while accounting for the externality that its policies impose on the other. The components of (2) and (3) that reflect the terms-of-trade motive for unilateral policy intervention do not appear in (4), because the exercise of monopoly power via an optimal tariff or export tax enhances aggregate welfare in one country at the expense of that in the other, and such beggar-thy neighbor policies have no place in an efficient bargain between governments, be they economically motivated or otherwise.

2.4 Is it All About the Terms of Trade?

To recap, Mayer (and subsequent authors) identified a terms-of-trade externality that arises when governments unilaterally pursue the maximization of constituents' aggregate welfare. This externality creates an opportunity for mutual gain from cooperation. Hillman and Moser (and others) argued that governments are motivated not only by economic concerns but also—or especially—by political concerns that reflect the distribution of income. In their view, a terms-of-trade externality is not the primary motivation for trade agreements. Rather, governments seek agreements in order to internalize a market-access externality. They argued that when institutional constraints preclude direct government support for export industries (for some unspecified reason), the governments can reap mutual political gains by jointly opening their markets, thereby capturing the political rewards that their respective export interests have to offer.

---

[k] The indeterminacy arises for much the same reason that all home and foreign tariff rates that satisfy (1) are efficient when tariffs are set by two welfare-maximizing governments.

So, is it a terms-of-trade externality that motivates trade agreements, or something else? Bagwell and Staiger (1999, 2002) make a strong claim that, even in a world with politically motivated governments, trade agreements are all about governments overcoming their temptation to manipulate the terms of trade. But they also claim that, when addressing the terms-of-trade externality, there is a sense in which governments are inexorably led to grant better market access. In short, they claim that there is no meaningful difference between a terms-of-trade externality and a market-access externality.

Bagwell and Staiger begin by specifying two governments' objective functions in reduced form. They write the governments' political objectives as $G(p,p_w)$ and $G^*(p^*,p_w)$, where p and p^* again are the internal (or "domestic") relative prices that producers and consumers face in the home and foreign countries, respectively, and p_w is the world relative price of the good imported by the home country, ie, the international terms of trade. The wedge between p and p_w reflects the home country's trade policies, while that between p^* and p_w reflects the foreign country's trade policies. A special case of these preferences arises when the governments maximize aggregate welfare, since all factor prices (and thus market incomes) and all consumption decisions depend on domestic prices, while a government's revenue depends on the difference between domestic and world prices. The Grossman and Helpman (1995b) specification yields a similar reduced form, once the contributions C and C^* that enter directly into the governments' objectives are replaced by the equilibrium first-stage contribution offers of the special interest groups. Indeed, the Bagwell-Staiger reduced form represents government preferences in a wide range of political-economy models with perfect competition, because in all such models the domestic prices determine the distribution of factor income and consumer surplus, while the wedges between the world price and the internal relative prices determine the intergovernmental distribution of tax revenues.

Consider the effects of a rise in the world relative price of the home country's import good, p_w, holding local prices in both countries constant. This will not alter factor incomes in either country, nor will it change the prices faced by any consumers. The only effect is a reduction in the home government's revenues from its trade policies and an equal increase in government revenues in the foreign country. Plausibly, this event should be viewed favorably by the foreign government and unfavorably by the home government. Accordingly, Bagwell and Staiger posit that $G^*_{p_w} > 0$ and $G_{p_w} < 0$. Concerning the economic environment, they assume only that the Lerner paradox and the Metzler paradox do not arise.[1]

---

[1] The Lerner paradox applies when an increase in a countries tariff leads to an increase in the world price of its imports, hence a deterioration in the terms of trade. This can happen only if the government spends a disproportionate share of its tariff revenues on the import good. The Metzler paradox applies when a tariff generates such a large improvement in an importing country's terms of trade that the domestic relative price of the import good actually falls there. For this to happen in the home country, the foreign excess demand for its import good must be sufficiently inelastic.

The market-clearing world price depends on the trade policies chosen by the two governments. Given the trade policies and the market-clearing world price, the pair of domestic prices are determined mechanically. In such circumstances, one might as well imagine that the governments choose their domestic prices directly and the respective trade policies are determined residually, once p_w is determined. Writing p_w as a function of p and p^* to reflect the dependence of equilibrium prices on trade policies, the first-order conditions for the governments' optimal choices of domestic prices at the Nash equilibrium imply

$$G_p(p, p_w) + G_{p_w}(p, p_w) \frac{\partial p_w(p, p^*)}{\partial p} = 0, \tag{5}$$

$$G_{p^*}^*(p^*, p_w) + G_{p_w}^*(p^*, p_w) \frac{\partial p_w(p, p^*)}{\partial p^*} = 0. \tag{6}$$

As before, this outcome is politically inefficient, inasmuch as both G and G^* could be increased by appropriate adjustments in the domestic prices away from those that prevail in the noncooperative equilibrium. This can be seen from the fact that the iso-utility curve for the home policy maker is perpendicular to that for the foreign policy maker at the Nash equilibrium, whereas political efficiency calls for tangency between these two curves.

Next, Bagwell and Staiger designate a benchmark that they term the "politically optimal tariffs." They define these tariffs implicitly as the wedges that arise between domestic and world prices when the internal prices satisfy

$$G_p(p, p_w) = 0, \tag{7}$$

$$G_{p^*}^*(p^*, p_w) = 0. \tag{8}$$

How should we understand these politically optimal tariffs? They are the tariffs the governments would choose if, for some unspecified reason, each were to ignore the effect on its political objective that results from changes in the terms of trade, and if each expected the other to do similarly; that is, if both acted as if $G_{p_w} \equiv G_{p_w}^* \equiv 0$. Were the governments hypothetically to behave in such a manner, there would be no scope for them to negotiate a trade agreement in pursuit of mutual political gains. To see why, consider the effect of a change in the foreign tariff, t^*, on the political welfare of the home government, starting from a pair of local prices that satisfy (7) and (8). A change in t^* would induce an equilibrium adjustment of the home price, p, but to first order this alone would neither benefit nor harm the home government, by (7). The change in t^* would also alter the terms of trade. But the induced change in p_w would generate a pure transfer of welfare between the two governments and so it could not be a basis for mutual gain. In short, if each government were to set its tariff equal to the political optimal, there would be nothing further on which they could agree.

The politically optimal tariffs refer to a thought experiment; Bagwell and Staiger view them as purely hypothetical and do not suggest that governments would have reason to behave this way in any set of circumstances. Since there is no behavioral justification for these tariffs, it is difficult to evaluate whether they provide a sensible benchmark to use in ascribing motives to the governments. Are terms-of-trade externalities an apt description of the motivation for trade negotiations, because no negotiations would take place if governments simply ignored their welfare effects? Perhaps, but without an explanation about why and in what circumstances the governments might do so, this is largely a matter of semantics. The semantic nature of the debate becomes clear when Bagwell and Staiger are asked, Is there no market-access externality such as the one identified by Hillman and Moser? Bagwell and Staiger (2002) in fact regard the terms-of-trade externality and the market-access externality as being two sides of the same coin. They associate the market access that a country affords to its trade partner at world prices p_w with the import demand function, for example, $M(p,p_w)$ for the home country. Now, starting from a non-cooperative equilibrium, suppose the home government were to contract its market access marginally by increasing the domestic relative price of the import good. In the absence of any Lerner paradox, this would have to decrease the world price, p_w. At the Nash equilibrium value of p^*, the effect on the political objective of the foreign government is unambiguously negative. So, a contraction of market access imposes a negative externality abroad, and a mutually beneficial trade agreement requires each government to shift out its import demand function, ie, to grant expanded market access to its trade partner.[m]

The important conclusion is that, with perfect competition in world markets, for a wide range of political objective functions governments have an incentive to negotiate a trade agreement that expands world trade. This is the essence of the Bagwell-Staiger insight, more so than whether we describe the agreement as being one in which each country offers a better world price for the initial volume of trade (improved terms of trade) or as one in which each offers greater import demand at the initial world prices (improved market access).

2.5 Market Distortions and Corrective Policies

We have seen that governments have an incentive to negotiate a trade agreement even when their objectives include the support of local special interests. The politically efficient agreement induces governments to take into account the international externalities from their policy decisions and generates improved market access for exporters in both

---

[m] Bagwell and Staiger (2002) make a global argument. They say that an agreement provides additional market access for a country if its trade partner's import demand function shifts out for *some* world prices. They prove that every mutually beneficial trade agreement must secure additional market access in this sense for both countries.

countries. What if local markets do not function perfectly and governments need to use the policy instruments at their disposal to overcome market inefficiencies? Or what if governments have idiosyncratic preferences for certain types of market outcomes, be they economic or noneconomic objectives? Trade policies are part of the arsenal that policy makers have to correct market failures and to generate preferred outcomes. And other policies besides trade policies—even if "legitimately" motivated—can generate externalities for other governments. How should we think about the purpose of trade agreements in a setting with market distortions, noneconomic objectives, and the possibility that governments might invoke all manner of domestic economic policies?

Bagwell and Staiger (2001, 2002, Chapter 8) offer an elegant answer to this question. Let us now write the objectives of the home and foreign governments as $G(p, p_w, s)$ and $G^*(p^*, p_w, s^*)$, respectively, where p and p^* are the relative prices faced by home and foreign consumers, and s and s^* represent the levels of two arbitrary domestic policies set by the home and foreign governments.[n] The domestic policies might be subsidies to local production of one good or the other, in which case the prices received by producers would differ from those paid by consumers. Or the policies might represent interventions in local factor markets, either in the form of taxes or subsidies for factor employment or factor supply, or else measures of direct regulation of factor usage. The policies could also represent limits on pollution, standards for product quality or safety, restrictions on the use of underage labor, minimum wage rates, etc. Meanwhile $G(\cdot)$ and $G^*(\cdot)$ could incorporate political and distributional objectives of the government, as before, as well as their idiosyncratic preferences over market outcomes, and the government objectives could reflect the extent to which market failings that can be traced to factor-market rigidities or product-market externalities. We rule out only the exercise of monopoly power by firms or households (which we will discuss later) and international nonpecuniary externalities that arise, for example, from cross-border pollution, induced climate change, or local concerns about market outcomes in the other country.[o] As before, we assume away conditions that give rise to the Lerner and Metzler paradoxes, and we assume that the Marshall-Lerner conditions for market stability (ie, that a rise in the relative price of a good causes world excess for the good to fall) are satisfied.

Now, governments set their trade policies and their "other" policies. Equivalently, they choose their domestic prices p and p^* along with s and s^*; in this conceptualization, the trade policies are determined residually. The choices of (p, s) and (p^*, s^*) determine

---

[n] This representation of government objectives is slightly different from the one used by Bagwell and Staiger (2001, 2002), but it captures the essence of their arguments about both standards and production subsidies provided that the local prices p and p^* are interpreted to be consumer prices and the governments do not have use of consumption taxes and subsidies. Bagwell and Staiger (2006) analyze WTO treatment of production subsidies in a setting that allows for domestic consumption policies.

[o] An example of a local concern for market outcomes in other countries arises when citizens disdain the use of child labor, even if it occurs outside the borders of their country.

home and foreign supplies and demands, given p_w, and so the world relative price must settle at the level that clears the world market. In other words, the equilibrium world price can be written as $p_w(p,s,p^*,s^*)$. Each government has two first-order conditions that guide its unilateral choice of trade and domestic policies; for example, for the home government, these are

$$G_p(p,p_w,s) + G_{p_w}(p,p_w,s)\frac{\partial p_w(p,s,p^*,s^*)}{\partial p} = 0, \tag{9}$$

$$G_s(p,p_w,s) + G_{p_w}(p,p_w,s)\frac{\partial p_w(p,s,p^*,s^*)}{\partial s} = 0. \tag{10}$$

On the other hand, global political efficiency requires that the home government set p and s to maximize $G(p,p_w,s) + \lambda G^*(p^*,p_w,s^*)$, where λ is the relative weight attached to the foreign government's objective in the efficient agreement, an indicator of its relative negotiating ability. Therefore, the globally efficient home policies satisfy

$$G_p(p,p_w,s) + \left[G_{p_w}(p,p_w,s) + \lambda G^*_{p_w}(p^*,p_w,s^*)\right]\frac{\partial p_w(p,s,p^*,s^*)}{\partial p} = 0, \tag{11}$$

$$G_s(p,p_w,s) + \left[G_{p_w}(p,p_w,s) + \lambda G^*_{p_w}(p^*,p_w,s^*)\right]\frac{\partial p_w(p,s,p^*,s^*)}{\partial s} = 0. \tag{12}$$

Clearly, the unilateral policies that the home government would choose in a noncooperative setting, as given by (9) and (10), do not satisfy the requirements for political efficiency in (11) and (12). The inefficiency of the Nash equilibrium arises again from an international externality, as reflected in the neglected terms $\lambda G^*_{p_w}(p^*,p_w,s^*)$ $[\partial p_w(p,s,p^*,s^*)/\partial p]$ and $\lambda G^*_{p_w}(p^*,p_w,s^*)[\partial p_w(p,s,p^*,s^*)/\partial s]$. And clearly the externalities travel to the foreign country via world prices; when the home government acts unilaterally, it ignores the effect that its choices have on world market prices and thereby on the objectives of the foreign government. The foreign government can react by setting its trade and domestic policies to further its own political objectives, to pursue its idiosyncratic preferences over market outcomes, and to offset its local market distortions, but ultimately the joint choices in a Nash equilibrium leave scope for mutual gain.

Bagwell and Staiger make a further observation. Suppose the governments negotiate over market access, as reflected in the location of each country's import demand schedule or, equivalently, as ultimately reflected in the world market price. Once they agree on a value of p_w, the governments can (and should) be left to determine their own mix of trade and domestic policies. That is, suppose the governments conclude that $p_w(p,s,p^*,s^*)$ should be equal to $\bar{p}_w$ under an international agreement. Then unilateral policy choices by the home government *subject to* $p_w(p,s,p^*,s^*) = \bar{p}_w$ will satisfy

$$G_p(p,\bar{p}_w,s) + \gamma\frac{\partial p_w(p,s,p^*,s^*)}{\partial p} = 0, \tag{13}$$

$$G_s(p,\bar{p}_w,s) + \gamma \frac{\partial p_w(p,s,p^*,s^*)}{\partial s} = 0, \tag{14}$$

where γ is the Lagrange multiplier on the terms-of trade (or market-access) constraint. By judicious choice of $\bar{p}_w$, γ can be made to equal $G_{p_w}(p,\bar{p}_w,s) + \lambda G^*_{p_w}(p^*,\bar{p}_w,s^*)$, and then the conditions for global political efficiency in (11) and (12) will be satisfied. In short, the international agreement can leave the details about policy mix to each country, as long as each provides the appropriate degree of market access.

Lest this tolerance for national sovereignty be misinterpreted, Bagwell and Staiger emphasize its limitation. Given an agreement about market access, their analysis shows that each government can be allowed to choose its own mix of trade and domestic policies. But this is not the same thing as saying that the governments can come to an agreement about trade policies while leaving each one free to choose whatever domestic policies it prefers. If the governments agree only about trade policies while making no commitments about their domestic policies, the home government, for example, will have an incentive to distort its choice of s to satisfy a condition like (10). That is, it will choose its policy not only to correct the domestic market failure or to achieve its non-economic objective, but also with an eyes towards the effect on the terms of trade. In so doing, it will partly undo any concession about providing market access that is implied by its restricted choice of trade policy. An agreement that restricts choices of trade policies may be better than no agreement at all, but without a commitment to prescribed levels of market access, the resulting outcomes will not be politically efficient.

2.6 Critiques of the Theory

I have presented a theory of trade agreements founded on the potential gains from cooperation among policy makers that have different constituencies and serve different interests. On the economic side, the theory assumes convex technologies and perfect competition, but it allows for various types of domestic market failures. On the political side, it assumes self-interested policy makers who may have purely benevolent motivations or political motivations and may pursue noneconomic objectives. The theory rests on the sole premise that a noncooperative Nash equilibrium is inefficient for the two sets of policy makers, because unilateral policy choices generate international externalities. The theory presumes governments negotiate trade agreements in order to internalize these externalities.

The theory has been criticized on various grounds, most notably by Ethier (2007, 2013) and Regan (2006, 2015). The criticisms take three, interrelated forms. First, whereas the theory highlights the role of terms-of-trade manipulation in motivating trade negotiations, the rhetoric surrounding actual negotiations makes virtually no reference to the terms of trade and focuses instead on governments' aims to reduce "protectionism." Second, whereas the theory assumes that governments value tariff revenue, the discussions surrounding trade agreements do not highlight such a concern. Finally, the theory takes the set of political actors that lobby for trade policy as given, whereas it seems that the prospect of a trade negotiation mobilizes export interests that might otherwise remain on the political sideline. In this section, I will describe these criticisms in more detail and outline potential responses.

Recall that Bagwell and Staiger (1999, 2002) identify terms-of-trade manipulation as *the problem* that trade agreements are meant to solve. They argue that, in a hypothetical situation in which governments act unilaterally but behave as if they see no benefit (political or otherwise) from any terms-of-trade improvement, the outcome would be politically efficient and admit no potential gains from cooperation. For this reason, they point to governmental concerns about terms-of-trade manipulation as the motivating force behind trade negotiations. Grossman and Helpman (1995b) make no such claim, but they do observe that the politically efficient trade policies strip away the optimum-tariff components of the noncooperative policies while preserving the components that reflect the difference in the political strengths of the special interests in the import-competing and exporting industries. One might say that the trade talks in Grossman and Helpman also are necessary only to rid the world economy of terms-of-trade manipulation.

Regan (2015) describes a "practitioner's understanding" of trade agreements, based loosely on his reading of historical accounts by participants in trade negotiations. Trade practitioners, he asserts, do not mention any concern about the terms of trade. The words never appear in their accounts of their bargaining experiences. Rather, the practitioners tell a story of reducing "protectionism," which he defines as "any unilateral trade policy that restricts imports to get political support for the government from import-competing producers." In his view, policy makers are willing to forego protectionism in exchange for similar concessions by their partners, because the political support each can attract from export interests exceeds what each stands to lose from its import-competing interests.[P] Regan further notes that a reduction of protectionism in this sense can play no role in motivating trade negotiations in Bagwell and Staiger (1999, 2002) or Grossman and Helpman (1995b), because protectionism remains unabated under the politically efficient agreement.

Next, Regan and Ethier (2013) point to tariff revenues. These are the other side of the coin from terms-of-trade improvements. When a trade tax causes the world price of a country's imports to fall or the world price of its exports to rise, and domestic prices move in the opposite direction in the absence of any Lerner paradox, the terms-of-trade gain is realized in the revenues collected by the government. Were the government not to care about these revenues, it also could not value the change in world prices. Put differently, a

---

[P] Regan (2015) cites Hillman et al. (1995) as an example of what he has in mind, although, as noted above, the welfare effects of term-of-trade changes are essential to the Hillman et al. demonstration that the political support gains from export interests exceeds the loss from import-competing interests.

policy that raises domestic prices while collecting no revenue (such as a "voluntary export restraint") can only worsen the terms of trade, not improve them. But Regan and Ethier see no evidence in their reading of practitioners' accounts of any negotiator's interest in the revenues generated by import and export taxes.

Finally, Regan and Ethier argue that the key to understanding trade agreements is the boon they provide to export interests. As they recognize themselves, their preferred account relies on an assumption that export interests have no way to capture policy rents in a world of unilateral policy setting in a manner akin to what import-competing interests manage to do. Import-competing interests exchange political support in the form of campaign contributions or otherwise for private benefits from protection. Export interests, they claim, cannot play this game. According to these authors, a trade negotiation is fundamentally about empowering export interests to counter protectionist forces.[q]

Let us evaluate these criticisms in terms of what they imply about the modeling of trade agreements. The fact that practitioners do not mention a concern about the terms of trade *per se* is not determinative about their role in the workings of formal models of international externalities. The terms of trade are instrumental in these models, not a direct policy goal. The Grossman-Helpman model assumes that policy makers are concerned with the welfare of their constituents and with campaign contributions, and that the latter are offered by interest groups to further their economic interests. The politicians need only recognize that a lower price of imports contributes to the welfare of consumers and that a higher price of exports adds to the income of (some) producers in order to behave "as if" they are concerned about the terms of trade. What policy maker would not prefer that imports be cheaper and that exports command higher prices, *all else the same?* This logic underlies the reduced-form specification of preferences in Bagwell and Staiger. The legitimacy of their rather general formulation of government preferences does not rest on whether practitioners use the words "terms of trade" to describe their bargaining goals.

The modeling of trade agreements by Grossman and Helpman and by Bagwell and Staiger does rely on the assumption that governments care about the fiscal consequences of their policy choices. To see why, consider a Grossman-Helpman world in which a negligible fraction of the population is represented by an interest group ($\alpha_L = 0$) and in which the government for some reason places no value of tax revenue, positive or negative. In such a setting, the equilibrium contribution schedules would induce the government to act as if it were maximizing $G = \sum (1 + aI_i)\Pi_i(p_i) + S_i(p_i)$, where a is the weight that the policy maker attaches to campaign contributions relative to producer-plus-consumer surplus (but with no revenue term), $\Pi_i(p_i)$ and $S_i(p_i)$ are producer and

---

[q] Neither Ethier nor Regan provides a logically consistent formal model of this process. Similar informal statements about this role of trade negotiations can be found in the writings of some trade-focused political scientists and legal scholars, such as, Hudec (1993), Destler (2005), and Pauwelyn (2008).

consumer surplus from the consumption of good i when the domestic price is p_i, and I_i again is a dichotomous variable that indicates whether industry i is politically organized or not. Note that $\partial G/\partial p_i = (1 + aI_i)x_i(p_i) - c_i(p_i)$, where x_i and c_i are output and consumption, respectively, and that $\partial^2 G/\partial p_i^2 = (1 + aI_i)x_i'(p) - c_i'(p) > 0$. Evidently, there can be no interior solution in this setting; each government tries to set as high a domestic price as possible, which it can do by raising toward infinity its export subsidy. Needless to say, this is not a sensible prediction of the model and does not provide a benchmark against which to consider governments' incentives for negotiating a trade agreement. In a political-economy setting in which governments literally do not care about the fiscal implications of their policies, their search for contributions or other forms of political support leads them to subsidize lavishly whichever group has more at stake in the policy decision and a better means of playing the political game.

Regan and Ethier recognize that an assumption of no governmental concern for fiscal deficits generates nonsensical predictions, so they argue instead for a formulation in which the government places no value on any positive revenues generated by trade taxes, but bears a prohibitive cost of making public outlays for import or export subsidies. Regan in particular argues that such an assumption—admittedly inconsistent with the belief that policy makers are "rational actors"—is descriptively realistic. But, even if we accept such irrationality, it is not clear how it would rescue the situation. Suppose a government acts unilaterally to maximize $G = \sum(1 + aI_i)\Pi_i(p_i) + S_i(p_i)$, but does so under the constraint that $R_i \equiv (p_i - p_{wi})[c_i(p_i) - x_i(p_i)] \geq 0$ for all i, where p_{wi} is the world price of good i and therefore R_i is the revenues collected from trade taxes on good i. The constraint says that the revenues from any trade tax cannot be negative, ie, that subsidies to trade are impossible. There are two cases to consider. Suppose first that $x_i(p_{wi}) > c_i(p_{wi})$, ie, that the country would export good i under free trade. In this case, $\partial G/\partial p_i = (1 + aI_i)x_i(p_i) - c_i(p_i) > 0$, so the government would like to raise the domestic price to benefit the exporters, but it cannot do so due to the fact that subsidies are forbidden. Alternatively, suppose that $c_i(p_{wi}) > x_i(p_{wi})$, ie, that the country would import good i under free trade. If $c_i(p_{wi}) > (1 + aI_i)x_i(p_{wi})$, it would wish to reduce the domestic price, but cannot do so without subsidizing imports. If $c_i(p_{wi}) < (1 + aI_i)x_i(p_{wi})$, it will instead wish to raise the domestic price, and will do so until imports are eliminated. So a government that acts unilaterally and that does not care about positive revenues from trade taxes but stays clear of trade subsidies has either zero or prohibitive trade taxes in every sector. This hardly seems a reasonable depiction of the counterfactual outcome in the absence of a trade agreement.

More promising, perhaps, is the Ethier-Regan suggestion that trade negotiations empower export interests that otherwise would be shut out of the political process. They offer no convincing reason why import-competing interests are able to organize themselves and lobby for protection in a noncooperative setting whereas export interests cannot do so. Nor do they offer any explanation as to why the situation suddenly changes when trade negotiations are contemplated.[r] But Grossman and Helpman (1995b) are silent about which industries are politically organized and which are not, and Bagwell and Staiger (2002) are silent about the stability of their reduced-form government preferences. It is certainly possible that new interest groups become organized when trade negotiations are active, so that the induced government preferences change.[s] Future research might uncover reasons why the onset of trade negotiations encourages the participation of export interests in lobbying that are otherwise unable to influence trade policy outcomes. If so, then policy makers might well wish to enter into trade agreements as a way of to mobilize these interests and thereby counter the forces of protectionism.[t]

Regan (2015) and others have offered another critique of the competitive theory of trade agreements, one that focuses on its predictions rather than its assumptions. The critique concerns the model's implications for how export subsidies ought to be treated in trade agreements and the reality of how modern agreements actually treat such subsidies. Indeed, (Bagwell and Staiger, 2002, Chapter 10) have been puzzled by this same issue.

Consider again the trade policies that result when the home and foreign governments choose t and t^* to maximize $G(W,C) = aW + C$ and $G^*(W^*, C^*) = a^* W^* + C^*$, respectively, in a noncooperative equilibrium of the Grossman-Helpman "trade wars" model.[u] Suppose that good i is an export good for the home country and that, contrary to the discussion in the previous paragraph, its export industry is politically active even before any trade talks take place, ie, $I_i = 1$. The home-country's trade policy in the Nash equilibrium might involve an export subsidy $(t_i > 1)$ or an export tax $(t_i < 0)$. The first term on the right-hand side of (2) captures the force for a subsidy, reflecting the influence bought by the domestic industry. The second term captures the force for a tax, inasmuch as an export tax improves the country's terms of trade and thus contributes to the

---

[r] Regan (2015) does offer the argument that government support for exporters in the noncooperative setting would require export subsidies and that governments find such subsidies politically intolerable, for some unexplained reason. But as we have just seen, the combination of indifference to positive tariff revenues and intolerance for any trade subsidies leads inexorably to the conclusion that either trade is free or none takes place.

[s] Mitra (1999) develops a model in the spirit of Grossman-Helpman (1994) in which interests group endogenously form prior to the lobbying game by bearing a cost of organizing. However, the equilibrium in his model does have endogenous organization by some export industries, just as it has endogenous organization by some import-competing industries.

[t] This potential argument for a trade agreement has the same flavor as the commitment theories that are discussed in Section 4. That is, a government that has benevolent intentions *ex ante* may anticipate that it will be tempted to cater to organized interests *ex post*. By entering into a trade negotiation, it encourages the participation of the exporters in the political process and thereby induces an outcome that is closer to its *ex ante* preferences.

[u] A similar argument can be made using instead the Bagwell-Staiger reduced-form specification of the governments' objectives, $G(p, p_w)$ and $G(p^*, p_w)$, for which the Nash equilibrium is described by (7) and (8).

country's aggregate welfare (note that $e_i^* < 0$ when the foreign country imports good i). The net effect reflects, *inter alia*, the size of a, the government's weight on contributions relative to welfare. When a is large, $t_i < 1$, as concerns about welfare carry the day. When a is small, $t_i > 1$, as the lobbyists prefer.

Suppose the Nash equilibrium policy involves an export subsidy and that the countries come together to discuss a cooperative trade agreement. A small change (up or down) in the home country's subsidy has no effect on the government's objective, G, because t_i was chosen by the home government to balance the marginal effects of a policy change on contributions and welfare. But a small *increase* in the home export subsidy (starting from the Nash equilibrium) raises the objective G^* of the foreign government. An increase in the subsidy rate conveys a positive externality to the foreign government inasmuch as it reduces the world price of one of that country's import goods, ie, it improves the foreign terms of trade. Since the foreign government has chosen t_i^* to balance the marginal influence of its import-competing industry against the marginal affect on aggregate welfare, dG^*/dt_i must be positive at the Nash equilibrium. In short, the model predicts that trade talks ought to encourage larger export subsidies than in the noncooperative equilibrium. But the actual rules of the GATT and WTO do much the opposite, in fact they forbid export subsidies entirely.[v]

Unfortunately, the literature offers no compelling reason why trade agreements should outlaw export subsidies in a trading environment characterized by perfectly competitive markets. Perhaps the world economy is better described by pervasive imperfect competition, in which case the analysis of Section 3 comes into play. There, as we shall see, limitations on export subsidies can more easily be explained. Or perhaps further research will uncover other ways to resolve what Maggi (2014) has termed the "export subsidy puzzle."

3. INTERNATIONAL EXTERNALITIES WITH IMPERFECT COMPETITION

Until now, I have focused on international externalities that arise in a perfectly competitive trading environment. These externalities give rise to gains from cooperation and so provide incentives for governments to negotiate a trade agreement. I now turn to environments with imperfect competition, where a wider set of externalities prevail.

---

[v] As noted previously, the national policies for industry i in the cooperative equilibrium are not well determined; only the difference in policies is pinned down by the requirements for political efficiency, as expressed in (4). Accordingly, t_i might fall as the result of trade talks, so long as t_i^* does so as well. Still, it is troubling that the model suggests that marginal increases in export subsidies starting from the Nash equilibrium would enhance the combined political objectives of the two governments and yet the trade agreement calls for zero subsidies.

3.1 Firm-Delocation Externalities

Delocation refers to the exit by producers from some locations coupled with entry by new firms in other locations. The mix of producers' locations in an industry can matter for national welfare whenever firms set prices above marginal cost and transport costs create price differences across markets. In such a setting, a government may have an incentive to pursue trade policies that encourage entry at home and exit abroad, thereby changing the mix of prices faced by local consumers. If the governments act unilaterally, they will neglect the harm that delocation causes to consumers elsewhere.

Venables (1985, 1987) studied the welfare effects of tariffs in models with imperfect competition and free entry. In Venables (1987), for example, two countries produce varieties of a differentiated product under increasing returns to scale. They also produce a homogeneous good under constant returns to scale. The varieties are CES substitutes, as in Krugman (1980), and trade in the differentiated varieties entails shipping costs. Labor is the only factor of production. A zero-profit condition determines the number of varieties produced in each country. Venables shows that when the home country levies a small import tariff, domestic welfare rises even if the tariff revenues confer no social value. The gains come at the expense of foreign consumers. The mechanism for these welfare transfers is that of delocation: The tariff raises the profitability of producing in the home market, which generates additional entry there. Foreign firms lose directly from the incidence of the tariff and indirectly from competition with a greater number of home firms. So, some firms exit abroad. Since home products do not bear tariffs or shipping costs in the home market, they are cheaper than the imports. Therefore, an increase in the relative number of domestic producers reduces the home price index, which raises real incomes at home. Just the opposite is true in the foreign country.

In the model developed by Venables (1987), an export subsidy also can be used to raise home welfare. A subsidy, like a tariff, enhances profitability for home firms while reducing that of foreign firms, so it induces entry at home and exit abroad. Again, the change in the composition of firms benefits consumers at home while harming those abroad. Although Venables does not discuss the net effect on foreign welfare, it is straightforward to show that welfare there might fall; the direct benefit that foreign consumers receive from the subsidized prices can be more than offset by the harm from delocation.

What are the incentives for forming a trade agreement in the presence of delocation externalities? Ossa (2011) addresses this question in a model based on Krugman (1980). He considers trade between two countries that have symmetric preferences and the same production technologies. The countries may differ in their labor endowments and in their trade policies. Consumers have Cobb-Douglas preferences over a homogeneous good and a CES composite of differentiated varieties. The homogeneous good is produced with constant returns to scale and is freely traded. Varieties of the differentiated product require a fixed input of labor as well as a constant per-unit variable input.

The differentiated varieties are traded subject to an iceberg shipping cost and an *ad valorem* import tariff. Firms earn zero profits in an equilibrium with free entry.

Ossa assumes that the iceberg trade costs are sufficiently high that both countries produce differentiated products. Also, the labor endowments are sufficiently large that both countries produce positive amounts of the homogeneous good. As in Venables (1987), he finds that the real price index in each country is decreasing in the country's own tariff and increasing in the tariff of its trading partner, for small enough tariffs. The explanation again is delocation: A tariff at home generates entry by home firms and exit by foreign firms and the direct effect of the higher import prices due to the tariff is more than offset by the indirect effect of the change in the mix of producers.

If tariff revenues do not enter the government's welfare calculus, then the pair of welfare-maximizing governments set prohibitive tariffs in a Nash equilibrium of the policy game. If the revenues do figure in welfare, then the Nash tariffs are positive but finite. The interior solution results from the fact that by further raising an already high tariff, the government sacrifices tax revenue. This cost must eventually outweigh the benefit from further delocation. As usual, the noncooperative tariffs are detrimental to the joint welfare of the two countries. The benefit that each country achieves by delocation comes at the expense of its trading partner and generates further deadweight loss. Efficiency requires tariff reductions; eg, in the case in which tariff revenue does not enter welfare, at least one country's tariff rate must be set to zero under an efficient trade agreement.

Ossa emphasizes that the externality that arises in the noncooperative Nash equilibrium of his model should not be called a terms-of-trade externality. Since the CES demand structure implies a constant markup over marginal cost, the ex-factory prices of export goods are independent of the tariff rate. If we define the terms of trade to be the ex-factory price of an imported variety divided by that of a domestic variety, then the terms of trade are, in fact, independent of trade policy. If, instead, we define the terms of trade as the price index for exported varieties divided by the price index for imported varieties, then—as Ossa shows—a tariff that improves a country's welfare via delocation actually generates a deterioration in its terms of trade. The purpose of a trade agreement, he argues, is to internalize the externality that results when countries use their import policies to alter the composition of domestic and foreign firms in the market.

Bagwell and Staiger (2012b) consider a different but related model with delocation possibilities, namely one based on Venables (1985). Their model has linear demands for a homogeneous product and no income effects on demand. Home and foreign firms engage in Cournot competition in the two markets, which are assumed to be segmented. Trade costs are positive. As in Venables (1985), the equilibrium features two-way trade in identical products. A small tariff in the home country increases the number of firms located there, decreases the number of firms in the foreign country, and by altering the intensity of Cournot competition in the two markets, it raises home welfare at the expense of foreign welfare. In this setting, if governments are limited to using import tariffs as instruments for delocation, then—just as in Ossa (2011)—the inefficient Nash equilibrium involves positive tariffs in both countries. Moreover, the countries have reason to negotiate a reduction in these tariffs, just as Ossa describes. In a symmetric setting, the efficient tariffs are zero.

In Bagwell and Staiger's model, just as in Ossa's, the countries also have incentive to introduce export policies. A small export subsidy starting from free trade raises a country's welfare just as does a tariff, and for much the same reason (see Venables, 1985). The entry of firms in the country with the subsidy and the exit of firms in the other country results in a change in the intensity of competition in the two markets that favors consumers in the country with the active policy.

Bagwell and Staiger proceed to consider the Nash equilibrium of a policy game in which the two governments can implement both import and export policies. They find, perhaps surprisingly, that in the Nash equilibrium, each country combines a tariff on imports with a *tax* on exports. The key to this finding is their observation that, when deviating from free trade, each government can always find a small tariff and a small export tax that together generate the same internal price and the same consumer surplus as are achieved under free trade but that yield positive tax revenue. In effect, import tariffs and export taxes are complements in their model, because a country that imposes a high tariff and thereby induces entry by a large number of local firms will want to avoid an export subsidy that would transfer a great deal of revenue to foreign consumers. Put differently, with an import tariff in place, an export tax by the home country that causes entry abroad will increase the volume of foreign exports on which the tariff is levied, thereby increasing the home government's revenues. Bagwell and Staiger conclude that, starting from a noncooperative equilibrium that has positive export taxes and high import tariffs, the countries might appear to have no reason to conclude an agreement that limits the use of export subsidies inasmuch as subsidies are absent from this equilibrium. Moreover, an efficient agreement is one in which any positive import tariff maintained by one country is exactly offset by an export subsidy in the other, so that the net effect of the offsetting trade policies on world prices is nil. In this sense, export subsidies must be tolerated (indeed encouraged) to achieve efficiency, unless import tariffs are fully eliminated. However, as the authors emphasize, an efficient agreement cannot leave governments free to choose whatever export subsidies they prefer; once tariffs have been reduced to low levels, the countries will have incentives to overuse these instruments to encourage delocation. While the model does not provide an explanation for bans on export subsidies, it does provide a reason why the use of subsidies should be regulated.

Finally, in Bagwell and Staiger (2015), the authors consider the nature of the externality that motivates a trade agreement in models of firm delocation. They show that the globally efficient policies coincide with the "political optimum," where the latter is defined as the vector of policies that would maximize $G(p, p^*, p_w)$ and $G^*(p, p^*, p_w)$ were the two countries for some reason to ignore the effect of its trade policy choices on the world price. In this sense, they argue, and contrary to the claim in Ossa (2011), the fundamental purpose of a trade agreement in the delocation model is really to eliminate manipulation of the terms of trade. Maggi (2014) points out, however, that their conclusion very much relies on their assumption of no income effects in the demands for the imperfectly competitive good. Moreover, the meaning of "terms-of-trade manipulation" in a model of Cournot competition with free entry is not entirely clear, at least not to me.

3.2 Profit-Extracting and Profit-Shifting Externalities

International externalities also arise in imperfectly competitive environments when governments can use trade policies to extract monopoly rents from foreign producers or to shift profits from such producers to their domestic rivals. Katrik (1977) and Svedberg (1979) were the first to demonstrate that a government might be able to raise national welfare by imposing a tariff on a good imported from a foreign monopolist. They assumed that the home country confronts the foreign monopoly with a linear demand. In such a setting, a small specific tariff reduces the ex-factory price charged by the monopoly. Although consumers pay more for the good with the tariff in place, part of their payment goes to the home government in the form of tariff revenue. The monopolist's reduction in the ex factory price corresponds to a terms-of-trade improvement, for the home country, which boosts its welfare. Brander and Spencer (1984a) extended the Katrik and Svedberg analyses to include more general demands. When the foreign monopolist operates subject to a constant marginal cost, a specific tariff induces a reduction in its ex-factory price if and only if the demand curve is not too convex. The condition for a terms-of-trade gain in the policy active country is $R \equiv mp''(m)/p'(m) > -1$, where $p(m)$ is the home inverse demand for imports m. If this condition is satisfied—or equivalently, if the inverse demand curve is flatter than the inverse marginal revenue curve—then a small tariff improves the home country's terms of trade and the country's optimal tariff is positive. Much like the tariff that arises from unilateral welfare maximization in a competitive setting, the optimal rent-extracting policy is a beggar-thy-neighbor policy. The revenues captured by the home government come entirely at the expense of the foreign producer's profits. Since global efficiency requires an output greater than what the monopolist sells under free trade and since the home country's tariff reduces the monopolist's output, the optimal tariff in fact reduces global welfare.

Brander and Spencer (1984b) extend the analysis by considering a market in which a pair of firms with different national origins compete as duopolists. The firms compete in segmented markets by simultaneously choosing their deliveries to the two destinations. In this setting with Cournot competition, not only does a unilateral tariff by some country have the potential to extract rents from the foreign firm, to the benefit of the domestic treasury, but it also changes the outcome of the strategic competition between the two firms, to the benefit of the domestic producer. Accordingly, if a tariff induces the foreign firm to reduce the ex-factory price of output destined for the home market, this is sufficient to ensure a welfare gain for the home country. But even if the ex-factory price rises, home welfare might rise due to the profit shifting that results from the changes in market shares.

Brander and Spencer go on to consider the Nash equilibrium of a noncooperative game between two welfare-maximizing governments. In the Nash equilibrium, each government sets a positive tariff on imports from the other's country's monopolist. In so doing, it captures revenue and shifts profits towards its domestic producer. But the profit-shifting effects in the two markets offset one another and, taken together, the pair of Nash tariffs reduce world output. The noncooperative tariffs exceed those that maximize world welfare. In this setting, the governments have an incentive to negotiate mutual trade liberalization and improved market access for their own national firms in the other country's market.

Brander and Spencer (1985) provide the cleanest analysis of the international externalities that arise from profit-shifting trade policies. They assume that there are single suppliers in each of two countries that produce a common good only for export to a third market. The governments can subsidize their local firm's exports in anticipation of the Cournot competition for third-country sales. Consider the unilateral incentives for the use of trade policy in one of the exporting countries. There is no consumption there, so no concern about consumer surplus. The subsidy payment represents a dollar-for-dollar transfer from the government to the domestic firm, which is neutral from the point of view of aggregate welfare, if tax revenues and firm profits are weighted equally. What remains, then, is only the strategic effect of the export subsidy on the outcome of the oligopolistic competition. When a government offers a subsidy, the local producer has a greater incentive to export than otherwise. For any given quantity of its rival's sales the local producer sells more than it would without the subsidy. In other words, the firm's best response function shifts outward in the space of the two output levels. If the foreign best-response function slopes downward—as is commonly assumed for Cournot competition—then the subsidy induces the rival producer to reduce its exports to the third market. This strategic response increases the market share for the subsidized firm and increases its export price relative to what it would be without the rival's retreat from the market. The price in the third-country market typically will be lower than what it would be absent the export subsidy—which implies a terms-of-trade loss for the subsidizing country. But the extra profits captured by the domestic firm at the expense of its foreign rival more than compensate for this. When both best-response functions slope downward, each government has a unilateral incentive to subsidize exports in a grab for oligopoly profits.

Again, we recognize an international externality. The profit gains for one producer come at the expense of the other. And the subsidy causes the price in the third country to fall, which means that joint profits for the two exporters also fall. If both governments were to pursue their unilateral incentives, the resulting pair of subsidies would roughly neutralize one another, leaving market shares about where they would have been without the interventions. The firms may benefit from their governments' largesse, but welfare inclusive of the subsidy costs must fall in at least one of the exporting countries. Therefore, the two governments of the exporting countries have a shared incentive to negotiate a trade agreement that limits the use of such strategic subsidies. Notice that the purpose of such an agreement would not be to limit manipulation of the terms of trade (since the noncooperative policies are subsidies that, in fact, worsen the exporters' terms of trade), but rather to prevent the unilateral pursuit of profit shifting.[w]

As Brander and Spencer (1985) point out, and Bagwell and Staiger (2012a, Section 5) further emphasize, the externality associated with profit shifting can explain a trade agreement that limits or prohibits export subsidies among a pair (or group) of exporting countries, such as the Boeing-Airbus pact between the United States and Europe that limited the countries' use of credit subsidies on foreign sales of large passenger aircraft. But the profit-shifting externality cannot explain a limitation on export subsidies in the context of a multilateral trade negotiation in which all countries participate. The benefit that exporting countries would capture from an agreement that restricts export subsidies comes at the expense of higher prices and reduced consumer surplus in the importing country or countries. Bagwell and Staiger examine a Nash equilibrium in a three-country model with symmetric exporting firms in two of the countries and all consumption confined to the third country, much as in Brander and Spencer (1985). The Nash equilibrium in the three-country policy game involves profit-shifting export subsidies in each of the two exporting countries and a rent-extracting import tariff in the importing country. An agreement that achieves efficiency for the three countries together does not pin down the tariff in the importing country or the subsidies in the exporting countries; efficiency only determines the magnitude of the combined policy wedge. However, it can be shown that the volume of trade is inefficiently low in the Nash equilibrium as compared to what is required for efficiency. Therefore, a negotiated agreement should either lower the tariff in the importing country or raise the subsidies in the exporting countries. Under

---

[w] Eaton and Grossman (1986) have pointed out that the optimality of subsidies in an export duopoly rests heavily on the assumption of Cournot competition. If, instead, the rival exporters engage in Bertrand (price) competition, the Nash equilibrium policies typical involve a pair of export taxes. A unilaterally imposed tax serves to temper competition in the third market and to generate a more collusive outcome. In a Bertrand competition—where a tax on one firm's exports typically induces its rival to raise its price—the strategic response can generate revenues for the taxing government that exceeds the loss in its firm's profits. Nonetheless, an international externality arises from unilateral policies, because the governments do not consider the profit gain that the foreign firm enjoys as a result of their export taxes. In fact, the joint welfare of the two exporting countries would be greater if the export taxes were raised above the levels in the Nash equilibrium.

an efficient agreement, the trade policies should be set so that the firms in the two export-ing countries receive the same cum-subsidy price as one another and the consumers in the importing country pay the same price as they would under perfect competition with free trade.

Bagwell and Staiger (2012a) revisit the question of what is the "fundamental purpose" of a trade agreement in settings with monopoly or oligopoly profits. In other words, they ask, What is the nature of the international externality that a trade agreement seeks to correct? Brander and Spencer might concede that rent extraction is a form of terms-of-trade manipulation inasmuch as the government captures revenue from its import tar-iff by inducing a foreign monopolist or oligopolist to lower its ex-factory price. But what about strategic subsidies that steal profits from other exporters and generate welfare gains despite causing a deterioration of the exporters terms-of-trade? Bagwell and Staiger con-clude that the identification of a profit-shifting motive for a trade agreement arises only when the governments lack full sets of trade policy instruments to tax or subsidize imports and exports and when the importing countries are, for some reason, left out of the cal-culus. They show that, in a variety of settings with excess profits—albeit all with quasi-linear utility—a country's welfare can be written in reduced form as a function $G(p, p^*, p_\mathrm{w})$ of local prices p at home and p^* abroad, and a world price, p_w.[x] They define again a "political optimum" as the policies that the governments would choose in a Nash equilibrium if, for some reason, they were to ignore the welfare enhancing effects of a terms-of-trade improvement, given local prices at home and abroad. That is, their bench-mark arises when all governments choose policies to satisfy their first-order conditions, but in the process act as if $G_{p_\mathrm{w}}(p, p^*, p_\mathrm{w}) \equiv 0$. They show that the efficient agreement coincides with this benchmark, which leads them to conclude once again that the fun-damental externality operates through the terms of trade.

It is not clear to me why their benchmark is appropriate, especially in a setting such as this one where the prices in each market are chosen by active players rather than resulting from market clearing. What does it mean—aside from the formal definition in terms of the first-order condition—that the government acts "as if the terms of trade do not affect aggregate welfare given the domestic prices?" And why is it so important that we pin a name to the externality, be it "profit shifting" or "terms of trade"? Be that as it may, an interesting insight emerges from Bagwell and Staiger's analysis. Namely, in a setting in which each traded good is subject both to an export tax or subsidy imposed by the exporting country and an import subsidy or tax imposed by the importing country, and when utility is quasilinear so that the traded good in question is not subject to any income effects, the policies in the importing and exporting countries become perfect substitutes in terms of their effects on quantities, consumer surplus, and profits. When one

[x] The competitive setting considered in Bagwell and Staiger (1999, 2002) is a special case in which the foreign price p^* does not enter the reduced-form government objective function.

government sets its policy at a level that the other takes as given, the second government can always "undo" the effects of this policy on local prices in each market by an appropriate choice of its own instrument. In so doing, it will impact its trade tax revenues or subsidy outlays, but it can achieve its chosen targets for consumer surplus and local producer profits. This means that the governments can each "get what they want" in the Nash equilibrium, except for the implied revenues and fiscal costs.[y]

3.3 Profit-Extracting Externalities in International Outsourcing Relationships

A recent paper by Antràs and Staiger (2012) addresses the inefficiencies that result from noncooperative policy setting in an environment with international outsourcing. In such circumstances, governments may use their trade policies both to correct allocative inefficiencies that result from incomplete contracting and to extract rents from foreign producers. The two governments share the former objective but not the latter, and a trade agreement may be needed to help them to achieve their common goals while avoiding the inefficiencies that result from conflict.

The economic environment has customized intermediate inputs, two-sided buyer-supplier relationships, and incomplete contracts that give rise to hold-up problems. Two countries, Foreign and Home, are small in relation to the world market for some final good. They take the world price of the final good as given. Foreign alone among the two can produce intermediate inputs, with a unit continuum of potential suppliers. Home alone among the pair can produce the final good, with a unit mass of potential buyers. Each potential supplier in Foreign is matched randomly with a potential buyer in Home and the two engage in bilateral bargaining in order to work out an outsourcing arrangement. If the bargaining breaks down, no final good can be produced and any customized inputs produced for the relationship become worthless. Either country can import the final good from the rest of the world at the fixed world price and Home can export the final good to the world market at this same price.

Imperfect contracting manifests in that the specifications of the input cannot be stipulated before production takes place. Instead, the supplier must produce some quantity of the intermediate good and then negotiate to sell it to its downstream partner. Given that the outside options are zero at the bargaining stage, the negotiation always results in a transaction, with a division of *ex post* surplus dictated by exogenous parameters. But the supplier in any relationship anticipates that it will bear the full cost of production while capturing only a fraction of the surplus; this hold-up problem generates

---

[y] As Maggi (2014) notes, this would not be true if the allocation of revenues had an effect on market demands, as they would in a demand system with income effects. It would also not be true if the international distribution of revenues and outlays had implications for efficiency, for example, if raising revenue entails deadweight losses from distorting taxes.

underinvestment in the intermediate input and an inefficiently low level of offshoring in a free-trade equilibrium.

Now consider the use of trade policies. The government of Foreign can encourage greater investment by subsidizing exports of the intermediate good. The government of Home can do likewise by subsidizing imports of the input or by subsidizing exports or taxing imports of the final product. But the combination of these three policies has implications for the distribution of rents among the two firms and the two governments.[z] And the governments care about national welfare, not global welfare; if they act unilaterally in a noncooperative equilibrium, they will take actions on the margin that benefit their local producers and their treasury at the expense of profits and revenues abroad.

Consider first the incentives facing the government of Home. If its goal were to maximize global welfare given the foreign export subsidy (or tax), it would allow free trade in the final good and subsidize imports of the intermediate good to induce the efficient level of input production. Such a policy would solve the hold-up problem without generating any by-product distortion of consumption decisions. But, by taxing exports or subsidizing imports of the final good, the government of Home can engineer a bargaining outcome that is more favorable to its local firms at the expense of their foreign suppliers. The best response of the government of Home to any policy in Foreign is to combine such a tax on exports or subsidy to imports with an import subsidy for intermediates that pushes the volume of input trade closer to the efficient level, but not fully there. The government of Foreign, in turn, finds it optimal to respond to this pair of policies with a tax on exports of the intermediate input. Two considerations explain why a tax is optimal. First, the foreign firms choose their output levels to maximize their own profits, which coincides with the goal that the foreign government has for its local industry. Second, the tax generates revenue for the foreign government and part of the tax burden is passed on to home firms in the bargaining process. As Antràs and Staiger (2012) show, the Nash equilibrium involves an inefficiently low volume of input trade and an inefficiently low price of the final good in Home, which creates the motivation for a trade agreement.[aa]

The requisite trade agreement in these circumstances is, however, rather subtle. First, efficiency requires intervention in the input market, not free trade. The governments

---

[z]   The government of Foreign has no reason to place a tariff on imports of the final good, inasmuch as this has no effect on the efficiency of the outsourcing relationships and it cannot alter its terms of trade vis-à-vis the rest of the world.

[aa] Antràs and Staiger proceed to introduce political-economic concerns in the form of a potential extra weight that the government attaches to profits relative to consumer surplus or tax revenues. They then ask whether the so-called "political optimum" in this setting, defined as elsewhere, achieves (political) efficiency for the two governments. They conclude in the affirmative if the governments place no extra weight on profits, but not otherwise. Accordingly, they describe the trade agreement that arises with political-economic concerns as addressing more than just a terms-of-trade externality.

must jointly subsidize the trade in intermediates to overcome the underinvestment asso-ciated with the hold-up problem. But, second, it is not enough that they agree to an appropriate level of joint subsidy to intermediate trade. If such a joint subsidy were agreed and the government of Home were left free to set its own trade policy for final goods—perhaps because Foreign does not sell this good to Home and it can always import this good at a fixed terms of trade from the rest of the world—then the government of Home would subsidize exports of the final good in order to tilt the bargaining between supplier and buyer in favor of the latter. In fact, an efficient agreement must constraint not only the policies that directly affect input trade, but also those that affect the outsourcing relationship in other ways.

3.4 International Agreements to Protect Intellectual Property

Most of the literature on the purpose of international agreements focuses on contracts aimed at limiting the opportunistic use of trade policies. But the externalities approach that I have outlined here can also be applied to international agreements that may arise in other policy areas. To illustrate, I will briefly discuss the purpose of international agreements to protect intellectual property, such as the TRIPS Agreement in the WTO. A similar approach has also been applied, for example, to externalities that arise from governments' choices of environmental policies; see the survey by Barrett (2005) for a review of this research.

Grossman and Lai (2004) consider two countries, North and South, that differ in the sizes of their populations and in their endowments of human capital. The countries use labor alone to produce varieties of a horizontally differentiated product and a homoge-neous good. They use labor together with human capital to develop new varieties of the differentiated product. North has a larger endowment of human capital. Preferences are quasilinear, with each differentiated product generating some consumer surplus for households. The differentiated products are sold at monopoly prices by their inventors until imitation takes place due to imperfect patent protection or until the patent runs out. Every product becomes obsolete after a fixed period of time. There is free entry into product development, so the dynamic equilibrium is characterized by equality between the expected profits from a new product over the course of its economic life and the cost of developing such a product. In the steady state, the rate of invention of new products exactly matches the rate of obsolescence of old products.

The welfare maximizing governments in North and South choose policies that deter-mine the degree of their protection of intellectual property. Grossman and Lai define a pair of policy variables as $\Omega_N \equiv \omega_N(1 - e^{-\rho\tau_N})/\rho$ and $\Omega_S \equiv \omega_S(1 - e^{-\rho\tau_S})/\rho$, where ω_J is the instantaneous probability that a patent used in country J will be violated due to lack of sufficient enforcement, τ_J is the duration of patent protection in country J, and ρ is the discount rate. Thus, Ω_J is a combination of the length and strength of patent protection in country *J*. By assumption, these policies are applied by each government with *national treatment*; ie, local and foreign producers are treated similarly by the patent enforcement authorities of each country.

There are two international externalities that arise in this setting. First, governments that maximize national welfare ignore the surplus that consumers in the other country derive from a new invention over the course of that product's subsequent economic life. Second, governments that are concerned only with national welfare neglect the loss of producer surplus (profits) that foreign monopolies suffer when imitation occurs or patents expire. Both of these externalities point in the same direction: patents are too short and too weakly enforced in a noncooperative regime of patent policies compared to the efficient level of protection of intellectual property. The externalities create the opportunity for a Pareto-improving patent agreement.

If the governments behave noncooperatively, their best-response functions are downward sloping curves in (Ω_N, Ω_S)-space, because the policies implemented by the two governments are strategic substitutes; when one country affords greater protection of intellectual property, this induces greater innovation by firms in both countries and reduces the incentive that the other country has to offer its own inducement for R&D. The Nash equilibrium occurs at the unique intersection of these downward sloping curves. Grossman and Lai show that, in a Nash equilibrium, if the size of the consumer population in North is at least as large as that in South and the endowment of human capital in North is larger that in the South, then $\Omega_N > \Omega_S$; ie, North provides greater protection for intellectual property than South. In such circumstances, North has greater incentive to protect intellectual property, because it has more consumers who can enjoy the surplus from new products and it has more monopolies that stand to lose profits by patent infringement or patent termination. Notice that these results do not rely on discrimination, because national treatment precludes any discrimination in the application of patent rules.

Grossman and Lai compare the patent policies that emerge in a Nash equilibrium with those that would be stipulated by an efficient agreement. The efficiency frontier lies uniformly outside the two best-response functions, because the two externalities imply that, given any policy of the other government, each government provides less protection of intellectual property than would maximize global welfare. Therefore, an international agreement must strengthen patent protection in at least one country and provide greater incentives for innovation worldwide. An efficient agreement need not strengthen patent protection in both countries in order to generate Pareto welfare gains and "harmonization" of national patent policies is not necessary for global efficiency. In fact, a continuum of combinations of Ω_N and Ω_S can be used to achieve efficiency; all that matters for efficiency is the aggregate protection of intellectual property in the world economy, whereas the policies required of each country under an efficient agreement govern the division of welfare between the two.

4. TRADE AGREEMENTS AS COMMITMENT DEVICES

In Sections 2 and 3, I reviewed a literature that treats trade agreements as a means to overcome international externalities. The externalities may arise from the incentives governments have to manipulate their terms of trade or from other externalities, such as the incentive to relocate firms to the local market or to shift profits to local oligopolists. Another strand of literature offers an alternative explanation for trade agreements, namely that they provide a means for governments to tie their own hands and resist the temptation to give in to local special interests that advocate polices inimical to the general good. I prefer to think of the commitment motive as explaining why a country might sign an existing trade agreement, rather than a reason for two countries to get together to negotiate an agreement *de novo*. It is not clear to me why governments would prefer to design a trade agreement to achieve commitment vis-à-vis their own special interests rather than to self commit by some other, simpler means. Negotiating a new agreement is a complicated process that involves many compromises; wouldn't it be easier to do so unilaterally by, for example, passing a constitutional amendment that restricts the use of trade policy instruments? However, if an agreement already exists in some form, a country may choose to take advantage of its existence by acceding to its terms. Be that as it may, the literature offers an interesting answer to the question, Why might a government be willing to sign a trade agreement?

Pre-commitment is desirable when a policy that the government regards as beneficial before the private sector takes some irreversible (or costly to reverse) action no longer is so afterwards. This situation creates a "time-inconsistency" problem, as famously described by Kydland and Prescott (1977). The literature offers several examples of economic environments where the trade policy that is optimal *ex ante* no longer is so *ex post*. I will describe informally a setting akin to that in Staiger and Tabellini (1987) as an example.

Suppose the world price of some import good falls, which depresses incomes for those who work in the import-competing sector. This creates an incentive for workers to move from the adversely impacted sector to others. Imagine that workers must make a decision at some point in time whether to move to a new job or not. Moving requires them to incur a sunk cost that cannot be recouped subsequently. Let there be a distribution of such costs among workers in the import-competing sector, so that all those with a personal cost below some critical level move, while the remainder stay in their original jobs, albeit at lower pay. Finally, suppose the government values high national income, but also has a preference for an equal distribution of that income.

Once the trade shock has occurred and workers have made their irreversible choices to stay or move, the government will see higher incomes in the export sector than in the import-competing sector. If resource allocation has been fully determined by this point, the policy makers may find it attractive to use trade policy as a means to redistribute income. The government can impose an import tariff that somewhat restores wages in the import-competing sector, thereby narrowing the income gap that results from the terms-of-trade shock.

However, if the government is free to use trade policy as a redistributive tool, the workers may anticipate such interventions when they make their decisions whether to move jobs or not. If the workers understand that the government's optimal policy will involve intervention that partly restores wages in the import-competing sector, fewer of them will move to the export sector than would be the case without such expectations. The government's *ex post* response to potential inequality will come at a high cost in terms of national income, because there will be less movement of workers than what efficiency requires. Herein lies the potential benefit from precommitment: a trade agreement that precludes tariff hikes in response to terms-of-trade shocks can increase allocative efficiency to such an extent as to more than offset the perceived social welfare cost from accepting greater inequality.[ab]

Maggi and Rodriguez-Clare (1998) extend a similar logic to a setting with political-economic forces at work. Consider a small country that faces given world prices and that has a fixed stock of capital. Initially, the capital is malleable and can be allocated to either of the economy's two, nonnumeraire sectors. Once allocated, however, the capital is specialized such that it no longer can be used to produce the other good. The timing is as follows. First, capital owners allocate their capital to one industry or the other. Then interest groups form (exogenously) and the organized groups lobby for trade policy.[ac] In a small departure from Grossman and Helpman (1994), suppose that the lobbying proceeds by Nash bargaining between the policy maker and the organized groups, with an exogenous fraction σ of the surplus accruing to the former. Finally, the government implements trade policies, competitive firms hire capital and mobile labor to produce output, and households devote their after-tax incomes (reflecting payments made or rebates received to balance the government's budget) to consumption of the three goods. The policy maker has an objective function of the form $G(W,C) = aW + C$, while the lobbies, which represent a small fraction of the total population, seek to maximize

---

[ab]   One might reasonably ask, In what sense does a trade agreement preclude a tariff hike? Mightn't a government that has signed a trade agreement decide anyway to raise its tariffs? Presumably, a government that is tempted to use trade policy to redistribute income might be dissuaded from doing so by its participation in a trade agreement only if it fears some sort of retaliation from its agreement partners. Moreover, the country's trading partners will not have any incentive to retaliate against an unauthorized tariff hike unless there are external effects of trade policies. In this general sense, the commitment power of a trade agreement also relies on the presence of international trade policy externalities.

[ac]   Mitra (2002) disallows intersectoral capital mobility both ex ante and ex post but introduces a fixed cost of political organization such that lobbies form endogenously. In his setting, as well, a government may wish to sign a trade agreement in order to precommit to free trade in anticipation of how the political economy will play out in the absence of commitment.

their industry's capital income in view of the owners' negligible stake in aggregate consumer surplus and in the government budget.

Suppose there is a multilateral trade agreement in effect, but that the government of the small country has not acceded to it, thereby retaining its sovereign right to set whatever trade policies it likes. Once the capital has been allocated and the lobbies have been formed, the organized groups bargain with the government over trade policies. At this stage, the fallback positions are zero contributions from any organized group and free trade; the latter policy maximizes aggregate welfare and therefore the government's objective G in the absence of any meeting of the minds about contributions and policies. Let $\Pi_i[(1 + t_i)p_i^*, K_i]$ be the payments to capital in industry i when the world price is p_i^*, the ad valorem tariff or export subsidy applied to this good is t_i, and the capital that has previously been allocated to the sector is K_i. The joint surplus of the organized lobbies and the policy maker is given by

$$J(\mathbf{K}) = \max_{[\mathbf{t}]} aW(\mathbf{t}, \mathbf{K}) + \sum_i I_i\Pi_i\big[(1 + t_i)p_i^*, K_i\big] - aW(\mathbf{0}, \mathbf{K}) - \sum_i I_i\Pi_i\big[p_i^*, K_i\big],$$

where $\mathbf{t}$ is the vector of trade policies applied to the two nonnumeraire industries, $\mathbf{K}$ is the vector of capital allocations to the two nonnumeraire industries, $W(\mathbf{t}, \mathbf{K})$ is aggregate welfare when the trade policies are $\mathbf{t}$ and the capital allocations are $\mathbf{K}$, $W(\mathbf{0}, \mathbf{K})$ is aggregate welfare under free trade when the capital allocations are $\mathbf{K}$, and I_i is an indicator variable that takes on a value of one if industry i is politically organized and zero otherwise. In these circumstances, the government achieves the political welfare $G = aW(\mathbf{0}, \mathbf{K}) + \sigma J(\mathbf{K})$, in view of the fact that it receives its fallback level of welfare plus the fraction σ of the surplus in the lobbying relationships. The net payoffs for the organized groups can be calculated similarly.

Still assuming that the government has not acceded to the multilateral trade agreement, we can solve for the capital allocations in a rational-expectations equilibrium. The equilibrium allocations, $\tilde{\mathbf{K}}$, are those that equalize the expected net incomes for capital allocated to the alternative uses, considering the trade policies that are anticipated as well as the contributions (if any) that are expected to be made.

Now suppose that the government has the opportunity at the outset to sign a trade agreement that commits the country to free trade. By doing so, it foregoes the surplus from its political relationships with the lobbies. Although the government sees free trade as a desirable outcome for aggregate welfare, given any $\mathbf{K}$ it prefers to enact protectionist or export-promoting policies in exchange for the valuable contributions it can extract from the lobbies. So why would the government potentially wish to precommit to trade freely? The answer, as before, has to do with the *ex ante* allocation of capital. With a trade agreement in place, the capital owners recognize that lobbying for protection or export subsidies will be futile. Accordingly, they anticipate earnings of $\Pi_i[p_i^*, K_i]$ in industry i.

The allocation that equates the returns in the two industries, $\mathbf{K}_{FT}$, is of course the one that is *ex ante* most efficient. Accordingly, $W(\mathbf{0}, \mathbf{K}_{FT}) \geq W(\mathbf{0}, \tilde{\mathbf{K}})$, with strict inequality whenever $\tilde{\mathbf{K}} \neq K_{FT}$. In deciding whether to accede to the trade agreement, the government compares $aW(\mathbf{0}, \mathbf{K}_{FT})$, its expected political welfare when it joins the agreement, to $aW(\mathbf{0}, \tilde{\mathbf{K}}) + \sigma J(\tilde{\mathbf{K}})$, the net payoff including contributions that it achieves when it opts not to join.

Maggi and Rodriguez-Clare (1998) observe that joining the trade agreement will be attractive to the government if $\sigma = 0$, but not so if $\sigma = 1$. If the policy maker captures none of the surplus in its relationship with the lobbies, then the comparison hinges on the aggregate welfare that results from the initial allocation of capital, and $aW(\mathbf{0}, \mathbf{K}_{FT}) > aW(\mathbf{0}, \tilde{\mathbf{K}})$. On the other hand, if the policy maker captures most of this surplus, then the capital owners will anticipate a net return after lobbying that differs little from what they would earn under government's fallback position of free trade; accordingly, the allocation $\tilde{\mathbf{K}}$ will be very close to $\mathbf{K}_{FT}$. Then $aW(\mathbf{0}, \tilde{\mathbf{K}}) + \sigma J(\tilde{\mathbf{K}}) \approx aW(\mathbf{0}, \mathbf{K}_{FT}) + \sigma J(\tilde{\mathbf{K}}) > aW(\mathbf{0}, \mathbf{K}_{FT})$. In short, the government prefers to tie its own hands when its bargaining position vis-à-vis domestic interest groups is weak, but not when it is strong; in the latter case, it can use the flexibility to implement trade policies to attract contributions from the lobbies that exceed (in its political assessment) the losses that it policies impose on the general public.

Brou and Ruta (2013) extend the model of Maggi and Rodriguez-Clare (1998) to allow for domestic subsidies. The government can transfer income to special interests in the import-competing sector either by affording protection or by providing production subsidies that are financed by distortionary taxation. An agreement that limits only the use of trade policies will not be very attractive to the government, because the value of precommitting the use of one instrument is limited when the interest group knows that the government can readily substitute another. Brou and Ruta use the model to analyze the Subsidies and Countervailing Measures Agreement in the WTO system; a government that wishes to tie its hands vis-à-vis domestic lobbies will be more inclined to accede to an international agreement that limits the use of production subsidies alongside the use of tariffs (or export subsidies) than one that restricts only trade policies.

Whereas an agreement that eliminates tariffs and export subsidies may not be attractive for commitment purposes if it leaves the government free to use good substitutes for trade policies like production subsidies as alternative means to redistribute income, a government may be willing to sign an agreement that does not constrain the use of more inefficient means of income transfer. Limão (2011) study a government's willingness to constrain the use of tariff policies when nontariff barriers (NTBs) are available as substitutes. They assume that NTBs, like tariffs, transfer rents to domestic special interests in the import-competing sectors. But these policies dissipate some of these rents, so they are strictly less efficient as tools of redistribution. The government may be willing to sign a trade agreement that constraints the use of tariffs for reasons akin to those offered by Maggi and Rodriguez-Clare while recognizing that the costliness of NTBs provides some assurance that it will not succumb to that temptation, or at least not do so to any great extent. Limão (2011) offer their analysis as an explanation for why the WTO system binds tariffs and prohibits production subsidies, but does not constrain the use of a variety of less efficient policies that can serve as (imperfect) substitutes for the tariffs and subsidies.

If governments have incentives to negotiate a trade agreement in order to mitigate international externalities, then the benefits from precommitment vis-à-vis domestic special interests can provide an added inducement for doing so. Maggi and Rodriguez-Clare (2007) incorporate the two distinct benefits of a trade agreement in a single model, which generates some interesting further insights. There are two symmetrically different countries and three goods. In the home country, capital endowment K_1 can be used to produce either the numeraire good or good 1. Capital endowment K_2 can only be used to produce good 2. In the foreign country, capital endowment K_1^* can be used only to produce good 1. Capital endowment K_2^* can be used either to produce good 2 or the numeraire good. Endowments and demands are such that the home country imports good 1 and exports good 2. Production technologies are linear in capital and only the import-competing sector in each country is politically organized. The governments have a political motive for providing protection and a terms-of-trade motive, as in Grossman and Helpman (1995b). The international externality lends value to a trade agreement, as does the capital misallocation that results from anticipated protection.

Let the initial allocations of capital and the initial tariff rates emerge from the Nash equilibrium of a noncooperative game, as in Grossman and Helpman's trade war. The resulting tariffs are larger than the welfare-maximizing rates, and so there is overinvestment in the import-competing industry. Initially there is no thought of a trade agreement and the allocations do not anticipate one being negotiated. But suddenly, that possibility arises.[ad] The lobbies and the governments negotiate over a campaign contribution and the terms of an agreement, which takes the form of an (endogenous) cap on tariff rates. The agreement maximizes the joint surplus of the two governments and the two lobbies. After an agreement is signed—if that happens—each owner of a unit of K_1 in the home country or of type K_2^* in the foreign country has the opportunity to move that capital to the numeraire sector with some exogenous probability z. The parameter z is meant to capture the degree of capital mobility in the import-competing industry, from complete specificity ($z = 0$) to perfect mobility ($z = 1$). After any capital reallocation takes place, the lobby in each country and its government negotiate again about the actual level of the

---

[ad] Maggi and Rodriguez-Clare (2007) show that their insights carry over to a version of the model in which the opportunity to negotiate a trade agreement is not a surprise, but rather is perfectly anticipated when the initial capital allocation takes place.

tariff, but this time subject to the constraints imposed by the international agreement. Finally, political contributions are paid and production, trade and consumption take place.

Maggi and Rodriguez-Clare show first that the governments and the lobbies (weakly) prefer an agreement that imposes caps on tariffs to one that explicitly determines their levels. If an agreement must stipulate exact levels of the policy instruments, a jointly efficient agreement will reduce tariffs from their noncooperative levels, but not to zero, and there will remain distortions in the allocation of capital and in consumption. Now suppose that there is an option instead to set that same tariff as a maximum, rather than as a requirement. Such an agreement would leave discretion for each government to set the actual tariff below the agreed ceiling, and so the lobbies would have to offer contributions to avoid such an outcome. Inasmuch as a tariff ceiling imposes an additional burden of contributions on the capital owners, it reduces the overinvestment in politically organized sectors. Joint surplus is raised by an agreement that reduces such distortions, and all parties (governments and lobbies) can share in the gains by appropriate adjustment of contributions in the initial round of lobbying. Accordingly, the model predicts that a trade agreement will designate tariff ceilings ("bindings") rather than tariff levels, if such a contract is possible.

The model links the size of tariffs cuts (from the initial Nash levels to ultimate policies that are set subject to the constraints of the agreement) to the degree of capital mobility, as captured by the parameter z. In the extreme, if $z = 1$, the owners of capital in the import-competing sector can always earn the return promised in the numeraire sector. There are no rents to be captured in the *ex post* stage of lobbying, hence the lobbies are not willing to pay anything to their governments to compensate for long-run distortions associated with protection. Accordingly, the trade negotiation cuts tariffs to zero. At the opposite extreme, if $z = 0$, there is no possibility to undo the misallocation of capital. The equilibrium agreement eliminates the terms-of-trade component of the Nash tariff—as in Grossman and Helpman's trade talks—but it cannot reduce the domestic-commitment problem. Maggi and Rodriguez-Clare show that the tariff cut relative to the initial, Nash equilibrium level is monotonically increasing in capital mobility, z. If we interpret this result as a cross-sectional prediction, it says that tariff cuts should be deeper in those industries where capital specificity is less and outward reallocation is easier.

Finally, the authors consider how the extent of trade liberalization varies with the extent of the governments' concern for aggregate welfare relative to campaign contributions. In a setting without precommitment considerations, such as Grossman and Helpman (1995b), the Nash equilibrium tariffs tend to be higher when the governments' concern for aggregate welfare is small. High initial tariffs limit the volume of trade and thus weaken the terms-of-trade externalities. We might expect, therefore that tariff cuts will be smaller when the government has a greater taste for contributions and when it places less weight on aggregate welfare. But in the model developed by Maggi and

Rodriguez (2007), the opposite can be true when capital is sufficiently mobile. In this setting, high initial tariffs in the Nash equilibrium (that emerge when the government has less concern for aggregate welfare) imply a large departure from allocative efficiency. If z is large, there is much to be gained by committing to low tariffs and thereby inducing a substantial reallocation of capital. Accordingly, the agreement should call for deep tariff cuts when a small government weight on welfare induces a large initial distortion and a high degree of capital mobility implies that the costs can be reduced greatly by a commitment to freer trade.

5. INCENTIVES TO FORM REGIONAL OR PREFERENTIAL TRADE AGREEMENTS

Until now, I have mostly discussed the purpose of trade agreements in the context of a two-country world economy. One exception concerned the incentives that exporting countries might have to limit their use of strategic export subsidies to third-country markets. But bilateral and plurilateral agreements take place in many other contexts. Indeed, the number of bilateral, regional, or other preferential trade pacts has been growing in leaps and bounds, giving rise to what Bhagwati (1995) has called the "spaghetti bowl" of international agreements. Baldwin and Venables (1995), Panagariya (2000), and Krishna (2005) have written excellent surveys of the theoretical literature on the economic effects of preferential trade agreements (PTAs), while Limão (2016) reviews the empirical research in Chapter 14. In this section, I will limit myself to those few articles that address the reasons that governments might choose to negotiate exclusive agreements—rather than, or in addition to, multilateral agreements—in a world economy with more than two countries.

5.1 The Ohyama-Kemp-Wan Theorem

Any discussion of the incentives for trade agreements among a limited set of countries should begin with the renowned Ohyama-Kemp-Wan theorem (see Ohyama, 1972; Kemp and Wan, 1976). These authors proved a striking result: If lump-sum transfers are feasible within a union, any group of countries can form a customs union and set a common external tariff in such a way that all member countries benefit and no excluded country is harmed. The logic of the argument is simple. Let the union choose an external tariff that leaves its members' aggregate vector of trades with the rest of the world unchanged. (We know this always is possible based on results about the existence of market-clearing prices in a competitive equilibrium.) Then markets will clear in the rest of the world at the prices that prevailed before the union. With the same prices and the same trades, these countries are exactly as well-off as before. As for the union members, we can treat their vector of trades as if it were an endowment vector. Efficiency within the union requires equalization of marginal rates of transformation and of marginal rates of substitution across member countries. This is achieved by a common vector of prices, which in turn is guaranteed by internal free trade. All that remains is to share the efficiency gains, which can be accomplished costlessly when the countries have access to lump-sum transfers between members.[ae]

Countries have an incentive to form customs union in order to achieve allocative efficiency. The same is true if the governments have noneconomic production targets (Krishna and Bhagwati, 1997). The result also extends to environments in which the policy makers have political objectives besides aggregate welfare, provided they have access to efficient instruments to redistribute income to favorite interest groups. However, as Richardson (1995) cautions, the Ohyama-Kemp-Wan theorem should be interpreted with care. It cannot be taken to imply that a group of countries can form a mutually beneficial customs union *no matter what is the response in the rest of the world*. The proof assumes that the rest of the world responds to the customs union by making the same vector of trades at the same prices; ie, the aggregate offer curve of the rest of the world is not affected by the formation of the union. If nonmembers can respond by, for example, setting a new vector of "optimal" or "politically guided" tariffs, then gains for union members are not assured.

5.2 Terms-of-Trade Gains

Just as a single country can gain at the expense of its trading partners by exploiting its monopoly power in world markets, so too can a group of large countries benefit by cooperating to exploit their joint market power in trade. In fact, two large countries stand to gain by forming a free-trade area (FTA) even if they do not alter their external tariffs vis-à-vis nonmember countries.

Consider a three-country world in which countries A and B form an FTA with distinct external tariffs and country C represents the excluded rest of the world. Suppose first that A imports some good from B and C, both of which have upward-sloping, competitive supply curves. Country A has an external tariff of t^A that applies initially to imports from all sources. Once it forms an FTA with B, the tariff applies only to imports from C. Let p^C represent the initial price received by exporters in both B and C for sales in country A, so that $p^C(1 + t^A)$ is the pre-FTA domestic price in A. When country A eliminates its tariff on imports from B, suppliers there can sell in A's market at the prevailing domestic price. There is excess supply in the world market at the original prices, as firms in B

[ae]   Dixit and Norman (1986) show that lump-sum transfers are not necessarily to share the gains from trade, if countries have access to a full set of consumption and factor taxes and subsidies. Panagariya and Krishna (2002) extend the Ohyama-Kemp-Wan result to include free trade areas in which member countries maintain separate external tariffs vis-à-vis imports from the rest of the world but trade freely within the area. In this case, member tariffs are chosen to preserve the initial vector of trades by each area country and resulting internal prices are not the same in these countries.

produce more at the higher delivered price. The price of imports from the rest of the world must fall to clear the world market. The fall in p^C benefits A while harming B, but since A's imports are larger than B's exports, the net effect must be positive. The members of the FTA capture a terms-of-trade gain as a result of trade diversion.

Now suppose instead that A and C both import from B. The initial price received by exporters in B is p^B and the domestic price in A is $p^B(1 + t^A)$. With the elimination of the barrier to internal trade, the price in country A falls. This creates excess demand. The supply price from B must rise to clear the world market. The increase in p^B benefits B while harming A, but since B's exports are larger than A's imports, again the gains outweigh the losses. In this case, trade creation generates a positive terms-of-trade effect for the members of the FTA.

Countries that forge a regional or preferential trading arrangement can gain even more by adjusting their external tariff or tariffs. The incentive for doing so is analogous to that for merger among competing oligopolists; whereas each country can exploit market power on its own, the joint influence over world prices is greater than for any one alone. The potential gains are evident as a corollary to the Ohyama-Kemp-Wan theorem (or the Panagariya-Krishna extension to FTAs): If a group of countries can benefit by forming a customs union with an external tariff that leaves the terms of trade the same as before, then they can benefit even more by adjusting their external tariff optimally.

Kennan and Riezman (1990) investigated whether countries can gain by forming a customs union, once the tariff response by nonmember countries is taken into account. They examined an endowment economy with three goods and three countries that are symmetric up to a relabeling of the endowment goods, with a linear expenditure system in all countries. In this setting, they compared the outcome in a Nash equilibrium in which two of the countries allow internal free trade while jointly choosing an optimal external tariff to the outcome in a Nash equilibrium without any cooperation, and the outcome in an equilibrium with global free trade. Whenever each country's endowments of its export good is not too large relative to the total world endowment, any pair of countries fares better in a customs union equilibrium than in one with global free trade. Therefore, the possibility of forming customs unions undermines the prospects for a multilateral trade agreement

Kennan and Riezman also examined how size affects the incentives that countries have to form a customs union and, in particular, whether a pair of smaller countries can gain by joining forces to enhance their collective market power once retaliation is taken into account. In their examples, welfare rises in each of a pair of smaller countries when they form a customs union compared to the outcome with no cooperation, but each fares less well than it would in an equilibrium with universal free trade. In contrast, larger countries fair better in a Nash equilibrium in which they are partners in a customs union compared to both the Nash equilibrium without any cooperation and the equilibrium with global free trade.

Of course, the motivation to form a customs union or FTA in order to exert collective market power relies on the same beggar-thy-neighbor calculus as does the unilateral imposition of optimal tariffs in a setting without trade agreements. The gains to the member countries come entirely at the expense of countries on the outside. Krugman (1991a) began a small literature that addresses the welfare implications of having a trading system with multiple, nonoverlapping blocs in which each bloc allows internal free trade but behaves noncooperatively vis-à-vis the others. He considers a world with a large number of symmetric countries divided into a smaller number of symmetric blocs. Each country produces a unique good and all such goods are CES substitutes for one another. He takes the number of such blocs as exogenous. Each bloc sets an external tariff that maximizes the joint welfare of its members, given the tariffs set by other blocs. In these circumstances, the height of each country's tariff grows with the size of the typical bloc. Consolidation of the world into larger blocs has offsetting effects on welfare in the typical country; between-bloc trade distortions grow monotonically larger with bloc size, but so does the fraction of world trade that takes place within blocs. Welfare is highest when the entire world comprises one bloc, but also is high when the world has small blocs that have little monopoly power and therefore impose low tariffs. In between, welfare is a nonmonotonic function of bloc size. Krugman notoriously found that, for many values of the elasticity of substitution, welfare is minimal when the trading systems comprises three symmetric blocs.

The findings in Krugman (1991a) rely heavily on the assumption that countries are symmetric and form their blocs arbitrarily. In a follow-up paper, Krugman (1991b) discusses informally a case with "natural trading blocs." In this setting, geography or other considerations give certain groups of countries a greater predilection to trade with one another than with those outside the group. If blocs form "naturally" among groups of countries that trade intensively, the free movement of goods within blocs will cover a majority of world trade and the external trade barriers will apply to a small volume of trade. In the limit, with very high costs of trade outside a natural grouping, the formation of trading blocs must be raise welfare for all involved.[af]

5.3 Political Incentives for Regional or Preferential Agreements

In addition to the potential improvements to allocative efficiency and to external terms of trade that can motivate countries to form preferential trade agreements such as FTAs and customs unions, there are political forces that can explain this outcome.

Grossman and Helpman (1995a) examine the political conflict between supporters and opponents of an FTA in a model with industry campaign contributions. There are two small countries that initially have the tariffs predicted by the lobbying model

---

[af]   In another extension of Krugman (1991a), Bond and Syropoulos (1996) examine more fully the relationship between bloc size and the market power exerted by trading blocs, by allowing for blocs of different sizes and by allowing for alternative endowment structures.

of Grossman and Helpman (1994). Each can trade with the rest of the world at fixed terms of trade. The countries have an opportunity to eliminate tariffs on their internal trade while retaining their initial external tariffs for imports from the rest of the world. Export industries offer contributions to encourage the government conclude an agreement in order to expand market access in the partner country. Import-competing interests offer contributions to discourage the agreement, in order to protect their local markets. Each government chooses a stance that maximizes a weighted sum of aggregate welfare and contributions. A FTA is politically viable if and only if it is favored by both governments. The question is, Under what conditions is an FTA most likely to form?

An FTA has no effect on industries in which both countries export to the rest of the world. So, Grossman and Helpman focus on industries in which at least one of the member countries has positive imports in the initial equilibrium. They distinguish two possible outcomes for such an industry once an FTA comes into being. First, the importer might expand its imports from its partner while continuing to import from the rest of the world. In this case, the internal price in the importing country remains equal to the world price augmented by the MFN tariff. There is no expansion of its total imports, only diversion of trade from the rest of world to the FTA partner. Second, the importing country might cease its imports from the rest of the world and import only from its FTA partner. In this case, the price falls in the importing country and total imports expand. The internal price in the exporting member of the FTA need not rise very much and might not rise at all. Grossman and Helpman refer to the former outcome as one with *enhanced protection*, which comes hand in hand with trade diversion. The latter outcome is one with *reduced protection*, together with trade creation.

Now consider the politics. In the case of enhanced protection, the industry in the exporting country gains producer surplus from preferential access to the higher internal prices in the partner country. Meanwhile, the import-competing industry suffers no losses, as the internal price there remains as before. On net, such industries contribute to political viability; the export interests lobby in favor of the agreement and the import-competing interests have no reason to oppose. In contrast, with reduced protection, the exporting interests stand to gain little or nothing, while the import-competing interests in the potential partner face the prospect of falling local prices. The existence of such industries bolster opposition to a potential agreement in one country with only modest (or no) support generated in the other. Overall, an FTA will be viable if most industries have the potential for enhanced protection and not so if most face the prospect of reduced protection. But trade creation enhances economic efficiency in the small countries, whereas trade diversion detracts from an efficient allocation of resources. This leads Grossman and Helpman to conclude that an FTA is most likely to be politically viable when it is also economically harmful. Krishna (1998) comes to much the same conclusion in a model with oligopolistic trade in which trade politics are driven entirely by effects on firms' profits.

However, Ornelas (2005a) provides a counterargument. He considers an economy much like the one in Krishna (1998), with quasilinear utility, constant returns production of a numeraire good, and oligopolistic competition in a second sector, with fixed numbers of firms in each country and segmented markets. But whereas Krishna assumes that MFN tariffs remain the same after any agreement is signed, Ornelas allows the FTA members to adjust their external tariffs. He shows that, in this setting, they have incentive to *reduce* their tariffs vis-à-vis nonmembers, for two reasons.[ag] First, a government's incentive to set high tariffs in order to extract profits from firms in nonmember countries is mitigated by the FTA, because firms in partner countries with improved access to the local market capture more of the profits that are extracted from the outsiders. Second, the political support for high tariffs vis-à-vis nonmember countries is reduced by the formation of an FTA, because politically active firms lose sales in their home market to rivals in partner countries, and so have less incentive to lobby for protection from outsiders. In the economic environment considered by Ornelas, the fall in external tariffs that results from an FTA always is deep enough to generate net trade creation with nonmember countries. Moreover, in his model, an FTA can be politically viable only if it is efficiency enhancing. Since the FTA reduces political contributions by local firms, it can be attractive to the policy makers only if aggregate welfare rises to more than compensate.

When FTAs cause trade diversion from nonmembers, the politics of preferential trade can be self-reinforcing, a phenomenon that Baldwin (1993) termed "domino regionalism." He considers a world with many potential members of a customs union. Each government's stance toward joining the union reflects an internal trade-off between consumer welfare and industry interests, but with an additional term that reflects the country's exogenous "resistance" (positive or negative) to being a member of the club. Countries differ in this regard, and those that are least resistant are the first to join. The economies produce a homogeneous good and a fixed set of differentiated varieties. The former good is traded freely, whereas the latter goods are traded subject to iceberg trading costs. These costs are higher for firms outside the region than for those that are potential members of the customs union. The political contributors in this setting are the owners of the differentiated varieties.

Baldwin imagines an initial equilibrium in which all countries in the region with resistance below some critical level are members of the union and those with greater resistance are not. Then, there is an exogenous shock that reduces trade costs within the region. The decline in within-group trade costs causes additional governments to apply for membership. But, as membership expands, firms in nonmember countries intensify their lobbying, as the potential profits for insiders expand at the expense of profits for outsiders. An initial round of union expansion alters the political balance in nonmember countries,

---

[ag] Richardson (1993) shows that countries also have an incentive to reduce their external tariffs after forming an FTA when markets are perfectly competitive.

such that further expansion follows. The ultimate growth in regionalism, then, is a multiple of what one might expect from the initial shock. In short, Baldwin argues that the trade diversion associated with preferential trade agreements can be politically contagious.[ah]

But once again, the conclusion can be different if an FTA results in a reduction of external tariffs that promotes trade with nonmember countries. Ornelas (2005b) considers one such setting, using the same economic model as in Krishna (1998) and Ornelas (2005a). The fact that firms in nonmember countries benefit from the reduction in external tariffs of the FTA partners without having to reduce their own tariffs means that they may have less incentive than before to enter into agreements with the member countries, either as partners to a PTA or as signatories to a multilateral agreement.

5.4 PTAs as Stepping Stones to Multilateral Free Trade

Another potential purpose of preferential trade agreements is to facilitate a process of multilateral trade liberalization. The literature identifies circumstances under which PTAs serve as "building blocks" for global free trade; that is, a multilateral agreement that implements free trade becomes achievable as an equilibrium outcome in a dynamic game when PTAs are negotiated along the way, when such an outcome would not be possible in a negotiation game that precludes preferential agreements. Of course, PTAs can also represent "stumbling blocks" in some circumstances; that is, they can impede or prevent the achievement of global free trade in situations where a multilateral agreement would emerge as an equilibrium if discriminatory trade were prohibited.[ai] Indeed, the Ornelas (2005b) paper mentioned above provides one such example. But, in such cases, one would not typically regard the "purpose" of the PTA as being to interfere with multilateral negotiations; rather, the impediment to free trade would be seen as an unintended consequence. Since this chapter deals with the purpose of trade agreements and not their unintended consequences, I will not review further the research that describes PTAs as stumbling blocks.

[ah] Chen and Joshi (2010) examine how the existence of FTAs affects the incentives that countries have to form new agreements. They consider a model with three countries and two goods. The numeraire good is competitively produced while the other good is produced by one firm in each country. Preferences are quasilinear, demands for the oligopoly good are linear, and the competition features Cournot behavior with segmented markets. In this setting, if one country in a pair has an existing FTA with the third country but the other does not, then the existing FTA strengthens the incentive for the member to form another FTA but weakens the incentive for the nonmember country to do so, compared to a benchmark with no pre-existing FTA. However, if both potential members of a new FTA participate in pre-existing agreements with the third country, the incentives that both have to conclude a new agreement are inevitably strengthened.

[ai] The terminology of building blocks and stumbling blocks was first introduced by Bhagwati (1991).

One way in which a PTA may facilitate the achievement of global free trade is by raising the cost of being left out. Saggi and Yildiz (2010) illustrate this idea in a three-country, three-good, endowment model with linear demands. Each country is endowed with two goods that it exports to the other two. It has no endowment of the third good, which it imports from its two trade partners. In a dynamic game that allows for "bilateralism," each country announces in a first stage the names of any trade partners with whom it is willing to engage in mutual free trade. In the second stage, the countries set external tariffs for any and all countries with whom they have not entered into an agreement in the first stage. In a game that precludes bilateralism, the countries can only agree to liberalize trade on a multilateral basis. If any country declines to do so, then the noncooperative tariffs ensue.[aj]

Saggi and Yildiz consider first a situation in which the countries are symmetric with respect to their endowment levels. In such circumstances, global free trade is the unique stable equilibrium under both bilateralism and multilateralism. Accordingly, with symmetry, PTAs have no role to play in the achievement of global free trade in their model; a multilateral agreement is reached even if bilateral agreements are not allowed. But the conclusion can be different with asymmetric countries. Then, global free trade emerges as a stable equilibrium for a wider set of parameter values with bilateralism than with multilateralism. In other words, for some endowment combinations, a multilateral agreement can be reached only if bilateral agreements represent a permissible alternative.

The finding is readily understood. Consider a country that fares better in a Johnson-like Nash equilibrium than under global free trade. In a multilateral process, such a country would decline to name any of its partners in the negotiation stage. By submitting a blank sheet, it could effectively block an agreement and achieve its first best. Suppose instead that bilateral agreements are possible. The country that fares best in the noncooperative equilibrium might not have this outcome as a viable option. If the other two countries can gain by forming a bilateral block compared to universal noncooperation, then the relevant comparison for the third country is between a multilateral agreement and a world with an PTA from which it is excluded. Since trade diversion within the member countries would hurt the excluded country, it might well prefer the multilateral agreement to being the one country on the outside.[ak]

[aj]   Saggi et al. (2013) compare bilateralism and multilateralism in a model in which countries are free to form customs unions but not FTAs. They show that customs unions, unlike FTAs, can prevent the achievement of global free trade, because two countries may prefer to exclude the third country from mutual free trade in order to exploit their joint market power. The incentive for exclusion is stronger under a customs union than under a FTA, so the former can be a stumbling block but not a building block for multilateral trade liberalization in their setting.

[ak]   Saggi and Yildiz (2011) reach much the same conclusion in a model with a different economic setting. There they consider a world economy with Cournot competition in segmented markets and one firm per country. In a symmetric setting in which all three firms have the same costs, global free trade emerges as the unique stable equilibrium with bilateral agreements are possible or not. However, the possibility of bilateral agreements is necessary for the achievement of global free trade in a setting in which one firm has much higher production costs than the others.

In Saggi and Yildiz (2010), the possibility of a PTA facilitates the conclusion of a multilateral agreement, but no PTAs need to form for global free trade to be realized. This is an inevitable consequence of the game structure, wherein either a bilateral agreement or a multilateral agreement is signed, but not both. Aghion et al. (2007) introduce a sequential structure in which PTAs may actually form along the equilibrium path. They consider a trade-negotiation process in reduced form, with the details of the economic environment suppressed. In particular, they specify payoffs for each of three countries under all possible coalition structures: with each country alone; with all combinations of bilateral agreements; and with a multilateral agreement. They allow for utility transfers between coalition members, so the relevant payoffs are those that accrue jointly to the parties to any trade agreement. The bargaining protocol features an agenda setter that makes take-it-or-leave offers to the other two countries. In a multilateral negotiation, the offers to engage in free trade are made simultaneously to the others and they can accept or reject. With bilateralism, the agenda setter makes the offers sequentially, in whatever order it prefers. If the first to receive an offer accepts, a bilateral agreement is formed. If the second also accepts, the agreement becomes multilateral. Aghion et al. (2007) ask, when does the agenda setter choose the sequential process? And, when is a sequential process necessary to achieve global free trade?

The authors distinguish several cases. If the payoffs exhibit "grand coalition superadditivity," then the sum of the payoffs under global free trade exceeds the sum of the payoffs under any other coalition structure. Grand coalition superadditivity necessarily applies in a neoclassical economy with welfare-maximizing governments. But it need not apply if there is imperfect competition in world markets, or if the governments have political motivations. With or without grand coalition superadditivity, there can be positive or negative coalition externalities. Payoffs are characterized by positive coalition externalities when the welfare of a country that is excluded from a PTA is higher than it would be without the bilateral agreement. Negative coalition externalities imply just the opposite.

With grand coalition superadditivity and transferable utility, the agenda setter always prefers a multilateral agreement to any alternative. Moreover, it can achieve such an outcome by offering payoffs to the others that make them indifferent between joining and not. The question remains, How do the structure of coalition externalities affect the agenda sender's choice between simultaneous and sequential negotiation? Aghion et al. show that, if at least one coalition externality is negative, the agenda setter will opt to negotiate sequentially. First it will form an agreement with the country (if any) that faces a positive externality. Then it will invite the participation of the remaining country. By the time the second country receives its offer, its fallback position is the lower level of welfare that it would suffer if excluded from a bilateral pact. So, the agenda setter can extract surplus from this country by confronting it with an inferior default option.

Even if the payoffs do not satisfy grand coalition superadditivity, a sequential negotiation process might lead to global free trade. A multilateral agreement can be reached even at a cost in terms of the collective (economic or political) welfare of the three countries under conditions that the authors describe. The outcome becomes possible, because the agenda setter's option to form a bilateral agreement first with one country allows it to extract enough surplus from the other that it is willing to begin these negotiations in preference to the *status quo*. More specifically, let C represent the agenda setter and A and B represent the other two countries. Suppose C prefers the *status quo* with no trade agreements to global free trade. In a simultaneous, multilateral negotiation, C must offer A and B their *status quo* payoffs. If the sum of the three status quo payoffs exceeds the joint welfare under a multilateral trade agreement, then C will not make any offers under multilateral bargaining, and the *status quo* will prevail. But suppose C has already negotiated a bilateral agreement with A and that the coalition externalities for B are negative. Then C will not need to offer B as much as its status quo level of welfare in order to induce it to join the existing agreement. With the lesser payment that is needed, C might prefer to have B join once an agreement with A has been established. Moreover, C might prefer this outcome (with the smaller payment to B) than what it can attain in the *status quo*. In these circumstances, C will approach A first and then B, and the bilateral agreement with A serves as a building block for a multilateral agreement with both A and B.[al] The authors develop in their appendix an example of an economic setting with the requisite payoff structure.

6. CONCLUSION

This chapter has reviewed research that asks about the purpose of trade agreements. Why do governments willingly give up their sovereign rights to set trade policies and enter into agreements that restrict their choices? A unifying theme in much of the literature is that they do so in order to help internalize international externalities. No matter what the governments' objectives, be they the welfare of the aggregate polities or of particular constituent groups, or even the interests and well-being of the politicians themselves, interdependence in the trading system implies that any government's actions affect outcomes abroad. Each government would like others to take its concerns into account when setting policy. The only way to secure such an outcome is to display a willingness to take account of other governments' concerns when setting ones own policies.

The literature has usefully identified a number of international externalities that can arise in different market settings and with different political institutions. Less fruitful, in my opinion, have been the efforts to pin labels on these externalities. Is the fundamental purpose of the agreement to eliminate manipulation of the terms of trade or to ensure that

---

[al]   An additional condition is needed to ensure that C prefers to approach A for a bilateral agreement before negotiating with b. Of course, there are analogous conditions on the payoffs for which multilateral free trade is achieved after an initial bilateral agreement between C and B.

domestic exporters are granted satisfactory access to foreign markets? It is not clear to me why this distinction is important, so long as we understand that noncooperative policy setting gives rise to inferior outcomes. We do want to understand why trade agreements have the features they do and what provisions must be added or modified to generate efficient outcomes and mutual gain. In my opinion, future research effort would be more productively spent understanding and improving the design of trade agreements (ie, extending the literature reviewed in Chapter 8) than in worrying about the words that best describe the purpose of trade agreements.

ACKNOWLEDGMENTS

I am grateful to Daniel Goetz for excellent research assistance and to Kyle Bagwell and Bob Staiger for comments on an earlier draft. I am also grateful to Henrik Horn, with whom I have discussed many of these issues before (see Grossman and Horn, 2013).

REFERENCES

Aghion, P., Antràs, P., Helpman, E., 2007. Negotiating free trade. J. Int. Econ. 73 (1), 1–30.
Antràs, P., Staiger, R.W., 2012. Offshoring and the role of trade agreements. Am. Econ. Rev. 102 (7), 3140–3483.
Ashley, P., 1904. Modern Tariff History: Germany, United States, France. John Murrary, London.
Aumann, R.J., 1985. Repeated games. In: Feiwel, G.R. (Ed.), Issues in Contemporary Microeconomics and Welfare. State University of New York Press, Albany, NY.
Bagwell, K., Staiger, R.W., 1999. An economic theory of GATT. Am. Econ. Rev. 89 (1), 215–248.
Bagwell, K., Staiger, R.W., 2001. Domestic policies, national sovereignty and international economic institutions. Q. J. Econ. 116 (2), 519–562.
Bagwell, K., Staiger, R.W., 2002. The Economics of the World Trading System. MIT Press, Cambridge, MA.
Bagwell, K., Staiger, R.W., 2006. Will international rules on subsidies disrupt the world trading system? Am. Econ. Rev. 96 (3), 877–895.
Bagwell, K., Staiger, R.W., 2012a. Profit shifting and trade agreements in imperfectly competitive markets. Int. Econ. Rev. 53 (4), 1067–1104.
Bagwell, K., Staiger, R.W., 2012b. The economics of trade agreements in the linear Cournot delocation model. J. Int. Econ. 88 (1), 32–46.
Bagwell, K., Staiger, R.W., 2015. Delocation and trade agreements in imperfectly competitive markets. Res. Econ. 69 (2), 132–156.
Bagwell, K., Staiger, R.W., 2016. The design of trade agreements. In: Bagwell, K., Staiger, R. (Eds.), Handbook of Commercial Policy, vol. 1A. North Holland, Amsterdam, pp. 435–529.
Baldwin, R.E., 1993. A Domino theory of regionalism. National Bureau of Economic Research, Cambridge, MA. NBER Working Paper 4465.
Baldwin, R.E., Venables, A.J., 1995. Regional economic integration. In: Grossman, G.M., Rogoff, K. (Eds.), Handbook of International Economics, vol. 3. North-Holland, Amsterdam.
Barrett, S., 2005. The theory of international environmental agreements. In: Mäler, K.G., Vincent, J.R. (Eds.), Handbook of Environmental Economics, vol. 3. North Holland, Amsterdam.
Bhagwati, J., 1991. The World Trading System at Risk. Princeton University Press, Princeton, NJ.
Bhagwati, J., 1995. U.S. trade policy: the infatuation with free trade areas. In: Bhagwati, J.N., Krueger, A.O. (Eds.), The Dangerous Drift to Preferential Trade Agreements, The AEI Press, Washington, D.C.
Bond, E.W., 1990. The optimal tariff structure in higher dimensions. Int. Econ. Rev. 31 (1), 103–116.

Bond, E.W., Park, J.H., 2002. Gradualism in trade agreements with asymmetric countries. Rev. Econ. Stud. 69 (2), 379–406.

Bond, E.W., Syropoulos, C., 1996. The size of trading blocks: market power and world welfare effects. J. Int. Econ. 40, 412–437.

Brander, J., Spencer, B., 1984a. Trade warfare: tariffs and cartels. J. Int. Econ. 16, 227–242.

Brander, J., Spencer, B., 1984b. Tariff protection and imperfect competition. In: Kierzkowski, H. (Ed.), Monopolistic Competition and International Trade, Clarendon Press, Oxford.

Brander, J., Spencer, B., 1985. Export subsidies and market share rivalry. J. Int. Econ. 18, 83–100.

Brou, D., Ruta, M., 2013. A commitment theory of subsidy agreements. The B.E. J. Econ. Anal. Policy 13 (1), 239–270.

Chen, M.X., Joshi, S., 2010. Third-country effects on the formation of free trade agreements. J. Int. Econ. 82 (2), 238–248.

Destler, I.M., 2005. American Trade Politics, fourth ed. Institute for International Economics, Washington, D.C.

Dixit, A.K., 1985. Tax policy in open economies. In: Auerbach, A., Feldstein, M.J. (Eds.), Handbook of Public Economics, vol. 1. North Holland, Amsterdam, pp. 313–374.

Dixit, A.K., 1987. Strategic aspects of trade policy. In: Bewley, T.F. (Ed.), Advances in Economic Theory: Fifth World Congress, Cambridge University Press, Cambridge, UK.

Dixit, A.K., Norman, V.D., 1986. Gains from trade without lump-sum compensation. J. Int. Econ. 21, 111–122.

Eaton, J., Grossman, G.M., 1986. Optimal trade and industrial policy under oligopoly. Q. J. Econ. 101 (2), 383–406.

Ethier, W.J., 2007. The theory of trade policy and trade agreements: a critique. Eur. J. Polit. Econ. 23, 605–623.

Ethier, W.J., Kim, N., 2013. The trade-agreement embarrassment. J. East Asian Econ. Integr. 17, 243–260.

Fukushima, K., Kim, N., 1989. Welfare improving tariff changes: a case of many goods and many countries. J. Int. Econ. 26, 383–388.

Graaf, J., 1949. On optimum tariff structures. Rev. Econ. Stud. 17, 47–59.

Grossman, G.M., Helpman, E., 1994. Protection for sale. Am. Econ. Rev. 84 (4), 833–850.

Grossman, G.M., Helpman, E., 1995a. The politics of free-trade agreements. Am. Econ. Rev. 85 (4), 667–690.

Grossman, G.M., Helpman, E., 1995b. Trade wars and trade talks. J. Polit. Econ. 103 (4), 675–708.

Grossman, G.M., Helpman, E., 1996. Electoral competition and special interest politics. Rev. Econ. Stud. 63 (2), 265–286.

Grossman, G.M., Horn, H., 2013. Why the WTO? An introduction to the economics of trade agreements. In: Horn, H., Mavroidis, P.C. (Eds.), Legal and Economic Principles of World Trade Law, Cambridge University Press, Cambridge, UK.

Grossman, G.M., Lai, E.L.-C., 2004. International protection of intellectual property. Am. Econ. Rev. 94 (5), 1635–1653.

Hillman, A.L., Moser, P., 1995. Trade liberalization as politically optimal exchange of market access. In: Canzoneri, M., Ethier, W.J., Grilli, V. (Eds.), The New Transatlantic Economy, Cambridge University Press, Cambridge, UK.

Hillman, A.L., Long, N.V., Moser, P., 1995. Modeling reciprocal trade liberalization: the political-economy and national welfare perspectives. Swiss J. Econ. Stat. 131, 503–515.

Hudec, R.E., 1993. 'Circumventing' democracy: the political morality of trade negotiations. Int. Law Polit. 25, 311–322.

Johnson, H.G., 1953. Optimum tariffs and retaliation. Rev. Econ. Stud. 21 (2), 142–153.

Katrik, H., 1977. Multi-national monopolies and commercial policy. Oxf. Econ. Pap. 29 (2), 283–291.

Kemp, M., 1967. Notes on the theory of optimal tariffs. Econ. Record 43, 395–403.

Kemp, M., Wan Jr., H., 1976. An elementary proposition concerning the formation of customs unions. In: Kemp, M. (Ed.), Three Topics in the Theory of International Trade: Distribution, Welfare and Uncertainty, North Holland, Amsterdam.

Kennan, J., Riezman, R., 1990. Optimum tariff equilibria with customs unions. Can. J. Econ. 23 (1), 70–93.

Krishna, P., 1998. Regionalism versus multilateralism: a political economy approach. Q. J. Econ. 113 (1), 227–251.

Krishna, P., 2005. The economics of preferential trade agreements. In: Choi, E.K., Harrigan, J. (Eds.), Handbook of International TradeBlackwell, Oxford.

Krishna, P., Bhagwati, J., 1997. Necessarily welfare improving customs unions with industrialization constraints: the Cooper-Massell-Johnson-Bhagwati proposition. Jpn. World Econ. 9, 441–446.

Krugman, P.R., 1980. Scale economies, product differentiation, and the pattern of trade. Am. Econ. Rev. 70 (5), 950–959.

Krugman, P.R., 1991a. Is bilateralism bad? In: Helpman, E., Razin, A. (Eds.), International Trade and Trade Policy, MIT Press, Cambridge, MA, pp. 9–23.

Krugman, P.R., 1991b. The move toward free trade zones. In: Policy Implications of Trade and Currency Zones: A Symposium Sponsored by the Federal Reserve Bank of Kansas CityFederal Reserve Bank of Kansas City, Kansas City, MO.

Kydland, F.E., Prescott, E.C., 1977. Rules rather than discretion: the inconsistency of optimal plans. J. Polit. Econ. 85 (3), 473–492.

Limão, N., 2016. Preferential trade agreements. In: Bagwell, K., Staiger, R. (Eds.), Handbook of Commercial Policy, vol. 1B. North Holland, Amsterdam, pp. 279–367.

Limão, N., Tovar, P., 2011. Policy choice: theory and evidence from commitment via international trade agreements. J. Int. Econ. 85 (2), 186–205.

Maggi, G., 1999. The role of multilateral institutions in international trade cooperation. Am. Econ. Rev. 89 (1), 190–2014.

Maggi, G., 2014. International trade agreements. In: Gopinath, G., Helpman, E., Rogoff, K. (Eds.), Handbook of International Economics, vol. 4. North Holland, Amsterdam.

Maggi, G., Rodriguez-Clare, A., 1998. The value of trade agreements in the presence of political pressures. J. Polit. Econ. 106 (3), 574–601.

Maggi, G., Rodriguez-Clare, A., 2007. A political-economy theory of trade agreements. Am. Econ. Rev. 97 (4), 1374–1406.

Mayer, W., 1981. Theoretical considerations on negotiated tariff adjustments. Oxf. Econ. Pap. 33 (1), 135–153.

Mitra, D., 1999. Endogenous lobby formation and endogenous protection: a long-run model of trade policy determination. Am. Econ. Rev. 89 (5), 1116–1134.

Mitra, D., 2002. Endogenous political organization and the value of trade agreements. J. Int. Econ. 57 (2), 473–485.

Ohyama, M., 1972. Trade and welfare in general equilibrium. Keio Econ. Stud. 9, 37–73.

Ornelas, E., 2005a. Endogenous free trade agreements and the multilateral system. J. Int. Econ. 67 (2), 471–497.

Ornelas, E., 2005b. Trade creating free trade areas and the undermining of multilateralism. Eur. Econ. Rev. 49 (7), 1717–1735.

Ossa, R., 2011. A new trade theory of GATT/WTO negotiations. J. Polit. Econ. 119 (1), 122–152.

Panagariya, A., 2000. Preferential trade liberalization: the traditional theory and new developments. J. Econ. Lit. 38 (2), 287–331.

Panagariya, A., Krishna, P., 2002. On necessarily welfare-enhancing free trade areas. J. Int. Econ. 57, 353–367.

Park, J.H., 2011. Enforcing international trade agreements with imperfect private monitoring. Rev. Econ. Stud. 78 (3), 1102–1134.

Pauwelyn, J., 2008. New trade politics for the 21st century. J. Int. Econ. Law 11 (3), 559–573.

Regan, D.H., 2006. What are trade agreements for? Two conflicting stories told by economists, with a lesson for lawyers. J. Int. Econ. Law 9, 951–988.

Regan, D.H., 2015. Explaining trade agreements: the practitioners' story and the standard model. World Trade Rev. 14 (3), 391–417.

Richardson, M., 1993. Endogenous protection and trade diversion. J. Int. Econ. 34 (3-4), 309–324.

Richardson, M., 1995. On the interpretation of the Kemp/Wan theorem. Oxf. Econ. Pap. 47 (4), 696–703.

Saggi, K., Woodland, A., Yildiz, H.M., 2013. On the relationship between preferential and multilateral trade liberalization: the case of customs unions. Am. Econ. J. Microecon. 5 (1), 63–99.

Saggi, K., Yildiz, H.M., 2010. Bilateralism, multilateralism, and the quest for global free trade. J. Int. Econ. 81, 26–37.

Saggi, K., Yildiz, H.M., 2011. Bilateral trade agreements and the feasibility of multilateral free trade. Rev. Int. Econ. 19 (2), 356–373.

Staiger, R.W., Tabellini, 1987. Discretionary trade policy and excessive protection. Am. Econ. Rev. 77 (5), 823–837.

Svedberg, P., 1979. Optimal tariff policy on imports from multinationals. Econ. Record 55 (1), 64–67.

Turunen-Red, A.H., Woodland, A.D., 1991. Strict Pareto-improving reform of tariffs. Econometrica 59, 1127–1152.

Venables, A.J., 1985. Trade and trade policy with imperfect competition: the case of identical products and free entry. J. Int. Econ. 19, 1–20.

Venables, A.J., 1987. Trade and trade policy with differentiated products: a Chamberlinian-Ricardian model. Econ. J. 97, 700–717.

CHAPTER 8

The Design of Trade Agreements

K. Bagwell*,‡, R.W. Staiger†,‡
*Stanford University, Stanford, CA, United States
†Dartmouth College, Hanover, NH, United States
‡NBER, Cambridge, MA, United States

Contents

Handbook of Commercial Policy, Volume 1A
ISSN 2214-3122, http://dx.doi.org/10.1016/bs.hescop.2016.04.005

Abstract

What does economics have to say about the design of international trade agreements? We review a literature on this question, providing detailed coverage on three key design features of the GATT/WTO: reciprocity, nondiscrimination as embodied in the MFN principle, and tariff bindings and binding "overhang." Each of these features is central to the design of the GATT/WTO and we argue that an economic perspective can go a long way toward revealing a consistent logic to the inclusion of these design features in trade agreements.

Keywords

Trade agreements, GATT, WTO, Reciprocity, MFN, Nondiscrimination, Tariff bindings, Binding overhang

JEL Classification Codes:

F02, F13

1. INTRODUCTION

What does economics have to say about the design of international trade agreements? In this chapter, we review a literature related to this question. We provide detailed coverage on three key design features of the General Agreement on Tariffs and Trade (GATT) and its successor the World Trade Organization (WTO).[a] The three design features on which we focus are reciprocity, nondiscrimination as embodied in the most-favored-nation (MFN) principle, and tariff bindings and binding "overhang." Each of these features is central to the design of GATT/WTO.

We adopt the view that design reflects purpose. We thus discuss the purpose of a trade agreement as a tool to set the stage for our discussion of design.[b] That is, we seek first to catalog the "problems" that a trade agreement may "solve" in the various formal models of trade agreements, where the problems lead to inefficiencies whose solutions can then generate increases in joint surplus that make a mutually beneficial trade agreement possible. With the problems identified and the inefficiencies characterized, we are then better able to assess whether according to these formal models the trade agreement is well designed to facilitate mutual gains for member governments.

We now provide the narrative for the organization of our chapter. At the broadest level, trade agreements could be designed following either of two standard traditions in economics for addressing inefficiencies (see Hoekman and Kostecki, 1995, pp. 59–60).

---

[a] Other design features are briefly mentioned in Section 6 and are treated in detail in other chapters of this Handbook.

[b] Our discussion of the purpose of trade agreements is thus narrow in scope. The broad literature on the purpose of trade agreements is considered by Grossman (2016).

A "top down" approach would create a supranational authority that sets trade policies for each member country. A "bottom up" approach would entail Coasean bargaining among governments, and a critical element to ensure efficiency would be the existence of secure property rights over the objects on which bargaining was to occur. In practice international trade agreements are typically designed according to the second approach: each government has property rights over its own policy instruments, but further rules may be needed to secure the relevant property rights (eg, to "market access"); governments negotiate first over the rules (multilaterally); and they then bargain over actual policies within rules (bilaterally, typically, though not always). The agreement must be self-enforcing.

From here, we can imagine how negotiators would start by agreeing that they should use policy instruments that are transparent, so that they know what is agreed upon and can monitor compliance. As we discuss below, if the diagnosis of the problem is a terms-of-trade problem at any rate, they would also focus on reciprocal liberalization. They would then need to confront the problem of third-party externalities, leading to consideration of nondiscrimination. Next, a basic question would be whether they are negotiating exact tariffs or bounds. At this point, they might have various "what-if" questions, concerning upward flexibility to shocks, opportunistic use of nonborder measures, the rules for settling disputes when unanticipated issues arise, export policy instruments, and the like. We refer to other Handbook chapters for full treatments of these important topics, and only briefly touch on them here. As indicated, our focus here is on evaluating and interpreting the design features of reciprocity, MFN and tariff bindings and overhang.

A natural question at this point is whether there is really any consistent logic to the design of trade agreements at all. Do the design features of these agreements appear to be sufficiently "purposeful" and deliberate to support the view that they can be usefully analyzed from an economic perspective? We argue in this chapter that the answer is yes.[c] To develop this argument, we present formal models that speak to the purpose and essential design of the GATT/WTO, and we also relate the implications of these models to legal and historical writings that concern the purpose and design of trade agreements.

The rest of the chapter proceeds as follows. In Section 2 we present a sequence of models and diagnose the problem that a trade agreement might solve. Building on our findings from Section 2, Section 3 then covers reciprocity, Section 4 covers MFN, and Section 5 covers bindings and overhang. Finally, Section 6 touches briefly on other important design features and concludes.

2. DIAGNOSIS OF THE PROBLEM

In this section, we present a sequence of two-country models and diagnose the problem that a trade agreement might solve. We describe each model in detail, and organize our discussion around three questions. First, is the Nash equilibrium inefficient? In effect, this

---

[c] See Krugman (1997) for an early dissenting view.

question asks whether there is a problem for governments that a trade agreement might solve. Second, if the Nash equilibrium is inefficient, then is reciprocal trade liberalization a necessary design feature for a mutually advantageous trade agreement among governments? By asking this question, we address an initial and basic design feature while postponing consideration of other design features until later sections. Finally, if governments were not motivated by the terms-of-trade implications of their trade policies, would the resulting noncooperative tariffs be efficient? This question acknowledges the central role played by the terms-of-trade externality in the trade-agreement literature and provides a means of categorizing models based upon whether this externality alone explains the purpose of a trade agreement.

Before proceeding, we pause to remark on the value of characterizing the purpose of a trade agreement. Why should we bother to identify the problem that a trade agreement solves? For our purposes in this chapter, the reason is this: by identifying the problem that a trade agreement may solve, we are better able to assess whether the trade agreement is well designed for facilitating mutual gains for member governments. Our discussion here thus serves as a foundation for later sections, where we consider trade-agreement design in greater detail.

We conclude the section by approaching issues of purpose and design from a different angle. Given the prominence played by the terms-of-trade externality in the formal literature on trade agreements, it is important to ask whether there is meaningful contact between the problems emphasized by this literature and those emphasized by economists and others who were directly involved in GATT's design. Drawing on an early GATT document, we describe some suggestive evidence consistent with a central role for terms-of-trade externalities.

2.1 Competitive General-Equilibrium Model of Trade Agreements

We begin with the standard perfectly competitive general-equilibrium model of trade agreements. This model provides a general framework in which to understand the basic terms-of-trade-driven Prisoners' Dilemma problem that a trade agreement may solve.

2.1.1 The Model

We consider a standard general-equilibrium model of trade between two countries in two goods. Each good is a normal good in consumption, and production is determined in perfectly competitive markets under conditions of increasing opportunity costs. The home country imports good x and exports good y, while the foreign country imports good y and exports good x. The local relative price facing domestic producers and consumers is denoted as $p \equiv p_x/p_y$, and similarly the local relative price in the foreign country is represented as $p^* \equiv p_x^*/p_y^*$, where here and throughout we use an "*" to denote foreign-country variables. The government of each country has available an ad valorem import tariff, and we assume that governments set tariffs at nonprohibitive levels.

Let $t > -1$ denote the ad valorem import tariff selection of the home government, with $t^* > -1$ representing the corresponding selection by the foreign government. It is convenient to define $\tau \equiv 1 + t$ and $\tau^* \equiv 1 + t^*$. We further define the relative world (ie, offshore or untaxed) price as $p^w \equiv p_x^*/p_y$. The world price is thus the relative price of the foreign country's export good to its import good on the "world" market and as such is the foreign country's "terms of trade." The home country's terms of trade is then $1/p^w$. With these definitions in place, we may now observe the following relationships: $p = \tau p^w \equiv p(\tau, p^w)$ and $p^* = p^w/\tau^* \equiv p^*(\tau^*, p^w)$.

Once a country's local price and terms of trade are determined, its production, consumption and tariff revenue are implied. In each country, the production of good i, where $i = x, y$, is determined by the point on the concave production possibilities frontier at which the marginal rate of transformation between x and y equals the local relative price. We may thus represent the domestic and foreign production functions as $Q_i(p)$ and $Q_i^*(p^*)$, respectively. Consumption in each country is determined by the local and world prices: $C_i(p, p^w)$ and $C_i^*(p^*, p^w)$. Intuitively, the local price determines the relative price faced by consumers and also the level and distribution of factor income, while tariff revenue is distributed lump sum to consumers and can be expressed as a function of the local and world prices.[d] We may now define import demand and export supply for the home country as $M(p, p^w) \equiv C_x(p, p^w) - Q_x(p)$ and $E(p, p^w) \equiv Q_y(p) - C_y(p, p^w)$, respectively. Similarly, we may represent the foreign country's import demand and export supply functions, respectively, as $M^*(p^*, p^w) \equiv C_y^*(p^*, p^w) - Q_y^*(p^*)$ and $E^*(p^*, p^w) \equiv Q_x^*(p^*) - C_x^*(p^*, p^w)$.

For any local and world prices, each country must satisfy budget or "trade balance" constraints. For the home country, the trade balance constraint is

$$p^w M(p, p^w) = E(p, p^w). \tag{1}$$

The foreign-country trade balance is similarly represented as

$$M^*(p^*, p^w) = p^w E^*(p^*, p^w). \tag{2}$$

We may think of these relationships as constraints that are embedded in the construction of the import demand and export supply functions.

The final ingredient in our model is a market-clearing requirement. Given τ and τ^*, we require that the world price is set so as to achieve market clearing in good x:

$$M(p(\tau, p^w), p^w) = E^*(p^*(\tau^*, p^w), p^w). \tag{3}$$

For given τ and τ^*, we notice that (3) describes one equation in a single unknown variable, p^w. Let $\tilde{p}^w(\tau, \tau^*)$ denote the market-clearing world price that satisfies (3). It is now straightforward to confirm that conditions (1), (2) and (3) ensure that market clearing is

---

[d] For further details, see Bagwell and Staiger (2002, pp. 14–15).

achieved in good y as well. In this general fashion, for any specification of τ and τ^*, we may determine the equilibrium world price and the associated local prices. All equilibrium quantities (production, consumption, tariff revenue, imports, exports) are then implied in turn.

The only assumption that we place upon the general-equilibrium model is that prices respond to tariffs in the "regular" way.[e] Specifically, we make the following assumptions:

$$\frac{dp(\tau, \widetilde{p}^w(\tau, \tau^*))}{d\tau} > 0 > \frac{\partial \widetilde{p}^w(\tau, \tau^*)}{\partial \tau}$$

$$\frac{dp^*(\tau^*, \widetilde{p}^w(\tau, \tau^*))}{d\tau^*} < 0 < \frac{\partial \widetilde{p}^w(\tau, \tau^*)}{\partial \tau^*}. \tag{4}$$

In short, when a country's tariff is increased, the relative price of its import good increases in the local market and falls in the world market. The latter (world price) effect amounts to an assumption that the country is "large" and can exercise monopsony power by raising its tariff. It also means that a country can improve its terms of trade—and thus cause a deterioration in its trading partner's terms of trade—by raising its tariff.

With the basic general-equilibrium model of trade described, we now consider the preferences of governments. In the *traditional approach* to trade agreements, governments are assumed to maximize national economic welfare. This is the approach explored by Dixit (1987), Johnson (1953-1954), Kennan and Riezman (1988), and Mayer (1981), for example. Following Bagwell and Staiger (1999, 2002), we adopt a *political-economic approach* which includes the traditional approach as a special case but allows as well that governments may have political or distributional concerns. We thus represent the preferences of a government as a general function of its country's local price and terms of trade. Formally, the home and foreign government preferences, respectively, are represented as $W(p, \widetilde{p}^w)$ and $W^*(p^*, \widetilde{p}^w)$, where all prices are evaluated henceforth at market-clearing levels. We note that each government's welfare is ultimately a function of the underlying tariff choices, since under market clearing we have that $p = p(\tau, \widetilde{p}^w)$, $p^* = p^*(\tau^*, \widetilde{p}^w)$ and $\widetilde{p}^w = \widetilde{p}^w(\tau, \tau^*)$. It is nevertheless convenient to represent government welfare functions in terms of local and world prices, as we are thereby able to identify the channel through which one government's tariff selection imposes an externality on the welfare of the other government.

Following Bagwell and Staiger (1999, 2002), the only assumption we make on government preferences is as follows: a government benefits from a terms-of-trade improvement, when the local price in its country is held fixed. Formally, our assumption may be stated as follows:

---

[e] Put differently, we assume that the model does not exhibit the Metzler or Lerner paradox.

$$W_{\widetilde{p}^w}(p, \widetilde{p}^w) < 0 < W^*_{\widetilde{p}^w}(p^*, \widetilde{p}^w). \tag{5}$$

Notice that no assumption is made as to the manner in which welfare varies with the local price, and so a wide variety of political and distributional motivations can be accommodated. It is important to reflect on the meaning of the preference assumption captured in (5). Imagine that the home government raises its tariff, τ, and that the foreign government cuts its tariff, τ^*. Under (4), this adjustment in tariffs results in a lower value for $\widetilde{p}^w$ and thus an improvement in the home country's terms of trade. Further, the tariff changes can be made in such a way as to maintain the local price, p, in the home country.[f] Such a change in tariffs does not alter the local price faced by producers and consumers in the home country; instead, it amounts to a transfer of tariff revenue from the foreign country to the home country. The meaning of the preference assumption in (5) is simply that a government benefits from being the recipient of such a transfer.

As Bagwell and Staiger (1999, 2002) discuss, assumption (5) is satisfied under the traditional approach where governments maximize national economic welfare. The assumption is also satisfied in the leading models that adopt the political-economic approach, including the lobbying models of Grossman and Helpman (1994, 1995) and the median-voter model of Mayer (1984).[g] As discussed below, the model presented here does not include, however, models in which governments face a "commitment problem" and have time-inconsistent preferences, since such models allow that government preferences may change over time.

2.1.2 Prisoners' Dilemma

We show next that the general-equilibrium model generates a terms-of-trade-driven Prisoners' Dilemma problem between governments. To begin, let us consider a simultaneous-move game in which governments select import tariffs. Assuming that a unique, interior Nash equilibrium exists, we represent the non-cooperative or *Nash* tariffs as a pair, (τ^N, τ^{*N}), satisfying the following first-order conditions:[h]

---

[f] Under (4), the increase in τ raises p and the decrease in τ^* further lowers $\widetilde{p}^w$ and thus decreases p.

[g] As noted earlier, work in the traditional approach includes Dixit (1987), Johnson (1953-1954), Kennan and Riezman (1988), and Mayer (1981). Work in which government preferences correspond to the preferences of the median voter includes Dhingra (2014), Dutt and Mitra (2002), and Mayer (1984), while work in which government preferences reflect the interests of lobbies includes Baldwin (1987), Brock and Magee (1978), Caves (1976), Feenstra and Bhagwati (1982), Findlay and Wellisz (1982), Grossman and Helpman (1994, 1995), Hillman (1982), and Olson (1965). The preference assumption in (5) is satisfied in all of these approaches.

[h] As Dixit (1987) establishes for a setting in which governments maximize national economic welfare, Nash equilibria with autarky also exist. The equilibrium upon which we focus here, by contrast, has positive trade volume and is in this sense "interior."

$$\frac{dW(p, \tilde{p}^w)}{d\tau} = W_p \frac{dp}{d\tau} + W_{\tilde{p}^w} \frac{\partial \tilde{p}^w}{\partial \tau} = 0$$

$$\frac{dW^*(p^*, \tilde{p}^w)}{d\tau^*} = W_{p^*}^* \frac{dp^*}{d\tau^*} + W_{\tilde{p}^w}^* \frac{\partial \tilde{p}^w}{\partial \tau^*} = 0.$$

(6)

The first condition in (6) defines the "optimal tariff" or the best-response tariff for the home government, while the second condition defines the analogous tariff for the foreign government.[i] Using (4) and (5), we may immediately observe that $W_p < 0$ when the home government selects its optimal tariff. Intuitively, the home government would welcome the lower local price and corresponding greater trade volume that a tariff reduction would induce; yet, the home government refrains from unilaterally lowering its tariff from the optimal level, since a lower tariff would worsen its terms of trade. Similarly, for the foreign government, (4) and (5) imply that $W_{p^*}^* > 0$ at the optimal tariff, where a higher value for p^* would result from a lower foreign tariff.

A trade agreement is an agreement between governments. To understand the rationale for a trade agreement, we thus consider whether a trade agreement could generate greater government welfare than governments enjoy under non-cooperative tariff setting (ie, in the Nash equilibrium). We are thus motivated to consider Pareto efficient tariff pairs, where efficiency is measured relative to government welfare. An *efficient* pair of tariffs is defined by a tangency condition for government indifference curves:

$$\frac{d\tau}{d\tau^*}\Big|_{dW=0} = \frac{d\tau}{d\tau^*}\Big|_{dW^*=0}.$$

(7)

This tangency condition that defines an efficient pair of tariffs can be rewritten as

$$\frac{[\tau W_p + W_{\tilde{p}^w}] \frac{\partial \tilde{p}^w}{\partial \tau^*}}{W_p \frac{dp}{d\tau} + W_{\tilde{p}^w} \frac{\partial \tilde{p}^w}{\partial \tau}} = \frac{W_{p^*}^* \frac{dp^*}{d\tau^*} + W_{\tilde{p}^w}^* \frac{\partial \tilde{p}^w}{\partial \tau^*}}{\left[\frac{1}{\tau^*} W_{p^*}^* + W_{\tilde{p}^w}^*\right] \frac{\partial \tilde{p}^w}{\partial \tau}}.$$

(8)

Notice that, in assuming that a trade agreement may deliver an efficient tariff pair, we are putting enforcement issues to the side for now.

Under the traditional approach, the optimal import tariff for each government is positive, and so $\tau^N > 1$ and $\tau^{*N} > 1$. This finding dates back to Torrens (1844) and Mill (1844) and was formalized by Johnson (1953-1954). It implies that free trade is not the optimal unilateral tariff for a government that maximizes national economic welfare and presides over a large country. As Mayer (1981) showed, the efficiency frontier under the traditional approach is defined by the locus $\tau = 1/\tau^*$. This tariff locus ensures that

---

[i] Throughout, we assume that all second-order conditions are globally satisfied and that all partial derivatives of W and W^* are continuous and finite.

local prices are equalized across countries (ie, $p = p^*$) and includes global free trade ($\tau = \tau^* = 1$) as a special case. As we raise the home-country tariff and lower the foreign-country tariff while moving along the locus of efficient tariffs, the home (foreign)-country experiences a terms of trade gain (loss). Hence, the world price and thus the distribution of income across countries varies along the efficiency frontier.

The traditional approach thus indicates that governments of large countries face a Prisoners' Dilemma problem. The Nash tariffs are too high, and governments could achieve a Pareto gain by forming an agreement in which tariffs are reduced in an appropriate reciprocal manner. If governments are symmetric, then Nash and efficient tariffs lie along the 45-degree line. In this case, governments can achieve efficiency and both gain relative to the Nash equilibrium by moving to global free trade. As Johnson (1953-1954), Kennan and Riezman (1988), and Mayer (1981) argue, however, if countries are sufficiently asymmetric, then a large country may prefer the Nash equilibrium to global free trade. Thus, reciprocal tariff reductions that lead to an efficient outcome do not always generate Pareto gains relative to the Nash equilibrium.

Adopting the more general political-economic approach, Bagwell and Staiger (1999, 2002) establish the following three findings. First, and as may be easily verified, the Nash equilibrium tariffs defined by (6) do not satisfy (8) and are thus inefficient. This finding is not entirely surprising, since a higher tariff from one country imposes a negative international externality in the form of a terms-of-trade loss on the other country. The second finding is that, starting at the Nash equilibrium tariffs (τ^N, τ^{*N}), governments can mutually gain from moving to a new pair of tariffs (τ, τ^*) only if the new tariffs entail *reciprocal trade liberalization*: $\tau < \tau^N$ and $\tau^* < \tau^{*N}$. A general form of reciprocity is thus necessary if governments are to achieve mutual gains from a trade agreement.

The second finding follows easily once it is established that a government experiences a strict welfare reduction along its best-response curve as its trading partner's tariff is increased. To establish this point, we focus on the home country and define its best-response function, $\tau = \tau^R(\tau^*)$, as the solution to the first equation in (6). Following Bagwell and Staiger (1999, 2002), we may now use (6) to find that

$$\frac{dW(p, \widetilde{p}^w)}{d\tau^*}\bigg|_{\tau=\tau^R(\tau^*)} = \left[(W_p\tau + W_{\widetilde{p}^w})\frac{\partial\widetilde{p}^w}{\partial\tau^*}\right]\bigg|_{\tau=\tau^R(\tau^*)}$$

$$= \left[(1 - \tau\lambda)W_{\widetilde{p}^w}\frac{\partial\widetilde{p}^w}{\partial\tau^*}\right]\bigg|_{\tau=\tau^R(\tau^*)} \tag{9}$$

$$< 0,$$

where $\lambda \equiv \dfrac{\partial\widetilde{p}^w}{\partial\tau} \bigg/ \dfrac{dp}{d\tau} < 0$ by (4). To complete the argument, we suppose that a trade agreement generates mutual gains and specifies a tariff pair (τ, τ^*) for which $\tau^* > \tau^{*N}$. Starting at this tariff pair, we may reposition the home tariff to the home best-response level, $\tau^R(\tau^*)$, and then reduce the foreign tariff from τ^* to τ^{*N} while adjusting the home tariff along the home best-response curve. It then follows from (9) that the home government experiences strictly higher welfare at the Nash tariffs than at the tariff pair specified by the agreement, which contradicts the supposition that the agreement generate mutual gains. A similar argument applies when the trade agreement specifies a pair (τ, τ^*) where $\tau > \tau^N$.

The third finding concerns the reason that the Nash tariffs are inefficient. To identify the source of the problem, Bagwell and Staiger (1999, 2002) define *politically optimal* tariffs as the tariff pair, (τ^{PO}, τ^{*PO}), that satisfies

$$W_p = 0 = W_{p^*}^*. \tag{10}$$

We may understand the politically optimal tariffs to be the tariffs that governments would choose if, hypothetically, they were not motivated by the terms-of-trade implications of their tariff selections (ie, if, hypothetically, they acted as if $W_{\tilde{p}^w} = 0 = W_{\tilde{p}^w}^*$). The third finding, which follows easily from (8) and (10), is that the politically optimal tariffs are efficient. Bagwell and Staiger (1999, 2002) interpret this finding as establishing that the terms-of-trade externality is the sole rationale for a trade agreement, even when governments have political-economic preferences. They note further that the politically optimal tariffs correspond to global free trade when governments maximize national economic welfare.

The three findings are captured in Fig. 1 (adopted from Bagwell and Staiger, 1999). As this figure illustrates, Nash tariffs are inefficient and too high. Further, reciprocal tariff liberalization (ie, $\tau < \tau^N$ and $\tau^* < \tau^{*N}$) is necessary but not sufficient for mutual gains

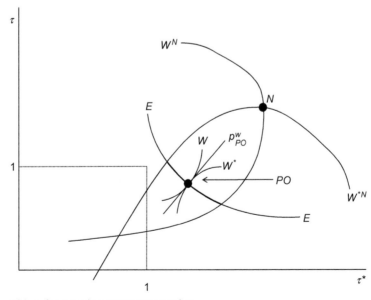

Fig. 1 The problem for a trade agreement to solve.

for governments relative to the Nash equilibrium. Finally, politically optimal tariffs are efficient. As depicted, when the home and foreign countries are sufficiently symmetric, the politically optimal tariffs reside on the contract curve (ie, they are efficient and generate greater-than-Nash welfares for both governments). The politically optimal tariffs may fall outside the contract curve, though, if countries are sufficiently asymmetric.

2.2 Competitive Partial-Equilibrium Model of Trade Agreements

In the preceding discussion, we use a competitive general-equilibrium model and show that the purpose of the GATT/WTO is to provide a means of escape from a terms-of-trade driven Prisoners' Dilemma problem. As we discuss further in later sections, however, some design features of the GATT/WTO are most easily captured in the context of a simple partial-equilibrium model which includes specific parameters relating to political ingredients in governments' preferences. We thus now prepare for this analysis by presenting a simple partial-equilibrium model of trade. An additional and important benefit of our partial-equilibrium analysis is that it provides a concrete framework within which to understand and further explore the purpose of trade agreements. In particular, and as we show below, this analysis leads to new insights regarding the existence of international externalities that do not travel through the terms of trade when the set of trade-policy instruments is incomplete.

2.2.1 Partial-Equilibrium Model

We now present a two-country partial-equilibrium model of trade. The home country imports good x from the foreign country and exports good y to the foreign country. A numeraire good, n, is also traded between the two countries.[j]

Consumers in each country share a common utility function, which is quasilinear and additively separable across goods. The numeraire good enters the utility function in a linear way. Within any country, the demand for good i, where $i = x, y$, thus depends on the local price of good i relative to that of the numeraire good. Each good is supplied under conditions of perfect competition; hence, within a given country, the supply of good i, $i = x, y$, is also a function of the local price of good i relative to that of the numeraire good. As is standard, the numeraire good is produced in each country under constant returns to scale and is sufficiently abundant in each country that it is consumed in positive quantities. The numeraire good is also freely traded across countries so as to ensure that trade balance is achieved. We may normalize the price of the numeraire good to unity.[k]

---

[j] For further details regarding the specific model presented here, see Bagwell and Staiger (2001b).

[k] The model can be further specified with a description of the underlying factor market. Assume that the numeraire good is produced from labor alone, with one unit of labor generating one unit of the numeraire good. Suppose further that, in each country, the supply of labor is perfectly elastic at a unitary wage. A unitary wage is then implied. In each country, good i, $i = x, y$, is produced from labor alone subject to diminishing returns.

With the general-equilibrium trade-balance requirement achieved through trade in the numeraire good, whose price is fixed, a convenient feature of this model is that the market outcomes for good x are independent of those for good y. The model is thus partial equilibrium in nature.

We assume that consumers possess symmetric preferences across goods x and y. For $i = x, y$, each good i is then demanded in each country according to a symmetric demand function, D. Letting p_x and p_y denote the home-country local prices of goods x and y, respectively, we may represent the home-country demand function for good i as $D(p_i)$.[1] We may represent foreign demand functions similarly in terms of foreign local prices, p_x^* and p_y^*. To establish a basis for trade, we assume that the countries have different supply functions. The domestic supply functions are represented as $Q_x(p_x)$ and $Q_y(p_y)$, while the foreign supply functions are denoted as $Q_x^*(p_x^*)$ and $Q_y^*(p_y^*)$. For prices that are associated with strictly positive volumes, we assume that the demand function is strictly decreasing and the supply functions are increasing.[m] In line with our assumption that the home country imports good x, we assume that $Q_x(p) = Q_y^*(p) < Q_y(p) = Q_x^*(p)$ for any p such that $Q_y(p) > 0$. The associated competitive profit functions are represented by the strictly increasing functions, $\Pi_x(p_x)$, $\Pi_y(p_y)$, $\Pi_x^*(p_x^*)$, and $\Pi_y^*(p_y^*)$.

We assume that each country has a specific (ie, per unit) trade-policy instrument with which to affect the volume of trade for each good i, $i = x, y$. In particular, the home country has an import tariff, τ_x, that is applied to imports of good x and an export subsidy, τ_y, that is applied to exports of good y. An import subsidy is used if $\tau_x < 0$, while an export tax is applied when $\tau_y < 0$. The foreign country similarly has an import tariff, τ_y^*, and an export subsidy, τ_x^*. The "net tariff" for good x is then $\tau_x - \tau_x^*$, and similarly the net tariff for good y is captured as $\tau_y^* - \tau_y$.

We may now determine local prices as functions of tariffs. Provided that the net tariff is not so high as to prohibit trade, local prices in each country must obey the following arbitrage and market-clearing conditions:

$$p_i = p_i^* + \tau_i - \tau_i^* \tag{11}$$

$$Q_i(p_i) + Q_i^*(p_i^*) = D(p_i) + D(p_i^*) \text{ for } i = x, y. \tag{12}$$

For each good i, conditions (11) and (12) constitute two requirements on two prices; thus, we may solve these equations to determine the market-clearing local prices as functions of the associated net tariffs: $p_x(\tau_x - \tau_x^*)$, $p_x^*(\tau_x - \tau_x^*)$, $p_y^*(\tau_y^* - \tau_y)$ and $p_y(\tau_y^* - \tau_y)$. Under our assumptions, and provided that trade is not prohibited, it is direct to confirm

---

[1] Let the utility of the representative consumer take the form $u(C_x) + u(C_y) + C_n$, where C_i and C_n, respectively, represent consumption levels of good i, $i = x, y$, and the numeraire good n. The demand for good i is implicitly defined by the consumption level that satisfies the first-order condition: $u'(C_i) = p_i$.

[m] We allow that supply functions may be constant in order to include the possibility of endowment economies.

that an increase in the net tariff for a given good strictly increases (decreases) the local price in the importing (exporting) country. We thus have that $p_x'(\tau_x - \tau_x^*) > 0 > p_x^{*\prime}(\tau_x - \tau_x^*)$ and $p_y^{*\prime}(\tau_y^* - \tau_y) > 0 > p_y'(\tau_y^* - \tau_y)$.

We next consider the world (ie, offshore) prices. Let p_x^w and p_y^w denote the world prices for goods x and y, respectively. The world prices are defined as follows: $p_i \equiv p_i^w + \tau_i$ for $i = x, y$. For a given good, we may thus think of the world price as the price that prevails after the export policy is applied but before the import policy is imposed.[n] Given that we have already solved for the market-clearing local prices, we may use the definition of world prices to represent the market-clearing world prices as functions of tariffs: $p_x^w(\tau_x, \tau_x^*)$ and $p_y^w(\tau_y, \tau_y^*)$. Under our assumptions, if tariffs are not so high as to prohibit trade on a given good, then the world price is strictly decreasing in each argument: the world price strictly falls when the import tariff increases and when the export subsidy increases. In what follows, it is convenient to express market-clearing local prices in a country as explicit functions of the world prices and the country's own trade policy. For $i = x, y$, we thus define the market-clearing local price functions as $\hat{p}_i(\tau_i, p_i^w(\tau_i, \tau_i^*)) \equiv p_i^w(\tau_i, \tau_i^*) + \tau_i$ and $\hat{p}_i^*(\tau_i^*, p_i^w(\tau_i, \tau_i^*)) \equiv p_i^w(\tau_i, \tau_i^*) + \tau_i^*$.

It is instructive to consider the price implications of trade policies in more detail. Consider the home-country import good. An increase in the home-country import tariff causes the local price of the import good to rise in the home country; however, this price increase is less than one for one, since an increase in the import tariff reduces the world price and thereby the price that foreign exporters receive. When the home country raises its import tariff, it thereby shifts some of the cost of the tariff hike onto foreign exporters, who receive a lower price for their good and thus earn lower profits. For the partial-equilibrium model, the terms-of-trade externality that is associated with an import tariff increase thus admits a simple interpretation and corresponds to a reduction in the world price of the import good. Notice further than an increase in the foreign export subsidy causes the world price of the home import good to fall as well. Thus, an increase in an export subsidy generates a positive terms-of-trade externality for the importing country, by enabling this country to import at a lower world price.

We next identify the trade volumes that are implied by tariffs in this model. For the home country, we may define the import demand and export supply functions as $M(\hat{p}_x) \equiv D(\hat{p}_x) - Q_x(\hat{p}_x)$ and $E(\hat{p}_y) \equiv Q_y(\hat{p}_y) - D(\hat{p}_y)$, respectively. The foreign import demand and export supply functions are, respectively, defined in an exactly analogous manner as $M^*(\hat{p}_y^*) \equiv D(\hat{p}_y^*) - Q_y^*(\hat{p}_y^*)$ and $E^*(\hat{p}_x^*) \equiv Q_x^*(\hat{p}_x^*) - D(\hat{p}_x^*)$. Of course, under (12), the import demand for any good must equal the export supply for this good.

---

[n] Thus, for good x, $p_x \equiv p_x^w + \tau_x$. Similarly, for good y, we know from (11) that $p_y^* = p_y + \tau_y^* - \tau_y$. Using the definition of p_y^w, it follows that $p_y^* = p_y^w + \tau_y^*$.

Our assumptions also imply that, provided trade is not prohibited, the import demand (export supply) functions are strictly decreasing (increasing).

We now define government welfare functions. As Baldwin (1987) observes, a wide range of political-economy models are included under the assumption that governments maximize a weighted sum of consumer surplus, producer surplus and tariff revenue.[o] Let us use $\gamma_m \geq 1$ and $\gamma_e \geq 1$ to denote the weight that the domestic government attaches to the producer surplus earned by its import-competing and exporting firms, respectively. The welfare functions that the domestic government uses for its import and export goods, respectively, are then defined as follows:

$$W_x(\hat{p}_x, p_x^w) \equiv \int_{\hat{p}_x}^{\bar{p}} D(p_x)dp_x + \gamma_m \Pi_x(\hat{p}_x) + [\hat{p}_x - p_x^w]M(\hat{p}_x)$$

$$W_y(\hat{p}_y, p_y^w) \equiv \int_{\hat{p}_y}^{\bar{p}} D(p_y)dp_y + \gamma_e \Pi_y(\hat{p}_y) - [\hat{p}_y - p_y^w]E(\hat{p}_y),$$

where $\bar{p}$ denotes the reservation price for the demand function, D.[P] The home-government welfare function is then the sum of its welfare functions for import and export goods:

$$W(\hat{p}_x, \hat{p}_y, p_x^w, p_y^w) \equiv W_x(\hat{p}_x, p_x^w) + W_y(\hat{p}_y, p_y^w).$$

Welfare functions for the foreign government may be defined in an exactly analogous way. For given welfare weights γ_m^* and γ_e^*, the foreign-government import and export welfare functions are

$$W_y^*(\hat{p}_y^*, p_y^w) \equiv \int_{\hat{p}_y^*}^{\bar{p}} D(p_y^*)dp_y^* + \gamma_m^* \Pi_y^*(\hat{p}_y^*) + [\hat{p}_y^* - p_y^w]M^*(\hat{p}_y^*)$$

$$W_x^*(\hat{p}_x^*, p_x^w) \equiv \int_{\hat{p}_x^*}^{\bar{p}} D(p_x^*)dp_x^* + \gamma_e^* \Pi_x^*(\hat{p}_x^*) - [\hat{p}_x^* - p_x^w]E^*(\hat{p}_x^*).$$

The foreign-government welfare function is thus

$$W^*(\hat{p}_y^*, \hat{p}_x^*, p_y^w, p_x^w) \equiv W_y^*(\hat{p}_y^*, p_y^w) + W_x^*(\hat{p}_x^*, p_x^w).$$

For simplicity, in this section, we suppose further that the welfare weights are symmetric across governments, so that $\gamma_m = \gamma_m^* \geq 1$ and $\gamma_e = \gamma_e^* \geq 1$.

---

[o] The lobbying models of Grossman and Helpman (1994, 1995) provide microfoundations for such preferences.

[P] In terms of the utility function detailed in footnote 1, we may understand that the tariff revenue term depicted in the welfare functions corresponds to consumer surplus that arises from the consumption of the numeraire good.

2.2.2 Prisoners' Dilemma

With the partial-equilibrium model now fully specified, we may briefly consider the basic Prisoners' Dilemma that arises in this model. We do so by considering the Nash, efficient and politically optimal tariffs in this model.

To characterize Nash trade policies, we first must consider the best-response or optimal trade policies for the domestic and foreign governments. The best-response policies are defined by

$$
\text{Home}: W_{\hat{p}_x}\frac{d\hat{p}_x}{d\tau_x} + W_{p_x^w}\frac{\partial p_x^w}{\partial \tau_x} = 0 = W_{\hat{p}_y}\frac{d\hat{p}_y}{d\tau_y} + W_{p_y^w}\frac{\partial p_y^w}{\partial \tau_y}
$$

$$
\text{Foreign}: W_{\hat{p}_y^*}^*\frac{d\hat{p}_y^*}{d\tau_y^*} + W_{p_y^w}^*\frac{\partial p_y^w}{\partial \tau_y^*} = 0 = W_{\hat{p}_x^*}^*\frac{d\hat{p}_x^*}{d\tau_x^*} + W_{p_x^w}^*\frac{\partial p_x^w}{\partial \tau_x^*}.
$$

(13)

Thus, when setting its best-response trade policies, each government considers the effects of its policies on its country's local prices and terms of trade. A higher import tariff, for example, raises the local price of the import good. The local-price increase in turn implies a redistribution from consumer surplus to producer surplus on domestically produced units, which is especially attractive to the domestic government when γ_m is large. A higher local price for the import good, however, also leads to lower trade volume and an associated loss in tariff revenue. The terms-of-trade effect of a change in trade policy encourages the use of import tariffs and discourages the use of export subsidies. For example, a higher import tariff depresses the world price and thereby shifts foreign surplus into domestic tariff revenue.

The home-government best-response trade policies satisfy the first set of equations in (13) and may be represented as $\tau_x^R(\tau_x^*)$ and $\tau_y^R(\tau_y^*)$, and the best-response trade policies of the foreign government satisfy the second set of equations in (13) and are represented as $\tau_y^{*R}(\tau_y)$ and $\tau_x^{*R}(\tau_x)$. An *interior Nash equilibrium* vector of tariffs, $(\tau_x^N, \tau_y^N, \tau_y^{*N}, \tau_x^{*N})$, satisfies all of the requirements in (13), so that each trade policy of each government is a best response. As Dixit (1987) observes, an *autarky Nash equilibrium* also exists for tariff games. In the present model, as Bagwell and Staiger (2001b) confirm, if for a given good the import tariff is sufficiently high and the export tariff is also sufficiently high, then trade is prohibited and neither government has incentive to cut its tariff sufficiently so as to induce positive trade volume.

To analyze efficient tariffs, we first observe that governments have adequate instruments in this model to generate direct transfers. Let us suppose that the domestic government raises its import tariff and that the foreign government raises its export subsidy by the same amount. The net tariff on the home-country import good is then unaffected. This means that local prices and thus trade volume are unaffected by the proposed change in trade policy. The change does, however, generate a lower world price for the home-country import good. As is evident from the welfare functions above, if $\hat{p}_x$ and $\hat{p}_x^*$ are unchanged and p_x^w falls by, say, one unit, then the domestic government enjoys a welfare gain in the amount of $M(\hat{p}_x)$ and the foreign government suffers a welfare loss in the amount $E^*(\hat{p}_x^*)$. Since the market-clearing condition (12) ensures that $M(\hat{p}_x) = E^*(\hat{p}_x^*)$, we may conclude that governments can make lump-sum government-to-government transfers through policy changes that preserve local prices and alter world prices.

This conclusion implies that a vector of tariffs is *efficient* if and only if it maximizes joint government welfare, $W(\hat{p}_x, \hat{p}_y, p_x^w, p_y^w) + W^*(\hat{p}_y^*, \hat{p}_x^*, p_y^w, p_x^w)$. Looking at the welfare functions defined above, we may also easily confirm that, at given local prices, joint government welfare is independent of world prices. Since joint welfare depends only on local prices, while local prices in turn depend only on net tariffs, we see that efficiency determines only the net tariff for each good. For example, if $\gamma_m = \gamma_x = 1$ so that each government maximizes national economic welfare, then efficiency requires that the net tariff is zero. For a given good, however, this requirement is met whenever the import tariff equals the export subsidy. If we start at free-trade policies and then increase the import tariff and export subsidy for this good in the same amount, then the outcome remains efficient. The joint increase in the import tariff and export subsidy, however, lowers the world price of the good and thus redistributes welfare from the exporting country to the importing country.

Given that joint government welfare depends only on net tariffs, we may fully characterize the set of efficient tariff vectors for any good by finding the net tariff for that good that maximizes joint government welfare. Furthermore, since the model is symmetric across goods, the efficient net tariff is common across goods. We may therefore focus on good x. Assuming that joint government welfare is strictly concave with respect to net tariffs, the associated first-order condition for an efficient tariff vector is

$$W_{\hat{p}_x} \frac{d\hat{p}_x}{d\tau_x} + W_{\hat{p}_x^*}^* \frac{d\hat{p}_x^*}{d\tau_x} = 0. \tag{14}$$

Thus, the set of efficient tariff vectors is the set of tariff vectors that deliver for each good the net tariff that satisfies (14). For any good, different combinations of tariffs that deliver the same net tariff vector simply indicate alternative international transfer patterns achieved through different world prices.

We now turn to the three questions raised at the start of the section. First, we consider the efficiency of Nash trade policies. We expect that Nash trade policies are inefficient, since governments are motivated by terms-of-trade considerations when setting Nash policies while efficiency imposes requirements only on local prices and thus the net tariff. We find that, at Nash policies,

$$W_{\hat{p}_x} \frac{d\hat{p}_x}{d\tau_x} + W_{\hat{p}_x^*}^* \frac{d\hat{p}_x^*}{d\tau_x} = W_{\hat{p}_x} \frac{d\hat{p}_x}{d\tau_x} - W_{\hat{p}_x^*}^* \frac{d\hat{p}_x^*}{d\tau_x^*} = -W_{p_x^w} \frac{\partial p_x^w}{\partial \tau_x} + W_{p_x^w}^* \frac{\partial p_x^w}{\partial \tau_x^*} < 0, \tag{15}$$

where the first equality follows since $\hat{p}_x^*$ ultimately depends on the net tariff, $\tau_x - \tau_x^*$, the second equality uses (13), and the inequality follows since $W_{p_x^w}^* = -W_{p_x^w} > 0$ and the world price is strictly decreasing in each of its arguments. Given our assumption that the joint government welfare function is strictly concave, (14) and (15) imply that the Nash net tariff is higher than efficient.

Second, we establish a general sense in which governments can achieve mutual gains relative to Nash policies only through reciprocal liberalization. In particular, suppose that governments start with Nash policies and then make mutual policy adjustments that change the net tariffs for goods x and y in a symmetric way. Importantly, while the net tariff changes under consideration are symmetric across goods, we are not assuming that the underlying policy adjustments are symmetric across governments. Since the net tariff under Nash policies is higher than efficient, total government welfare rises—and thus mutual gains to government welfare are feasible—only if the net tariff falls. Furthermore, given that each government selects its best-response policies at the Nash equilibrium, mutual gains are possible only if each government makes adjustments to its policies that contribute to some degree to the fall in net tariffs.

Finally, we confirm that terms-of-trade motivations provide the sole rationale for trade agreements in the partial-equilibrium model just as in the general-equilibrium model of the previous section. For the partial-equilibrium model, we follow Bagwell and Staiger (2001b) and define the *politically optimal* tariffs as the vector of tariffs satisfying

$$W_{\hat{p}_x} = W_{\hat{p}_y} = 0 = W_{\hat{p}_y^*}^* = W_{\hat{p}_x^*}^*. \tag{16}$$

The four requirements in (16) determine values for all four trade-policy instruments. In the symmetric model considered here, a common net tariff is thereby determined for both goods. Using (14) and (16), it is now clear that the net tariff is also efficient. In other words, the politically optimal tariffs are efficient. Following Bagwell and Staiger (2001b), we may interpret this finding to mean that the terms-of-trade externality is the sole rationale for a trade agreement in the partial-equilibrium model as well.

Bagwell and Staiger (2001b) also consider a "linear-quadratic" version of the above model in which demand is linear with a reservation price of unity and supply functions are linear. Specifically, they posit that $D(p) = \bar{p} - p$, $\bar{p} = 1$, $Q_y(p) = Q_x^*(p) = p$ and $Q_x(p) = Q_y^*(p) = p/2$. The associated profit functions are quadratic: $\Pi_y(p) = \Pi_x^*(p) = p^2/2$ and $\Pi_x(p) = \Pi_y^*(p) = p^2/4$.[q] If the political-economy weights are not

---

[q] Under the assumption that labor supply is perfectly elastic at a unitary wage, the domestic supply and profit functions can be derived from the following production functions: $Q_x = \sqrt{L_x}$ and $Q_y = \sqrt{2L_y}$, where L_i units of labor are used in the production of good i, $i = x, y$. Analogous remarks apply to the foreign functions. The demand functions can be derived from a representative consumer with utility function $U = C_n + (C_x - C_x^2/2) + (C_y - C_y^2/2)$, where C_n and C_i denote consumption of the numeraire good and good i, $i = x, y$.

too large, so that $\gamma_m \in [1, 3]$ and $\gamma_e \in [1, 3]$, then second-order conditions hold and best-response trade-policy functions are strictly increasing. Intuitively, when the foreign export subsidy increases, the home country imports a larger volume and domestic production falls. The former effect magnifies the terms-of-trade benefit of raising the import tariff. The latter effect, however, weakens the political-economy benefit of using a higher import tariff to raise the local price, since the higher price would apply to a smaller volume of domestic production. The finding that trade policies are strategic complements indicates that, in the linear model at least, the magnification of the terms-of-trade effect dominates the weakening of the political-economy effect.

Under the maintained assumption that the political weight on the import-competing sector is not too large relative to that on the export sector, in the specific sense that $5/8 + 9\gamma_e/8 > \gamma_m$, Bagwell and Staiger (2001b) establish that the interior Nash equilibrium is unique and has positive trade volume. The Nash import tariff is always positive; however, the sign of the export subsidy is ambiguous.[r] Intuitively, the Nash import tariff is strictly positive even for a government that maximizes national economic welfare, since the government of a large country can use a positive import tariff to improve its country's terms of trade. If $\gamma_m > 1$ so that the government receives political benefits from raising the local price of the import good, then the case for a positive Nash import tariff is reinforced. An export tax is likewise optimal for a government that maximizes national economic welfare; however, the Nash export subsidy is positive when γ_e is sufficiently large, since the government then enjoys a large benefit from using an export subsidy to elevate the local price of the export good. Bagwell and Staiger also report that the politically optimal import tariff and export subsidy are nonnegative and correspond to free trade when political economy effects are absent.[s] Finally, they confirm that joint government welfare is strictly concave in the net tariff and that the Nash trade policies are too restrictive, as the trade volume in the interior Nash equilibrium is strictly less than would be efficient for the governments.

The partial-equilibrium model presented here provides a simple and concrete framework with which to understand and explore the terms-of-trade driven Prisoners' Dilemma problem. Like the general-equilibrium model presented above, the partial-equilibrium model indicates that a mutually beneficial trade agreement between governments must entail reciprocal reductions in trade barriers. Thus, the partial- and general-equilibrium frameworks generate the same broad conclusions regarding the purpose of trade agreements.

---

[r] Grossman and Helpman (1995) present a related finding in a more sophisticated model in which political-economic preferences are endogenously determined by lobbying of politically organized sectors. In their model, the ad valorem import tariff is positive for a good with an organized import-competing industry, and the ad valorem export subsidy is negative (ie, an export tax is used) for a good in an export sector that is not organized. In other cases, the sign of the optimal policy is ambiguous, since terms-of-trade and political considerations pull in opposite directions.

[s] The politically optimal import tariff and export subsidy are zero when $\gamma_m = 1$ and $\gamma_e = 1$, respectively.

2.2.3 Missing Instruments in the Partial-Equilibrium Model

We now consider the purpose of trade agreements when the partial-equilibrium model is modified so that some trade-policy instruments are "missing." Recall that the politically optimal trade-policy vector is a vector with four policies—an import tariff and an export subsidy for each country—such that each country achieves its preferred local price on each good: $W_{\hat{p}_x} = W_{\hat{p}_y} = 0 = W^*_{\hat{p}^*_y} = W^*_{\hat{p}^*_x}$. Intuitively, if policies satisfy these requirements, then a small change in any one trade policy cannot generate a Pareto improvement, since the first-order welfare effects of the resulting local-price changes are zero and since the resulting change in any world price constitutes a pure transfer from one government to the other and thus cannot be a source of mutual gain.

Suppose now, however, that export policies are prohibited. In this restricted-instrument setting, let us assume that each government selects its import tariff in a politically optimal fashion. The resulting politically optimal import tariffs are those tariffs that deliver $W_{\hat{p}_x} = 0$ and $W^*_{\hat{p}^*_y} = 0$ when all export subsidies are set to zero. In general, the politically optimal import tariffs for the restricted-instrument setting differ from the politically optimal import tariffs for the setting in which both import and export instruments are available.[t] When the politically optimal import tariffs for the restricted-instrument setting are used, we may easily verify that $W_{\hat{p}_y} > 0$ and $W^*_{\hat{p}^*_x} > 0$ when $\gamma_e > 1$. Thus, when these import tariffs are used and $\gamma_e > 1$, each government would prefer a higher local price for its export good. A government is unable to deliver such a price on its own, however, when export subsidies are prohibited.

We now claim that the resulting four-tuple of policies, where import tariffs are politically optimal in the restricted-instrument setting and export subsidies are zero, is inefficient. To establish this claim, we need only note that each government would strictly gain if the governments were to reciprocally and symmetrically exchange small import tariff cuts. A small import tariff cut by the home government would change the local price of good x in the home country, but this has no first-order effect on the welfare of the home government since $W_{\hat{p}_x} = 0$. The tariff cut would also raise the world price and thus the local price of the good in the foreign country; furthermore, when $\gamma_e > 1$, this local-price effect would generate a first-order welfare gain for the foreign government since $W^*_{\hat{p}^*_x} > 0$. Symmetrically, a small import tariff cut by the foreign government would change the local prices of good y in a manner that would generate no first-order effect on the welfare of the foreign government (since $W^*_{\hat{p}^*_y} = 0$) and a first-order gain in the welfare of the domestic government when $\gamma_e > 1$ (since $W_{\hat{p}_y} > 0$). Finally, each tariff

---

[t] When the foreign government provides an export subsidy at level τ^*_x, the import tariff for the home government that satisfies $W_{\hat{p}_x} = 0$ is given by $\tau_x = 4(\gamma_m - 1)(1 - \tau^*_x)/(25 - 4\gamma_m)$. Thus, if $\gamma_m > 1$, then the politically optimal selection for the home import tariff differs depending on whether export subsidies are prohibited ($\tau^*_x = 0$) or the foreign export subsidy is set at its politically optimal level ($\tau^*_x > 0$ when $\gamma_e > 1$).

cut would induce a terms-of-trade loss for the importing country and a terms-of-trade gain for the exporting country. In a symmetric setting, a country imports as much as it exports, and the overall welfare effect for each government of the resulting changes in world prices is zero.[u] It follows that each government gains from a small and symmetric exchange of reciprocal tariff cuts.

In the restricted-instrument setting, therefore, when governments are not motivated by the terms-of-trade implications of their trade-policy selections, a problem may remain for a trade agreement to solve. The problem is fundamentally a missing-instrument problem. When $\gamma_e > 1$, a domestic government that ignores the terms-of-trade implications of its policies would like to subsidize its exports so as to achieve its preferred local price. Since the domestic government does not have an instrument with which to perform this subsidization, the local price for its export good may be lower than it prefers. A *local-price externality* then arises: an import tariff reduction by the foreign government can generate a positive international externality for the domestic government by raising the local price of the domestic export good. Interestingly, mutual improvements for governments are again achieved in this setting through reciprocal reductions in import tariffs. It is also interesting to note that the local-price externality arises in the competitive setting, even though the domestic government then has no direct interest in the foreign local prices. As we argue below, related findings occur in imperfect competition settings, although in that case the domestic government also has a direct interest in foreign local prices.

2.3 Monopolistic Competition Model of Trade Agreements

Our discussion to this point diagnoses the purpose of a trade agreement from the perspective of models that assume perfectly competitive markets. A large literature, however, suggests that unilateral trade policies have novel implications in imperfectly competitive markets.[v] We thus turn our attention next to the possible implications of imperfectly competitive markets for the purpose of trade agreements. To focus our discussion, we develop a variant of the monopolistic competition model used by Venables (1987). The variant that we explore is also examined by Helpman and Krugman (1989) and further developed by Bagwell and Staiger (2015).[w] The model features integrated markets, "iceberg" transport costs, monopolistically competitive firms which produce differentiated varieties under increasing returns, CES preferences for differentiated products, free entry in both the home and foreign countries, and a homogeneous "outside" good that is produced under constant returns to scale. As before, we first develop the model and then

---

[u] When export subsidies are set equal to zero, the local price of the export good is the same as the world price of this good. It is nevertheless useful to break this price change into local- and world-price components, as captured for general trade policies in the welfare functions above.

[v] See, eg, Brander (1995) and Helpman and Krugman (1989).

[w] Our presentation here is closely related to that found in Bagwell and Staiger (2015).

consider the three questions raised at the start of the section. We conclude with a brief discussion of related research that uses other models of imperfect competition.

2.3.1 Monopolistic Competition Model

We again consider a two-country model. The utility functions for consumers in the home and foreign countries are symmetric and are, respectively, given by

$$U = (C_D)^\theta \left(\frac{1}{\theta}\right) + C_Y$$

$$U^* = (C_D^*)^\theta \left(\frac{1}{\theta}\right) + C_Y^*,$$

(17)

where $\theta \in (0, 1)$, C_D is a home-country index of consumption of a bundle of differentiated goods, C_Y is home-country consumption of a homogeneous good Y, and where C_D^* and C_Y^* are defined analogously in the foreign country. At this point, we respectively treat C_D and C_D^* as home and foreign consumption of a single composite good, which we refer to as good D. We assume that good Y is a numeraire good that is produced in each country from labor, where each unit of labor produces a single unit of good Y. The home and foreign countries, respectively, are endowed with large supplies of labor, L and L^*. Each country then produces good Y, which is freely traded across countries. Under these assumptions, we may fix the wage and thus the price of good Y in each country at unity.

In each country, utility maximization establishes an equality between the ratio of marginal utilities across goods D and Y and the ratio of prices between goods D and Y, where we recall that the price of good Y is unity. Letting P and P^*, respectively, denote the price of good D in the home and foreign countries, we thus have that

$$C_D = P^{-\epsilon}$$

$$C_D^* = (P^*)^{-\epsilon}$$

(18)

where in each country $\epsilon \equiv 1/(1 - \theta) > 1$ is the price elasticity of demand for good D. Letting I and I^* denote income in the home and foreign country, respectively, we may use (17) and (18) to derive the home- and foreign-country indirect utility functions:

$$V(P,I) = P^{-\epsilon\theta} \left(\frac{1}{\epsilon\theta}\right) + I$$

$$V^*(P^*,I^*) = (P^*)^{-\epsilon\theta} \left(\frac{1}{\epsilon\theta}\right) + I^*$$

(19)

where income is measured in terms of the numeraire good Y.

We assume now that C_D is a consumption index that takes a CES form. Specifically, we assume that $C_D = [\sum_i (c_i)^\alpha]^{1/\alpha}$, where $\alpha \in (0, 1)$ and c_i is the consumption level in the home country of variety i of the differentiated good. We may similarly represent

$C_D^* = [\sum_i (c_i^*)^\alpha]^{1/\alpha}$, where c_i^* is the consumption level in the foreign country of variety i of the differentiated good. Letting p^i and p^{*i} denote the prices of variety i in the home and foreign countries, respectively, it can be shown (see Dixit and Stiglitz, 1977) that

$$P = \left[\sum_i (p^i)^{\alpha/(\alpha-1)} \right]^{(\alpha-1)/\alpha}$$

$$P^* = \left[\sum_i (p^{*i})^{\alpha/(\alpha-1)} \right]^{(\alpha-1)/\alpha} \qquad (20)$$

are the associated home- and foreign-country price indices for good D.

Letting $\sigma \equiv 1/(1-\alpha) > 1$, we may now represent the demand for variety i in the home and foreign countries, respectively, as

$$c^i = C_D \left(\frac{p^i}{P} \right)^{-\sigma}$$

$$c^{*i} = C_D^* \left(\frac{p^{*i}}{P^*} \right)^{-\sigma}. \qquad (21)$$

Combining (18) with (21) yields

$$c^i = (p^i)^{-\sigma} P^{\sigma-\epsilon} \equiv c^i(p^i, P)$$

$$c^{*i} = (p^{*i})^{-\sigma} (P^*)^{\sigma-\epsilon} \equiv c^{*i}(p^{*i}, P^*), \qquad (22)$$

which completes the description of the demand side.

We now consider the costs confronted by firms. Production of any variety i entails a fixed cost of labor, $F > 0$, and a constant marginal cost of labor, $\lambda > 0$. The positive fixed cost ensures that no variety is produced by more than one firm; thus, if variety i is produced somewhere, then exactly one firm in the world supplies this variety. In addition, firms confront trade costs. Let $\phi > 0$ denote the "iceberg" transport cost associated with international trade. An exporting firm also faces trade costs in the form of ad valorem export and import tariffs. Let the home-country ad valorem import and export tariffs, respectively, be denoted as τ_h and τ_h^*, and let the foreign-country ad valorem import and export tariffs similarly be denoted as τ_f^* and τ_f, respectively. Notice that an export subsidy by the home country, for example, is captured by a negative value for τ_h^*.

We assume that the markets are integrated and that tariffs are not prohibitive. It then follows that price wedges across countries for any given variety are determined by the total trade costs. Letting $\iota \equiv 1 + \phi + \tau_h + \tau_f$ and $\iota^* \equiv 1 + \phi + \tau_f^* + \tau_h^*$, we have that

$$p_h^{*i} = \iota^* p_h^i$$

$$p_f^i = \iota p_f^{*i}, \qquad (23)$$

where p_h^i and p_h^{*i} are the respective prices of home-produced variety i in the home and foreign countries and where p_f^{*i} and p_f^i are the respective prices of foreign-produced variety i in the foreign and home countries.[x]

The profit for a home-country firm that produces variety i is now given by

$$\pi^i = (p_h^i - \lambda)[c^i(p_h^i, P) + (1 + \phi)c^{*i}(p_h^{*i}, P^*)] - F, \tag{24}$$

where the number of varieties in each country enters profit only through the price indices.[y] Each firm selects its profit-maximizing price while taking as given the price indices, P and P^*. Using (22), (23) and (24), the profit-maximizing prices for home-produced variety i are

$$p_h^i = \frac{\sigma}{\sigma - 1}\lambda \equiv \hat{p}$$
$$p_h^{*i} = \iota^* \hat{p} \equiv p_h^*(\iota^*). \tag{25}$$

Similarly, the profit for a foreign-country firm that produces variety i is given by

$$\pi^{*i} = (p_f^{*i} - \lambda)[c^{*i}(p_f^{*i}, P^*) + (1 + \phi)c^i(p_f^i, P)] - F, \tag{26}$$

and the profit-maximizing prices are

$$p_f^{*i} = \frac{\sigma}{\sigma - 1}\lambda \equiv \hat{p}$$
$$p_f^i = \iota \hat{p} \equiv p_f(\iota). \tag{27}$$

Our next step is to represent the price indices that result from profit-maximizing pricing. Using (20), (25) and (27), we obtain

$$P = [n_h(\hat{p})^{\alpha/(\alpha-1)} + n_f(p_f)^{\alpha/(\alpha-1)}]^{(\alpha-1)/\alpha} \equiv P(n_h, n_f, p_f)$$
$$P^* = [n_f(\hat{p})^{\alpha/(\alpha-1)} + n_h(p_h^*)^{\alpha/(\alpha-1)}]^{(\alpha-1)/\alpha} \equiv P^*(n_h, n_f, p_h^*), \tag{28}$$

where n_h and n_f are the number of firms producing differentiated varieties in the home and foreign countries, respectively, and where we suppress the dependence of p_f on ι and of p_h^* on ι^* here and henceforth. Using (28), we observe that, for given n_h and n_f, the price index in any one country is rising in the total trade costs faced by exporters from the other country but is independent of the total trade costs faced by its own

[x] This formulation assumes that a foreign importer of variety i, for example, purchases at the home-country factory gate at price p_h^i and then pays the export tax, $\tau_h^* p_h^i$, import tax, $\tau_f^* p_h^i$, and transport cost, ϕp_h^i.

[y] This expression reflects the fact that a foreign importer must purchase $1 + \phi$ units at the home-country factory gate in order that 1 unit may be delivered for consumption in the foreign country. Our formulation assumes that international shipping services are freely traded.

exporters. It is also interesting to consider the implications of a reallocation of firms across countries. Referring again to (28), if the total trade costs are positive (ie, $\iota > 1$ and $\iota^* > 1$), then an increase in n_h that is matched by a reduction in n_f results in a fall in the home-country price index P and a rise in the foreign-country price index P^*.

We are now prepared to determine n_h and n_f using free-entry conditions. The free-entry conditions are defined as follows:

$$c(\hat{p}, P(n_h, n_f, p_f)) + (1 + \phi)c^*(p_h^*, P^*(n_h, n_f, p_h^*)) = F/(\hat{p} - \lambda)$$
$$c^*(\hat{p}, P^*(n_h, n_f, p_h^*)) + (1 + \phi)c(p_f, P(n_h, n_f, p_f)) = F/(\hat{p} - \lambda), \tag{29}$$

where we exploit the symmetry of the differentiated sector and now eliminate variety i superscripts. The resulting values for n_h and n_f may be expressed as $n_h(p_f, p_h^*)$ and $n_f(p_f, p_h^*)$. After inserting these expressions into (28), we may abuse notation somewhat and write the free-entry values for the price indices as $P(p_f, p_h^*)$ and $P^*(p_f, p_h^*)$.

As first noted by Venables (1987), the monopolistic competition model exhibits an interesting "firm-delocation effect" from trade protection. To illustrate the point, suppose that we begin at global free trade and then introduce a small and positive import tariff in the home country (ie, $\tau_h > 0$). We see from (25) and (27) that p_h^* is unaltered while p_f rises; thus, for given values of n_h and n_f, it follows from (28) that P^* is unchanged and that P rises. This in turn implies that $c(\hat{p}, P(n_h, n_f, p_f))$ and thus the LHS of the first expression in (29) rises. In addition, since it can be confirmed that p_f rises more than does P, it follows as well that $c(p_f, P(n_h, n_f, p_f))$ and thus the LHS of the second expression in (29) falls. Therefore, for given values of n_h and n_f, the introduction of a small and positive import tariff in the home country generates positive profits for home firms and negative profits for foreign firms. The restoration of zero profits in each country then requires a decrease in P and an increase in P^*.[z] The final step is to note from (28) that these changes in the price indices in turn require an increase in n_h and a decrease in n_f, that is, a "delocation" of firms from the foreign to the home country. A related argument establishes that the introduction of a small export subsidy in the foreign country (ie, $\tau_f < 0$) leads to a rise in P and a fall in P^*, which in turn require a decrease in n_h and an increase in n_f, that is, a "delocation" of firms from the home to the foreign country.

More generally, the firm-delocation effect indicates that a slight increase in the home-country import tariff "delocates" foreign firms to the home-country market, which benefits home-country consumers who enjoy the lower price index that derives

---

[z]   Intuitively, home and foreign profits can adjust in different directions only if the price indices also move in different directions; furthermore, given the positive trade cost $\phi > 0$ and the symmetry of the model, local sales contribute relatively more to the profits of each country's firms than do export sales. See Bagwell and Staiger (2015) and Helpman and Krugman (1989) for additional discussion.

from reduced trade costs and harms foreign-country consumers who experience increased trade costs and thus a higher price index. By a similar logic, a slight increase in the foreign-country export subsidy "delocates" home firms to the foreign-country market, which benefits foreign-country consumers while harming home-country consumers.

As our preceding discussion suggests, trade policy affects welfare through the firm-delocation effect and the associated impact on price indices. But trade policy may also generate tariff revenue and impact income and thus welfare through this channel as well. In the model that we consider here, where profits are zero due to free entry, income in a given country is given by its labor force (which receives a wage of unity) plus the country's net trade tax revenue. To formally represent income, we use M to denote the imports in the home country and E to represent exports from the home country, where by market-clearing home-country imports (exports) are equal to foreign-country exports (imports). We have that

$$
\begin{aligned}
M &= n_f(p_f, p_h^*)c(p_f, P(p_f, p_h^*)) \equiv M(p_f, p_h^*) \\
E &= n_h(p_f, p_h^*)c^*(p_h^*, P^*(p_f, p_h^*)) \equiv E(p_f, p_h^*),
\end{aligned}
\tag{30}
$$

and so income levels in the home and foreign countries are given as[aa]

$$
\begin{aligned}
I &= L + \tau_h^* \hat{p} E(p_f, p_h^*) + \tau_h \hat{p} M(p_f, p_h^*) \\
I^* &= L^* + \tau_f \hat{p} M(p_f, p_h^*) + \tau_f^* \hat{p} E(p_f, p_h^*).
\end{aligned}
\tag{31}
$$

To express welfare as a function of local and world prices, we must first define world prices. Consider first varieties that are exported from the home to the foreign country. We define the world price for these varieties as

$$
p^{*w} = (1 + \tau_h^*)\hat{p} \equiv p^{*w}(\tau_h^*),
\tag{32}
$$

from which it follows that $\tau_h^* \hat{p} = p^{*w} - \hat{p}$. Using also that $p_h^* = \iota^* \hat{p}$ from (25), we then further have that $\tau_f^* \hat{p} = p_h^* - \phi \hat{p} - p^{*w}$. Consider now varieties that are exported from the foreign to the home country. The world price for these varieties is defined as

$$
p^w = (1 + \tau_f)\hat{p} \equiv p^w(\tau_f),
\tag{33}
$$

from which we see that $\tau_f \hat{p} = p^w - \hat{p}$. We may use $p_f = \iota \hat{p}$ from (27) to further derive that $\tau_h \hat{p} = p_f - \phi \hat{p} - p^w$.

With these pricing relationships in hand, we may rewrite the expressions for income in (31) as

---

[aa]   As indicated in footnote y, we assume that international shipping services are freely traded and earn zero profit.

$$I = L + [p^{*w} - \hat{p}]E(p_f, p_h^*) + [p_f - \phi\hat{p} - p^w]M(p_f, p_h^*) \equiv I(p_h^*, p_f, p^w, p^{*w})$$

$$I^* = L^* + [p^w - \hat{p}]M(p_f, p_h^*) + [p_h^* - \phi\hat{p} - p^{*w}]E(p_f, p_h^*) \equiv I^*(p_h^*, p_f, p^w, p^{*w}).$$

(34)

It is instructive to compare the expressions for incomes given by (31) and (34). The advantage of the expressions for incomes in (34) is that the price channels through which trade policies transmit international externalities are directly identified.

With (34) in place, we may now refer to (19) and (with some abuse in notation) write each country's indirect utility function in terms of local and world prices:

$$V(p_h^*, p_f, p^w, p^{*w}) = P(p_f, p_h^*)^{-\epsilon\theta}\left(\frac{1}{\epsilon\theta}\right) + I(p_h^*, p_f, p^w, p^{*w})$$

$$V^*(p_h^*, p_f, p^w, p^{*w}) = P^*(p_f, p_h^*)^{-\epsilon\theta}\left(\frac{1}{\epsilon\theta}\right) + I^*(p_h^*, p_f, p^w, p^{*w}),$$

(35)

where as noted earlier we may express price indices as functions of p_f and p_h^*. Since free entry ensures that profits are zero in this model, an obvious role for political motivations does not arise. We thus associate a country's welfare with its indirect utility function.

The monopolistic competition model considered here admits an interesting pattern of international externalities. As Helpman and Krugman (1989) note, one special feature of the model is that a country's import tariff does not generate an international externality that travels through world prices. For example, we may use (32) and (33) to confirm that the import tariff of the home country, τ_h, affects neither p^{*w} nor, more surprisingly, p^w. As Helpman and Krugman (1989) discuss, this feature arises because of CES preferences (which result in a constant markup) and the existence of a freely traded outside good (which ensures that the marginal cost λ is constant). By contrast, and as Bagwell and Staiger (2015) emphasize, these same features imply that a country's export tariff has an extreme impact on world prices, in that 100% of an export tariff is passed through to consumers abroad. For instance, using (32) and (33), we see that the export tariff of the home country, τ_h^*, has no effect on p^w but is fully passed through in p^{*w}.

We note, too, that the pattern of international externalities is more complicated in the monopolistic competition model than in the perfectly competitive models considered above. In the models with perfect competition, the welfare function of the home government, for example, is determined by the local and world prices, where the relevant local prices are those that prevail in the home country. In the model with monopolistic competition, however, and as (35) confirms, the home-country welfare depends directly also on the price of home-produced varieties in the foreign market (ie, on $p_h^* = p_h^*(\iota^*)$). Thus, the monopolistic-competition model admits a richer set of international externality channels. The key question for our purposes here, however, is whether these new channels lead to new rationales for a trade agreement. This question is addressed below.

2.3.2 Prisoners' Dilemma

We now briefly consider the basic Prisoners' Dilemma that arises in the monopolistic competition model. As with the models above, we characterize the Nash, efficient and politically optimal tariffs.

To characterize Nash trade policies, we begin by representing the best-response or optimal trade policies for the home and foreign governments. We assume in this discussion that the relevant second-order conditions hold. The home-country best-response import and export policies are then determined by the following two first-order conditions:

$$V_{p_f} \frac{dp_f}{d\iota} = 0$$

$$V_{p_h^*} \frac{dp_h^*}{d\iota^*} + V_{p^{*w}} \frac{dp^{*w}}{d\tau_h^*} = 0,$$

(36)

where the home-country import tariff τ_h affects p_f via ι, the home-country export tariff affects p_h^* via ι^*, and the indirect utility function V is given in (35). Similarly, the foreign-country best-response import and export policies satisfy the first-order conditions

$$V_{p_h^*}^* \frac{dp_h^*}{d\iota^*} = 0$$

$$V_{p_f}^* \frac{dp_f}{d\iota} + V_{p^w}^* \frac{dp^w}{d\tau_f} = 0.$$

(37)

We may now define the *Nash trade policies*, $(\tau_h^N, \tau_h^{*N}, \tau_f^{*N}, \tau_f^N)$, as the tariffs that simultaneously satisfy (36) and (37).

Consistent with our discussion earlier, we note that terms-of-trade effects are absent from the conditions that determine the best-response import policies (the top expressions in (36) and (37)) but present in the conditions that determine the best-response export policies (the bottom expressions in (36) and (37)). As Bagwell and Staiger (2015) discuss further, the optimal export policy for a given country thus represents a balance between the terms-of-trade gain that is associated with an export tariff and the firm-delocation benefit that is associated with an export subsidy.

Our next goal is to characterize efficient trade policies. Since this model also has sufficient trade-policy instruments with which to effect lump-sum transfers, efficient trade policies are those which maximize $V + V^*$. Using (34), we observe that total income can be written as

$$I(\cdot) + I^*(\cdot) = L + L^* + [p_f - \phi\hat{p} - \hat{p}]M(p_f, p_h^*) + [p_h^* - \phi\hat{p} - \hat{p}]E(p_f, p_h^*) \equiv T(p_f, p_h^*).$$

(38)

Notice in particular that world prices do not affect total income, which is to say that we can express total income as the function $T(p_f, p_h^*)$. Using (35) and (38), we can now also represent joint welfare as a function $J(p_f, p_h^*)$ where

$$V(\cdot) + V^*(\cdot) = P(p_f, p_h^*)^{-\epsilon\theta}\left(\frac{1}{\epsilon\theta}\right) + P^*(p_f, p_h^*)^{-\epsilon\theta}\left(\frac{1}{\epsilon\theta}\right) + T(p_f, p_h^*) \equiv J(p_f, p_h^*). \quad (39)$$

As this expression confirms, any trade-policy induced change in world prices corresponds simply to pure international rent shifting and does not affect efficiency.

Efficient trade policies thus maximize the joint welfare function $J(p_f, p_h^*)$ given in (39). By (25) and (27), respectively, we also know that $p_h^* = p_h^*(\iota^*)$ and $p_f = p_f(\iota)$; thus, joint welfare is a function of the four tariffs only through ι and ι^*. Assuming that the joint welfare function is strictly concave when treated as a function of ι and ι^*, the set of *efficient tariffs* is thus characterized by the following two first-order conditions:

$$[V_{p_h^*} + V_{p_h^*}^*]\frac{dp_h^*}{d\iota^*} = 0$$
$$\quad (40)$$
$$[V_{p_f} + V_{p_f}^*]\frac{dp_f}{d\iota} = 0.$$

Bagwell and Staiger (2015) further explore the two conditions in (40) and show that efficiency requires a net subsidy to trade along each trade channel (ie, $\tau_f^* + \tau_h^* < 0$ and $\tau_h + \tau_f < 0$).[ab] The intuition is that a net subsidy is desirable due to the positive markup in the differentiated sector.

We now turn again to the three questions raised at the start of the section. First, we consider the efficiency of Nash trade policies. Once again, we expect that Nash trade policies are inefficient, since governments are motivated by world-price considerations when setting Nash policies but not when maximizing joint welfare. More formally, after adding the bottom Nash condition in (36) to the top Nash condition in (37), and likewise adding the top Nash condition in (36) to the bottom Nash condition in (37), we arrive at the following:

$$[V_{p_h^*} + V_{p_h^*}^*]\frac{dp_h^*}{d\iota^*} = -E\frac{dp^{*w}}{d\tau_h^*} < 0$$
$$\quad (41)$$
$$[V_{p_f} + V_{p_f}^*]\frac{dp_f}{d\iota} = -M\frac{dp^w}{d\tau_f} < 0$$

[ab]   See Helpman and Krugman (1989) for related discussion.

where we use (34) and (35) to obtain that $V_{p^{*w}} = E$ and $V_{p^w}^* = M$. Comparing (40) and (41), it is now immediate that Nash trade policies are inefficient.

Given the assumed second-order conditions and the symmetry of the model, we know that Nash and efficient tariffs are each such that the total tariffs satisfy $\iota = \iota^*$. Starting at the Nash equilibrium, if we were to undertake any change in underlying tariffs that delivered a symmetric increase in $\iota = \iota^*$, then the change in joint welfare would be given by the sum of the terms on the LHS of the equalities in (41), when evaluated at $\iota^N \equiv 1 + \phi + \tau_h^N + \tau_f^N = 1 + \phi + \tau_f^{*N} + \tau_h^{*N} \equiv \iota^{*N}$. As is evident from (41), starting at the Nash equilibrium, a symmetric change in $\iota = \iota^*$ increases joint welfare if and only if $\iota = \iota^*$ is decreased. It thus follows that the total trade cost, $\iota = \iota^*$, is strictly higher at Nash tariffs than at efficient tariffs.

We turn now to our second question and explore whether a mutually beneficial trade agreement requires reciprocal trade liberalization. Our preceding discussion already establishes that a trade agreement that delivers symmetric changes in total trade costs can generate greater joint welfare if and only if total tariffs are reduced from Nash levels. Thus, at least in the context of trade policy adjustments that maintain symmetric total trade costs, $\iota = \iota^*$, mutual gains are possible starting at Nash only if reciprocal trade liberalization occurs in the sense that $\tau_h + \tau_f = \tau_f^* + \tau_h^*$ is reduced. Just as in our discussion of the partial-equilibrium model with perfect competition, such efficiency-enhancing paths may involve adjustments in underlying tariffs that are asymmetric across countries. Mutual gains are again possible, however, only if each government makes adjustments to its policies that contribute to some degree to the fall in total tariffs.

Finally, we consider whether terms-of-trade motivations represent the sole rationale for trade agreements in the monopolistic competition model. To explore this issue, we again define the politically optimal tariffs to be those tariffs that hypothetically would be chosen by governments unilaterally if they did not value the pure international rent-shifting associated with the terms-of-trade movements induced by their unilateral tariff choices. For the monopolistic competition model under consideration here, when making their respective politically optimal tariff selections, the home-country government acts as if $V_{p^{*w}} = 0 = V_{p^w}$ while the foreign-country governments acts as if $V_{p^w}^* = 0 = V_{p^{*w}}^*$.[ac] Formally, and following Bagwell and Staiger (2015), we define the *politically optimal tariffs* for the monopolistic competition model as the vector of tariffs satisfying

$$V_{p_f} \frac{dp_f}{d\iota} = V_{p_h^*}^* \frac{dp_h^*}{d\iota^*} = 0 = V_{p_h^*}^* \frac{dp_h^*}{d\iota^*} = V_{p_f}^* \frac{dp_f}{d\iota}. \tag{42}$$

[ac]   As noted previously, in the monopolistic competition model considered here, a country cannot use its import policy to change the world price of varieties produced abroad. For consistency, in our definition of politically optimal tariffs, we nevertheless include the requirement that such a change would not be valued.

The four equations in (42) determine the politically optimal tariff vector, $(\tau_h^{PO}, \tau_h^{*PO}, \tau_f^{*PO}, \tau_f^{PO})$. In the symmetric model considered here, a common total tariff is determined for each direction of trade, $\tau_h^{PO} + \tau_f^{PO} = \tau_f^{*PO} + \tau_h^{*PO}$, so that the resulting total trade cost is also symmetric: $\iota^{PO} \equiv 1 + \phi + \tau_h^{PO} + \tau_f^{PO} = 1 + \phi + \tau_f^{*PO} + \tau_h^{*PO} \equiv \iota^{*PO}$. Using (40) and (42), it is now immediate that the politically optimal tariffs are efficient. Thus, in the monopolistic competition model as well, the terms-of-trade externality is the sole rationale for a trade agreement.

Intuitively, in the Nash equilibrium of the monopolistic competition model, each government is mindful of the beneficial firm-delocation effect that import tariffs and export subsidies offer, and each government is also attentive to the terms-of-trade gain that export tariffs provide. The effects of trade policies on trade volumes and thereby tariff revenue are also considered. By contrast, when governments select politically optimal policies, they ignore the terms-of-trade impacts of trade (namely, export) policies and focus on the local-price implications of trade policies. The local prices that can be influenced by trade policy in this model are the domestic prices of varieties produced abroad, p_h^* and p_f, where these prices in turn are determined by total trade costs, $\iota = 1 + \phi + \tau_h + \tau_f$ and $\iota^* = 1 + \phi + \tau_f^* + \tau_h^*$. A key point is that, when a government selects its politically optimal export policy, it does so to deliver its preferred local price abroad for its domestically produced varieties, which in turn *neutralizes* the externality that travels from the trading partner's import tariff through this price. Likewise, a government's politically optimal import tariff delivers its preferred local price in the domestic market for varieties produced abroad, which in turn neutralizes the externality that travels from the trading partner's export policy through this price.

Thus, while the monopolistic competition model admits a rich set of local-price externalities that complement the traditional terms-of-trade externality, the local-price externalities are "shut down" when each government selects its politically optimal import and export policies, leaving only the terms-of-trade externality, which by itself amounts simply to a lump-sum transfer between governments. In this sense, the terms-of-trade externality remains the sole rationale for a trade agreement. From this perspective, it is also apparent that politically optimal trade policies would not in general be efficient were governments to possess an incomplete set of trade-policy instruments. For example, if export policies were unavailable, then a government would not be able to use its export policy to deliver its preferred local price abroad for domestically produced varieties, and its trading partner's import tariff would then induce a local-price externality through this channel.[ad] As in the partial-equilibrium perfect competition model discussed earlier, the

---

[ad] Indeed, in this model, import tariffs do not generate a terms-of-trade externality, and so the inefficiency that emerges under Nash policies when export policies are unavailable clearly does not derive from this externality.

efficiency of politically optimal policies relies deeply on the assumption that governments possess a complete set of trade-policy instruments.[ae]

The finding just described—that politically optimal policies are efficient in the monopolistic competition model when governments have a complete set of trade-policy instruments—extends to a range of other imperfect competition settings. For example, Bagwell and Staiger (2015) show that this finding holds as well in the Cournot delocation model considered by Venables (1985), wherein firms engage in Cournot competition and markets are segmented. In complementary work, Bagwell and Staiger (2012b) show that the finding holds as well in various "profit-shifting" models, where the number of firms is fixed and trade policy can shift profits from one country to another. An important direction for future research concerns the extent to which this finding extends to settings with multiple countries, domestic policies and other forms of imperfect competition.[af] Another extension, which we discuss below, concerns whether this finding extends in "offshoring" settings where prices may be determined through bilateral bargaining between sellers and buyers.

Finally, while the results summarized here indicate that the terms-of-trade externality remains the sole rationale for a trade agreement in important imperfect-competition settings, non-terms-of-trade externalities may nevertheless be important for understanding key features of actual trade agreements. First, actual trade agreements may constrain the trade-policy instruments that are available to governments, so that local-price externalities are not neutralized when politically optimal policies are selected. As one important example, we note that the WTO prohibits export subsidies. As Ossa (2011) argues and as

---

[ae]   The argument here is distinct from standard arguments that governments may need a complete set of policy instruments in order to achieve a first-best outcome in the presence of market imperfections. The argument here instead concerns whether governments can achieve an efficient outcome while using politically optimal policies, when efficiency and political optimality are defined relative to a fixed set of policy instruments.

[af]   In this regard, Campolmi et al. (2014) extend the study of trade agreements within a Venables (1987) delocation-type model to include domestic policies as well as trade policies. They argue in this setting that the choice of domestic policies introduces a novel motive for non-cooperative trade policy choices; and they further claim that politically optimal policies are not efficient in this setting, implying the possibility of a trade agreement whose purpose extends beyond the internalization of terms-of-trade externalities. However, the characterization of politically optimal policies employed by Campolmi et al. does not conform to the definition of such policies that we have described here—Campolmi et al. impose the restriction that governments act as if their unilateral policy choices had no impact on world prices, while as described earlier (see also Bagwell and Staiger, 2015) we impose the restriction that governments act as if they did not *value* the world price impacts of their unilateral policy choices; and they evaluate their political optimum conditions at reciprocal free trade policies, which do not correspond to the politically optimal policies in this setting according to our definition—and so we view the purpose of trade agreements in this setting as still an open question. See also Costinot et al. (2015), who consider a modeling framework that includes that of Campolmi et al. as a special case, and who argue that the motives for policy intervention can indeed be understood to reflect only terms-of-trade considerations in this setting.

we discuss further in a later section, in such a restricted-instrument setting, novel externalities may influence trade-agreement purpose and design. Second, and relatedly, models with imperfect competition may deliver novel interpretations of certain design features of trade agreements. For instance, as Bagwell and Staiger (2012a) show, the Cournot delocation model can provide a novel interpretation of the WTO's restrictions on export subsidies.[ag] Finally, our discussion here emphasizes international externalities that travel through prices. Trade policies also may be associated with international nonpecuniary externalities, such as global warming. The purpose and design of trade agreements in settings characterized by pecuniary and nonpecuniary international externalities is a very important direction for future research.[ah]

2.4 Offshoring Model of Trade Agreements

In all of the models that we describe earlier, prices are determined by market-clearing mechanisms. A growing volume of trade, however, involves intermediate inputs, with firms "offshoring" production and frequently customizing inputs to reflect the needs of buyers. In the presence of such "relationship-specific" investments, hold up is a natural concern. Since contracts involving international transactions may be difficult to enforce, the resulting prices may be determined by bilateral negotiations rather than market-clearing mechanisms: that is, while it is natural to think that market clearing is still a feature of the equilibrium in settings where offshoring is prevalent, the discipline that market-clearing places on the determination of international prices is likely to be diminished. An interesting issue is whether the rise of offshoring impacts in some fundamental way the purpose and design of trade agreements. Antràs and Staiger (2012a,b) examine this issue in detail. Here, we develop the basic model used by Antràs and Staiger (2012a), characterize the Nash, efficient and politically optimal policies, and emphasize in particular their finding that the politically optimal policies are not efficient when governments have political-economic motivations and seek to use trade policies for the purposes of redistribution. The key implication of this finding is that the inefficiency associated with the terms-of-trade externality is not necessarily the only problem for a trade agreement to solve when intermediate inputs are traded and the resulting prices are determined by bilateral negotiations.

[ag] See also Bagwell and Lee (2015) for a recent effort that interprets these restrictions from the perspective of the monopolistic competition model with heterogeneous firms developed by Melitz and Ottaviano (2008).

[ah] Related existing research that emphasizes the presence of international nonpecuniary externalities includes Limão (2005) and Spagnola (1999a,b). Related research on trade agreements in the presence of *domestic* nonpecuniary externalities includes Ederington (2001) and Lee (2007, 2014).

2.4.1 Offshoring Model

Following Antràs and Staiger (2012a), we consider two countries that are small in the market for a final good, which is called good 1 and is traded on world markets at a price of unity. Consumers in the home (H) and foreign (F) countries share identical preferences, which take the quasi-linear form

$$U^j = c_0^j + u(c_1^j), \tag{43}$$

where c_i^j is the consumption of good $i \in \{0, 1\}$ in country $j \in \{H, F\}$ and where $u' > 0 > u''$. As is standard, the numeraire good, which here is good 0, is costlessly traded and consumed in positive quantities in both countries. With p_1^j denoting the price of good 1 in country j, we let $D_1(p_1^j) \equiv u'^{-1}(p_1^j)$ indicate the demand for good 1 in country j. The corresponding consumer surplus function is then represented as

$$CS(p_1^j) = \int_{p_1^j}^{\bar{p}} D_1(p)dp, \tag{44}$$

where $\bar{p}$ is the choke price (if any).

Good 1 is produced by the home country using a customized input x sourced in the foreign country, where the good-1 production function $y(x)$ satisfies $y(0) = 0, y'(x) > 0 > y''(x), \lim_{x \to 0} y'(x) = \infty$ and $\lim_{x \to \infty} y'(x) = 0$.[ai] The marginal cost for a foreign input supplier is normalized to unity.

The home country H has a unit mass of producers of the final good 1, while the foreign country F has a unit mass of suppliers of the intermediate input good x. Importantly, an input requires customization for its intended final good producer and is thus specific to the particular supplier–producer relationship. A simplifying assumption is that a given input in fact has no outside value to other suppliers. As well, Antràs and Staiger assume that contracts are infeasible so that the price at which each supplier in F sells its inputs to a producer in H is determined ex post (after the cost of producing x is sunk) according to the generalized Nash bargaining solution, where $\alpha \in (0, 1)$ is the weight attached to the home producer and $1 - \alpha \in (0, 1)$ is thus the weight attached to the foreign supplier.

Before supplier–producer relationships are established, trade policies are determined. Let τ_x^H denote the specific trade tax imposed by H on imports of x from F, where $\tau_x^H > 0$ ($\tau_x^H < 0$) indicates an import tariff (import subsidy). Similarly, τ_x^F denotes the specific trade tax imposed by F on exports of x to H, where $\tau_x^F > 0$ ($\tau_x^F < 0$) indicates an export tariff (export subsidy). It is convenient also to define the total trade tax on the intermediate input x as $\tau_x \equiv \tau_x^H + \tau_x^F$. The model allows that the home country H may import or export final good 1. Let the specific trade tax imposed by H on the final good

---

[ai]   An important implication of concavity is that $y(x)/x > y'(x)$ for $x > 0$.

1 be represented as τ_1^H, where $\tau_1^H > 0$ ($\tau_1^H < 0$) indicates an import tariff or export subsidy (import subsidy or export tariff).[aj]

Formally, Antràs and Staiger (2012a) consider a game with the following stages:

stage 0: Trade policies τ_x^H, τ_x^F and τ_1^H are determined.

stage 1: Each supplier in F is randomly matched to a unique producer in H.

stage 2: Each supplier decides on an amount x of the customized input to produce.

stage 3: Each producer–supplier pair bargains over the price of the intermediate input.

stage 4: Each producer imports x units and produces the final good, and payments and trade taxes are settled.

To begin, let us consider the bargaining game in *stage* 3, at which point the trade policies are fixed, the volume x is determined, and the associated production costs for x are sunk. The joint surplus over which a producer–supplier pair bargains in *stage* 3 can be represented as

$$J(\tau_1^H, \tau_x, x) = (1 + \tau_1^H)\gamma(x) - \tau_x x, \tag{45}$$

where $p_1^H = 1 + \tau_1^H \equiv p_1^H(\tau_1^H)$ is the price of final good 1 and we recall that $\tau_x \equiv \tau_x^H + \tau_x^F$ is the total trade tax on the intermediate good x. The producer in H and the supplier in F thus obtain the respective bargaining payoffs of $\alpha J(\tau_1^H, \tau_x, x)$ and $(1 - \alpha)J(\tau_1^H, \tau_x, x)$.

Foreseeing this bargaining payoff, a supplier in F chooses the volume x in *stage* 2 so as to maximize $(1 - \alpha)J(\tau_1^H, \tau_x, x) - x$, where we recall that the marginal production cost of x is unitary. Let us denote the profit maximizing volume as $\hat{x} = \hat{x}(\tau_1^H, \tau_x)$, where this volume is defined by the first-order condition for profit maximization:

$$(1 - \alpha)(1 + \tau_1^H)\gamma'(\hat{x}) = (1 - \alpha)\tau_x + 1. \tag{46}$$

Given the maintained assumptions that $1 + \tau_1^H > 0$ and $\gamma'' < 0$, it is straightforward to verify that $\partial\hat{x}/\partial\tau_1^H > 0 > \partial\hat{x}/\partial\tau_x$. Intuitively, a tariff change elicits a higher profit-maximizing value for x when the tariff change results in a higher joint surplus for bargaining.

It is instructive to pause at this point and highlight the hold-up problem that is embedded in the model. If the producer–supplier pair could contract over x with the objective of maximizing the sum of their joint payoffs inclusive of the cost of producing x, then they would choose x to maximize $J(\tau_1^H, \tau_x, x) - x$. The associated first-order condition is

---

[aj]   As Antràs and Staiger (2012a) argue, the foreign country F has no incentive to deviate from free trade in the final good, and so for our discussion here we simply assume that F maintains free trade in the final good.

$$(1 + \tau_1^H)\gamma'(x) = \tau_x + 1. \tag{47}$$

Comparing (47) with (46), we conclude that $\hat{x}$ is lower than the level that would be contracted upon. The key point, of course, is that the cost that the foreign supplier incurs in producing the intermediate input is treated as sunk once the Nash bargaining process commences in *stage* 3.

Continuing with our analysis of the Antràs and Staiger (2012a) game, we now roll back to *stage* 1 to determine payoffs for the home producer and foreign supplier. We define these payoffs as follows:

$$\begin{aligned}
\pi^H &= \alpha J(\tau_1^H, \tau_x, \hat{x}(\tau_1^H, \tau_x)) \equiv \pi^H(\tau_1^H, \tau_x) \\
\pi^F &= (1 - \alpha) J(\tau_1^H, \tau_x, \hat{x}(\tau_1^H, \tau_x)) - \hat{x}(\tau_1^H, \tau_x) \equiv \pi^F(\tau_1^H, \tau_x).
\end{aligned} \tag{48}$$

Our next step is to represent welfare functions for the governments of the home and foreign countries. Letting $\gamma^j \geq 1$ denote the welfare weight that the government of country j attaches to the payoffs enjoyed by its firms, the home- and foreign-country government welfare functions may be, respectively, represented as follows:

$$\begin{aligned}
W^H(\tau_1^H, \tau_x^H, \tau_x^F) &= CS(1 + \tau_1^H) + \gamma^H \pi^H(\tau_1^H, \tau_x) + \tau_1^H[D_1(1 + \tau_1^H) - \gamma(\hat{x}(\cdot))] + \tau_x^H \hat{x}(\cdot) \\
W^F(\tau_1^H, \tau_x^H, \tau_x^F) &= CS(1) + \gamma^F \pi^F(\tau_1^H, \tau_x) + \tau_x^F \hat{x}(\cdot)
\end{aligned} \tag{49}$$

where $\hat{x}(\cdot) \equiv \hat{x}(\tau_1^H, \tau_x)$. Notice that the foreign country imports final good 1 at the world price, whereas the home-country government may be tempted to use its final-good tariff τ_1^H so as to influence the joint bargaining surplus and thus the determination of $\hat{x}$. The final two terms in the top line of (49) and the final term in the bottom line of (49) are tariff-revenue terms.

We may now represent world welfare, W^w, as the sum of W^H and W^F. Formally:

$$\begin{aligned}
W^w &= W^H(\tau_1^H, \tau_x^H, \tau_x^F) + W^F(\tau_1^H, \tau_x^H, \tau_x^F) \\
&= CS(1 + \tau_1^H) + CS(1) + \gamma^H \pi^H(\tau_1^H, \tau_x) + \gamma^F \pi^F(\tau_1^H, \tau_x) \\
&\quad + \tau_1^H[D_1(1 + \tau_1^H) - \gamma(\hat{x}(\cdot))] + \tau_x \hat{x}(\cdot) \\
&\equiv W^w(\tau_1^H, \tau_x).
\end{aligned} \tag{50}$$

Observe that W^w depends on τ_x^H and τ_x^F only through their sum, τ_x.

Having described the basic model, we now show that the welfare functions can be written as functions of local and world prices. As in the models described earlier, such a formulation is useful, since it enables us to define politically optimal policies. We begin by defining the implied prices for the offshoring model.

We may think of a supplier in F as delivering $\hat{x}$ units to a producer in H at the home-country local price p_x^H, where p_x^H is thus defined by

$$p_x^H \hat{x} - (1 + \tau_x^H + \tau_x^F)\hat{x} \equiv \pi^F(\tau_1^H, \tau_x). \tag{51}$$

Using (45) and (48), we may now rewrite (51) equivalently as

$$p_x^H = \frac{(1-\alpha)(1+\tau_1^H)\gamma(\hat{x}(\cdot))}{\hat{x}(\cdot)} + \alpha\tau_x \equiv p_x^H(\tau_1^H, \tau_x). \tag{52}$$

Next, we let p_x^* represent the international or world price for the intermediate good x. This is the implied price that prevails prior to the application of H's import policy:

$$p_x^* = p_x^H - \tau_x^H = \frac{(1-\alpha)(1+\tau_1^H)\gamma(\hat{x}(\cdot))}{\hat{x}(\cdot)} + \alpha\tau_x^F - (1-\alpha)\tau_x^H \equiv p_x^*(\tau_1^H, \tau_x^H, \tau_x^F). \tag{53}$$

Finally, we may define the foreign-country local price p_x^F as the implied price that prevails before the application of F's export policy:

$$p_x^F = p_x^* - \tau_x^F = \frac{(1-\alpha)(1+\tau_1^H)\gamma(\hat{x}(\cdot))}{\hat{x}(\cdot)} - (1-\alpha)\tau_x \equiv p_x^F(\tau_1^H, \tau_x). \tag{54}$$

We now make a few observations. First, we observe from (53) and (54) that $p_x^H - p_x^F = \tau_x$. Second, we recall that $p_1^H = 1 + \tau_1^H$. Next, using these observations, we note that we may think of $\hat{x}(\tau_1^H, \tau_x)$ as a function of local prices. Formally, we may define the function $\bar{x}$ as follows:

$$\bar{x}(p_1^H, p_x^H - p_x^F) = \hat{x}(\tau_1^H, \tau_x). \tag{55}$$

Finally, with $\bar{x}$ defined in terms of prices as indicated in (55), we can likewise express firm payoffs and tariff revenues in terms of prices. For instance, using (51) and replacing $\hat{x}$ with $\bar{x}$ as allowed via (55) and $\tau_x^H + \tau_x^F \equiv \tau_x$ with $p_x^H - p_x^F$, π^F can be expressed as a function of p_1^H, p_x^H and p_x^F. While firm profit depends only on total tariffs, tariff revenue is also influenced by the world price. For example, H's tariff revenue on the intermediate good, $\tau_x^H \hat{x}$, can be written as $(p_x^H - p_x^*)\bar{x}(p_1^H, p_x^H - p_x^F)$.

Proceeding in this general manner, we may now represent the home and foreign government welfare functions, and thus the world welfare function, in terms of the local and world prices that the underlying trade policies imply. We begin with the welfare function of H's government:

$$W^H = CS(p_1^H) + \gamma^H[p_1^H \gamma(\bar{x}(\cdot)) - p_x^H \bar{x}(\cdot)] + (p_1^H - 1)[D(p_1^H) - \gamma(\bar{x}(\cdot))] + (p_x^H - p_x^*)\bar{x}(\cdot)$$

$$\equiv \overline{W}^H(p_1^H(\tau_1^H), p_x^H(\tau_1^H, \tau_x), p_x^F(\tau_1^H, \tau_x), p_x^*(\tau_1^H, \tau_x^H, \tau_x^F)), \tag{56}$$

where $\bar{x}(\,\cdot\,) \equiv \bar{x}(p_1^H, p_x^H - p_x^F)$. And next, the welfare function of F's government:

$$
\begin{aligned}
W^F &= CS(1) + \gamma^F[p_x^F - 1]\bar{x}(\,\cdot\,) + (p_x^* - p_x^F)\bar{x}(\,\cdot\,) \\
&\equiv \overline{W}^F\big(p_1^H(\tau_1^H), p_x^H(\tau_1^H, \tau_x), p_x^F(\tau_1^H, \tau_x), p_x^*(\tau_1^H, \tau_x^H, \tau_x^F)\big).
\end{aligned}
\tag{57}
$$

Finally, the world welfare function can now be defined as follows:

$$
\begin{aligned}
\overline{W}^w &= \overline{W}^H + \overline{W}^F = CS(p_1^H) + \gamma^H[p_1^H y(\bar{x}(\,\cdot\,)) - p_x^H \bar{x}(\,\cdot\,)] \\
&\quad + (p_1^H - 1)[D(p_1^H) - y(\bar{x}(\,\cdot\,))] + CS(1) + \gamma^F[p_x^F - 1]\bar{x}(\,\cdot\,) \\
&\quad + (p_x^H - p_x^F)\bar{x}(\,\cdot\,) \\
&\equiv \overline{W}^w\big(p_1^H(\tau_1^H), p_x^H(\tau_1^H, \tau_x), p_x^F(\tau_1^H, \tau_x)\big).
\end{aligned}
\tag{58}
$$

We note that the welfare functions of the governments of H and F each depend on the terms of trade, p_x^*. The government of H (F) enjoys a terms-of-trade gain when p_x^* is lower (higher):

$$
\overline{W}_{p_x^*}^H = -\bar{x}(\,\cdot\,) < 0 \text{ and } \overline{W}_{p_x^*}^F = \bar{x}(\,\cdot\,) > 0.
\tag{59}
$$

But the world welfare function is independent of the terms of trade: for given local prices, and thus for a given value of $\bar{x}(\,\cdot\,)$, a change in p_x^* simply amounts to an international transfer.

2.4.2 Prisoners' Dilemma

With the offshoring model developed and the welfare functions presented in terms of local and world prices, we are prepared now to characterize the Nash, efficient and politically optimal trade policies. To this end, we first present the associated first-order conditions and then describe the main findings. For each optimization problem, we assume that the corresponding second-order conditions are satisfied.

The *Nash trade policies* for the offshoring model, $(\tau_1^{HN}, \tau_x^{HN}, \tau_x^{FN})$, satisfy the following first-order conditions:

$$
\overline{W}_{p_1^H}^H + \overline{W}_{p_x^H}^H \frac{\partial p_x^H}{\partial \tau_1^H} + \overline{W}_{p_x^F}^H \frac{\partial p_x^F}{\partial \tau_1^H} - \bar{x}(\,\cdot\,)\frac{\partial p_x^*}{\partial \tau_1^H} = 0
$$

$$
\overline{W}_{p_x^H}^H \frac{\partial p_x^H}{\partial \tau_x} + \overline{W}_{p_x^F}^H \frac{\partial p_x^F}{\partial \tau_x} - \bar{x}(\,\cdot\,)\frac{\partial p_x^*}{\partial \tau_x^H} = 0
\tag{60}
$$

$$
\overline{W}_{p_x^H}^F \frac{\partial p_x^H}{\partial \tau_x} + \overline{W}_{p_x^F}^F \frac{\partial p_x^F}{\partial \tau_x} + \bar{x}(\,\cdot\,)\frac{\partial p_x^*}{\partial \tau_x^F} = 0,
$$

where we use $p_1^H = 1 + \tau_1^H$, $\tau_x = \tau_x^H + \tau_x^F$ and (59). Next, the *efficient trade policies* for the offshoring model, (τ_1^{HE}, τ_x^E), satisfy the following first-order conditions:

$$\overline{W}^w_{p_1^H} + \overline{W}^w_{p_x^H}\frac{\partial p_x^H}{\tau_1^H} + \overline{W}^w_{p_x^F}\frac{\partial p_x^F}{\tau_1^H} = 0$$

$$\overline{W}^w_{p_x^H}\frac{\partial p_x^H}{\tau_x} + \overline{W}^w_{p_x^F}\frac{\partial p_x^F}{\tau_x} = 0.$$

(61)

Finally, the *politically optimal trade policies* for the offshoring model, $(\tau_1^{HPO}, \tau_x^{HPO}, \tau_x^{FPO})$, satisfy the following first-order conditions:

$$\overline{W}^H_{p_1^H} + \overline{W}^H_{p_x^H}\frac{\partial p_x^H}{\tau_1^H} + \overline{W}^H_{p_x^F}\frac{\partial p_x^F}{\tau_1^H} = 0$$

$$\overline{W}^H_{p_x^H}\frac{\partial p_x^H}{\tau_x} + \overline{W}^H_{p_x^F}\frac{\partial p_x^F}{\tau_x} = 0$$

(62)

$$\overline{W}^F_{p_x^H}\frac{\partial p_x^H}{\tau_x} + \overline{W}^F_{p_x^F}\frac{\partial p_x^F}{\tau_x} = 0.$$

We now consider the efficiency of the Nash and politically optimal policies. Looking at (60) and (61), it is natural to expect that the Nash trade policies are inefficient. After all, when setting their Nash policies, governments are mindful of the impact of their policies on the terms of trade, p_x^*, even though for fixed local prices the terms of trade has no impact on world welfare. Antràs and Staiger (2012a) show that the Nash policies are indeed inefficient, and thus that a problem exists for a trade agreement to solve.

But is the terms-of-trade externality the only problem for a trade agreement to address in this setting? Antràs and Staiger show that politically optimal trade policies are efficient when $\gamma^F = 1$, so that the foreign-country government maximizes national income; however, they find that, if $\gamma^F > 1$, then politically optimal trade policies are inefficient. Thus, in the offshoring model and when governments have political-economic motivations and value redistribution, it follows that the terms-of-trade externality is not the only problem for a trade agreement to address.

At a broad level, why might politically optimal policies be inefficient in the offshoring model?[ak] Notice that the bottom two conditions in (62) can be added to deliver the bottom condition in (61); thus, the underlying source of the potential inefficiency of politically optimal policies is connected to the top conditions in (61) and (62) and thus to the determination of H's final-good trade tax, τ_1^H. Let us thus follow Antràs and Staiger (2012a) and contemplate a small increase in τ_1^H that is coupled with a change in τ_x^H that leaves the world price p_x^* fixed. This policy adjustment results in a higher value for p_x^H but leaves p_x^F fixed (since τ_x^F is unaltered). Starting at the politically optimal policies, Antràs and Staiger show that the resulting changes in p_1^H and p_x^H lead only to a second-order loss

---

[ak]   Antràs and Staiger (2012a) also provide a more detailed explanation that clarifies the role played by $\gamma^F > 1$ in the inefficiency of the political optimum in the offshoring model.

for H's government welfare but can generate a first-order effect for the government welfare of F. Intuitively, F's government does not have an "offsetting" instrument with which to position $p_1^H = 1 + \tau_1^H$ at its preferred level and thereby "shut down" the associated local-price externality; hence, F's government may experience a first-order welfare change at politically optimal policies when H's government alters p_1^H by changing τ_1^H.[al] In fact, as Antràs and Staiger show, the described policy adjustment generates a first-order gain for F's government welfare when $\gamma^F > 1$. Politically optimal policies are thus inefficient, since τ_x^H and τ_x^F can then be adjusted while holding τ_x fixed so as to effect a transfer (via the resulting world-price change) that compensates H's government for its second-order welfare loss while still delivering a first-order welfare gain to F's government.

Our preceding discussion provides answers to the first and third questions that motivate this section. Specifically, for the offshoring model, Nash tariffs are inefficient, and if $\gamma^F > 1$ an inefficiency remains even when governments are not motivated by the terms-of-trade implications of their trade policies. We have not addressed for this model the second motivating question about the role of reciprocity. We postpone our discussion of reciprocity in the offshoring model until Section 3.3.

2.5 Summary

At this point, we have reviewed four models of trade agreements, and each model features a terms-of-trade externality.[am] We have also argued that the first three models can be interpreted as indicating that the sole purpose of a trade agreement is to help governments escape from a terms-of-trade driven Prisoners' Dilemma, at least when governments possess a complete set of trade policy instruments, in the particular sense that politically optimal policies are efficient in these models. We may therefore regard these first three models as falling within the "class" of terms-of-trade theories of trade agreements.

Are there some general features of these models that can be used to identify models that fall within the terms-of-trade class? Maggi (2014) makes some progress in providing

[al] Antràs and Staiger (2012a) work within a benchmark model where the offshoring of inputs occurs between H and F who are both small countries on world markets for the final good. It might be thought that this small country assumption is responsible for the inefficiency of the political optimum in this setting, because it generates a "missing instrument" problem for F's government with respect to the final good price in H's market. However, in their Online appendix G Antràs and Staiger confirm the inefficiency of the political optimum in a three-large-country extension of their benchmark model, while in their Online appendix H they show that when international prices are determined in their benchmark model by standard market-clearing conditions rather than bilateral bargaining the political optimum is indeed efficient. Together these results indicate that the missing-instrument problem described in the text is associated with the nature of international price determination rather than the small-country assumption.

[am] Below we will also discuss the commitment theory of trade agreements, which does not feature a terms-of-trade externality. We do so in the context of our evaluation of reciprocity as a design feature of trade agreements.

an answer to this question. He identifies three conditions that together are sufficient for efficiency of the political optimum: (i) there are only two countries; (ii) there are no income effects; and (iii) governments choose only (a complete set of) trade taxes. Indeed, each of the first three models we have reviewed earlier satisfies the sufficient conditions that Maggi identifies.[an] However, it is important to realize that this set of sufficient conditions is by no means necessary. On the contrary, the literature includes a number of findings that the political optimum is efficient also when these sufficient conditions are not met, and specifically in general equilibrium models with income effects (see for example Bagwell and Staiger, 1999 and DeRemer, 2012, appendix E), in models featuring domestic policy instruments in addition to a complete set of trade policy instruments (see for example Bagwell and Staiger, 2001a, 2002; Staiger and Sykes, 2011, and DeRemer, 2013), and in models with more than two countries (see for example Bagwell and Staiger, 1999, 2001b).

We emphasize two take-away points from our discussion just above. First, it is not a simple matter to generate models of trade agreements that fall outside the terms-of-trade class (beyond the commitment theory of trade agreements which we discuss below). We have described here two ways that such models have been generated: missing instruments, and international prices determined by bilateral bargaining.[ao] There may well be other possibilities, but thus far they have not been identified in the literature. And second, while it is useful to identify sets of sufficient conditions for models to fall within the terms-of-trade theory class, working through the details of models that may satisfy these sufficient conditions is nevertheless illuminating for gaining a deeper understanding of the features that ultimately dictate whether or not escape from a terms-of-trade driven Prisoners' Dilemma can be said to be the sole purpose of a trade agreement.

2.6 GATT's Designers and the Terms-of-Trade Externality

As reflected in the previous sections, the terms-of-trade theory provides an important benchmark in the literature for interpreting and evaluating the design of trade agreements. And as we have indicated, the design of a trade agreement is likely to reflect its purpose. In this light, it is important to ask whether there is meaningful contact between the problems emphasized by this theory and those emphasized by the designers of the institution it is supposed to illuminate. If the problems to be addressed as perceived by those involved in the design of a trade agreement make little or no substantive contact with the problems that the terms-of-trade theory suggests should be at the forefront of their thinking, then findings that the design features of the agreement should work well or poorly to solve the problems at the center of the theory are less meaningful,

---

[an] And as Maggi (2014) emphasizes, surprisingly, politically optimal policies can be efficient even in models that feature nonpecuniary international externalities as long as these sufficient conditions are satisfied.

[ao] A third way, which we discuss below, arises when there are many countries and MFN is not imposed.

and the position that the agreement's successes or failings can be understood on these terms is less tenable.

Before moving on with our survey, we therefore pause here and ask: Did the designers of GATT, or at least economists at the time including those directly involved in GATT's design, emphasize the terms-of-trade externality associated with commercial policy? And if so, did they view GATT as a forum for addressing these terms-of-trade externalities?

Some suggestive evidence on these questions is contained in what became known as the *Haberler Report*, commissioned by GATT and written by a Panel of Experts composed of Roberto de Oliveira Campos, Gottfried Haberler, James Meade and Jan Tinbergen.[ap] The Panel's terms of reference were to investigate the prevalence of agricultural protectionism and "...the failure of the export trade of the under-developed countries to expand at a rate commensurate with their growing import needs." (GATT, 1958, foreword).

The Haberler Report provides a wide-ranging discussion of the economic issues of the day and their impacts on the exports of developing countries, emphasizing business cycle fluctuations and balance of payments constraints as well as commercial policy concerns. But when it comes to commercial policy and the topic of agricultural protectionism, terms-of-trade externalities, albeit expressed not in the simple two-country context that we have considered above but rather in the context of a more complex multicountry setting along the lines that we introduce in a later section of this chapter, appears to be at the center of the Report's discussion:

> The problem of the interests of different primary producing countries outside industrialized Western Europe and North America is ... not only a question which of the other countries would gain by a moderation of agricultural protectionism in these two great industrialized regions; there are undoubtedly cases in which an increase in agricultural protectionism in these two regions, while it would be to the disadvantage of some of the unindustrialized countries, would actually be to the advantage of others. Two examples will serve to illustrate the point. An increased stimulus to the production of wheat in any of the countries of North America or of Western Europe by increasing the exportable surplus of North America and decreasing the import requirements of Western Europe would depress the world market for wheat. This might mean that a country like India or Japan would obtain cheaper imports of wheat (either because of a fall in the world price or because of a development of special sales or gifts for the disposal of surplus wheat by the United States), but a country like Australia or the Argentine which competed in the world export market for wheat would be damaged. Another example of the same principle would be provided by measures which stimulated the export of raw cotton from the United States: this might increase the plenty and cheapness of raw cotton in world markets; an importing country like Japan would gain but competing exporters like Egypt, the Sudan, and Brazil would lose.

[ap] James Meade was a member of the British delegation to the London and Geneva conferences in 1946 and 1947 which produced the charter for the International Trade Organization and GATT. Along with Keynes, Meade was widely regarded as a central figure in these conferences (see for example Penrose, 1953, pp. 89–90).

> *In general, if one considers any particular agricultural product, a protective stimulus to its pro-*
> *duction in any one country by increasing supplies relatively to the demand for that product will tend*
> *to depress the world market for that product. This will damage the interests of other countries which*
> *are exporters of the product on the world market. But it will be to the national interest of countries*
> *which import the product from world markets. Whether the initial protective stimulus confers a net*
> *benefit or a net damage to all other countries concerned depends, therefore, upon whether the*
> *country giving the protective stimulus to its own production is an exporter or an importer of the*
> *product; if it is an exporter it is conferring a benefit on the world by giving its supplies away at*
> *a cheap price; if it is an importer it is damaging the rest of the world by refusing to take their supplies.*
>
> *This general principle can be applied to a single country or to a whole region. It is because*
> *Western Europe and North America in combination are net importers of agricultural produce that*
> *we reach the general conclusion that a reduction of agricultural protectionism in these areas will*
> *on balance benefit the rest of the world...(GATT, 1958, pp. 93–94, original emphasis, footnotes*
> *omitted).*

In describing the impacts of agricultural protectionism in Western Europe and North America on various countries in the rest of the world, the Report's references to "depress the world market," "fall in the world price," gains for other importing countries from "cheaper imports" and losses for countries who are "competing exporters" hew quite closely to a terms-of-trade logic. And the references to the protective policies of "any of the countries of North America or of Western Europe," "any one country" and "a single country" suggest that the Report's authors did not find implausible the notion that a single country's protective choices could have world price impacts; indeed, the general principle for signing the international externalities associated with commercial policy intervention is couched in terms of "the country giving the protective stimulus." Hence, in these paragraphs the authors of the Haberler Report appear to be describing the terms-of-trade externality that is at the heart of the terms-of-trade theory of trade agreements.

Moreover, the Haberler Report makes recommendations to GATT that are based on these terms-of-trade externality patterns. For example, the following recommendation, taken from the Report's executive summary, reflects the application of the international externality signing principle as articulated in the quoted excerpt above:

> *Since in North America and Western Europe as a whole net imports of agricultural products rep-*
> *resent the relatively narrow margin by which their large domestic consumption exceeds their large,*
> *but not quite so large, domestic production, a relatively small restraint on domestic production or*
> *stimulus to domestic consumption could lead to a large percentage increase in their net imports.*
> *For this reason much could be achieved by some moderate change in the direction of the*
> *agricultural policies of the highly industrialized countries. (GATT, 1958, p. 9).*

There are many other such examples throughout the commercial policy portion of the Report. It appears as well, then, that the authors of the Haberler Report viewed GATT as a forum for addressing these terms-of-trade commercial policy externalities.

This, of course, does not establish that GATT is well designed to solve the terms-of-trade driven Prisoners' Dilemma, or even necessarily that there is a terms-of-trade driven

Prisoners' Dilemma to be solved: though implicit in its recommendations, the Haberler Report is silent on its position about a key step in the terms-of-trade logic, that in not valuing the terms-of-trade externalities imposed by their commercial policy choices governments were led to make unilateral commercial policy choices that were overly protective from an international efficiency perspective. And in any event these quotes are not a substitute for systematic empirical evidence (some of which we survey below) relating to the terms-of-trade theory's relevance for interpreting GATT/WTO outcomes. But in suggesting that the designers of GATT placed emphasis on the terms-of-trade externalities associated with the commercial policy choices of individual countries, and that they viewed GATT as a forum for addressing these externalities, the statements quoted above lend credence to the view that GATT *could* be especially well designed to solve the terms-of-trade problem—in part perhaps as a result of experimentation and purposeful engineering and in part perhaps by luck—that the GATT/WTO may in large part owe its successes to these design features, and that its failings might also be understood at least in part from the perspective of this theory.

A final observation is also relevant: while we have presented the terms-of-trade theory using the "world price" and "terms-of-trade" language that economists typically employ to describe the relevant policy externalities, the theory can easily be translated into the language of "market access" that real-world trade-policy negotiators prefer. When a country raises its import tariff and thereby shifts in its import demand curve, the resulting price effect under which it enjoys a terms-of-trade improvement is accompanied by a volume effect under which its trading partner experiences a reduction in access to its market. Once this link between price and volume effects is forged, the terms-of-trade theory can be reexpressed in the market access language that trade-policy negotiators adopt.[aq]

We now turn to the literature on the key design features of trade agreements. We emphasize three prominent features of the GATT/WTO: the principle of reciprocity, the principle of nondiscrimination as embodied in MFN, and tariff caps that allow for "binding overhang."

3. RECIPROCITY

In this section we consider the GATT principle of reciprocity. We begin with a discussion of reciprocal liberalization, define the principle of reciprocity in GATT, describe its applications in the GATT/WTO, consider its implications for sustainable bargaining outcomes, and consider its impacts on the GATT tariff bargaining process. Our initial discussion of the implications of reciprocity adopts the perspective of the terms-of-trade theory. We then consider as well the implications of reciprocity when a number of the

[aq] Bagwell and Staiger (2002) provide a formal definition of market access and further development of the relationship between the terms-of-trade theory and the language of market access.

standard assumptions which typically accompany analyses based on the terms-of-trade theory are relaxed. Finally, we close this section with a discussion of reciprocity from modeling perspectives that fall outside the terms-of-trade theory.

3.1 Reciprocal Liberalization

At a general level, reciprocity in trade agreements can be thought of as a norm or rule stating that negotiated tariff changes should result in tariff movements in the same direction across the participating countries. When negotiations are aimed at liberalizing market access, as is the focus of multilateral GATT/WTO negotiating rounds under GATT Article XXVIII bis, the reciprocity norm is that the tariffs of each negotiating partner should be reduced. And if one country increases its tariff, as in the context of *re*-negotiations under GATT Article XXVIII or the settlement of disputes about negotiated market access commitments under GATT Article XXIII, then the tariffs of its trading partners should rise as well. The expectation that reciprocity in market access commitments will be achieved and maintained in the GATT/WTO is fundamental to the institution.[ar]

But the reciprocity principle in GATT is more specific than simply a general complementarity in the direction of tariff changes across countries: it refers to a balance of tariff changes (in either a downward direction or an upward direction) that leads to changes in the volume of a country's exports that are commensurate with the changes in the volume of its imports.[as] In the context of negotiations over market access, therefore, GATT's principle of reciprocity is a negotiation norm that defines an idealized *terms of exchange* of market access, and it sets this terms of exchange at one for one: if country A wishes to acquire for its exporters a certain amount of additional access to the markets of country B, then under the GATT reciprocity norm it is expected that country A will in exchange provide to country B's exporters the same amount of additional access to its own markets; and the same terms of exchange applies to country B if country B seeks to obtain additional access for its exporters to the markets of country A.[at]

[ar] Indeed, GATT's reciprocity principle was thought to be critical to ensuring the constitutionality of US participation in GATT. See United States Council of the International Chamber of Commerce (1955, pp. 74–76).

[as] For example, in calibrating the magnitude of the Canadian tariff increase aimed at reducing exports from the EU that would be consistent with reciprocity and therefore permissible in response to the EU ban on imports of hormone-treated beef in the EC-Hormones dispute, the arbitrators (WTO, 1999, paragraph 41) stated: "To do so…, we have to focus on trade flows. We must estimate trade foregone due to the ban's continuing existence…".

[at] As we discuss in detail below, the principle of reciprocity arises as a negotiation norm when governments negotiate tariff reductions under GATT Article XXVIII bis, and the principle of reciprocity arises in GATT rules when tariffs are increased under GATT Article XXVIII renegotiations. See also Bagwell and Staiger (1999, 2002).

Two questions naturally follow. A first question is: Why did governments adopt the particular (one for one) terms of exchange embodied in the reciprocity principle of GATT? And a second question is: What advantage would there be for governments in choosing to fix the terms of exchange in GATT market access bargains in the first place?

3.1.1 The GATT Principle of Reciprocity

Why did this particular notion of reciprocity take hold in GATT? Put differently, what accounts for the feature that in the GATT/WTO the "price" of "purchasing" one additional unit of export market access is set equal to one additional unit of import market access?[au] Even if the price is to be fixed, why not a different price or terms of exchange, such as two additional units of exports for one additional unit of imports, or one additional unit of exports for three additional units of imports? In fact, there is an immediate and simple answer to this question, as long as governments are committed to adopting a *common* terms of exchange applied uniformly across all countries: the adding-up constraint imposed by market clearing makes any other terms of exchange infeasible. Of course, this is just the observation that one country's exports are another's imports, and hence together all countries cannot increase their exports more (or less) than they increase their imports.

Formally, this point can be confirmed very simply in any model that exhibits market clearing as a feature of the equilibrium outcome. Here we illustrate the point in a two-good two-country general equilibrium setting, remaining agnostic for now about the other features of the model economy (eg, the nature of competition or of international price determination).[av] For the purposes of defining reciprocity, we use the equilibrium terms of trade at original tariffs, $\tilde{P}_0^w$, to convert "apples to oranges." [aw] With "Δ" in front of a variable denoting the change in that variable induced by a change in tariffs, let us begin with the home country, and consider a general version of reciprocity defined as

---

[au] As is well known, much of the design of GATT was inspired by the US Reciprocal Trade Agreements Act of 1934, and this included the particular notion of reciprocity adopted in GATT (see, for example, the discussion of this point in Penrose, 1953, p. 93), though as we discuss later in our chapter GATT allowed for an important multilateralization of the reciprocity principle. So although we pose our questions here in the context of GATT, they should be interpreted more broadly to include GATT's antecedents.

[av] In the Online Appendix (http://dx.doi.org/10.1016/bs.hescop.2016.04.005), we show how the points we emphasize below regarding GATT's principle of reciprocity and its implications within GATT/WTO practice extend to a many-good general equilibrium setting.

[aw] As long as countries agree to use the same conversion factor of apples to oranges in their assessments of reciprocity, for our purposes here the conversion factor can be anything they want, but the original world prices are a natural choice. Using world prices (original or new) as the conversion factor is important for the fixed-terms-of-trade property that we highlight next.

any change in tariffs that leads to a change in home-country export and import volumes satisfying

$$\Delta E = \gamma \tilde{P}_0^w \Delta M \tag{63}$$

where E and M denote home-country export and import volumes, and γ is a parameter specifying the terms of exchange of market access. Next observe that market clearing implies

$$\Delta E = \Delta M^* \tag{64}$$

$$\Delta E^* = \Delta M \tag{65}$$

where E^* and M^* denote foreign-country export and import volumes. But (63) and (65) imply $\Delta E = \gamma \tilde{P}_0^w \Delta E^*$, which using (64) then implies $\Delta M^* = \gamma \tilde{P}_0^w \Delta E^*$ or

$$\tilde{P}_0^w \Delta E^* = \frac{1}{\gamma} \Delta M^*, \tag{66}$$

which describes the foreign-country terms of exchange of market access that must accompany (63) according to the market-clearing requirements. Evidently, if a common terms of exchange is to be applied to both the home and the foreign country, then (63) and (66) imply $\gamma = 1$, which is to say a one-for-one exchange of import volumes for export volumes. Hence, if governments wish to adopt a common terms of exchange for all countries, the adding-up constraint imposed by market clearing makes it inevitable that they must adopt the one-for-one terms of exchange that characterizes GATT's reciprocity principle.

The essence of the first question posed above, then, is not why GATT's reciprocity principle reflects a one-for-one exchange, but rather why a common terms of exchange was adopted for all countries.[ax] This is a question that to our knowledge has not received specific attention in the trade agreements literature, but at a general level it seems plausible that part of the explanation may reflect a desire for fairness: there are reasons to think that fairness might originate as a social norm in a wide variety of bargaining settings (see, for example, Binmore, 2014), and ensuring a common terms of exchange for each country participating in GATT market access bargains resonates with a norm of fairness. In the context of answering the second question posed above, we will also suggest that the link between a common terms of exchange and fairness can be given a more specific representation in the trade agreements context, and as well that there may be additional efficiency benefits to adopting a common terms of exchange, provided that governments

---

[ax] An important exception to the reciprocity norm was granted to developing countries in the GATT/WTO. We touch on some of the implications of this "special and differential treatment" exception below (see Ornelas, 2016 for a comprehensive treatment).

seek (at least in part) to solve the terms-of-trade driven Prisoners' Dilemma problem described in Section 2.[ay]

We now turn to the second question: What advantage would there be for governments in choosing to fix the terms of exchange in GATT market access bargains in the first place? As we next describe, a number of potential benefits can be appreciated, once it is observed that negotiations that achieve the balance described by the GATT reciprocity principle leave the terms of trade unchanged. In this way, GATT's principle of reciprocity helps to create a bargaining forum within which, for each government, terms-of-trade manipulation is effectively removed from the calculus of preferred tariffs.[az]

The terms-of-trade fixing property of reciprocity can also be shown simply in any model that exhibits market clearing as a feature of the equilibrium outcome, provided that countries also satisfy a balanced trade condition. In fact, it is easy to show that reciprocity fixes the terms of trade even in the presence of nonzero trade imbalances, provided only that the size of the trade imbalances are not impacted by the tariff changes, but for simplicity we adopt here the assumption that trade is balanced.[ba] Staying within the two-good two-country general equilibrium setting described just above, and with reciprocity now defined by any set of tariff changes that satisfies

$$\Delta E = \tilde{P}_0^w \Delta M \tag{67}$$

$$\tilde{P}_0^w \Delta E^* = \Delta M^*, \tag{68}$$

for our present purposes we may focus on the home country, and we next introduce the home country's balanced trade condition. The balanced trade condition must hold both at the original and at new tariffs (as before, $\tilde{P}_0^w$ denotes the equilibrium terms of trade at original tariffs, and we now denote the equilibrium terms of trade at the new tariffs by $\tilde{P}_1^w$):

$$E_0 = \tilde{P}_0^w M_0 \text{ and } E_1 = \tilde{P}_1^w M_1. \tag{69}$$

Using $\Delta E \equiv E_1 - E_0$ and $\Delta M \equiv M_1 - M_0$, it then follows from (69) that (67) may be rewritten as

---

[ay] We have in mind that such benefits could help explain why a particular design feature might have been included in a trade agreement, either because the specific benefits suggested by the theory were understood to flow from the feature in question, or because the feature was incorporated by chance in some earlier agreement that performed well as a result of the benefits suggested by the theory.

[az] Bagwell and Staiger (1999) derive this property of reciprocity and highlight the benefits that we discuss below.

[ba] What is required is that the size of the new trade imbalance, measured at the new equilibrium world prices, must be the same as the size of the original trade imbalance, measured at original equilibrium world prices.

$$[\widetilde{P}_1^w - \widetilde{P}_0^w]M_1 = 0. \tag{70}$$

Hence, according to (70) and assuming only that a strictly positive volume of trade takes place at the new tariffs so that $M_1 > 0$, reciprocity exhibits a striking property: mutual changes in trade policy conform to the principle of reciprocity if and only if they leave the terms of trade unchanged.

We thus arrive at the following general conclusion. If governments wanted to create a forum for the exchange of market access commitments in which the terms of exchange were fixed at a common level for all countries, then they would have had to fix the terms of exchange of export market access for import market access at one for one, the same terms of exchange described by GATT's reciprocity principle. And having enshrined into the GATT reciprocity principle the only common terms of exchange available to them and provided that their trade was balanced (or if unbalanced, provided that the magnitude of the imbalances were independent of the outcome of tariff negotiations), governments would have, with GATT's reciprocity principle, directed the focus of GATT market access negotiations toward the volumes of trade desired by the participating governments rather than the terms of trade.

3.1.2 The Applications of Reciprocity in the GATT/WTO

Armed with this general conclusion, we consider next the specific applications of reciprocity within GATT/WTO practice. We highlight the potential implications of reciprocity with regard to addressing the terms-of-trade driven Prisoners' Dilemma problem; and for this purpose we now return to our benchmark two-good two-country perfectly competitive general equilibrium trade model described in Section 2. We first express our formal definition of reciprocity in terms of the notation introduced in that model. From an initial pair of tariffs, (τ^0, τ^{*0}), suppose that a tariff negotiation results in a change to the new pair of tariffs, (τ^1, τ^{*1}). Denoting the initial world and home local prices as $\widetilde{p}^{w0} \equiv \widetilde{p}^w(\tau^0, \tau^{*0})$ and $p^0 \equiv p(\tau^0, \widetilde{p}^{w0})$, and the new world and home local prices as $\widetilde{p}^{w1} \equiv \widetilde{p}^w(\tau^1, \tau^{*1})$ and $p^1 \equiv p(\tau^1, \widetilde{p}^{w1})$, we say that the tariff changes conform to *the principle of reciprocity* provided that

$$\widetilde{p}^{w0}[M(p^1, \widetilde{p}^{w1}) - M(p^0, \widetilde{p}^{w0})] = [E(p^1, \widetilde{p}^{w1}) - E(p^0, \widetilde{p}^{w0})], \tag{71}$$

where changes in trade volumes are valued at the existing world price.[bb] We next use the balanced trade condition (1)—which must hold at both the initial tariffs and the new tariffs—to confirm that (71) may be rewritten as

---

[bb] We have defined reciprocity here only for the domestic country, but as should now be clear in our two-country setting tariff changes conform to reciprocity for the domestic country if and only if they conform to reciprocity for the foreign country as well.

$$[\tilde{p}^{w1} - \tilde{p}^{w0}]M(p^1, \tilde{p}^{w1}) = 0. \tag{72}$$

As (72) reflects and as stated above, mutual changes in trade policy conform to the principle of reciprocity if and only if they leave the terms of trade unchanged. We are now ready to consider the specific applications of reciprocity within GATT/WTO practice.

A first application of reciprocity can be found when negotiations are aimed at liberalizing market access, as is the focus of multilateral GATT/WTO negotiating rounds under GATT Article XXVIII bis. Suppose that governments begin with Nash tariffs. A key observation follows from a property of the Nash point that we emphasized earlier, namely, that using (4) and (5) the Nash first-order conditions (6) imply that $W_p < 0 < W_{p*}^*$. The structure of international cost-shifting therefore implies that, beginning from their Nash tariff choices, each government would desire greater trade volume if this could be achieved at a fixed terms of trade. But if governments were to reduce tariffs according to reciprocity, then by (72) the terms of trade *would* be fixed, while the home local price p would fall and the foreign local price p^* would rise, allowing each government to achieve greater trade volume. Hence, as long as their tariff cuts are not too large, both the home-government welfare and the foreign-government welfare would then rise. In other words, starting at the Nash equilibrium and for tariff cuts that are not too large, liberalization under the principle of reciprocity is sufficient for mutual gains.[bc] Evidently, by directing the focus of GATT market access negotiations toward the volumes of trade desired by the participating governments at a fixed terms of trade, the principle of reciprocity provides a recipe for efficiency-enhancing gains from tariff liberalization.

A second application of reciprocity in the GATT/WTO can also be identified, in this case applying to situations where protective measures are being reimposed rather than liberalized. Such situations can arise in the GATT/WTO, both in the context of dispute resolution and in the context of the renegotiation of GATT tariff bindings. We focus here on renegotiation.[bd] The rules for renegotiation of GATT tariff bindings,

---

[bc] This sufficiency finding for the principle of reciprocity may be contrasted with our discussion in Section 2, where we show for various models that a general form of reciprocity is necessary for mutual gains.

[bd] Our focus is on the implications of reciprocity and whether it can be interpreted as serving a useful purpose rather than on its optimality per se. Maggi and Staiger (2015a) explore the optimal design of trade agreements in the presence of renegotiation more generally, and argue that reciprocity exhibits features that under certain conditions can be part of an optimal compensation rule in the event of disagreement. A related literature (eg, Lawrence, 2003; Bagwell, 2008; Beshkar, 2010; Grossman and Sykes, 2010; Maggi and Staiger, 2015b; and Staiger and Sykes, forthcoming) evaluates reciprocity in the context of GATT/WTO dispute resolution. As Mavroidis (2016) emphasizes, a distinguishing feature of reciprocity as it arises under dispute settlement is that the associated retaliation is prospective in nature and is available to the complainant only after the judicial process has run its course.

contained in GATT Article XXVIII, apply when one country reopens negotiations with its trading partners on a tariff binding to which it had earlier agreed, for the purpose of modifying (in an upward direction) or withdrawing the original tariff binding. These rules explicitly provide for the possibility that agreement might not be reached; and when this possibility arises, the country is permitted to modify or withdraw its original tariff binding anyway, with the understanding that the trading partners may then reciprocate. Here, the principle of reciprocity puts a lid on the response of the trading partners, who are allowed to withdraw "substantially equivalent concessions" of their own. And accordingly, the country initiating the renegotiation (ie, the country desiring less trade volume at the existing terms of trade) can anticipate that it can achieve its desired trade volume at the existing terms of trade. This suggests in turn that incentives to renegotiate a GATT tariff binding will arise any time that, at the existing terms of trade, some government desires less trade volume than its existing tariff commitments imply.

This second application of reciprocity points to a potentially attractive feature of the political optimum: the political optimum is the only point on the efficiency frontier where each government has achieved its preferred local price—and hence its desired trade volume—at the existing terms of trade. At all other points on the efficiency frontier, some government would want more trade volume at the existing terms of trade and some government would want less. In light of the explicit provisions that govern renegotiations of GATT tariff bindings, the political optimum is therefore also the only point on the efficiency frontier where governments would have no reason to attempt to renegotiate their tariff commitments. In this sense, once achieved, the political optimum can be viewed as a particularly robust and stable bargaining outcome of GATT tariff negotiations.

Fig. 2 (adapted from Bagwell and Staiger, 1999) illustrates the point. With the home tariff τ on the vertical axis and the foreign tariff τ^* on the horizontal axis, Fig. 2 depicts the locus of efficient tariff combinations labeled as EE. The point on EE labeled as PO is the political optimum. At the political optimum the iso-welfare contours of the home country (labeled W) and the foreign country (labeled W^*) are tangent to each other *and* to the iso-terms-of-trade locus passing through the point PO and labeled p_{PO}^w, reflecting the property that each government has achieved its preferred local price and desired trade volume at the existing terms of trade. Now consider the possibility of renegotiation subject to reciprocity beginning from the political optimum. As we have observed, in such renegotiations any country desiring less trade volume at the existing terms of trade can achieve the trade volume it desires; but beginning from the point PO, each country already achieves its desired trade volume at the existing terms of trade. Clearly then, and as Fig. 2 illustrates, there is nothing to be gained for either government from such renegotiations: once achieved the political optimum is robust to the possibility of renegotiation subject to reciprocity.

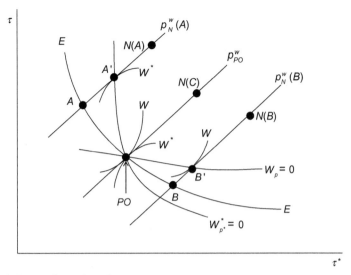

Fig. 2 Renegotiation under reciprocity.

Next consider a point on EE that does not correspond to the political optimum, such as point B in Fig. 2. Point B is also efficient, but relative to the political optimum point PO the foreign tariff is higher while the home tariff is lower, with these tariff adjustments orchestrating a terms-of-trade improvement for the foreign country which efficiently transfers surplus toward the foreign country relative to the political optimum. Beginning from an efficient point such as B, the possibility of renegotiation subject to reciprocity will be exercised. This is because in such renegotiations, the home government can be assured of achieving no less than its welfare level at the point B' in Fig. 2, where it has achieved its desired trade volume at the existing terms of trade (corresponding to a point on the home government's politically optimal reaction curve where $W_p = 0$); and this is a welfare level that is higher than the welfare level that the home government achieves at the efficient point B. Analogous statements apply to an efficient point such as A and its counterpart A' in Fig. 2, with the roles of the home and foreign governments reversed. Hence, in light of the explicit provisions that govern renegotiations of GATT tariff bindings, any point on the efficiency frontier EE other than the efficient political optimum PO is susceptible to renegotiation. And for this reason we can think of the points B', PO and A' in Fig. 2 as tracing out the "reciprocity-constrained" efficiency frontier for GATT tariff negotiations.

We have described these two properties of the applications of reciprocity in the GATT/WTO within our benchmark two-good two-country perfectly competitive general equilibrium trade model, but these properties have also been shown to hold in each of the other models described in Section 2 that fall within the terms-of-trade theory class. Consider for example the monopolistic competition model of firm delocation presented in Section 2.[be] As demonstrated in Bagwell and Staiger (2015), in this model as well these applications of reciprocity both provide a recipe for mutually advantageous liberalization and suggest that, once achieved, the political optimum can be viewed as a particularly robust and stable bargaining outcome of GATT tariff negotiations.

To illustrate these features in the monopolistically competitive model of firm delocation, we follow Bagwell and Staiger (2015) and again define tariff changes that conform to reciprocity as those that bring about equal changes in the volume of each country's imports and exports when valued at existing world prices, but in this partial equilibrium setting we now also take into account trade in the numeraire good. Letting a superscript "0" denote original trade tax levels and a superscript "1" denote new trade tax levels, Bagwell and Staiger show that in this model tariff changes conforming to reciprocity must satisfy[bf]

$$[p^w(\tau_f^0) - p^w(\tau_f^1)]M(p_f^1, p_h^{*1}) = [p^{*w}(\tau_h^{*0}) - p^{*w}(\tau_h^{*1})]E(p_f^1, p_h^{*1}). \tag{73}$$

As with the benchmark competitive model, in the monopolistically competitive model tariff changes that conform to reciprocity remove terms-of-trade manipulation from the calculus of preferred tariffs. Here, according to (73), such tariff changes imply either that world prices are left unchanged as a result of the tariff changes, or if world prices are altered, that they are altered in a way that leaves net trade–tax revenue unchanged.

With the terms-of-trade fixing property of reciprocity now recorded for the monopolistically competitive model, it follows that, starting at the Nash equilibrium, the home and foreign countries must each gain from an adjustment in trade taxes that reduces total trade barriers (ι and ι^*, and hence by (25) and (27), p_h^* and p_f) and satisfies reciprocity, as long as the reduction in total trade barriers is not too large. Consider for example a small reduction in ι and ι^* that is brought about by reciprocal reductions in the home and foreign export taxes τ_h^* and τ_f from their Nash levels.[bg] From (73) it follows that the reduction in τ_f that is required to satisfy reciprocity in response to a small reduction in τ_h^*, which

we denote by $\frac{d\tau_f}{d\tau_h^*}\big|_{rec}$, is defined by

---

[be] Bagwell and Staiger (2015) also demonstrate that these same properties of reciprocity hold in the Cournot model of firm delocation with segmented markets first introduced in Venables (1985). See Bagwell and Staiger (2012b) and (2001b), respectively, for the demonstration that these properties of reciprocity hold in the profit-shifting model of trade agreements and the competitive partial equilibrium model of trade agreements described in Section 2.

[bf] The steps to derive (73) use the balanced trade condition at the original and the new world prices, and are identical to those described in note 19 of Bagwell and Staiger (2001b). See also Bagwell and Staiger (2012b) for a related application.

[bg] See Bagwell and Staiger (2015) for the case of a reduction in ι and ι^* that is engineered with a small reduction in the home and foreign import tariffs τ_h and τ_f^*.

$$\frac{d\tau_f}{d\tau_h^*}\Big|_{rec} = \frac{E^0}{M^0}, \tag{74}$$

where M^0 and E^0 denote the initial levels of home-country imports and exports, respectively.[bh] But then, evaluated at the Nash conditions given by (36) and (37) and using (74), the impact on home and foreign welfare of a small reciprocal reduction in τ_h^* and τ_f is given, respectively, by

$$-\Big\{V_{p_f}\frac{dp_f}{d\tau_f}\frac{d\tau_f}{d\tau_h^*}\Big|_{rec} + V_{p_h^*}\frac{dp_h^*}{d\tau_h^*} + V_{p^{*w}}\frac{dp^{*w}}{d\tau_h^*} + V_{p^w}\frac{dp^w}{d\tau_f}\frac{d\tau_f}{d\tau_h^*}\Big|_{rec}\Big\} = E^N\frac{dp^w}{d\tau_f} > 0, \text{ and}$$

$$-\Big\{V_{p_h^*}^*\frac{dp_h^*}{d\tau_h^*} + V_{p_f}^*\frac{dp_f}{d\tau_f}\frac{d\tau_f}{d\tau_h^*}\Big|_{rec} + V_{p^{*w}}^*\frac{dp^{*w}}{d\tau_h^*} + V_{p^w}^*\frac{dp^w}{d\tau_f}\frac{d\tau_f}{d\tau_h^*}\Big|_{rec}\Big\} = E^N\frac{dp^{*w}}{d\tau_h^*} > 0.$$

Consider next the impact of reciprocity in the monopolistically competitive model when reciprocity is applied in response to the reintroduction of trade barriers. As with our benchmark competitive model, if countries negotiate to the political optimum, then neither country can gain from unilaterally raising its import tariff or export tax as long as such behavior would result in a reciprocal action from its trading partner, and hence the political optimum is robust to the possibility of renegotiation subject to reciprocity. To see this, suppose we begin at the politically optimal policies defined by (42), and let us focus again on export policies.[bi] Beginning from the political optimum, if the home country were to raise τ_h^* and the foreign government were to reciprocate according to $\frac{d\tau_f}{d\tau_h^*}\Big|_{rec}$, the impact on home-country welfare would be

$$V_{p_f}\frac{dp_f}{d\tau_f}\frac{d\tau_f}{d\tau_h^*}\Big|_{rec} + V_{p_h^*}\frac{dp_h^*}{d\tau_h^*} + V_{p^{*w}}\frac{dp^{*w}}{d\tau_h^*} + V_{p^w}\frac{dp^w}{d\tau_f}\frac{d\tau_f}{d\tau_h^*}\Big|_{rec} = V_{p_f}\frac{dp_f}{d\tau_f}\frac{d\tau_f}{d\tau_h^*}\Big|_{rec} + V_{p_h^*}\frac{dp_h^*}{d\tau_h^*} = 0,$$

where the first equality uses (74) and the fact that $\frac{dp^{*w}}{d\tau_h^*} = \hat{p} = \frac{dp^w}{d\tau_f}$, and the second equality follows according to the conditions for the home-country's politically optimal tariff choices given in (42). An analogous argument applies for the foreign country's incentive to raise τ_f in the face of a reciprocal response from the home country.

Finally, it is straightforward to show that, as in the competitive benchmark model, in the monopolistically competitive model the political optimum is the only point on the efficiency frontier that exhibits this robustness feature. Hence, like the competitive benchmark model, the monopolistic competition model of firm delocation (as well as

---

[bh] The expression in (74) may be derived in the same way as (73) by considering small tariff changes and dropping second-order terms, and using $\frac{dp^w}{d\tau_f} = \hat{p} = \frac{dp^{*w}}{d\tau_h^*}$.

[bi] See Bagwell and Staiger (2015) for the arguments related to import tariffs.

the Cournot firm delocation model and the profit-shifting model) suggests that the points B', PO and A' in Fig. 2 can be thought of as tracing out the (reciprocity constrained) efficiency frontier for GATT tariff negotiations.[bj]

3.1.3 The Political Optimum as a Focal Outcome of GATT/WTO Negotiations

Our preceding discussion indicates that under GATT Article XXVIII governments will end up on the reciprocity-constrained efficiency frontier as a result of their GATT tariff negotiations. And as Fig. 2 depicts, this implies an efficiency penalty away from the political optimum. The political optimum may therefore be viewed as a possible focal outcome for negotiations of reciprocity-constrained efficient points, in addition to being an idealized outcome for the purpose of undoing the terms-of-trade problem. According to this perspective, deviations from the political optimum to other points on the reciprocity-constrained efficiency frontier are then desirable only to the extent that the implied redistribution of the gains from tariff bargaining across countries makes such deviations desirable, where this redistribution is effected through the implied movements in the terms of trade away from the terms of trade associated with the political optimum.

Is there evidence that the political optimum describes an outcome which is viewed as focal in GATT/WTO discussions, or which is actually delivered in GATT/WTO negotiations, as our theoretical discussion earlier suggests might be the case? This is an important question whose answer has practical implications. It is related to the often-heard claim that the rules-based outcomes of the GATT/WTO protect small and weak countries from the exploitation they would otherwise suffer at the hands of larger and stronger countries if trade negotiations took place outside the GATT/WTO forum, a claim that if true would help to strengthen the link suggested above between GATT's adoption of a common terms of exchange (from which, according to the terms-of-trade theory, the features we have emphasized here then follow) and fairness in the context of trade agreements.[bk] And it is related to the policy debate concerning the performance of the WTO in general and the benefits for developing countries of GATT/WTO membership in particular.

Some broadly suggestive evidence on the focal nature of the political optimum in GATT/WTO discussions can be found in the many references to the GATT/WTO

[bj] See Bagwell and Staiger (2012b, 2015) for further discussion.

[bk] On the rules-based nature of GATT/WTO bargaining, see for example Jackson (1969, pp. 85–86) and Bagwell and Staiger (1999). As we discuss further below, Bagwell and Staiger suggest an added efficiency benefit that, in guiding governments toward the political optimum, GATT's reciprocity norm may help powerful countries commit not to exploit weaker countries at the tariff bargaining table, and in this way encourage the participation of weaker countries in GATT/WTO rounds of negotiation. On whether developing countries benefit from GATT/WTO membership, see for example Jawara and Kwa (2003) and the review of Jawara and Kwa in Staiger (2006), and see Bagwell et al. (forthcoming) for a more general assessment of issues relating to the WTO's performance.

as a "member-driven" organization that leaves room for countries with different needs to pursue different trade policies. Certainly this would be a necessary feature of an institution designed to deliver the political optimum—and thereby to simply strip away the terms-of-trade motivations from the policy choices of governments with diverse policy goals—rather than, say, laissez faire. A suggestive discussion in this regard can be found in the Haberler Report's description of GATT's accommodation of the different needs of industrialized and developing country members:

> We recognize that there are special considerations affecting the position of under-developed primary producing countries which justify a rather greater use of trade controls by them than by the highly industrialized countries. Industries may need special promotion during the first stages of industrialization when the process of learning industrial techniques is in its early stages and when the promotion of one industry may set a general background which is favourable to the successful growth of others. Special measures to promote industry may be desirable in order to bring into productive employment labour which is under-employed in agriculture. Where the whole or the greater part of a luxury product comes from imports, the restriction of such imports may be administratively the best way of discouraging luxury consumption and promoting savings. Under-developed primary producing countries may be more likely to be in genuine balance-of-payments difficulties than the majority of highly industrialized countries, in which case they will need more often to control imports on these grounds. Finally, insofar as import restrictions can turn the international terms of trade in favour of the restricting countries, it can be argued that poorer countries should have a somewhat greater freedom in their use than richer countries (GATT, 1958, p. 125).

Rather than advocating laissez faire policies for all, the Panel of Experts for the Haberler Report appears instead to offer as a benchmark a member-driven set of policies where an expansive list of motives for trade controls are seen as potentially justified depending on the needs of individual countries as perceived by their governments, but where terms-of-trade motives are absent from this list.[bl] And with this benchmark established, the

---

[bl]   The excerpt quoted above lists a number of potential rationales for protection that might be interpreted as consistent with the political optimum, but it does not explicitly mention the use of import protection for distributional purposes. This use, too, however, appears to be acknowledged in the Haberler Report, as is confirmed by the following qualification to the Report's statement that a fall in the world price of its import good caused by the policy interventions of its trading partners will benefit an importing country:

It will, of course, tend to depress the market for the domestic producers in the importing country; but this tendency *can* be offset by protective measures in the importing countries which support the incomes of their producers. The importing country, in any case, purchases its imports on better terms (GATT, 1958, p. 93, footnote 1, emphasis in the original).

> On the other hand, it should be noted that while the Report lists a number of points that could legitimize greater use of trade controls in less developed as compared to highly industrialized countries, it also emphasizes that "...there have certainly been cases in which the trade control policies of the under-developed countries have gone far beyond these points in discouraging exports of their primary products and in encouraging import-competing industries" and notes that these policies have probably hurt both the less-developed and the industrialized countries.

potential desirability of a movement away from the benchmark trade policies in the direction that permits terms-of-trade considerations to reenter the determination of policies so as to improve the terms of trade of developing countries and thereby transfer surplus from richer to poorer countries is then suggested for consideration.[bm]

As to whether politically optimal outcomes are actually delivered in GATT/WTO negotiations, at a broad level there are features of the outcomes that have emerged from nearly 70 years of GATT/WTO negotiations that are consistent with the political optimum. For example, it is the policies of the countries which are large in world markets that should be most constrained by a trade agreement that delivers the political optimum, with the policies of the smallest countries left largely or even completely unconstrained. Consistent with this feature, most of the significant market-access concessions have been made by the large industrialized countries, a feature that is in some sense almost guaranteed by the exporter-driven process through which governments identify the markets of their trading partners which they would most like GATT/WTO negotiations to open, and which is further accentuated by special and differential treatment clauses that exempt developing countries and especially the least developed countries from a host of GATT/WTO obligations to which other countries must conform.[bn] And even where a country that is small in a given market accepts on paper obligations that apply to that market, the GATT/WTO enforcement procedures operate "on demand," and so a small player in a market can often expect to violate GATT/WTO obligations in that market with impunity in any event. But beyond these broad observations, there is little available evidence one way or another as to whether GATT/WTO outcomes are well described by the

---

[bm] Interestingly, in its discussion of agricultural export subsidies the Haberler Report develops this particular point further and advocates that, where possible, the best form for aid from industrialized to less-developed countries is direct financial aid, rather than aid orchestrated indirectly through the terms-of-trade consequences of trade policy intervention and thereby attached to transactions in particular commodities, summarizing with:

> For these reasons we would wish to combine our general recommendation in favour of a moderation of policies for agricultural protectionism with the recommendations (i) that such policies should be moderated in importing and exporting countries simultaneously; and (ii) that economic aid from the richer and more developed to the poorer and less-developed countries—which, as we have argued above (paragraph 148), is certainly much needed—should as far as possible take the form of direct financial aid from the former to the latter. In this way aid can flow in the desired direction and at the same time production can be undertaken where it is most economic. Aid which is indirectly attached to transactions in particular commodities will inevitably make it difficult for the world resources to be used in the most productive manner... (GATT, 1958, pp. 96–97).

> From the perspective of Fig. 2, this statement can be interpreted as an argument that a position such as B' can be improved upon by eliminating the use of terms-of-trade movements for purposes of aid to the foreign country, repositioning trade policies at the political optimum point PO, and providing aid directly to the foreign country in the form of direct financial transfers.

[bn] Of course, to the extent that special and differential treatment clauses in the GATT/WTO lead developing countries with significant market power, such as the emerging economies of the BRICS, to not engage in meaningful tariff cutting negotiations of their own in the GATT/WTO, this would interfere with attainment of the political optimum, a point emphasized by Staiger (2006) and Bagwell and Staiger (2014).

political optimum, a fact that is surprising in light of the potential importance of such evidence both in relation to the theory and to the policy debate. Here we discuss several papers that provide some partial evidence on this question.

One way to shed light on this question is to look for evidence that GATT/WTO negotiating outcomes differ significantly from "power-based" bargaining outcomes such as those predicted by the Nash bargaining solution. Baldwin and Clarke (1987) offer an early attempt to gauge the ability of the Nash bargaining solution to track actual bargaining outcomes in the GATT/WTO, focusing on the Tokyo Round of GATT negotiations concluded in 1979. As Baldwin and Clarke note, in the Tokyo Round and the earlier GATT Kennedy Round, an initial bargain occurred over the formula by which each county would in principle cut its tariffs; and then once the formula was agreed, countries engaged in essentially bilateral tariff-item-by-tariff-item negotiations over *exceptions* to the formula cuts. Baldwin and Clarke focus only on the outcomes for the US and the (then) European Community, so their results cannot speak directly to our question here. But their findings are still interesting for the present discussion. They find that the Nash bargaining solution does reasonably well at matching the tariff cuts that would have been implemented under the negotiated formula, but that the Nash bargaining solution performs relatively poorly in predicting the actual tariff cuts that emerged from the Tokyo Round (ie, the cuts that resulted once the exceptions to the formula cuts were taking into account). Baldwin and Clarke conclude (p. 281) that the while concepts such as the Nash bargaining solution "may be successful at predicting the outcome of formal GATT negotiations, they are less accurate in describing the subsequent, more political, process of requesting exceptions from the general formula." Interestingly, Baldwin and Clarke (p. 282) also observe that "[m]any of the pullbacks in both the Kennedy and Tokyo Rounds were on items on which there was not much domestic political pressure for less–than–formula cuts, and hence, were made for reciprocity purposes only... The main point to emphasize is that the process of determining exceptions and achieving reciprocity resulted in a considerably different outcome than would have occurred if the cutting rules were followed strictly." This suggests the possibility that GATT's reciprocity principle may have played an important role in moving the negotiating outcomes of the Tokyo Round away from power-based outcomes such as those predicted by the Nash bargaining solution. What is left unanswered by the Baldwin and Clarke analysis is whether the Tokyo Round outcomes were moved in the direction of the political optimum.[bo]

[bo]   Ossa (2014) undertakes a quantitative multicountry analysis of the potential losses from trade wars and potential gains from trade talks while incorporating into his model both inter- and intra-industry trade as well as political economy motives for trade policy intervention. Ossa's analysis of negotiated tariffs focuses on the Nash bargaining solution, but he does not offer a comparison of model predictions under the Nash bargaining solution relative to the actual tariff levels that have emerged from GATT/WTO tariff negotiations (what Ossa terms the "factual" tariffs). Ossa does consider how the MFN principle alters the bargaining outcomes predicted by his model relative to the model's predicted Nash bargaining outcomes in the absence of MFN. We discuss further some of Ossa's findings later in our chapter in the context of our consideration of MFN.

Some suggestive evidence that the political optimum is useful for understanding GATT/WTO negotiating outcomes is provided from a different perspective by the findings of Bagwell and Staiger (2011) and Bagwell et al. (2015). Bagwell and Staiger study the tariff cuts agreed in WTO accession negotiations by 16 countries that joined the WTO as new members after its creation in 1995. They ask whether the pattern of agreed tariff cuts for these countries correspond to the pattern that would be predicted by the terms-of-trade theory if the cuts moved each acceding country from its reaction curve (pre-WTO membership) tariff to its politically optimal reaction curve, and find strong support for this prediction. Bagwell et al. study the recently declassified GATT bargaining records from 1950 to 1951 Torquay Round. They ask whether the pattern of tariff cuts offered by the US in this round, and the probability that the US offers were successful (ie, led to an agreed US tariff binding in the round), can be understood from the perspective of the terms-of-trade theory under the assumption that the US offers correspond to its politically optimal reaction curve tariffs.[bp] Bagwell et al. too, find support for the terms-of-trade theory and the view that the US made tariff offers at Torquay that resided on its politically optimal reaction curves. These two papers do not yield direct evidence on whether GATT/WTO outcomes deliver the political optimum, because they merely suggest that the tariff bindings of individual countries agreed in GATT/WTO negotiations can be understood with reference to their politically optimal reaction curves, but the findings are nonetheless suggestive. In terms of Fig. 2, the distinction here is between, on the one hand, whether GATT delivers the political optimum as defined by the point PO, and on the other hand whether the politically optimal reaction curve as depicted for example by the point B' is helpful for predicting the negotiated tariff choices of individual countries. Our question posed above concerns the first point, but the supporting evidence on the second point provided by these two papers is still encouraging, in the sense that a lack of support on this second point would have cast doubt on an affirmative answer to the question of interest.

3.1.4 Reciprocity and the GATT/WTO Bargaining Process

Thus far we have considered separately the two applications of reciprocity that arise in GATT practice, one relating to market access liberalizing tariff negotiations and the other relating to renegotiation of tariff commitments for the purpose of reintroducing tariffs. The second of these applications of reciprocity constitutes a fairly rigid rule in GATT/WTO practice, but the first is in principle simply a norm of behavior.

There is evidence, however, that supports an important role for even this first application of reciprocity in the GATT/WTO practice. Finger (1979) describes the central role that the desire to achieve reciprocity as felt by GATT member governments played in determining the outcomes of each GATT round through the 1964–67 Kennedy

---

[bp] As Bagwell et al. (2015) demonstrate and as we describe further below, according to the terms-of-trade theory a country's tariff-cutting offers should correspond to its politically optimal reaction curve under strict adherence to reciprocity and MFN.

Round, focusing on how this desire and the exception from reciprocity granted to less-developed countries prevented the less-developed countries from achieving meaningful increases in access to the markets of their trading partners as a result of these rounds (see also Hoda, 2001, pp. 52–63). And in an early analysis of the 1950–51 Torquay Round prepared for the US International Chamber of Commerce (1955, p. 33), the need for reciprocity in GATT tariff negotiations was viewed as sufficiently rigid to constitute an impediment to further negotiated tariff liberalization in light of existing tariff asymmetries across the bargaining countries. More recently, Shirono (2004) finds that the tariff-cutting results of the Uruguay Round conform well with the reciprocity norm. Focusing on US tariff cuts in the Uruguay Round and constructing a measure of market-access concessions while instrumenting to address the potential endogeneity issues, Limão (2006, 2007) also finds evidence consistent with reciprocity, reporting that a decrease in the tariff of a US trading partner that exports a given product leads to a decrease in the US tariff on that product, and that a significant determinant of cross-product variation in US tariff liberalization is the degree to which the US received reciprocal market-access concessions from the corresponding exporting countries. A similar exercise for the EU tariff cutting behavior in the Uruguay Round is carried out by Karacaovali and Limão (2008), who find analogous support for the importance of reciprocity in explaining the pattern of EU tariff cuts. Evidence of reciprocity may be stronger for some sectors than others, however. Examining tariff liberalization by the US in the Uruguay Round, Gulotty (2014) reports evidence that sectors with high contract-intensive products do not exhibit reciprocity.

While more evidence is needed and findings may differ across sectors, the empirical work described above is broadly supportive of an important role for the reciprocity norm in actual GATT/WTO tariff negotiations. In combination with our earlier observation that the application of reciprocity in the context of renegotiations constitutes a fairly rigid rule in GATT/WTO practice, it is then relevant to consider the ramifications for the GATT/WTO bargaining process of a rigid application of reciprocity *both* in the context of tariff liberalizing negotiations *and* in the context of renegotiation to higher tariff levels. To this end, we return to Fig. 2, and illustrate a simple point: the first application of reciprocity focuses bargaining on the volume of trade rather than the terms of trade; and together with the first application, the second application of reciprocity in GATT effectively eliminates (strategic) bargaining on the volume of trade as well. In fact, as we now describe, together the two applications of reciprocity in GATT simplify the market access bargaining process and leave each country with a dominant "truth-telling" strategy to offer to adopt its politically optimal reaction curve tariffs in exchange for reciprocal cuts from its trading partners.[bq]

[bq]   For a more complete presentation of these points, see Bagwell and Staiger (1999) and Bagwell et al. (2015). Bagwell et al. extend these arguments to a multicountry setting in the presence of MFN; we discuss their extended results further in the next section.

That the first application of reciprocity focuses bargaining on the volume of trade rather than the terms of trade follows directly from the terms-of-trade fixing property of reciprocity highlighted above. In terms of Fig. 2, this is manifested in the fact that, beginning from any pair of initial tariffs, tariff liberalizing negotiations that conform to reciprocity must lead to an outcome on the iso-terms-of-trade locus passing through the initial tariff pair. In Fig. 2 we take the initial tariffs to be the pair of Nash tariffs and illustrate with three possible Nash points labeled in the figure as $N(A)$, $N(B)$ and $N(C)$. Notice that, beginning from any of these Nash points and with the terms-of-trade pinned down by the requirement of reciprocity, the preferred trade volume of each government corresponds to the point on the government's politically optimal reaction curve at this terms-of-trade (ie, the tangency of the government's iso-welfare contour with the relevant iso-terms-of-trade locus). Any bargaining that occurs in the presence of this first application of reciprocity would then be over trade volumes at the fixed terms of trade, with each government attempting to achieve its preferred volume. Next notice from Fig. 2 that, together with the first application, the second application of reciprocity in GATT effectively eliminates (strategic) bargaining on the volume of trade as well. This is because under the second application of reciprocity, no government can be forced to accept more trade volume than it desires at the existing terms of trade, and so the government whose preferred volume is lowest will ultimately get its way.

As Bagwell and Staiger (1999) argue, the implications of the two applications of reciprocity in GATT can together then be captured in the following stylized game. An initial pair of tariffs, say the Nash point $N(C)$ in Fig. 2, corresponds to a particular iso-terms-of-trade line. Governments simultaneously make tariff proposals, where any proposal must conform to reciprocity and therefore amount to a tariff pair that lies along the iso-terms-of-trade line passing through the point $N(C)$. If the proposals agree, then the common proposal is implemented, while if the proposals disagree then the proposal implying the least trade volume (the higher tariff pair) is implemented. In this game, as Bagwell and Staiger demonstrate, it is a dominant strategy for each government to propose the tariff pair that if implemented would deliver its preferred trade volume at the existing terms of trade (ie, its politically optimal reaction curve tariff paired with the reciprocity-consistent tariff for its trading partner). And importantly, it is easy to see that this conclusion holds whether or not governments possess private information about their preferred trade volumes.

This discussion suggests a potential benefit from strict adherence to reciprocity in the two applications where it arises in GATT: strict adherence to reciprocity can induce governments to reveal their politically optimal reaction curves, and thereby allow governments to avoid costly bargaining delays that might otherwise be associated with the presence of private information (see, for example, Admati and Perry, 1987 and Cramton, 1992). But the costs of strict adherence to reciprocity are also evident from Fig. 2: whenever the negotiating environment is asymmetric, in the particular sense that the Nash terms of trade differ from the politically optimal terms of trade, negotiations under strict adherence to reciprocity fails to reach the efficiency frontier. In Fig. 2 this is illustrated by the fact that the stylized game described just above would deliver governments to the political optimum in the symmetric case corresponding to the Nash pair $N(C)$, where the Nash and the politically optimal tariffs both lie on the same iso-terms-of-trade line.[br] Asymmetric cases are illustrated in Fig. 2 by the Nash points $N(A)$ and $N(B)$:[bs] for these asymmetric cases, the stylized game described earlier would deliver governments to the inefficient points A' and B', respectively, in Fig. 2. In general, as Fig. 2 illustrates, the performance of strict adherence to reciprocity in GATT/WTO tariff negotiations as measured by its ability to deliver governments to the efficiency frontier deteriorates with the asymmetry of the environment.

As is known from the Myerson and Satterthwaite Theorem (Myerson and Satterthwaite, 1983), in the presence of private information it is generally not possible to design an institution or mechanism that satisfies certain attractive constraints (Bayes–Nash incentive compatibility, interim individually rationality and budget balancing) and yet achieves ex-post efficient (first-best) outcomes. Still, given these constraints, the optimal or second-best mechanism would typically out-perform the strict adherence to reciprocity that we have described earlier. But in this regard the observations of Hagerty and Rogerson (1987) concerning shortcomings of this Bayesian approach to second-best mechanisms seem relevant:

> The key shortcoming of this approach is that it relies heavily on the assumption that there exists a common prior over traders' valuations known to all participants. In particular, an institution which produces a very efficient outcome for one prior might perform very poorly under some other prior. This creates two related problems. First, a social planner may not be able to ascertain exactly what traders' priors are when choosing an institution. Second, given the costs of creating new institutions, a trading institution (such as a stock exchange, for example) is often chosen with the intention that it will be used by a variety of traders over a long period of time. A variety of priors might be expected to occur over this time. These problems suggest that an important concern when choosing a trading institution is that it work "fairly well" over a broad range of priors, ie, that it be robust with respect to changes in the information structure of the market (Hagerty and Rogerson, 1987, p. 95).

On this basis, Hagerty and Rogerson advocate the consideration of mechanisms under which each player has a dominant strategy, which they argue can then avoid these

---

[br] In the symmetric case, beginning from their politically optimal tariffs at the point PO in Fig. 2, if a trade war were to break out and move the countries back to the Nash point $N(C)$, neither country would succeed in pushing the terms-of-trade in its favor.

[bs] In these asymmetric cases, if a trade war were to break out beginning from PO the home country would succeed in pushing the terms of trade in its favor in the case corresponding to the Nash point $N(A)$ and the foreign country would succeed in pushing the terms of trade in its favor in the case corresponding to the Nash point $N(B)$.

shortcomings. Interestingly, Hagerty and Rogerson show for the simple bilateral trade setting that "posted-price" mechanisms, whereby a price is posted in advance and trade occurs if and only if all traders agree to trade, are essentially the only mechanisms such that each trader has a dominant strategy. The general-equilibrium model that we consider differs from a simple bilateral trade setting. Nevertheless, together the two applications of reciprocity in GATT can be interpreted as working like a posted price mechanism for tariff bargaining and therefore exhibiting these robustness benefits.[bt] From this perspective, strict adherence to reciprocity may be understood to be a potentially attractive design feature of the GATT/WTO.

It thus appears that, in the context of trade agreements and from the perspective of the terms-of-trade theory, fixing the terms of exchange of market access at a common level for all countries—from which GATT's one-for-one definition of reciprocity and each of the features we have described earlier then follows—produces a number of potentially desirable properties, and the more so the more symmetric is the underlying tariff bargaining environment. Notice, too, that these properties should remain desirable as long as terms-of-trade manipulation is an important problem for trade agreements to solve, even if it is not the *only* problem as the terms-of-trade theory suggests.

We close this section with a brief consideration of a question we have thus far ignored: Why are the terms of exchange of market access in the GATT/WTO expressed in barter terms; that is, why is there no role for cash? This is an important question that has received little attention in the trade agreements literature. Greater use of cash transfers in the WTO system offers potential benefits. As the Haberler Report well describes (see note bm), cash payments may be attractive as a relatively efficient instrument with which to achieve transfers across countries.[bu] From this perspective, monetary compensation is a potentially attractive means of offering compensation in bilateral disputes.[bv] Furthermore, and especially as asymmetries in the GATT/WTO system become increasingly prominent (for example, between the advanced industrialized countries and the BRICS), the findings we have described earlier suggest that the GATT/WTO reliance on reciprocity could become increasingly problematic, and other methods of orchestrating

---

[bt] An interesting direction for future research concerns the conditions under which dominant strategy implementation in the general-equilibrium model of trade necessitates that an exchange of tariff changes must satisfy the principle of reciprocity.

[bu] As Bagwell and Staiger (2005a) confirm, in a partial-equilibrium model with privately informed governments, governments can achieve first-best efficient policies when cash transfers are available.

[bv] In a self-enforcing, repeated-game context, Limão and Saggi (2008) argue that a system in which retaliatory tariffs enforce the payment of monetary fines does not offer greater cooperation than a system that relies directly on retaliatory tariffs. A system with fines offers an advantage when (unanticipated) shocks result in actual disputes, however. Bagwell et al. (2007) demonstrate that the auctioning of retaliation rights in the GATT/WTO could serve as a third-party mechanism for enforcing the payment of cash compensation to countries injured by GATT/WTO inconsistent policies of their trading partners.

internationally efficient trade liberalization—such as holding auctions for reductions in tariffs and increased market access in exchange for cash payments—may in principle become relatively more attractive.

At the same time, the use of cash transfers raises potential concerns as well. One potential drawback is suggested by the finding in Bagwell and Staiger (1999) that, in guiding governments toward the political optimum and away from power-based outcomes, GATT's reciprocity norm may help more powerful countries commit not to exploit weaker countries at the tariff bargaining table, and thereby help to solve a potential hold-up problem that could otherwise reduce the participation of weaker countries in GATT/WTO rounds of negotiation. The availability of monetary transfers at the negotiation stage would make such commitments less meaningful, because direct monetary transfers can be used to undo the transfers implied by the terms-of-trade movements of tariff choices; and this could be one potential downside of facilitating a greater role for such transfers in exchange for trade liberalization. In the broader bargaining literature, Harstad (2007) makes the argument that the availability of cash side-payments in settings of bargaining with private information can exacerbate the reasons for delay and lead to worse outcomes in some situations than if the cash payments were not available. We discuss further in the context of our consideration of MFN an additional potential reason suggested by the literature that cash payments are not more prominent in the GATT/WTO, but we see this as an understudied and fruitful area for further research.

3.2 Reciprocity and the Terms-of-Trade Theory Under Alternative Assumptions

We now return to the first application of reciprocity in the GATT/WTO with which we began our discussion, namely, the application that arises when negotiations are aimed at liberalizing market access as in multilateral GATT/WTO negotiating rounds under GATT Article XXVIII bis. We described in our earlier discussion how the structure of international cost-shifting implies that, beginning from their Nash tariff choices, each government would desire greater trade volume if this greater trade volume could be achieved at a fixed terms of trade. And we argued that tariff-cutting according to reciprocity is a way to achieve such fixed-terms-of-trade increases in trade volume, and that liberalization under the principle of reciprocity thus delivers mutual gains.

Here we comment on how this conclusion must be modified when a number of the standard assumptions that usually accompany the terms-of-trade theory of trade agreements are relaxed. And for this purpose we now return to our benchmark two-good two-country perfectly competitive general equilibrium trade model described in Section 2.

A first and critical assumption is contained in (5), which states that $W_{\tilde{p}^w} < 0$ and $W^*_{\tilde{p}^w} > 0$ and indicates that each government benefits from a terms-of-trade improvement, when the local price in its country is held fixed. As we observed, this assumption is satisfied by each of the leading models of trade policy formulation. But as Blanchard

(2007a, 2010) shows, there is an important qualification to this statement that can arise in the presence of international ownership. Blanchard (2007a) considers the impact that export-platform foreign direct investment can have on the unilateral tariff choices of the investment-source country, while Blanchard (2010) extends the analysis of optimal tariffs to international ownership more generally. In both cases, Blanchard demonstrates that international ownership can mitigate the unilateral incentive to use tariffs for purposes of manipulating the terms of trade, and thereby can have important effects on the inefficiency of unilateral tariff setting, serving to reduce Nash tariffs closer to their internationally efficient levels and possibly even to lead to Nash tariffs that are efficient (in a knife edge case) or too *low* from an international perspective. In relation to the Nash conditions described by (6), the key difference here is that international ownership operates to diminish the absolute value of $W_{\tilde{p}^w}$ and $W^*_{\tilde{p}^w}$, possibly all the way to zero, and may even reverse the sign of these terms.[bw]

As Blanchard (2007a, 2010) demonstrates and as the Nash conditions in (6) confirm, if international ownership ends up reversing the signs of $W_{\tilde{p}^w}$ and $W^*_{\tilde{p}^w}$, then in the Nash equilibrium we would have $W_p > 0$ and $W^*_{p^*} < 0$ and a trade agreement would need to *raise* tariffs to reach the international efficiency frontier; this can be seen most clearly by considering a trade agreement that satisfies reciprocity and therefore fixes $\tilde{p}^w$, and where it is then clear that both countries gain by reciprocally raising their tariffs. And if the

[bw] In addition to this international-ownership effect, Blanchard (2010) identifies a second effect, according to which the domestic local price can be manipulated to extract rents from foreign investors; and with this second effect she demonstrates that in the presence of international ownership the terms of trade is not the only channel through which externalities travel. As we describe earlier, local price externalities also arise in the profit shifting and delocation models analyzed by Bagwell and Staiger (2012a,b, 2015), but Bagwell and Staiger show for these models that the terms-of-trade externality is nevertheless the only source of policy inefficiency in the Nash equilibrium (ie, at the political optimum these local price externalities are "shut down"). In her working paper (see Blanchard, 2007b, appendix 5.3), Blanchard establishes a related result in the presence of international ownership. Exploiting the fact that market clearing allows p^* to be expressed as $p^*(p, \tilde{p}^w)$ and p to be expressed as $p(p^*, \tilde{p}^w)$, thereby allowing the home and foreign objectives to be written as $W(p, \tilde{p}^w) \equiv w(p, p^*(p, \tilde{p}^w), \tilde{p}^w)$ and $W^*(p^*, \tilde{p}^w) \equiv w^*(p^*, p(p^*, \tilde{p}^w), \tilde{p}^w)$, respectively, even in the presence of local price externalities, and defining the political optimum with respect to the W and W^* functions (ie, politically optimal home and foreign tariff selections are made "as if" $W_{\tilde{p}^w} \equiv 0$ and $W^*_{\tilde{p}^w} \equiv 0$ respectively), Blanchard shows that at the political optimum the local price externalities vanish—and therefore that the political optimum remains efficient—and in this sense that the terms-of-trade externality remains the only source of policy inefficiency in the Nash equilibrium in the presence of international ownership. It is important to note, however, that the political optimum defined by Blanchard is related to but different than the political optimum as we have defined it above. According to the definition employed by Blanchard, not valuing movements in $\tilde{p}^w$ implies not valuing the pure international transfers associated with such movements *and* the trade volume changes associated with the implied local price movement (ie, the implied movement of p^* in the case of $W_{\tilde{p}^w}$ and of p in the case of $W^*_{\tilde{p}^w}$), whereas according to the definition of the political optimum that we have described earlier it is only the pure international transfer associated with movements in $\tilde{p}^w$ that is assumed not to be valued.

pattern of international ownership happened to deliver $W_{\tilde{p}^w} = 0 = W^*_{\tilde{p}^w}$ then governments would adopt the efficient politically optimal tariffs (defined by $W_p = 0 = W^*_{p^*}$) in the Nash equilibrium and the pattern of international ownership would obviate the need for a trade agreement completely. More generally, even absent these extreme cases, it is clear that by reducing the absolute magnitude of $W_{\tilde{p}^w}$ and $W^*_{\tilde{p}^w}$, international ownership can reduce the magnitude of the terms-of-trade driven policy inefficiencies associated with unilateral tariff choices.[bx] Finally, whether the pattern of international ownership requires governments to agree to lower or rather to raise their tariffs beginning from Nash to reach the international efficiency frontier, Blanchard argues that the principle of reciprocity continues to serve as an important guide to efficient outcomes, once the definition of market access reflects ownership positions.

A second important assumption that is usually made in the context of the terms-of-trade theory is contained in (4), which states that $\dfrac{dp}{d\tau} > 0 > \dfrac{\partial \tilde{p}^w}{\partial \tau}$ and $\dfrac{dp^*}{d\tau^*} < 0 < \dfrac{\partial \tilde{p}^w}{\partial \tau^*}$ and indicates that prices respond to tariffs in the "regular" way and therefore do not exhibit either the Lerner or the Metzler paradox. How must the conclusion above be qualified if this assumption fails? An initial observation is that, as long as international markets are integrated, the Lerner and Metzler paradoxes cannot both hold at once.[by] To see this, consider the home country, where existence of the Metzler and Lerner paradoxes would imply $\dfrac{dp}{d\tau} < 0 < \dfrac{\partial \tilde{p}^w}{d\tau}$.

As the assumption of integrated markets implies $p = \tau \tilde{p}^w$ for nonprohibitive tariffs, it follows immediately that we can not simultaneously have Metzler and Lerner paradoxes in this setting. Hence, there are two remaining cases to consider.

A first case is where the Metzler paradox arises but there is no Lerner paradox. Focusing on the domestic country, this corresponds to the case where $\dfrac{dp}{d\tau} < 0$ and $0 > \dfrac{\partial \tilde{p}^w}{d\tau}$. This can happen if a tariff hike pushes $\tilde{p}^w$ down to such an extent as to overwhelm the direct effect on p of the tariff hike. For this case, the domestic government's Nash first-order condition recorded in (6) then implies $W_p > 0$, where we assume that $W_{\tilde{p}^w} < 0$. This means that, under the principle of reciprocity (ie, holding the world price fixed), the domestic government would want to raise $p = \tau \tilde{p}^w$, and similarly for the foreign government.

[bx] Assessing the impact of US multinational firms' affiliate offshoring behavior on US tariff preferences, Blanchard and Matschke (2015) find evidence consistent with this effect. Gulotty (2014), however, argues that greater international ownership does not similarly lead to reductions in regulatory barriers. He argues that regulatory barriers raise fixed costs, and that the associated reduction in entry may lead to net gains for efficient, globalized firms.

[by] With segmented markets, the Lerner and Metzler paradoxes can coexist (see for example the discussion of export policies in the Cournot delocation model in Bagwell and Staiger, 2015).

Therefore, when the Metzler paradox is present, mutual gains under the principle of reciprocity are achieved via reciprocal tariff *increases*. To understand why, consider the externality on W of a change in τ^*:

$$\frac{dW}{d\tau^*} = W_p \frac{dp}{d\tau^*} + W_{\tilde{p}^w} \frac{\partial \tilde{p}^w}{d\tau^*} = [W_p \tau + W_{\tilde{p}^w}] \frac{\partial \tilde{p}^w}{d\tau^*}$$

$$= [\tau(\frac{-W_{\tilde{p}^w} \dfrac{\partial \tilde{p}^w}{d\tau}}{\dfrac{dp}{d\tau}}) + W_{\tilde{p}^w}] \frac{\partial \tilde{p}^w}{d\tau^*} = [\tilde{p}^w] W_{\tilde{p}^w} \frac{\partial \tilde{p}^w}{d\tau^*} \frac{1}{\dfrac{dp}{d\tau}} > 0,$$

where the third equality uses the domestic government's Nash first-order condition and the inequality follows since $\tilde{p}^w > 0$, $W_{\tilde{p}^w} < 0$, $\dfrac{\partial \tilde{p}^w}{d\tau^*} > 0$ (no Lerner paradox for foreign, either) and $\dfrac{dp}{d\tau} < 0$. With this, an envelope argument suggests that mutual gains can be achieved starting at Nash if each country slightly increases its tariff, since its trading partner thereby enjoys a first-order positive externality despite the fact that the trading partner suffers a terms-of-trade loss. Intuitively, if home were to cut τ slightly from the Nash level, it would receive a small increase in p, and under the Nash first-order condition the value of this increase would be exactly offset by home's consequent terms-of-trade loss. Let us then fix this p increase and consider an alternative way of achieving it, namely through a small increase in τ^*, which induces a higher p by raising $\tilde{p}^w$. While the same p is achieved under both approaches, notice that $\tilde{p}^w$ is higher under the first approach, since τ is reduced in this scenario (and $p = \tau\tilde{p}^w$ always holds). So, if home were indifferent about achieving a higher p while suffering a high value for $\tilde{p}^w$, then home will strictly benefit by getting the same higher p in the company of a lower value for $\tilde{p}^w$. The externality is therefore positive, even though it generates a terms-of-trade loss for the recipient.[bz]

The second case is where the Lerner paradox arises but there is no Metzler paradox. Focusing again on the domestic country, this corresponds to the case where $\dfrac{dp}{d\tau} > 0$ and $0 < \dfrac{\partial \tilde{p}^w}{d\tau}$. For this case, the domestic government's Nash first-order condition in (6) then implies $W_p > 0$, where again we assume that $W_{\tilde{p}^w} < 0$. This means that, under the principle of reciprocity (ie, holding the world price fixed), the domestic government would again want to alter tariffs so as to raise $p = \tau\tilde{p}^w$, and similarly for the foreign government.

For the case where the Lerner paradox is present, therefore, mutual gains under the principle of reciprocity are thus again achieved via reciprocal tariff *increases*. To

---

[bz] This intuition is similar to that described for the case of export taxes in the linear Cournot delocation model analyzed by Bagwell and Staiger (2012a).

understand why, consider again the externality on W of a change in τ^* beginning from Nash. Following the same steps as above, we find that:

$$\frac{dW}{d\tau^*} = [\widetilde{p}^w] W_{\widetilde{p}^w} \frac{\partial \widetilde{p}^w}{d\tau^*} \frac{1}{\dfrac{dp}{d\tau}} > 0,$$

where the inequality now obtains since $\widetilde{p}^w > 0$, $W_{\widetilde{p}^w} < 0$, $\dfrac{\partial \widetilde{p}^w}{d\tau^*} < 0$ (Lerner paradox for foreign, too) and $\dfrac{dp}{d\tau} > 0$. So, once again, starting at Nash, a higher foreign tariff generates a positive externality for home. In this case, though, the higher foreign tariff also gives home a terms-of-trade gain, due to the Lerner paradox.

It therefore appears that when either the Metzler or the Lerner paradox is present, the terms-of-trade theory's implication that liberalization under the principle of reciprocity delivers mutual gains must be modified: it is still the case that reciprocal tariff changes deliver mutual gains, but now the sign of these changes is reversed, with reciprocal tariff increases pointing the way to the international efficiency frontier. Finally, we note that when the assumption of integrated markets is relaxed and segmented markets are instead considered, the standard reciprocal import-tariff-liberalizing predictions of the terms-of-trade theory can survive both the Metzler and the Lerner paradox, though new predictions can also arise regarding export policies in such settings.[ca]

3.3 Reciprocity Beyond the Terms-of-Trade Theory

In the preceding sections we have considered reciprocity from the perspective of a variety of models that fall within the terms-of-trade theory of trade agreements, as well as a number of extensions to those models. We close this section with a brief discussion of reciprocity from modeling perspectives that fall outside the terms-of-trade theory, including environments where governments have a limited set of trade policy instruments, where offshoring is prevalent, and where governments seek to make commitments to their own private sectors through trade agreements.

A first observation is that, in each of these environments, we may continue to expect that tariff changes conforming to reciprocity as we have defined reciprocity above will hold the terms of trade fixed. This is because, as we noted above, we have derived this property of reciprocity in a modeling framework that features little more than market clearing and trade balance, and that is thus general enough to include each of the environments that we consider below.

[ca]   See Bagwell and Staiger (2012a, 2015) and Bagwell and Lee (2015) for theoretical explorations of the design of trade agreements in settings that feature Metzler and Lerner paradoxes, and see Ludema and Zhi (2015) for recent empirical evidence relating to the existence of the Metzler paradox.

We therefore turn to the remaining two questions around which we have organized our discussion of reciprocity above. First, beginning from their Nash tariffs, can both countries gain from reciprocal liberalization in these alternative modeling environments provided they do not go too far? And second, in these environments can the political optimum still be singled out as the only point on the efficiency frontier that is robust to renegotiation subject to reciprocity?

Consider first the case of missing trade policy instruments. For this case we return to the competitive partial equilibrium model with missing instruments described in Section 2, where we assumed that export policies are prohibited so that the home government has only an import tariff τ_x and the foreign government has only an import tariff τ_y^*. In this environment, the Nash tariffs are defined by the first-order conditions

$$\text{Home}: W_{\hat{p}_x} \frac{d\hat{p}_x}{d\tau_x} + W_{p_x^w} \frac{\partial p_x^w}{\partial \tau_x} = 0$$

$$\text{Foreign}: W_{\hat{p}_y^*}^* \frac{d\hat{p}_y^*}{d\tau_y^*} + W_{p_y^w}^* \frac{\partial p_y^w}{\partial \tau_y^*} = 0.$$

With $W_{\hat{p}_x} < 0$ and $W_{\hat{p}_y^*}^* < 0$ implied, an immediate observation is then that, beginning from their Nash import tariffs, both countries can gain from at least a small amount of reciprocal liberalization, because such tariff reductions lower $\hat{p}_x$ and $\hat{p}_y^*$ without inducing any welfare-relevant changes in p_x^w and p_y^w and therein raise home and foreign welfare according to $W_{\hat{p}_x} < 0$ and $W_{\hat{p}_y^*}^* < 0$. So our earlier answer to the first question above is unchanged by the limitation we have imposed here on the set of trade instruments. But our earlier answer to the second question is overturned in this environment. This follows directly from the result reported earlier, that with missing trade policy instruments it is no longer generally the case that politically optimal policies are internationally efficient, because there is a local price externality that now persists at the political optimum. In fact, as we argued above, when export policies are missing the political optimum will be inefficient whenever export industries enjoy political support in the objective functions of their governments.

We may therefore conclude that in an environment with missing trade policy instruments, the political optimum cannot in general be singled out as the only point on the efficiency frontier that is robust to renegotiation subject to reciprocity, because the political optimum does not itself generally rest on the efficiency frontier in this environment. Moreover, in light of the fact that any efficient point that does not correspond to the political optimum is susceptible to such renegotiation, we can make a stronger statement: in general for this missing-instrument setting, *no* point on the efficiency frontier is robust to renegotiation subject to reciprocity. This suggests that the attractive features of reciprocity that hold in the context of the terms-of-trade theory and that we have emphasized above are substantially diminished in environments where trade policy instruments are missing.

A key question, then, is how to interpret the possibility of missing trade policy instruments. One possible interpretation is that countries do not in fact possess complete sets of trade policy instruments, with a possible candidate for missing instruments being export subsidies whose funding needs might make these policies simply inaccessible to all but the richest countries. Under this interpretation a trade agreement must be designed to both internalize the terms-of-trade externality and provide the missing trade policy instruments. A second possible interpretation is that these trade policy instruments are not truly missing, but rather their use has been prohibited by international agreement. Under this second interpretation the problem to be solved by a trade agreement is still *fundamentally* the terms-of-trade problem, but as part of the approach to solving the terms-of-trade problem the agreement has altered the nature of the policy externalities with which the agreement itself must contend. From this perspective an important question is whether the increasingly stringent prohibition on the use of export subsidies as this prohibition has evolved from GATT to the WTO (see, for example, Sykes, 2005) creates such a missing-instruments environment for WTO member governments; and if so, whether the GATT/WTO traditional reliance on reciprocity is growing increasingly at odds with an institution well designed to solve the terms-of-trade driven Prisoners' Dilemma problem.[cb]

Ossa (2011) provides an interesting answer to this question. He demonstrates that, in a general equilibrium monopolistic competition model of firm delocation where export policies are ruled out, an adaptation of the definition of reciprocity can be found which largely preserves the properties of reciprocity we have emphasized above. Ossa's model has both a manufacturing and a nonmanufacturing sector, with the manufacturing sector composed of many firms producing differentiated manufacturing goods and representing the sector where firm delocation effects occur. In Ossa's model the terms-of-trade manipulation problem is completely absent because, as in the partial equilibrium monopolistic competition model of firm delocation we described in Section 2, only export policies can have terms-of-trade impacts, and as we noted in Ossa's model the use of export policies is ruled out by assumption. This allows Ossa to highlight the firm-delocation problem that is then transmitted across countries though local-price channels. Ossa shows in this setting that if reciprocity is defined to cover only changes in manufacturing exports and imports, and not also changes in the trade of the nonmanufacturing good as would be consistent with our definition of reciprocity above, then tariff changes that conform to this adaptation of reciprocity keep the numbers of firms in each country unchanged and hence will be free of the firm delocation externality that countries would otherwise

---

[cb]   There is also the related question of how to interpret the increasing stringency of GATT/WTO rules on export subsidies and subsidies more generally. On attempts to interpret these developments, see for example Bagwell and Staiger (2001c, 2006, 2012a), Potipiti (2012), Brou and Ruta (2013), and Bagwell and Lee (2015).

impose on one another with their trade policy choices; and for this reason reciprocity in Ossa's model behaves much like the terms-of-trade fixing property of reciprocity that we have emphasized above in the context of the terms-of-trade theory.

In particular, Ossa (2011) demonstrates that, beginning from Nash and under the restriction of nonnegative import tariffs, countries can gain from reciprocal tariff liberalization if they abide by this definition of reciprocity. And he shows that any point on the efficiency frontier is robust to renegotiation subject to reciprocity when reciprocity is defined in this way. More broadly, Ossa's findings point to the possibility that the principle of reciprocity can constitute a sensible design feature of trade agreements in environments that extend beyond the terms-of-trade theory, and at the same time suggest that in the absence of a full set of trade policy instruments it may be important to adopt a flexible view about the precise definition of reciprocity.[cc]

We consider next how the answers to the two questions above must be modified in environments where offshoring is prevalent. To begin, starting from their Nash tariffs, can both countries gain from at least a small amount of reciprocal liberalization? As it turns out, in the presence of offshoring this is no longer assured.

To see why, we return to the model of Antràs and Staiger (2012a). Recall that in (53) we defined the international input price p_x^*; and as the world price of the final good is fixed on world markets by assumption, p_x^* represents the terms of trade between the home and foreign country in this model. Hence, reciprocal reductions in τ_1^H, τ_x^H and τ_x^F are defined by any set of tariff reductions that hold p_x^* fixed. Next recall that Nash policies are indeed inefficient in this model. But as Antràs and Staiger show, the Nash inefficiencies take a particular and interesting form: both the volume of input trade ($\hat{x}^N$) *and* the local price of the final good in the home-country market (p_1^{HN}) are inefficiently low. From this vantage point, it can now be seen that, beginning from the Nash point, even small reciprocal tariff cuts can lead to losses in this setting for a simple reason: if the home

---

[cc]   In this light it is interesting to observe that, while reciprocity in the GATT/WTO has a specific definition in the context of the reintroduction of protective measures and what constitutes a reciprocal response to that reintroduction (see note as), the precise definition of what constitutes reciprocity in the context of negotiations aimed at liberalizing market access, as is the focus of multilateral GATT/WTO negotiating rounds under GATT Article XXVIII bis, has been left up to each country to decide. Hoda (2001) provides an illuminating account:

As mentioned earlier, neither the provisions of GATT 1994 nor the procedures of the eight rounds of tariff negotiations indicate how reciprocity is measured or defined. At the [1955 GATT] Review Session, Brazil had proposed a formula for measurement of concessions for determining reciprocity. On this 'the Working Party noted that there was nothing in the Agreement, or in the rules for tariff negotiations which has been used in the past, to prevent governments from adopting any formula they might choose, and therefore considered that there was no need for the CONTRACTING PARTIES to make any recommendation in this matter' [GATT, BISD, Third Supplement, p. 22]. No further attempt has been made to give greater definition to the manner in which reciprocity is to be measured and it has been left to each county to develop its own yardsticks (Hoda, 2001, p. 53).

country is an exporter of the final good, then a reduction in τ_1^H raises p_1^H and therefore moves this price in the direction of the efficient level; but if the home country is an importer of the final good, then a reduction in τ_1^H reduces p_1^H and moves this price *further away* from the efficient level. Whether the resulting first-order loss in joint surplus can be made up with additions to joint surplus associated with the other elements of the reciprocal liberalization depends on circumstances, but with respect to the impact on p_1^H it is clear that reducing τ_1^H (reciprocally or otherwise) reduces joint surplus when the home country is an importer of the final good.

Hence, in the presence of offshoring our earlier answer to the first question above must at a minimum be qualified. And our earlier answer to the second question is overturned in this environment, for the same reason that it is overturned in the missinginstruments environment: as with missing instruments, in the presence of offshoring it is no longer generally the case that politically optimal policies are internationally efficient, because as Antràs and Staiger (2012a) show and as we have described earlier, there is a local price externality that may now persist at the political optimum. In fact, as we have discussed, Antràs and Staiger argue that in the presence of offshoring the political optimum will be inefficient unless government objectives correspond to national income maximization. And with the inefficiency of the political optimum in the presence of offshoring comes as well the conclusion that no point on the efficiency frontier is robust to renegotiation subject to reciprocity. We therefore conclude that the attractive features of reciprocity that hold in the context of the terms-of-trade theory and that we have emphasized above may be substantially diminished in environments where offshoring is present.

Finally, notice that at one level all the models we have reviewed thus far share a common perspective on the purpose of a trade agreement: the trade agreement exists to address an international externality that is associated with unilateral policy choices. As we have described, regarding their stance on the question of purpose, where these models sometimes differ is in the form that the externality takes. The "commitment theory" of trade agreements is in this respect quite different, in that the central role for an international externality is absent. According to the commitment theory governments value trade agreements as a way to tie their hands (make commitments) against their own lobbies and citizens.[cd] Does reciprocity look attractive when viewed from the perspective of the commitment theory?

To answer this question, we begin by observing that as an international externality plays no fundamental role in the commitment theory, it is natural that the theory would

---

[cd] Expressions of the commitment theory of trade agreements can be found in a variety of early papers (see, for example, Carmichael, 1987; Staiger and Tabellini, 1987; Lapan, 1988; Matsuyama, 1990; Tornell, 1991; and Brainard, 1994), but Maggi and Rodriguez-Clare's (1998) extension of the lobbying model of Grossman and Helpman (1994) provides what has become the workhorse model of the commitment theory in the trade agreements literature.

predict no *international* inefficiencies associated with the unilateral policy choices of governments. Rather, in the commitment theory the inefficiencies associated with unilateral policy setting are *domestic* in nature: they reflect domestic distortions that are created when governments have incentives to surprise domestic private actors (producers and/or consumers) with unexpected policy intervention, and lack the ability to precommit on their own not to engage in such behavior. In the context of trade policy the incentive to surprise is especially likely to be present, owing to the second-best nature of trade-policy intervention and the incentive governments have to bring such intervention closer to the first best through the element of surprise (see, for example, Staiger and Tabellini, 1989). The point can be seen clearly in the case where a government uses a tariff to address a domestic consumption distortion, say, a negative externality (that does not cross borders) associated with domestic consumption. As a tariff is a combination production subsidy and consumption tax, it is a second-best instrument for addressing the consumption distortion; and it is for this reason that the government would have an incentive to surprise, announcing a policy of nonintervention until domestic production decisions had been made, and then following through with a tariff once production decisions are sunk so as to discourage consumption. In equilibrium domestic producers would not likely be fooled, and as a result the government might be better off if it could commit not to use the tariff at all. And if it cannot manage this commitment on its own, a trade agreement may serve as a useful external commitment device.

It should be fairly clear from this discussion that where governments seek to make commitments to their own private sectors through trade agreements, the attractive features of reciprocity that we have emphasized above in the context of the terms-of-trade theory are likely to lose their luster. This can be most directly appreciated by considering the case of a truly small country that seeks trade agreements as a way to make commitments to its private sectors. For such a country, reciprocity has no bite whatsoever, because by definition the trade policy choices of this country cannot alter the terms of trade; and so, if this country were allowed to renegotiate out of its commitments subject to reciprocity, its commitments would become meaningless. Put slightly differently, according to the logic of the commitment theory, governments care about their own tariff commitments but have no particular reason to care about the tariff commitments of their trading partners, whether those commitments are reciprocal or not. The one potential caveat to this statement arises in regard to how the commitments will be enforced. As trade agreements must generally be self-enforcing, and as commitments have no value if they are not enforced, it is possible that some form of reciprocity would be desired even by governments who saw the trade agreement as valuable to themselves only in so far as the agreement helped them to make commitments to their own private sectors. The logic is that only with reciprocity in some form would these governments (and their private sectors) expect that the commitments they undertook in a trade agreement might actually be enforced. We see this logic as a possible route along which reciprocity might be shown to play an important role in the commitment theory of trade agreements, and in that light as an interesting avenue for further research.

4. NONDISCRIMINATION

We have focused thus far on two-country modeling environments, but real-world trade agreements operate in a multicountry setting. With multiple countries, an important design feature of a trade agreement is whether it allows its member countries to adopt discriminatory tariffs against each other. In the GATT/WTO, such discriminatory tariff behavior is discouraged by the most-favored-nation (MFN) principle contained in GATT Article I, which prohibits any WTO member from applying its tariff on imports of a given good (a "like product") in a way that discriminates across exporters from different WTO member countries (or at a level that is higher than it applies to imports of the good from nonmember countries).[ce] Exceptions to the MFN principle are provided in GATT/WTO rules, however, and can be invoked by GATT/WTO member governments in certain circumstances. The most important exception to MFN is contained in GATT Article XXIV, which allows GATT/WTO members to form preferential trade agreements provided that the members of such agreements eliminate tariffs on "substantially all trade" between them. The coexistence of the GATT/WTO on the one hand, which is built on the foundation of the MFN principle, and on the other hand preferential trade agreements, of which there are now nearly 400 in force, raises the question: What are the advantages and disadvantages of the MFN principle as a design feature of a trade agreement? This is the question we address in this section.

4.1 A Three-Country Model, Discriminatory Tariffs, and MFN

To proceed, we begin by describing a three-country extension of the two-country two-good general equilibrium trade model developed in Section 2.[cf] In the three-country extension, the home country now imports good x from two foreign countries who for simplicity do not trade with each other, and exports good y to each of them. We denote foreign-country 1 and foreign-country 2 variables with the superscripts "$*1$" and "$*2$," respectively. Each foreign country can impose a tariff on its imports of good y from the home country, and we represent the tariff of foreign country i by τ^{*i}. The home country can set tariffs on its imports of good x from the two foreign countries; we represent the home-country tariff on imports from foreign country i by τ^i. An

---

[ce] In addition to the MFN principle, the National Treatment principle, contained in GATT Article III and prohibiting discriminatory treatment against foreign produced goods once they have cleared customs, is the other major leg of the nondiscrimination principle in the GATT/WTO.

[cf] Bagwell and Staiger (1999, 2005a, 2010b) provide details of this model and develop most of the themes we describe here. See also Bagwell et al. (2015).

important observation is that there can only be one local price in the home economy, and the pricing relationships $p = \tau^1 p^{w1}$ and $p = \tau^2 p^{w2}$ therefore imply $p^{w1} \neq p^{w2}$ whenever $\tau^1 \neq \tau^2$. That is, if the home country applies *discriminatory* tariffs $\tau^1 \neq \tau^2$ against the imports from foreign countries 1 and 2, then separate equilibrium world prices $\tilde{p}^{w1}(\tau^1, \tau^2, \tau^{*1}, \tau^{*2})$ and $\tilde{p}^{w2}(\tau^1, \tau^2, \tau^{*1}, \tau^{*2})$ apply to its trade with foreign countries 1 and 2, respectively. Alternatively, if the home country applies a *nondiscriminatory* (MFN) tariff $\tau^1 = \tau^2 \equiv \tau$ against the imports from foreign countries 1 and 2, then a single equilibrium world price $\tilde{p}^w(\tau, \tau^{*1}, \tau^{*2})$ applies to its trade with both foreign countries.

4.1.1 Discriminatory Tariffs

Let us start with discriminatory tariffs. Owing to our assumption that each foreign country trades only with the home country, it is clear that the objectives of the foreign governments can be represented in this three-country model in a completely analogous fashion to that of the two-country model: with discriminatory home-country tariffs, foreign government welfares can be written as $W^{*1}(p^{*1}, \tilde{p}^{w1})$ and $W^{*2}(p^{*2}, \tilde{p}^{w2})$ with $W^{*1}_{\tilde{p}^{w1}} > 0$ and $W^{*2}_{\tilde{p}^{w2}} > 0$. But discriminatory tariffs complicate the expression for the welfare of the home government relative to that in the two-country model. In particular, we cannot simply express home government welfare as a function of the home local price and the two world prices, because the home government is not indifferent to the foreign source of its imports of x when p^{w1} and p^{w2} are not equal: the home government would prefer to have more of its imports of x coming from the foreign country with which its tariff is higher and its terms of trade more favorable (p^{wi} lower), and the share of its imports coming from each foreign source depends on the local prices in each foreign country. For this reason, as Bagwell and Staiger (1999) show, when the home government adopts discriminatory tariffs its welfare can now be represented by $W(p, T)$ with $W_T < 0$, where T is the home country's multilateral terms of trade defined as a trade-weighted average of the bilateral world prices with each of its trading partners and is therefore a function of both world prices *and* foreign local prices.

Hence, in the presence of discriminatory tariffs the channels through which externalities travel extend beyond world prices to include local prices. A number of conclusions relevant to trade agreements that permit tariff discrimination then follow. First, as Bagwell and Staiger (1999) show, these local price externalities are not neutralized at the political optimum, and so politically optimal tariffs are not efficient in the presence of discriminatory tariffs. As can be expected from our discussion in the previous section, this implies in turn that the attractive features of reciprocity that we emphasized above fail to survive in a multicountry world with discriminatory tariffs. Second, as Bagwell and Staiger (2005b) show, trade agreements that permit discriminatory tariffs are susceptible to an extreme form of bilateral opportunism through "concession erosion": beginning from any point on the efficiency frontier, the home government and the government of either of its trading partners can gain from a bilateral agreement in which each agrees to lower its tariff against the other and worsen the terms of trade of the third country, converting the third-country loss into their own gain.[cg] This suggests that trade agreements that allow for discriminatory tariffs may have particular difficulty reaching and maintaining *any* position on the efficiency frontier.

4.1.2 MFN

Next consider the impact of the MFN principle, which in this setting requires that the home government apply a common tariff level $\tau^1 = \tau^2 \equiv \tau$ to the imports of x, regardless of whether these imports originate from foreign country 1 or 2. As we have observed, this implies that a single equilibrium world price $\tilde{p}^w(\tau, \tau^{*1}, \tau^{*2})$ must then prevail. But then, in complete analogy to the two-country model, the objectives of the three governments may be written as $W(p, \tilde{p}^w)$, $W^{*1}(p^{*1}, \tilde{p}^w)$ and $W^{*2}(p^{*2}, \tilde{p}^w)$, with $W_{\tilde{p}^w} < 0$, $W^{*1}_{\tilde{p}^{w1}} > 0$ and $W^{*2}_{\tilde{p}^{w2}} > 0$.

Evidently, in a multicountry environment, the MFN principle ensures that the international externality continues to exhibit the same structure as in the simpler two-country setting. And as a result, in the company of MFN the attractive properties of reciprocity described in the previous section extend to the multicountry setting as well. In particular, under the MFN principle and beginning from noncooperative tariffs, each country can gain from reciprocal liberalization that does not go too far; and MFN politically optimal tariffs (which are efficient) are the only efficient tariffs that are robust to renegotiation under the reciprocity rule, suggesting that, once achieved, the political optimum can be viewed as a particularly robust and stable bargaining outcome of GATT tariff negotiations.[ch]

4.2 MFN Plus Reciprocity

The MFN principle can be understood to offer a further advantage when it is joined with reciprocity in a multicountry world. As we next describe, together reciprocity and MFN can neutralize third-party externalities of bilateral tariff bargaining.

[cg]   With previous concessions exchanged to position the three countries initially on the efficiency frontier, and with the deterioration in foreign country 2's terms of trade synonymous with a reduction in its access to the home-country market, it is natural to use the term "concession erosion" to describe the impact on foreign country 2 of the bilateral bargain between the home country and foreign county 1.

[ch]   It is also straightforward to extend to the multicountry MFN setting our earlier finding that, if governments wish to adopt a common terms of exchange of market access for all countries, the adding-up constraint imposed by market clearing requires that they adopt the one-for-one terms of exchange embodied in GATT's reciprocity principle. A different view of the benefits of the MFN principle than we have emphasized in the text is offered by McCalman (2002). In McCalman's model private information plays a central role, and if the number of small countries is sufficiently great, MFN helps to diminish the ability of a large country to hold an agreement hostage and extract rents from its small trading partners, thereby enhancing both global efficiency and the payoffs of small countries. Other implications of the MFN principle are explored in Ludema (1991), Choi (1995), and Saggi (2004).

4.2.1 The Bilateral Opportunism Problem and the Free-Rider Problem

To appreciate the additional advantage of MFN when it is combined with reciprocity, we first return to the bilateral opportunism problem raised above in the presence of discriminatory tariffs, and note that the MFN restriction by itself mitigates against this problem (as Schwartz and Sykes, 1997, point out) but does not completely prevent it (as emphasized by Bagwell and Staiger, 2005b). Suppose for example that the home country and foreign country 1 engage in a bilateral bargain to cut their tariffs, with the home-country tariff constrained to abide by MFN. If foreign country 1 agrees to cut its tariff unilaterally, this will worsen its terms of trade, which under MFN is to say it will also worsen the terms of trade of foreign country 2 (who experiences concession erosion) while improving the terms of trade of the home country. Under this agreement, the bilateral bargain between the home country and foreign country 1 would impose a negative externality on Foreign country 2. Of course, unless foreign country 1 begins the negotiations with its tariff above its own reaction curve, it would lose from such a unilateral tariff cut, but it *could* gain from the bargain if the home country agrees to cut its tariff as well, and it *might* gain even if the agreed changes to the two tariffs together still result in a deterioration of the foreign (country 1 and country 2) terms of trade. Bagwell and Staiger show that the MFN restriction would prevent the home country and foreign country 1 from jointly gaining in such a bilateral bargain beginning from some points on the efficiency frontier (the MFN political optimum included among them), thereby confirming the position of Schwartz and Sykes that MFN can help protect against concession erosion; but Bagwell and Staiger show that there are also points on the efficiency frontier from which, even under the MFN restriction, the home country and foreign country 1 *can* jointly gain from engineering concession erosion and the associated terms-of-trade deterioration suffered by foreign country 2.

Hence, the negative third-party externality problem associated with concession erosion is mitigated under the MFN restriction, but only partly so.[ci] At the same time, it is also true that MFN introduces a new concern associated with a *positive* externality to third parties: the free rider problem. This is the familiar weakness of the MFN principle, which in our three-country model requires that any tariff cut given by the home country to one foreign country must be automatically (and unconditionally) extended as well to the other foreign country. In the context of the bilateral bargain between the home country and foreign country 1 that we considered just above, the free-rider problem associated with MFN arises when the home country agrees to cut its tariff, because in so doing the home country is then worsening its own terms of trade and conferring a terms-of-trade

---

[ci] And as Bagwell and Staiger (2010a, note 10) point out, this partial mitigation is further weakened if international transfers are possible, providing a potential reason to discourage the use of transfers in the GATT/WTO system.

benefit to foreign country 1, which under MFN is to say it is also conferring a terms-of-trade benefit to foreign country 2, who "free rides" on the additional market access that the home country's tariff cut implies. The free-rider problem is typically viewed as the Achilles heel of the MFN principle.

4.2.2 MFN Plus Reciprocity

Notice, however, that what we describe above is in the first instance the possibility that a bilateral MFN tariff bargain might impose a *negative* externality on third parties; there the negative externality arises when foreign country 1 cuts its tariff on imports of good y in a bilateral bargain with the home country, and the externality is transmitted to competing importers of good y (foreign country 2). And what we describe in the second instance is a *positive* third-party externality that arises when the home country cuts its tariff on imports of good x in a bilateral bargain with foreign country 1 and is transmitted to competing exporters of good x (foreign country 2). Suppose, then, that the home country and foreign country 1 were to engage in a bilateral MFN tariff bargain that cut the tariff of foreign country 1 and the tariff of the home country in a way that just *balanced* these two opposing third-party externalities; in principle, the home country and foreign country 1 could then neutralize the third-party externality of their bilateral tariff bargain. As Bagwell and Staiger (2005b) show, this balance is precisely what GATT's principle of reciprocity achieves in a multicountry MFN world, because the balance requires nothing more than ensuring that the terms of trade does not move in either direction as a result of the bilateral bargain, and that is what MFN tariff changes that abide by reciprocity deliver.

It bears emphasis that, following a bilateral reciprocal MFN tariff bargain between the home country and foreign country 1, exporters from foreign country 2 experience a reduced MFN tariff from the home country and yet do not enjoy any increase in their export volume. How can this be? The reason is that the exports from foreign country 2 must compete for sales in the domestic market with the exports from foreign country 1, and exports from foreign country 1 are stimulated by the negotiated reduction in foreign country 1's import tariff (Lerner symmetry).[cj] Put another way, what we are describing here is the possibility that tariff adjustments in one country (the home country) that, in isolation, would have altered the local prices in a second country (foreign country 2) and as a consequence triggered changes in that country's export volumes, might be matched by the tariff adjustments of a third country (foreign country 1) in a way that ultimately left the local prices of the second country, and hence its export volumes, unchanged. This reasoning is admittedly subtle, and there is as yet scant evidence available on its empirical

[cj]   In this light, it is also easy to see that in a many-good setting where reciprocity could lead to changes in individual world prices but not the overall terms of trade, the third country could experience changes in the export volumes of individual goods but not in its overall export volume.

relevance.[ck] There is, however, ample evidence on the empirical relevance of Lerner symmetry, and the point we describe here is simply an application of Lerner symmetry to the context of bilateral MFN tariff bargaining.[cl]

Finally, we note that Ossa (2014) provides an important qualification to the claim that reciprocity and MFN can neutralize the third-party externalities of bilateral tariff bargaining, arguing that the existence of differentiated products can interfere with this claim. Intuitively, in a setting with differentiated products, even if it imposes an MFN tariff a country can trade at distinct world prices for (differentiated) products exported from distinct foreign sources, contrary to the homogeneous-good case; and in this setting, negotiating reciprocal tariff changes with one foreign partner that leave unchanged the terms of trade with that partner will generally alter (and as Ossa demonstrates, in fact improve) the terms of trade with the other foreign partner.[cm] Of course, with product differentiation the definition of "like products" takes center stage in the application of the MFN principle: At what point do differentiated products cease to become like products and hence not demand a common tariff treatment under MFN? The answer to this question is especially important here, because as Ossa demonstrates and as is intuitively clear, the magnitude of the third-party externality imposed by bilateral bargains that respect reciprocity and MFN is proportional to the degree of product differentiation within the scope of the like-product determination over which the MFN restriction applies; in the GATT/WTO this scope is typically constrained to fall within narrow product classifications. And as Ossa observes, for his quantification exercises he must impose MFN at the level of broad industry categories. Nevertheless, with this caveat noted Ossa reports

---

[ck]   But we note here that, though with the purpose of making a different point, the Haberler Report (GATT, 1958, pp. 95–96) includes discussions that mirror a key part of the reasoning we sketch above, namely, that multiple tariff adjustments can have offsetting impacts on local prices with no consequence for trade volumes.

[cl]   See Bagwell and Staiger (2014) for further discussion of empirical studies reporting evidence that a country's own tariff cuts stimulate its exports. Two recent papers provide evidence on the extent of the free-rider problem in GATT/WTO tariff negotiations more generally, though neither provides specific evidence on the contribution of reciprocity in mitigating the problem. Ludema and Mayda (2013) report evidence of significant free-riding effects in the pattern of tariff commitments implemented as a result of the 1986–94 Uruguay Round of GATT negotiations, while Bagwell et al. (2015) fail to find evidence of a free-rider problem in their analysis of the detailed bargaining records of the 1950–51 Torquay Round of GATT negotiations.

[cm]   In this sense, Ossa's (2014) finding shares similarities with the finding of Bagwell and Staiger (2005b), that with discriminatory tariffs across trading partners—and hence multiple world prices for the same good—reciprocity does not eliminate third-party externalities. A difference, though, is that with discriminatory tariffs (and homogeneous goods) Bagwell and Staiger show that reciprocal tariff liberalization between two parties will hurt the third party via a terms-of-trade deterioration, while Ossa shows with MFN tariffs and differentiated products that the third party benefits via a terms-of-trade improvement. See also Suwanprasert (2014), who reports an analogous result to that of Ossa (2014) in the firm-delocation model of Ossa (2011).

that in the presence of differentiated products the third-party externality associated with MFN can be substantial, even when negotiations conform closely to reciprocity.[cn]

4.3 Multilateral Reciprocity

Overall, the preceding discussion suggests an important insight: broadly speaking, the MFN principle permits the liberalizing force of reciprocity to be harnessed in an essentially bilateral manner even in a multicountry world. Indeed, in the context of reciprocity's implications for the GATT/WTO bargaining process discussed in the earlier two-country setting, it can be shown that when that setting is extended to a multicountry world, reciprocity and MFN together work to eliminate bargaining externalities across bargaining pairs, and at the same time induce truth-telling on the part of governments, and in this way convert a potentially complex multilateral bargaining problem with private information into a comparatively simple set of full-information bilateral bargains (albeit with difficulties encountered in the face of asymmetries as we described earlier).[co]

But this observation raises a further question: If MFN and reciprocity can together essentially "decentralize" the tariff problem in a multicountry world into a collection of bilateral bargains, why, then, is there a need for GATT/WTO multilateral rounds? Why not simply let countries negotiate a web of bilateral reciprocal MFN tariff agreements on their own, much as was the practice of the United States during the 1930s under the US Reciprocal Trade Agreements Act (RTAA)?

One answer to this question is that, at least in the later GATT/WTO rounds, writing and elaborating on agreed common codes of behavior has been an important function, and for this the multilateral features of the negotiations are no doubt crucial. A second answer to this question is provided by Maggi (1999). Maggi demonstrates that, even in a world without externalities across bilateral relationships, multilateral tariff bargaining yields a Pareto-superior outcome to bilateral tariff bargaining whenever there are bilateral imbalances of power across bargaining pairs. As Maggi explains, bilateral bargains generate outcomes that are biased in favor of the "strong" country in each bilateral relationship, and unless countries can make international lump sum transfers this results in an inefficiency at the global level that multilateral tariff bargaining can avoid.

Here we suggest a third answer to the question why multilateral rounds of negotiation might be desirable: the GATT/WTO multilateral rounds relax the requirement of

---

[cn] In their analysis of the Torquay bargaining records, Bagwell et al. (2015) report evidence which they interpret as consistent with Ossa's (2014) result that third-party externalities should be larger where products are more differentiated. In addition, Ossa (2014) reports results from counterfactuals that are designed to illuminate how the MFN principle by itself impacts GATT/WTO bargaining outcomes. Again as Ossa notes, imposing MFN at the broad industry categories used in his quantification exercise is problematic, but with this caveat he reports that the MFN restriction appears to have little quantitative impact on bargaining outcomes.

[co] See Bagwell and Staiger (1999, 2010b) and Bagwell et al. (2015).

bilateral reciprocity and allow countries to seek instead only *multilateral reciprocity* in their bargaining outcomes. And as we explain, in a multicountry MFN world, multilateral reciprocity is sufficient to deliver all of the properties that we have above attributed to the pairing of reciprocity with MFN.[cp]

To see the point, it is helpful to return to the three-country two-good general equilibrium model described earlier, with the home government restricted to an MFN tariff. As we observed, this implies that there is a single equilibrium world price $\tilde{p}^w(\tau, \tau^{*1}, \tau^{*2})$, and under standard conditions $\tilde{p}^w$ is decreasing in the home tariff τ and increasing in each of the foreign tariffs τ^{*1} and τ^{*2}. Let us suppose, then, that the tariff reductions $\Delta\tau$, $\Delta\tau^{*1}$ and $\Delta\tau^{*2}$ together satisfy reciprocity, in the sense that together they leave $\tilde{p}^w$ unchanged.

One way to structure these tariff changes is to proceed sequentially through the bilaterals and demand bilateral reciprocity at every stage. Under this approach, the home country could split its tariff reduction $\Delta\tau$ into two parts: a $\Delta\tau_1$ that was matched with $\Delta\tau^{*1}$ so that $\tilde{p}^w$ remained unchanged under the tariff reductions $\Delta\tau_1$ and $\Delta\tau^{*1}$; and a further $\Delta\tau_2$ that was matched with $\Delta\tau^{*2}$ so that $\tilde{p}^w$ remained unchanged under the tariff reductions $\Delta\tau_2$ and $\Delta\tau^{*2}$ (and by construction, $\Delta\tau_1 + \Delta\tau_2 = \Delta\tau$). "Split concessions" of this kind were a common tactic used by the United States to maintain reciprocity in each of its bilaterals under the RTAA (see Beckett, 1941).

An alternative way to structure these tariff changes, however, is to not worry about achieving bilateral reciprocity in each bilateral bargain, as long as overall *multilateral* reciprocity is achieved once the direct-plus-indirect impacts of all the bilateral bargains on each country's trade are taken into account. Under this approach, in its bilateral with foreign country 1 the home country could offer its entire tariff cut $\Delta\tau$ in exchange for the tariff cut $\Delta\tau^{*1}$ from foreign country 1, creating a positive spillover for foreign country 2 from this bilateral; and in its bilateral with foreign country 2, the home country could then ask for the tariff cut $\Delta\tau^{*2}$ and offer nothing directly in return, with the tariff cut $\Delta\tau^{*2}$ serving as compensation for the indirect benefit that foreign country 2 would be receiving from the bilateral between home and foreign country 1. Neither of these bilaterals satisfies bilateral reciprocity, but each country nevertheless achieves reciprocity—and $\tilde{p}^w$ is left unchanged—once the direct and indirect effects of all the tariff cutting agreed in the round are added up.

It is not hard to see that the second approach would be facilitated by a multilateral round of bilateral negotiations in which all participants in the bilaterals could assess both what they were obtaining directly in their own bilaterals and also what they would be obtaining indirectly from the bilaterals of other pairs of countries. In the simple model here, there is nothing to gain from relaxing the restriction of bilateral reciprocity and replacing it with the weaker requirement of multilateral reciprocity. But it is easy to see with more complicated trade patterns that the relaxation of the constraint from

---

[cp] This is a point emphasized by Bagwell et al. (2015).

one of bilateral reciprocity to one of multilateral reciprocity could make possible some deals that would otherwise not be possible.[cq]

In a four-country version of this model with one home and three foreign countries, Bagwell et al. (2015) show that if the home country and foreign countries 1 and 2 engage in negotiations that conform to MFN and multilateral reciprocity, then foreign country 3 is unaffected by their bargain. And with this result they also establish that multilateral reciprocity is sufficient to deliver all of the properties attributed above to the pairing of reciprocity with MFN. Bagwell et al. then use these properties to guide their empirical analysis of GATT bargaining records from the Torquay Round, and find evidence consistent with a number of themes developed above. But for our purposes here their findings concerning multilateral vs bilateral reciprocity are the most relevant. Exploiting the "quasi experiment" created by the breakdown of the United States–United Kingdom bilateral in the middle of the Torquay Round, Bagwell et al. report evidence of rebalancing in the offers and counter-offers made by the United States and its other bilateral bargaining partners subsequent to the news of this breakdown that would not have been required to maintain reciprocity if countries had been achieving bilateral reciprocity in each of their bargains all along. These findings support the view that the bilateral reciprocity restriction that might otherwise have constrained negotiations was indeed relaxed in the GATT multilateral bargaining forum, where the weaker restriction of multilateral reciprocity could instead be achieved.[cr]

5. BINDINGS AND OVERHANG

Governments in the GATT/WTO negotiate bound tariff rates, or tariff caps, rather than exact tariff levels. When a government agrees to a tariff cap for some product, the government is permitted under GATT/WTO rules to set any (nondiscriminatory) tariff below that cap but is not allowed to apply a tariff above the cap unless certain contingencies arise.[cs] Binding overhang occurs when the applied tariff is below the bound level.

[cq] Indeed, the relaxation of this constraint was seen by early GATT practitioners as a key innovation of GATT relative to the RTAA (Interim Commission for the ITO, 1949). Notice, too, that our point here is distinct from that made by Maggi (1999), as our point relates to the ability to balance spillovers across bilaterals in the presence of MFN whereas Maggi's point addresses power asymmetries in bilaterals with no spillovers and no essential role for MFN.

[cr] A remaining question is why, given the multilateral bargaining forum, the organizing principle of GATT/WTO tariff negotiations remained focused on bilaterals. In fact, in several of the GATT Rounds (the Kennedy Round and the Tokyo Round) countries first negotiated on a multilateral basis over a tariff cutting rule (or rules) to be adopted by all, and the bilaterals then reemerged in these rounds as a way of introducing exceptions to the agreed rules and to establish and maintain reciprocity. In the now-stalled WTO Doha Round, a mixture of these approaches was being utilized. Especially with the recent declassification of the GATT bargaining records for many of the GATT rounds, we see the choice of bargaining protocols to be an important topic for future theoretical and empirical research.

[cs] Tariff caps play a central role in GATT/WTO design. This role is highlighted, for example, in the World Trade Report 2009 (World Trade Organization, 2009, p. 105), which argues that the "concept of a tariff binding—ie, committing not to increases a duty beyond an agreed level—is at the heart of the multilateral trading system."

In practice, the extent of binding overhang varies markedly across countries and products, but is a prominent feature of tariff policies for many WTO members.[ct] Thus, GATT/WTO rules allow for substantial "downward flexibility" but impose significant constraints on "upward flexibility."

Does the GATT/WTO tariff-cap approach make sense in light of the trade-agreement models described in Section 2? The terms-of-trade theory of trade agreements clearly suggests that an effective trade agreement must include some constraints against opportunistic tariff hikes. A tariff cap is one such constraint. From the perspective of this theory, we can also appreciate that a well-designed trade agreement might provide substantial downward flexibility; after all, if a government applies a (nondiscriminatory) tariff that is below the bound level for a given product, then the trading partners that export this product enjoy a terms-of-trade gain. A further consideration is that the nature of tariff flexibility may impact the negotiated baseline tariff; for example, a higher baseline tariff may be more attractive in the presence of downward flexibility. To address these and other considerations and to thereby assess the optimality of the GATT/WTO tariff-cap approach, we require a model of tariff negotiations in which shocks occur so that flexibility would sometimes be exercised if permitted.

Bagwell and Staiger (2005a) analyze tariff caps and binding overhang in the context of a model in which governments are exposed to preference shocks in the form of political pressure. They posit that at the time of negotiation governments face at least some uncertainty about the political pressures that they might later face. After the trade agreement is negotiated, governments privately observe their respective political pressure realizations and select their preferred import tariffs from those that are permitted by the trade agreement. Bagwell and Staiger develop their analysis in the context of the linear-quadratic partial-equilibrium model presented in Section 2.2.1, under the assumptions that only import tariffs are selected (ie, export policies are exogenously set at free trade), the political-economy weights attached to export interests are unitary, and the political-economy weights that governments attach to import-competing interests are independently drawn from the interval $[\underline{\gamma}, \overline{\gamma}]$ according to the continuously differentiable distribution function $F(\gamma)$ and where $\underline{\gamma} = 1 < \overline{\gamma} < 7/4$.[cu]

Given the separable structure of the linear-quadratic model and the absence of export policies, the tariff policy of one government has no direct interaction with the tariff selection of the other government. We therefore focus on the home-country import good,

[ct]   See, for example, WTO (2009, p. xix) for a related description. Recent empirical work includes Bacchetta and Piermartini (2011) and Beshkar et al. (2015).

[cu]   Thus, in terms of the model presented in Section 2.2.1, Bagwell and Staiger (2005a) assume that $\gamma_e = \gamma_e^* = 1$ while γ_m and γ_m^* are independently determined according to the distribution function $F(\gamma)$. Recall now the assumption that $5/8 + 9\gamma_e/8 > \gamma_m$ for the linear-quadratic model in Section 2.2.1, which ensures that trade volume is positive at Nash (and efficient) tariffs. In the present context, with $\gamma_e = 1$, this assumption requires that $7/4 > \gamma_m$, which explains the assumption that $\overline{\gamma} < 7/4$.

which we denote as good x in Section 2.2.1.[cv] To simplify our presentation, we drop the good x subscript in our notation here.

Consider then the import tariff policy of the home country. For the linear-quadratic model, the optimal tariff for the government of the home country is the same as its Nash tariff.[cw] As Bagwell and Staiger (2005a) confirm, the *Nash tariff function* for the linear-quadratic model takes the form $\tau^N(\gamma) = (8\gamma - 5)/[4(17 - 2\gamma)]$, where γ is the political-economic welfare weight attached to profit in the import-competing industry. As illustrated in Fig. 3 (adapted from Bagwell and Staiger, 2005a), the Nash tariff function is strictly increasing. This simply reflects the fact that a home-country government with a greater welfare weight on import-competing interests derives greater benefit from the higher local price that a tariff hike implies. Similarly, we let $\tau^E(\gamma)$ denote the import tariff for the home-country government that maximizes joint government welfare, $W + W^*$. Bagwell and Staiger show that $\tau^E(\gamma) = 4(\gamma - 1)/(25 - 4\gamma)$. This function is strictly increasing as well, and it is also strictly lower than the Nash tariff: $\tau^E(\gamma) < \tau^N(\gamma)$. The difference between the two tariffs is attributable to the terms-of-trade externality. A final feature illustrated in Fig. 3 is that the difference between $\tau^N(\gamma)$ and $\tau^E(\gamma)$ shrinks as γ rises. The intuition is that the incentive to manipulate the terms of trade diminishes at higher values for γ, since $\tau^N(\gamma)$ and $\tau^E(\gamma)$ then take higher values and thus generate lower trade volumes. Of course, $\tau^N(\gamma)$ and $\tau^E(\gamma)$ also characterize the tariff policies for the foreign government, when γ is interpreted as the welfare weight that the foreign government attaches to its import-competing industry (for good y).

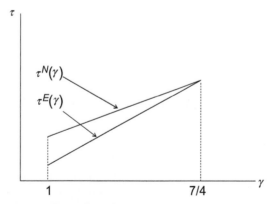

Fig. 3 Nash and efficient domestic tariff levels.

[cv] Even though the model has a separable structure, in the private-information setting under consideration here, gains may exist from "linking" tariff decisions over time or across products. We return to this issue below.

[cw] Amador and Bagwell (2013) refer to this tariff as the flexible tariff, since it is the tariff that a government would select if it were granted full flexibility under the trade agreement.

Since we have ruled out export policies, governments do not have sufficient trade-policy instruments with which to effect lump-sum transfers. The relationship between efficient tariffs and the function $\tau^E(\gamma)$ thus requires some additional discussion. We make two points. First, if governments have available an ex ante (noncontingent) lump-sum transfer instrument, then they achieve efficiency by maximizing $W + W^*$, and so $\tau^E(\gamma)$ then indeed defines the efficient tariff function. Second, if such an instrument is not available, then the Pareto frontier includes other tariff functions as well; however, in the symmetric environment under consideration here, a focal point on the efficiency frontier is arguably where governments use the same tariff function, $\tau^E(\gamma)$. We therefore refer below to the tariff function $\tau^E(\gamma)$ as the *efficient tariff function*, and we evaluate a trade agreement relative to the objective of maximizing the expected value of $W + W^*$. The efficient tariff function is the first-best function for this objective, since it maximizes the objective pointwise.

Unfortunately, however, the efficient tariff function is not feasible in this private-information setting, since it fails to be incentive compatible. To see the issue, we may refer again to Fig. 3 for a given value of γ, the home-country government prefers $\tau^N(\gamma)$ to $\tau^E(\gamma)$. If the governments were to attempt to implement the efficient tariff function, then the home-country government with true political pressure γ would have incentive to claim that its type is $\gamma' > \gamma$ where $\tau^E(\gamma') = \tau^N(\gamma)$. Thus, if governments are unable to observe and write verifiable contracts that condition on political pressure realizations, and if governments do not have available contingent transfer functions with which to make the efficient tariff function incentive compatible, then a trade agreement cannot deliver the efficient tariff function.[cx]

Bagwell and Staiger (2005a) compare a *strong tariff binding*, whereby a government must select the same tariff for all political-pressure realizations, with a *weak tariff binding*, whereby a government can apply any tariff so long as the applied tariff does not exceed the bound tariff level (ie, the tariff cap). Given that political pressure enters welfare in a linear way, they find that the optimal strong tariff binding is at the tariff $\tau^E(E(\gamma))$, where $E(\gamma)$ is the expected value of political pressure. Imposing the assumption that $E(\gamma) > 5/4$ so that $\tau^E(E(\gamma)) > \tau^N(\underline{\gamma})$, they further show that the optimal weak binding, τ^w, strictly exceeds $\tau^E(E(\gamma))$ and corresponds to the efficient tariff level for the average political pressure among those types that are constrained by the binding (ie, among those higher types for which $\tau^N(\gamma) > \tau^w$). Intuitively, when a weak binding is used, lower types automatically satisfy the binding while selecting their Nash tariffs; thus, the bound rate is actually selected only by higher types, and so the optimal weak binding is efficient on average conditional on the realization of higher types.

[cx]   As Bagwell and Staiger (2005a) discuss, since the efficient tariff function is strictly increasing, it could be implemented were lump-sum and contingent transfers feasible. In practice, however, state-contingent and monetary transfers are not a prominent feature of GATT/WTO practice.

For both the strong and weak tariff bindings, the induced applied tariff schedules are incentive compatible and thus correspond to a feasible trade agreement.[cy] Furthermore, and as Bagwell and Staiger (2005a) show, the optimal weak binding generates strictly greater expected joint welfare than does the optimal strong binding.[cz] In this sense, their analysis provides a rationalization for the GATT/WTO tariff-cap approach, while also providing an interpretation of binding overhang (by lower types for which $\tau^N(\gamma) < \tau^w$). At the same time, the analysis is not fully complete in that it does not establish that the trade agreement defined by the optimal weak binding offers greater expected joint welfare than does any other incentive-compatible trade agreement.

Amador and Bagwell (2013) develop a theory of optimal delegation that completes and extends this analysis. In a delegation problem, a principal selects a set of permissible actions from which a privately informed agent selects.[da] The principal faces a trade off when selecting this set, since the agent has superior information (which argues in favor of giving the agent substantial discretion) but has biased preferences (which argues in favor of limiting the agent's discretion). Amador and Bagwell characterize optimal delegation for a general family of preferences for the principal and agent, and they then apply their characterizations to the trade-agreement problem. Specifically, they show that the trade-agreement problem can be understood as a delegation game in which the "principal's" objective corresponds to the ex ante expected joint welfare of the two governments, the privately informed "agent's" objective corresponds to the ex post welfare of the government of the importing country, the state of the world about which the agent obtains private information corresponds to the level of political pressure that this government ultimately faces, and the set of permissible actions corresponds to the set of tariffs that are allowed under the trade agreement.

Formally, Amador and Bagwell (2013) analyze the following *delegation problem*:

$$\max_{\pi:\Gamma\to\Pi} \int_\Gamma w(\gamma,\pi(\gamma))dF(\gamma) \text{ subject to}$$
$$\gamma \in \arg\max_{\widetilde{\gamma}\in\Gamma}[\gamma\pi(\widetilde{\gamma}) + b(\pi(\widetilde{\gamma}))] \text{ for all } \gamma \in \Gamma, \tag{75}$$

where $\Gamma \equiv [\underline{\gamma},\overline{\gamma}] \subset \mathfrak{R}$, F is continuous with an associated continuous and strictly positive density f, Π is an interval of the real line with nonempty interior where, without loss of generality, $\inf\Pi = 0$ and $\overline{\pi}$ is in the extended reals such that $\overline{\pi} = \sup\Pi$. Their maintained

---

[cy] The applied tariff schedule induced by the strong tariff binding is trivially incentive compatible, since all types apply the same tariff. The applied tariff schedule induced by the weak tariff binding entails lower types selecting their Nash tariffs and higher types pooling at the weak binding, τ^w. This applied tariff schedule is also incentive compatible, since each type applies the permitted tariff that is as close as possible to its Nash tariff.

[cz] To establish this point, suppose that governments were to use a weak binding where the cap is set at the optimal strong tariff binding, $\tau^E(E(\gamma))$. Given $\tau^N(\underline{\gamma}) < \tau^E(E(\gamma))$, it follows that the weak binding leads to strictly lower tariffs for lower types, with both governments strictly gaining as a result. The optimal weak binding is then an even better alternative for governments.

[da] See Holmstrom (1977) for an original statement and analysis of the delegation problem.

assumptions are that: (i) $w : \Gamma \times \Pi \to \mathfrak{R}$ is continuous on $\Gamma \times \Pi$; (ii) for all $\gamma_0 \in \Gamma$, $w(\gamma_0, \cdot)$ is concave on Π and twice differentiable on $(0, \overline{\pi})$; (iii) $b : \Pi \to \mathfrak{R}$ is strictly concave on Π and twice differentiable on $(0, \overline{\pi})$; (iv) there exists a twice-differentiable function $\pi_f : \Gamma \to (0, \overline{\pi})$ such that, for all $\gamma_0 \in \Gamma$, $\pi_f'(\gamma_0) > 0$ and $\pi_f(\gamma_0) \in \arg\max_{\pi \in \Pi} [\gamma_0 \pi(\gamma) + b(\pi(\gamma))]$; and (v) $w_\pi : \Gamma \times (0, \overline{\pi}) \to \mathfrak{R}$ is continuous on $\Gamma \times (0, \overline{\pi})$.[db]

The objective of the principal is thus to maximize the expected value of the function w, where w depends on the state variable γ and the associated action, $\pi(\gamma)$. The agent privately observes the state γ and chooses over actions π to maximize $\gamma \pi + b(\pi)$. The principal, however, selects the set of permissible actions, and is thereby able to match states to actions provided that the incentive compatibility constraint is met (so that an agent that observes state γ does not prefer to choose a permissible action $\pi(\widetilde{\gamma})$ intended for a different state). Amador and Bagwell (2013) provide sufficient and necessary conditions under which an *interval allocation* solves the delegation problem defined in (75), where an interval allocation π is defined by bounds γ_L and γ_H with $\gamma_L, \gamma_H \in \Gamma$ and $\gamma_L < \gamma_H$ and satisfies $\pi(\gamma) = \pi_f(\gamma_L)$ for $\gamma \in [\underline{\gamma}, \gamma_L], \pi(\gamma) = \pi_f(\gamma)$ for $\gamma \in (\gamma_L, \gamma_H)$, and $\pi(\gamma) = \pi_f(\gamma_H)$ for $\gamma \in [\gamma_H, \overline{\gamma}]$. Thus, when the principal selects an interval allocation, an agent that observes an intermediate value of γ selects the optimal (ie, flexible) action $\pi_f(\gamma)$ while an agent that observes a higher (lower) value of γ selects the highest (lowest) permissible action. A *cap allocation* is an interval allocation for which $\gamma_L = \underline{\gamma}$.

A case of particular interest for trade-agreement applications occurs when $w(\gamma, \pi(\gamma)) = v(\pi) + b(\pi) + \gamma \pi$. For example, consider again a partial equilibrium model of trade in which only import tariffs are available. For a given traded good, the interpretation here is that π is the profit that is delivered to the import-competing industry, with γ then indicating the welfare weight that the government of the importing country ultimately places on π. Since a higher import tariff results in a higher profit level in the import-competing industry, there is a one-to-one relationship between import tariffs and import-competing industry profit. The optimal import tariff, for example, is the unique tariff that delivers the corresponding optimal profit level, $\pi_f(\gamma)$. More generally, a trade agreement that specifies permissible import tariffs can be understood equivalently as specifying permissible levels of profit for the import-competing industry. We then may use $b(\pi)$ to capture the consumer surplus and tariff revenue in the importing country as a function of the delivered profit, so that the welfare function for the government of the importing country can be represented as $b(\pi) + \gamma \pi$. Finally, when the two governments design the trade agreement, they seek to maximize their ex ante expected welfare, $w(\gamma, \pi(\gamma)) = v(\pi) + b(\pi) + \gamma \pi$, where the function $v(\pi)$ captures the impact of π on welfare in the exporting country. In other words, $v(\pi)$ represents export-industry profit and consumer surplus for the traded good in the exporting country, when these values are expressed as functions of the profit that is enjoyed on this good in the importing country.

[db] Amador and Bagwell (2013) also analyze and apply a version of the delegation problem that allows for a nonnegative money-burning variable.

For trade-agreement applications, cap allocations correspond to tariff caps and are thus of particular interest. Under the assumption that $v'(\pi_f(\gamma)) < 0$ for all $\gamma \in \Gamma$, Amador and Bagwell (2013) show that, within the family of cap allocations, the optimal value for γ_H is *interior* (ie, satisfies $\gamma_H \in (\underline{\gamma}, \overline{\gamma})$) provided that $v'(\pi_f(\underline{\gamma})) + E(\gamma) - \underline{\gamma} > 0$. The assumption that $v'(\pi_f(\gamma)) < 0$ is quite natural in trade-agreement applications, where a higher import tariff imposes a negative international externality on a country's trading partner. For example, in the linear-quadratic partial equilibrium model that Bagwell and Staiger (2005a) use, the assumption that $v'(\pi_f(\gamma)) < 0$ for all $\gamma \in \Gamma$ is satisfied, and the requirement that $v'(\pi_f(\underline{\gamma})) + E(\gamma) - \underline{\gamma} > 0$ holds given $\underline{\gamma} = 1$ if and only if $E(\gamma) \geq 5/4$.[dc] The tariff cap implied by the optimal cap allocation in this example corresponds to the optimal weak binding, τ^w, that Bagwell and Staiger (2005a) characterize.

For the case where $w(\gamma, \pi(\gamma)) = v(\pi) + b(\pi) + \gamma\pi$, Amador and Bagwell (2013) further provide a simple set of sufficient conditions under which the optimal cap allocation solves the delegation problem defined in (75) and is thus the optimal allocation among *all* incentive-compatible allocations. The sufficient conditions are those just mentioned— that $v'(\pi_f(\gamma)) < 0$ for all $\gamma \in \Gamma$ and $v'(\pi_f(\underline{\gamma})) + E(\gamma) - \underline{\gamma} > 0$—as well as two additional conditions. The additional conditions are that the density f is nondecreasing on Γ and that

$$\kappa \equiv \inf_{(\gamma, \pi) \in \Gamma \times \Pi} \left\{ \frac{w_{\pi\pi}(\gamma, \pi)}{b''(\pi)} \right\} \geq \frac{1}{2}. \tag{76}$$

The latter condition allows that v may be convex but ensures that the magnitude of any convexity in v is not too large relative to the magnitude of the concavity in b. The stated conditions are sufficient to ensure that the optimal cap allocation generates higher expected welfare for the principal than does any other incentive-compatible allocation.[dd]

As Amador and Bagwell (2013) show, these conditions can be easily applied to trade models. As a first application, they apply their analysis to the linear-quadratic partial equilibrium model studied by Bagwell and Staiger (2005a) and show that the optimal tariff-cap allocation is optimal in the full set of incentive-compatible allocations given $\underline{\gamma} = 1$ if $E(\gamma) \geq 5/4$ and f is nondecreasing. For this model, $\kappa = 2/3$ and so the condition that $\kappa \geq 1/2$ is automatically satisfied. Amador and Bagwell also show for this model that the monotonicity restriction on the density can be relaxed to allow for differentiable densities that are decreasing over ranges or even over the whole support, provided that the rate of decrease is not too great.[de] Thus, under the described conditions, the optimal weak

---

[dc] As Amador and Bagwell (2013) show, for the linear-quadratic model, $b(\pi) = (1/2)(-1 + 9\sqrt{\pi} - 17\pi)$ and $v(\pi) = (1/4)(2 - 6\sqrt{\pi} + 9\pi)$, where π is the profit in the import-competing industry and $\overline{\pi} = 1/9$ is the maximal profit obtained when the prohibitive tariff of $1/6$ is applied.

[dd] Alternative incentive-compatible allocations must be nondecreasing and include a large family of allocations with points of discontinuity, where the allocation hurdles the flexible allocation $\pi_f(\gamma)$.

[de] The specific condition is that $f(\gamma) + (7/4 - \gamma)f'(\gamma) \geq 0$ for all $\gamma \in \Gamma$. To establish this point, Amador and Bagwell (2013) refer to the sufficient conditions that they provide for the optimality of interval allocations in the general version of their model.

binding τ^{w} that Bagwell and Staiger (2005a) characterize indeed describes the optimal trade agreement in the full set of incentive-compatible allocations for this model.[df]

In a second application, Amador and Bagwell (2013) consider a model closely related to the monopolistic competition model described in Section 2.3. Specifically, they consider a short-run version of the model in which the number of home- and foreign-country firms is fixed at the exogenous value $n_h = n_f > 1$, so that firms may enjoy positive profits, and in which the utility functions in (17) are replaced by $U = \log(C_D) + C_Y$ and $U^* = \log(C_D^*) + C_Y$, where as before $C_D = [\sum_i (c_i)^{\alpha}]^{1/\alpha}$, $C_D^* = [\sum_i (c_i^*)^{\alpha}]^{1/\alpha}$, $\alpha \in (0, 1)$, and c_i and c_i^* are the respective consumption levels in the home and foreign countries of variety i of the differentiated good. Relative to the partial equilibrium model with perfect competition, a novel feature of this model is that trade is two-way within the differentiated sector, and so the profit earned by each home-country firm depends on the import tariffs in both countries.[dg] To simplify that analysis, Amador and Bagwell assume that the private information is one-sided and concerns the welfare weight that the home-country government attaches to the producer surplus enjoyed by home-country firms.[dh] Despite the more complex trade setting, Amador and Bagwell show that the simple sufficient conditions described earlier can be applied once π is appropriately defined.

In particular, Amador and Bagwell (2013) establish conditions under which the optimal tariff-cap allocation is optimal in the full set of incentive-compatible allocations for the (short-run) monopolistic competition model. The simple sufficient conditions for this model are satisfied if the density is nondecreasing and the parameters are such that $1 > \alpha \geq 2/3$, $\alpha(1-\alpha)\overline{\gamma} < 1$ and $E(\gamma) - \alpha\underline{\gamma} - (2-\alpha)/\alpha > 0$, where $\alpha \geq 2/3$ ensures that $\kappa \geq 1/2$, the role of the latter condition is to generate an interior value for γ_H, and the other parameter restrictions ensure that the model satisfies the basic assumptions of the general delegation problem.[di]

The work described earlier provides a foundation for other recent analyses of tariff caps and binding overhang. Beshkar et al. (2015) extend the linear-quadratic partial-equilibrium

---

[df]   Amador and Bagwell (2013) show also that related results hold in a partial equilibrium model with perfect competition that features log utility and endowments (inelastic supply).

[dg]   The dependence takes a separable form, since the import tariff in one country does not affect the terms of trade and nor thereby the price index in the other country. See also Ossa (2012) for a complete-information analysis of trade negotiations in a monopolistic competition model where profits matter due to a fixed number of firms.

[dh]   The foreign-country government is assumed to maximize national income. An alternative would be to assume a second differentiated sector and let the foreign government be privately informed about its preferences as well.

[di]   Amador and Bagwell (2013) represent home-country government welfare as $W = CS + TR + \gamma PS$, where CS is the consumer surplus enjoyed by home-country consumers, TR is home-country tariff revenue, and PS is the producer surplus enjoyed by home-country firms. They then define π as a specific function of $n_h = n_f$ and the home-country import tariff, τ, where π influences PS but is distinct from PS, and they show that the corresponding formulation of the delegation problem satisfies $v'(\pi) < 0 < v''(\pi)$.

model in an important direction to allow for countries with asymmetric sizes. They focus on tariff caps and provide theoretical and empirical support for the prediction that a higher tariff cap, and thus a greater probability of binding overhang, is optimal when the market power of the importing country is lower. To gain some insight, consider the extreme case of a small country. Since the import tariff for such a country does not generate a terms-of-trade externality, an optimal trade agreement would grant such a country full discretion to respond to its preference shocks. A tariff cap that is sufficiently high accomplishes this objective. Amador and Bagwell (2012) consider the possibility that governments have private information about the value of tariff revenue. They provide an approach under which this problem can be solved using Amador and Bagwell's (2013) propositions for the delegation problem with money burning. For the linear-quadratic model, they then give conditions under which an optimal trade agreement again takes the form of a tariff cap.[dj]

Tariff caps can also be rationalized in other modeling frameworks. Horn et al. (2010), for example, consider a model with contracting costs and show that a weak-binding rule is preferred to a rigid (ie, strong)-binding rule, due to the downward flexibility that the former allows. As in the discussion above, binding overhang occurs with positive probability when a weak-binding rule is used. Maggi and Rodriguez-Clare's (2007) work is also related. They consider a model in which a trade agreement addresses both terms-of-trade and a domestic-commitment problems. While binding overhang does not occur in equilibrium in their model, the potential to apply a tariff below the bound level gives rise to ex post lobbying and thereby helps to diminish the extent of excess investment that occurs in the ex ante stage.[dk]

We also highlight a new literature on the trade effects of tariff bindings, as distinct from reductions in applied tariffs, for settings characterized by policy uncertainty.[dl] As Handley (2014) and Handley and Limão (2015) argue, exporters may be sensitive to policy uncertainty, and tariff caps may thus stimulate entry into export markets by reducing the risk of future increases in protection. Their empirical analyses indicate large trade effects of tariff bindings in trade agreements, both in the context of WTO bindings (for Australia, in Handley, 2014) and preferential-agreement bindings (for Portugal joining the EC, in Handley and Limão, 2015). We view the study of tariff caps in the presence of policy uncertainty as a promising direction for future research.

[dj]   In other related work, Bagwell (2009) considers the linear-quadratic model but assumes that the political pressure variable, γ, can only take two values. The optimal trade agreement in the two-type setting does not take the form of a tariff cap. Frankel (forthcoming) is also related. He considers delegation problems with multiple decisions, where each decision has its own underlying state variable, and describes a constant-bias setting where a cap (defined as a ceiling on the weighted average of actions) is optimal. A key theme is that linking decisions can soften incentive constraints. See Athey and Bagwell (2001) and Jackson and Sonnenschein (2007) for broadly related themes in different contexts.

[dk]   Another approach is taken by Bowen (2015). Working with a dynamic legislative bargaining model, she considers how tariff caps affect the domestic legislative process and thereby the resulting applied tariffs.

[dl]   Other recent contributions to this literature include Limão and Maggi (2015) and Pierce and Schott (2015).

6. CONCLUSION

What does economics have to say about the design of international trade agreements? In this chapter, we have reviewed a literature on this question, providing detailed coverage on three key design features of the GATT/WTO: reciprocity, nondiscrimination as embodied in the MFN principle, and tariff bindings and binding "overhang." Each of these features is central to the design of the GATT/WTO, and we have argued that an economic perspective can go a long way toward revealing a consistent logic to the inclusion of these design features in trade agreements.

We conclude by briefly mentioning several other topics relating to trade-agreement design that are examined in detail elsewhere in this Handbook. A broad theme of our chapter is that the design features of trade agreements are sufficiently deliberate and connected to economic tradeoffs that they can be usefully analyzed from an economic perspective. A good further illustration of this theme can be found in early discussions of the role of dispute settlement procedures to be included in GATT. GATT's dispute settlement procedures raise remarkably subtle tradeoffs between completion of the contract, compliance and compensation that were at the heart of the discussions surrounding these procedures at the time of their initial design.[dm] Themes developed in this chapter provide a foundation for understanding economic aspects of enforcement and dispute settlement procedures in trade agreements, and for understanding as well the manner in which trade agreements can provide upward flexibility to shocks. The themes raised in this chapter also suggest that a properly designed trade agreement must ensure that nontariff and behind-border measures are not used opportunistically, so as to undermine the value of negotiated tariff commitments. Similarly, in multicountry settings, the work described above suggests that discriminatory liberalization may give rise to third-party externalities, a consideration that informs the debate over preferential vs multilateral liberalization. More broadly, other design issues include the treatment of investment and intellectual property in trade agreements; indeed, it is natural to ask what criteria may be put forth to determine which policies are "linked" through trade agreements. These and other design issues are treated in later chapters of this Handbook. These chapters, as they relate to design issues, reinforce the main message of our chapter: economic arguments provide valuable tools for evaluating and interpreting the design of trade agreements.

[dm] For example, in his proposal for a commercial union which would lay much of the groundwork for the design of GATT, James Meade emphasized the tradeoff between writing a more detailed and precise contract vs relying on the dispute settlement system to interpret the contract when disputes inevitably arise (see Meade, 1942, as reproduced in Culbert, 1987, p. 404). And in an early analysis of the 1950–51 GATT Torquay Round, it was suggested that measured compensatory adjustments to restore reciprocity might require on-equilibrium-path authorization of retaliation by GATT at the same time that the possibility of further retaliation and an all-out trade war was to be held as an off-equilibrium threat (see US International Chamber of Commerce, 1955, pp. 63–64).

ACKNOWLEDGMENTS

We thank Emily Blanchard and Giovanni Maggi as our discussants and for detailed comments on an earlier draft and participants at the Handbook of Commercial Policy Conference held at Dartmouth College June 4–June 6 2015 for helpful discussion. K. Bagwell thanks the Center for Advanced Studies in the Behavioral Sciences for support and hospitality.

REFERENCES

Admati, A.R., Perry, M., 1987. Strategic delay in bargaining. Rev. Econ. Stud. 54, 345–364.

Amador, M., Bagwell, K., 2012. Tariff revenue and tariff caps. Am. Econ. Rev. Pap. Proc. 102 (3), 459–465.

Amador, M., Bagwell, K., 2013. The theory of optimal delegation with an application to tariff caps. Econometrica 81 (4), 1541–1599.

Antràs, P., Staiger, R.W., 2012a. Offshoring and the role of trade agreements. Am. Econ. Rev. 102 (7), 3140–3183.

Antràs, P., Staiger, R.W., 2012b. Trade agreements and the nature of price determination. Am. Econ. Rev. Pap. Proc. 102 (3), 470–476.

Athey, S., Bagwell, K., 2001. Optimal collusion with private information. Rand J. Econ. 32 (3), 428–465.

Bacchetta, M., Piermartini, R., 2011. The Value of Bindings. World Trade Organization, Geneva.

Bagwell, K., 2008. Remedies in the WTO: an economic perspective. In: Janow, M.E., Donaldson, V.J., Yanovich, A. (Eds.), The WTO: Governance, Dispute Settlement & Developing Countries. Juris Publishing, Huntington, NY, pp. 733–770 (Chapter 40).

Bagwell, K., 2009. Self-enforcing trade agreements and private information. NBER Working Paper No. 14812.

Bagwell K., Bown C., Staiger R.W., forthcoming. Is the wto passé? *J. Econ. Lit.*

Bagwell, K., Lee, S.H., 2015. Trade Policy Under Monopolistic Competition with Firm Selection (Mimeogr.). Stanford University.

Bagwell, K., Mavroidis, P.C., Staiger, R.W., 2007. Auctioning countermeasures in the WTO. J. Int. Econ. 73 (2), 309–332.

Bagwell, K., Staiger, R.W., 1999. An economic theory of GATT. Am. Econ. Rev. 89 (1), 215–248.

Bagwell, K., Staiger, R.W., 2001a. Domestic policies, national sovereignty, and international economic institutions. Q. J. Econ. 116 (2), 519–562.

Bagwell, K., Staiger, R.W., 2001b. Reciprocity, non-discrimination and preferential agreements in the multilateral trading system. Eur. J. Polit. Econ. 17 (2), 281–325.

Bagwell, K., Staiger, R.W., 2001c. Strategic trade, competitive industries and agricultural trade disputes. Econ. Polit. 13 (2), 113–128.

Bagwell, K., Staiger, R.W., 2002. The Economics of the World Trading System. The MIT Press, Cambridge, MA.

Bagwell, K., Staiger, R.W., 2005a. Enforcement, private political pressure and the GATT/WTO escape clause. J. Leg. Stud. 34 (2), 471–513.

Bagwell, K., Staiger, R.W., 2005b. Multilateral trade negotiations, bilateral opportunism and the rules of GATT/WTO. J. Int. Econ. 67 (2), 268–294.

Bagwell, K., Staiger, R.W., 2006. Will international rules on subsidies disrupt the world trading system? Am. Econ. Rev. 96 (3), 877–895.

Bagwell, K., Staiger, R.W., 2010a. Backward stealing and forward manipulation in the WTO. J. Int. Econ. 82 (1), 49–62.

Bagwell, K., Staiger, R.W., 2010b. The WTO: theory and practice. Annu. Rev. Econ. 2, 223–256.

Bagwell, K., Staiger, R.W., 2011. What do trade negotiators negotiate about? Empirical evidence from the World Trade Organization. Am. Econ. Rev. 101 (4), 1238–1273.

Bagwell, K., Staiger, R.W., 2012a. The economics of trade agreements in the linear cournot delocation model. J. Int. Econ. 88 (1), 32–46.

Bagwell, K., Staiger, R.W., 2012b. Profit shifting and trade agreements in imperfectly competitive markets. Int. Econ. Rev. 53 (4), 1067–1104.

Bagwell, K., Staiger, R.W., 2014. Can the Doha Round be a development round? Setting a place at the table. In: Feenstra, R.C., Taylor, A.M. (Eds.), Globalization in an Age of Crisis: Multilateral Economic Cooperation in the Twenty-First Century. University of Chicago Press for the NBER, Chicago, IL, pp. 91–124.

Bagwell, K., Staiger, R.W., 2015. Delocation and trade agreements in imperfectly competitive markets. Res. Econ. 69 (2), 132–156.

Bagwell, K., Staiger, R.W., Yurukoglu, A., 2015. Multilateral Trade Bargaining: A First Look at the GATT Bargaining Records (Mimeogr.). Stanford University

Baldwin, R., 1987. Politically realistic objective functions and trade policy PROFs and tariffs. Econ. Lett. 24 (3), 287–290.

Baldwin, R.E., Clarke, R.N., 1987. Game-modeling multilateral trade negotiations. J. Policy Model 9 (2), 257–284.

Beckett, G., 1941. The Reciprocal Trade Agreements Program. Columbia University Press, New York, NY.

Beshkar, M., 2010. Trade skirmishes and safeguards: a theory of the WTO dispute settlement process. J. Int. Econ. 82 (1), 35–48.

Beshkar, M., Bond, E.W., Rho, Y., 2015. Tariff binding and overhang: theory and evidence. J. Int. Econ. 97 (1), 1–13.

Binmore, K., 2014. Bargaining and fairness. Proc. Natl. Acad. Sci. USA 111 (Suppl. 3), 10785–10788.

Blanchard, E.J., 2007a. Foreign direct investment, endogenous tariffs, and preferential trade agreements. BE J. Econ. Anal. Policy 7 (1)(Advances), Art. no. 54.

Blanchard, E.J., 2007b. Reevaluating the Role of Trade Agreements: Does Investment Globalization Make the WTO Obsolete? (Mimeogr.). University of Virginia.

Blanchard, E.J., 2010. Reevaluating the role of trade agreements: does investment globalization make the WTO obsolete? J. Int. Econ. 82 (1), 63–72.

Blanchard, E.J., Matschke, X., 2015. US multinationals and preferential market access. Rev. Econ. Stat. 97 (4), 839–854.

Bowen, T.R., 2015. Legislated protection and the World Trade Organization. Int. Econ. Rev. 56 (4), 1349–1384.

Brainard, L., 1994. Last one out wins: trade policy in an international exit game. Int. Econ. Rev. 35 (1), 151–172.

Brander, J.A., 1995. Strategic trade policy. In: Grossman, G.M., Rogoff, K. (Eds.), Handbook of International Economics, 3. North-Holland, Amsterdam, NL, pp. 1395–1455.

Brock, W.A., Magee, S.P., 1978. The economics of special interest politics. Am. Econ. Rev. 68 (2), 246–250.

Brou, D., Ruta, M., 2013. A commitment theory of subsidy agreements. BE J. Econ. Anal. Policy 13 (1), 239–270.

Campolmi, A., Fadinger, H., Forlati, C., 2014. Trade policy: home market effect versus terms-of-trade externality. J. Int. Econ. 93, 92–107.

Carmichael, C.M., 1987. The control of export credit subsidies and its welfare consequences. J. Int. Econ. 23 (1-2), 1–19.

Caves, R.E., 1976. Economic models of political choice: Canada's tariff structure. Can. J. Econ. 9 (2), 278–300.

Choi, J.P., 1995. Optimal tariffs and the choice of technology: discriminatory tariffs vs. the most favored nation clause. J. Int. Econ. 38 (1-2), 143–160.

Costinot, A., Rodriguez-Clare, A., Werning, I., 2015. Micro to Macro: Optimal Trade Policy with Firm Heterogeneity (Mimeogr.). MIT.

Cramton, P., 1992. Strategic delay in bargaining with two-sided uncertainty. Rev. Econ. Stud. 59 (1), 205–225.

Culbert, J., 1987. War-time anglo-american talks and the making of the GATT. World Econ. 10 (4), 381–408.

DeRemer, D.R., 2012. Essays on International Trade Agreements Under Monopolistic Competition (Dissertation). Columbia University.

DeRemer, D.R., 2013. Domestic Policy Coordination in Imperfectly Competitive Markets (Mimeogr.). Hungarian Academy of Sciences.

Dhingra, S., 2014. Reconciling observed tariffs and the median voter model. Econ. Polit. 26 (3), 483–504.

Dixit, A., 1987. Strategic aspects of trade policy. In: Bewley, T.F. (Ed.), Advances in Economic Theory: Fifth World Congress. Cambridge University Press, New York, NY, pp. 329–362.

Dixit, A., Stiglitz, J.E., 1977. Monopolistic competition and optimum product diversity. Am. Econ. Rev. 67 (3), 297–308.

Dutt, P., Mitra, D., 2002. Endogenous trade policy through majority voting: an empirical investigation. J. Int. Econ. 58 (1), 107–133.

Ederington, J., 2001. International coordination of trade and domestic policies. Am. Econ. Rev. 91 (5), 1580–1593.

Feenstra, R.C., Bhagwati, J.N., 1982. Tariff seeking and the efficient tariff. In: Bhagwati, J.N. (Ed.), Import Competition and Response. University of Chicago Press for the NBER, Chicago, IL, pp. 245–262.

Findlay, R., Wellisz, S., 1982. Endogenous tariffs, the political economy of trade restrictions, and welfare. In: Bhagwati, J.N. (Ed.), Import Competition and Response. University of Chicago Press for the NBER, Chicago, IL, pp. 223–244.

Finger, J.M., 1979. Trade liberalization: a public choice perspective. In: Amacher, R., Haberler, G., Willett, T. (Eds.), Challenges to a Liberal International Economic Order. American Enterprise Institute, Washington, DC, pp. 421–453.

Frankel A., forthcoming. Delegating multiple decisions. Am. Econ. J. Microecon.

GATT, 1958. Trends in International Trade: A Report by a Panel of Experts. GATT, Geneva.

Grossman, G.M., 2016. The purpose of trade agreements. In: Bagwell, K., Staiger, R.W. (Eds.), The Handbook of Commercial Policy, vol. 1A. Elsevier, Netherlands, Chapter 7, pp. 379–434.

Grossman, G.M., Helpman, E., 1994. Protection for sale. Am. Econ. Rev. 84 (4), 833–850.

Grossman, G.M., Helpman, E., 1995. Trade wars and trade talks. J. Polit. Econ. 103 (4), 675–708.

Grossman, G.M., Sykes, A.O., 2010. Optimal retaliation in the WTO–a commentary on the upland cotton arbitration. World Trade Rev. 10, 133–164.

Gulotty, R., 2014. Governing Trade Beyond Tariffs: The Politics of Multinational Production and Its Implications for International Cooperation (Dissertation). Stanford University.

Hagerty, K.M., Rogerson, W.P., 1987. Robust trading mechanisms. J. Econ. Theory 42, 94–107.

Handley, K., 2014. Exporting under trade policy uncertainty: theory and evidence. J. Int. Econ. 94 (1), 50–66.

Handley, K., Limão, N., 2015. Trade and investment under policy uncertainty: theory and firm evidence. Am. Econ. J. Econ. Policy 7 (4), 189–222.

Harstad, B., 2007. Harmonization and side payments in political cooperation. Am. Econ. Rev. 97 (3), 871–889.

Helpman, E., Krugman, P.E., 1989. Trade Policy and Market Structure. The MIT Press, Cambridge, MA.

Hillman, A.L., 1982. Declining industries and political-support protectionist motives. Am. Econ. Rev. 72 (5), 1180–1187.

Hoda, A., 2001. Tariff Negotiations and Renegotiations under the GATT and the WTO: Procedures and Practices. WTO and Cambridge University Press, New York.

Hoekman, B., Kostecki, M., 1995. The Political Economy of the World Trading System. Oxford University Press, Oxford.

Holmstrom, B., 1977. On Incentives and Control in Organizations (Ph.D. dissertation). Stanford University.

Horn, H., Maggi, G., Staiger, R.W., 2010. Trade agreements as endogenously incomplete contracts. Am. Econ. Rev. 100 (1), 394–419.

Interim Commission for the ITO, 1949. The Attack on Trade Barriers: A Progress Report on the Operation of the General Agreement on Tariffs and Trade, Geneva, August.

Jackson, J.H., 1969. World Trade and the Law of GATT. Bobbs-Merrill, New York, NY.

Jackson, M.O., Sonnenschein, H.F., 2007. Overcoming incentive constraints by linking decisions. Econometrica 75 (1), 241–257.

Jawara, F., Kwa, A., 2003. Behind the Scenes at the WTO: The Real World of International Trade Negotiations. Zed Books, London.

Johnson, H.G., 1953-1954. Optimum tariffs and retaliation. Rev. Econ. Stud. 21 (2), 142–153.

Karacaovali, B., Limão, N., 2008. The clash of liberalizations: preferential vs. multilateral trade liberalization in the European Union. J. Int. Econ. 74 (2), 299–327.

Kennan, J., Riezman, R., 1988. Do big countries win tariff wars? Int. Econ. Rev. 29 (1), 81–85.

Krugman, P.R., 1997. What should trade negotiators negotiate about? J. Econ. Lit. 35 (1), 113–120.

Lapan, H.E., 1988. The optimal tariff, production lags, and time consistency. Am. Econ. Rev. 78 (3), 395–401.

Lawrence, R.Z., 2003. Crimes and Punishments? Retaliation Under the WTO. Institute for International Economics, Washington, DC.

Lee, G.M., 2007. Trade agreements with domestic policies as disguised protection. J. Int. Econ. 71 (1), 241–259.

Lee, G.M., 2014. Optimal International Agreement and Restriction on Domestic Efficiency (Mimeogr.). Singapore Management University.

Limão, N., 2005. Trade policy, cross-border externalities and lobbies: do linked agreements enforce more cooperative outcomes? J. Int. Econ. 67 (1), 175–199.

Limão, N., 2006. Preferential trade agreements as stumbling blocks for multilateral trade liberalization: evidence for the U.S. Am. Econ. Rev. 96 (3), 896–914.

Limão, N., 2007. Are preferential trade agreements with non-trade objectives a stumbling block for multilateral liberalization? Rev. Econ. Stud. 74 (3), 821–855.

Limão, N., Maggi, G., 2015. Uncertainty and trade agreements. Am. Econ. J.: Microecon. 7 (4), 1–42.

Limão, N., Saggi, K., 2008. Tariff retaliation versus financial compensation in the enforcement of international trade agreements. J. Int. Econ. 76 (1), 48–60.

Ludema, R.D., 1991. International trade bargaining and the most-favored nation clause. Econ. Polit. 3 (1), 1–20.

Ludema, R.D., Mayda, A.M., 2013. Do terms-of trade effects matter for trade agreements? Theory and evidence from WTO countries. Q. J. Econ. 128 (4), 1837–1893.

Ludema, R.D., Zhi, Y., 2015. Tariff Pass-through, Firm Heterogeneity and Product Quality (Mimeogr.). Georgetown University.

Maggi, G., 1999. The role of multilateral institutions in international trade cooperation. Am. Econ. Rev. 89 (1), 190–214.

Maggi, G., 2014. International trade agreements. In: Gopinath, G., Helpman, E., Rogoff, K. (Eds.), The Handbook of International Economics. vol. 4. Elsevier, Amsterdam.

Maggi, G., Rodriguez-Clare, A., 1998. The value of trade agreements in the presence of political pressures. J. Polit. Econ. 106, 574–601.

Maggi, G., Rodriguez-Clare, A., 2007. A political-economy theory of trade agreements. Am. Econ. Rev. 97 (4), 1374–1406.

Maggi, G., Staiger, R.W., 2015a. Optimal design of trade agreements in the presence of renegotiation. Am. Econ. J. Microecon. 7 (1), 109–143.

Maggi, G., Staiger, R.W., 2015b. Trade Disputes and Settlement (Mimeogr.). Yale University.

Matsuyama, K., 1990. Perfect equilibria in a trade liberalization game. Am. Econ. Rev. 80 (3), 480–492.

Mavroidis, P.C., 2016. Dispute settlement in the WTO: mind over matter. In: Bagwell, K., Staiger, R.W. (Eds.), The Handbook of Commercial Policy, vol. 1A. Elsevier, Netherlands, Chapter 6, pp. 333–377.

Mayer, W., 1981. Theoretical considerations on negotiated tariff adjustments. Oxf. Econ. Pap. 33 (1), 135–153.

Mayer, W., 1984. Endogenous tariff formation. Am. Econ. Rev. 74 (5), 970–985.

McCalman, P., 2002. Multi-lateral trade negotiations and the most-favored nation clause. J. Int. Econ. 57 (1), 151–176.

Melitz, M., Ottaviano, G., 2008. Market size, trade, and productivity. Rev. Econ. Stud. 75 (1), 295–316.

Mill, J., 1844. Essays on Some Unsettled Questions of Political Economy. Parker, London.

Myerson, R.B., Satterthwaite, M.A., 1983. Efficient mechanisms for bilateral trading. J. Econ. Theory 29, 265–281.

Olson, M., 1965. The Logic of Collective Action: Public Goods and the Theory of Groups. Harvard University Press, Cambridge, MA.

Ornelas, E., 2016. Special and differential treatment for developing countries. In: Bagwell, K., Staiger, R.W. (Eds.), The Handbook of Commercial Policy, vol. 1B. Elsevier, Netherlands, Chapter 7, pp. 369–432.

Ossa, R., 2011. A 'new-trade' theory of GATT/WTO negotiations. J. Polit. Econ. 119 (1), 122–152.

Ossa, R., 2012. Profits in the new trade approach to trade negotiations. Am. Econ. Rev. Pap. Proc. 102 (2), 466–469.

Ossa, R., 2014. Trade wars and trade talks with data. Am. Econ. Rev. 104 (12), 4104–4146.

Penrose, E., 1953. Economic Planning for the Peace. Princeton University Press, Princeton, NJ.

Pierce, J., Schott, P.K., 2015. The Surprisingly Swift Decline of U.S. Manufacturing Employment (Mimeogr.). Yale University.

Potipiti, T., 2012. Import Tariffs and Export Subsidies in the WTO: A Small Country Approach (Mimeogr.). Chulalongkorn University.

Saggi, K., 2004. Tariffs and the most favored nation clause. J. Int. Econ. 63 (2), 341–368.

Schwartz, W.F., Sykes, A.O., 1997. The economics of the most favored nation clause. In: Bhandari, J.S., Sykes, A.O. (Eds.), Economic Dimensions in International Law: Comparative and Empirical Perspectives. Cambridge University Press, Cambridge, UK, pp. 43–79.

Shirono, K., 2004. Are WTO Tariff Negotiations Reciprocal? An Analysis of Tariff Liberalization (Mimeogr.). Columbia University.

Spagnola, G., 1999a. Issue Linkage, Delegation and International Policy Coordination (Mimeogr.). Stockholm School of International Economics.

Spagnola, G., 1999b. On interdependent supergames: multimarket contact, concavity and collusion. J. Econ. Theory 89 (1), 127–139.

Staiger, R.W., 2006. What can developing countries achieve in the WTO? J. Econ. Lit. 44, 779–795.

Staiger, R.W., Sykes, A.O., 2011. International trade, national treatment, and domestic regulation. J. Leg. Stud. 40 (1), 149–203.

Staiger, R.W., Sykes, A.O., forthcoming. How important can the non-violation clause before the GATT/WTO? Am. Econ. J. Microecon.

Staiger, R.W., Tabellini, G., 1987. Discretionary trade policy and excessive protection. Am. Econ. Rev. 77 (5), 823–837.

Staiger, R.W., Tabellini, G., 1989. Rules and discretion in trade policy. Eur. Econ. Rev. 33 (6), 1265–1277.

Suwanprasert, W., 2014. The Role of MFN in the 'New Trade' Model (Mimeogr.). University of Wisconsin.

Sykes, A.O., 2005. The economics of WTO rules on subsidies and countervailing measures. In: Appleton, A.E., Macrory, P.F.J., Plummer, M.G. (Eds.), The World Trade Organization: Legal, Economic and Political Analysis, Springer-Verlag, USA.

Tornell, A., 1991. On the ineffectiveness of made-to-measure protectionist programs. In: Helpman, E., Razin, A. (Eds.), International Trade and Trade Policy. MIT Press, Cambridge, pp. 66–79.

Torrens, R., 1844. The Budget: On Commercial Policy and Colonial Policy. Smith, Elder, London.

United States Council of the International Chamber of Commerce, 1955. G.A.T.T.: an analysis and appraisal of the General Agreement on Tariffs and Trade. Prepared by the William L. Clayton Center for International Economic Affairs of the Fletcher School of Law and Diplomacy, February.

Venables, A.J., 1985. Trade and trade policy with imperfect competition: the case of identical products and free entry. J. Int. Econ. 19 (1-2), 1–19.

Venables, A.J., 1987. Trade and trade policy with differentiated products: a Chamberlinian-Ricardian model. Econ. J. 97 (387), 700–717.

WTO, 2009. World Trade Report 2009: Trade Policy Commitments and Contingency Measures. WTO, Geneva.

WTO Arbitrators, 1999. European communities–measures concerning meat and meat products (hormones); original complaint by Canada; recourse to arbitration by the European communities under article 22.6 of the DSU: decision by the arbitrators. WT/DS48/ARB, 12 July.

INDEX

Note: Page numbers followed by "*f*" indicate figures, "*t*" indicate tables, and "*np*" indicate footnotes.